The demographic shockwaves of the nineteenth and early twentieth centuries in Europe produced tremendous change in the national economies and affected the political, social, and cultural development of these societies. Within the past two decades, migration historians began to connect the various European migratory streams during this period with transcontinental migration to North America. This volume contains empirical studies on German in-migration, internal migration, and transatlantic emigration from the 1820s to the 1930s, placed in a comparative perspective of Polish, Swedish, and Irish migration to North America. Special emphasis is placed on the role of women in the process of migration. By looking specifically at contemporary Germany, Klaus J. Bade underscores the relevance of this history in a concluding essay.

PUBLICATIONS OF THE GERMAN HISTORICAL INSTITUTE
WASHINGTON, D.C.

Edited by Detlef Junker
with the assistance of Daniel S. Mattern

People in Transit

THE GERMAN HISTORICAL INSTITUTE, WASHINGTON, D.C.

The German Historical Institute is a center for advanced study and research whose purpose is to provide a permanent basis for scholarly cooperation between historians from the Federal Republic of Germany and the United States. The Institute conducts, promotes, and supports research into both American and German political, social, economic, and cultural history, into transatlantic migration, especially in the nineteenth and twentieth centuries, and into the history of international relations, with special emphasis on the roles played by the United States and Germany.

Other books in the series

Hartmut Lehmann and James J. Sheehan, editors, *An Interrupted Past: German-Speaking Refugee Historians in the United States after 1933*

Carol Fink, Axel Frohn, and Jürgen Heideking, editors, *Genoa, Rapallo, and European Reconstruction in 1922*

David Clay Large, editor, *Contending with Hitler: Varieties of German Resistance in the Third Reich*

Larry Eugene Jones and James Retallack, editors, *Elections, Mass Politics, and Social Change in Modern Germany*

Hartmut Lehmann and Guenther Roth, editors, *Weber's Protestant Ethic: Origins, Evidence, Contexts*

Catherine Epstein, *A Past Renewed: A Catalog of German-Speaking Refugee Historians in the United States after 1933*

Hartmut Lehmann and James Van Horn Melton, editors, *Paths of Continuity: Central European Historiography from the 1930s to the 1950s*

Jeffry M. Diefendorf, Axel Frohn, and Hermann-Josef Rupieper, editors, *American Policy and the Reconstruction of West Germany, 1945–1955*

Henry Geitz, Jürgen Heideking, and Jürgen Herbst, editors, *German Influences on Education in the United States to 1917*

Peter Graf Kielmansegg, Horst Mewes, and Elisabeth Glaser-Schmidt, editors, *Hannah Arendt and Leo Strauss: German Emigrés and American Political Thought after World War II*

R. Po-chia Hsia and Hartmut Lehmann, editors, *In and Out of the Ghetto: Jewish–Gentile Relations in Late Medieval and Early Modern Germany*

People in Transit

GERMAN MIGRATIONS IN COMPARATIVE PERSPECTIVE,
1820–1930

Edited by

DIRK HOERDER
and
JÖRG NAGLER

GERMAN HISTORICAL INSTITUTE
Washington, D.C.

CAMBRIDGE
UNIVERSITY PRESS

Published by the Press Syndicate of the University of Cambridge
The Pitt Building, Trumpington Street, Cambridge CB2 1RP
40 West 20th Street, New York, NY 10011-4211, USA
10 Stamford Road, Oakleigh, Melbourne 3166, Australia

First published 1995

Printed in the United States of America

Library of Congress Cataloging-in-Publication Data
People in transit : German migrations in comparative perspective,
1820–1930 / edited by Dirk Hoerder, Jörg Nagler.
p.   cm. − (Publications of the German Historical Institute)
Includes bibliographical references and index.
ISBN 0-521-47412-4

1. Germany − Emigration and immigration − History.   2. Germans −
United States − History.   3. United States − Emigration and
immigration − History.   4. German Americans − History.   5. Germans −
Foreign countries.   I. Hoerder, Dirk.   II. Nagler, Jörg.
III. Series.
DD68.P46   1995
973'.0431 − dc20   94–34289
                                                                CIP

A catalog record for this book is available from the British Library.

ISBN 0-521-47412-4 Hardback

Contents

v

Preface

In the past two decades, historical migration research has undergone a profound change. Several factors account for this development: an extended scope of inquiry, a shift in focus, the inclusion of neglected topics, and the use of new methods and tools – all of which have noticeably raised the level of scholarly sophistication. Individual migration processes are no longer studied in isolation but are understood as part of population movements situated within changing local, regional, national, and international contexts. Intersocietal population flows, formerly often interpreted as unidirectional and haphazard, are now seen as informed, intentional, and multidirectional. The concept of uprootedness has been replaced by that of cultural transfer. Individual and family migration, chain migration, and return migration attest to the existence and impact of a well-informed, interpersonal communications system and to migrants' shrewd utilization of labor markets that extended beyond national boundaries. The new approach has also brought into sharper focus the role of specific groups, as well as the impact of gender, in the migration process.

German immigration research in particular has profited considerably from these innovations. Beginning in the late 1970s, projects funded by the Volkswagen Foundation took a fresh look at German emigrants to the United States and their acculturation into American society. Adopting a social historical and often interdisciplinary approach, these studies placed German migration into a comparative framework through collaboration with foreign scholars and through analysis of interethnic as well as intragroup experiences. As a result, the new immigration research in Germany has made valuable contributions to the historical study of international migration flows, shedding the ugly memory of the late 1920s and the 1930s when immigration research was a willing tool of Nazi propaganda and ideology.

Ironically, at a time when it has again been recognized as a serious scholarly discipline, historical immigration research is faced with new challenges arising from the profound political changes that have taken place in Europe. The perennial question, "[What] can we learn from history?" may perhaps legitimately be asked of immigration historians now that peoples in Europe have become uprooted and European countries, including the Federal Republic of Germany, have become the destination for many refugees. Can historians point to precedents elsewhere and at other times for at least tentative answers to burning current issues?

For these myriad reasons a conference taking stock of the state of German immigration history research seemed timely. In August 1991, the German Historical Institute, Washington, D.C., and the Labor Migration Project at the University of Bremen, in cooperation with the Friends of the German Emigration Museum, Bremerhaven, and the Cultural Office of the City of Bremerhaven, invited European and American scholars to Bremerhaven, the port of embarkation from which many German and eastern European emigrants sailed across the Atlantic. The institute would like to thank the conference conveners, Dirk Hoerder and Jörg Nagler, as well as their co-workers who helped in the preparations. We also would like to thank the chairs, presenters, and commentators for their innovative and stimulating contributions, the majority of which are included in this volume. Reflecting the new reality of a unified country, it also includes essays by young scholars from eastern Germany. Finally, we would like to thank the series editor Daniel S. Mattern for his help in the preparation of this volume for publication.

We hope that these essays will answer some questions and raise many more that may give direction to future research. Specifically, immigration historians might want to compare the legal and administrative mechanisms that immigration countries, including the United States, adopted at various times in order to allow and/or control the flow of immigration. In addition they might wish to study the prerequisites of acculturation both in terms of the openness and constraints of the receiving societies and the goals of individuals and groups entering these host societies. What, for example, were the levels of tolerance and repression at specific historical moments, when did resentment and antagonism turn into violence, how was conflict diffused, what was the role of education and information in preparing the ground for positive encounters between groups? These are questions clearly defined by contemporary concerns; they have had, and will continue to have, a major impact on relations between countries and ethnic groups well into the twenty-first century. This seems to be a point in time when immigration historians have an obligation and an opportunity perhaps to help shape the outcome – something historians cannot often claim for themselves or for their work.

September 1994   Hartmut Keil
Washington, D.C.   Former Acting Director of the
                                                  German Historical Institute

Contributors

Klaus J. Bade is a professor of history and director of the Institute for Migration Research and Intercultural Studies (IMIS) at the Universität Onsabrück. His fields of research comprise modern economic and social history, including the history of migration, imperialism, and colonialism. He is the author of several books and the editor of numerous collections.

Karl Marten Barfuss is a professor of economics in the business department at the Hochschule Bremen. He is a specialist on the modern history of the German Northwest and has published widely on economic history. His publications include *Problemaspekte: Beiträge zu Wirtschaft, Politik, Gesellschaft* (1976), *Geld und Währung* (1983), *Gastarbeiter in Nordwestdeutschland, 1884–1918* (1985).

Sven Beckert is completing a dissertation entitled "The Formation of New York City's Bourgeoisie, 1850–1896" at Columbia University. He is the author of *Bis zu diesem Punkt und nicht weiter: Arbeitsalltag während des Zweiten Weltkriegs in einer Industrieregion* (1990). With Dieter Plehwe he has written *Energy Privatization and Deregulation, Restructuring, and Internationalizing the World's Energy Industries* (1992). He has also written frequently on labor issues and on German Jewish history in the United States, Germany, and the Netherlands.

Monika Blaschke is a research assistant at the Deutsche Presseforschung Institut at the Universität Bremen. She studied at Bremen, Freiburg, Cork (Ireland), and Eugene, Oregon. She is finishing her dissertation on the German American women's press in the twentieth century. In 1992 she contributed to the exhibition "Fame, Fortune, and Sweet Liberty" at Ellis Island, New York.

Dirk Hoerder teaches North American social history at the Universität Bremen, where he is director of the Labor Migration Project. His publications include *Labor Migration in the Atlantic Economies* (1985), *"Struggle a Hard Battle": Essays on Working-Class Immigrants* (1986), and a three-volume bibliography of the non-English-language labor and radical immigrant press (1840s to 1970s). Presently, he is working with autobiographies to reconstruct the personal experiences of migrants.

James H. Jackson, Jr. is a professor of history at Point Loma College, San Diego. He is the author of *Migration and Urbanization in the Ruhr Valley, 1850–1900* (1980).

Walter D. Kamphoefner is an associate professor of history at Texas A & M University. He has authored *Westfalen in der Neuen Welt* (1982) and *The Westfalians: From Germany to Missouri* (1987). He coedited *Briefe aus Amerika* (1988) and *News from the Land of Freedom: German Immigrants Write Home* (1991). He has also written numerous articles and essays on German immigration to the United States. He is currently working on an anthology of German American Civil War letters.

Joy K. Lintelman is an assistant professor of history at Concordia College in Moorhead, Minnesota. She has published several articles on Swedish immigrant women and on immigrant children, most recently, " 'On My Own': Single, Swedish, and Female in Turn-of-the-Century Chicago," in Phillip J. Anderson and Dag Blanck, eds., *Swedish American Life in Chicago* (1992).

Axel Lubinski studied history and German language and literature at the Universität Rostock, 1983–88, and has since completed a doctorate on overseas emigration from Mecklenburg in the nineteenth century. He is currently assistant researcher with the project "Ostelbische Gutsherrschaft" in the Max-Planck-Gesellschaft at the Universität Potsdam.

Deirdre M. Mageean is an assistant professor of public administration and research fellow at the Margaret Chase Smith Center for Public Policy, both at the University of Maine, Orono. She is currently working on the role of Irish Catholic women, lay and religious, in charity work. Her most recent publications are "Catholic Sisterhoods and the Immigrant Church," in Donna Gabaccia, ed., *Seeking Common Ground* (1992), and "From Ulster Countryside to American City: The Settlement and Mobility of Ulster Migrants in Philadelphia," in Colin G. Pooley and Ian Whyte, eds., *Emigrants, Migrants, and Immigrants: A Social History of Migration* (1991).

Susanne Meyer is currently the director of the Textile Industry Museum in Bramsche, Germany. Her publications include *Schwerindustrielle Insel und ländliche Lebenswelt: Georgsmarienhütte 1856–1933* (1991) and with Jürgen Boldt et al., *Freiheit – Krise – Diktatur: Zur Zerschlagung der Gewerkschaften in Osnabrück 1933* (1983). She is presently working on an economic, technical, and social history of the wool industry in early nineteenth-century Germany.

Rainer Mühle currently teaches and researches in the history department at the Universität Rostock. He has written on Swiss migration history and is presently involved in a project on East Elbian migration in the nineteenth century. His most recent publication is "Zum historischen Hintergrund von ostelbischen Migrationsbewegungen im 19. Jahrhundert," *Jahrbuch für Wirtschaftsgeschichte* (1992).

Jörg Nagler is currently the director of the Kennedy Haus in Kiel and a guest lecturer in history at the Universität Kiel. He has written books, articles, and essays on nineteenth- and twentieth-century U.S. political, social, cultural, and ethnic history. His most recent publication is "Victims of the Home Front: Enemy Aliens in the United States during the First World War," in Panikos Panayi, ed., *Minorities in Wartime: National and Racial Groupings in Europe, North America and Australia during the Two World Wars* (1993). He is currently preparing a study on national minorities and the American home front in the First World War.

Sibylle Quack is currently a senior civil servant at the German Federal Press and Information Office (Bundespresse- und Informationsamt) in Bonn. She is the author of *Geistig frei und Niemandes Knecht: Paul Levi – Rosa Luxemburg* (1986). She is currently finishing a book about the emigration of Jewish women from Germany to the United States after 1933.

Uwe Reich is a research assistant for American history in the department of English and American languages and literatures at the Universität Potsdam. He has completed a dissertation on the social history of German emigrants to the United States in the nineteenth century.

Horst Rössler was a researcher with the Labor Migration Project at the Universität Bremen. He is a specialist in immigration from Britain and Germany to the United States during the nineteenth century. He is the author of *Literatur und Arbeiterbewegung: Studien zur Literaturkritik und frühen Prosa des Chartismus* (1985). With Dirk Hoerder, he has coedited *Distant Magnets: Expectations and Realities in the Immigration Experience* (1993).

Karen Schniedewind is currently a research associate at the Universität Bremen. Her interests include German emigration and re-migration in the nineteenth century. She is at work on a study of social policy in France in the nineteenth and twentieth centuries. She has published an essay in Klaus J. Bade, ed., *Deutsche im Ausland – Fremde in Deutschland* (1992). Her dissertation, "Begrenzter Aufenthalt im Land der unbegrenzten Möglichkeiten: Sozialgeschichte deutscher Rückwanderer aus den USA nach Bremen, 1850–1914," was published in 1993.

Suzanne M. Sinke is a doctoral student and instructor in the history department of the University of Minnesota. She is the coeditor, with Rudolph J. Vecoli, of *A Century of European Migrations, 1830–1930* (1991) and the author of several articles on immigrant women, including "A Historiography of Immigrant Women in the Nineteenth and Twentieth Centuries," *Ethnic Forum* 9 (1989), and "Give Us This Day: Dutch Immigrant Women in Two Protestant Denominations," *Amerikastudien* (1993).

Adam Walaszek is a professor of history in the Polonia Institute of Jagiellonian University, Cracow. In addition to numerous articles, he has published two studies of Polish emigration to and from the United States: *Reemigracja ze Stanow Zjednoczonych do Polski po I wojnie swiatowej, 1919–1924* [Return Migration from the United States to Poland after World War I] (1983) and *Polscy robotnicy, praca i zwiazki zawodowe w Stanach Zjednoczonych Ameryki, 1880–1922* [Polish Workers, Work, and the Labor Movement in the United States of America] (1988). He is currently working on a history of the children of immigrants to the United States, 1880 to 1930.

Silke Wehner recently completed a dissertation on "Deutsche Dienstmädchen in Amerika: Akkulturation junger alleinstehender Auswanderinnen von 1850 bis 1914," at the Universität Münster. She has published an essay in Monika Blaschke and Christiane Harzig, eds., *Frauen wandern aus: Deutsche Migrantinnen im 19. und 20. Jahrhundert* (1990).

Introduction

DIRK HOERDER

Germany is a country of emigration and immigration. The vast number of departures from port cities was obvious to any nineteenth-century observer. That the German states needed immigrants before the nineteenth century was also self-evident to mercantilist princes and their advisors. Accordingly, Huguenots as well as Salzburg and Bohemian Protestants were welcomed. Only in the twentieth century, or, to be more exact, from the 1880s onward, did attitudes toward in-migrants become ambivalent: Germany needed workers but did not want immigrants. Poles, Ruthenians, Italians, Belgians, and Danes were admitted only as "foreign workers." While German emigrants to Russia, southeastern Europe, North and South America, and elsewhere were proud of their contributions to and economic achievements in other lands, emigrants from other countries to Germany were treated like pariahs, required to carry "legitimizing cards," and forced to leave Germany every autumn. The situation improved after World War II, though in-migrants to Germany were never accepted in the same way as German out-migrants expected to be treated when they went abroad.

In the nineteenth century, Germany had high rates of internal migration. As a consequence, by the 1880s about one-half of the German population did not reside at its place of birth. Changes in agriculture as well as industrialization demanded migration – within a system of changing labor markets – to places where social life was not constricted by marriage regulations, remnants of feudal relations, or the absence of recreational possibilities.

Migration was one of the topics at a 1983 conference in Philadelphia organized on the occasion of the tricentennial of German immigration to the United States. Scholars specializing in the political and cultural history of Germans in America provided a survey of the state of the art.[1] Since

1 Frank Trommler and Joseph McVeigh, eds., *America and the Germans: An Assessment of a Three-Hundred-Year History,* 2 vols. (Philadelphia, 1985). The notes will, with a few exceptions, list studies

1983 scholars have advanced considerably our knowledge of migration into and out of Germany. Several large projects on German emigration have been completed, two surveys of foreign in-migration to Germany now exist, numerous specialized studies have appeared in print, and, recently, a massive analysis of all migration flows has been concluded. At the end of this volume we will review these projects and the body of work derived from them in a bibliographical essay.

This volume focuses on westward migration from Europe to North America, covers the long century from the 1820s to the 1930s, and takes a broad comparative approach. The three types of migration – in-migration, internal migration, and out-migration – are assumed to be interrelated processes. In addition, German migrants are placed in perspective with Polish, Swedish, and Irish migrations. Moreover, gender is given special emphasis. For organizational purposes, the present volume has been broken into four parts of roughly equal length.

Part I of the volume covers out-migration from Germany. The first contribution, by Walter Kamphoefner, deals with questions of method, findings, and approaches to migration history. This methodological piece is followed by three essays that explore the historical terrain of the East Elbian region of Germany. A comparative study by a Polish scholar on Polish migration patterns concludes this part.

In his essay, Kamphoefner introduces a theme that recurs in many of the later pieces, namely, the causes of migration. The three types of landholding in the German states – large estates, independent peasantry with impartible inheritance, and independent peasantry with equal division of land among inheritors – determined socioeconomic status of the different social strata in the agrarian world. This status and its changes over time help explain the propensity to migrate. The direction of migration depended on proximity to or distance from German centers of industrialization and the emerging labor markets. Whereas agents and guidebooks facilitated rather than caused emigration, personal letters played an extremely important role in promoting this process. The analysis here is mainly concerned with emigration from agricultural sectors. During the last wave of emigration, from 1878 to 1893, however, many migrants came from urban areas. Their role in the United States is analyzed in a case study by Sven Beckert as well as by other essays in Parts III and IV of the volume.

that have appeared since. Only German migrations are covered; publications on Austrians and the Swiss are thus excluded.

Most studies in this volume strongly emphasize economic factors in the motivation of potential migrants to seek their fortunes elsewhere. Yet an important but often overlooked additional factor must be considered, namely, the economic conditions in the place of origin, which provided the structural framework for migration processes. But the decision to depart remained with individuals and/or their families, each assessing the relative opportunities or total absence thereof. There was nothing deterministic about it. Similarly, on the receiving end, the analysis leads many authors to stress the importance of labor markets. Again, knowledge of markets provides only the general framework. Information from the ethnic communities abroad guided immigrants to certain segments of the labor markets. At stake was the securing of material existence in the new world, establishing a material culture, a family "economy," and a community. It is the strength of many of the essays in this collection that the economic framework is related to individual decisions, cultural factors (like religion), gender spheres, traditions of work, and governmental regulations, for example, marriage restrictions or the legal right of estate owners to punish hired hands physically.

Into the mid-1980s scholars in the Federal Republic of Germany neglected the eastern territories of various German states and, since 1871, of the German Reich, areas of considerable in-migration. A seminal essay by Klaus J. Bade and research by the scholars involved in the Chicago project on the German working class as well as the comparative project on female immigrants to Chicago provided a beginning.[2] Most of the German migrants living in the United States during the last third of the nineteenth century came from the German northeast. But until recently, Polish archives in the territories once under German domination were not open to German researchers from either East or West. The situation improved when three scholars from the universities of Rostock and Potsdam developed a research program to study migration in Mecklenburg, Brandenburg, and Pomerania in the nineteenth century (1815–1914) using sophisticated sociohistorical microstudies.

The three essays on East Elbian migration include Rainer Mühle's look at three cases of emigration from West Brandenburg and Pomerania – continental migration from the Potsdam area to Russian Poland (1817–19), from Ruppin County to Russian Poland (1817–19), and overseas migration of Old Lutherans from Uckermark and the "Oderbruch" to the United

---

2 Klaus J. Bade, "Massenwanderung und Arbeitsmarkt im deutschen Nordosten von 1880 bis zum Ersten Weltkrieg: Überseeische Auswanderung, interne Abwanderung und kontinentale Zuwanderung," *Archiv für Sozialgeschichte* 20 (1980): 265–323.

States in 1843; Axel Lubinski's study of Mecklenburg-Strelitz with its 80,000 inhabitants in 1871 and the emigration of 16,000 people between 1846 and 1914; and Uwe Reich's exploration of continental and overseas migration from East Brandenburg from 1818 to the 1850s. All three studies succeed in presenting references to the complex migration history of these territories. In-migration followed the devastation of the Thirty Years' War (1618–48) and later military conflicts. Swiss colonists and French Huguenots were attracted by settlement subsidies and by privileges for their religious practices. Bohemian dissenters and Salzburg Protestants also came.[3] Out-migration was short-distance, from Mecklenburg to Prussia, medium-distance into Russian Poland – and, in some cases, in secondary long-distance eastward movements to the South Russian plains – or long-distance, intercontinental emigration to Australia and the Americas. There was return migration from Russian Poland and, from the 1890s onward, in-migration of seasonal Polish workers.

In the nineteenth century, war-related underpopulation in the Germanies was replaced by relative overpopulation. The demographic developments, particularly the high rates of reproduction, complicated the transition from feudal and communal arrangements to capitalist agriculture. Commons were divided, and work for rural laborers became more seasonal. Interference of the large landowners and the state in private lives of servants and laborers (*Gesinde*), however, continued. Men and women were subject to corporal punishment by their employers; to marry they had to get permission from the authorities. While the old order remained dominant in social relations, the economic sphere changed under the influence of new forces. Competition with the United States and Russia in the production of grain began to influence the possibilities for earning a living. Decisions about the importation of cloth made in Moscow or elsewhere influenced the amount of food a weaver in an East Elbian village could bring to his family's table. In addition, the revocation of religious privileges granted to colonists who left their culture of origin led to discontent. But these migrants knew that their capability to pay taxes and thus support state interests was sought after. They petitioned the authorities for redress, announcing their intention to migrate further if no improvement in their living conditions was achieved through governmental action. Migration was therefore conceived as a means of escape from oppressive spiritual conditions, constriction of social

3 Stefi Jersch-Wenzel, *Juden und "Franzosen" in der Wirtschaft des Raumes Berlin-Brandenburg zur Zeit des Merkantilismus* (Berlin, 1978); Frédéric Hartweg and Stefi Jersch-Wenzel, eds., *Die Hugenotten und das Refuge: Deutschland und Europa* (Berlin, 1990); *Das Böhmische Dorf in Berlin-Neukölln, 1737–1987: Dem Kelch zuliebe Exulant* (Berlin, 1987).

life, generalized exploitation, and the reality of larger economic cycles. The scholarly debate over the question whether migration is flight as well as militancy – conducted with reference to South Italian peasants – need not be continued for East Elbia.[4] Migration was part of a process of bargaining over the allocation of resources and the resistance to unacceptable conditions imposed either by demographic and economic developments or by political and social systems, as the villagers' petitions show.

To a large extent, the decision to migrate depended on the economic position within the communities. In particular, persons dependent both on wages and on small garden plots were among those who left. They no longer had a place in agriculture that permitted a regular and sufficient income from land as agricultural laborers. It was not always clear whether wages were needed to supplement income from agriculture or whether small plots helped laborers survive on below-subsistence wages. In the first half of the century from 1815 to 1914 much of the migration was family migration; later individual migration dominated. But since the "individuals" were parts of family migration chains, both as regards stem family and family of procreation (marriage migration), this was in fact part of a sequential family migration. These case studies of out-migration from East Elbian areas show the complexity of local social and economic conditions, the impact of international economic down- or upswings, and the range of destinations from which potential migrants selected the one that best suited their aspirations.

Adam Walaszek's analysis of the impact of migration on the Polish economy takes into account the consequences of emigration for the society of origin. Was emigration beneficial or detrimental to the villages and regions in the Polish territories? Given the enormous output of Polish migration research in the last two decades,[5] Walaszek uses microstudies on Ropczyce County and the parish of Zaborow, both in Galicia, in order to achieve an evaluation of, first, the changes in Polish society that led to out-migration, whether temporary or permanent, and, second, the changes that these mass migrations produced. While larger capital flows and investments influenced the overall economic development in the Polish territories, the small flows of emigrant remittances changed living conditions on the local level. Again,

---

4 Donna R. Gabaccia, *Militants and Migrants: Rural Sicilians Become American Workers* (New Brunswick, N.J., 1988).
5 For further information, see the worldwide surveys by Celina Bobinska and Andrej Pilch, eds., *Employment-Seeking Emigrations of the Poles Worldwide in the 19th and 20th Centuries* (Cracow, 1975), and Ewa Morawska, "Labor Migrations of Poles in the Atlantic World Economy, 1880–1914," *Comparative Studies in Society and History* 31 (1989): 237–72.

migration was also part of resistance movements. Return migrants no longer showed the deference expected of them by priests or (land)lords. Women realized that they had options other than working in subservient positions on the family farm. Communities extended over continents. This localism, so well researched for Italian migrants, led a Polish journalist to comment on a Cleveland Polish neighborhood: "This is not America! It's Tarnów!" It also led Jews in the Russian Pale of Settlement to greet each other with "Next year in America!" rather than "Next year in Jerusalem!" However, even the mass migrations of Poles worldwide, brilliantly analyzed by Ewa Morawska, wrought only limited changes in the society they left. Return migrants could not influence larger social structures, and often were content with visible consumption. Only the much larger rural-to-urban migration of the post–World War II years profoundly changed the countryside.[6]

In the second part of the volume, four authors look at internal migration in Germany and the demand for labor that had to be externally met. In fact, the traditional artisanal migrations were internal to a central European German-language craft and town culture, extending beyond areas settled exclusively by Germans. Subsequently, as Horst Rössler shows, such migrations were continued by skilled workers. The growth of urban areas and the formation of company towns in the settling of the rapidly changing agricultural areas are the subject of the studies by James Jackson and Susanne Meyer. Karl Barfuss's study of the in-migration of Polish and Ruthenian workers to Bremen and its surroundings from 1884 to 1914 concludes this section and posits the existence of ethnic substratification in a native-born labor force.

From the artisanal migrations of earlier centuries, in the nineteenth century the tradition of taking to the road was transferred to workers, their organizations, and trade unions. Migration was undertaken before "strikes" were widely practiced and before trade organizations had been established. Aims varied: to spread ideas of solidarity, to exert a (limited) control over labor markets, to resist exploitative employer demands, and to ease the strain on strike funds. Workers' migrations indicated resistance to poor working conditions and low wage levels. Collective withdrawal of parts of the labor force was a means of struggle. Thus, as Horst Rössler argues, travel aid was more important than other aid features of organized labor. Regional disparities could be eased in this way. But when disparities appeared elsewhere,

---

6 Dirk Hoerder, "Labour Migrants' Views of 'America,' " *Renaissance and Modern Studies* 35 (1992): 1–17; essay by Mary Cygan in Dirk Hoerder et al., eds., *Roots of the Transplanted* (New York, 1994).

the migrants had no sensible destination – in periods of general recession or structural crisis, migration could not alleviate unemployment or under-employment. Furthermore, by bringing in migrant workers to undercut labor's demands, employers could turn migration to their advantage. Röss-ler's case study of Germany is supported by research in trade union-assisted emigration from England and Scotland. His emphasis on the differences of behavior and strike strategies between single, mobile and married, and set-tled workers is supported by a study of labor militancy in Marseilles.[7] In the 1850s migration still could be used as a form of resistance; by 1900 it was more a program of keeping the surplus labor on the move.

Although better labor markets were the primary destination for migrants in search of support for themselves and their families, the visible physical setting and associated urban concentrations have received more attention from historians. These were, of course, shaped not only by migration but also by investment and natural resources or transport facilities. Duisburg, at the confluence of the Rhine and Ruhr Rivers, provides the setting for James H. Jackson, Jr.'s study of gross and net migration flows in preindustrial and industrial eras. Economic cycles, new realities in the farm economy of the surrounding countryside, and the coming of heavy industry established the framework. But religion, family status, and gender determined migration rates and, in conjunction with family relations and personality factors, de-termined who migrated, who stayed, and who migrated repeatedly. With unusually rich sources, the author illustrates the high mobility of people in preindustrial times as well as the local roots of the majority of the migrants in a circle of 150 kilometers in the 1860s and – with a slight increase of average distance per migrant from 105 to 118 kilometers – in 1890. But in later years, the "locals" could no longer meet the demands of the labor markets. By 1910 foreigners accounted for one out of every ten Duisbur-gers. In addition, this local migration was – for some people – one of several stages in the process of international migration.

While Duisburg was about to celebrate its four hundredth anniversary, planners in Hanover decided to add a town to a recently established mine and smeltery. Georgsmarienhütte, about 120 kilometers north of Duisburg, was established in 1860 and within a decade grew to 1,600 inhabitants. Susanne Meyer studies this industrial island surrounded by an agrarian

---

7 John H. M. Laslett, *Nature's Noblemen: The Fortunes of the Independent Collier in Scotland and the American Midwest, 1855–1889* (Los Angeles, 1983); William H. Sewell, Jr., "Natives and Migrants: The Work-ing Class of Revolutionary Marseilles, 1848–1851," in Dirk Hoerder, ed., *Labor Migration in the Atlantic Economies: The European and North American Working Classes during the Period of Industrialization* (Westport, Conn., 1985), 225–52.

ocean. Skilled miners and foundry workers were needed as were large numbers of unskilled and semiskilled construction workers. Just as for East Elbia, Poland, and the Duisburg area, a detailed analysis of social structure and changing patterns of production explains which socioeconomic groups were prone to leave home for industrial workplaces. Almost 70 percent came from below-subsistence plots and ranked socially below independent peasants. This new industrial center provided an alternative to overseas migration. In fact, the geographical distance of rural work from industrial work was so short that flight from agriculture did not necessarily involve migration but might have required simply a daily commute. Skilled workers had to be imported over medium distances from the mines in the Harz Mountains. These, however, were hard-rock miners and reluctant to change to coal. Consequently, the factory had to begin to train local men. One result of this development was the feminization of agriculture. The tiny plots were worked by wives, children, and sometimes by hired boys and girls. Another result was the increasing monetarization of economic relations through an influx of cash from wages. These changes did not imply higher standards of living; industrial workers were as bad off as agricultural laborers and smallholders. Thus, many workers continued to debate the opportunities provided by overseas migration.

Where wages were low and working conditions extremely poor, employers were unable to attract labor from either the lowest strata of the immediately surrounding regions or from areas farther away. They then started recruitment in areas where industry offered even less and could not absorb the surplus agrarian labor. Foreign workers from the East were brought in: Poles from the territories incorporated into the German Reich during the eighteenth and nineteenth centuries; Poles, Russians, and Ruthenians from the Russian Empire; and Croats from Austria-Hungary.

Using textile factories in and around Bremen for a case study, Karl Marten Barfuss analyzes the reaction of trade unions as well as national and local governments to migration driven by industrialization. This inmigration created a conflict for the internationally minded German labor organizations concerned as well as for their immediate constituencies. It also created problems in the relations between private enterprise and governments. On the one hand, employers typically wanted a stable labor force; the government, on the other hand, resented colonies of foreign workers on German soil and demanded a constantly changing labor force. The responses of local governments varied widely: In some places, Ruthenians or others replaced Polish workers; in some, toleration of Polish workers was stressed; in others, paternalistic measures were taken toward foreign labor, especially with regard to housing. But the general lot of these "foreign workers" was difficult and in wartime it deteriorated to the point where they became forced labor. Beginning in the 1880s, the in-migration from the East initiated a tradition of importing labor that continued for nearly a century. By the early 1970s, however, Germany had switched its reservoir of labor to the Mediterranean basin. Thus, the rotation of the labor force was and remained at the core of governmental policies.

After about eighty years of emigration, 1815–93, the German Reich joined the ranks of labor-importing countries in western Europe: England, France, and Switzerland. While England drew workers from its Irish colony, and France and Switzerland relied on surrounding countries and especially Italy, Germany tapped not only the Italian worker reservoir but also recruited far into the east and southeast. Europe was now divided into a labor-importing core and a labor-exporting periphery. In the German case, foreign workers became forced labor during the two world wars.[8]

The authors represented in Part III focus on questions of gender in the emigration from Germany and other European countries. This subject requires special care since it is not always possible statistically to account for gender differences. Women were, of course, part and parcel of all family migrations. In some cases, such as Duisburg, it was even possible to learn their marital status. Until the 1930s, women emigrants were in the minority; since that time, however, the pattern of migration to North America shows a slight preponderance of women over men. Nonetheless, even before the mid-twentieth century women accounted for approximately two-fifths of all migration to North America. Furthermore, they also had a considerably lower return rate than men.

At the start of most labor migrations more males than females left or were permitted to leave. As a consequence, sex ratios became unbalanced in the society of origin and in the receiving society. Accordingly, those looking for jobs in international labor markets had to turn to international marriage markets when looking for potential partners. Since much of the communication was by mail, the term "mail-order brides" was sometimes used, either with emphasis on personal letters (Europe) or on pictures (Asia). Eligible women were sent by the shipload to the early English colonies and to French Quebec; later on they were exported for specific groups. What might seem a crude way of finding a partner to the modern observer, be-

8 See the references to the work by Lothar Elsner, Ulrich Herbert, and Joachim Lehmann in the bibliographic essay.

lieving in romantic coupling and conveniently overlooking high divorce rates, was common practice a century ago.

The situational variants that Suzanne M. Sinke analyzes in her essay are neatly summarized in the autobiography of an Italian woman who traveled to the United States in order to join her husband. She left their only child behind with her mother. On the ship she met another woman, accompanied by all of her children, who was also en route to join her husband and thereby reunite the family. A third woman sailed toward a prospective husband she had never met, while a fourth was going to meet a man she had last seen seven years before.[9] Because women had less access to money, that is, to travel funds, or were not permitted to leave on their own initiative, marriage became a way for these women to enter the flow of migration. Both sides of these equations considered their respective advantages and self-interests. When faced with scarce resources, earlier migrants were willing to invest in prepaid tickets to tap the home reservoir of potential partners.

A second reason women migrated was to find work. In keeping with socially ascribed roles, one of the most important workplaces was the home. Immigrant women worked in the growing field of paid domestic service. While native-born North American women were said to shun live-in domestic service because of the constraints on their private lives, for immigrant women domestic work held several advantages. They either used skills they already possessed or improved their "domestic skills"; they achieved control over their income and could start a family without having to rely on a dowry provided by parents; they received an introduction to new life-styles and to a new language; they came into a working life that implied dependence but to a lesser extent than in Europe. As servants or as spinsters in the households of relatives, domestics in Europe worked long hours and were "on call" for the rest of the twenty-four hours. They had no free weekends or afternoons, made do with low wages, and had to remain submissive in their attitude. Given that in North America no expenses for food had to be incurred and that clothing often consisted of their mistresses' discarded dresses, the income–expenditure balance was considerably better than the wage level suggests. Furthermore, given that there was an abundance of jobs, domestic servants achieved a measure of self-determination by leaving or threatening to leave employers who insisted on too much control.

As Joy Lintelman shows in her essay, Swedish, German, and other immigrant women in domestic service combined strategies for a remunerative

9 Marie Hall Ets, *Rosa: The Life of an Italian Immigrant* (Minneapolis, 1970), 162–71.

working life and a satisfactory private life. They were thus able to move between the labor and marriage markets. This observation applies equally to female migrants of the turn of the century as much as to those of the 1980s. Silke Wehner concentrates on single working women. Just as artisans in European villages became the harbingers of urban life-styles, so domestics in America translated the life-styles of native-born middle classes to the immigrant working population.

Until the establishment of women's studies as part of the university curriculum, the study of labor history, with its emphasis on union formation, class consciousness, and male working-class culture, has generally overlooked domestic service. Research on immigrant women shows the importance of domestic service in the house of labor. Most of the tasks combined here – cooking, child care, sewing – were skilled in the general sense of the term; other tasks required some skill, for example, laundry work, whereas some jobs, such as cleaning, required no skill. Arranging for the best position available, via labor agents or informal networks, combined with the freedom to quit and the right to bargain for better wages or working conditions, provided experience in the democratization of work relationships. Finally, the double change in economic status – out of the dowry system in which parents had to invest to get their daughters into the marriage market and into a wage system that permitted young women to develop (modestly) independent economic life courses – shows the degree of change that these women experienced.

The extensive changes that migration engendered is also the subject of a comparative research project, coordinated by Christiane Harzig, on women from German, Irish, Swedish, and Polish backgrounds in turn-of-the-century Chicago. The women were studied first in the culture of origin, that is, in the regions from which migration to Chicago occurred, and then they were studied in various Chicago neighborhoods. The American urban industrial environment brought about a homogenization as well as the loss of rural material culture that might surprise those who argue for the persistence of strong cultural ties. But developments in labor market behavior and changes in marriage patterns present differences from ethnic group to ethnic group.

Migration permitted rational choices between marriage and economic independence, as Deirdre Mageean points out in her summary of some of the major project results. But, on the level of emotions and social practices, many prospective marriage partners wanted little change. Almost half of the women from Zaborow, Poland, married men from the same parish of origin. If rural material culture itself could not be transplanted, persons of similar socialization were sought out. The separation from the land and from the agrarian pattern of inheritance and family formation permitted migrants to marry younger and – except for Swedish men and women – they did. The Old World status of married women was still a desirable goal in the new societal context. Younger women spent the years between migration and marriage in wage work and after marriage often supplemented the income of their husbands by taking in work or lodgers. Single women, in contrast, could choose from a range of employment opportunities, yet they mostly gravitated to domestic service.

Many of these women contributed to the development of a public sphere in their new surroundings, which was often considered to be the sole domain of men. Churches, schools, orphanages, hospitals, and old people's homes were either organized or supported by women. Women also established recreational, educational, and intellectual organizations. Thus, they helped shape the community as well as their own lives in a way they never could have done in their villages of origin. Even if men dominated most formal organizations, women played a much larger role than often assumed and did so consciously, redefining as they went the boundaries of what was considered their sphere.

The essays in Part IV explore some of the ways in which women and men experienced their settling into a new society differently. Acculturation in the United States or elsewhere or return to Germany occurred after a long process of coming to terms with the new society. This is reflected in the ethnic press, in labor organizations, in the churches, or in the choice to return to the home country. In cases where return was not possible, or the hope for it proved illusionary, as in the case of Jews from Germany in the 1930s and 1940s, the process of acculturation became obligatory.

In the context of increasing attention paid by the English-language press to women and parallel to the emergence of a Jewish and Finnish American women's press, Monika Blaschke analyzes the role played by the German American women's press. The papers were established to create income for publishers and to introduce women to the merchandise of a paper's advertisers. But female journalists were able to fashion lives of their own and these papers fared best when they addressed women's interests on a grassroots level. The press also reached out to women in rural areas. To rural and urban women two models were presented: a traditional one concerned mainly with family life and a modern one that assigned women a place in the public sphere, whether in politics in general or in working-class struggles in particular. As a result, a debate emerged over whether gender or class issues should take precedence. Women took the space allotted to them in socialist papers under their own direction rather than echoing male views. Finnish women in particular assumed a radical stance. But more important than larger class issues or distant goals were the small issues of daily life, which had an immediate impact on women and their families. Letters, advice columns, and readers reporting on social events not only transformed the female readership into part of the process but also helped the papers survive commercially. Because of this interaction the women's press is an invaluable source for observing the changing roles and outlooks of immigrant women.

Whereas the ethnic press addressed those who remained and functioned within stable ethnic communities, a segment of the German migrants chose to return. Karen Schniedewind's pioneering research on return migration is based on city directories and citizenship files. Using these sources, Schniedewind traces the migration of merchant sons and clerks who wished to acquire business connections and training in a foreign environment. But success was certain only for those who, on both ends of out-migration and return, ended up in established family firms or partner firms. For artisans and workers, who generally lacked these contacts and connections, social and economic advance was rare. As in earlier journeymen migrations, artisans increased their qualifications while abroad and after their return some achieved a rise to master artisan and a few established their own small businesses. For most, however, the stay in North America permitted them to earn a living for a few years but did not improve their status. The same has been found to be true for Swedes and South Italians. Even among those who returned with modest savings, with new ideas, or with new qualifications, these gains were neither consciously applied in nor sought by the society of origin.

The migration of Bremen merchants to corresponding firms in the United States had its parallel in the migration of skilled workers to German-owned and managed enterprises there. In his essay, Sven Beckert shows how from the 1880s onward German skilled workers in Passaic, New Jersey, held advantageous positions as foremen or supervisors. Most of the unskilled or semiskilled workers, approximately 23,000 in 1910, came from southern and eastern Europe. In that year, 2,100 Germans were registered in Passaic. Many had migrated among various textile mills within Europe before moving on to Passaic, often solicited directly by the managers of one of the German-owned firms. They were considerably better off than the workers they supervised. Whereas on the average Polish, Ruthenian, and Slovak workers earned $400 a year, German workers, foremen, and managers

annually earned $800 (1909 figures). Women workers earned considerably
less. Neighborhoods and ethnic organizations were divided by class but
German millowners and managers controlled the ethnic community. As a
result of this advantageous position, no class-based solidarity with other
workers evolved during strikes or organization drives.

In 1919, however, employers decided to lay off the skilled workers who
only then flocked to the union where they were accepted as members. In
1926 workers of many ethnic backgrounds joined in a year-long strike. In
this case, class solidarity triumphed over ethnic loyalties. The study of
German workers, initiated by the Chicago Project, is only now beginning
to take shape. Moreover, the imbalance in the study of rural and urban
German immigrants still stands in need of correction.

Migration implied a change in status and gender roles. Perhaps nowhere
was this change as great as among German Jewish refugees from Nazi Germany. An educated middle-class group, active mainly in trade and commerce with the traditional view of women's role in the family, it was jolted
by the Nazi ascent to power. Suddenly, men had no jobs and women had
to search for employment. Flight from National Socialist Germany was
often belated. The men of this well-integrated group in particular could
not imagine or even accept clear signs that mistreatment awaited them in
these years. In the United States, the role reversal for women proceeded
even further. Women found jobs more easily than men and, for the sake
of their family, seemed to have accepted the inevitable with greater ease.
However, many of them considered the changes only temporary. Men
witnessed the changes but were slow to react. Taking responsibilities in the
household was done – if at all – hesitatingly and reluctantly. As their exile
grew longer, some men regained their social status. But as Sibylle Quack
argues, women retained their new self-confidence and some also remained
in careers outside the home.

Collectively, these essays dispel the notion that migration in the context of
the Germanies consisted merely of the journeymen's *tour d'Europe* and, later,
of large-scale, one-way emigration. Even these two forms are no longer
part of living, public memory. Emigration from Sweden, much of which
occurred parallel to emigration from Germany, is considered part of that
nation's heritage as expressed in museums, novels, and films. One finds in
the German case, in contrast, almost a conspiracy of silence. Why do people
forget about this aspect of their past? Why do current cases of migration fail
to activate memories? These questions cannot be answered here, but, in his

concluding survey, Klaus J. Bade summarizes most of the in- and out-migration from the German territories over the past three centuries.

When immigration to British and French North America began in the first half of the seventeenth century, Germany was embroiled in the Thirty Years' War, 1618–48, and thus the Germans could not participate in this movement across the Atlantic. That war killed large numbers of Germans directly, while others succumbed to hunger and disease. Whole areas had to be repopulated by in-migration. Religious schism provided the reason for Huguenots, Salzburgers, Bohemians, and others to migrate to Germany in the late seventeenth and eighteenth centuries. In these centuries, then, Germany was – if on a comparatively small scale – an immigration country. These religious refugees became much sought-after immigrants. Their skills, capital, and economic potential were needed in the budding mercantilist economies. But toward the end of the eighteenth century, overpopulation, particularly in the German Southwest with its divisible inheritance, began to take its toll. As a result, emigration, mainly to the east, commenced among the peasantry. The period from 1815 to 1893 was characterized by the gross out-migration of about five million men, women, and children.

With unification and industrial takeoff after 1871, wages remained low and workers continued to leave. To fill the demands of the labor market, workers from eastern Europe and in smaller numbers from Denmark and Belgium were recruited or came of their own volition. Half a million were counted in Germany in 1914 and to these a similar number of Poles and Mazurians in the Ruhr District who had German citizenship have to be reckoned. Among other reasons, the two world wars were conducted by the Second and Third Reichs to secure a supply of cheap and docile labor, namely, forced labor from eastern Europe. During both wars, forced labor was extracted from the occupied territories. The aftermath of the wars forced the migration of millions of Germans and other peoples, as borders and populations were shifted. But only ten years later, those relocated to West Germany no longer provided a sufficient labor supply. Then, Germany began the recruitment of the so-called "guest workers" from southern Europe and Turkey.

The German people experienced as much – or perhaps more – migration than most other people in the North Atlantic economies. However, it never was accepted as a way of life, nor was an equality of cultures part of German thinking. Germans exported their assumedly sophisticated culture and considered in-migrants as coming from a lower cultural level, people who had to be segregated from the main population. Germans assumed that they would be welcomed wherever they went but they rarely welcomed those who came to them. Down to the present day, the history of German in- and out-migration is full of such contradictions.

Contemporary figures tell part of the story: 4.5 million "guest worker" immigrants to Germany, their German-born children and grandchildren remain foreigners; 3 million ethnic Germans from eastern Europe, many of whom no longer speak German, are entitled to immediate citizenship; between 100,000 and half a million people from Third World countries apply for asylum each year. Still, the German government reiterates that Germany is not an immigration country. Part of the population supports this stance. It remains a fascinating question why some nations accept ethnic pluralism and multiculturalism as part of their heritage, while other nations – with almost as many shifts in population and with histories of in- as well as out-migration – continue to resist the very idea.

Continuity and Complexity: Migrations from East Elbian Germany and Galician Poland

1

German Emigration Research, North, South, and East: Findings, Methods, and Open Questions

WALTER D. KAMPHOEFNER

Germany, like Caesar's Gaul, *est omnia divisa in partes tres,* as far as agricultural history is concerned. The areas of *Gutsherrschaft* east of the Elbe, dominated by great estates, contrast in important ways with the areas of *Grundherrschaft* in the west, with their more independent peasantry. These in turn are roughly divided between areas of impartible inheritance (*Anerbenrecht*) and of equal division among heirs (*Realteilung*) north and south of the Main, respectively. Obviously these are oversimplifications, but they help us to recognize commonalities in socioeconomic and particularly agrarian patterns that form the background for nineteenth-century emigration.

The heavy emigration from southwest Germany has usually been seen as a result of its custom of partible inheritance, which gradually led to splintering of holdings too small to be economically viable. Although this view is not entirely wrong, it is misleading unless further qualified. Partible inheritance was neither a necessary nor a sufficient condition for heavy emigration. Some areas of northwest Germany with systems of impartible inheritance had emigration rates rivaling those anywhere in the German Southwest. Moreover, areas with partible inheritance had emigration rates ranging from the highest to among the lowest throughout Germany.

Statistics gathered in 1895 for all counties (*Kreise*) in the German Empire show that among the areas with the highest proportion of "dwarf agriculture" (holdings under two hectares), three of the first five and six of the first twenty were indeed in Württemberg. But those in first and third place, Zellerfeld in the Harz and Siegen in southern Westphalia, both traditional centers of mining and metalworking, had rather low emigration rates. Moreover, among the six Württemberg counties, none was in the top quintile of net out-migration for the period 1813–67, and four were at or below the Württemberg average. And they showed similar trends for the period 1856–95. Five of the six lay within a thirty-kilometer radius of Stuttgart, and no doubt reflect the combination of part-time agriculture with industrial employment, a more modern version of the "handwerkende Bauern und verbauerte Handwerker" whom Wilhelm Heinrich Riehl observed back in the 1850s. These patterns reflect less the mechanistic operation of inheritance systems than the influence of specific local economic factors on both population density and migration patterns.[1]

In fact, all three regions of Germany show a wide range of migration behavior independent of inheritance systems (see Table 1.1). Varying quality of record keeping over time and place makes it difficult to obtain reliable direct measures of emigration. Instead, Table 1.1 shows net migration balances (the difference between the expected population growth between censuses based on the balance between births and deaths and the actual change) for districts in various regions of Germany.[2] While the southwest German areas of the Palatinate and the Schwarzwald as well as the Jagst districts of Württemberg suffered the heaviest exodus, next in line, far surpassing the other two districts of Württemberg, was the Minden District in the Northwest, an area of impartible inheritance. And after 1840, in fact, Minden moves up to third place. Moreover, the adjacent Osnabrück District probably suffered even heavier losses. Even if one overlooks the distorting population gains before 1840, Trier, the district with the heaviest losses in Rhineland Prussia, falls far behind Minden.

One of the most important factors affecting population density and emigration in the Northwest, and one that deserves greater attention for other regions of Germany as well, was the rise and subsequent demise of cottage textile production and other forms of rural industry. In the Minden and Osnabrück areas, the decline of the handloom linen industry was the prime factor in precipitating the mass exodus of the 1840s and 1850s. It undoubtedly played an important role in the Schwarzwald region of Württemberg and other areas of southwest Germany as well.[3]

---

1 Hans Lang, *Die Entwicklung der Bevölkerung in Württemberg* (Tübingen, 1903), 19; Wolfgang von Hippel, *Auswanderung aus Südwestdeutschland: Studien zur württembergischen Auswanderung und Auswanderungspolitik im 18. und 19. Jahrhundert* (Stuttgart, 1984), 202–3, 278.

2 Sources for Table 1.1: for the Palatinate, see Hippel, *Auswanderung aus Südwestdeutschland,* 144; post-1871 figures calculated from *Beiträge zur Statistik des Königreichs Bayern* 69 (1912): 52, 262; for Württemberg, calculated from Hippel, *Auswanderung aus Südwestdeutschland,* 172; *Württembergisches Jahrbuch* (1900): 2:61–67, 3:3–7; for Prussia, calculated from Alexis von Markow, *Entwicklung der Aus- und Einwanderung, Ab- und Zuzüge in Preussen* (Tübingen, 1889), 212–17. Quite similar results were obtained by an entirely different calculating method. See Walter Kamphoefner, *The Westfalians: From Germany to Missouri* (Princeton, N.J., 1987), appendix C. At most there were two or three other southwest German districts that may have had higher emigration rates than Minden. Baden as a whole had slightly lower rates than Württemberg, and Hesse-Darmstadt surpassed it only after 1865. Cf. Hippel, *Auswanderung aus Südwestdeutschland,* 144; Klaus-Jürgen Matz, *Pauperismus und Bevölkerung: Die gesetzlichen Ehebeschränkungen in den Süddeutschen Staaten während des 19. Jahrhunderts* (Stuttgart, 1980), 153–57.

3 The most sophisticated treatment of demographic and economic interrelationships is found in Peter

Table 1.1. *Net annual migration per 1,000 inhabitants by district*

	'34 – '37	– '40	– '43	– '46	– '49	– '52	– '55	– '58	– '61	– '64	– '67	– '71	– '75	– '80	– '85	Sum
Pfalz	−7	−6	−5	−9	−8	−16	−19	−6	−5	−4	−12	−14	−6	−5	−9	−131
Neckar	−1	−4	−3	+1	−9	−7	−18	−1	−4	−1	−4	+1	−3	−3	−7	−63
Schwarzwald	−4	−6	−3	−7	−5	−17	−19	−1	−7	−8	−4	−10	−9	−5	−10	−115
Jagst	−1	−4	0	−4	−4	−14	−10	−5	−3	−5	−9	−7	−8	−4	−11	−100
Donau	+5	0	−4	+3	−1	−6	−10	−2	−2	−2	−2	−2	−4	−1	−6	−34
Trier	+29	+3	−3	−5	−3	−3	−9	0	−1	−2	−5	−3	−5	−4	−7	−18
Minden	−4	+6	−3	−4	−7	−6	−15	−12	−5	−3	−13	−11	−7	−4	−7	−95
Münster	0	−1	−1	−3	−4	−1	−2	−3	−4	−5	−8	−6	−3	+2	−1	−40
Arnsberg	+1	+5	0	−1	−1	+1	+4	+10	0	+5	+9	+11	+15	−3	+4	+60
Düsseldorf	+5	+7	+4	+3	−3	+5	+6	+6	+1	+6	+6	+6	+8	+3	+4	+67
Stadt Berlin	+20	+27	+42	+47	+7	−14	+19	+9	+46	+44	+33	+42	+33	+19	+24	+398
Oppeln	+6	+27	−2	+2	−4	0	−2	+6	−1	−1	−2	−2	−3	−6	−5	+13
Erfurt	+11	+1	0	−4	−5	−7	−6	−8	−4	−6	−13	−10	−4	−6	−8	−69
Coeslin	+4	+10	−1	0	−2	−2	−2	−3	−5	−6	−9	−13	−16	−7	−20	−72
Stettin	+1	+6	+1	+3	+1	0	−3	−5	−3	−5	−10	−12	−8	−4	−15	−53
Stralsund	+2	+11	−4	0	0	0	−3	−3	−3	−5	−11	−18	−12	−6	−16	−68
Danzig	+6	+9	+5	+4	−5	−5	+2	+4	+1	+4	0	−4	−7	−5	−11	−2
Marienweder	+4	+23	+1	+3	−3	+4	−3	+1	−2	0	−5	−6	−12	−8	−17	−20
Königsberg	+6	+15	0	0	−3	+4	0	+3	0	+1	0	−2	−7	−3	−9	+5
Gumbinnen	+2	+13	+3	−1	−8	+3	−2	+3	−2	+1	−4	−5	−8	−4	−9	−18

By contrast, the areas with the lowest rates of emigration in Germany were those where modern, mechanized industry developed (sometimes but not necessarily on the foundations of cottage industry). By 1860, population losses slowed considerably in the Neckar District of Württemberg (including the city of Stuttgart) as modern industrialization got underway. The Ruhr industrial districts of Arnsberg and Düsseldorf showed minor population outflows in only a couple of crisis periods, and the single loss sustained by Berlin occurred in the cholera years around 1850. The transition from cottage industry to more mechanized forms of production was not without temporary setbacks in Silesian Oppeln, but it was successful enough to keep population losses low. Other eastern industrial areas such as the rest of Silesia and also Saxony had quite low emigration rates throughout the era under consideration.[4]

The more rural areas of East Elbia also varied considerably in their migration behavior. Through 1840, all areas show migration gains probably resulting from the positive effects of agricultural reforms. The period from 1840 to 1864 is characterized overall by stagnation, or more precisely by minor gains and losses alternating across time and place. Erfurt, an area of declining cottage industry, shows greater similarity to Minden than to other East Elbian districts in its migration pattern – in fact it had the highest losses in the region between 1843 and 1867. Only after 1864 did East Elbian population losses exceed 1 percent annually, a level that can be equated with mass migration. One can also see the eastward spread of "migration fever" in the region, affecting first Pomerania, then West Prussia, and only belatedly East Prussia.

One factor needing further investigation is the concentration of landholdings in the hands of great estate owners, whether from the nobility or the bourgeoisie. It is probably not coincidental that the heaviest emigration rates in the east were from areas such as Pomerania and Mecklenburg where property concentration was greatest. It was not that peasant agriculture was unable to compete – the largest estates showed the heaviest levels of indebtedness per acre. Rather, the old semifeudal elite was propped up by the state, which showed full sympathy for the complaint of one such owner: "Our estates would become a kind of hell for us if our neighbors were

Kriedte, Hans Medick, and Jürgen Schlumbohm, *Industrialization before Industrialization: Rural Industry in the Genesis of Capitalism* (Cambridge, 1981); see also Hans Pohl, ed., *Gewerbe- und Industrieland-schaften vom Spätmittelalter bis ins 20. Jahrhundert* (Wiesbaden, 1986), esp. the chapter by Elizabeth Harder-Gersdorff, "Leinen-Regionen im Vorfeld und im Verlauf der Industrialisierung (1780–1914)," 203–53.

4 See Harder-Gersdorff, "Leinen-Regionen," 216–28; Kamphoefner, *The Westfalians*, 208.

independent peasant proprietors." The Prussian bureaucracy in the east was largely recruited from such circles, and Prussian law greatly hindered or in some cases forbade the subdividing of estates.[5] The end result was that peasant proprietors and the rural lower classes were left to compete for the small amount of remaining agricultural land. Just how this interacted with emigration patterns has, however, yet to be worked out in detail.[6]

Another development that deserves closer attention in its relation to emigration is the agrarian reforms commonly known as the *Bauernbefreiung*. One obvious way in which they promoted emigration was by helping to make land just another freely disposable commodity that could be turned into cash at any time in order to finance the journey. More important, however, were the structural changes within the rural population precipitated by these reforms, particularly by the division of common lands. This issue has received greater attention east of the Elbe (particularly from East German historians) than it has in the west. In Northwest Germany the division of common lands (*Gemeinheitsteilung*) was often mentioned as a factor in emigration by the *Heuerling* (tenant cottager) class. This is not to say that they clung to a precapitalistic, communal ethos that was being undermined by such new developments. Instead, what they opposed was the way the reforms were carried out. In the Northwest, division was usually carried out according to the biblical principle: "To him that hath shall be given; to him that hath not shall be taken away even that which he hath." Grazing a cow on the common pasture, gathering wood, or cutting peat for heating and gathering leaf mulch for livestock bedding and fertilizer were customary privileges but not legal rights for *Heuerleute* (tenant cottagers), and were usually disregarded in the process of division. Contemporary descriptions echo a standard refrain: "The *Heuerleute* went away empty-handed."[7]

In contrast to the bimodal social structure – relatively prosperous peasant proprietors and propertyless tenants – in northwest Germany, in regions of partible inheritance in the Southwest there was a much broader range of property holding. Nevertheless, in view of the degree to which village self-administration was dominated by the peasant elite, it would appear that the division of the commons followed similar patterns as in the Northwest.[8] In

5 Hans-Jürgen Puhle, *Politische Agrarbewegung in kapitalistischen Industriegesellschaften: Deutschland, USA und Frankreich im 20. Jahrhundert* (Göttingen, 1975), 42–47.
6 Axel Lubinski's essay in this volume marks an important beginning.
7 Little attention has been given the division of common lands, but one of the few modern studies, focusing on eastern Westphalia, found that the prime beneficiaries were peasant proprietors, the biggest losers the *Heuerleute*. Stefan Brakensick, "Markenteilung in Ravensberg 1770 bis 1850," *Westfälische Forschungen* (1990): 45–85.
8 Cathleen S. Catt, "Farmers and Factory Workers: Rural Society in Imperial Germany: The Example

fact, even in areas where the commons remained undivided, there was a tendency to restrict the access of the rural lower classes, resulting in polarization despite a surface impression of traditional continuity.[9] Similarly, recent research on East Elbia has somewhat downplayed the harmful effects of land cessions to the nobility during peasant emancipation, and stressed the growing class differentiation within the peasantry instead of the conflict between peasant and noble. But even for the rural lower classes in the east the reforms had at least a short-term positive effect, making possible the founding of new households on marginal land that peasants or nobles obtained through the division of commons but could not efficiently use themselves. These groups of *Neubauer* supplied the dynamics behind the peasant emancipation as *Landesausbau,* a process, however, that had its greatest effect before 1840 and by 1865 had fully run its course and exhausted the possibilities of further intensification. What looked like a way out to the first generation experiencing peasant emancipation turned out to be a blind alley for the second. And it was at this point in time that the locus of German emigration shifted eastward, the first time any East Elbian districts showed exodus rates over 1 percent annually.[10]

While regional patterns of emigration can be quite revealing, any explanation of the phenomenon is incomplete without an examination of which people actually left, and where they fit into the socioeconomic structure of their places of origin. How literally is one to take an officially recorded emigration motive: "Kann nicht mehr leben" (Can no longer make a living)? Were emigrants responding to absolute or only to relative deprivation, or indeed merely to the fact that expectations were rising even more quickly than living standards? Regardless of whether one takes the more pessimistic estimates of Kuczynski or the more optimistic ones of Gömmel, real wages of German artisans and industrial workers were higher in the 1820s than for the next three decades. The harvest failures of the mid-forties and the

of Maudach," 129–57, 147–48, and Wolfgang Kaschuba, "Peasants and Others: The Historical Contours of Village Class Society," 235–64, 243–44, 259–60, both in Richard J. Evans and W. R. Lee, eds., *The German Peasantry* (New York, 1986); and Sigrid Faltin, *Die Auswanderung aus der Pfalz nach Nordamerika im 19. Jahrhundert* (Frankfurt/Main, 1987), 85–90. According to Christof Dipper, day laborers in Hesse were often "forced to emigrate, once the division of the commons had taken away their last chance of existence." See Dipper's *Die Bauernbefreiung in Deutschland* (Stuttgart, 1980), 76, 82. Similarly in Hanover, "the rural lower classes were the biggest losers" in the agricultural reforms.

9 Robert von Friedeburg, "Bauern und Tagelöhner: Die Entwicklung gesellschaftlicher Polarisierung in Schwalm und Knüll im Gewand der traditionellen Dorfgemeinde, 1737–1855," *Zeitschrift für Agrargeschichte und Agrarsoziologie* 39 (1991): 44–68.

10 Hartmut Harnisch, *Kapitalistische Agrarreform und Industrielle Revolution* (Weimar, 1984), 268–310, esp. 292–95.

early fifties hit especially hard.[11] Devising an equivalent index of living standards for the rural populations is difficult, but a measure used by Prussian statisticians, livestock units per capita, may provide some indication. For two emigration-prone areas of Westphalia the results are contradictory, but at least show no decline in per-capita ratios.[12] In East Elbian Prussia, however, the pattern is unambiguous. Between 1816 and 1840, the number of livestock, though increasing in absolute terms, did not keep pace with population. The number of livestock units increased by 37 percent, whereas the total population grew by 51 percent, and the rural population by 54 percent. Of the five eastern provinces, Posen was the only one that saw an increase in the livestock-per-capita ratio. Although this to some extent reflects changes from a more extensive grazing economy to more intensive crop production, it at least does not suggest rising rural living standards.[13] Moreover, as was the case in Westphalia, even improvement in livestock ratios overall does not preclude falling standards of living among the rural lower classes, that is, those not owning land.

One of the paradoxes of the emigration movement is that apparently those suffering the most serious deprivations hardly had the resources for the journey, whereas those who could afford the trip had no real reason to leave. However, one should not overstate this point. In the course of the nineteenth century the nominal and real costs of travel declined, and the speed, comfort, and reliability of both ocean and land travel greatly improved.

Getting at the question of precisely who emigrated presents the serious problem of sources. Although aggregate level official statistics are of considerable value for investigating the economic, demographic, and social structures that produced the heaviest emigration, they are of limited use in constructing a social profile of the emigrants themselves. For one thing, they were based not on socioeconomic criteria but on narrow minded *raison d'état*. Before 1871, a move from Brandenburg to Anhalt counted as emigration for Prussian statisticians, whereas a migration from Posen to the Ruhr District was not registered at all. Although the various non-Prussian destinations are listed separately in the statistics, the information on dem-

11 Rainer Gömmel, *Realeinkommen in Deutschland: Ein internationaler Vergleich (1810–1914)* (Nuremberg, 1979), 12 and passim.
12 Calculated from information in Albin Gladen, *Der Kreis Tecklenburg an der Schwelle des Zeitalters der Industrialisierung* (Münster, 1979); Regine Krull, "Das Amt Enger im 19. Jahrhundert," *Wittekindsland* 1 (1987): 62–71. The Prussian formula is 1 cow = ⅔ horse = 4 hogs = 10 sheep = 12 goats.
13 Harnisch, *Kapitalistische Agrarreform*, 243–59.

ographic characteristics, family status, and, most important, occupation, lumps all emigrants together – intra-German, intra-European, and overseas. Moreover, the occupational categories are hopelessly broad and undiffer-entiated. All agricultural occupations are squeezed into just three boxes: *Gutsbesitzer, Pächter, Inspektoren, Verwalter; Winzer, Gärtner, Jäger, Fischer; Gesinde und Arbeiter bei der Land- und Forstwirtschaft.*[14] Even for East Elbian conditions, this is woefully inadequate; for the western parts of Prussia it is practically useless. Fortunately, the secondary sector follows roughly the same categories as the Prussian occupational census; unfortunately it omits the crucial distinctions between dependent and independent workers.

Another source of aggregate statistics is those from the ports of Hamburg and Bremen, which have the advantage of being restricted only to overseas emigrants, and of including clandestine emigrants not enumerated by local authorities. But these too have serious limitations, even in their unaggre-gated form. From the perspective of the Hanseatic cities, the rural popu-lation seemed to be an undifferentiated mass, and is usually subsumed under a single term, *Ackermann* (literally, small-scale farmer). Nor is there an ad-equate distinction made between laborers in agriculture and in other eco-nomic sectors; the fact that the category *Arbeiter* (worker) is highest among the Mecklenburgers and the (primarily East Elbian) Prussians suggests that many, perhaps a majority of, emigrating laborers came from the agricultural sector. Information on females is even more unsatisfactory in the Hamburg lists than that for males. No occupations are given; in their place is a tally of whether women were married or single.[15]

Thus, an adequate treatment of the socioeconomic selectivity of migra-tion can only be attained by recourse to the original emigrant lists and permits, where this archival material has survived. This allows the researcher to take into account the differentiated, and often very localized terminology of various types of agricultural ownership and rental and labor conditions, and to classify occupations by modern social scientific criteria. It also allows the occupational data to be used in correlation with age and, where it exists, data on wealth to construct a more differentiated occupational profile. Even these lists often fail to register women's occupations or, if they do, the information is often quite sketchy. In some cases the father's occupation is

---

14 Estate owner, tenant farmer, overseer, administrator, vintner, gardener, hunter, fisher, and agricul-tural and forestry wage laborers and workers.

15 T. Bödicker, "Die Einwanderung und Auswanderung des preussischen Staates," *Preussische Statistik* 26 (1874); *Zeitschrift des Preussischen Statistischen Bureaus* (1874–87); *Statistik des Hamburgischen Staats* 4 (1872): 109; Peter Marschalck, *Deutsche Überseewanderung im 19. Jahrhundert* (Stuttgart, 1973), 79–80.

given, which allows one at least to compare the social origins of emigrating women and men.[16]

One remaining disadvantage of data from emigration lists is that they omit all or some of the clandestine emigrants, though local officials often were able to supply such information retrospectively. Since these emigrants tended to be younger, poorer, and more often unmarried than officially registered emigrants, a profile from emigrant lists can be considered a "best-case scenario" on the socioeconomic status of emigrants. Moreover, by comparing the surplus of births over deaths with the actual population increase between censuses, one can estimate how much of the total out-migration (including internal migration) went unrecorded.

Of course, motivating factors were not exclusively economic, neither for women nor for men. Often social, economic, and what were ultimately political grievances became so intertwined with one another as to be practically inseparable. One example bears further investigation. Into the 1860s, most German states outside Prussia imposed marriage restrictions in an attempt to prevent "pauper weddings," which would burden poor relief funds. But if they managed to prevent marriages, they were less successful in preventing pauper births. How important a motive for emigration was illegitimate birth or parentage, particularly for women but perhaps also for men? Emigrant applications and permits often include such information, and for Württemberg and Braunschweig there is even published material on the subject, but it has yet to be exploited by migration researchers.[17]

There are other areas of inquiry where even information on an individual level on the German side is inadequate; only a transatlantic perspective can provide an adequate understanding. Such a perspective is especially crucial for interpreting time trends of emigration. Peter Marschalck has pointed out that the American Civil War had a retarding effect on emigration from 1861 to 1865, and that heavy emigration rates for the rest of the decade can to some extent be explained as a "catch-up" effect. Moreover, in various areas across Germany, the Civil War diverted more of the emigration than normal to destinations other than the United States.[18] Similarly, without a transatlantic perspective one would be at a loss to explain why the

---

16 One published source containing such data is Fritz Gruhne, *Auswandererlisten des ehemaligen Herzogtums Braunschweig, ohne Stadt Braunschweig und Landkreis Holzminden, 1846–1871* (Braunschweig, 1971).

17 The standard treatment of marriage restrictions is Matz, *Pauperismus und Bevölkerung,* which largely ignores the factor of emigration. For examples of emigration where illegitimacy played a role, see Walter D. Kamphoefner, Wolfgang Helbich, and Ulrike Sommer, eds., *News from the Land of Freedom: German Immigrants Write Home* (Ithaca, N.Y., 1991), 532–36, 589–90.

18 Marschalck, *Überseewanderung,* 42–44; Kamphoefner, *The Westfalians,* 55–56.

year 1855, which recorded the highest grain and potato prices of the century in many regions, saw such little emigration.[19] The answer lies in the nativist movement in the United States, which reached its peak in terms of electoral support and riot casualties in 1854 and 1855. No doubt many recent immigrants warned off potential followers, as did Christian Lenz, who had witnessed a riot in Louisville that had produced twenty casualties: "Now dear brother should anyone else move to America, no – stay where you were born . . . even if there's nothing besides bread and potatoes and salt that is still better than meat three times a day in a foreign country."[20]

For the post-1865 period, when migration activity in East Elbia comes especially to the fore, a transatlantic perspective is all the more important since the emigration curve follows ever more closely the roller-coaster ride of the American business cycle. The same principle applies in reverse as well. The Panic of 1893 in the United States depressed immigration rates for all nationalities. But the steadily climbing real wages in Germany explain why – despite the American economic recovery after 1896 – immigration rates for other nationality groups rebounded much more strongly than for Germans, who found opportunities in their own expanding economy.[21]

Another area where a transatlantic perspective can clear up many misconceptions is in evaluating which factors were most important in precipitating emigration and influencing destinations. In older German literature, a prominent place is accorded emigration agents and propaganda, as if these were of great influence and seduced many to emigrate without good reason. Such claims should be treated with great skepticism, even if they can be supported by numerous statements from government officials, pastors, and the like. After all, these were the elements in society who perceived emigration as a rejection of their authority and of the existing social order, and rightly so. For them, agents served as scapegoats, a way of denying that the mass exodus resulted from genuine social and economic problems.[22]

In reality, agents should be seen as mediators and facilitators, who eased the process of emigration. But they could do little to promote it where a predisposition did not already exist or a firm decision to emigrate had not already been made. Statistics from Westphalia in the 1850s show that only

---

19 See the annual price data in *Jahrbuch für die Amtliche Statistik des Preussischen Staats* 2 (1867): 117ff.
20 Kamphoefner et al., *News From the Land of Freedom,* 134; on the nativist movement, see also 16–17, 126–27.
21 Ibid., 10–11.
22 See, e.g., Faltin, *Auswanderung,* 181. An important first step in revising the image of emigration agents was taken by Agnes Bretting and Hartmut Bickelmann, *Auswanderungsagenturen und Auswanderungsvereine im 19. und 20. Jahrhundert* (Stuttgart, 1991), 25–90.

about one-third of emigrants booked with agents. Such figures should also be available for other areas of Prussia. Another reason for agents' negative image in the older literature is that agents were often Jewish. But once again, the majority of Westphalian agents had Christian sounding names and came from such prominent families as Diepenbrock and Delius. What such agents had in common with their Jewish counterparts was their involvement in commerce; running an emigration agency was a popular sideline for merchants and storekeepers.[23]

The influence of immigrant guidebooks has also been exaggerated. Before the 1850s, there were only two references to guidebooks (those of Duden and Chevalier) found in the large collection of letters and other material on Palatinate emigration at the Heimatstelle Palatinate. References to guidebooks are equally rare in the six-thousand-odd letters in the collection at Bochum. Agents appear somewhat more frequently, but primarily as facilitators, not as promoters of emigration. Potential followers were often advised as to the dependability of a particular agent. Emigration societies were seldom mentioned except by their actual participants, and their appeal seems to have been largely restricted to the educated bourgeoisie.[24]

The few references in immigrant letters to guidebooks and colonization societies bespeak anything but confidence. Writing back to his brother-in-law in 1839, Dr. Bernhard Bruns, one of the early settlers of Westphalia, Missouri, vented his spleen at the books of Nicholas Hesse and Heinrich von Martels: "Which of the two authors knows best how to lie . . . the interested reader may determine for himself – both stray too often from the path of truth, neither gained any experience as a farmer. . . . Mr. von Martels is a shameless braggart, Mr. Hesse a miserable complainer, but at bootlicking they give one another quite a run for the money." Bruns, of an educated bourgeois background, was clearly not a typical immigrant, but there is evidence that his opinion of Hesse was shared also by the rank and file of his countrymen. Westphalian peasants applying for emigration permits in 1840 were routinely asked whether they had read Hesse's rather pessimistic advice. They just as routinely replied that they had but would not change their minds on that account. However, the uniform wording of question and answer for case after case suggests that this was a mere formality. Perhaps most of the emigrants actually did know the book at least

---

23 Kamphoefner, *The Westfalians,* 57–58; Faltin, *Auswanderung,* 241.
24 Karl Scherer, "Die Auswanderung aus der Pfalz und die Quellenbestände der Heimatstelle Pfalz," in Willi Paul Adams, ed., *Die deutschsprachige Auswanderung in die Vereinigten Staaten: Forschungsstand und Quellenbestände* (Berlin, 1980), 108.

from hearsay, but this was not what they relied upon in making their de-cisions.[25]

Emigration societies, too, have gotten more than their share of attention in the historical literature. They often made headlines and their well-educated, articulate leaders left behind more primary accounts than ordinary immigrants. But most Germans traveled to America alone or in small, un-organized groups of family or friends. Nevertheless, there are several secular or religious group migration projects during the first half of the nineteenth century that deserve to be mentioned. The Giessen Emigration Society and the Solingen Emigration Society, both led by liberal democratic members of the *Bildungsbürgertum,* attempted in 1834 to found colonies in the area of Missouri made famous by Gottfried Duden's writings. Both fell apart almost before they arrived at their destination, and neither retained more than a couple dozen settlers at their original location.[26]

In 1831 forty-four members of the Thuringian Emigration Society, led by Johann and Karl Roebling from Mühlhausen, established the colony of Saxonburg about forty kilometers from Pittsburgh. It was no more suc-cessful than most of the other group endeavors. The most prominent mem-ber of the group of followers that was recruited the next year, Carl Angelrodt, a former state parliamentarian in Prussian Saxony, was dissatis-fied with the site, denounced Roebling as a swindler, demanded his money back, and effectively discredited the colony back home. The site of Sax-onburg was in fact not exactly propitious and, despite its proximity to Pitts-burgh, still numbered only 1,330 inhabitants in 1980. But its fate was rather typical of such organized efforts to establish settlements of emigrants.[27]

The largest migration project, and not coincidentally the biggest catas-trophe, was the so-called *Adelsverein* (Society of Nobles), an attempt to colonize Texas in the mid-1840s. Over seven thousand people were trans-ported to Texas between 1843 and 1846, before the society went bankrupt in 1847. Promises of free land went largely unfulfilled, and few preparations were made for the arriving newcomers, so that many of them died from the hardships of the trip inland from the port of Galveston. From that point on, immigration societies were regarded with deserved skepticism.

25 Letter of June 6, 1839, copy in Bochumer Auswandererbriefsammlung; Kamphoefner, *The West-falians,* 99.
26 Kamphoefner, *The Westfalians,* 94–96, 100–01.
27 D. B. Steinman, *The Builders of the Bridge* (New York, 1945), 21–42; Gustav Körner, *Das Deutsche Element in den Vereinigten Staaten, 1818–1848* (Cincinnati, 1880; reprint, Frankfurt/Main, 1986), 93–94, 307–8. Happier than that of Saxonburg was the fate of the two adversaries: Angelrodt became a merchant and German consul in St. Louis; Roebling went on to fame as the builder of suspension bridges, above all the Brooklyn Bridge.

Writing in 1845, another university-educated, politically liberal immigrant made no bones about his disdain for colonization schemes in general and the *Adelsverein* in particular: "Prince Solms, the director of this company, seems to have made himself totally laughable and hated through his ignorance of democratic conditions. On my tour I met a knowledgeable man from Texas. He said, 'We will cowhide him when he comes again.' "[28] The mistrust exhibited by ordinary immigrants toward such emigration societies was perhaps even greater than that shown by the more educated. Nor did religious societies fare much better than secular ones in this respect.

Religious minorities in general had a stronger propensity for emigration than the rest of society. This was particularly true for Jews but also for Mennonites from Bavaria.[29] But in terms of size, the most important religious group migration was that of the so-called Old Lutherans in the 1830s and 1840s. In protest against the forced merger of the Lutheran and Reformed denominations, some Germans sought refuge in Australia. Three main groups, however, looked to America for religious freedom. One group from Pomerania and Silesia, led by Pastor William Grabau, settled in Buffalo, New York, and the Milwaukee area of Wisconsin; a second from Bavarian Franconia settled in Michigan. A group from Saxony, often called Stephanites after their bishop Martin Stephan, settled on an isolated site of several thousand acres purchased in Missouri.[30]

One should not overemphasize the significance of any of these projects, religious or secular. The occupational profile of religious refugees differed little from that of ordinary emigrants, suggesting that economic motives also came into play. Among the largely Wendisch and Old Lutheran emigration from Kottbus county, the seventy-six *Häusler* (cottagers) far outnumbered the thirty farmers with appreciable holdings, and even of those only four were *Vollbauern* (farmers in the American sense). Similarly, the Saxon Old Lutherans included a disproportionately high number from the educated classes, particularly candidates of theology. Yet three-fifths were artisans and of those the beleaguered weaver's trade made up the largest contingent.[31] Even in the peak year of 1843, no more than sixteen hundred Old Lutherans

28 Carl von Gimborn, ed., *Aus der Neuen Welt. Familienbriefe, 1844–1869* (Emmerich, 1968), 35.
29 Avraham Barkai, "German-Jewish Migrations in the Nineteenth Century, 1830–1910," *Leo Baeck Institute Yearbook* 30 (1985): 301–18; Friedrich Blendinger, "Die Auswanderung aus dem Regierungsbezirk Oberbayern in den Jahren 1846–1852," *Zeitschrift für bayerische Landesgeschichte* 17 (1964): 431–87.
30 Wilhelm Iwan, *Die Altlutherische Auswanderung um die Mitte des 19. Jahrhunderts,* 2 vols. (Ludwigsburg, 1943); Walter O. Forster, *Zion on the Mississippi: The Settlement of the Saxon Lutherans in Missouri, 1839–1841* (St. Louis, 1953).
31 George R. Nielsen, *In Search of a Home: Nineteenth-Century Wendish Immigration* (College Station, Tex., 1989), 17–18; Forster, *Zion,* 562–63.

emigrated to America, thus comprising only a tenth of the total migration volume for that year. They made up a rather large proportion of migrants from East Elbia during that era, however, though the trails they blazed were followed by many other, not primarily religiously motivated emigrants from eastern Germany. Secular organizations had if anything an even less significant impact. Despite the low levels of emigration in the early years, the organized migrants from Giessen and Solingen made up only 3 percent of the total immigration in 1834. Only 6 percent of all immigrants coming over between 1843 and 1846 were transported by the *Adelsverein,* although they did make up a large share of those going to Texas.

Another indication of the relatively small impact of such organized migrants is the regional composition of the German population in the states where the colonies were located. Despite the settlement of the Giessen Society from Hesse and Old Lutherans from Saxony, Hessians and Saxons made up a lower proportion of Germans in Missouri than in the United States as a whole. Despite the homogeneous settlement of (Bavarian) Franconians in the Frankenmuth area of Michigan, the state as a whole attracted less than its share of Bavarians. Wisconsin, a leading destination of the Old Lutherans, continued to attract a large contingent from eastern Germany, but this was just as true of Mecklenburgers, who did not suffer any religious grievances, as of Prussians, who did. About the only state where organized immigration had a visible impact on the makeup of the German population as a whole was Texas. This was particularly reflected in the large number of settlers from Nassau, home of *Adelsverein* leader Prince Solms-Braunfels. But here, too, the number of people actually transported by the society was outnumbered by the relatives and friends who followed.[32]

Much more decisive for the process of migration than emigration societies were families or lone individuals who were sometimes accompanied by relatives, friends, or neighbors. Such small groups migrated without a common treasury or any formal organizational framework. But the risks involved in such an undertaking were greatly reduced through chain migration, that is, choosing an initial destination where one already had personal contacts. Family and friends in such locations could provide temporary lodgings, arrange a job, and generally ease the shock of confronting a new society, culture, and economy. When American immigration authorities in the early twentieth century began to pose the question whether arriving immigrants were coming to join relatives or friends, only 6 percent of all Germans said no. Friends provided the initial point of contact for some 15

32 Kamphoefner, *The Westfalians,* 72–77.

percent and nearly four-fifths were awaited by relatives. In fact, over one-third of all Germans traveling across the Atlantic during this era had their passages prepaid by someone in America. It would, of course, be unwarranted to extrapolate such figures to the early nineteenth century, but Swedish figures show little change in the proportion of prepaids between the 1880s and 1910.[33]

The establishment of informal colonies in various locales in America is one clear indication that such chain migration was operating earlier as well. Without having been steered by any organized colonization efforts, one-twelfth of all former Braunschweigers in the whole United States in 1860 lived in one single Missouri county, where they made up a quarter of the German population, compared with 0.3 percent nationally.[34] The letters of immigrants contain much evidence of chain migration and the concentration of immigrants in certain localities. There was a regular transatlantic exchange of gossip, greetings, and advice on immigration that bears witness to settlers surrounded, sometimes literally, by friends and acquaintances from the old country.[35]

In conclusion, immigration history will be best served by a combination of micro- and macroperspectives. Aggregate statistical approaches are important to understand how local and regional migration patterns fit into the big picture. Existing studies have not yet exhausted potential sources, both for cross-sectional and for time-series analysis. But above all, it is important to get closer to the actual migrants and to ask questions that contemporary bureaucrats and observers did not. For investigations of this kind there is often no substitute for the arduous but rewarding work with emigration permits and other personal data, supplemented by the letters of ordinary immigrants. Needless to say, perspectives from both the source and the destination of migrants need to be combined and integrated. What is needed most of all for emigration research on Germany, be it from the north, south, or east, are scholars who are at the same time both cosmopolitan and "provincial."

33 Ibid., 188.
34 Walter D. Kamphoefner, "Chain Migration and Local Homogeneity of Immigration: Cape Girardeau County Germans in Comparative Perspective," in Michael Roark, ed., *French and Germans in the Mississippi Valley* (Cape Girardeau, Mo., 1988), 179–89.
35 See, e.g., Walter D. Kamphoefner, *Westfalen in der Neuen Welt* (Münster, 1982), 195–99; Kamphoefner et al., *News from the Land of Freedom.*

2

Colonist Traditions and Nineteenth-Century Emigration from East Elbian Prussia

RAINER MÜHLE

I

Modern history, which is characterized by the genesis and development of capitalism, witnessed numerous and diverse regional, national, and international migrations. These migrations differ in their dominant motives, their scope, their origins and destinations, their structure, forms, and organization. They took place simultaneously, consecutively, or flowed into each other within a certain geographical space.[1] In their totality, their relationships to each other and to their underlying social contexts, such migrations constitute the subject matter of historical migration research.[2]

Rostock University is home to a research project on the history of East Elbian migration during the nineteenth century. The project is investigating different streams of migration and their historical interrelationship in certain territories. It is concentrating on migrations varied in direction, structure, intensity, duration, and scope, from selected small areas, namely, county, town, districts of the landed nobility (*Gutsbezirke*), and village. These migrations are considered in their relationship to each other, to the underlying social conditions, and to migration traditions in each historical area. The participants in this project essentially use the same archival basis and the same research methods and cover the following regions in their studies: Mecklenburg, Pomerania, and Brandenburg.[3] These regions were selected

---

1 Klaus J. Bade, "Massenwanderung und Arbeitsmarkt im deutschen Nordosten von 1880 bis zum Ersten Weltkrieg: Überseeische Auswanderung, interne Abwanderung und kontinentale Zuwanderung," *Archiv für Sozialgeschichte* 20 (1980): 269.
2 Rainer Mühle, "Einige konzeptionelle Gedanken zur Erforschung der Massenemigrationen aus Deutschland von 1815 bis 1914," *Migrationsforschung* 21 (1989): 13; Rainer Mühle, "Arbeitshypothesen zur Erforschung der Sozialgeschichte von Emigrationen aus ausgewählten Territorien Ostelbiens im 19. Jahrhundert," *Migrationsforschung* 24 (1990): 6–10.
3 At Rostock University, two historians are involved in this project: Axel Lubinski, whose research focuses on selected areas of Mecklenburg-Strelitz, and Rainer Mühle, who deals with the emigration from Prignitz, Ruppin County, Uckermark, West Brandenburg, and from Randow and Lauenburg

because they constitute a coherent research area. Other criteria that led to this choice, and thus opened up the possibility of a comparative study of nineteenth-century East Elbian migration, include a substantial archival base, the significance of these areas in the overall migration process, and similar socioeconomic conditions among them.

A part of the larger project, this essay will attempt to place nineteenth-century continental and transatlantic migration within the context of the emigration history of East Elbian Prussia. Although it focuses on transatlantic emigration, especially to North America, continental migrations will also be considered. Insofar as sources will permit, both streams of migration will, in turn, be examined in their relation to other types of migration, especially to internal short- and long-distance migrations, to continental labor migrations, and to possible migration traditions in the regions under study. In general, the individual forms of migration will be analyzed in terms of scope, structure, causes, and organization.

The time frame for this study covers the period from 1815 to 1914. The first date coincides with the Congress of Vienna and marks the end of Napoleonic-era restrictions on emigration, which were lifted in many member states of the German Federation (Deutscher Bund). In the years 1818–19 an emigration surge into the areas of partitioned Poland that were part of the Russian Empire also took place. The second date, the start of World War I, signals a turning point in the history of migration within the German Reich.

The analysis of the structure, causes, and organization of the migrations to and from the selected East Elbian areas, and of the migrant's behavioral patterns is based on primary and secondary sources. The main archival sources are the so-called *Konsensakten,* that is, files pertaining to applications for permits to emigrate. They are stored in Prussian archives located in the former East Germany, in Polish archives,[4] and in the Mecklenburgisches Landeshauptarchiv in Schwerin. Large numbers of such files are extant for several Prussian administrative districts (*Regierungsbezirke*) within the provinces of Brandenburg and Pomerania, and for both Mecklenburgs, although gaps in the records exist. These sources contain documents related to the individual emigrants, such as copies of emigration permits, applications for emigration, statements by state authorities and employers, officially regis-

---

counties, Pomerania. Also involved in this project is Uwe Reich, now at Universität Potsdam. The focus of his study is Arnswalde and Cottbus counties in eastern Brandenburg.

4 Besides the sources recorded in the Geheimes Staatsarchiv in Berlin-Dahlem and the relevant sources in the *Landeshauptarchive* in Potsdam and Greifswald, documents found in the Polish state archives in Stettin and Köslin were also used.

tered estimates of the emigrants' wealth, and the like. In addition, these studies use sources from different provincial and central government agencies, church registers, and sources found in the archives of large estates, as well as printed and manuscript migration statistics. The selection of relevant sources was also stimulated by Wolfgang von Hippel who, in his book on the history of emigration from southwest Germany, recommends that "future studies . . . should at least try to combine emigration lists and citizenship renunciations in order to include their additional information, for example, on the emigrant's wealth, and means spent on the journey."[5]

The sources mentioned here, especially *Konsensakten,* provide a wide range of information about individual emigrants, their social and economic situation, the status of eligibility for military service, and about how emigration was organized. Additional information on each individual emigrant could be gathered if, in addition to *Konsensakten,* which were created by royal district administrations, the parallel files of the respective county supervisors' offices could also be located.[6] Produced by the state and by the church, in total these sources yield information that enables the creation of a sociostatistical data base. This solid statistical base allows a structural analysis of migrations from the selected territories. The results of this analysis are an indispensable prerequisite for examining the causes of migration.

Precise information on the structure of migrations from or to a small area – county, town, *Domänenamt* (administrative unit of state-owned areas), districts of landed nobility, and village – combined with an analysis of its social conditions opens the way to the actual causes of migration. In addition to these results, this study uses many diverse sources and special literature dealing with these selected areas. These include, for example, emigration reports produced by government and church institutions as well as general reports produced by authorities (*Zeitungsberichte*). The latter contain excellent descriptions of social conditions, reports on the development of agriculture and trade, on the results of agrarian reforms, on states of emergency and on catastrophes, official transcripts, and letters by emigrants. The facts gleaned from these sources can be arranged into a mosaic, which in composite contains important information on the causes of these migrations. This methodological approach was inspired by an opinion formulated in 1860 by the former director of the Statistical Bureau in Berlin, Ernst Engel. He wrote that only a person who is familiar with the local conditions (of emigration) can find the key to migration causes amid the raw data of the

5 Wolfgang von Hippel, *Auswanderung aus Südwestdeutschland: Studien zur württembergischen Auswanderung und Auswanderungspolitik im 18. und 19. Jahrhundert* (Stuttgart, 1984), 120.
6 Mühle, "Einige konzeptionelle Gedanken," 16, 17.

Prussian immigration and emigration statistics.[7] Finally, using source material located in state archives, an attempt will be made to gain insight into how migrations were organized. Thus, to answer the question of how different migrations were organized, researchers involved in this project must use many diverse sources, including private ones.

The following five hypotheses constitute the heuristic guidelines for my research. First, during the nineteenth century there were no mass emigrations from East Elbia in the sense of a general phenomenon covering all areas with similar or equal socioeconomic structures. In relation to the total number of inhabited places and the total population of a given territory, the overwhelming majority of emigrants came from a relatively small number of rural communities and small towns.

Second, from the beginning of the nineteenth century laborers constituted the majority of emigrants from East Elbia. It was the mostly proletarian and semiproletarian elements who, because of clearly ascertainable social grievances, broke away from their native, mostly rural soil. This holds true for the stormy prelude, which was marked by the emigration wave to Russian Poland and to Russia proper in the years 1818–19, as well as for the overseas migrations in the second half of the nineteenth century.[8]

Third, hard times belong to a multilayered set of factors causing migrations, including transatlantic emigration. This does not mean, however, that famines, rising food prices, and war are the only causes of migrations; hardships alone are insufficient to trigger migrations. In order to penetrate the complicated interwoven web of causes, it is necessary to analyze a precisely defined social context within small areas, which are the emigrant's starting point and his destinations. The schematic separation of religious, political, economic, social, and other causes from each other does not appear to be the most promising method to investigate the underlying factors of migration.

Fourth, mobility was an elementary part of the existence of rural lower classes in the nineteenth century. In this respect migration, including transatlantic emigration, was a normal and accepted means to secure and improve one's existence, and was not a romantic longing for the far away places or for adventure.

---

7 Ernst Engel, "Die Aus- und Einwanderungen im Preussischen Staate (insoweit Nachrichten darüber zur Kenntnis der Königlichen Regierungen gekommen sind)," *Zeitschrift des Königlichen Preussischen Statistischen Bureaus* 1 (1861): 67.

8 Between 1862 and 1871 about 90 percent of Pomeranian emigrants belonged to the categories defined by the *Preussische Statistik* as farmhands, maidservants, and laborers in agriculture and forestry, factory workers, day laborers, and other laborers. See *Preussische Statistik* 26 (1874): 214–15.

Fifth, migrations as an expression of peasant resistance to feudal rule have a long tradition. The threat of out-migration as well as its actual realization belonged to a set of instruments of peasant politics, which were often brilliantly implemented. It essentially aimed to defend existing rights and to acquire new ones. For centuries, migrations were an integral part of the political consciousness of the peasant and lower rural classes. The threat of migration was a means of bringing pressure to bear on the authorities and was also a practical measure to be carried out in case their demands were not met.

Agricultural laborers and wage-earning small-scale farmers, the predominant social elements of nineteenth-century East Elbian migration, inherited a variety of mental and behavioral patterns. This was due to their peasant social origins and to the fact that since the end of the seventeenth century the areas of the Prussian monarchy considered in this study had been the destination of strong in-migrations sponsored by the state. Governmental promotion of immigration and internal colonization long provided favorable conditions for the solution of social problems by means of out-migration. State sponsored internal colonization absorbed the surplus population of previously colonized villages (*Kolonistendörfer*). Since resources became insufficient to support everyone in these villages, strain on resources was relieved through short-distance migration. This meant that those descendants who were not eligible to inherit the parental farm moved on to other places where they could establish a new settlement or at least a small farm in an already existing village. In this way, the ideas of emigration and of establishing a new existence in another place – as appropriate means of providing for one's family – were passed from generation to generation. These inherited mental and behavioral patterns continued to play a role under the fundamentally changed social conditions of the nineteenth century. Consequently, the East Elbian immigrant population became an essential part of the social basis of ever new internal migrations as well as emigrations. The following sections of this essay should be considered an initial attempt to discuss the second and fifth hypotheses in particular.

II

What were the scope, social structure, and causes of the emigration from District Potsdam to Congress Poland between 1817 and 1819? In his still relevant book, Wilhelm Mönckmeier stated categorically that immediately following the Congress of Vienna (1815) "emigration on a larger scale was impossible in the eastern and northern parts of Prussia because of the then existing agricultural system, the bonds of the agricultural population to their native soil, and because of the lack of the means of transportation."[9] The following thesis sets forth a counterpoint to Mönckmeier's assumption, which no longer can be sustained in light of the latest findings of migration research.

Between 1817 and the early 1820s there was a strong emigration wave from various central and eastern Prussian territories to Russia and Russian Poland. It was followed by subsequent family migrations to these areas until the 1830s. This emigration can be compared to the continental emigration from southwest Germany taking place at the same time. The core areas of this "emigration fever," as contemporaries frequently called it, were the western and eastern parts of Brandenburg, Upper Silesia, West and East Prussia, and the districts of Bromberg and Köslin. My thesis is based entirely on sources that have only recently been discovered. These sources have been long overlooked, because modern sociohistorical research to a large extent neglected eighteenth- and nineteenth-century German continental emigration.[10]

The following quotations are taken from reports written by the Prussian county supervisors von Kroecher and von Petersdorf of East and West Prignitz counties, respectively, who were personally involved in these significant events in migration history. On August 26, 1818, when the emigration from Prignitz was about to reach its climax, von Kroecher reported to the royal administration in Potsdam that

the desire to emigrate to Poland has become epidemic in my country. The announcement of the Royal Ministry of Foreign Affairs dating back to June 15, 1817 (*Berliner Zeitung,* no. 74), was generally spread by shady lawyers, and since there is hope to acquire real estate, and for propertied men even the chance of acquiring large plots of land in Poland, nothing can make them change their . . . minds. Each day laborer wants to become an owner of land. The people who desire to emigrate come here in droves, almost besieging my house, and if I don't listen to them and drop everything . . . they get impatient, pushy, and presumptuous. Because I am a peace-loving man, I have meanwhile borne all that and the troubles connected with it patiently and have so far not punished anybody.[11]

9 Wilhelm Mönckmeier, *Die deutsche überseeische Auswanderung* (Jena, 1912), 73.
10 Dirk Hoerder, ed., *Labor Migration in the Atlantic Economies: The European and North American Working Classes during the Period of Industrialization* (Westport, Conn., 1985), 8; Klaus J. Bade, "Die deutsche überseeische Massenauswanderung im 19. und frühen 20. Jahrhundert: Bestimmungsfaktoren und Entwicklungsbedingungen," in Klaus J. Bade, ed., *Auswanderer – Wanderarbeiter – Gastarbeiter: Bevölkerung, Arbeitsmarkt und Wanderung in Deutschland seit der Mitte des 19. Jahrhunderts,* 2 vols. (Ostfildern, 1984), 1:263.
11 Brandenburgisches Landeshauptarchiv (BLHA) Potsdam, Pr. Br. Rep. 2 A, Regierung Potsdam, I St. Nr. 60, 427, and 428.

Table 2.1. *Family emigration from* Regierungsbezirk *Potsdam to Russian Poland, 1818 (by counties)*

County	Families receiving permits			Families actually emigrating		
	Prussia	Foreign born	Total	Prussia	Foreign born	Total
E. Prignitz	370	63	433	163	23	186
W. Prignitz	223	77	300	113	45	158
Ruppin	182	17	199	45	8	53
Templin	1	—	1	—	—	—
Niederbarnim	1	—	1	—	—	—
Total	777	157	934	321	76	397

Source: BLHA Potsdam, Pr. Br. Rep. 2 A Regierung Potsdam, I St. Nr. 65, 52.

In another part of his report, von Kroecher stated that the news about the advantages waiting for prospective emigrants to Poland "has spread like a brush fire and that the mere word 'Poland' . . . penetrates the excited souls like an electric spark."[12] His fellow civil servant from neighboring Prignitz County reported to Potsdam on March 13, 1819, that

I can't protect myself any longer against those who wish to emigrate and who are impetuously besieging me. Every day they urge me to grant them an emigration permit and the necessary passports in order to give them the opportunity to emigrate to Poland, the object of their desires. . . . All these people are so full of ideas about the good fortune awaiting them in Poland that nothing can make them change their minds. They go around doing nothing, spend their money in pubs, and mislead otherwise reasonable people. This situation can't be tolerated much longer. Unless rigid measures are taken to stop this mischief, serious consequences are to be expected.[13]

What was the actual background for these dramatic reports issued by two Prussian county supervisors?

Between 1817 and 1819 about 1,100 families applied to the county supervisors' and magistrates' offices in District Potsdam for permits to emigrate to the Kingdom of Poland. About 1,000 applicants actually received an emigration permit or a passport (see Table 2.1). But only approximately 450 families eventually emigrated. Families who received official permission to emigrate to Poland, as well as those who actually did emigrate, came with few exceptions from neighboring Prignitz and Ruppin counties.

12 Ibid.
13 BLHA Potsdam, Pr. Br. Rep. 2 A, Regierung Potsdam, I St. Nr. 65.

About 20 percent of the families who actually carried out their decision to emigrate had earlier immigrated to Prussia, the majority coming from Mecklenburg.[14] With the exception of a few cases, all the emigrants went to Poland with their families.

In the second half of 1817 the emigration of a few families from the Oderbruch – a swampy area northeast of Berlin on the Oder River that was cultivated under King Friedrich II of Prussia – constituted the opening scene of our emigration drama on the stage of history. In August, September, and October 1818 there was a dramatic increase in emigration, which sharply declined between January and July in 1819. Between January 1 and July 31, 1819, about 150 families applied for emigration permits with royal officials in Potsdam. Of these, 127 actually received their permits. The majority of families came from East Prignitz (42), West Prignitz (45), and Ruppin counties (9). The remaining families were from the western part of the Havelland (17), from Templin (2), from Teltow-Storkow (2), and from Prenzlau counties (1).[15] If one considers that about 5,500 people applied for emigration from District Potsdam and relates this figure to the total population of 128,994 (1816) living in the core areas of emigration, namely, East Prignitz, West Prignitz, and Ruppin counties, the portion of those desiring to emigrate was 4.26 percent.

Although the overwhelming majority of the emigrants stemmed from the countryside, some came from a few rural towns, namely, from Wittstock, Kyritz, Lenzen, Neuruppin, and Pritzwalk. In 1818, for example, 236 inhabitants of Pritzwalk applied to the magistrate of this small town of weavers for permits to emigrate to Russian Poland. This represented 9.2 percent of the total population of 2,562.[16] Even when compared with the rates of emigration from the East Elbian core areas, mainly to the United States, in the second half of the nineteenth century, these figures are significant as historical evidence of a strong readiness to migrate.[17]

The overwhelming majority of those 1,100 families, who applied for emigration at their county supervisors' offices, as well as the bulk of those families who actually emigrated, were tenants (day laborers or live-in laborers) or small-scale farmers and cottagers, who, like the tenants, were

14 The exact number of the emigrants from District Potsdam to Russian Poland cannot be determined with any precision, since the statistics of this emigration could not be found and gaps in recording the issuance of emigration permits prevent their approximation.
15 BLHA Potsdam, Pr. Br. Rep. 2 A, Regierung Potsdam, I St. Nr. 66, 56, and 290.
16 BLHA Potsdam, Pr. Br. Rep. 8, Stadt Pritzwalk, Nr. 2715, 20–31.
17 Between 1862 and 1871, e.g., about 8.2 percent of the total population living in Prenzlau County in 1864 left for overseas destinations.

mostly dependent on wages or a trade. There were almost no peasants among these emigrants.

When asked about why they intended to emigrate, the tenants and wage-earning small-scale farmers and cottagers mentioned time and time again the shortage of jobs and the lack of opportunity to acquire property. They also complained about the housing shortage. Such reasons appear frequently in numerous recorded petitions and official transcripts. For example, take the petition of the day laborer Dietrich Gragert of Gandow near Lenzen, West Prignitz County. In his application, which he sent to the royal administration of Brandenburg on April 12, 1819, he pleaded for an emigration permit at the earliest possible date, because, he implored, there

are no jobs available for me and my fellow laborers in this area, since shipping and wood cutting are depressed. I am only able to do farm work and similar manual jobs, but I as well as my fellow laborers cannot support a family on this. If we don't want to starve and end up as beggars . . . we have to migrate to another place where we will get the necessary food without undue efforts and obtain free land. This is what I owe to my family.[18]

The few peasants who applied for emigration permits were mostly heavily indebted and hoped with their remaining wealth to acquire unmortgaged farms in Russian Poland.

Let us now turn our attention to the remarkable fact that with only a few exceptions those people who wanted to emigrate came from East Prignitz, West Prignitz, and Ruppin counties. Why the concentration of emigrants from these few counties? In 1819 the Potsdam senior civil servant, Weil, sent a report to the Prussian cabinet that helps to answer this question. Referring to this core area of continental migration, Weil draws attention to the following circumstance:

In these three counties, agriculture has made such remarkable progress in comparison to all the other counties that they can serve as a model of rural activity. Long before the agrarian reform bill of 1807 was passed . . . all manors had already been separated from the peasants' farms; many peasants had acquired consolidated farms on which they built new houses and outbuildings, even small-scale farmers, colonists, etc. had parcels of land at their disposal, which had come from the former commons. After the war, new villages were established out of dissolved farms. Tenants bought the expansive old farmhouses with potato patches in the villages. Only recently five day laborers bought a farm in East Prignitz County, divided it,

18 BLHA Potsdam, Pr. Br. Rep. 2 A, Regierung Potsdam, I St. Nr. 66, 123.

and built new homes on their plots. In the remaining counties, there are only rare signs of such an activity.[19]

In its 1818 annual report, the royal administration in Potsdam indicated that during the previous eight years 150 peasants had subdivided and consolidated their fields in conjunction with the construction of new farmhouses and outbuildings. These subdivisions mainly took place in East Prignitz and Ruppin counties. Further evidence of the relatively rapid progress of agricultural development in the three counties was the construction activity closely connected with the division of the commons, discontinuation of forced labor, and property adjustments.[20]

Between 1808 and the end of 1818, about 64.9 percent of all so-called family homes were built in Prignitz and Ruppin counties. And 58.4 percent of the total number of new *établissements* were constructed in these counties, which had a 49.8 percent share in the total growth in the number of tenant and propertied families of District Potsdam during the same period.[21]

The connection between the increase in construction activities and the practical consequences of the agrarian reforms can be explained (see Table 2.2). The large number of subdivisions in conjunction with farm consolidation, and the construction of new farm buildings, provided favorable legal and material prerequisites for selling many old farmyards (*Hofstellen*), predominantly to persons who did not yet possess their own houses in these villages. Since large-scale parceling of private or state-owned estates was uncommon in District Potsdam at this time, the acquisition of farmland was only possible in this way. Many of these subdivisions of land would not have been possible if forced labor done by those peasant proprietors on large estates had not been discontinued in connection with property adjustments. Another precondition was the subdivision and consolidation of their farms. On the other hand, without a strong demand among tenants, who were mostly day laborers and live-in laborers, for small holdings, the abandonment of old and the construction of new farm buildings would have been infrequent. The peasant proprietors used the financial means gained from the sale of their old farm buildings, including the surrounding garden patches, for the construction of new buildings.

The desire of day laborers and live-in laborers to acquire small parcels of land, and the desire of small-scale farmers to acquire enough land to become independent of the uncertainty of wage earning, were not caused solely by

19 BLHA Potsdam, Pr. Br. Rep. 2 A, Regierung Potsdam, I St. Nr. 65, 55.
20 BLHA Potsdam, Pr. Br. Rep. 2 A, Regierung Potsdam, I P. Nr. 136, 13.
21 See Table 2.2.

Table 2.2. *Construction of family homes*[a] *and new "establishments":*[b] *population growth in* Regierungsbezirk *Potsdam, 1808–18*

County	No. of family homes	No. of tenant families	New *établissements*	Families with own home	Total of new *établissements*	Increase in no. families
E. Prignitz	56	103	165	193	211	296
W. Prignitz	151	227	92	99	263	326
Ruppin	227	211	173	173	400	384
E. Havelland	31	83	44	44	75	127
W. Havelland	24	82	9	22	33	104
Prenzlau	38	115	10	21	48	136
Templin	18	48	18	18	36	66
Angermünde	51	130	13	15	64	145
Oberbarnim	29	99	47	53	76	152
Niederbarnim	10	10	27	42	37	52
Teltow-Storkow	22	38	40	66	62	104
Zauche-Belzig	12	20	71	74	83	94
Jüterbogk-Luckenwalde	—	—	27	33	27	33
Total	699	1,166	736	853	1,395	2,019

[a]Rental houses built by landlords for mostly day laborers.
[b]All new owner-occupied houses.
Source: BLHA Potsdam, Regierung Potsdam, I. St. Nr. 65, 53.

the wish to improve their social position. Such striving was much more an expression of an effort to establish a basis for the long-term economic security of the family, which in turn would provide security in old age and for their descendants. In September 1818, for example, County Supervisor von Petersdorff referred to this difficult social problem in one of his official reports.

Eager and good day laborers have . . . a relatively decent income and there is always a demand for them as long as they are industrious. But they mostly have large families and this makes it very difficult for them to gain enough wealth to provide for old age. Many a village community often treats old and needy live-in laborers callously. Only administrative orders induce care. As soon as these laborers get old and weak, village communities try to get rid of them with the result that they often have to move from one place to another.[22]

22 BLHA Potsdam, Pr. Br. Rep. 2 A, Regierung Potsdam, I St. Nr. 62, 7.

The high rates of population growth among rural laborers in East Prignitz, West Prignitz, and Ruppin counties, particularly in a few peasant and colonist villages, were caused above all by the absence of restrictions on marriage, by strong immigration from Mecklenburg, and by a rise in the construction of rented apartments. It should be noted that tenants as well as small-scale farmers were partially or totally dependent on wage earning. Progress in agriculture in these counties had deep social and economic consequences, which particularly affected the life of rural wage laborers.

The following effects are especially apparent. First, the division of the commons, which first took place in state-owned villages, over time deprived laborers and small-scale farmers of opportunities to keep livestock, and thus provide their families with meat and milk, and to produce manure, which was a precondition for successful potato cultivation. Second, population growth among rural laborers, especially in a few peasant and colonist villages, resulted in increased competition for jobs in the rural labor market. This situation brought about declining or stagnating wages, an ever higher demand, and consequently higher prices for real estate, and a noticeably stronger demand for rented apartments. This led to a decline in the living standards of agricultural laborers and their families, made worse for a short time by economic depression. One result of this situation was the placement of several announcements in the *Berliner Zeitung* by the Russian embassy in Prussia offering opportunities to acquire land in Russian Poland.[23] In sum, the social conditions of the rural laborers living in Ruppin, East Prignitz, and West Prignitz counties created a favorable climate for increased emigrations.

III

This attempt to place two emigrations, the continental emigration from Ruppin County to Russian Poland between 1817 and 1819 and the overseas emigration of the Old Lutherans from the Uckermark and the Oderbruch to the United States in 1843, within the context of East Elbian migration history is to a large extent guided by the agenda Klaus J. Bade set for sociohistorical migration research.[24] Consciously disregarding simultaneous migrations, which because of their scope and diversity cannot be dealt with in this essay, this section focuses primarily on the influence

---

23 BLHA Potsdam, Pr. Br. Rep. 2 A, Regierung Potsdam, I St. Nr. 38.
24 Klaus J. Bade, "Sozialhistorische Migrationsforschung und 'Flüchtlingsintegration,' " in Klaus J. Bade, ed., *Flüchtlinge und Vertriebene in der westdeutschen Nachkriegsgeschichte: Bilanzierung der Forschung und Perspektiven für die künftige Forschungsarbeit* (Hildesheim, 1987), 138–43.

and the normative power of experiences shared by groups of people as well as on traditions and the resulting behavioral patterns, which in turn influenced migrations to a considerable extent. The Swedish scholar Åkerman has already emphasized the important role that pioneers may have played in the migration process. This was the basis for his recommendation to migration historians to pay more attention to such migration pioneers.[25]

It was precisely in the Kurmark (the western part of Brandenburg) where the mercantilistic settlement policy pursued by the Brandenburg-Prussian rulers in their state after the Thirty Years' War had remarkable consequences. More specifically, both the Great Elector and Friedrich the Great stimulated the immigration and subsequent settlement of tens of thousands of foreign colonist and artisan families in Brandenburg-Prussia, lasting to the end of the eighteenth century. According to Beheim-Schwarzbach's estimate, in 1786 "about one third of the Kurmark's total population of 683,145 were foreign colonists."[26] The majority had immigrated from Mecklenburg, Saxony, the Palatinate, Württemberg, France, Switzerland, the Netherlands, and Poland to the Kurmark.[27] Mecklenburgers, Saxons, Walloons, Swiss, and natives of the Palatinate first settled in the territory of what later became Ruppin County. They established their settlements predominantly in the state-owned areas, and the geographic core areas of their settlements were in the western, northwestern, central, and northeastern parts of Ruppin County.[28]

In order to draw immigrants to Brandenburg-Prussia, its rulers repeatedly published announcements abroad, inviting foreigners to immigrate to their state. Since the reign of the Great Elector, this activity had become a virtual campaign aimed at attracting foreign colonists, at times competing directly with similar efforts by the Austro-Hungarian Empire and by Russia. In order to draw as many colonists as possible to Brandenburg-Prussia, a number of privileges were promised. These privileges were by no means always of the same nature. It was only in 1769 that they were summarized and published as five points: first, freedom from conscription; second, freedom from public taxes for a fixed period, which was not the same in all parts of the state; third, freedom from import duties for all belongings; fourth, free-

---

25 Sune Åkerman, *Historisk forskning på migrationsområdet – några utvecklingslinjer och karaktärsdrag, in Omflyttningen* (Stockholm, 1980), 43.
26 Max Beheim-Schwarzbach, *Hohenzollernsche Colonisationen: Ein Beitrag zu der Geschichte des preussischen Staates und der Colonisation des östlichen Deutschlands* (Leipzig, 1874), 365.
27 Heinrich Berger, *Friedrich der Grosse als Kolonisator,* Giessener Studien auf dem Gebiet der Geschichte, vol. 8 (Giessen, 1896), 82–83.
28 Friedrich Wilhelm August Bratring, *Die Grafschaft Ruppin in historischer, statistischer und geographischer Hinsicht: Ein Beitrag zur Kunde der Mark Brandenburg* (Berlin, 1799), 48–59.

dom of religion; and, fifth, the granting of subsidies for the construction of
new farm buildings.

Without cost, the colonists received title to property in full inheritable
ownership, but they had to pay an annual tax after a fixed time. In case
they did not acquire landed property of different size as independent owners
in state-owned areas, they became serfs.[29] In addition to general privileges,
that is, those promised to prospective colonists in announcements published
abroad, a number of special privileges were granted, which were carried in
such announcements but which had to be fixed in a written or oral form
later in the new settlement.[30] This procedure led to endless disputes between
the authorities responsible for internal colonization and the colonists themselves. The colonists' struggle for the preservation of the once granted rights
and for gaining new, including legal, concessions from the state became an
integral part of the internal colonization history – and not just in Brandenburg-Prussia. The colonists' experiences in this struggle led to the development of special behavioral patterns among them.

Two examples from the seventeenth and eighteenth centuries, involving
Swiss colonist villages in Ruppin County, will draw attention to a phenomenon that also influenced migration and migration behavior in other
Prussian territories settled by colonists in a similar way. In a 1694 petition
to the elector signed by Swiss peasants living in the village of Vielitz, the
inhabitants demanded in the case of the possible expulsion from a farm of
a Swiss peasant who did not work properly that he be replaced by a compatriot. They asked the village teacher to draft their petition.

If the [Prussian] authorities don't support and protect us as they used to, we will
write to our former authorities in Switzerland to send us money for the journey
and we will then leave this place altogether. But if they give us assistance in this
respect, we will be absolutely subservient so God help us.[31]

Only a few years after establishing a Swiss settlement in Brandenburg,
the Vielitz colonists threatened to remigrate to Switzerland if their demand
was not met. Unfortunately, the answer of Elector Friedrich III to this
petition has not been recorded. But one might expect that the demand of
the self-conscious Swiss was in fact met since the elector, like his predecessor, was very interested in increasing the number of Brandenburg's in-

29 Beheim-Schwarzbach, *Hohenzollernsche Colonisationen,* 289–98.
30 Ibid.
31 Hermann Schneider, *Die Schweizer Kolonie in der Mark, ein ländliches Kulturbild aus dem Ende des 17.
   Jahrhunderts,* in *Beilage zum Programm des Königlichen Wilhelms-Gymnasiums 1906* (Berlin, 1906), 17.

habitants. This becomes even more probable because a senior civil servant evidently revised the first draft of the petition and moderated its tone.

The Lindow parish of the German Reformed Church, to which the Swiss colonist villages Vielitz, Glambeck, and Klosterheide also belonged, registered 267 marriages, 820 births, and only 466 deaths between 1690 and 1765, an excess of 354 births over deaths.[32] This rapid population growth in the Swiss villages, which was probably similar in other Swiss villages, prompted the community of all Swiss colonist villages in Ruppin County to address a number of petitions to King Friedrich II in 1747–48. Encouraged by the generous settlement policy pursued by the Hohenzollern dynasty, the Swiss peasants presented the following request on January 17, 1748.

We honor His Royal Majesty's grandfather's memory, who at the end of the last century gave us Swiss colonists the order to establish on the once deserted fields, marches, and outlying farms the villages of Schultzendorff, Königstedt, Lüdersdorff, Vielitz, Glambeck, Closterheide, Storbeck, and Lünow located in the *Domänen-ämter* Ruppin and Lindau, which we have done successfully assisted by His Royal Majesty's grandfather, whose memory we honor. Meanwhile the great Lord has blessed our parents, who immigrated to His Royal Majesty's country, with so many children that in some villages they have to build twice as many day laborer homes as there are farmhouses to provide their children with housing. But these day laborers have to earn their living by working in Mecklenburg.

But we, who are also blessed with many children, are not able to provide new prospects for our children. We plead with His Royal Majesty for some of those deserted field marches, which could be changed into the most beautiful villages or outlying farms, to give our children and unemployed day laborer fellows the opportunity to establish their own farms so that they won't be forced to go begging, but to earn their living by cultivating deserted fields and outlying farms . . . [33]

When the answer of the government administration of the Kurmark, evidently already announced in advance, did not arrive quickly enough (in the opinion of the petitioners), they complained in a new petition to the king on August 26, 1748, that

there has been so far no response and our poor social condition has become even worse. Since it is totally impossible for us to subsist any longer, unless we are relieved, we in our greatest misery shall be either forced to end our lives or to look for our bread abroad . . . [34]

32 Erich Wentscher, "Die Schweizer Kolonie in der Mark Brandenburg," *Archiv für Sippenforschung* 7 (1930): 388–89.
33 BLHA Potsdam, Pr. Br. Rep. 2, Kurmärkische Kriegs- und Domänenkammer, D. 16521, 2.
34 Ibid., 58, 59.

Confronted with the long delay in an official response to their petition, these colonists again threatened to emigrate as a way of putting additional pressure on the authorities. Since the colonists finally achieved their goal of acquiring several settlement opportunities for their children, they did not carry out the threat. Many more examples of such behavior in the history of internal colonization in Brandenburg-Prussia were found in the sources and could be mentioned here. But the cases described here already indicate that the Ruppin County colonists showed the following behavioral pattern in certain critical socioeconomic situations:

1. They petitioned the administration of state-owned areas in order to be granted title to property and benefits for the establishment of farmsteads, particularly for children, who were not eligible to inherit the parental farm.
2. In case of a positive response, the colonists moved within Prussia to where the state authorities had granted them the requested title to property and assistance. There they settled and cultivated the arable land.
3. But if even the threat of emigration, which was sometimes expressed in petitions sent directly to the king, did not bring the desired results, there was a high probability that the colonists would indeed emigrate to another country with more favorable conditions.

In the seventeenth and eighteenth centuries the colonists were often successful in disputes with the Prussian state, which was at that time very interested in population growth and in agricultural progress.

Let us now take a look at the 1817 events that took place at the beginning of the emigrations from Ruppin County to Russian Poland. Facing bad harvests, rising food prices, a commercial crisis, and widespread unemployment among the rural lower classes, which together decisively influenced the socioeconomic conditions in the countryside, the pioneers of the emigration to Russian Poland resorted to the already well-practiced means of bringing pressure to bear, the use of which had certainly already become traditional.

The first group of people desiring to emigrate from Ruppin County, a group that had already applied for emigration in the middle of September 1817 at County Supervisor von Zieten's office, consisted of six day-laborer families from two neighboring colonist villages in the northwestern section of the county. They were joined by seven live-in laborer families and two colonist families by the middle of December 1817 – all of them came from five neighboring colonist villages, which had a maximum distance from each other of ten kilometers. Moreover, they all belonged to the same parish.

On December 15, 1817, County Supervisor von Zieten stated in his report to the president of the royal administration, von Bassewitz:

Your Honor knows that several heads of families from Bienenwalde, Basdorff, Glienicke, Steinberge, and Storbeck applied for emigration permits in order to emigrate to the Grand Duchy of Warsaw. Hereupon I received . . . the order to ask these heads of families about their reasons for leaving. They replied that they would stay if they were given parts of the forest land on inheritable lease, free grazing rights for their livestock, and assistance in the construction of farm buildings. . . . I myself wish nothing more than to issue some of the required emigration permits in order to solve this problem. But as long as these permits are withheld from them, these people believe that the government is very interested in keeping them home and will reward them for that. They also believe that they can expect an easier life in Poland.[35]

Potential emigrant pioneers traditionally expected rewards for their readiness to stay in the country in the form of titles to the property they would settle, privileges, and state support, all of which the government had granted in the second half of the eighteenth century. The long delay in issuing the emigration permits as well as the readiness of lower-level state authorities to negotiate and to reach compromises seemed to indicate to the colonists that the state had a strong interest in keeping them within the country. This experience also corresponded to their ancestors' experience with the Prussian state. Some of the colonists interpreted this as a sign of hope and decided to stay in the country for the time being. A group of twelve out of seventeen families, the most determined colonists, honored their intention to emigrate and left for Russian Poland as soon as they received their emigration permits or passports in the spring of 1818. County Supervisor von Zieten's repeated warnings and the very vague prospect of receiving both property titles and privileges finally led these colonists to abandon their hopes. On October 3, 1817, only one day after day laborer Johann Holz had petitioned for a plot of land in the state-owned forest in order to establish a farm, County Supervisor von Zieten replied categorically

that he could not make such a deal and that, if he and the others actually received plots of land, they would soon be dissatisfied again and would ask for some thing or another; there are thousands of other live-in laborer families, who are able to earn a decent living. If he and his fellows would only accept their fate, they too could live in a similar way.[36]

35 BLHA Potsdam, Pr. Br. Rep. 2 A, Regierung Potsdam, I St. Nr. 58, 156.
36 Ibid., 134.

And to add insult to injury, von Zieten assured Holz on the same day that "they should not believe that the king would be particularly interested in keeping them; they would be allowed to leave."[37]

Von Zieten's warnings not to emigrate to Russian Poland had little effect on those wishing to emigrate. By August 22, 1818, 652 Ruppin County inhabitants had applied for emigration permits. Whereas nearly 75 percent of the emigrants came from colonist villages, the readiness to emigrate was remarkably lower in the towns. The colonists lived mostly in state-owned areas. Only a few came from villages under the jurisdiction of landed nobility. By September 15, 1818, the number of willing emigrants had grown by 416, for a total of 1,068 individuals.

The conclusion can be drawn that the idea to emigrate spread especially rapidly in the colonist villages and that in these villages the readiness to emigrate was very high, which in turn reinforced preparations for emigration. It has to be added that the fourteen old villages and manors, in which the remaining 25 percent of the rural emigrants lived, were located – almost without exception – in the immediate vicinity of those colonist settlements with high emigration rates.

In the District Potsdam, the core area of transoceanic emigration, particularly to the United States, was the Uckermark. Between 1862 and 1871 the share of Prenzlau (36.14 percent), Templin (19.49 percent), and Angermünde (17.14 percent) counties, the Uckermark, in the total emigration from District Potsdam was 72.77 percent. The proportion of people in the two Prignitz counties (13.07 percent) and Barnim County (3.22 percent) was much lower, namely, 16.29 percent.[38]

The 1843 decision of the Old Lutherans from the eastern area of Prenzlau County, from Angermünde County, and from some communities located in the Oderbruch to leave for America was the most remarkable event in the early emigration to an overseas destination. They were the pioneers of emigration to America. The local and personal structure of their emigration from the Uckermark and the Oderbruch to America between the 1840s and the 1870s clearly shows that those Old Lutheran pioneers triggered subsequent emigrations to the so-called New World.

In 1843 the Old Lutheran emigrants from the Oderbruch came from colonist villages; only two families lived in other nearby villages. Concerning the local composition of the Old Lutheran emigration from the eastern section of Prenzlau County in that year, it is striking to note that the ma-

37 Ibid.
38 *Preussische Statistik* 26 (1874): 200–207.

jority of the emigrants came from villages in which French Huguenots had settled at the end of the seventeenth century. This observation is further substantiated by the repeatedly occurring French family names among the Old Lutherans from this area.[39]

Descendants of the French refugees occupied leading positions in these emigration groups and also financially sponsored the passage of compatriots. Thus, the peasants Logé, Johann William, and Johann Salingré from Bergholz near Löcknitz were undoubtedly descendants of those French religious refugees who became the spokesmen, organizers, and financial sponsors of this momentous emigration. Peasant Christian Krull, who also belonged to this elite and whose wife's maiden name was Beccü, agreed to guarantee 5,000 taler, out of a travel fund totaling 21,500 taler. The peasants William and Salingré agreed to guarantee 16,500 taler.[40]

In his report to the royal administration of April 16, 1843, the supervisor of Prenzlau County, von Stülpnagel, emphasized that the peasants William, Logé, and Salingré

belonged to the French Reformed Church in earlier times and have been converted to the Old Lutheran faith by Ehrenström. Their ancestors left France because they did not want to practice Calvin's religious teachings and now they leave Prussia, because, guided by Ehrenström, they don't consider the teachings of Calvin as being right and leading to eternal salvation. All efforts to calm these confused souls were totally in vain. It is probably desirable to get rid of them as soon as possible since their minds are completely spoiled and they have been brought up to be unruly and rebellious.[41]

But this attitude expressed by the county supervisor is misleading. His description of the Old Lutheran pastor, Ehrenström, which went so far as to portray him as a demon of sorts, is subjective and his denigration of the Old Lutherans is tendentious. A remarkable number of the Huguenot descendants living in the Uckermark had already converted to the Lutheran Church long before the middle of the nineteenth century.[42] The latter was united with the Reformed Church after 1817. The united church was then called United Evangelical Country Church. Von Stülpnagel was evidently a convinced hard-liner in dealing with Old Lutheran pastors and members of the congregation. King Frederick William III supported this attitude, which since the 1830s led to exaggerated persecutions of and discrimination

---

39 Wilhelm Iwan, *Die Altlutherische Auswanderung um die Mitte des 19. Jahrhunderts,* 2 vols. (Ludwigsburg, 1943), 2:261–65.

40 BLHA Potsdam, Pr. Br. Rep. 2 A, Regierung Potsdam, I St. Nr. 44, 99.

41 Ibid., 60.

42 Werner Lippert, *Geschichte der 110 Bauerndörfer in der nördlichen Uckermark* (Cologne and Vienna, 1968), 140.

against the Old Lutherans. This intolerant behavior and the massive restrictions placed upon the freedom of religion by the Prussian state particularly
upset the inhabitants of the Uckermark of French origin. The roots of their
remarkable commitment to the defense of Old Lutheran principles and
interests had deep roots in their own history. Their ancestors had been
granted freedom of religion in the Edict of Potsdam in 1685. This guaranteed privilege was so deeply rooted in their consciousness, even after they
had left the French Reformed Church, that its violation provoked their
active resistance. Given this background, and considering the radical-
democratic sentiments in the prerevolutionary period, the intransigent demands of Old Lutherans from the Uckermark expressed in many petitions,
declarations, and the like can be better understood.

It was because of such a petition, which the peasants Krull, Salingré,
Logé, and William addressed to the king in the name of the Lutheran
congregations including that of the Uckermark on March 21, 1843, that
they were questioned in the county supervisor's office in Prenzlau on April
15, 1843. They gave the following reasons for their decision to emigrate:

We consider the contemporary Evangelical Country Church not to be a pure one
because its principles are deviant from the principles of the Augsburg Confession,
in which we strongly believe. Although on February 25 the county supervisor
well-meaningly informed us about the privileges regarding religious beliefs, which
His Royal Majesty in his fatherly kindness granted to us, and warned us to accept
gratefully the will of our gracious king, these concessions are not sufficient to calm
our consciousness. We demand either the full recognition of the old pure Lutheran
faith as laid down in the principles of the Augsburg Confession or we have to leave
our native land in order to find a refuge for our pure old faith. Only in case His
Royal Majesty would return to us the churches including their income, the parishes
including their income, and the schools including their income in the entire country, leave the election of our clergymen and schoolteachers to us alone without
any interference either with the services or with the schools by a secular power,
would we consider our conscience to be clear and would refrain from emigration.
Since we have no hope that our wishes will be fulfilled, our decision to emigrate
is unshakable . . . [43]

It was certainly no coincidence that these petitions were analogous to
the colonists' applications for emigration, though the latter were formulated
in earlier times for different reasons. Also in this case, privileges granted
earlier were defended and even expanded by using the threat of emigration
as a means of bringing pressure to bear upon the authorities. As for the Old
Lutherans, it was freedom of religion that was to be defended in the tra-

---

43 BLHA Potsdam, Pr. Br. Rep. 2 A, Regierung Potsdam, I St. Nr. 44, 63.

ditional way. When they recognized that their comprehensive and extensive demands could not be realized, they emigrated. This emigration was initiated by the most determined descendants of immigrant colonists.

In the initial phase of both emigrations, the people who left Ruppin County for Russian Poland between 1817 and 1819 and the first Old Lutherans, who lived in the Uckermark and the Oderbruch and who decided to migrate to the United States in the 1840s, came from colonist villages or from villages with a certain portion of colonist population. These pioneers of emigration from colonist villages, which were established or partially newly settled, clearly determined the migration patterns in the initial phase of the massive emigrations of the nineteenth century. Information on emigration projects and their realization was spread from these core areas via personal and church ties to neighboring colonist villages. Later on, the notion to emigrate was also spread by rumors and emigration agents. These pioneer emigrations significantly influenced subsequent migrations.

As I have demonstrated in the preceding, there is ample evidence for the historical relevance of the "spirit of the colony," that is, of a colonial consciousness based on historical and contemporary experiences – and its normative effects on the mental and behavioral patterns of emigration pioneers in particular. This spirit was characterized by a colonist tradition that used migration as an appropriate means to secure or improve their socioeconomic conditions and as an instrument to defend and expand privileges already granted.

3

Overseas Emigration from Mecklenburg-Strelitz: The Geographic and Social Contexts

AXEL LUBINSKI

In the second half of the nineteenth century, the Grand Duchy of Mecklenburg-Strelitz was one of those northeast German regions from which emigration to North America was especially intensive and massive (see Map 3.1).[1] Emigration to America from this region started in 1846–47; that is, it should be noted, before the revolution of 1848 in Germany. The core areas of early emigration were located on the border to the Uckermark (Brandenburg). This fact points to the initiating and stimulating role of information from this area that subsequently directed emigration to North America. Even before this emigration began, Mecklenburg-Strelitz experienced a sharp decline in population due to migrations principally to Prussia and, increasingly, especially to Berlin. Within this context, migration patterns can be identified on the village level as well and extrapolated to the larger entities examined in this essay: the duchy, state-owned areas (*Domanium*), local administrative units of the state-owned areas (*Domanialämter*), and groups of villages. Although neither substantive factors of a more complex structural and causal analysis nor the problems of chain migrations can be dealt with here, this essay will examine the emigration patterns of various groups of agricultural laborers, paying particular attention to their geographical differences and social conditions.

SCOPE, COURSE, AND STRUCTURE OF EMIGRATION

The Duchy of Mecklenburg-Strelitz, which in 1871 had a population of 79,976, encompassed an area of 2,547 square kilometers. This does not include the Principality of Ratzeburg, which was also part of the Grand Duchy. To the west, the duchy was bordered by Mecklenburg-Schwerin,

---

1 This essay presents initial results from my dissertation, which will be published under the title "Aus dem Untertanenverband entlassen: Die Amerikaauswanderung aus Mecklenburg-Strelitz" in 1995.

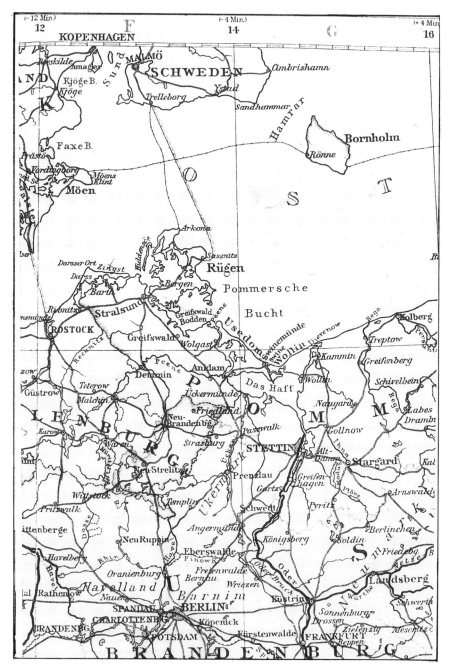

Map 3.1. North central Germany.

Table 3.1. *Overseas emigration from the Duchy of Mecklenburg-Strelitz, 1846–1914*[2]

Destinations	Emigrants (N)
North America	15,793
South and Central America	21
South Africa	104
Australia	26
Other overseas destinations	9
Overseas emigration	15,953
Russia	232
Other European states	180

Source: Emigration lists, passport lists, and files containing emigration permits in Mecklenburgisches Landeshauptarchiv Schwerin.[3]

to the east and south by Brandenburg, and to the north by Pomerania. Between 1846 and 1914, 15,953 persons in possession of either an emigration permit or a passport emigrated from the duchy to overseas destinations.[4] North America was the destination that the overwhelming majority of these migrants (96.5 percent) set for themselves (see Table 3.1). Overseas emigration from the area reached its peak in 1872, when 1,275 people left, that is, 1.57 percent of the total population.

A comparison of Mecklenburg-Strelitz, Mecklenburg-Schwerin, and

2 Emigration to other German states belonging, since 1871, to the German Reich was not considered.
3 Mecklenburgisches Landeshauptarchiv Schwerin (hereafter cited as MLHAS), Mecklenburg-Strelitzsche Landesregierung (hereafter cited as MSLR), vols. 1/277–1/286, 4/24, 4/27, 4/37, 4/45–4/113, 4/131–4/160; Mecklenburg-Strelitzsches Ministerium (hereafter cited as MSM), Abteilung des Innern (hereafter cited as AdI), 1571.
4 This study relies substantially on the statistics of the German Reich, which are reliable because they tried to register German overseas emigration via the ports of Bremen, Hamburg, and Antwerp and later also via Stettin, Le Havre, Rotterdam, and Amsterdam. I have also consulted official publications after 1872 that deal with naturalization and loss of citizenship of those persons who legally emigrated from German states to non-European countries and embarked in Bremen, Hamburg, or Antwerp for countries across the Atlantic. For the years between 1872 and 1882, see *Statistik des Deutschen Reiches,* ser. 1, vols. 2, 8, 14, 20, 25, 30, 37, 43, 48, 53, 59. In this analysis it turned out that the Grand Duchies of Mecklenburg-Schwerin and Mecklenburg-Strelitz had a relatively high rate of emigrants who applied for emigration before they left (about 70 percent for both Mecklenburgs; the average for Prussia and the German Reich was between 20 and 30 percent). Emigration with a passport was uncommon after 1853. For further information on sources and on emigration law of the Mecklenburgs, see A. Lubinski, "Zur Auswanderung aus Mecklenburg: Perspektiven der Forschung," *Wissenschaftliche Zeitschrift der Wilhelm-Pieck-Universität Rostock* 38, no. 2 (1989); Axel Lubinski, "Zu auswanderungsrechtlichen Grundsätzen Mecklenburgs in der 2. Hälfte des 19. Jahrhunderts," *Migrationsforschung* 24 (1990).

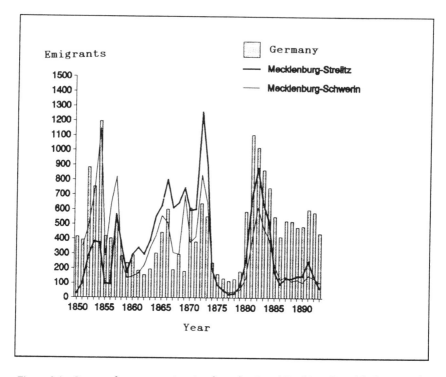

Figure 3.1. Course of overseas emigration from the Grand Duchies of Mecklenburg-Strelitz, Mecklenburg-Schwerin, and Germany between 1850 and 1893. The numbers from Mecklenburg-Schwerin figures have to be multiplied by a factor of ten; those for Germany by a factor of two hundred. *Source*: Data on Mecklenburg-Strelitz, see n. 4; data on Mecklenburg-Schwerin, see Lindig[5] and Mönckmeier;[6] data on Germany, see Marschalck.[7]

Germany generally reveals a startlingly apparent overlapping of the various waves of transatlantic emigration (see Figure 3.1). This fact in turn throws light on the importance of national and international factors underlying the migration process.

Although emigration to America rose rapidly in the early 1850s, this increase did not occur immediately after the failed revolution of 1848–49. Before the middle of the nineteenth century it was mainly the neighboring Prussian provinces and Berlin that received the bulk of the emigrants from

5 Lindig, "Entwicklung und gegenwärtiger Zustand des Auswanderungswesens in Mecklenburg," in Eugen von Philippovich, ed., *Auswanderung und Auswanderungspolitik in Deutschland, Schriften des Vereins für Sozialpolitik*, vol. 52 (Leipzig, 1892): 348.
6 Wilhelm Mönckmeier, *Die deutsche überseeische Auswanderung* (Jena, 1912), 78, 79, 86–89.
7 Peter Marschalck, *Deutsche Überseewanderung im 19. Jahrhundert: Ein Beitrag zur soziologischen Theorie der Bevölkerung* (Stuttgart, 1973), 36, 37.

Mecklenburg-Strelitz. This led to a loss of population of about 7,800 people in total from the Grand Duchy between 1817 and 1850.[8] As production for cash profits became the aim of Mecklenburg agriculture, landowning nobility, leaseholders, and peasants became more determined to hold their labor force to a minimum. This development in turn exerted strong pressure on a rapidly growing population.[9] A contemporary, Pastor Bohm from Neuenkirchen, who was a member of the Agricultural Society (*landwirtschaftlicher Verein*) Woldegk, described the situation as follows:

The enlarged estates and the rapid development of more efficient agricultural practices increased the need for labor. But since there were at the same time sufficient, and indeed too many, laborers who worked for lower wages than the estates' own day [contracted] laborers, no estate owner thought about employing more day laborers.[10] On the contrary, they tore down old small cottages without building new ones. It was about that time (1830–40) that the contracted laborers were forced to hire other laborers (often members of their own family) to work on the large estates. This was not difficult in a situation, when there was an abundant supply of young people, who were not able to establish their own households as a direct consequence of the housing shortage. . . . Thus, many young people, journeymen, farmhands, and maidservants crossed the border into Prussia and most went to Berlin to find a job there.[11]

Thus, emigration from Mecklenburg-Strelitz played an important role in economic and social developments in the region already prior to the middle of the nineteenth century.

EMIGRATION, INTENSITY, AND LIVING CONDITIONS OF DIFFERENT SOCIAL GROUPS

Analysis of emigration from Mecklenburg-Strelitz in relation to the places the emigrants came from confirms the already well known patterns of Mecklenburg emigration.[12] The area of the landowning nobility (*ritterschaftliches Gebiet*) had the highest rates of emigration.[13] However, its lower

---

8 Lindig, "Entwicklung und gegenwärtiger Zustand des Auswanderungswesens in Mecklenburg," 346.
9 Population development of the Grand Duchy of Mecklenburg-Strelitz: 1817: 72,675; 1822: 77,232; 1831: 84,796; 1840: 90,065; 1851: 99,628. Source: MLHAS, MSM, AdI, 506.
10 See section on contracted laborers.
11 MLHAS, MSLR 4/10, 89.
12 See Lindig, "Entwicklung und gegenwärtiger Zustand des Auswanderungswesens in Mecklenburg," 293–94.
13 The area of the landowning nobility consisted of all estates owned by the nobility and middle-class capitalists. The ownership of a large estate entitled the respective person to political and economic privileges, rights as well as commitments, e.g., seat in the legislature, patrimonial jurisdiction, obligation to poor relief and to provide old-age benefits. Besides the area of the landowning nobility there were state-owned and town areas.

Table 3.2. *Overseas emigration from individual parts of the Duchy Mecklenburg-Strelitz and* Domanialämter, *1846–1914*

Part of the Duchy/*Domanialamt*	Inhabitants 1871	Emigrants 1846–1914	Relation of emigrants to inhabitants (%)
State-owned	32,711[14]	7,114	21.7
Domanialamt			
Feldberg	8,475	2,594	30.6
Mirow	7,426	611	8.2
Stargard	9,140	3,287	36.0
Strelitz	6,523	410	6.3
"Kabinettsamt"	1,044	212	20.3
Area of landowning nobility	15,055	6,362	42.3
Villages	32,210	2,289	7.1
Duchy	79,976	15,953[15]	19.9

Source: Hof- und Staatshandbuch des Grossherzogtums Mecklenburg-Strelitz für 1875 (Neustrelitz); for emigration figures, see n. 4.

proportion of land and population accounts for the fact that, in terms of absolute numbers, there were fewer emigrants from this part of Mecklenburg-Strelitz than from the state-owned areas or *Domanium*.[16] In addition, the role of the towns in the migration process was only important at the early stage of overseas migration (see Table 3.2).

As was the case when viewing the emigration pattern in relation to the geographic pattern, an analysis of the emigrants' social and occupational backgrounds confirms the high proportion of agricultural laborers and rural artisans in comparison to the corresponding social groups in the towns (see Table 3.3).

The internal structure of employment for agricultural laborers as well as the underlying conditions and causes for their emigration, however, are

14 The 103 inhabitants of *Domanialamt* Fürstenberg have to be added to the total number of inhabitants living in the *Domanialämter* listed in the table.
15 Since the localities of 180 overseas migrants could not be determined, there is a difference between the number of emigrants from the Duchy of Mecklenburg-Strelitz and the total amount of the emigrants from its individual parts.
16 The owner of the *Domanium* was the grand duke. The *Domanium* was subdivided into districts that were administered by local departments. The grand duke leased his property either in the form of large estates to lease holders or to peasants and smallholders. Although the large estates of the *Domanium* and the landowning nobility were clearly separated by administrative lines they were spread all over the territory of the duchy.

Table 3.3. *Social and occupational composition of the overseas emigration,*
1846–1914[17]

	Domanium	Domanialämter	Villages	Duchy
"Arbeiter"	406	271	126	803
"Tagelöhner"	349	535	17	898
Farmhands and other laborers	713	667	143	1,523
Women	571	457	136	1,173
"Mädchen"	241	272	77	590
Artisans, all	353	188	407	948
Master artisans	16	10	53	79
Journeymen	198	109	199	506
Apprentices	16	3	23	42
Clerks, intellectuals, artists, soldiers, officers	37	12	47	96

Source: See n. 4.

much more clearly revealed by a microanalysis on the local level and by
their differentiated social frames of reference.

As one moves beyond the regional level of the duchy and the higher
administrative units – the *Domanium,* area of landowning nobility, and
towns – one discovers many and diverse variations to the original picture
of emigration from Mecklenburg-Strelitz.

RURAL EMIGRATION

An examination of the *Domanium* and individual *Domanialämter* provides an
exemplary illustration of this diversity. Analysis of the emigration from the
Domanium reveals that emigration rates were high in the eastern part of the
duchy, which encompassed *Domanialämter* Feldberg and Stargard, and rel-

17 Since the sources usually contain the occupation of the applicant for an emigration permit, these
data refer only to these persons. Consequently, all those female persons without husbands, who applied for emigration for themselves and their family members (if there were any), belong to the category "women." Separately registered is the category "girl" (*Mädchen*), whose status was denoted as
Mädchen in the sources. In contrast to the category "women," who could be married, widowed, or
divorced, these *Mädchen* were single at any rate. There is a high probability that they worked as
maidservants or in similar occupations. Persons who belonged to the middle or upper class were not
called *Mädchen*. The designations *Arbeiter* and *Tagelöhner* also reflect the corresponding terms used in
the sources. It is often the case that both designations were used for the same person by different
authorities as synonyms. Whether they were workers in towns, live-in laborers (*Einlieger*), or contracted laborers (*Hoftagelöhner*) can be determined almost certainly by considering their residences.
Persons specialized in certain dependent jobs, e.g., coachmen, shepherds, "Holländer," waiters,
sailors, were categorized as "other laborers," listed together with the farmhands in row three.

atively low in the western part, which included *Domanialämter* Mirow and Strelitz (see Table 3.2).

In order to determine the causes of these contrasting emigration patterns, we must examine some of the essential socioeconomic structures and conditions of these *Domanialämter*. There are striking differences in the size of the agricultural units and in the cultivation patterns (agriculture and forestry), which seem to indicate a relationship to the contrasting emigration patterns. While the majority of the state-owned property leaseholds (*domaniale Pachthöfe*) were located in an area of fertile loamy soil in the northeast section of the *Domanium,* the sandy southwestern part of the duchy, which included *Domanialämter* Strelitz, Mirow, and the southern part of Feldberg, was the location of the large forests owned by the duke.

The size of the seventy-five state-owned demesne property leaseholds was between 300 and 1,000 hectares. In November 1848 these estates employed about 1,200 contracted laborers and their families.[18]

In the course of the distribution of village lands, which were part of the land reforms beginning in 1792, the last fifty-one peasants who originally lived in state-owned villages (*domaniale Gutsdörfer*) had been moved to peasant villages. Significantly fewer cottagers lived in the state-owned villages than in the peasant villages.[19]

In 1848 there were 332 peasants, 733 so-called *Häuschen-Leute* (cottagers), and 2,670 live-in laborers (*Einlieger*) staying in rented accommodations in the duchy's peasant villages (Table 3.4 shows the situation in 1880).[20]

The figures in Table 3.4 show several features of *Domanialämter* that need to be highlighted. First, 81 percent of the areas cultivated by leaseholders were located in *Domanialämter* Feldberg and Stargard. Moreover, the concentration of farms (*Bauernstellen*) in *Domanialamt* Stargard, which had the largest and most fertile agricultural areas, is remarkable. Second, a relatively high concentration of farms existed in *Domanialamt* Mirow. The thirty-two *Kolonisten* (settlers) were small peasants, occupying an ambiguous position between the small peasantry and the rural lower classes. The extraordinarily high proportion of cottagers in *Domanialamt* Mirow also belonged to the latter category.

The following report, issued on January 3, 1866, by *Domanialamt* Mirow and sent to the government in Mecklenburg-Strelitz, shows that the existence and accessibility of small plots of land had an immediate effect on the emigration rate in the area of its jurisdiction.

18 MLHAS, MSLR 7/46, 105–25.
19 Ibid.
20 Ibid.

Table 3.4. *Structure of the size of agricultural and property units in the* Domanium *in 1880*

	Domanialamt Feldberg	Domanialamt Mirow	Domanialamt Stargard	Domanialamt Strelitz
Overseas emigration, 1846–1914	2,594	611	3,287	410
Population 1880	8,503	7,555	9,135	6,664
Leased area (hectare)[21]	12,692	2,748	16,455	3,994
Peasants and leaseholders	78	79	143	48
"Kolonisten"	2	32	4	13
Smallholders	—	—	2	8
Cottagers	—	31	—	4
Homeowners	275	462	214	305

Source: *Hof- und Staatshandbuch des Grossherzogtums Mecklenburg-Strelitz für 1885* (Neustrelitz).

The tendency to emigrate to North America, which was relatively high in *Domanialamt* Mirow, has recently decreased remarkably. We believe that this is related to the fact that the people are more and more convinced that they can acquire small plots of land in their own country on which to settle. Ever since the acquisition of such small plots of land by the rural lower classes became possible, they have stopped migrating to America.[22]

Viewing the duchy as a whole, however, these settlement measures were an exception to the rule. The exertions to expand, in particular, the number of small and middling peasants were much more effective and reached greater dimensions, for example, in neighboring Mecklenburg-Schwerin than in Mecklenburg-Strelitz.

To clarify further the possible correlation between the size of the agricultural units and the emigration rates, the Stargard *Domanialamt,* which had the highest absolute and relative emigration in the *Domanium,* needs to be studied more closely (see Table 3.5).

The figures for the individual villages of one *Domanialamt* in Table 3.5 further substantiate the correlation that has already been indicated, that is, the emigration rates in state-owned villages were generally much higher than in peasant villages. There were, however, a number of exceptions to this rule. The following section focuses on the specific nature of this correlation by comparing the social situation of the contracted laborers with

21 This area encompassed the property leaseholds owned by the grand duke of Mecklenburg-Strelitz (*Domanium*). Besides, small plots of land were leased to cottagers and "free laborers." Formally in Mecklenburg-Strelitz, almost all peasants in the *Domanium* were tenant farmers until 1922.
22 MLHAS, MSLR 4/2.

Table 3.5. *Emigration rates and property sizes in the Domanialamt Stargard*

Place	Population, 1871	Overseas emigrants	Relation emigrants/inhabitants	Property leasehold, 1871 (hectares)	Peasants, colonists, and smallholders	Homeowners, 1871
Badresch	231	089		529,81		6
Ballin	276	149		782,17		
Broda	109	047		365,69		
Klein Daberkow	118	067		520,32		
Dewitz	321	113		840,71	4 colonists	
Friedrichshof	077	—		351,85		
Golm	233	154		797,57		3
Katzenhagen	070	026		311,67		
Krickow	093	005		296,42		
Küssow	094	059		458,80		
Alt Käbelich	307	126		991,97		1
Neu Käbelich	117	076		428,28		
Lindow	206	067		671,37		5
Loitz	159	113		517,42		1
Marienhof	068	029		299,58		
Neetzka	233	173		873,83		
Klein Nemerow	145	045		473,18		
Pragsdorf	273	210		923,72		
Quastenberg	172	106		657,99		
Neu Rhäse	101	023		251,69		
Rosenhagen	066	038		359,61		
Rowa	173	054		456,26		4

Sabel	136	037		423,89		1
Sponholz	201	047		669,81		
Teschendorf	270	177		877,06		1
Warlin	230	183		622,95		
Zirzow	304	165		843,68		6
Estate villages	4,785	2,378	0,497	15,599	4	28
Ballwitz	239	7			10	10
Bargensdorf	236	42			9	9
Georgendorf	131	62				14
Glienke	287	104			10	11
Holldorf	145	19			4	4
Kublank	349	51			14	15
Gross Nemerow	378	33			14	16
Neuendorf	213	38			4	15
Pasenow	391	86			19	8
Petersdorf	257	29			16	5
Rühlow	294	101			13	8
Weitin	429	82			19	23
Wulkenzin	497	139			11	32
Peasant villages	3,846	793	0,206	—	143	170
Schönbeck	373	101		872		15
Stargard Bauhof	136	15			10	
Sum total	9,140	3,287	0,36	16,471	157	213

Source: Hof- und Staatshandbuch des Grossherzogtums Mecklenburg-Strelitz für das Jahr 1875 (Neustrelitz); for emigration figures, see n. 4.

that of the so-called free laborers in the countryside. In addition to these two main categories of agricultural laborers, the social status of the farm-hands and maidservants in the village community of midcentury Mecklen-burg will also be described.

THE "FREE LABORERS"

The "free laborers," those agricultural laborers who had no contract with an employer covering a longer period of employment, were for the most part cottagers or tenants in the peasant villages (live-in laborers). They found employment not only on farms but also on state-owned property leaseholds, especially in seasons of high labor demand (harvests, etc.). The live-in la-borers lived in the houses of peasants or cottagers.

   The cottagers owned a plot of land that had a maximum size of 700 square rods (1 square rod = 21.7 square meters). In the first half of the century the cottagers had been able to cultivate leased plots of land and were allowed to take advantage of free grazing on common lands (*Allmende*) of the respective village. To a large extent these opportunities vanished with distribution of land to the village households in the course of the land reforms. The small compensation in land they received for the loss of free grazing on the common lands was often not sufficient to graze a single cow, which was of vital importance for the existence of the cottager's family. On March 21, 1848, twenty-seven cottagers from the villages of Priepert and Radensee, *Domanialamt* Strelitz, petitioned the grand duke of Mecklen-burg-Strelitz: "Six to eight years ago the *Kammer- und Forstkollegium* gave the order to take away some of our land with the result that each of us was left in possession of only 150 square rods. Our land was given to the present leaseholder."[23] The petitioners added that they could not survive without additional land.[24]

   In the spring of the revolutionary year of 1848, the ducal government's attention was directed particularly to the social plight of the common people in the peasant villages, that is, the tenants and cottagers. The officials as-sumed that the greatest potential for conflict was located here. On April 6, 1848, the government informed the *Domanialämter* that:

Serenissimus [the duke] has decided to lease a plot of land at a reasonable rent to those cottagers in the peasant villages of our estates who, with the exception of

23 According to their own information, some of them had owned only 200 but most of them 500 to 1,000 square rods of arable land.
24 MLHAS, MSLR 7/46, 4, 5.

their land compensation for the former grazing rights on the common lands, own no other land. The same measure shall be taken for the tenants, who live in peasant villages.[25]

In this way the affected cottagers received 700 and the tenants 150 square rods of good land. If the soil was deemed less fertile, they received even more. The cottagers thus received sufficient land to enable them to keep a cow. The remaining land was used to grow potatoes and flax to support the household, although it was not enough to reach subsistence level. The tenants as well as the cottagers and home owners were thus dependent mainly or almost exclusively on earning outside wages. They had no annual contracts like the contracted laborers and were therefore forced to find a job for the harvest season, for a week, or even for the day. These so-called "free laborers" found work, for example, on large property leaseholds, large estates, on farms, in the forest, as peat cutters, in road construction, on soil improvement projects. They received higher wages as contracted laborers, but in contrast to the estate-contracted laborers their year-round permanent employment was not guaranteed.

In May 1851 the ducal government ordered *Domanialamt* Feldberg to investigate employment opportunities for tenants within the district. The subsequent report concluded that those tenants who lived or worked in the state-owned villages usually found work on the state-owned property lease-holds only from May until October, unless they got a permanent job such as feeding livestock.[26]

The situation in the peasant villages, where the majority of the tenants lived, was similar. In 1851 a report was issued from Triepkendorf, a large peasant village with a total of forty-five tenants located in *Domanialamt* Feldberg, that stated: "At present the people [tenants] in Triepkendorf usually find work for eight months and there is no employment for four months. . . ."[27]

This situation was also typical for laborers who found work on the large estates in Mecklenburg and Prussia. Only a small percentage of the laborers found winter work as woodcutters.[28]

THE FARMHANDS AND MAIDSERVANTS

In Mecklenburg villages, sons and daughters of peasants, smallholders, and day laborers – from their confirmation to their marriage – traditionally

25 Ibid., 3.
26 MLHAS, DA Feldberg 199, 25–45.
27 Ibid., 46.
28 Ibid., 46–74.

belonged to the category of farmhands (*Knechte*) and maidservants (*Mädge*). These young people worked in the field and as domestic servants on the state-owned property leaseholds or large estates. Children of peasants often worked on their parents' farms. The farmhands and maidservants had very little leisure time, were constantly used for all kinds of jobs, and had to work Sundays performing farm chores such as feeding livestock and servicing the households. In turn they were entitled to free board and lodging. They also received a certain wage, which in the middle of the century was about twenty-three taler for maidservants and about forty-six taler for farmhands and some payment in kind such as cloths, wool, or linen.[29]

By the second half of the century, this occupation became less and less attractive for the younger generation. Even rising wages, a consequence of an increasing shortage of farmhands and maidservants, could not compensate for the personal and social disadvantages of this kind of work. These disadvantages included rigid regimentation and regulation not only of the working day but of leisure time as well, brought about by both the rhythm of farming and the law (*Gesindeordnung*) itself. The result was that there was literally no privacy for farmhands and maidservants.

Under these circumstances it is not surprising that young people looked for alternatives to satisfy their desire for personal freedom, which in the spirit of the times influenced and conditioned their values and mentality to an ever increasing degree. On December 10, 1864, the meeting of the Mecklenburg Patriotic Society in the town of Waren came to the conclusion that, unlike in the past, single young men were increasingly looking for jobs in road and railroad construction and in the summer harvests. "They no longer like the contractual relationship to their employers, although in the above-mentioned jobs they have to work harder and longer hours and they don't get paid better."[30]

But, for a long period of time, such alternatives were not easily realized in Mecklenburg-Strelitz. In 1855, moreover, the ducal government actually instructed *Domanialämter* to enforce the law on farmhands and maidservants (*Gesindeordnung*), which dated back to 1654. These instructions, which were issued on June 2, 1855, stated:

The children of the day laborers, shepherds, contracted laborers, artisans, smallholders . . . in the *Domanium* are obliged to engage in a contractual relationship from their confirmation to the time they get a residence permit [*Niederlassungs-*

29 See Theodor Freiherr von der Goltz, *Die Lage der ländlichen Arbeiter im Deutschen Reich: Bericht an die vom Congress deutscher Landwirthe niedergesetzte Commission zur Ermittelung der Lage der ländlichen Arbeiter im Deutschen Reich* (Berlin, 1875), 70, 71, 453, 454.
30 MLHAS, Mecklenburg-Schwerin, Ministerium des Innern (hereafter cited as MdI) 10829/5, 142.

schein], unless they learn a trade or find another occupation that allows them to support themselves without ordinary wage earning and to acquire a residence permit some day.[31]

The impact of such and similar instructions on the social situation of the rural population and the way local officials in the *Domanium* used their discretionary authority to administer them is illustrated by their assessment and treatment of the problem of common-law marriage.

In the 1850s and 1860s almost every sixth child born in Mecklenburg-Strelitz was illegitimate. The proportion of these children had risen since the beginning of the century but dropped rapidly after 1867 when legal restrictions on marriages were lifted. These restrictions prohibited marriage unless the prospective groom could prove that he had a home. To do so he was required to submit a residence permit to the local authorities. A place to live, be it an apartment or a house, was either provided by the *Domanialamt* or it granted construction permits (especially for artisans or for tenant farmers). In addition, the leaseholders in the *Domanium* and the noble owners provided their contracted laborers with accommodations. The existing living units, however, could not meet the demand for housing, particularly since the leaseholders and noble owners were interested in keeping the number of their contracted laborers low in order to minimize wage costs, their expenditures for the poor and for old age benefits. This is the reason why *Domanialämter* tolerated only a limited number of tenements. At the end of 1848, alderman Franz Schroeder, who was from *Domanialamt* Mirow, estimated that the housing shortage in the demesne area was 1,100 units.[32]

Under these circumstances, illegitimate births were everyday occurrences in Mecklenburg and the rural lower classes did not view illegitimacy as immoral. Another local official in *Domanialamt* Stargard, *Oberlanddrost* (chief bailiff) Bernhard von Kamptz, reported to the ducal government on April 17, 1852:

Things have gone so far that out in the country the principle has established itself in public opinion that extramarital pregnancy is no longer a scandal for the weaker sex and that the male sex can get away with impertinence and thoughtlessness when it sires illegitimately and also finds an excuse in the fact that housing cannot always be found right away.[33]

31 MLHAS, DA Feldberg 104.
32 MLHAS, MSLR 7/67, 44.
33 MLHAS, MSLR 1/8.

Whereas von Kamptz and his government demanded that steps be taken to correct this development, and asked other local officials to register their opinion on this issue, the latter responded only cautiously. Official Franz Schroeder from *Domanialamt* Mirow "was not able to suggest any measures that promised the least bit of success."[34] Official Hermann Held from Feldberg argued against law enforcement:

Here in the district in most of the cases by far, the parents of the child want to marry, but they can't because no one will house them. . . . The parents remain true to one another and support the child, who is often followed by a second one, without the parents being able to obtain a place to live so they can marry. Measures of law enforcement and punishment against the parents can easily lead to disadvantages for the child. Dishonorable punishments have led to infanticide. Fines . . . hit the parents at a time when child care takes up all their means. Imprisonment, at least for the mother, usually could be imposed only a good deal later.[35]

Despite all reservations, in April 1856 the governments of Mecklenburg-Schwerin and Mecklenburg-Strelitz adopted a marriage law punishing lewdness and concubinage. In accordance with this law, concubinage was punished by fines of between 3 and 100 taler, or incarceration for up to four weeks. Among other things, the law makes the following points:

In determining the sentence one should consider: (a) How long the immoral intercourse has been going on, how often it is practiced, the more or less mitigating circumstances, and the degree of public outrage; (b) The character of those involved, their previous conduct, and the degree to which they have been corrupted.[36]

Today, it is hard to determine the extent to which this law actually affected the life of the rural lower classes. The Select Committee of the landowning nobility in Rostock in a declaration from March 23, 1855, claimed that the essential factor in the marriage question was a simple matter of strictly enforcing the existing law: "The cause for the increasing tendency of couples to live together out of wedlock is that these offenses have not been adequately and consistently punished."[37]

Not all local officials shared this opinion. On August 24, 1869, Bailiff Franz Schroeder reported to the ducal government:

---

34 Ibid.
35 Ibid.
36 *Grossherzoglich Mecklenburg-Strelitzscher Officieller Anzeiger für Gesetzgebung und Staatsverwaltung* (Neustrelitz, 1856), 43–47.
37 MLHAS, MSLR 1/8.

Stringent and prompt enforcement of the 1856 law against lewdness and concubinage was so repulsive and unbearable that – I don't deny it – mainly for this reason the administration here has become laxer in its practice . . . in no branch of police administration was there a clearer conviction that despite any strict application of this law this evil could never be controlled, in fact it couldn't even be reduced.[38]

In detailing the differing official positions on this law as well as with the law itself, my purpose has been to illustrate how differing official attitudes and patterns of behavior concerning an issue of vital concern to young people in nineteenth-century Mecklenburg-Strelitz either generated or avoided social pressures and conflicts. Similar constellations arose – not only in dealings with governmental authorities or in the case of young people – and influenced the social climate at the local level. This in turn stimulated or inhibited geographic mobility. The situation of the contracted laborer was to a great extent dependent on the leaseholder's and noble owner's character and value system.

CONTRACTED LABORERS

Since the social situation of the contracted laborer's family was determined by a multilayered system of labor obligations and income in the form of wages and payment in kind, I will forgo describing it in great detail. This has already been accomplished in numerous studies of the social situation of agricultural laborers in East Elbia.[39]

In this context I want to emphasize those factors, which in my opinion were especially relevant to the migration process. First, a relatively large proportion of the contracted laborer's household income consisted of payment in kind and leases for land on which potatoes and flax were grown. The family was able to keep a cow, pigs, geese, chickens, and sometimes also sheep. In Mecklenburg-Strelitz in 1848 each contracted laborer was entitled to receive one bushel of rye, one bushel of oats, and one taler every three weeks. During the threshing season his payment consisted of grain (every seventeenth bushel); in the fall, he received two bushels of dried peas or rye and two bushels of barley or oats, in addition to the small plot of land he leased. A portion of this payment in kind was at times paid in cash.

---

38 Ibid.
39 Max Weber, *Die Verhältnisse der Landarbeiter im ostelbischen Deutschland, Schriften des Vereins für Socialpolitik,* vol. 55 (Leipzig, 1892), 9–31, 697–735; Alexander von Lengerke, *Die ländliche Arbeiterfrage,* (Berlin, 1849); von der Goltz, *Die Lage der ländlichen Arbeiter im deutschen Reich.*

In addition, the contracted laborer was supplied with firewood or bales of peat.[40]

In 1853 Mecklenburg-Schwerin senior civil servant Friedrich von Bassewitz, who had previously served in the Prussian royal civil service before his current appointment on August 2, 1837, compared the income of Mecklenburg contracted laborers with that of agricultural laborers in Prussia in general and with that of other categories of laborers. He reported that

> whereas in the Prignitz area (West Brandenburg) a contracted laborer's family has an annual income in kind that equals 120–150 taler in cash, the annual income in kind of our contracted laborers on the large estates is equivalent to 150 and 200 taler in cash. Thus, as a rule, it is often more than double the annual income that our remaining urban and rural laborers and the majority of our artisans are able to obtain, and this does not take into consideration the fact of the regularity and security this income provides to the contracted laborer.[41]

Contemporary studies concluded that in the 1870s[42] and 1890s[43] the annual income of the contracted laborers in Mecklenburg, when compared with that in other German provinces, was above the national average. In his 1892 survey, Max Weber stated that "the social situation of the agricultural laborers in Mecklenburg can be described as being the most favorable in the whole German east."[44] Although the annual net income of the contracted laborer in Mecklenburg was relatively small, he still was evidently able to save some money and this situation improved with the rising wages in the second half of the nineteenth century.

Because the contracted laborers could satisfy the basic needs of their families through payment in kind (accommodation, food, firewood, clothes), they were much less threatened by the effects of agricultural and economic crises than "free laborers" in the countryside, urban workers, or artisans. The latter were forced to pay for all of their living costs out of their wages. During times of unemployment, caused either by seasonal labor market fluctuations or economic downturns, as well as during times of rising food prices, their existence was immediately threatened. Between 1847 and 1855 governmental efforts to relieve extreme social hardship by creating jobs in road construction, woodcutting, and the like, and by selling subsidized food, were directed at the "free laborers" in rural areas and in the towns but not at the contracted laborers.[45]

40 MLHAS, MSLR 7/46, 100–101.
41 MLHAS, MdI 10829/5, 20.
42 Von der Goltz, *Die Lage der ländlichen Arbeiter im Deutschen Reich,* 143.
43 Max Weber, "Die Verhältnisse der Landarbeiter im ostelbischen Deutschland."
44 Ibid., 762.
45 MLHAS, MSLR 1/109, 3–29; MSLR 1/77.

Second, the relationship between employer and contracted laborer was characterized by fundamental, "patriarchal" remnants of the former feudal society, which survived the abolition of serfdom in Mecklenburg in 1820. It was not until 1848 that contracted laborers on large estates could enforce the claims that resulted from their contracts with a landowner or leaseholder. After this time their opportunities improved but recourse to any appeals process remained limited. Payment took place in accordance with agreement and local custom, which sometimes varied widely from village to village and affected such matters as differences in the quality of the payment in kind, or of the allotted pasture and arable land, or differences in the amount of time and the date when the contracted laborer was allowed to till his land (he was often allowed to do so only on Sundays). Differences also arose over the issue of just how sick a contracted laborer or one of his family members had to be in order to be exempted from work on the large estate, or just when the estate owner was forced to send for a doctor.

In the summer of 1848 the leaseholders in *Domanialämter* of Mecklenburg-Strelitz asked for regulation of the relationship with their contracted laborers by the government, especially in relation to the amount and quality of firewood they had to provide their laborers "to avoid further conflicts."[46] The appropriate authorities refused to intervene in the relationship between employers and laborers, stating:

Only the leaseholder can know the special situation of his laborers and take it into account. And only to him should be left the responsibility of how to satisfy all the basic needs of his laborers. In general we would consider a state to be most unfortunate, which hardheartedly sets the lord and the laborer in opposition to one another. . . . A coming together like father and child is in our opinion what these times demand. A mere *Rechtsstaat* [legalistic state] is the product of an ice-cold imagination.[47]

Nevertheless, following the example set in Mecklenburg-Schwerin, juries were convened in 1848 in Mecklenburg-Strelitz as well. Their task was to determine what payment "in accordance with local custom" meant in so-called normal contracts (*Normalkontrakten*). This measure did not, however, ease the tensions between both parties. The quality of the lives of the contracted laborers was directly affected by their relationships with the employer – either good or bad – precisely because the contractual relationship extended into every sphere of the former's lives.

During a period of rising geographic mobility in which more and more

---

46 MLHAS, MSLR 7/46, 16.
47 MLHAS, MSLR 4/46, 21.

people enjoyed their freedom to choose their domicile, a period of increasing public debate on current political events and of open disputes among opposing interests, the pressure of the patriarchal relationship with the landowner became ever more intolerable to an increasing number of contracted laborers. At its meeting in December 1865, the local branch of the Mecklenburg Patriotic Society in Crivitz drew the following conclusion:

The contracted relationship between landowner and laborer, which stems from the feudal society, has, despite all of its material advantages, a lot of disadvantages. As a result people don't want to engage in such a relationship. Only in rare cases, that is, when forced by extreme hardship, will day laborers living in peasant villages decide to become contracted laborers.[48]

Third, unlike the cottager in the *Domanium,* the contracted laborer did not own the home in which he lived. Friedrich von Bassewitz described the possible consequences of this fact in a memorandum on emigration. Turning his attention to "the widows and those men unfit for work who live in quite a large number on the manors," he wrote:

It is the exception to the rule that they live with their families. This is only the case as long as the landowner allows it. As a rule, and who could deny it, the landowner considers them a burden. Whether their social situation is considered bearable or not depends totally on the degree of the landowner's philanthropy.[49]

As an alternative to this situation, many day laborers strove to acquire their own houses and land. And this alternative could be realized much more easily in America than in Mecklenburg.

Fourth, many landowners and leaseholders financially supported emigration at the beginning of the 1850s, before a shortage of agricultural contracted laborers occurred, due to strong emigration to America. Their efforts to increase agricultural efficiency by employing a minimum number of laborers, thus enabling them to compete with Americans and Russians on the world grain market, led to the increasing use of farm machines in Mecklenburg, especially after 1870.[50] The threshing machine in particular contributed to the increasingly seasonal character of agricultural labor. The seasonal demand for labor conflicted more and more with the chronic and painful labor shortage caused by emigration and internal migration of Mecklenburg laborers. The landowners tried to solve this problem by employing foreign laborers. By the early 1890s the immigration of seasonal migrants

48 MLHAS, MdI 10829/5, 77–78.
49 MLHAS, MdI 10829/5, 25.
50 Ulrich Bentzien, *Landbevölkerung und agrartechnischer Fortschritt in Mecklenburg vom Ende des 18. bis zum Anfang des 20. Jahrhunderts* (Berlin, 1983), 95, 122–76.

assumed massive proportions. In 1914 foreigners made up about 34 percent of the agricultural laborers in Mecklenburg-Schwerin.[51]

CONCLUSIONS

Upon analyzing the emigration intensity and the socioeconomic structures within the *Domanium* of Mecklenburg-Strelitz, it becomes evident that the overseas migration from the state-owned villages was more than twice as intensive as that from the villages of the independent peasantry. Contracted day laborers on the large estates received higher wages than other categories of agricultural laborers and were therefore in a much better situation to fulfill the material preconditions for participating in any migration overseas.

The factors determining this population transfer can be found in the difficult social conditions at home, standing in sharp contrast to alternatives abroad. These conditions can be summarized as follows:

First, large estate owners, leaseholders, and administrators imposed constraints like marriage restrictions, forced labor of servants (*Gesindezwangsdienst*), and patrimonial jurisdiction (*Patrimonialgerichtsbarkeit*) on agricultural laborers, especially servants and contracted laborers, that had been carried over from feudal society.

Second, and related to the first condition, agricultural laborers found it impossible to acquire small plots of arable land, which would have allowed them to gain a greater measure of independence and, in turn, to improve their social status.

Third, decreasing employment opportunities as a consequence of the land reforms played a role until the middle of the 1850s. This was an especially important factor in villages within the *Domanium* and the area controlled by the landed nobility. But it was also true for those villages of the independent peasantry that experienced above average population growth. Since the middle of the 1850s the demand for agricultural labor had been increasing, but this demand became simultaneously more and more seasonal. Decreased income resulting from seasonal labor or unemployment had a stimulating effect on the readiness to migrate. However, in the case of the so-called free laborers, who had smaller financial resources at their disposal, the alternative of emigration was more or less not feasible. It can therefore be assumed that this category of agricultural laborers was overrepresented in the internal migration.

---

51 Reno Stutz, "Landwirtschaft und ausländische Arbeitskräfte im Grossherzogtum Mecklenburg-Schwerin zwischen 1850 und 1914," Ph.D. diss., Universität Rostock, 1990, 142.

Thus, emigration from the Grand Duchy of Mecklenburg-Strelitz in the second half of the nineteenth century also documents that "the export of the social question was an inherent feature of German overseas emigration." As such it functioned as a safety valve for the social crisis that resulted from the transition of an agrarian society to an industrial one.[52] It has to be emphasized, however, that the specifics of the social question in Mecklenburg-Strelitz were to a large extent determined by the preservation of semifeudal customs and constraints in so-called patriarchal relations. Such phenomena can be documented on the legislative and executive levels as well as observed in the relations among large estate owners, leaseholders, and agricultural laborers.

52 Klaus J. Bade, "Die deutsche überseeische Massenauswanderung im 19. und frühen 20. Jahrhundert: Bestimmungsfaktoren und Entwicklungsbedingungen," in Klaus J. Bade, ed., *Auswanderer – Wanderarbeiter – Gastarbeiter: Bevölkerung, Arbeitsmarkt und Wanderung in Deutschland seit der Mitte des 19. Jahrhunderts,* 2 vols. (Ostfildern, 1984), 1:267–68.

4

Emigration from Regierungsbezirk Frankfurt/Oder, 1815–1893

UWE REICH

I

In 1979 the German Society for American Studies organized a conference on German emigration to North America in the nineteenth and twentieth centuries. Held in Stuttgart, the conference examined the results of the past two decades of German migration research. One of the conclusions reached at the conference was the need for more historical research on the migration process at the local and regional levels.[1] This approach has since guided my own research on emigration from several counties in eastern Brandenburg within the administrative district or *Regierungsbezirk* of Frankfurt an der Oder between 1815 and 1893.

Located to the east of Berlin, these counties now straddle the present German–Polish border. As an example of regional migration history, my case study forms part of the emigration project at Rostock University, the focus of which is East Elbian emigration between 1815 and 1914.[2] This essay looks at the social structure and causes of emigration from *Regierungsbezirk* Frankfurt/Oder as well as at factors that determined the emigrant's choice of destinations and settlement patterns. But prior to discussing the main topic, I would like to introduce briefly the goals, methods, and the sources used in this project.

A detailed study of emigration from *Regierungsbezirk* Frankfurt/Oder has been underway since 1987. The ultimate goal of this research is to examine

---

1 "Zusammenfassung der Diskussion nach den Vorträgen von Peter Marschalck und Günter Molt-mann," in Willi Paul Adams, ed., *Die deutschsprachige Auswanderung in die Vereinigten Staaten: For-schungsstand und Quellenbestände* (Berlin, 1980), 31.
2 Rainer Mühle, "Arbeitshypothesen zur Erforschung der Sozialgeschichte von Emigrationen aus aus-gewählten Territorien Ostelbiens im 19. Jahrhundert," *Migrationsforschung* 24 (1990): 6–10; Axel Lubinski, "Zu auswanderungsrechtlichen Grundsätzen Mecklenburgs in der 2. Hälfte des 19. Jahr-hunderts," ibid., 14–18; Uwe Reich, "Einige Bemerkungen zum methodischen Herangehen und Gegenstand der Untersuchung kontinentaler und überseeischer Auswanderungen aus ausgewählten neumärkischen Kreise im Verlaufe des 19. Jahrhunderts," ibid., 11–13.

the migration's structure, causes, motives, and organization. In order to
avoid a one-sided perspective on overseas emigration, continental and internal migrations were also taken into account. This approach opens up a
perspective on the decision to emigrate as one of several possible choices.
Thus, emigration is not seen as a one-way street without junctures, turning
points, and countercurrents.[3] Nevertheless, this study concentrates on overseas migration from those areas of *Regierungsbezirk* Frankfurt/Oder that had
the highest emigration rate in the nineteenth century: Arnswalde and Cottbus counties. Between the 1840s and the 1890s, about nine thousand inhabitants of these two counties left Prussia with the permission of their
government.[4] This number of emigrants was nearly 32 percent of all the
officially registered emigration from *Regierungsbezirk* Frankfurt/Oder,
which was administratively subdivided into seventeen counties.

Limiting the scope of research to these few counties allows the study to
descend to the microlevel of the migration process. It also permits inclusion
of sources that historians have hitherto neglected when dealing with emigration from East Elbia. Among these sources are detailed transcripts of
interviews done with applicants for emigration as well as *Entlassungsurkunden,* that is, permits to emigrate issued by the royal administration in Frank-
furt/Oder. These sources contain a wide range of information about
individual emigrants. For example, the *Entlassungsurkunden* provide information on occupation, name, age, sex, date of birth, place of birth, residence, military standing, and financial means. Additional information on
spouses, children, or others traveling together is also included. I have collected the personal data of approximately 12,000 emigrants, and these data
provide a solid basis for an analysis of the emigration structure. Of course,
such a large amount of information required the application of quantitative
methods.

Besides structural data, both the interview transcripts of prospective emigrants and the applications for emigration contain detailed information on
the following: an emigrant's family situation, his or her local environment,
motivation behind emigration, proposed travel plans, travel agents, ports of
emigration, and connections to relatives in the place(s) of destination. The
sources mentioned previously, together with emigration reports generated

3 Klaus J. Bade, "Sozialhistorische Migrationsforschung," in Ernst Hinrichs and Henk van Zon, eds.,
   Bevölkerungsgeschichte im Vergleich: Studien zu den Niederlanden und Nordwestdeutschland (Aurich, 1988),
   68.
4 Geheimes Staatsarchiv (hereafter cited as GStA), Merseburg, Ministerium des Innern, Rep. 77, 226,
   Nr. 68, 2 vols.; *Preussische Statistik* 26 (1874): 212; 36 (1876): 274; 42 (1876): 207; 45 (1878): 211;
   48 (1877): 355–56; 51 (1880): 15, 355–56; 56 (1881): 22–23; 61 (1882): 244–45; 68 (1883): 370–
   71; 74 (1884): 243; 79 (1884): 247; 86 (1885): 247; 89 (1886): 247; 94 (1888): 459.

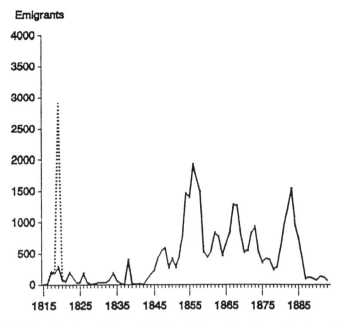

Figure 4.1. Emigration from *Regierungsbezirk* Frankfurt/Oder, 1815–93. The solid line indicates actual emigration; the dotted line, potential emigration. *Source*: See n. 23.

by the county supervisors and the royal administration of *Regierungsbezirk* Frankfurt/Oder, form a substantial basis for the reconstruction of the migration process. Methodologically, this approach situates emigration within its sociohistorical context. Thus, county supervisors' reports on the social, economic, and demographic developments in the counties as well as statistics (including census lists and local registers of changes in property distribution), county histories, and similar sources are also exploited.

II

Immediately after the end of the Napoleonic Wars, emigration from *Regierungsbezirk* Frankfurt/Oder increased. People migrated exclusively toward other continental destinations, above all to Russian Poland. Continental emigration peaked in 1818–19 (Figure 4.1), when the so-called *Auswanderungsfieber* (emigration fever), "that highly infectious social malady,"[5] swept through Friedeberg, Landsberg, Soldin, Küstrin, Sternberg,

---

5 Robert Ostergren, *A Community Transplanted: The Transatlantic Experience of a Swedish Immigrant Settlement in the Upper Middle West, 1835–1915* (Madison, Wis., 1988), 109.

Map 4.1. *Regierungsbezirk* Frankfurt/Oder, Prussian Province of Brandenburg, county lines as of 1815. *Source: Brandenburgische Kreiskarte, 1815,* ed. Historische Kommission für die Provinz Brandenburg und die Reichshauptstadt Berlin.

and Königsberg counties (see Map 4.1).[6] In January 1819 the supervisor of Friedeberg County, von Köller, reported to royal officials in Frankfurt/ Oder that within eight days about six hundred persons had applied for emigration to Russian Poland or to Russia. "The people who wish to emigrate come here in flocks of twenty, thirty, or more persons," he wrote, "and taken together it looks very much like a 'migration of peoples' [*Völkerwanderung*]."[7]

Shortly after this date, that is, on February 27, 1819, Landsberg county supervisor von Sturm sent the royal administration in Frankfurt/Oder a list of 869 people who wanted to emigrate. On March 7, 1819, he described the situation in his county as follows:

6 The information on continental emigration from *Regierungsbezirk* Frankfurt/Oder was obtained from the following sources: Brandenburgisches Landeshauptarchiv (hereafter cited as BLHA), Potsdam, Pr. Br. Rep. 3 B, Regierung Frankfurt/Oder, I St. Nr. 688, 689, 692, 694, 698, 702–8, 710–12.
7 Ibid., Nr. 544.

There is widespread unrest among the lower rural classes. . . . As soon as these people receive their permits to emigrate, without first having to prove that they are in the possession of 100 guilders, they will gather in the street and leave. And unless these crusaders are escorted by soldiers through the Grand Duchy of Posen, they will maltreat the peace-loving peasant and proprietor.[8]

In 1819 several hundred families, representing between four and five thousand individuals, signaled their intention to emigrate. Of these, 2,890 were officially registered. But only a small portion of this group was able to realize the decision to emigrate.

The discrepancy resulted from restrictive measures imposed by the Prussian government, which aimed to prevent a mass emigration. Unless the potential emigrant could prove that he was in the possession of at least 100 guilders, he was denied an emigration permit. Only those persons who were assisted by relatives at home or abroad were exempted from this requirement. Since the overwhelming majority of the potential emigrants did not possess the necessary means, they were forced to remain.

Almost 70 percent of the heads of the families who desired to emigrate were *Hausleute* or "live-in laborers." They came predominantly from colonist villages situated in the swampy areas (*Bruchgegenden*) of the Netze, Warthe, and Oder Rivers, as well as from Soldin County.[9] Only a very small number came from towns.

Four main underlying factors account for this emigration wave: First, the core areas of emigration had been settled by colonists only in the 1760s and 1780s at the invitation of the Prussian government under Frederick the Great. They were independent proprietors from the beginning. Their colonist status exempted them from forced labor on large estates and other services.[10] These privileges led to an increasing dissatisfaction among the established peasants in neighboring villages, who demanded the same privileges. As a consequence, in the Netze and Warthe areas, agrarian reforms were already initiated in the 1760s and 1770s, which resulted in increasing population growth, predominantly among day laborers.[11] This population growth was stimulated by the uneven distribution of property in the form of land among colonists during the settlement period. Of all colonists, 43.9 percent received 80.7 percent of the land, which required the draining of swampland along the Netze and Warthe rivers before it could be culti-

8 Ibid.
9 Ibid., Nr. 702–7.
10 Erich Neuhaus, *Die Friederizianische Kolonisation im Warthe- und Netzebruch* (Landsberg a.W., 1906), 92–99.
11 Hans-Heinrich Müller, *Märkische Landwirtschaft vor den Agrarreformen von 1807* (Potsdam, 1967), 34, 35.

vated.[12] Thus, many small farmsteads between four and twelve *Morgen* were established.[13] When land became scarce and land prices rose, the descendants of these smallholders were able to support themselves only as wage earners.

By the middle of the second decade of the nineteenth century there were clear indications of an increasing gulf between the growth of the rural lower classes and limited or even decreasing employment opportunities and inadequate housing. This development, in turn, increased the pressure on labor and housing markets, which resulted in stagnant wages and rising rents. It also caused a "hunger for land" (*Landhunger*) among the rural lower classes. A number of reports issued by the Landsberg County and the Friedeberg County supervisors to the royal administration in Frankfurt/Oder referred to complaints by day laborers about unemployment, housing shortages, prohibitively high rents, and shortages of land beginning about 1816.

Second, the elimination of common village land to the detriment of live-in laborers and cottagers, which took place in the demesne villages of Soldin County, deprived these social groups of the opportunities to keep livestock and consequently to provide their families with meat and milk.[14]

Third, a series of bad harvests in 1817 and 1818 caused an extreme, short-term contraction of the labor market and a rise in food prices, which put the rural lower classes in desperate social straits.[15]

Fourth, both long-term and short-term developments created a favorable climate for emigration. By the end of 1817, rumors spread – for the first time – in the Warthe, Netze, and Oder areas about opportunities to acquire landed property in Russian Poland and Russia proper.[16] But it was only at the beginning of 1819 that the readiness to emigrate gained momentum. Nevertheless, financial barriers, bad news about settlement conditions in Russian Poland (brought home by emissaries who had been sent to perspective destinations by potential emigrants in the spring of 1819), and improving conditions at home led to a sudden decrease in the readiness to emigrate.[17]

12 Neuhaus, *Friederizianische Kolonisation,* 90.
13 One morgen equals 0.25 hectare.
14 BLHA, Potsdam, Pr. Br. Rep. 3 B, Regierung Frankfurt/Oder, I St. Nr. 544.
15 The price of rye rose from 63.4 silbergroschen per bushel in 1816 to 81.3 silbergroschen per bushel in 1817. See *Mitteilungen des Statistischen Bureaus* 6 (1853): 94.
16 These rumors had essentially two sources. One was the official announcement of the Russian government in 1817 in the *Berliner Zeitung* wherein colonists were invited to settle in Russian Poland, if they could prove that they were in the possession of at least 100 guilders. Another source was letters of people from the Oder, Netze, and Warthe areas, who had already emigrated to Poland and Russia.
17 At the end of March, live-in laborer Wollenberg returned from Congress Poland with an official

During the 1820s and 1830s the scope of continental emigration was rather modest. On March 21, 1822, Tsar Alexander I ordered the raising of protective trade barriers against cloth imported into Russia and the Russian part of Poland. Three years later cloth imports from Prussia were prohibited altogether. These measures severed traditional trade relations between cloth weaving centers in eastern Brandenburg, for example, Züllichau and Schwiebus, and their markets to the east. As a result, they caused a deep depression in the local weaving industry.[18] At the same time, the Polish government and landowners encouraged the immigration of Prussian weavers to Polish weaving towns via the granting of privileges.[19] Between 1821 and 1829 more than one hundred cloth weavers and their families left eastern Brandenburg for Poland.[20] A depression in the Polish weaving industry and the insurrection of 1830–31, however, caused a decline in this immigration in the late 1820s and early 1830s.[21]

In 1832 the Prussian king repealed the military service exemption for Mennonites living in eastern Brandenburg.[22] Given this assault on their religious principles, Wilhelm Lange, the alderman of the Mennonite congregation of Brenkenhofswalde and Franzthal in Friedeberg County petitioned the Russian tsar to allow their immigration to southern Russia. On January 10, 1834, the Russian consulate general in Danzig announced the tsar's decision to permit their immigration. Consequently, between 1833 and 1836 forty Mennonite families, totaling 279 individuals, left the towns of Brenkenhofswalde and Franzthal.[23]

The period between 1816 and the early 1830s had been but a prelude, as emigration from *Regierungsbezirk* Frankfurt/Oder resumed by the end of the decade. But the character of this emigration gradually shifted from continental to overseas migration. Moreover, by the 1850s the readiness to emigrate had spread to all areas of the district.

Overseas emigration from *Regierungsbezirk* Frankfurt/Oder may be divided into three phases. The first, which lasted from the middle of the 1840s to the end of the 1850s, carried more than 13,000 emigrants across the

letter from a senior civil servant in the Warsaw government, von Baykoff, addressed to the German colonists in Soldin County. In this letter, von Baykoff denied allegations that the Warsaw government would subsidize immigration to Congress Poland by means of granting title to property. BLHA Potsdam, Pr. Br. Rep. 3 B, Regierung Frankfurt/Oder, I St. Nr. 704, 386.

18 Albert Breyer, *Deutsche Tuchmachereinwanderung in den ostmitteleuropäischen Raum von 1550 bis 1830* (Leipzig, 1941), 116–22.
19 Kurt Lück, *Deutsche Aufbaukräfte in der Entwicklung Polens* (Plauen, 1934), 334.
20 BLHA, Potsdam, Pr. Br. Rep. 3 B, Regierung Frankfurt/Oder, I St. Nr. 688, 710–12.
21 Breyer, *Tuchmachereinwanderung*, 235, 236.
22 BLHA, Potsdam, Pr. Br. Rep. 3 B, Regierung Frankfurt/Oder, I St. Nr. 689, 2.
23 Ibid., Nr. 689, 692.

Table 4.1. *Occupational structure of emigrants, Cottbus and Arnswalde counties (1838–93)*

	Arnswalde Co., 1848–93		Cottbus Co., 1838–88	
	Number	Percent	Number	Percent
Peasants	44	1.9	27	5.7
Smallholders	121	5.4	35	7.4
Cottagers	0	0.0	107	22.8
Subtotal	165	7.3	169	35.9
Contracted/live-in laborers	912	40.4	70	14.9
Farmhands	449	19.9	82	17.4
Maidservants	129	5.7	14	3.0
Subtotal	1,490	66.0	166	35.3
Artisans	485	21.5	111	23.6
Other	119	5.3	24	5.1
Total	2,259	100.0	470	100.0

Source: See n. 23.

ocean. Emigration peaked in 1857–58 and declined rapidly the following year. The second phase began in the first half of the 1860s and came to an end in 1874, reaching its climax of roughly 11,000 emigrants in 1867–68. The last phase extended from 1880 to 1887. Although only 7,174 emigrants were officially registered between 1880 and 1893, their actual number must have been much higher, due to an increasing rate of clandestine emigration.[24]

These overseas emigrants came predominantly from rural areas and consisted mainly of contracted laborers, cottagers, farmhands, live-in laborers and artisans, and their families. As Table 4.1 indicates, the proportion of the rural lower classes in the occupational structure of Cottbus and Arnswalde counties, for example, was more than 60 percent. If one takes into consideration the fact that the majority of the rural artisans were often forced

24 GStA, Merseburg, Ministerium des Innern, Rep. 77, 226, Nr. 68, 2 vols.; *Preussische Statistik* 26 (1874): 212; 36 (1876): 274; 42 (1876): 207; 45 (1878): 211; 48 (1877): 355–56; 51 (1880): 15, 355–56; 56 (1881): 22–23; 61 (1882): 244–45; 68 (1883): 370–71; 74 (1884): 243; 79 (1884): 247; 86 (1885): 247; 89 (1886): 247; 94 (1888): 459; T. Bödicker, "Die Auswanderung und die Einwanderung des preussischen Staates," *Zeitschrift des Königlich Preussischen Statistischen Bureaus,* nos. 1–2 (1873): 2–3; BLHA, Potsdam, Pr. Br. Rep. 3 B, Regierung Frankfurt/Oder, I St. Nr. 728, 732, 741, 745, 751, 753, 754, 757, 760; the information on emigration from Cottbus County was obtained from the following sources: ibid., Nr. 729, 730; ibid., Rep. 6 B, Cottbus, Nr. 13–18; the information on emigration from Arnswalde County was obtained from the following sources: Rep. 3 B, Regierung Frankfurt/Oder, I St. Nr. 720–27; Archiwum Panstwowe Szczecin, Rep. 6 B, Arnswalde, Nr. 45–72.

to supplement their income by additional wage earning, the percentage of the lower classes in the social structure would be even higher. One might argue that these numbers do not cover the relative share of the individual social groups in the occupational structure. An analysis of this relationship in Cottbus and Arnswalde counties, however, revealed that agricultural laborers without property, farmhands, and artisans were clearly overrepresented, whereas peasants were underrepresented.

The similarity between the emigration curves for *Regierungsbezirk* Frankfurt/Oder and for Germany as a whole suggests that emigration was essentially caused by the same push and pull factors on the regional and national levels. Changing conditions on both sides of the ocean generated simultaneous fluctuations in the emigration curve in most parts of Germany.[25]

A detailed analysis of the factors underlying overseas emigration from *Regierungsbezirk* Frankfurt/Oder falls beyond the scope of this essay. Instead, I will briefly summarize only the most important long-term developments and short-term factors in *Regierungsbezirk* Frankfurt/Oder.

Changes in the agricultural structure of the region, as a consequence of the agrarian reforms in the first half of the nineteenth century, led to rapid population growth, particularly among agricultural laborers. But the need for laborers began to stagnate or even decrease by the end of the 1840s.[26] This development resulted in a structural relative overpopulation by the middle of the 1840s.[27]

Overpopulation, in turn, led to an increasing competition in the labor market and to conditions of social insecurity. The agricultural laborers' hunger for land, which became a common phenomenon by the middle of the 1840s, was an indirect result of the relative overpopulation. Agricultural laborers considered the possession of a small plot of land to be a means of supplementing their income and also a means to satisfy the basic subsistence

---

25 See Mönckmeier, *Auswanderung*, 113, 130.

26 In a number of reports dating back to 1847 and 1848, the county supervisors of *Regierungsbezirk* Frankfurt/Oder, for the first time, suggested measures to create jobs in order to combat increasing unemployment among the rural lower classes.

27 Peter Marschalck and Klaus J. Bade argue that East Elbia started to experience a relative overpopulation only in the 1860s. This would not, however, explain the high emigration rates that occurred in *Regierungsbezirk* Frankfurt/Oder already in the 1850s. Peter Marschalck, *Deutsche Überseewanderung im 19. Jahrhundert* (Stuttgart, 1973), 66; Klaus J. Bade, "Massenwanderung und Arbeitsmarkt im deutschen Nordosten von 1880 bis zum Ersten Weltkrieg: Überseeische Auswanderung, interne Abwanderung und kontinentale Zuwanderung," *Archiv für Sozialgeschichte* 20 (1980): 291. Hartmut Harnisch, who analyzed the relationship between agrarian reforms and the industrial revolution in Prussia's eastern provinces, concluded that the relative overpopulation of many East Elbian villages emerged as early as the late 1830s. See his *Kapitalistische Agrarreform und Industrielle Revolution: Agrarhistorische Untersuchungen über das ostelbische Preussen zwischen Spätfeudalismus und bürgerlich-demokratischer Revolution von 1848/49 unter besonderer Berücksichtigung der Provinz Brandenburg* (Weimar, 1984), 270.

needs of their families. But rising land prices as a consequence of an increasing agricultural output, higher demand for land, and the inflexible distribution of property ownership, particularly in the areas of the landed nobility, made the acquisition of land by the rural lower classes more and more difficult.

The capitalist transformation of agriculture toward intensified and rationalized forms of production, especially on large estates, caused agricultural employment to become increasingly seasonal in character. The introduction of the threshing machine gave a technological push to this trend. Whereas, on the one hand, the growing seasonal character of agricultural labor led to a rise in the mobility of "free laborers," on the other, the intensification and subsequent rationalization of agricultural production undermined the patriarchal relationship between the large estate owners and their contracted laborers. Their half-independent status was gradually abolished and their payment in kind was replaced by a wage.[28] Thus, the position of a contracted laborer on large estates lost its attractive force for rural laborers.

Times of depression in *Regierungsbezirk* Frankfurt/Oder, especially in the mid-1850s, mid-1860s, and at the beginning of the 1880s, often worked in harmony with transatlantic pull factors to produce migration waves. In the 1880s, for example, a crisis in agriculture, caused by the introduction of cheap American and Russian grain into the German market, in combination with a period of general prosperity in the United States, triggered a sharp increase of overseas emigration from the district.

But demographic, economic, and social developments alone can hardly explain why people made the decision to emigrate and why they chose particular destinations. The focus of the following section is on factors that determined the genesis of emigration routes and the emigrants' pattern of settlement in their new homeland.

III

As already indicated, continental emigration from *Regierungsbezirk* Frankfurt/Oder went mainly to Russian Poland.[29] Between 1815 and 1820 almost all those who actually emigrated ended up there. More than 49 percent of

28 Bade, "Massenwanderung und Arbeitsmarkt," 295–302; Max Weber, "Die Verhältnisse der Landarbeiter im ostelbischen Deutschland," *Schriften des Vereins für Socialpolitik* 55 (1892): 36, 37, 661.
29 Although almost 40 percent of the potential emigrants between 1815 and 1820 told the authorities that they wanted to emigrate to Russia, only 0.4 percent actually did. BLHA, Potsdam, Pr. Br. Rep. 3 B, Regierung Frankfurt/Oder, I St. Nr. 702–7.

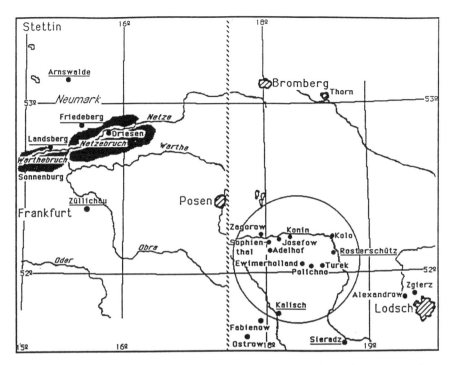

Map 4.2. Settlements of immigrants from *Regierungsbezirk* Frankfurt/Oder in Russian Poland. *Source*: Field research by author.

these people settled in a few colonist villages in the vicinity of Konin,
Zagórów, and Kolo (see Map 4.2).

The overwhelming majority of overseas emigrants from *Regierungsbezirk*
Frankfurt/Oder went to North America and South Australia. North America became the primary destination for emigrants from the northern part of
the district, whereas people from the southern counties predominantly left
for Australia. More than 50 percent of the emigration from Cottbus County
went to South Australia; only one-third of the county's emigrants went to
the United States and Canada.[30] This emigration pattern stands in sharp
contrast to that of Arnswalde County. Almost 99 percent of its emigrants
left for North America (94.3 percent to the United States and 4.4 percent
to Canada).

Thanks to the very detailed information provided by the emigration permits, destinations within the United States can be specified further. The

30 See n. 24.

following states are mentioned in these documents: Wisconsin, Minnesota, Ohio, Illinois, Michigan, New York, Pennsylvania, the Dakotas, Indiana, Iowa, Arkansas, Maryland, Nebraska, Texas, Virginia, California, and Montana. Although emigrants from Arnswalde County settled in all of the states previously named, they were clearly concentrated in the Midwest, and in one state in particular. More than 62 percent of the Arnswalde County emigrants bound for the United States informed the Prussian authorities that their destination in North America was the far-off state of Wisconsin.[31] What were the factors that may have caused these emigration routes? To answer this question it is first necessary to examine the initial migration phase.

It has already been mentioned that the Warthe and Netze areas were settled between the 1760s and 1780s: 61.2 percent of the immigrants to the Warthe area and 71.8 percent of the new settlers in the Netze area were German remigrants from that part of Poland later acquired by Russia.[32] Germans from eastern Brandenburg, Pomerania, and Silesia began migrating to Polish areas already in the seventeenth century. The German "frontier" in Poland moved further eastward in the eighteenth century and reached Kalisch County (central Poland) in the 1750s. But the Catholic Church put increasing pressure on Protestant Germans. When Frederick the Great invited immigrants to settle the Netze and Warthe areas after the Seven Years' War, many Germans decided to return to Prussia.[33]

Since immigrants often left behind relatives in Poland, contacts to their original settlements were as close as eighteenth-century conditions allowed. There were also occasional migrations between German villages in central Poland and the Warthe or Netze areas.[34]

When Germans from central Poland started to migrate to southern Russia in 1814, to escape the hardships of the Napoleonic Wars, they left open spaces behind.[35] This emigration continued until the end of the century's second decade and, in turn, triggered migration to colonist villages in the Netze and Warthe areas. A civil servant named Seiffert, who was sent to

---

31 Ibid.

32 Wilhelm Scheer, "Ansiedler im Warthebruch im Jahre 1775," *Der Neumärker* 3 (1943): 1; Scheer, "Ansiedler im Netzebruch, 1763–1769," *Der Neumärker* 2 (1943): 13.

33 Oskar Eugen Kossmann, *Die Deutschen in Polen seit der Reformation* (Marburg, 1978), 88–89; Lück, *Aufbaukräfte*, 313.

34 With the second partition of the country in 1793, the remnants of Greater Poland fell to Prussia. Central Poland then became "South Prussia." From that time, the Prussian government encouraged migrations to these newly acquired territories.

35 This emigration was triggered by generous land offers made by Tsar Alexander I in an edict adopted on November 29, 1813. See Karl Stumpp, *The Emigration from Germany to Russia in the Years 1763 to 1862* (Lincoln, Neb., 1982), 106.

the core areas of emigration to investigate its causes, reported to the royal administration on March 1, 1819, that the majority of the emigrants wanted to settle in the areas around Konin and Kolo, because

a number of families had already migrated to these areas when they still belonged to the Prussian monarchy. Some of these families intend to look for better places to settle in Bessarabia. They tried to sell their landed property in Poland as soon as possible and this is the reason why land can be acquired at very low prices in the areas.[36]

It is obvious that a tradition of migration, prompted by a deterioration in the economic situation at home and/or the opening up of opportunities to improve their social condition somewhere else, had become an integral part of the colonists' way of life. The migration history of the colonists who settled in the Netze and Warthe areas suggests a relatively high degree of geographic mobility even before the nineteenth century. Long-term kin-ship connections between inhabitants of the Netze and Warthe areas and the German settlements in central Poland, which had been generated by migrations dating back to the seventeenth and eighteenth centuries, clearly determined the choice of the migration destination at the beginning of the nineteenth century.

In Cottbus County yearly emigration did not occur until 1848 and it was predominantly directed toward South Australia from the very beginning. There is substantial documentary evidence that the choice of this destination was mainly influenced by the preceding Old Lutheran emigration from Züllichau, Crossen, and also Cottbus counties.

First, a group of six hundred Old Lutherans from Züllichau County, which left Prussia for religious reasons in 1838, settled a few miles north of Port Adelaide, South Australia.[37] Their letters, which contained positive descriptions of life in their new homeland, circulated in the following years in the southern counties of *Regierungsbezirk* Frankfurt/Oder.[38] It is very probable that a group of twenty-two Old Lutherans from Cottbus County was influenced by these letters, since it left Cottbus in 1844 and, as a matter of course, settled near the Old Lutheran settlements north of Port Adelaide. The same is true for the group of seven families that left Cottbus County in 1848 and for the bulk of those who followed it in the 1850s and 1860s as well.[39]

36 BLHA, Potsdam, Pr. Br. Rep. 3 B, Regierung Frankfurt/Oder, I St. Nr. 544.
37 Wilhelm Iwan, *Die altlutherische Auswanderung um die Mitte des 19. Jahrhunderts,* 2 vols. (Ludwigsburg, 1943), 2:301.
38 Ibid., 1:113–14.
39 George R. Nielsen, *In Search of a Home* (College Station, Tex., 1989), 32, 41.

Second, the South Australian Company, which had already provided passage for many Old Lutherans seeking a new home, tried to recruit potential emigrants from several southern counties in *Regierungsbezirk* Frankfurt/Oder. To this end, it publicized the glowing recommendations of the Old Lutherans from Züllichau who already lived there. In a letter written by one of the Old Lutheran leaders, Fiedler, to his friends and relatives back home, he indicated that he wanted to come back to Prussia to recruit more emigrants. His wife's death, however, prevented him from doing so. Instead, one of the South Australian Company's agents, a man named Flaxman, would go to Prussia in his stead. There is evidence that a man named Hackert, another agent of the company recruited some emigrants from Cottbus County in the late 1840s.[40]

But what about the northern part of the district, where emigration in the nineteenth century went mainly to America? A brief examination of the initial phase of emigration from Arnswalde County may help to clarify this pattern.

The Old Lutherans played an important role in determining the emigrants' destinations in later years. It was mostly Old Lutherans from neighboring Pomerania who emigrated in the late 1830s to upstate New York and Wisconsin. In 1839 a group of about one thousand Old Lutherans from several Pomeranian counties departed Germany. They landed in New York City and continued on to Buffalo. From here, a group of five hundred individuals decided to go via the Great Lakes to Milwaukee, which subsequently became a distribution center for later Lutheran arrivals in Wisconsin. As Wilhelm Iwan puts it: "What Buffalo was for the east, Milwaukee became for the west – the starting point from which arriving Lutherans sought their prospective settlements."[41]

Radiating outward from Milwaukee, Old Lutherans established the nuclei of Pomeranian settlements in today's Milwaukee, Ozaukee, Washington, and Dodge counties between 1839 and 1846 (see Map 4.3). Later migrations from Pomerania followed the path paved by the Old Lutherans. Starting in 1854, a significant number of Pomeranians immigrated and either joined the original settlements or settled in Fond du Lac, Green Lake, Manitowoc, Marathon, and other counties.[42] By 1880 the U.S. Federal Census revealed a substantial Pomeranian population in Wisconsin.

The emigration pattern from Arnswalde County, which bordered on

40 Ibid., 17.
41 Iwan, *Altlutherische Auswanderung*, 1:260.
42 Kate Everest Levi, "Geographical Origin of German Immigration to Wisconsin," *Wisconsin Historical Collections* 14 (1898): 351.

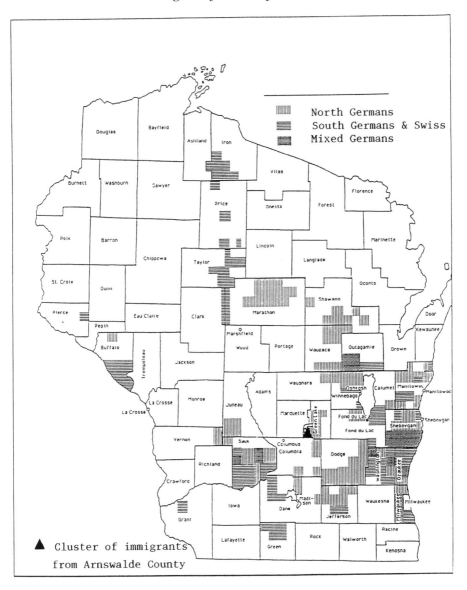

Map 4.3. Distribution of Germans in Wisconsin, according to U.S. Federal Census of 1890. *Source*: Kate Everest Levi, "Geographical Origin of German Immigration to Wisconsin," *Wisconsin Historical Collections* 14 (1898): 341.

Pomerania, was determined primarily by the Pomeranian emigration just described. The Arnswalde County supervisor issued reports that indicate the existence of extensive family connections between inhabitants of Arnswalde County and bordering Pomeranian counties, especially Pyritz County. Beginning in the late 1840s, these relationships in turn triggered emigration from Arnswalde County to Pomeranian destinations in America.[43] On February 2, 1854, the mayor of Reetz reported to the Arnswalde County supervisor on the emigration of individuals from his town that "[Arnswalders'] emigration was stimulated by their relatives from Pyritz County."[44] Thus, one can conclude that the Old Lutheran pioneers paved the way for later migrations from the southern and northern parts of *Regierungsbezirk* Frankfurt/Oder to South Australia and North America. These findings correspond to the results of Scandinavian and German migration research.[45]

If personal relationships influenced the choice of migration destinations, what effects did they have on settlement patterns? Emigration from Arnswalde County to Wisconsin provides the most striking example of their influence. Abundant documentary evidence found in the archives of Arnswalde County and in the U.S. Federal Census lists reveals the crucial role relatives and friends played in establishing a certain settlement pattern of Arnswalde County emigrants in North America.

The stable relationships between those who had already left their homes and those left behind formed the basis for the genesis of chain migrations. According to one sociologist, it is "that movement in which prospective migrants learn of opportunities, are provided with transportation, and have initial accommodations and employment arranged by means of primary social relationship with previous migrants."[46]

But it is difficult for the historian to ascertain the extent of services provided by chain migration in the nineteenth century. The evidence is fragmentary and indirect.[47] In this case study the first empirical documentation of chain migration comes from emigrant lists and transcripts made with prospective emigrants compiled by the Arnswalde County supervisors. Since the middle of the 1850s, emigrants' statements like the following were

43 GStA, Merseburg, Ministerium des Innern, Rep. 77 Tit. 226 Nr. 78, vol. 6, 172.
44 Archiwum Panstwowe Szczecin, Rep. 6 B, Arnswalde, Nr. 46.
45 Hans Norman and Harald Runblom, *Transatlantic Connections: Nordic Migration to the New World after 1800* (Oslo, 1988), 52; Walter D. Kamphoefner, *The Westfalians: From Germany to Missouri* (Princeton, N.J., 1987), 71; Ostergreen, *A Community Transplanted*, 109, 173, 174.
46 John S. MacDonald and Leatrice D. MacDonald, "Chain Migration, Ethnic Neighborhood Formation, and Social Networks," in Charles Tilly, ed., *An Urban World* (Boston, 1974), 227.
47 Kamphoefner, *The Westfalians,* 71.

found with increased frequency: "We have decided to follow our son to America."[48] Or: "Together with my family I want to emigrate to North America, where my son-in-law is living under comfortable circumstances."[49] Or: "My bridegroom, shepherd Krentzke, emigrated to North America last year and has sent me a letter asking me to follow him."[50] Obviously, the destination of these individuals in North America was clearly determined by their relatives or prospective relatives in the United States.

Favorable news about life in America sent home by some persons could trigger not only the emigration of close relatives, but also of friends and friends of friends, as the following example shows.[51] In 1854 August Wilhelm Hermann Volgmann, a journeyman bricklayer from Reetz, emigrated together with his wife Christine Louise to Watertown, Jefferson County, Wisconsin. Only one year later his widowed mother, Florentine Volgmann, applied for permission to emigrate:

> My son August Wilhelm Hermann Volgmann . . . emigrated to the North American Free States in 1854 and lives in Watertown in the state of Wisconsin. He makes a good living there and has asked me to follow him together with my five children so that he can take care of me as he has always done before he emigrated. . . . I am not able to pay the passage, but my oldest son and wealthy relatives from here have promised to provide me with the necessary financial means.[52]

A thorough official investigation of the causes for the increased emigration from Arnswalde County in 1855 revealed that this widow and proud mother actively spread the news she got from her successful son to several villages in Arnswalde County, which is an interesting note on the role of women in the migration process.

Her active role in this case is documented in the testimony of Ernestine Buchholz, a twenty-four-year-old domestic servant on a large estate in Pammin, and W. Page, a shepherd servant. Ernestine Buchholz told the county supervisor:

> It has often been told here that girls do well in America and so it also occurred to me that I should emigrate there, also widow Volkmann [*sic*] from Reetz brought a letter, which her son had written from America and cook Krebs read it to us, he has also read several letters to us, which he received from Ziegenhagen and Butow (Pomerania). Also the shepherd servant W. Page, whenever he came to see us in

48 Archiwum Panstwowe Szczecin, Rep. 6 B, Arnswalde, Nr. 46.
49 Ibid.
50 Ibid.
51 Jon Gjerde comes to the same conclusion. He points to the importance not only of kinship networks but also of friends and neighbors in the migration process. See his *From Peasants to Farmers: The Migration from Balestrand, Norway, to the Upper Middle West* (Cambridge, 1985), 132.
52 Archiwum Panstwowe Szczecin, Rep. 6 B, Arnswalde, Nr. 46.

the kitchen, told us a lot about America and it was praised so much that the desire
to emigrate was also awakened in me. . . . [53]

This statement also reveals an image of America as the promised land or a
garden of Eden that prevailed among common people in Arnswalde
County.

W. Page, when asked about the reasons for his intention to emigrate,
replied:

I already made the decision to emigrate to North America two years ago, this
decision has been determined by several reports that I got orally or in a written
form from Germans who have already settled there. The letters were from Haenke
of Ziegenhagen, which shepherd Suckow from Kleinsilber informed me about, a
second was sent by Volkmann [sic] to his mother in Reetz, widow Volkmann [sic],
who gave it to joiner Stabenow, he gave it to me and I have read it to several
people at my home.[54]

As the 1855 emigrant list shows, all of the people who were included in
the county supervisor's investigation and had learned about Volgmann's
and other letters from Wisconsin, emigrated that very year.[55] Another indicator of chain migration was the growing frequency of prepaid tickets
sent from individuals in the United States to relatives in Arnswalde County,
beginning around 1855. The emphasis on chain migration does not mean
that economic considerations somehow did not play an important role in
migration decisions, "but rather that economic information was channeled
through the filter of personal ties."[56]

It is not new that immigrants from Germany and other European countries did not scatter randomly across the United States. On the contrary,
they formed ethnic clusters in certain areas. But these patterns have scarcely
been documented in detail for the German Americans. Walter D. Kamphoefner's case study on the Westphalians is one of the few exceptions.[57]
One of his major conclusions is that chain migrations resulted in the genesis
and development of ethnic clusters in North America.[58] This conclusion is
echoed in my own findings.

I want to verify this in the emigration from Arnswalde County to Wis-

---

53 Ibid.
54 Ibid.
55 BLHA, Potsdam, Pr. Br. Rep. 3 B, Regierung Frankfurt/Oder, I St Nr. 720.
56 Kamphoefner, *The Westfalians,* 71.
57 Ibid., 70–105. Recent exceptions in Scandinavian migration research include Ostergreen and
   Gjerde.
58 This is also one of the major conclusions Robert Ostergreen and Jon Gjerde draw in their case
   studies on Rättvik and Balestrand emigrants to the Upper Midwest. Ostergreen, *A Community
   Transplanted,* 176–89; Gjerde, *From Peasants to Farmers,* 143–67.

consin. Linking the Arnswalde County data on individuals, taken from emigration permits, to that of the 1880 and 1900 federal census lists of Dodge, Fond du Lac, Winnebago, Jefferson, Green Lake, Rock, Marathon, Monroe, Green, and Jackson counties allowed me to trace a group of 140 families totaling over 450 individuals who emigrated between the 1850s and the 1880s from Arnswalde County to Wisconsin.[59] The effects of chain migration can be seen in the concentration of the Arnswalde County immigrants in a few townships in Green Lake, Jefferson, and Fond du Lac counties (Map 4.4). Nearly 83 percent (82.4 percent) of the Arnswalders I traced settled in these few counties. Green Lake stands out as the county with the greatest concentration of Arnswalders. Almost 60 percent of those Arnswalders who were traced went there. Smaller numbers could be identified also in Dodge, Marathon, and Winnebago counties. All counties had a substantial Pomeranian population, a fact that supports my hypothesis on the importance of early migrations for determining the path of later migrants.[60]

Taking a closer look at the distribution of the Arnswalders on the local level reveals a high degree of clustering. Of the 267 Arnswalders who chose Green Lake County as their destination, 184 (almost 70 percent) were found in three adjoining townships: Brooklyn, Princeton, and Green Lake. Moreover, their settlements were tightly clustered; sometimes two or even three families follow successively in the census lists.

As Map 4.4 shows, the migration chain from Arnswalde County to Brooklyn, Princeton, and Green Lake townships extended to a few villages spread out over an area of approximately 20 to 30 square miles in its northwestern section. A number of these villages belonged to the same parish. The main sources of the migration chain were Klein Silber, Zühlsdorf, Stolzenfelde, and Cürtow – the communities from which more than one-half of all the Arnswalders whom I traced to Brooklyn, Princeton, and Green Lake townships came.

IV

After the end of the Napoleonic Wars, emigration from *Regierungsbezirk* Frankfurt/Oder to continental destinations, above all to Russian Poland,

59 The source of data for the American side was the U.S. Federal Manuscript Censuses of 1880 and 1900.

60 Although Map 4.3 does not further specify northern Germans, Kate Everest Levi found out that Pomeranians were almost always among them.

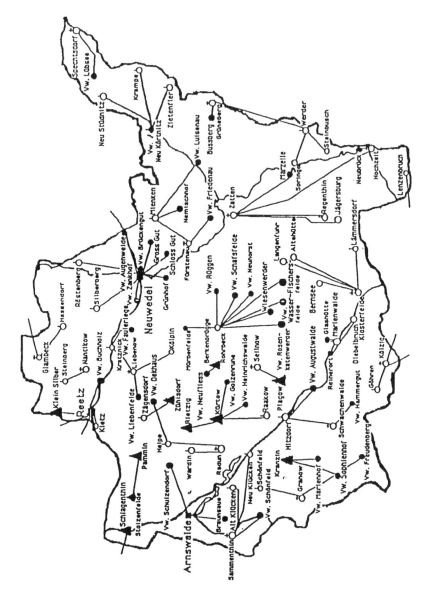

Map 4.4. Places of residence of Green Lake County immigrants from Arnswalde County. Triangle symbol equals villages from which more than ten people emigrated to Princeton, Brooklyn, and Green Lake township, Green Lake County. *Source*: Field research by author.

increased. After the climax of 1818–19 the scope of continental emigration was rather modest.

Following the period from 1816 to the early 1830s, emigration from *Regierungsbezirk* Frankfurt/Oder resumed. At this time, however, the pattern gradually shifted from continental to overseas migration. Moreover, the readiness to emigrate spread in the 1850s to all areas of the district. In addition, both continental and overseas emigrants belonged predominantly to the rural lower classes.

Changes in the agricultural structure, as a consequence of the agrarian reforms, led to a rapid population growth, particularly among agricultural laborers. But the need for laborers began to level off or even decrease. This development resulted in a structural relative overpopulation, which occurred for the first time in the Warthe, Netze, and Oder areas and, by the middle of the 1840s, in most rural sections of *Regierungsbezirk* Frankfurt/Oder. It placed growing pressure on the labor and housing markets, which resulted in stagnating wages and rising rents. Another consequence was an increasing hunger for land among the rural lower classes.

By the end of the 1860s, the capitalist transformation of agriculture toward intensified and rationalized forms of production, especially on large estates, caused agricultural employment to become increasingly seasonal in character. Moreover, it undermined the patriarchal relationship between the large estate owners and their contracted laborers. Consequently, there was a rising geographic mobility among both free and contracted laborers.

The genesis of emigration routes and the emigrants' settlement pattern in their new homeland were determined by a combination of economic considerations and sociopsychological factors. Early migration and migration traditions were of primary importance because they highly influenced the choice of future destinations by subsequent emigrants from a particular area. The emigration from Arnswalde County clearly shows that the key to the explanation of this phenomenon is the concept of chain migration. Chain migration on the basis of kinship networks and ties between friends strongly influenced the migration route of Arnswalde County emigrants and also the settlement patterns in their new home area to a remarkable extent. It resulted in a high degree of clustering in a few townships in Wisconsin. Green Lake County stands out as the most important receiving area of Arnswalde County immigrants in Wisconsin. Nevertheless, more studies are required to verify further the importance of sociopsychological factors for the understanding of the migration process in general and of the development of settlement patterns in particular.

5

Preserving or Transforming Role?
Migrants and Polish Territories in the
Era of Mass Migrations

ADAM WALASZEK

After 1795, Polish territories belonged to the Russian Empire, the Austrian Empire, or to the Kingdom of Prussia.[1] A complex set of factors motivated many inhabitants of Polish territories to migrate. First and foremost was the desire to better one's material situation. Rapid population growth, over-population, and lack of land characterized emancipated Polish villages (en-franchisement of peasants took place earliest in Prussia, in Austrian Poland in 1848, in Russian Poland in 1864). In this essay, I focus mainly on de-velopments in Russian and Austrian Poland.

"From all possible angles [emigration] affected peasants' personalities, their view of the world, people, and social relations, created a new attitude toward work and material goods, modernized their attitudes toward life, their goals and their wishes, and changed the appearance of people, houses, whole villages. Emigration caused a revolutionary transformation of peas-ants' personality," Jan Borkowski has emphasized.[2] Wincenty Witos, peas-

---

1 I would like to thank Dr. Pat Ryan from Saupstad, Norway, for helping to give this essay some sense in English. The lack of space does not allow discussion of the complexities of migration causes. Apart from the traditional push–pull interpretation, recent migration studies "have reconceptualized this problem, recasting the unit(s) of analysis from separate nation-states, linked by one-way transfer of migrants between two unequally developed economies, to a comprehensive economic system com-posed of a dominant core and dependent periphery – a world system that forms a complex network of supranational exchanges of technology, capital, and labor"; see Ewa Morawska, "Labor Migrations of Poles in the Atlantic World Economy, 1880–1914," *Comparative Studies in Society and History* 31 (1989): 237–72. For Polish history, see Norman Davies, *God's Playground: A History of Poland* (New York, 1982), vols. 1 and 2. On the causes of migration, see Andrzej Pilch, "Trendy migracji zarob-kowej ludności Galicji w XIX i XX w. (do 1918 r.)" [Labor migration trends in 19th- and 20th-century Galicia], in *Mechanizmy polskich migracji zarobkowych* [Mechanisms of Polish labor migrations] (Warsaw, 1976), 68–70; Zbigniew Stankiewicz, "Procesy migracyjno-twórcze na ziemiach polskich w okresie zaborów" [Migration processes on Polish territories in the times of partition], in *Mechan-izmy;* Władysław Grabski, *Materiały w sprawie włościanskiej* [Materials on Polish peasants] (Warsaw, 1919), 3:96; Stanisław Głąbinski, *Emigracja i jej rola w gospodarstwie narodowym* [Emigration and its role in national economy] (Warsaw, 1931), 9.
2 Jan Borkowski, *Chłopi polscy w dobie kapitalizmu* [Polish peasants in the era of capitalism] (Warsaw, 1981), 47. S. Grabski held a similar opinion: "Emigration was the main cause of cultural, economic,

ant leader and politician, was more moderate: "If the Polish village took a big step toward progress, if it rose out of the fetters of political dependence and backwardness of former economic poverty, the change was due to emigration."[3] Władysław Orkan, a Polish writer, hesitated: "It is so difficult to strike a proper balance and ascertain whether America brought our village greater assets or liabilities. But it seems to me that the benefits have predominated."[4] Which of these authors is right?

EMIGRATION

Plagues and economic crises toward the end of the nineteenth century, along with other factors, compounded the problems of peasants in the countryside. In the emancipated villages, money was scarce. One had to pay debts, buy more land and cattle, and take precautions against possible crop failures. Rich and poor villagers alike became participants in the market economy. Galician villagers' indebtedness increased twelvefold between 1885 and 1905. Money became a new reality and a new value in the life of Polish peasants. Banks and savings and loan associations eventually appeared. But it was difficult to acquire money in the countryside. Thus, people started seeking it abroad.[5] "Migration, like any other social phenomenon with an economic background, is conditioned by a rise of new needs among people, and by a knowledge that these needs can be fulfilled," wrote Florian Znaniecki.[6]

The idea of migration as well as the act itself broadened peasants' horizons. During fairs and in the market squares, the people heard about migrants' adventures and other such marvels of the outside world. Then a

and, I dare say, political and national progress of Galician villages." Quoted in Halina Janowska, *Emigracja zarobkowa z Polski, 1918–1939* [Polish labor migration, 1918–1939] (Warsaw 1980), 320.
3 Wincenty Witos, *Moje wspomnienia* [My memoirs] (Paris, 1964), 1:191.
4 Władysław Orkan, *Listy ze wsi i inne pisma społeczne* [Letters from the village and the other social writings] (Warsaw, 1934), 96.
5 Maria Misińska, *Podhale dawne i współczesne: Wybrane zagadnienia* [The old and contemporary Podhale: Selected topics] (Łódz, 1971), 26–46; Ewa Morawska, " 'For Bread with Butter': Life-Worlds of Peasant Immigrants from East Central Europe, 1880–1914," *Journal of Social History* 17 (1984): 388–89; Krzysztof Groniowski, *Uwłaszczenie chłopów w Polsce: Geneza – realizacja – skutki* [Enfranchisement of Polish peasants] (Warsaw, 1976), 179–89; Józef Kantor, "Czarny Dunajec," in *Materiały Antropologiczne, Archeologiczne i Etnograficzne* [Anthropological, archeological, and ethnographic materials] (1907), part 2: 57; Zygmunt Gargas, "Bank polsko–amerykański" [Polish–American bank], *Atheneum Polskie* [Polish atheneum] 2 (1908): 400; Władysław Bronikowski, *Drogi postępu chłopa polskiego* [The ways of progress of Polish peasants] (Warsaw, 1934), 156–58.
6 Florian Znaniecki, "Wychodźtwo a położenie ludności wiejskiej zarobkującej w Królestwie Polskim," [Migration and situation of village population in the Kingdom of Poland], quoted in Zygmunt Dulczewski, *Florian Znaniecki redaktor Wychodźcy Polskiego* [Florian Znaniecki editor of Polish emigrant] (Warsaw, 1982), 125.

gration was a topic of lively conversation in village taverns. It was the same story everywhere, though at different times. Wojciech Łagowski was, in the 1880s, the first resident from Krzywa, a Galician village in Ropczyce County, to cross the Atlantic:

There was so much talk in the village, so much fear. A year later the second, and then a third one left, and after these sent back a few dollars to their families a real hysteria started, everybody borrowed money wherever he could, and left for the golden country.[7]

Emigration was an act of struggle against fate but sometimes also a revolt against one's way of life, against oppression, military service, the authorities, and family and elders as well. Someone recalled: "Finally I revolted against my fate and my parents . . . I escaped from the house." In 1907, during the Twelfth Conference of Deaneries, priests noticed that among the reasons for emigration was "a wish for freedom, a desire to escape from parents' supervision."[8]

7 Jerzy Fierich, *Przeszłość wsi powiatu ropczyckiego w ustach ich mieszkańców* [The past of Ropczyce County in the words of its inhabitants] (Ropczyce, 1936), 58. I will often use examples from Ropczyce County (Galicia), which might be considered as a typical migration county – because people from that area had rather limited opportunities to seek employment in close proximity, and were forced to migrate abroad. Cf. also *Pamiętniki emigrantów: Stany Zjednoczone* [Emigrants' memoirs: United States] (Warsaw, 1977), 1:229; Ewa Morawska, "Motyw awansu w systemie wartości polskich imigrantów w Stanach Zjednoczonych na przełomie wieku: O potrzebie relatywizmu kulturowego w badaniach historycznych" [The motive of social rise in the system of values of Polish immigrants in the United States at the turn of century: About the necessity of cultural relativism in historical investigations], *Przegląd Polonijny* [Polonia review] 4, no. 1 (1978): 61–62; Stanisław Szczepanowski, *Pisma i przemówienia* [Writings and speeches] (Cracow, 1912), 1:190–91; Krystyna Duda-Dziewierz, *Wieśmałopolska i emigracja amerykańska* [Malopolska's village and American emigration] (Warsaw, 1938), 30.

8 Marian Czuła, "W niewoli życia i polityki: Pamiętnik" [In the slavery of life and politics: Memoirs], manuscript no. 12400II, Biblioteka Zakładu Narodowego im. Ossolińskich, Wrocław, 65; A. Pilch, "Trendy," 131; Zjazd 12ty XX Dziekanów w 1907 r. [12th Conference of Deaneries in 1907], Archiwum Kurii Metropolitalnej Kraków [Archive of Archdiocese Cracow], file Wychodźstwo [Emigration], 25. Emigration motives were complex. For example, an old woman from Chicago, who left Poland before World War I, recalled: "I wanted to go to America, I wanted to know, but my mother used to say: 'You don't know what the world is, but go, see.'" Her parents were rather wealthy (the girl had six coral strings), and they employed some agricultural workers. A daughter of one of these workers left the village for America: "After six months she mailed back a photograph; what a lady, a hat, feathers, beautifully dressed. . . . Her mother came to mine to show her. And my mother calls: Józia, come, you'll see Filomencia, look what a lady. I looked: Filomencia! So, here, you were such a beggar and your father worked for my parents just for food, and now you're such a lady! I said nothing but later to my mother: 'Mother I go to America . . . I don't want to work on a farm, I go to America.' I wanted to be a lady, like this companion of mine . . . I wanted to be here, send a photograph, see," Cis-049, vols. 1–2: 17, 20–22, Oral History Archives of Chicago Polonia, Chicago Historical Society, Chicago.

In the case of America, a "positive motivation" always existed. People were pushed out not only by the need for a better life but also by the desire for social improvement. The notion of advancement – a better future, prestige – was, of course, understood in the context of people's own culture. For better or worse, work in the fields afforded a living. Using cash received from outside the village, migrants could thus build a house, achieve greater authority, buy more land. Emigration created a chance, the means toward a personal career. The expansive economic situation in the United States at the end of the nineteenth century offered peasants an opportunity to fulfill "their aspiration for social rise defined by their own hierarchy of values." They saved, worked like oxen, and became members of the proletariat – all in order to buy land. During two weeks in America one could earn as much as during a whole season in German or Hungarian agriculture.[9]

Emigration was typically organized by families, relatives, or friends. Recent emigrants to America invited their relations and friends to follow in their shoes. Close ties existed between those who left for America and those who remained in European villages. Letters were constantly crossing the ocean. The everyday dialogue was conducted at a very great distance with the help of agents, who were able to write letters. Such letters concerned all interesting or boring but necessary matters. The migrants not only sent money to the old country, but they also gave advice and persuaded their friends that they, too, should leave. "And if you are going to lease the land, then let the lessee have it, but for years; and let him pay for the lease in advance if he can. . . . And if you have straw to sell, leave it on the land and the dung as well. Tear down the fence and chop it up for firewood unless he wants to pay you for it," one man wrote to his wife. And the most common statement was: "I will send you a steamship ticket if you

9 Morawska, "Motyw," 61–67; James A. Dunlevy and Henry A. Gemery, "Economic Opportunities and the Responses of 'Old' and 'New' Migrants to the United States," *Journal of Economic History* 38 (1978): 917; Kazimiera Zawistowicz-Adamska, *Społeczność wiejska: Wspomnienia i materiały z badań terenowych, Zaborów, 1938–1939* [Village society: Reminiscences and materials from the field work, Zaborów, 1938–1939] (Warsaw, 1958), 19; K. Duda-Dziewierz, *Wieś*, 79–86, 109–16, 135; Zbigniew T. Wierzbicki, *Żmiąca pół wieku później* [Zmiaca a half century later] (Wrocław and Warsaw, 1963), 158; Zygmunt Gargas, "W sprawie ruchu pieniężnego między Ameryką a Galicją" [About monetary transfers between America and Galicia], *Przegląd Polski* [Polish review] (1906): 518; Bronikowski, *Drogi postępu*, 150–53; Kantor, "Czarny Dunajec," 57; Caroline Golab, *Immigrant Destination* (Philadelphia, 1977), 48; Artur Benis, "Emigracja" [Emigration], in *IV Zjazd prawników i Ekonomistów Polskich* [IV Congress of Polish lawyers and economists], *Czasopismo Prawnicze i Ekonomiczne* [Law and economic review] (1907): 8–15; Z. Gargas, "Bank," 400; Barbara Golda, "Konsekwencje emigracji w życiu wiejskiej społeczności polskiej" [The effects of the emigration on a rural community's life], *Przegląd Polonijny* 2, no. 1 (1976): 114–15; Wierzbicki, *Żmiąca*, 70; Morawska, " 'For Bread,' " 390; Morawska, "Labor," 262–66; Adam Walaszek, *Reemigracja ze Stanów Zjednoczonych do Polski po I wojnie światowej, 1919–1924* [Return migration from the United States to Poland after World War I] (Warsaw and Cracow, 1984), 5–14, 149–54.

wish." Possibilities and dangers were considered in these "conversations": "As regards Wladek, I'd like to ask you to help him come overseas, as you are his uncle, and I will try to get a steamship ticket for him if he sends the money. For one must have at least 40 rubles for this journey; for the trip to Cleveland, one may need over 47." The agents bringing families to America and making trip arrangements also gave information about all de- tails of the journey. "When you are in Prussia and when they ask you where you come from, you should tell them you come from some little town or village in Prussia; thanks to that, you will have an easier journey. . . . Only ask God that the Lord Jesus will allow you to cross the border safely so that they will not catch you." Once in America: "When they ask you where you are going, you should say you are going to Cleveland, and if they ask you whether you have a job there, you should answer in the negative and say that you will take up any job they give you." Finally, the husband instructed:

You should take with you on the trip thick bread, smoked dried fatback, sugar, and vinegar. . . . take the nicer pictures out of their frames and bring them with you; sell the frames and glass. . . . Take the iron with you, the large pieces, too. But do not waste space on the bedding.[10]

Before World War I, return migration and the transatlantic circulation of migrants were common phenomena. A significant proportion of Polish migrants, perhaps the majority of them, intended their stay in America to

---

10 Relatives and friends helped each other in America. They helped each other find housing and often first jobs. In addition, train tickets were sent to the poorer relatives; cf. Witold Kula, Nina Asso- rodobraj-Kula, and Marcin Kula, *Listy emigrantów z Brazylii i Stanów Zjednoczonych, 1890–1891* [Letters of emigrants from Brazil and the United States, 1890–1891] (Warsaw, 1973), 424; Witold Kula, Nina Assorodobraj–Kula, and Marcin Kula, *Writing Home: Immigrants in Brazil and the United States, 1890–1891,* ed. Josephine Wtulich (Boulder, Colo., 1986), 264, 355, 365; also Theodore Olstyn to his sister, Feb. 26, 1910: Olstyn v.f., Western Reserve Historical Society, Cleveland, Ohio (hereafter cited as WRHS); Michael Kniola to A. Nowicki, June 8, 1893: Kniola Travel Bureau Collection, WRHS (hereafter cited KTB), ser. I, cont. 1, fold. 1; cf. F. Pachulski to J. Nasielewski, Sept. 12, 1912: KTB, ser. I, cont. 1, fold. 22; S. Groncki to his uncle, May 13, 1905: KTB, fold. 21. When he arrived at the Cleveland railway station, Stanley Radzyminski recollected: "Of course my sister-in-law and an uncle that we had here . . . all came for us, it was like salvation, coming to put sad immigrants into a strange country. So, we went home with them and . . . there were my brother and uncle, and, ah . . . my brothers' wives, and we lived there." When another immigrant, John Gallka, arrived at St. John Cantius parish in Cleveland everybody who once lived in his village or its vicinity, came to ask for local gossip. With great astonishment, the journalist Emil H. Duni- kowski commented while in America: "This is not America! It's Tarnów, Stanisławów!" Interview with S. Radzyminski, Immigrant Experience Project, Greater Cleveland Ethnographic Museum, Cuyahoga County College, Cleveland, Ohio, 8; John Gallka Collection, vol. 1: 18: WRHS; Emil H. Dunikowski, *Wśród Polonii w Ameryce: Druga Seria 'Listów z Ameryki'* [Among the Poles in America] (Lwów, 1893), 41; cf. E. Morawska, " 'T'was Hope Here': The Polish Immigrants in Johnstown, Pennsylvania, 1890–1930," in Frank Renkiewicz, ed., *The Polish Presence in Canada and America* (Toronto, 1982), 33.

be a temporary one. People went there, like the mountaineers of the Tatra Highlands, "to make their pile of krutzers" in order to "buy a farm to run" in Poland.[11] In their intention to return, Poles were not different from many other groups migrating to America from central, eastern, and southern Europe in the 1880s, 1890s, and ensuing years.[12] In the United States, these people were then labeled "birds of passage." If we place them in the context of the Atlantic economy we might better call them "migrant workers."[13] The available data enable us to calculate that the returnees amounted to nearly 30 percent of the total emigration.[14]

11 Kantor, "Czarny Dunajec," 57; Andrzej Brożek, *Polonia amerykańska, 1854–1939* [Polish-Americans, 1854–1939] (Warsaw, 1977), 21. See also n. 6. About the terms, cf. Frank Bovenkerk, *The Sociology of Return Migration: A Bibliographic Essay* (The Hague, 1974), 9–10.

12 Golab, *Immigrant;* Walaszek, *Reemigracja;* Betty Caroli, *Return Migration from the United States to Italy, 1900–1914* (New York, 1973); Francesco Cerase, "Nostalgia or Disenchantment: Considerations on Return Migration," in Silvano Tomasi and S. H. Engel, eds., *The Italian Experience in the United States* (Staten Island, N.Y., 1970); Dino Cinel, "Land Tenure Systems, Return Migration and Militancy in Italy," *Journal of Ethnic Studies* 12 (1984); Keijo Virtanen, *Settlement or Return: Finnish Emigrants (1860–1930) in International Overseas Migration Movement* (Turku, 1979); Reino Kero, "American Immigrants as Bearers of Entrepreneurial Ideas and Technology during the Early Stages of Industrialization in Finland," in Michael G. Karni, Olavi Koivukangas, and Edward W. Laine, eds., *Finns in North America: Proceedings of Finn Forum III* (Turku, 1988); Lars G. Tedebrand, "Remigration from America to Sweden," in Harald Runblom and Hans Norman, eds., *From Sweden to America: A History of the Migration* (Minneapolis, 1976); Frances Krajlic, *Croatian Migration to and from the United States, 1900–1914* (Palo Alto, Calif., 1978); Theodore Saloutos, *They Remember America: The Story of Repatriated Greek Americans* (Berkeley, Calif., 1956).

13 Golab, *Immigrant,* 48; terminology is explained in Bovenkerk, *Sociology,* 9–10.

14 Leopold Caro, *Statystyka emigracji polskiej i austro-węgierskiej do Stanów Zjednoczonych Ameryki Północnej* [Statistics of Polish and Austro-Hungarian emigration to the United States of America] (Cracow, 1907), 54; Leopold Caro, *Emigracja i polityka emigracyjna ze szczególnym uwzględnieniem ziem polskich* [Emigration and emigration policy with regard particularly to the Polish territories] (Poznan, 1914), 145; Brozek, *Polonia,* 22, 226–27; Andrzej Pilch, "Emigracja z ziem zaboru austriackiego (od polowy XIX w. do 1918 r.)" [Emigration from Austrian Poland from the beginning of 19th century to 1918], in Andrzej Pilch, ed., *Emigracja z ziem polskich w czasach nowożytnych i najnowszych (XVIII–XX w.)* [Emigration from Polish territories in modern times] (Warsaw, 1984), 272–75; Morawska, "Labor," 263; *Annual Report of the Commissioner General of the Immigration to the Secretary of Labor,* 1908–18, (Washington, D.C., 1909–19). For the other ethnic groups, cf. John Bodnar, *The Transplanted: A History of Immigrants in Urban America* (Bloomington, Ind., 1985), 53–54; Tedebrand, "Remigration," 209; J. E. Becker, "Norwegian Migration, 1856–1960," *International Migrations* 4, nos. 4–5 (1966): 174; Caroli, *Italian,* 8; Kraljic, *Croatian,* 29, 34; Mark Stolarik, "From Field to Factory: The Historiography of Slovak Immigration to the United States," *Slovakia* 28 (1978–79): 85; Monika Gletter, *Pittsburgh – Wien – Budapest: Programm und Praxis der Nationalitatenpolitik bei der Auswanderung der ungarischen Slowaken nach Amerika um 1900* (Vienna, 1980), 10; Saloutos, *They Remember,* 29–30. The size of migration seemed to be determined by the economic fluctuations in the United States (bigger waves of migrants from the United States always occurred during the economic depressions in the years 1884–85, 1894–95, 1904, 1907, 1908); Harry Jerome, *Migration and Business Cycles* (New York, 1926), 121–23, 141–46, 151; Tedebrand, "Remigration," 209–10; Saloutos, *They Remember,* 32; J. S. Lindberg, *The Background of Swedish Emigration to the United States and Economic and Sociological Study in the Dynamics of Migration* (Minneapolis, 1930), 245. The decision about the return was also determined by other factors connected both with the country of origin and the country of settlement, as well as by personal ones (Walaszek, *Reemigracja,* particularly chaps. 2 and 4), such as homesickness ("Before the outbreak of the war, the First World War, before I got married, I only wished to go [back]. I cried, I cried after my mother for a year. I was homesick

ECONOMIC EFFECTS OF MIGRATIONS ON THE
AREA OF ORIGIN

People went abroad mainly to earn money. In the rural villages, the inflow of money was one of the first effects of transatlantic migrations. The money earned abroad was spent on immediate needs: It stabilized the ownership and operation of small properties, had an impact on the distribution of landholding, and increased agricultural wages. In this section, I discuss the monetary and economic effects of these migrations.

The influx of "American" money to Poland "can be construed as yet another dimension of the incorporation of the periphery into the extended economic system."[15] In 1902 $3.5 million in money orders was sent from the United States to Austrian Galicia; an additional $4 million was brought back by the returnees; and $3.5 million was sent to Russian Poland. Another $12 million was probably mailed home in private letters. Thus, during one year perhaps $20 million reached two zones of the partitioned country. Whereas in 1900 5.5 million crowns were sent to Austria from the United States, in 1904 the amount was 15.8 million. In a single Galician village, Ropczyce, each household in one year received an average of $140 from relatives in America. During the period 1919–24, $220 million was sent or brought into Poland. Later, "emigration started to lose its importance in our balance of payments."[16] Nevertheless, short-term migrations had a "spectacular" impact on the economic situation of the village and on peasants' attitudes. In 1900 migrant laborers returned from Germany to Congress Poland with the equivalent of $4 million; in 1901, with $4.5 million; and in 1904, with $5,712,587.

The money brought in from abroad was spent on necessities, on immediate needs, in order to secure survival. Because of American dollars, the consequences of the disastrous flood of 1903 in Galicia were less drastic than had been expected.[17] Money was used for food and, during the winter,

and I could not find a place for myself. At night I always dreamed that I die, I was extremely homesick"; Chicago Historical Society, Oral History Archive of Chicago Polonia, JED 070, 27–28). What also inclined people to leave the New World were calculations and expectations evoked by gossip and news coming from the old country (cf. letters from the old country published by the Polish ethnic press in America), the lack of possibilities to adapt to the new conditions, and difficulties with the assimilation and eventual barriers to upward mobility. The returns were interrupted by the European and world military operations.

15 Morawska, "Labor," 263.
16 Morawska, "Labor," 257–63; Gargas, "W sprawie," 518–25; Gargas, "Bank," 401; Grabski, *Materiały,* 3: 91; A. Walaszek, "Działalność przekażowo-pieniężna polskich konsulatów w Stanach Zjednoczonych w latach, 1919–1922" [Money transfer activity to Polish consulates in the U.S.A., 1919–1922], *Studia Historyczne* 24 (1981): 409–21.
17 *Stenograficzne Sprawozdania Sejmu Krajowego,* Alegat 274, 21 posiedzenie, Sept, 15, 1903, VIII period,

for heat. Migrants had left the poorest sectors of villages, and to these places they returned. When the money was spent, people migrated again.[18] These huge sums of money were a great boon for the villages. "It is almost difficult to imagine what kind of poverty we would have faced without emigration and without money from America and from Boryslaw [an oil industry center in southeastern Galicia]," one correspondent wrote.[19]

In the 1860s people from small towns and villages in Prussian Poland migrated to Germany, in particular, to work in Saxony during the harvest season. Others migrated to Bavaria, Hanover, and the Ruhr Valley, in order to work in industry. Seasonal migrations created a lack of agricultural workers in western Prussia. Laborers from Russian Poland and Galicia replaced them. In 1890 17,275 people migrated from Russian Poland to Germany; in 1900 the figure was 119,284; and in 1903 it was 141,700. In the agriculture of Russian Poland they were replaced by workers from Galicia. Galicians also migrated toward the industry of Upper Silesia or Pest, or into the agriculture of Moravia, Bukovina, Bohemia, and Lower Austria. From

Wniosek posla J. Stapinskiego, Dec. 29, 1902 [Galician Diet Stenographic Protocols, 21 Session, Annex 274, Jan Stapiński's motion], 1312–18.

18 Benjamin Murdzek, *Emigration in Polish Social-Political Thought, 1870–1914* (Boulder, Colo., 1977), 152–53; Morawska, " 'For Bread,' " 388; Franciszek Bujak, *Maszkienice, wieś powiatu brzeskiego: Stosunki gospodarcze i społeczne* [Maszkienice, village of Brzesko County: Social and economic relations] (Cracow, 1902), 132; Irena Lechowa, "Tradycje emigracyjne w Klonowej (pow. Sieradz)" [Emigration traditions in Klonowa (Sieradz County)], *Prace i Materiały Muzeum Archeologicznego i Etnograficznego w Łodzi: Seria Etnograficzna* [Works and materials of the Archeological and Ethnographic Museum in Łódz: Ethnographic series] no. 3 (Łódz, 1960), 64; Misińska, *Podhale,* 56; Bohdan Kopeć, *Wychodźstwo sezonowe z ziemi wileńskiej do Łotwy* [Seasonal migration from Vilnius area to Latvia] (Wilno, 1938), 158. Other authors confirm that returned migrants were spending their savings mainly on personal needs. Orkan, *Listy ze wsi,* 1:119, wrote that seasonal migration to Prussia, which continued in the southern, mountainous region of Podhale for a dozen or so years, was "a real catastrophe for our village . . . pfennigs earned did to the village nothing, they disappeared and only the devil profited from them." Cf. also Kazimierz Fiedor, *Polscy robotnicy rolni na Śląsku pod panowaniem niemieckim na tle wychodźstwa do Rzeszy, 1918–1932* [Polish agricultural workers in German Silesia and the emigration to Germany, 1918–1932] (Wrocław, 1968), 180; Apoloniusz Zarychta, *Emigracja polska, 1918–1931, i jej znaczenie dla państwa* [Polish Emigration, 1918–1931, and its significance for the country] (Warsaw, 1933), 65; W. Skowron, *Emigracja sezonowa do Niemiec jako zagadnienie społeczne i gospodarcze* [Polish seasonal migration to Germany as a social and economic problem] (Warsaw, 1931), 21–22. Different were the opinions of Józef Frejlich, *Polskie wychodźstwo zarobkowe w obwodzie przemysłowym westfalsko-nadreńskim* [Polish labor migrants in the Westphalien and Rhine districts] (Cracow, 1911), 58; Ludwik Landau, *Wychodźstwo sezonowe na Łotwę i do Niemiec w 1938 r. na podstawie ankiety Instytutu Gospodarstwa Społecznego* [Polish seasonal labor migration to Latvia and Germany based on the questionnaire of the Institute of Social Economy] (Warsaw, 1966), 151–57.

19 Letter from Wietrzno, near Równe, *Ojczyzna* [Homeland] (Cracow), Jan. 24, 1909, 74; Franciszek Bujak, "Rozwój gospodarczy Galicji, 1772–1914" [Economic development of Galicia, 1772–1918], in his *Wybór Pism* [Selected papers], ed. Helena Madurowicz-Urbanska, 2 vols. (Warsaw, 1976), 2: 377; Jan Stapinski, *Pamiętniki* [Memoirs] (Warsaw, 1959), 254; Wierzbicki, *Żmiąca,* 63; Stanisław Pigoń, *Z Kamborni w świat: Wspomnienia młodości* [From Kambornia to the world: Memoirs from youth] (Cracow, 1957), 55.

all over others were embarking for the United States, Brazil, and, later, Canada, France, or other places. As a result, the cost of labor jumped. Newspaper correspondents complained:

The ranks of our population have been so depleted by emigration to America, that for hoeing potatoes or other work like weeding one cannot find a worker for less then 40 to 45 cents a day, and later, in harvest time, that will be twice as much. One won't find a servant for housework, not to mention a capable cooking lady.

And in 1912 someone from Bobowa in Ropczyce County wrote: "When someone wishes to finish up all tasks, he has to hire laborers; . . . but landless people are away, they have all emigrated into the world." Similar trends were observed in Russian Poland. In Zamosc County plowboys demanded pay raises, warning employers that otherwise they could go to Paraná.[20]

Migration made improvements in living conditions possible and allowed the purchase of tools and fertilizers. Between 1903 and 1937, 230 persons emigrated to America from the Galician village of Babica, and 36 percent of them returned. (The influence of American emigration on the village was researched in detail before World War II.) During these thirty-four years twenty-one individuals earned only enough to purchase a return ticket; twelve built houses (one very luxurious); thirty-eight bought land; two paid debts; and six invested in various properties, buying respectively a saloon (*karczma*), two tenement houses in town, a motorcycle, and books (!). Before World War I and immediately thereafter, "American" money helped accelerate parceling of manorial farms, yet restrained the excessive subdivision of plots. Such influxes also stimulated the rise of land prices and wage scales. When, in 1908, returning migrants did not bring with them sufficient sums of money, land prices dropped quickly. The money brought by returnees was used mainly for buying land to enlarge parcels. One-half of those who returned to Babica from America bought some land. On the average, the holdings were enlarged by a few hundred acres (one acre equals 100 square meters).[21]

---

20 *Pogoń*, no. 46, June 10, 1900; Krzysztof Groniowski, *Polska emigracja zarobkowa do Brazylii, 1871–1914* [Polish labor migration to Brazil, 1871–1914] (Wrocław, 1972), 141; Hupka, "Przyczynek," 41–42.
21 Zawistowicz-Adamska, *Społeczność*, 19; Wierzbicki, *Żmiąca*, 158; Duda-Dziewierz, *Wieś*, 79–86, 135; F. Bujak, *Wieś zachodnio-galicyjska u schyłku XIX wieku* [Village of western Galicia at the end of the 19th century] (Cracow, 1905), 79–80; W. Grabski, *Materiały*, 3:101–3; Kantor, "Czarny," 164; Anna Kowalska-Lewicka, "Badania etnograficzne na Podhalu [Research on Podhale]," *Etnografia Polska* [Polish ethnography] 1 (1958): 245; "Emigracja" [Emigration], *Gazeta Lwowska*, May 17, 1903, 1; "W sprawie emigracji [About emigration]," *Przyjaciel Ludu* [People's friend] 24, no. 14 (1912): 24; "Interpelacja posla Stapinskiego" [Interpellation of Deputy Stapinski], *Przyjaciel Ludu* 26, no. 13 (1914): 3; "Bp. Pelczar, Dyskusja" [Bishop Pelczar, discussion], *Przegląd Powszechny* [Common review] (1912): 159.

Whereas the number of smallest and biggest properties in the villages declined, the number of medium size grew.[22] Franciszek Bujak described the situation in Ropczyce County. Big farms, big properties were disappearing in the district. From 9,088 manorial farms before World War I, only 1,595 (17.5 percent) remained. The rest had been parceled out. At least 80 percent of families in the country "had someone in America" at the beginning of this century. If each of them had sent only 250 crowns yearly (in years like 1907 the equivalent of 1,500 crowns were sent), the village of Brzeziny alone would have received funds worth 350,000 crowns. Most of this money was used for the purchase of land through the parceling of manorial farms. In the summer of 1912 only 310 morgues (one Austrian morgue, or *Joch,* equaled 5,755.4 square meters; one Polish morgue equaled 5,598.7 square meters) were available for parceling. Owners of small farms (two to five morgues) were enlarging their properties and entering the category of owners of five to ten morgues. Bujak called this process "a victory of smallholders" and attributed this outcome to the American migration. Since the owners of marginal farms (up to two morgues) were able only to go to Prussia or Moravia, at least initially, they did not contribute much financially.

For peasants, the main indicator of social status was the amount of land owned. But in the villages from which people emigrated, the quantity of land available for purchase was limited.[23] Thus, the wealthiest returnees and those who wanted to change their social position, visibly and radically, had to look for it elsewhere. In post–World War I Poland this land was found in the northwestern (formerly Prussian Poland) and eastern voivodeships. Among the farms bought by the return American migrants originally from Babica, the biggest (thirty morgues) was located in Pomerania, hundreds of kilometers north of the village.[24] After World War I returnees were enthusiastic about their purchases in Pomerania and in the east. They wrote to America:

22 Stanisław Hupka, *Über die Entwicklung der westgalizischen Dorfzustände in der zweiten Hälfte des 19. Jahrhunderts* (Teschen, 1910); Review by Franciszek Bujak in *Ekonomista* [Economist] 4 (1911): 217–24; Franciszek Bujak, *Kilka przyczynków i sprostowań do pracy dra St. Hupki o rozwoju stosunków włosciańskich w Galicji Zachodniej (pow. Ropczyce)* [Some contributions and corrections to Dr. St. Hupka's work on the rural relations in western Galicia (Ropczyce County)] (Warsaw, 1913), offprint from *Ekonomista,* 80–85; Stanisław Hupka, *Przyczynek do metodycznonaukowejł strony badan stanu i rozwoju współczesnej wsi polskiej w Galicji Zachodniej* [Contribution to the methodological aspects of contemporary state and development of Polish villages in western Galicia] (Cracow, 1912).

23 Bujak was predicting that because there was a limited quantity of land available for parcelation just before World War I, the return migration to western Galicia would stop. People would have no reason to come back. Bujak, *Kilka przyczynków,* 84.

24 Bujak, *Wieś,* 30; Duda-Dziewierz, *Wieś,* 46, 108–16, 135; Wierzbicki, *Zmiąca,* 69–70; Zawistowicz-Adamska, *Społeczność,* 223–24.

Please announce in our paper, *Ameryka Echo,* that those who want to buy something in Poland should come to Pomerania. Here one can buy an excellent parcel from Germans . . . I have for a thousand dollars bought a tavern with 10 rooms, one two-family house, 20 morgues and garden of two morgues.[25]

Considered in social terms, migrants could only return to their previous social positions, and could strengthen the social roles they had played before in the village. The community did not favor promotion of its poor inhabitants to the ranks of the rich.[26] It would rather tolerate wealthy newcomers. Those who did not emigrate profited from the process as well. They invested money borrowed from emigrants, and they had a chance for better jobs – for example, the postwar construction boom caused a higher demand for labor.[27]

"Existing evidence on effects of capital inflow into the Polish countryside from international labor migrations of its inhabitants supports the general conclusion . . . that in structural terms this capital played a predominantly preserving rather than transforming role," Ewa Morawska summarizes.[28] Return migration increased the number of moderately wealthy households; thus it acted as a stabilizing factor. Inhabitants of the poorest, peripheral parts of the villages were not often among recipients of emigration assets. American savings helped to place the former migrants back in their previous social positions.[29]

WERE RETURN MIGRANTS INNOVATIVE IN THEIR FARMING?

Those migrants who had worked in industry in the West or in Budapest could have popularized new capitalist attitudes. The impact of migrants who had worked in German agriculture or elsewhere theoretically should have helped raise the level of agricultural knowledge. Historians Jan Borkowski and Krzysztof Dunin-Wasowicz are convinced that this really happened, that migrants modernized Polish agriculture.[30]

---

25 *Ameryka Echo,* Jan. 8, 1922, 11 (a very popular, liberal weekly published in Toledo, Ohio); *Przyjaciel Ludu,* May 7, 1922, 3; Dec. 18, 1921; *Praca* [Work] (Tarnow), May 11, 1924, 4.
26 Stefan Czarnowski was of a different opinion; cf. "Podłoze ruchu chłopskiego" [The base of the peasant movement], in his *Dzieła* [Works], vol. 2 (Warsaw, 1956), 173.
27 Lechowa, "Tradycje," 66; Misińska, *Podhale,* 56.
28 Morawska, "Labor," 267.
29 Zawistowicz-Adamska, *Społeczność,* 223–24; Duda-Dziewierz, *Wieś,* 135.
30 Jan Borkowski, *Chłopi,* 47–56. The statement refers to the whole of Poland, but Borkowski notices that modernization was most significant in Prussian Poland. Dunin-Wasowicz, "Głos w dyskusji" [Panel remarks], *Mechanizmy polskich,* 88, is the only author to claim that before World War I the returnees "were propagators of new methods of farming, including the use of machines." His statements, however, are not convincing.

Detailed studies, however, do not necessarily support this view. Franci-szek Bujak noticed earlier that the returnees did not use their migrant ex-periences, even if the knowledge gained abroad could be beneficial, in the old country (e.g., draining swamps). Social and economic historians, eth-nographers, anthropologists, and social workers mostly agree on the rela-tively limited impact this knowledge had on agricultural practices. Applied knowledge was limited to sporadic attempts to cultivate new crops, and usage of some new tools or techniques that migrants could have encoun-tered abroad. The sole exceptions (though after World War I) were prob-ably migrations to Germany, Denmark, and Latvia, which brought about the introduction of some innovations in agriculture, particularly near the western borders. In Babica, moreover, the most progressive peasant farmers did not migrate. They did not need to. Rather, they introduced new ma-chines and new tools into their village and also started planting fodder and root crops.

Thus, the impact of returnees or migrants was relatively insignificant. One has to remember that in America the majority of migrants lived and worked in big cities and in industry, not in the countryside. After their return, however, in some places migrants tried to grow lettuce, alfalfa, wal-nuts, tomatoes, leeks, and celery. Rarely did they make attempts to intro-duce such techniques as new forms of potato and cabbage cultivation or cow dung preparation. Usually such efforts ended unsuccessfully. The land-scape and climate were unfavorable. Modernizers also faced resistance from the tradition-oriented village community. Only in cases when a bigger group of people returned to one village had such innovations any chance of diffusion. They always met with some opposition from more conserva-tive community members. Successful new methods of farming introduced by returnees could have shaken the social positions of local authorities. Thus, they were bound to be resisted.[31]

MATERIAL CULTURE

Equally rare was the introduction of objects brought from abroad. Seasonal, short-distance migrations could not and did not increase the number of

31 Bujak, *Maszkienice . . . Stosunki,* 130–32; Franciszek Bujak, *Maszkienice wieś powiatu brzeskiego: Roz-wój od r. 1900 do r. 1911* [Maszkienice, a village in Brzesko County: Development from 1900 to 1911] (Cracow, 1914), 100, 107–8; Misińska, *Podhale,* 59–60; Wierzbicki, *Żmiąca,* 71; Lechowa, "Tradycje," 66–67; Landau, *Wychodźstwo,* 130, 149; Maria Wieruszewska-Adamczyk, "Rola kon-troli społecznej środowiska lokalnego w procesie zmiany kulturowej na wsi" [The role of local social control in the process of cultural change in the village]," in *Zmiany kultury chłopskiej* [Changes of peasants' culture] (Wrocław and Warsaw, 1973), 190–91; Duda-Dziewierz, *Wieś,* 85, 87, 129.

objects. Even if brought in, very few of them were found to be so useful that they became indispensable. In Babica emigration did not produce many material traces: a shirt worn on holidays, some photographs, or perhaps a wall calendar. Maria Biernacka, a Polish ethnographer, referring to peasants, notes: "Those who left for America, backward and ignorant, came back to the previous life-style of their families."[32] When migrants were found using some gadgets brought back from abroad, for example, coffee mills and mincing machines, these objects were treated only as curiosities and assumed no local importance. Relatively few were accepted in the villages.[33] After World War I, when people often returned from America with considerable amounts of savings, they also brought with them the simplest tools and the most basic foods.

There was one thing that most of the returnees certainly wanted to do, if only their savings allowed: to build or to modernize their houses. The "American" houses that mushroomed in the villages were more sumptuous and comfortable, were made of bricks and cement, had tiled roofs and coal stoves. Admiring neighbors often tried to imitate the returnees' example. A housing boom was doubtless stimulated by migration. In 1869 there were 100 houses in Galicia for 138 families. Twenty years later, in 1890, 100 houses served 102 families – American money enabled peasants to build new houses.[34]

TRADITION VERSUS MODERNIZATION

Migration was only one of many ongoing processes transforming villages and having an impact on peasants' attitudes, behaviors, and mentality. At the end of the nineteenth century, and in the beginning of the twentieth, contacts with the cities expanded in many districts. Education for different social groups was also either established or enlarged. Polemicizing with Stanisław Hupka's opinion on the near total isolation of Ropczyce County villages, Franciszek Bujak argued that in the mid-nineteenth century peasants had "quite wide" relations with the outside world. "Right after the enfranchisement they knew distant areas, and ways to them." Such as existed in the eighteenth and nineteenth centuries, protoindustry – for ex-

---

32 Maria Biernacka, *Potakówka, wieś powiatu jasielskiego 1890–1960: Z badań nad współdziałaniem* [Potakówka, a village of Jaslo County, 1890–1960: Investigation of Cooperation] (Warsaw, 1960), 71; Duda-Dziewierz, *Wieś*, 85.

33 Only Irena Lechowa, writing about the mountain area, mentioned some innovations that came to be widely accepted by villagers – a rarity in Polish circumstances. Lechowa, "Tradycje," 85.

34 Wierzbicki, *Żmiąca*, 70, 89; Borkowski, *Chłopi*, 48; Jan Stanisław Bystroń, *Kultura ludowa* [Folk culture] (Warsaw, 1947), 335; Misińska, *Podhale*, 58–59.

ample, linen and wood products – occasioned some travels. The products (even if their numbers were limited) were sold during the fairs. Onions cultivated in some parts of that county were later marketed in towns as far away as Debica, Rzeszów, Tarnów, and even Cracow. Bricklayers from Góra Ropczycka could be found searching for jobs in small Galician towns and villages in the summer months.

Village craftsmen, for example, coopers from Czarna, had to go from one place to the another. Peasants traveled to manorial farms with their grain and served in the army. From such journeys these people did not profit much economically but they encountered different cultures. Soldiers returned home from the army, attained authority in the villages, and became their leaders during the conflicts with the manor. Thus, villages were never completely isolated and the migrations did not radically alter the previous pattern of contacts with the outside. The modernization process could and did start from the bottom up. It went also via local leaders, clergy, and infrequent visitors.[35]

Nevertheless, migration could accelerate the rationalization of people's attitudes and could popularize nonconformist ideas and behaviors. Abroad, migrants could take notice that some behaviors and attitudes not accepted by the village community were accepted and esteemed elsewhere. This discovery might sometimes facilitate a diffusion of cultural innovations. Migrants could both directly and indirectly erode the traditional order, but such processes were by no means revolutionary. Obviously, those whose hierarchy of values changed during the migration more often stayed abroad permanently.[36] It has also been pointed out that the migration process comprised a kind of "emergency exit" from the villages for the discontented. Consequently, conservative politicians of the time might have been (though they were not) favorably disposed toward emigration.[37]

Migrants coming back to the old country tried to transplant certain elements of American fashion. Yet, the hostile responses of village communities toward such attempts and "the slavery of traditions, customs, and forms" determined that the "Americans" relinquish wearing American "lordly caps, gaiters and braces," the fashion "according to which everyone

35 Hupka, *Über die Entwicklung,* 390; Bujak review from Hupka, 222–23; Bujak, *Kilka przyczynków,* 85–89; Hupka, *Przyczynek,* 58–64; Bujak, *Maszkienice . . . Stosunki,* 133; Bujak, *Maszkienice . . . Rozwój,* 106–7; Duda-Dziewierz, *Wieś,* 118–29; Misińska, *Podhale,* 60–61; Seweryn Udziela, "Lud polski w powiecie ropczyckim" [Polish people in Ropczyce County], *Zbiór Wiadomości do Antropologii Krajowej* [Collection of information on country's anthropology] 14 (1890): 26–29.
36 Bujak, *Maszkienice . . . Rozwój,* 98–99, 108; Bujak, *Wieś,* 28; Duda-Dziewierz, *Wieś,* 119–21; Lechowa, "Tradycje," 70; Misińska, *Podhale,* 60–61.
37 Znaniecki, "Wychodźstwo," 126–27.

pretended to be a landowner." Before entering the Galician village of Ochotnica, peasants returning there from seasonal works in Budapest took off shoes purchased in Hungary and put on a local type of moccasin, due to concern for their kinsmen's disapproval. In the villages clothing differences were often read as negative, nonconformist behavior. Traditional folk attire could not be abandoned without a price. Thus persons wore "American" clothing not only when they wanted to stress their uniqueness and their superiority, but also when, as villagers might describe it, "they did not want to deal with dunghills."[38]

It was mainly the everyday rituals that changed. A head of the village of Zmiaca, upon returning from America, did not allow women to kiss his hand, saying that "one may kiss the pastor's hand but not mine."[39] Some family relations also changed. Migration offered women the chance to collect a dowry and for couples to save for a better marriage start. These factors might delay marriages as well. When migration gained popularity in Maszkienice (and elsewhere), marriages were contracted by older people. It has also been pointed out that the number of childbirths declined. This argument may be misleading, since children born abroad, during migration, did not appear in the vital statistics, though some of these later returned with their parents.[40] The stability of marriage plans could be shaken; plans were sometimes curtailed when a migrant abandoned the idea of his return.[41]

A change in the role of the woman (wife) might also change individual fates. Women took over many functions formerly performed by men, including the hiring of laborers and utilizing their help. Husbands tried to control their wives' activities and work, though, providing them with information and instructions, dictating from abroad what should be done, and asking relatives to help keep an eye on the farm. After their return, however, husbands often reestablished the old traditions and divisions of labor.[42] Children's participation in migrations and active involvement in earning some of the family income emancipated them, too.

38 Kazimierz Dobrowolski, *Studia nad życiem społecznym i kulturą* [Studies on social life and culture] (Wrocław, 1966), 94; Duda-Dziewierz, *Wieś*, 79; Misińska, *Podhale*, 59; Zawistowicz-Adamska, *Społeczność*, 69–70; *Ekonomia* [Economy] (Warsaw) 5, no. 3 (1920): 15; Danuta Markowska, *Rodzina w społeczności wiejskiej: Ciągłość i zmiana* [Family in a village community: Continuity and change] (Warsaw, 1976), 137.

39 Zbigniew T. Wierzbicki, "Pół wieku przemian wsi małopolskiej" [Half century of changes of a Malopolska Village], *Kultura i Społeczeństwo* [Culture and society] 2, no. 3 (1958): 89; Golda, "Konsekwencje," 119; some returnees damned water dousing – a very popular custom of Easter Monday; cf. Bystroń, *Kultura,* 338.

40 Bujak, *Maszkienice . . . Stosunki,* 107; Lechowa, "Tradycje," 70–72. Cf. school registers from the turn-of-century Village Community School in Chocholow, Podhale.

41 Duda-Dziewierz, *Wieś,* 61, 74; Kula, *Listy emigrantów,* 53–62.

42 Kula, *Listy emigrantów,* 57, 58.

THE FAILURE OF "RETURNS OF INNOVATION" FROM
THE UNITED STATES AFTER WORLD WAR I

In the late nineteenth and early twentieth centuries one could observe among peasants the growing fascination with the city. The city attracted and amazed, while at the same time "the spirit of the gentry" repudiated them. Years spent in the cities during one's migration enlarged the fascination for urban culture. After returning to Poland, the most venturesome migrants were not satisfied with the limits imposed by traditional village society. Some of them tried to lift their villages to a small-town level. Those less enterprising and less socially active simply moved to the cities and bought properties there, mainly tenement houses, believing that the best investment of their savings.[43] During the first years after World War I, when people were preparing to return from the other side of the ocean, city houses and lots were advertised in the newspapers. In the city of Bydgoszcz, for example, seventy real-estate agents served return migrants. One emigrant who bought a tenement house in Poznan for $4,000 wrote: "After so many years of migration, after such hard work abroad, now I will finally have my future secure!" Of course many persons made serious mistakes. Out of 130 returnees who had bought tenement houses in Grudziadz, only a few were really satisfied.[44]

Attempts to organize stores and enter trade might be understood as a return of innovation. In America emigrants had dreamed: "If I could only save few hundreds, and perhaps two hundred for a ship, then I would go back to the country and could organize a business. I could do anything, I could buy and sell, and I could change everything in the house, to make it all good."[45] Many persons did so. After they had returned, they organized small craftshops, bought and operated mills, sawmills, and taverns. These exemplified small investments connected with a rural economy.[46]

In spite of many similarities, the American "return fever" after World War I was different from previous return waves. About 100,000 persons returned to Poland in the years between 1919 and 1924. During the postwar

43 Jan Borkowski, "Problemy badawcze historii chłopów polskich w epoce kapitalizmu" [History of Polish peasants in the epoch of capitalism research problems], *Dzieje Najnowsze* [Contemporary history] 8, no. 1 (1976): 64; Duda-Dziewierz, *Wieś*, 108; W. Witos, *Jedna wieś* [One village] (Chicago, 1955), 40.

44 *Przyjaciel Ludu*, Oct. 2, 1921, 14; *Kurier Lwowski* [Lwów's courier], March 28, 1922, 7; *Pamiętniki . . . Stany*, 1: 165; Duda-Dziewierz, *Wieś*, 130–31.

45 Voivodeship Archive in Cracow, Sąd Okręgowy Karny Krakowski [Criminal District Court Collection], file 33, 731.

46 Orkan, *Listy*, 1:95; Zawistowicz-Adamska, *Społeczność*, 55, 177–78; *Pamiętniki emigrantów: Kanada* [Emigrant memoirs: Canada] (Warsaw, 1971), 328.

years the decision to leave America was often made spontaneously. People wanted to see the old country as quickly as possible, to help relatives with whom there often had been no contact throughout the war, and to boast of one's success in front of former neighbors. These seem to have been among the most common reasons. People were also disposed to return due to the decline in industrial production in the United States and by the recession, which had been deepest in the years 1920 to 1921. These crises were, of course, accompanied by a sharp decline in these return migrants' savings. Among Polish migrants, a specific image of future Poland was also beginning to crystallize: a free, democratic, and just country. It was assumed, moreover, that their country – destroyed by the war and deprived of industry – awaited the return migrants' collective initiative. Return to their homeland was viewed as almost a pioneer crusade of progress. Patriotic watchwords called for the reconstruction of the homeland, whereby simultaneously "You will help Poland industrially, but you will not do harm to yourself either." Such was the propaganda emanating from some Polish American political circles and economic groups, and presented by the contemporary ethnic press.

Many became convinced that the return to Poland might mean material success, the salvation of their savings.[47] It soon became evident, however, that the imagined Poland and the real one were not one and the same. While in the United States, the emigrants did not think about the confrontation between their "New World" and the old country. When leaving Poland, peasants from the rural areas "jumped from feudalism to capitalism" all within the space of one month. Conversely, after 1918, return migrants were suddenly faced with the realities of life in the old country. Their decision to return owed itself partly to practical reasons and partly to the general desire to make a pilgrimage to their native land, the land they had abandoned years before. What they had not realized was what it meant to return. The history of return migration from America to Poland after World War I is a history of the sudden death of the myth that had originated in and was created by the Polish communities in America, that of an affluent peasants' Poland, that of a modernized country like America. Yet attempts to transplant innovations from America to the old country failed. In reality,

47 Cf. Walaszek, *Reemigracja,* chaps. 1 and 4. Cf. also Adam Walaszek, "Stowarzyszenie Mechaników Polskich w Ameryce: 1919–1945" [Polish Mechanics Association in America: 1919–1945], *Przegląd Polonijny* 12, no. 2 (1986): 25–36; Adam Walaszek, "Polska Żegluga Morska i inne spółki okrętowe Polonii amerykańskiej po I wojnie światowej" [Polish Navigation Corporation and other ship corporations of American Polonia after World War I], *Przegląd Polonijny* 5, no. 4 (1979): 25–36; Walaszek, "Działalność przekazowo-pieniężna," 409–20.

neither the returnees nor the inhabitants of the new Polish Republic were prepared or able to fulfill such a task.[48]

"DEVILS COME FROM AMERICA":[49]
VILLAGES, AUTHORITIES, CLERGY, AND RETURNEES

A returnee's potential for leadership was determined by his previous, pre-migration status. A higher level of education and experience gained abroad, validated by a migrant's "fortune," could only help him succeed to a previous leader's position. In Babica "leadership ambitions of returnees were not coincidental [but] were tightly linked to leadership traditions of the part of the village they came from," as Duda-Dziewierz noticed.[50] Accustomed to working in various organizations in America, former emigrants could now become active socially, organizing societies, associations, and institutions. That activity was also often met with hostility, criticism, and open ridicule, which hurt even more. People mocked activists ("they call me a bureaucrat here!" one returnee complained).[51] Neighbors, returnees' "own" people, "pulled me to pieces. It was entirely different from Holyga [New York]. . . . The people here are so dumb and mean! They looked upon the Polish Americans as if they were criminals." Thus, those who returned began to entertain doubts whether they really belonged among their own kinsmen in their own villages. To the returnees, the American environment had become more familiar than Poland. It understood them better. Hence, bitter personal confessions poured forth: "I greatly regret that I ever left America. There is terrible poverty here, and I do not advise any one to come back here, especially if he or she has stayed a long time in America. There is nothing here to come back to."[52] Nostalgia and longing after the abandoned land were deeply felt:

There, in America, the Polish sons and daughters have a chance to become government officials. . . . and here they will perish. . . . America was a better mother

48 Adam Walaszek, " 'How was it possible to see it all in such rosy colors?' Return Migrants from the United States in Poland, 1919–1924," *Polish American Studies* (forthcoming); Kula, *Listy emigrantów,* 110–12; Tadeusz Radzik, *Społeczno-ekonomiczne aspekty stosunku Polonii amerykanskiej do Polski po I wojnie światowej* [Social-economic aspects of American Polonia relations to Poland after World War I] (Wrocław and Warsaw, 1989), 146–55.
49 *Ameryka Echo,* Jan. 13, 1924, 11.
50 Duda-Dziewierz, *Wieś,* 46, 108; Zawistowicz-Adamska, *Społeczność,* 224.
51 J. Cierniak, *Wieś Zaborów i zaborowski Dom Ludowy* [The village of Zaborów and Zaborovian people's home] (Zaborów, 1936), 52–53, 159–61; W. Stasiński, "Pamiętnik" [Memoirs], MS, Pamiętniki wiejskich Działaczy Społecznych [Memoirs of Village Social Activists Collection] Instytut Gospodarstwa Społecznego [Institute of Social Economy], Szkola Główna Handlowa, Warsaw (hereafter cited Pamiętniki wiejskich), 18; Duda-Dziewierz, *Wieś,* 85.
52 *Ameryka Echo,* Jan. 8, 1922, 11; Dec. 5, 1920, 17.

to us, and the law protected us, whereas here in our sovereign motherland we are pestered by parasites. It is enough to drive one mad.[53]

Migrations could change habits and morality. It is clearly visible from the collection of sermons of Rev. Sychowski. He warned migrants on various occasions, defended traditional morality and traditional habits, and he condemned sexual freedom and the rise in immorality, caused by a lack of family control. Yet, the clergy's laments were often perceived as exaggerated.[54] When migrations became everyday phenomena, the clergy of course, too, felt its impact. Before leaving their villages, migrants traditionally went to confession, took communion, and kissed the priest's hand. After returning to Poland, these habits slowly disappeared. Following World War I, few went to confession; and they stopped kissing the priest's hand.[55]

Migrants became critical about traditional beliefs and religious attitudes.[56] As workers abroad, peasants had to obey foremen's rules and were not allowed to observe traditional Polish church holidays. The religious views of some emigrants had changed under the influence of American rationalist ways of thinking. Skeptical, critical attitudes toward religion, cults, rituals, dogmas, and especially priestly authority increased. These types of attitudes triggered strong reactions from the Polish clergy. Priests openly criticized and stood against labor migrations, arguing that they contributed strongly to the rise of immorality and an equally devastating decline of piety. In Germany, the Diocese of Tarnów complained, laborers were forced to accept Protestantism. The piety of migrant laborers in Latvia was also considerably diminished.[57]

But it could be far worse in America. Under the influence of their migration experience, peasants who returned took on the status of benefactors (in the nineteenth century a role performed by nobles). Beginning with the migrations, donations and small church foundations stressed the social role of peasant families. Donations won dignity and respect for migrants and their families. The parish was now viewed as a common good, not merely as the church's property. The social distance between priests and parishion-

53 Duda-Dziewierz, *Wieś*, 152.
54 Stanisław Sychowski, *Praktyczny podręcznik dla opiekujących się wychodźcami* [Practical manual for those who help migrants] (Poznan, 1913); Lechowa, "Tradycje," 70–71; Orkan, *Listy*, 1:93; Maria Gliwcówna, "Drogi emigracji" [Ways of emigration], *Przegląd Socjologiczny* 4, nos. 3–4 (1936).
55 Gliwcówna, "Drogi emigracji," 511–12.
56 Duda-Dziewierz, *Wieś*, 121–22; Lechowa, "Tradycje," 69–70; Misińska, *Podhale*, 61.
57 Bujak, *Maszkienice . . . Stosunki*, 133; M. Biernacka, *Potakówka*, 70–73; Duda-Dziewierz, *Wieś*, 45–49, 121; cf. remarks of the Bishop of Tarnów Leon Wałęga, *Archaniol Rafał, czyli list pasterski o wychodźstwie* [Archangel Raphael or pastoral epistle about emigration] (Tarnów, 1906), 1–27; Leon Wałęga, bishop of Tarnów, Nov. 2, 1910, *Currenda*, no. 15 (1910): 154–58; also no. 2 (1912): 33–35; Landau, *Wychodźstwo*, 135.

ers diminished. This was the result of a process of democratization that Polish migrants witnessed on the other side of the ocean.[58] "The Poles in America have stopped being obedient lambs and no longer allow anyone to clip their hard-earned savings."[59]

Migrants' skepticism toward religion, cults, dogmas, and priestly authority precipitated swift rebuttal from the Polish clergy. Their vehement attacks were directed particularly against the returnees. Roman Moskala's remarks, significantly entitled "The Danger Coming from the U.S.A.," illustrate this clash. He worried about the possibility of great numbers of Polish National Catholic Church members returning to Poland after World War I. His fears were confirmed by an action launched in Poland by *Straż (The Guard),* an American weekly representing the Polish National Catholic Church. And they were underscored by the radical social agitation of new religious groups, which Moskala considered dangerous enough to contemplate stopping the return migration movement. The syndrome of secularized, religiously indifferent returnees, sympathetic to leftist peasant movements, was labeled "The American danger."[60] In a Bernardine church at Leżajsk the returnees heard from the pulpit: "You left for America. You made dollars there, but you have lost your faith, the mother of Poland . . . you should have been struck down by the first bullet, you scoundrels."[61] In another village a priest "exhorted the women of his parish . . . not to let their husbands returning from America back into their homes . . . since they had lost their faith."[62]

The clergy's fears did not relate merely to questions of faith. They also contemplated a radicalization of the villagers' views and the dismantling of existing social structures.[63] The return migrants were obviously trying to win people over to their side. In any case, they described the American way of life with great enthusiasm. They were disgusted with the depend-

58 Tadeusz Makarewicz, "Emigracja amerykańska a macierzysta grupa parafialna" [American emigration and the mother parochial group], *Przegląd Socjologiczny* [Sociology review] 4, no. 2 (1936): 522–35.

59 *Przyjaciel Ludu,* Oct. 14, 1923, 5. Cf. Antoni Kolaszewski's letter to Cleveland's bishop Ignatius Horstmann: "Now Bishop, please read this, that you may know that we are no longer your cattle, your dirty swine, your mad dogs. We declare to you that we are men, American citizens and you and every one of your bishops will have to treat us like men." Joseph H. Lackner, "Bishop Ignatius F. Horstmann and the Americanization of the Roman Catholic Church in the United States," Ph.D. diss., St. Louis University, 1977, 90.

60 *Przegląd Powszechny* [Universal review], nos. 145–46 (1920): 76–80; Charszewski, "Niebezpieczeństwo amerykańskie" [American danger], *Miesięcznik Pasterski Płocki* [Plock pastoral monthly], no. 9 (1919): 161–66.

61 *Przyjaciel Ludu,* Jan. 22, 1922, 10.

62 *Dziennik dla Wszystkich* [Everyone's daily], March 31, 1923.

63 "There is a gentleman here who is corrupting the whole village and has made them all read *Wyzwolenie* [Liberation – a Polish leftist peasant paper]," said a priest, *Ameryka Echo,* Jan. 13, 1924, 11.

ence of local authorities on the rectories. For their part, the clergy were "slow but consistent" in their reaction. In highly critical sermons they exhorted their flocks "to distrust the migrants and shun their company as that of unbelievers and corrupt people." "Our faith is unshaken," migrants vehemently countered. They were hurt that their donations for constructing churches, rectories, for buying bells were now being forgotten.[64]

The impact of return migrants on peasants' political and social consciousness was probably more important and significant than that on material life (although these factors are difficult to measure and trace). While abroad peasants sent their families books and newspapers. Going back, they often continued to subscribe to them.[65] Returnees read such papers to others, and this practice became another source of clashes with the clergy. Such instances were described in the American press to warn and shock their readers. One of the returnees was summoned by the local priest and was asked "why I've subscribed to *Ameryka Echo* and why I read articles to the local people and corrupt them." The priest forbade the migrant to read this weekly, alleging it to be "an infernal paper." He charged the unhappy parishioner with mortal sin, but to no avail. "I continue to read the paper to everyone and they all listen with great interest."[66] Somebody else complained that he was getting *Ameryka Echo* in tatters, with some articles cut out and torn away as a consequence of the priest's censorship.[67] This hurt. It was with considerable difficulty and cost that people obtained *Ameryka Echo,* that reminder of the country that had become a part of their lives. It was their paper.[68]

Had returnees' horizons been considerably broadened? Emigrants in their letters and return migrants in their stories related anecdotes about curiosities of that distant world, and described "how people work and live elsewhere." But did they have anything to tell? The tale of a man who after a dozen years or so in Chicago "knew only the way to the factory and to the church" was not so unusual. People wanted to listen, but what they heard was often another matter.[69] They wanted to hear about things consonant with their

64 *Przyjaciel Ludu,* July 15, 1923, 8.
65 Duda-Dziewierz, *Wieś,* 122.
66 *Ameryka Echo,* July 24, 1921, Oct. 8, 1922, Jan. 6, 1924, April 17, 1924; Biernacka, *Potakówka,* 88; Duda-Dziewierz, *Wieś,* 122–23.
67 *Ameryka Echo,* Oct. 22, 1922, 13.
68 *Ameryka Echo,* Jan. 6, 1924, 13.
69 Misińska, *Podhale,* 57–62; Stanisław Szerpak, "Stosunki społeczno – ekonomiczne i polityczne w północno-zachodniej Galicji w latach poprzedzających wybuch I wojny światowej" [Social and economic relations in northeast Galicia in the years before World War I], *Studia Historyczne* 19 (1976): 376; Jan Bukowski, "Życiorys tułacza syna Podhala" [Biography of a migrant, son of Podhale], MS, Pamiętniki Wiejskich, 1:11.

own cultural bearings. They could comprehend only their own cultural "texts." The peasant leader and later Prime Minister Wincenty Witos, for instance, noticed:

Soldiers on leave . . . would tell of marvels they had seen, and of things they usually did not understand. . . . They reported houses made of glass, golden churches, tenement houses as high as our Tatras, cows with stomachs ten times as big, with such an abundance of wine that people wash and bathe themselves in it, instead of using water. Curious, that in relating such stupidities none of them ever mentioned existing local arrangements, or working conditions, which they, as farmers, should have noticed first of all.[70]

NATIONAL CONSCIOUSNESS AND POLITICS

Finding themselves in new, unfamiliar surroundings emigrants were prompted to ask the question: Who are we? A youngster from Czarny Dunajec, who went with his parents to Budapest in 1893, wrote:

And here I find various nationalities Magyars, Germans, Talians, Croats, Slovaks, Czechs, and ourselves. Poles from all over Galicia . . . , each one sticking together at work and afterward. Only during disputes or misunderstandings they would divide into two camps. Magyars, Germans, and Talians together, and Poles, Slovaks, and Czechs together. . . . We are closer, because we can communicate more easily.[71]

Another wrote: "When I came to France I knew nothing, except how to plod along with plow and harrow what else could I know? Here my eyes opened and I realized what I had known was not enough."[72] Their feeling of having been exploited and badly treated (e.g., in Germany or Hungary) also had an impact on migrants' national rather than class feelings. Jan Borkowski claims: "mass migration at the end of the nineteenth century – labor migration – had the strongest impact on the rise of national consciousness."[73] Helena Brodowska, however, stresses that at the time of major migrations the peasants' activity was already quite visible, and levels

70 Quoted after Ludwik Stomma, *Antropologia kultury wsi polskiej XIX wieku* [Anthropology of a Polish 19th-century village] (Warsaw, 1986), 86, 142; cf. also a beggar's song that depicted Brazil, 79: A Brazilian was "also Christian. / But, God, mercy, what a man! / Sleeps and work fully armed. / All around are hanging knives, / Which they use to kill their wives. / When at children he gets mad, / Chops heads off, such a dad." The other charms of that country of immigration were: "Crocodile there day and night / In the swamps, in the lake / Sits and watches what you take." / "You take fruit, and you're slaughter / By a wild dog, big like stark / With wings, black, it eats pig."
71 Bukowski, "Życiorys," 1–2.
72 *Pamiętniki emigrantów: Francja* [Emigrants memoirs: France] (Warsaw, 1939), 232.
73 Borkowski, "Problemy," 67–68; Walaszek, *Reemigracja,* 147.

of political and national consciousness were quite high.[74] Other authors, whose assertions seem more balanced, also point out the major role migrations played in processes of developing national consciousness.[75] In any case, peasant leaders, before and after World War I, agreed that migrations and return migration visibly strengthened political movements in the old country. Returnees became active members of the Polish Peasant Party and contributed to its successes. They also supported goals of other peasant movements in Poland, especially in Galicia.[76]

The complex process of achieving national consciousness on the part of migrants has been described by various authors, and is known from recent literature on the subject, mainly sociological writings.[77] This process reached its peak during World War I, when Polish communities abroad contributed significantly and variously to Polish independence. Patriotic slogans in the Polish American press and from ethnic organizations pressed people to return. These efforts, as we have seen, were fated to end in disillusionment.[78]

Without further studies, the problems mentioned here can only be generalized or dealt with abstractly. Yet it cannot be denied that the migration process (among other factors) helped to reconstruct, indeed, to transform "traditional" village culture – all resistance notwithstanding.

Migrations deeply affected peasants' weltanschauung. Various authors have asserted that villagers' conscious isolation was thus broken.[79] Was this

74 Helena Brodowska, "Dyskusja" [Discussion], in *Mechanizmy,* 189–90.
75 See Tadeusz Łepkowski, "Naród polski w epoce rozbiorów" [Polish nation in the period of partitions], in Roman Heck, ed., *Studia nad rozwojem narodowym Polaków, Czechów i Słowaków* [Studies on national development of Poles, Czechs, and Slovaks] (Wrocław and Warsaw, 1976), 62–63; Andrzej Chojnowski, "Naród u progu niepodległości" [Nation on the eve of independence], in *Rok 1918: Tradycje i oczekiwania* [Year 1918: Traditions and expectations] (Warsaw, 1978), 137, 148; Zbigniew T. Wierzbicki, "Na drogach rozwoju świadomości narodowej ludności wiejskiej w Małopolsce na przykładzie wsi Żmiąca" [The roads of development of national consciousness among peasants of Małopolska, the example of a village of Zmiaca], *Przegląd Socjologiczny* 16 (1961): 122–23, 136.
76 Stapiński, *Pamiętnik,* 254; Witos, *Jedna,* 44; Józef Putek, *Miłosciwi panowie i krnąbrni poddani* [Gracious lords and stubborn subjects] (Cracow, 1959), 389–90.
77 See Hieronim Kubiak and Jerzy J. Wiatr, "Tendencje dominujące procesu formowania się i przeobrażeń Polonii amerykańskiej" [Dominant tendencies in the process of formation and transformations of the American Polonia], in Hieronim Kubiak, Eugeniusz Kusielewicz, and Tadeusz Gromada, eds., *Polonia amerykańska: Przeszłość i współczesność* [American Polonia: Past and present] (Wrocław and Warsaw, 1988), 757–809, for a list of the literature.
78 Walaszek, *Reemigracja.*
79 Kula, *Listy emigrantów,* 113–15; Wierzbicki, "Na drogach rozwoju," 132–33; Wierzbicki, *Żmiąca,* 200–201; Chałasiński, *Drogi,* 183; Duda-Dziewierz, *Wieś,* 135, 146–47; Józef Chałasiński, "Związek z parafią a świadomość narodowa emigranta" [Parish ties and the national consciousness of the emigrant], *Przegląd Socjologiczny* 4, no. 2 (1936): 547; Bujak, *Kilka przyczynków,* 85–89.

really the case? How important were emigration processes for Polish villages? A historian, Krzysztof Dunin-Wąsowicz, would strongly support the thesis of the innovative spirit of return migrants. He argues that returnees "brought with them a capitalist mentality."[80] The anthropologist Ludwik Stomma, however, opposed Wierzbicki's, Brodowska's, and others' opinions in that direction.

In the nineteenth century, destruction of conscious isolation barriers, undoubtedly occurred, but was specific and sporadic. Thus, neither the anthropologist who describes the culture of villages during that time, nor the ethnologist whose duty is to present his object's perspective from within, has any right under the peril of falsehood to move such cases beyond their bounds, to put them into his model or to enlarge them, since he knows what happened later.[81]

It is commonplace for the historical and sociological literature on migrations to mention the consequences. Undoubtedly, the most significant of these, in the case of Poland after World War I, was the impact of migratory movements on the economic life of the villages (broadly understood: money, land distribution and land prices, wages of agricultural workers, etc.). The picture remains less clear when one tries to investigate social, cultural, or psychological changes caused or influenced by migration movements. What is needed is thoroughgoing, systematic research that would show and explain the significant differences between territories or among villages.

80 Dunin-Wąsowicz, "Głos w dyskusji," 88.
81 Stomma, *Antropologia,* 148.

PART II

Internal German Migrations and In-Migrations

6

Traveling Workers and the German Labor Movement

HORST RÖSSLER

Research on the attitude of the German labor movement toward migrating working men has largely concentrated on either labor's stance on workers emigrating abroad, particularly to the United States in the second half of the nineteenth century,[1] or on the position of trade unions and the socialist party toward the in-migration of workers from southern and eastern Europe at the turn of the century.[2] By comparison, the working-class movement's attitude toward migrating workers within Germany has been much neglected.[3] The only exception is Christiane Eisenberg, who gave some attention to this problem in her important comparative study of the development of English and German trade unionism up to the late 1870s.

1 Hartmut Keil, "An Ambivalent Identity: The Attitude of German Socialist Immigrants towards American Political Institutions and American Citizenship," in Marianne Debouzy, ed., *In the Shadow of the Statue of Liberty: Immigrants, Workers and Citizens in the American Republic* (St. Denis, France, 1988), 247–63; Dirk Hoerder, "German Immigrant Workers' Views of 'America' in the 1880s," in ibid., 17–37; Horst Rössler, "Attitudes of German Socialists and Their Forerunners towards Emigration and Colonization Projects in the Nineteenth Century," paper presented at the German-American conference *Emigration and Settlement Patterns of German Communities in North America,* New Harmony, Ind., Sept. 28–Oct. 1, 1989. All quotations from the German in this essay were translated by the author.
2 Dirk Hoerder, "The Attitudes of German Trade Unions towards Migrant Workers, 1880s to 1914," *Migracijske Teme* 4 (1988): 21–33; Martin Forberg, "Ausländerbeschäftigung, Arbeitslosigkeit und gewerkschaftliche Sozialpolitik: Das Beispiel der Freien Gewerkschaften zwischen 1890 und 1918," *Archiv für Sozialgeschichte* (hereafter *AfS*) 27 (1987): 51–81; Christoph Klessmann, "Klassensolidarität und nationales Bewusstsein: Das Verhältnis zwischen der polnischen Berufsvereinigung (ZZP) und den deutschen Bergarbeitergewerkschaften im Ruhrgebiet, 1902–1923," *Internationale Wissenschaftliche Korrespondenz zur Geschichte der deutschen Arbeiterbewegung* (hereafter *IWK*) 10 (1974): 149–78.
3 For Great Britain and the United States, however, see the following studies from which the present essay has greatly profited: Eric Hobsbawm, "The Tramping Artisan," in Eric Hobsbawm, *Labouring Men: Studies in the History of Labour* (London, 1964), 34–63; Robert A. Leeson, *Travelling Brothers: The Six Centuries Road from Craft Fellowship to Trade Unionism* (London, 1979); Humphrey Southall, "Towards a Geography of Unionization: The Spatial Organization and Distribution of Early English Trade Unions," *Transactions of the Institution of British Geographers,* n.s. 13 (1988): 466–83; Jules Tygiel, "Tramping Artisans: The Case of the Carpenters in Industrial America," *Labor History* 22 (1981): 348–76; Patricia A. Cooper, *Once a Cigar Maker: Men, Women, and Work Culture in American Cigar Factories, 1900–1919* (Urbana, Ill., 1987), esp. 75–93.

Nevertheless, in the following I will challenge her argument that the tradition of artisan migrations and travels organized by labor obstructed the emergence of the trade union movement.[4]

This essay is only a first attempt to discuss some of the major aspects of the complex relationship between labor migration and the development of the working-class movement in Germany. It is largely based on an examination of some of the more important nineteenth-century trade union journals, socialist newspapers, and a selection of workers' autobiographies, all of which cover a broad range of skilled occupations. In particular, I focus on two aspects neglected by Eisenberg: the role of tramping journeymen and skilled workers in the spatial expansion of labor organizations as well as in the spread of socialist ideas and union principles; and the various tasks traveling working men performed during labor struggles. The first section examines the tradition of craft migration and the diffusion of radicalism by traveling working men and their organization-building activities. The second discusses labor's efforts at regulating the labor market by assisting itinerant workers. The third section deals with the relevance of traveling workers in the context of industrial disputes. Next, light is cast on the debates within labor's ranks about the use of traveling benefits in the trade union movement in the era of internal mass migration. A short biographical sketch illustrating the travels of a cigarmaker at the beginning of this century concludes the article.

I

Tramping had been part of the journeymen's work culture for a very long time. It started in the late Middle Ages and was compulsory in many crafts, according to whose customs and rules craftsmen were obliged to leave home and take to the road for a number of years after they had finished their apprenticeship. In their migrations they were supported by the masters as well as by journeymen brotherhoods, which, as relatively autonomous bodies within the guilds dominated by masters, had their own mutual benefit network. Originally, the purpose of these craft migrations was additional training and the transfer of "know-how" within the closed guild structure.[5]

---

4 Christiane Eisenberg, *Deutsche und englische Gewerkschaften: Enstehung und Entwicklung bis 1878 im Vergleich* (Göttingen, 1986), esp. 77–82, 101–15, 204–12; in his review of Eisenberg's study, Friedhelm Boll briefly notes that she fails to notice the positive aspects of traveling traditions in the emergence of national, centralized trade unions in Germany. "Gesellenwandern und verspätete Gewerkschaftsentwicklung," *IWK* 25 (1989): 86–87.

5 Dirk Hoerder, "An Introduction to Labor Migration in the Atlantic Economies, 1815–1914," in Dirk Hoerder, ed., *Labor Migration in the Atlantic Economies: The European and North American Working Classes during the Period of Industrialization* (Westport, Conn., 1985), 5–6.

In the first years of the nineteenth century, the old journeymen brotherhoods were dissolved in most of the German states through government
action. At the same time the state of handicraft production deteriorated
more and more due to the development of modern, industrial capitalism.
The guild system increasingly eroded and was abolished in all German states
after midcentury. Small craft shops became dependent on the putting-out
system of merchant capitalists or were threatened by the competition of
factories. Still, traveling continued well into the twentieth century as a
custom among journeymen and workers in those sectors of industry with
a craft tradition. Craftsmen had migrated along established traveling routes
for a very long time and, as bricklayer August Winnig recalled, as late as
the 1880s young journeymen in the trade did exactly the same tours as their
fellow craftsmen had done in the 1830s.[6]

However, while traveling continued, its purpose and character changed
decisively. Demographic pressure and the slow advancement of free trade
had resulted in a continuous surplus of labor in many crafts. Thus, from the
late eighteenth century onward, traveling on the part of artisans and skilled
workers changed into labor migration. Although the traditional motivation
to improve one's skills and knowledge still played a role, it was the search
for work that now dominated among the reasons for setting out on the
road.

The traditional mass crafts – like tailoring, shoemaking, cabinetmaking,
and locksmith trades – were particularly affected by the development of
industrial capitalism. It was journeymen in these occupations, along with
building trades workers, the highly skilled printers, and the nonguilded
cigarmakers, who largely made up the social basis of the trade union and
socialist labor movement. Among these groups of workers the craft tradition
of traveling was particularly marked (the cigarmakers were an exception
but otherwise strongly imitated artisan customs).[7]

It was during their *tour d'Europe* in the 1830s and 1840s that German
artisans came into contact with early socialist and communist ideas. In fact,
as the *Sozialdemokrat* stated in the mid-1890s, the German proletariat's

---

6 August Winnig, *Frührot: Ein Buch von Heimat und Jugend* (Hamburg, 1950), 204–5, 260.
7 Frolinde Balser, *Sozial-Demokratie, 1848/49–1863: Die erste deutsche Arbeiterorganisation*, 2 vols. (Stutt-
gart, 1962), 1:84; Klaus Tenfelde, "Die Enstehung der deutschen Gewerkschaftsbewegung: Vom
Vormärz bis zum Ende des Sozialistengesetzes," in Ulrich Borsdorf, ed., *Geschichte der deutschen Ge-
werkschaften: Von den Anfängen bis 1945* (Cologne, 1987), 113–14; Rudolf Knaack and Wolfgang
Schröder, "Gewerkschaftliche Zentralverbände, Freie Hilfskassen und die Arbeiterpresse unter dem
Sozialistengesetz," *Jahrbuch für Geschichte* 22 (1981): 355, 362; Reinhold Raith, "Arbeitsmigration und
Gruppenkultur im städtischen Handwerk vom 18. bis ins frühe 19. Jahrhundert," paper presented to
the conference *Städtische Bevölkerungsentwicklung in Deutschland im 19. Jahrhundert im internationalen
Vergleich*, Bremen, Jan. 1989.

struggle for emancipation had, out of necessity, begun on foreign soil.[8] While, for the time being, a wave of reaction in the German states frustrated the efforts of a liberal democratic movement, which had been set off by the July Revolution in France (1830), tramping journeymen started founding radical political societies abroad – in Switzerland, Belgium, France, and England – a process that culminated in the establishment of the Communist League in London in 1847.[9]

Itinerant artisans returning to Germany carried these radical ideas into the various artisans' and workers' educational associations, which were being hesitantly established at that time and which, politically and ideologically, were usually still dominated by liberal influences. In the mid-1840s, for example, "traveling journeymen returning from Paris to their German homeland" took the new socialist doctrines to the Berlin Artisans' Association, as Stephan Born, a widely traveled compositor, member of the Communist League and leading figure in the General German Workers' Brotherhood, recalled. Authorities and police supervised this tiny faction of secretly operating radical activists. They were probably not wrong in suspecting a spirit of rebelliousness in many tramping journeymen and workers. In the revolutionary year of 1848 the *Deutsche Arbeiter-Zeitung* asserted that the police knew well "that it was particularly the foreign workers who bear and spread the greatest spirit of freedom."[10]

A federation of various artisans' and workers' associations, the General German Workers' Brotherhood (1848–50), was the most influential national organization of the early German labor movement. Its program combined social, economic, trade union, and political objectives. Widely traveled journeymen artisans, including a considerable number of those who had been members of the early communist associations abroad, were prominent in the Brotherhood's leadership. The federation tried to organize all workers and artisans, male and female alike,[11] whether organized in guilds

---

8 *Sozialdemokrat: Wochenblatt,* Feb. 3, 1894.

9 Wolfgang Schieder, *Anfänge der deutschen Arbeiterbewegung: Die Auslandsvereine im Jahrzehnt nach der Julirevolution von 1830* (Stuttgart, 1963); Otto Büsch and Hans Herzfeld, eds., *Die frühsozialistischen Bünde in der Geschichte der deutschen Arbeiterbewegung: Vom "Bund der Gerechten" zum "Bund der Kommunisten,"* 1836–1847 (Berlin, 1975); Christine Lattek, "Die Entwicklung des deutschen Frühsozialismus in London, 1840–1852," in Gregory Claeys and Liselotte Glage, eds., *Radikalismus in Literatur und Gesellschaft des 19. Jahrhunderts* (Frankfurt/Main, 1987), 39–64.

10 Stephan Born, *Erinnerungen eines Achtundvierzigers* (1898; reprint, Berlin, 1978), 21; *Deutsche Arbeiter-Zeitung,* April 22, 1848; see also Tenfelde, "Die Entstehung der deutschen Gewerkschaftsbewegung," 36–39, 51.

11 The Brotherhood's positive attitude toward the organization of women was quite exceptional; in fact, along with the requirement of traveling, the prohibition of marriage was regarded as the central virtue of journeymen. Both were essential to the formation of the old journeymen association's group identity. From this originated an opposition to women working in guild shops, which con-

or not. In any case, its support was strongest among those in traditional crafts, where their economic and social status was threatened, as well as among printers and cigarmakers,[12] that is, in occupations in which traveling was an important element. In fact, the share of travelers among the membership of the early workers' associations was extremely high,[13] and thus, typically enough, it was only when the Brotherhood succeeded in establishing a nationwide traveling system – in summer 1850 ninety-four associations affiliated with the Workers' Brotherhood paid a traveling benefit to itinerant members – that larger numbers of artisans and workers joined the organization.[14]

Traveling funds were not only essential to broaden the Brotherhood's basis and to integrate travelers into the organization and thus attempt to overcome the division of the labor movement into resident and tramping working men.[15] As the Workers' Association in Freiburg stated in 1848, the traveling benefit "was one of the easiest yet most important means to bringing about the union of all workers." Through traveling journeymen the radical ideas of the Workers' Brotherhood were spread into regions with no affiliated local societies. In addition to special organizers, "traveling workers" were required by the Central Committee of the Workers' Brotherhood "to establish new associations."[16]

After the failure of the revolution and the ban on the Workers' Brotherhood and its journal in 1850, traveling aid societies served as important

tinued into the nineteenth century labor movement when most trade unions were hostile toward female labor and unwilling to organize women. See Merry E. Wiesner, "Wandervogels and Women: Journeymen's Concepts of Masculinity in Early Modern Germany," *Journal of Social History* 24 (1991): 767–82.

12 Horst Schlechte, ed., *Die allgemeine deutsche Arbeiterverbrüderung, 1848–1850: Dokumente des Zentralkomitees für die deutschen Arbeiter in Leipzig* (Weimar, 1979), introd., 17–21, 25–45, 82; Balser, *Sozial-Demokratie, 1848/49–1863,* 1:75–86, 155–98.

13 In 1846 more than 50 percent of the members of the Hamburg Workers' Educational Association were traveling artisans and workers who had left the city by the end of the year; in 1853, 48 out of 103 members of the Braunschweig Workers' Association did not have their primary place of residence in the city; more than 50 percent of the cabinetmakers, cigarmakers, and tailors were travelers; see John Breuilly, "Kontinuität in der Hamburgischen Arbeiterbewegung von 1844 bis 1863?" in Arno Herzig, Dieter Langewiesche, and Arnold Sywottek, eds., *Arbeiter in Hamburg: Unterschichten, Arbeiter und Arbeiterbewegung seit dem ausgehenden 18. Jahrhundert* (Hamburg, 1983), 139–40; Georg Eckert, *100 Jahre Braunschweiger Sozialdemokratie: Von den Anfängen bis zum Jahre 1890* (Berlin, 1965), 42–48.

14 Balser, *Sozial-Demokratie, 1848/49–1863,* 1:103–17, 2:521–22.

15 This segmentation was real; in 1848, for example, at a large meeting of workers in Berlin, one of the local cigarmakers railed against the "foreigners" from Hamburg and Bremen and insisted that if they only left "there would be enough work for us." Quoted in Willy Buschak, *Von Menschen, die wie Menschen leben wollten: Die Geschichte der Gewerkschaft Nahrung-Genuss-Gaststätten und ihrer Vorläufer* (Cologne, 1985), 24.

16 Printed in Schlechte, *Arbeiterverbrüderung,* 228, 369; see also Jutta Schindlmayr-Reyle, "Die Arbeiterbewegung in der Rheinprovinz, 1850–1862," Ph.D. diss., Universität Köln, 1969, 39–40.

mutual self-help institutions. They helped maintain worker solidarity in the face of political repression and provided communication between the once affiliated associations for a number of years. Reporting on the city's workers' association at the end of 1852, the Braunschweig police, for example, wrote: "This association, too, is in close touch with the respective associations from other places in Germany and these connections are maintained by so-called informed traveling journeymen." Moreover, like many others, the traveling aid society in Hamburg served as a cover organization for continuing radical political activity and, in addition, organized the emigration of political refugees and radical journeymen artisans and workers to England and America.[17] The first national trade unions of the printers and cigarmakers, both founded in 1848 and banned at the beginning of the 1850s, also had extensive traveling aid systems, which they, too, used as a means to expand their organizations, maintain their supralocal networks, and survive the years of reaction.[18]

For the emergence of the modern socialist parties and the trade unions in the 1860s, these organizational structures and the widespread tradition of tramping among the workers were of critical importance, and traveling members were of special relevance. For example, when in the spring of 1864 members of the socialist General German Workers' Association were forced to leave Hamburg due to a lack of work, the party organ remarked: "It may well be assumed that in their new homes they will try to found new branches. This kind of activity is absolutely essential, as it will make a continuous diffusion of our association possible." This was no easy task, however, and it often took the traveling socialists some time to overcome the negative attitude of resident workers toward "foreigners."[19]

Similarly, the trade unions discussed the necessity of sending off members "to go to work in a particular place in order to establish a union lodge there."[20] In fact, it was above all in the modern trade union movement that traveling was of great importance, although labor was not able to reestablish a uniform nationwide traveling system of all trades as in the days of the Workers' Brotherhood. The tradition remained alive and in 1877 the trade

17 Printed in Georg Eckert, *Braunschweiger Arbeiterbewegung unter dem Sozialistengesetz* (Braunschweig, 1961), 42; see also Schlechte, *Arbeiterverbrüderung,* 29–30, 84; Toni Offermann, "Arbeiterbewegung, Bürgertum und Staat in Hamburg, 1850–1862/63," in Herzig et al., *Arbeiter in Hamburg,* 124–25.
18 *Gutenberg,* Dec. 9, 1848; Gerhard Beier, *Schwarze Kunst und Klassenkampf: Geschichte der Industriegewerkschaft Druck und Papier und ihrer Vorläufer seit dem Beginn der modernen Arbeiterbewegung* (Frankfurt/Main, 1966), 101; Toni Offermann, *Arbeiterbewegung und liberales Bürgertum in Deutschland, 1850–1863* (Bonn, 1979), 120–23, 156.
19 *Nordstern,* April 9, 1864; Winnig, *Frührot,* 201–2.
20 *Volksstaat,* May 29, 1874.

union paper *Pionier* described traveling funds as a means "of convincing those fellow workers who still held back of the advantages of union." Traveling assisted by unions was described as essential "since it would especially contribute to the general brotherhood [*sic*] of corporations involved in the same struggle."[21]

When the antisocialist law (1878–90) took effect, most trade unions were banned. But many of them, like the workers' associations at the beginning of the 1850s, reestablished themselves as traveling aid societies. It was through these allegedly unpolitical associations (and through sick and death benefit societies) that socialists continued their political activities. Moreover, the support given to tramping workers was "for years the basis of the new trade union organizations" and organized traveling was a major instrument in establishing links among local unions and in rebuilding national associations.[22] In fact, through traveling labor activists, trade unionism spread to the remotest outposts of the German Reich. With the consolidation of a national movement in the 1890s, after the antisocialist law expired, though, traveling seems to have lost some of its significance for building organizations. In the course of time organized traveling by special union agitators and officials as well as the union press became increasingly relevant for the diffusion and consolidation of labor unions.[23]

II

As has been stated, from the turn of the nineteenth century onward, traveling increasingly turned into migration in search of work. Moreover, in nineteenth-century Germany tramping on the part of artisans and skilled workers became a generally approved form of self-help against unemployment. As a historian of the cigarmaker's movement put it: "Whoever lost his job packed up and traveled until he found employment."[24]

On the one hand, traveling aid as provided by the associations affiliated with the General German Workers' Brotherhood continued the mutual help traditions of the old journeymen brotherhoods; on the other, the

---

21 *Pionier*, Nov. 3, 1877.
22 Walter Frisch, *Die Organisationsbestrebungen der Arbeiter in der deutschen Tabakindustrie* (Leipzig, 1905), 89; see also Knaack and Schröder, "Gewerkschaftliche Zentralverbände," 352, 362, 382; *Neue Tischler-Zeitung*, Nov. 23, 1884; *Deutsche Metall-Arbeiter-Zeitung*, Nov. 12, 1887.
23 *Buchbinder-Zeitung*, Jan. 24, 1891; Klaus Schönhoven, *Expansion und Konzentration: Studien zur Entwicklung der Freien Gewerkschaften im Wilhelminischen Deutschland, 1890 bis 1914* (Stuttgart, 1980), 40, 188–221.
24 Frisch, *Organisationsbestrebungen*, 150; see also Klaus J. Bade, "Altes Handwerk, Wanderzwang und Gute Policey: Gesellenwanderung zwischen Zunftökonomie und Gewerbereform," *Vierteljahrschrift für Sozial- und Wirtschaftsgeschichte* (hereafter *VSWG*) 69 (1982): 25–26.

Brotherhood's intention went beyond that in attempting to establish a traveling system for all workers and thus transcend the sectional spirit of the traditional societies. The aim of traveling aid was not only to protect traveling journeymen artisans and workers from the fate of becoming beggars but also to provide an exchange of labor. The Workers' Brotherhood felt it was essential to inform the workers about the state of the trade and to assist them in their search for work through traveling benefits and labor exchange bureaus and thus regulate the labor supply in the various local labor markets.[25] But since the state authorities put an end to the Brotherhood in 1850, these plans could never be realized.

Until the mid-1890s traveling benefits were of the utmost importance for the modern trade union movement. In 1877 seventeen of thirty socialist unions (including twenty-four national organizations) paid travel money. In 1886 twenty-four of thirty-five and in 1895 thirty-five of forty-nine national unions provided their members with such benefits, which along with strike pay were the essential benefits. The unions that paid were usually those with the most members and local branches and continuing craft and craftsmanlike traditions. In the 1880s and 1890s, however, unions of unskilled factory operatives and building laborers also started to set up traveling funds. Traveling aid was used to assist members in their search for work and, more generally, was regarded as a means of regulating the labor market.[26]

In fact, the idea of exerting control over the labor market through traveling aid lived on in the modern trade union movement. For the *Pionier* the provision of traveling benefits was a way of enabling the unemployed "to leave the place lest they become a dangerous burden as a [wage] depressing surplus of labor."[27] But since only a small proportion of the working class was unionized, particularly from the 1860s to the early 1890s,[28]

---

25 Balser, *Sozial-Demokratie, 1848/49–1863,* 1:105–7, 115; 2:515, 522. Similar conceptions were developed by the printers; see *Gutenberg,* April 6, 1850.

26 Statistische Tafel der Gewerkschaften in Deutschland (1877), printed in August Bringmann, *Geschichte der deutschen Zimmererbewegung* (Hamburg, 1909), 233–34; *Deutsche Metall-Arbeiter-Zeitung,* March 20, 1897; Klaus Schönhoven, "Selbsthilfe als Form von Solidarität: Das gewerkschaftliche Unterstützungswesen im Deutschen Kaiserreich bis 1914," *AfS* 20 (1980): 149, 151–52, 186–89; Knaack and Schröder, "Gewerkschaftliche Zentralverbände," 423–31.

27 *Pionier,* Nov. 3, 1877; the same stance on this question was taken, for example, by the cigarmakers' union, "Delegirten-Versammlung des Cigarrenarbeitertages in Leipzig, Dezember 1865," printed in Buschak, *Menschen, die wie Menschen leben wollten,* 523, and by the bookbinders' union, *Buchbinder-Zeitung,* Oct. 1, 1873 and Jan. 1, 1881; Eisenberg, *Deutsche und englische Gewerkschaften,* 207, falsely asserts that the argument to regulate the local labor supply through union-organized traveling was never put forward by contemporary trade unions.

28 Whereas in 1875 1.5 percent of the German labor force was unionized, 4 percent had joined a union by 1895; however, the rate of unionization not only varied from place to place but also from trade to trade; in 1877, e.g., 50 percent of the printers, 12.5 percent of the cigarmakers, 6 percent

plans to exert any decisive pressure on the labor market through traveling assistance were to remain a mere intention. Nevertheless, travel benefits put the individual unionist in a position where he was not compelled to take work at any price and undercut local wages since he was able to tramp on in search of a better-paid job.[29]

III

Following the centuries-old tradition of journeymen struggles,[30] traveling was very often used during strikes as a form of collective protest. It was in the context of industrial disputes that traveling as a means of influencing labor market conditions in favor of the workers was most important. From the 1860s onward, tramping organized by unions, often financed by extra levies in the 1860s and 1870s, performed various functions during disputes.[31] It was used as a means of threatening employers with withdrawal of the work force. As the journal of the woodworkers' union argued, as soon as the employers realized that groups of workmen were ready to leave, "they will get scared and certainly prefer to give in" to the workers' demands since they would otherwise be faced with losing a large portion of their experienced work force.[32] It also served to relieve the strike fund. A metalworker recalled his first strike in Breslau in 1896, when he was seventeen years old:

I had been among the ranks of the strikers for two weeks . . . [then] the strike committee informed us that we, the unmarried colleagues had to take to the road as the strike fund had to be used frugally . . . [thus] I made preparations for traveling into the wide world.[33]

of the carpenters, and 2.5 percent of the tailors were members of labor unions. See Knaack and Schröder, "Gewerkschaftliche Zentralverbände," 373; Statistische Tafel der Gewerkschaften.

29 *Buchbinder-Zeitung,* Feb. 8, 1891; *Holzarbeiter-Zeitung,* May 30, 1897.
30 Helmut Bräuer, "Gesellenstreiks in Sachsen im Zeitalter der frühbürgerlichen Revolution," *Jahrbuch für Regionalgeschichte* 14 (1987): 183–99; Rüdiger Lison, "Produktion – Proletariat – Protest: Zum Konstitutionszusammenhang in Streik und Gewerkschaft," in Lars Lambrecht, ed., *Entstehung der Arbeiterbewegung* (Berlin, 1981), 158–59; *Gut Gesell und du musst wandern: Aus dem Reisetagebuch des wandernden Leinewebergesellen Benjamin Riedel, 1803–1816,* extract in Wolfgang Emmerich, ed., *Proletarische Lebensläufe: Autobiographische Dokumente zur Entstehung der Zweiten Kultur in Deutschland* (Reinbek, 1974), 1:67–69.
31 Ulrich Engelhardt, "Zur Entwicklung der Streikbewegungen in der ersten Industrialisierungsphase und zur Funktion von Streiks bei der Konstituierung der Gewerkschaftsbewegung in Deutschland," *IWK* 15 (1979): 555; Lothar Machtan, *Streiks und Aussperrungen im Deutschen Kaiserreich: Eine sozialgeschichtliche Dokumentation für die Jahre 1871 bis 1875* (Berlin, 1984), gives numerous references on workers collectively taking to the road during disputes.
32 *Holzarbeiter-Zeitung,* May 16, 1897. In the same year the metalworkers' union made the same point defending the necessity of the traveling benefit; see Schönhoven, "Selbsthilfe," 164.
33 Otto Buchwitz, *Fünfzig Jahre Funktionär der deutschen Arbeiterbewegung,* extract in Emmerich, *Proletarische Lebensläufe,* 347.

In cases like these, the union endeavored to place the leaving strikers into jobs elsewhere. Thus in 1872 the local strike committee of Berlin cigarmakers requested all colleagues outside of the capital "to inform us about how many workers will find employment there without running into the danger of creating a surplus of labor."[34] As will be shown later, however, the travelers were frequently thrown back on themselves in finding employment, or relied on informal information channels, that is, on the help and advice of kin or workmates in their search for a job.

The decision to depart was made at public meetings right at the start of many strikes. In the 1860s and 1870s the departure of workmates sometimes took on a festive form, which recalled the traditional strike culture of journeymen.[35] For example, during a strike of six hundred cigarmakers in Leipzig (1869) many workers were ready to leave the town in order to "teach the manufacturers a lesson for the future." Hundreds of fellow workers answered the strike committee's appeal to escort their "emigrating brothers." A band, composed of striking cigarmakers who played music to supplement their income, marched in front of the procession, which led the workers to a tavern outside of the town. Here the assembled cigarmakers had one for the road to the sounds of a vocal and instrumental concert. Similarly, after a central strike meeting during a turnout of one thousand Berlin cabinetmakers (1873), several hundred journeymen "left the assembly room cheering the cause of labor and singing the Marseillaise." Then in a long demonstration they "marched through the Brandenburg Gate to the tents where they had a beer before parting."[36] Such actions reinforced solidarity between the strikers who left and those who stayed; it was an ostentatious manifestation of the struggling workers' stamina; it openly demonstrated the strength of organized labor, particularly against the employers; and it also aimed at gaining the sympathy of the public for the "just" demands of the workers.

At their new workplaces and during their journeys, in taverns and hostels, it was up to the travelers to inform their fellow workers about the strike and to warn them to steer clear of the site of the dispute. Moreover, the woodworkers' union, for example, held it as "a matter of honor" for trav-

---

34 *Botschafter,* June 15, 1872.
35 Andreas Griessinger, *Das symbolische Kapital der Ehre: Streikbewegungen und kollektives Bewusstsein deutscher Handwerksgesellen im 18. Jahrhundert* (Frankfurt/Main, 1981), 411–14.
36 *Botschafter,* June 26, 1869; Machtan, *Streiks und Aussperrungen,* 320–21. The Marseillaise referred to here was very probably the "Workers' Marseillaise" written by the Lassallean Jakob Audorf in 1864, the quasi-official song of the social-democratic labor movement of the time. For further examples, see the strikes of Hanover shoemakers and Würzburg cabinetmakers in 1872, Machtan, *Streiks und Aussperrungen* 153, 194.

eling strikers "to transplant the principles of organization," to enlighten fellow workers "on the purpose and aims of the trade union movement," to enlist new members and to establish new union lodges.[37] Those who had found a job elsewhere were asked to pay part of their wages into the strike fund.[38] Those who remained had to continue negotiating with the employer and prevent strikebreaking by arranging for the return of workers who had been lured into town by the employer. It was also the duty of local unionists to organize support for the family members of departed strikers.[39]

Those who moved on during turnouts were primarily unmarried, non-resident, mobile young males. It had been the custom for decades that during industrial disputes single workers were morally obliged to take to the road while the married ones only went on the tramp in cases of extreme need.[40] The importance of mobile workers for labor struggles is indicated by the fact that during disputes employers sometimes deliberately tried to hire married workers since they "were not able easily to depart," as a strike committee of Hamburg basketmakers stated in 1873. Besides, indications in reports of strike committees, as in the case of Mainz tailors in 1872, that "too many married workers are involved in the strike" showed that the conditions for waging a struggle were particularly difficult right from the beginning, that higher support benefits had to be raised, and that the chances of success were not especially good.[41] As late as 1897 the executive of the bricklayers' union only sanctioned strikes if "the unmarried workmates were prepared to take to the road."[42] They played a special role in labor struggles, as the example of the metalworker Carl Severing shows. In 1896 his fellow workers at a Bielefeld factory made him the spokesman of the strike committee at the age of twenty and told him:

---

37 *Holzarbeiter-Zeitung,* May 16, 1897; see also *Volksstaat,* May 29, 1874. Due to the agitation of traveling molders who were forced to leave Hamburg during a lockout in 1899, "a considerable number of new branches" of the metalworkers' union were said to have come into existence; see *Deutsche Metall-Arbeiter-Zeitung,* Sept. 21, 1889.

38 Such as in the case of a Berlin cigarmakers' strike during which two-thirds of the 2,200 workers involved in the dispute left town. Some of the strikers emigrated to the United States; see *Neuer Social-Demokrat,* Aug. 7, 1872.

39 This occurred, for example, during a lockout of molders in Braunschweig; when 130 out of 169 workers had left town, the union supported families until the latter were able to follow those who had departed, *Deutsche Metall-Arbeiter-Zeitung,* Oct. 19, 1889. See also *Botschafter,* July 3, 1869; *Holzarbeiter-Zeitung,* May 16, 1897.

40 *Gutenberg,* July 22, 1848; *Volksstaat,* Nov. 23, 1873; *Holzarbeiter-Zeitung,* May 16, 1897; Beier, *Schwarze Kunst,* 100.

41 *Volksstaat,* Feb. 28, 1872. During the basketmakers' strike, one-third of the 180 workers left Hamburg; see Machtan, *Streiks und Aussperrungen,* 299.

42 *Protokoll des vierten ordentlichen Verbandstages des Zentralverbandes der Maurer Deutschlands* (Hamburg, 1897), 12.

You are still young and unmarried; if things turn out badly and the committee is penalized, it will not fall upon the head of a family in your case. You learned a craft and you can start traveling and search for another job elsewhere. Besides, the union is behind you.[43]

As in the struggles of traditional journeymen, the proportion of unmarried workers was an important factor in the strategy of labor. Their mobility and independence from local and family ties were powerful weapons that were decisive in enabling unions to escalate industrial conflicts. Repeatedly, strike committees reported that it was the great number of workers who had taken to the road that had made a (partial) victory possible.[44] For example, in the 1890s the bricklayers' union could report that strikes in Zwickau were successful since many workers had left the town, thus creating a demand for bricklayers and forcing the employers to give in to the union's demands. "The strikers could be placed with jobs elsewhere with no trouble at all and thus the boycotted employers had to give in willy-nilly as they wanted to have their work finished."[45]

Thus, leaving the locality was usually an integral part of the unions' strike policy. Until the mid-1870s, however, there were voices, particularly in the unions influenced by Lassalle, that questioned the significance of (expensive) strikes on principle. Here taking to the road was declared to be *the* means of struggle. In 1872, for instance, the cigarmakers' union called on the workers to stop striking and leave the manufacturers one by one if they thought that the wages they received were too low. For the cigar manufacturers, however, this was clear proof of labor protest that had "to be regarded all the more as a *strike.*"[46] It was not always possible to use the strategy of collectively taking to the road as an offensive weapon in labor struggles. If the organization was weak and a struggle was, from the beginning, likely to fail or if an industrial dispute was lost, many workers moved on rather than yielding to the employers' dictates. But even in these cases tramping was an expression of the workers' independence and self-confidence and of labor protest. Thus, after a lost turnout, Barmen shoe-

---

43 In fact, Severing lost his job and took to the road. His travelings brought him to Switzerland where he joined the German Workers' Educational Association, the union, and the socialists. See Carl Severing, *Mein Lebensweg: Vom Schlosser zum Minister* (Cologne, 1950), 48–65 (the quotation is from p. 43).

44 As in the case of Leipzig and Wiesbaden shoemakers at the end of their strikes in 1874; in Wiesbaden the great majority of the 150 workers had immediately left the city when the dispute broke out. See Machtan, *Streiks und Aussperrungen,* 420–21; *Volksstaat,* Aug. 12, 1874.

45 *Protokoll des vierten ordentlichen Verbandstages,* 55. In 1897 35.7 percent and in 1898 47 percent of all bricklayers involved in trade disputes took to the road; see *Protokoll des fünften ordentlichen Verbandstages* (Hamburg, 1899), 27–28.

46 *Deutsche Tabak-Zeitung,* Oct. 11, 1872.

makers reported in 1871: "We have no other weapon against the inhuman behavior of the masters than to pack up and turn our back on the city"; and the motto of their striking Offenbach colleagues in 1878 was, "All take to the road rather than give in to the employer."[47]

The limitations of tramping as means of trade union struggle should not be overlooked, however. Traveling was by no means a panacea in labor struggles. With the increasing nationalization and internationalization of labor markets, employers were, in many cases, able to replace strikers with imported (foreign) workers despite the endeavors of labor organizations to prevent scabbing by in-migrating workers.[48] Also, in times of a general recession and/or if strikes in a trade were waged in many places simultaneously, traveling lost its rationale since traveling workers could not expect to find work elsewhere. There was a danger that through large scale in-migration the conditions of struggle would worsen or would lead to a surplus on the local labor market to which the workers had moved, a situation employers could use to cut wages.[49] The unions were quite aware of these problems and under such conditions usually advised workers against tramping. Sometimes a local union branch had to close down since all or most of its members had taken to the road during an industrial dispute. In such cases traveling even resulted in a (temporary) weakening of trade unionism.[50]

IV

Until the antisocialist law expired, traveling hardly seemed a disputed question among the more important unions. From the mid-1890s onward trade unionism expanded rapidly, though fluctuation in membership was also very high. In a way, this reflected the enormous rise in internal migration in Germany, which was due to an extraordinarily rapid population growth, urbanization, and the expansion of the industrial labor market. Rapid industrialization during this boom period was accompanied by unstable con-

---

47 Quoted in Machtan, *Streiks und Aussperrungen*, 87; *Vorwärts*, April 7, 1878.
48 See, e.g., the nine-month strike and lockout of 360 molders in Hamburg and vicinity during which two-thirds of the workers left for other places in the German Reich and some even migrated to the United States. The strike failed because the employers were able to import strikebreakers from abroad. See *Deutsche Metall-Arbeiter-Zeitung*, Aug. 3 and 24, 1889.
49 E.g., during the Berlin bricklayers' strike of 1889 about two-thirds of the 19,000 workers left the area causing a surplus of labor in the vicinity of the capital. In Potsdam, e.g., this migration resulted in wage cuts; see Dirk H. Müller, "Syndicalism and Localism in the German Trade Union Movement," in Wolfgang J. Mommsen and Hans-Gerhard Husung, eds., *The Development of Trade Unionism in Great Britain and Germany, 1880–1914* (London, 1985), 243.
50 See, e.g., *Botschafter*, Aug. 19, 1871; *Holzarbeiter-Zeitung*, April 25, 1897.

ditions of employment for the great mass of the workers. In search of work, more and more unionists were forced to claim travel money. On the one hand, the unions' expenditure for such benefits increased enormously while, on the other, fluctuation among the younger, tramping members was disproportionately high. Therefore, traveling benefits became a vexed question among unionists.[51]

The debates in the German Metalworkers' Union, which annually spent large sums for assisting its traveling members, are a case in point.[52] In these debates traveling assistance was criticized and it was argued that it actually contributed to union instability: "The young colleagues, whose presence is often only transitory, are not suitable for strengthening the union." According to the critics this benefit met only the needs of the young and mobile members, many of whom ceased paying their dues and left the organization once they had been successful in finding a job or after they had completed their traveling years and got settled. Claims were even made that many workers would only join the union in order to finance their desire for travel (*Wanderlust*). Such members would turn the union "into a *benefit society for rovers* [*Reiselustige*]!" Besides, it was put forward that as long as traveling aid was not supplemented by unemployment benefits, it only increased the potential conflict of interests between local and tramping colleagues since the latter "does not care about the *conditions* in a place which he intends to leave anyway."[53]

Obviously, this left room for potential conflict between local and itinerant workmen (a conflict that had already played a role in the prenineteenth-century journeymen struggles).[54] The latter, for example, evaded more easily employer repression as well as local recessions. As has already been shown, however, it had always been the task of the labor movement to organize both tramping and settled workers. So the leadership of the metalworkers' union vigorously defended the payment of traveling

51 Schönhoven, "Selbsthilfe," 163, 165–66; Schönhoven, *Expansion und Konzentration,* 150–98. In the years 1894 and 1895 the major German unions spent more money in support of their traveling members than on any other benefits; see *Deutsche Metall-Arbeiter-Zeitung,* March 20, 1897.

52 For similar debates in the bricklayers' union, see *Verhandlungen des sechsten ordentlichen Verbandstages des Zentralverbandes der Maurer* (Hamburg, 1901), 203–12. For each year from 1899 to 1907 around 7.5 percent of all members of the metalworkers' union received traveling benefits. According to a union inquiry in 1895, 73.7 percent of those who applied for traveling pay were younger than twenty-five years old. See Schönhoven, "Selbsthilfe," 162–63.

53 *Deutsche Metall-Arbeiter-Zeitung,* Jan. 30 and Feb. 6, 1897; also see April 1, 1893. The argument that traveling benefits increased fluctuation in membership as well as the conflict between resident workers and travelers is also put forward by Eisenberg, *Deutsche und englische Gewerkschaften,* 208.

54 Andreas Griessinger, "Streikbewegungen im deutschen Baugewerbe an der Wende vom 18. zum 19. Jahrhundert: Eine vergleichende Analyse," in *II. International Symposium of Handicraft History* (Vesprem, 1983), 317, 327.

aid, arguing that it was of advantage to both traveling and local unionists: "Unmarried members were able immediately to leave the town in case of disagreements with the employers, thus strengthening the resistance of the local members."[55] Moreover, throughout the 1890s the union leadership demanded the adoption of unemployment benefits as a means of checking the high membership fluctuation and extending the union's base. This benefit was regarded as a way for resident, older, married working men to be won over or kept in the organization. It was adopted by the metalworkers' union in 1899 and was explicitly to serve married, immobile workmen as a substitute for traveling aid, which, as we have seen, primarily met the needs of the young and mobile. Besides, from 1903 onward, the union also provided its members with removal allowances, which helped families to migrate if they had to. Equally important, the payment of traveling benefits was more strictly controlled to prevent tramping members from misusing union money.[56]

It is doubtful that traveling assisted by unions increased the workers' *Wanderlust,* as the critics argued, since migration was caused mainly by the necessity of finding a better job or any kind of work at all. During this period of industrial boom and internal mass migration there was real segmentation of the urban working class into young, single and unsettled workers on the one hand and an older, settled majority of workers, on the other. Under such conditions, the provision of traveling benefits was an effective way of attracting migrating workers, particularly in skilled occupations, into the union movement. These migrants did not belong to an uprooted, helplessly drifting proletariat, to "the failures in the urban economy," but to a group of craftsmen and skilled workers for whom migration was a planned move in order to escape unemployment and poor working conditions or a rational pursuit of more favorable work and living conditions elsewhere.[57] In this they were greatly helped by labor's traveling benefits, which offered unionists better opportunities on the (skilled) labor

55 *Deutsche Metall-Arbeiter-Zeitung,* March 27, 1897; however, the departure of the unmarried was not only of advantage to the local worker during labor struggles as the union cigarmaker Fritz Pauk recalled in his autobiography: "I was working together . . . with a married colleague. The manufacturer's stocks were full and he wanted to dismiss the older worker. I could not permit such a thing to happen. Thus, I offered to temporarily beat a retreat and tramp for a longer period of time." *Jugendjahre eines Tabakarbeiters* (Jena, 1930), 31.

56 *Deutsche Metall-Arbeiter-Zeitung,* Jan. 30, 1897; Schönhoven, "Selbsthilfe," 164–65, 171.

57 David Crew, "Definitions of Modernity: Social Mobility in a German Town, 1880–1901," in Peter N. Stearns and Daniel J. Walkowitz, eds., *Workers in the Industrial Revolution: Recent Studies of Labor in the United States and Europe* (New Brunswick, N.J., 1974), 307; Walter D. Kamphoefner, "Soziale und demographische Srukturen der Zuwanderung in Deutsche Grossstädte des späten 19. Jahrhunderts," in Hans Jürgen Teuteberg, ed., *Urbanisierung im 19. und 20. Jahrhundert: Historische und Geographische Aspekte* (Cologne, 1983), 95–116.

market. With the assistance and information provided by their organization they were able to look for work more purposefully than the great mass of working men. Generally, the high mobility of the working class presented the trade union movement with immense organizational problems, an aspect of labor history that needs much more detailed research. As the development of the German union movement before 1914 shows, the high mobility rate among workers may have impeded the extension of labor organizations, but it did not prevent it.[58]

V

Although economic reasons were decisive for the migrations of artisans and workers, it would be wrong to reduce traveling to these factors. As workers' autobiographies show, going on the tramp was also an expression of personal independence and freedom, often the only opportunity to break out of oppressive local and family relationships; to escape, if only temporarily, the monotony and routine of work; to protest individually against the tyranny of foremen and employers, against low wages and bad working conditions. Traveling was also a way of acquiring new experiences, both generally and politically, and of improving one's training and seeing the world. For some, tramping doubtlessly became a way of life.[59] For most workers, however, *Wanderlust* was embedded in economic pressures, in the sorrows and troubles of an everyday life which to a great extent was shaped by job problems.

Cigarmaker Fritz Pauk's biography is a good case in point. Born in 1888

58 Friedrich Lenger, "Migration und Arbeiterbewegung: Erklärungsansätze und methodische Probleme," in Brigitte Kepplinger, ed., *Geschichte der Arbeiterbewegung/ITH-Tagungsberichte* (Vienna, 1988), 23:80–86; Dieter Langewiesche and Friedrich Lenger, "Internal Migration: Persistence and Mobility," in Klaus J. Bade, ed., *Population, Labour and Migration in 19th- and 20th-Century Germany* (Leamington Spa, England, 1987), 87–100; Dieter Langewiesche, "Wanderungsbewegungen in der Hochindustrialisierungsperiode: Regionale, interstädtische und innerstädtische Mobilität in Deutschland, 1880–1914," *VSWG* 64 (1977): 1–40; David Crew, "Regionale Mobilität und Arbeiterklasse: Das Beispiel Bochum, 1880–1901," *Geschichte und Gesellschaft* 1 (1975): 99–120.

59 See the autobiographies of cigarmaker Franz Bergg, *Ein Proletarierleben* (1913), and butcher Alois Lindner, *Abenteuerfahrten eines revolutionären Arbeiters* (1924), extracts in Emmerich, *Proletarische Lebensläufe*, 274, 374–75; shoemaker Joseph Belli, *Die rote Feldpost unterm Sozialistengesetz* (1912; reprint: Berlin, 1978), 51–94; printer Fritz Wartenberg, *Erinnerungen eines Mottenburgers: Kindheits- und Jugendjahre eines Arbeiterjungens* (reprint: Hamburg, 1983); bricklayer August Winnig, *Frührot*, 321–50; metalworker Carl Severing, *Mein Lebensweg*, 48–65; engineering worker Rudolf Wissell, *Aus meinen Lebensjahren* (Berlin, 1983), 30–35, and *Des Alten Handwerks Recht und Gewohnheit* (Berlin, 1971), 1:458–75; cabinetmaker Wilhelm Steinmeyer, "Kindheit, Lehrjahre, Wanderjahre 1899–1923," *Beiträge zur Sozialgeschichte Bremens*, no. 7 (Bremen, 1984), esp. 197–227; painter Johann Reiners, *Erlebt und nicht vergessen: Eine politische Biographie* (Fischerhude, 1982), 31–44; and the cobbler Sassenbach, Otto Schengenpflug, *Johann Sassenbach: Ein Beitrag zur Geschichte der deutschen und internationalen Arbeiterbewegung nach Aufzeichnungen Sassenbachs* (Hanover, 1959), 15–56.

as the illegitimate son of a traveling carpenter in a small village in the Lippe region, Pauk was apprenticed to a small cigar manufactory in 1902. Traveling journeymen who told him about the "sunny sides" of the tramping life aroused his desire to take to the road himself when his apprenticeship was over. What finally made him put his wish into practice was bullying from his workmates. However, a closer look at his regional, social, and family background reveals that other factors underlying this decision were also of critical importance.

In the seventeenth century labor migration was already common among many small cottagers and laborers in the principality of Lippe. Since that time many of these had traveled seasonally to work as brickmakers, until the early nineteenth century mainly to Holland, then later to northern Germany and even as far as Scandinavia and Russia. In 1905 almost every second able-bodied man in Lippe – among them, indeed, Pauk's stepfather – took part in these labor migrations.[60] At the same time, the women who remained either worked the family's own small plot of land or, like Pauk's mother, also left the village and worked as seasonal laborers on the large landed estates in the vicinity. Given this long tradition of widespread labor migration and the structure of the family economy, Pauk must have been no stranger to the idea of traveling in search of work.

Moreover, the end of the apprenticeship marked an important turning point in the workers' life cycle, the passage from adolescence to manhood, a time when young people were striking out on their own and becoming independent of their families. Leaving home and going on the tramp was still common among young journeymen and skilled workers and, as has been shown, particularly so in the cigarmaking trade. This custom, then, obviously also lay behind Pauk's decision.

In 1906 Pauk left home for the neighboring Minden-Ravensburg area, a center of cigar production in Westphalia, where his unsettled life as a tramping cigarmaker began. A mixture of voluntary and involuntary moves characterized his travels in the following years but at the bottom of these was the bare necessity to earn a living, which made Pauk take to the road time and again. To escape from miserable working conditions, low wages, or threatening unemployment and in search of better work, he frequently changed his place of employment. In this he was no exception, for fluctuation in the cigarmaking trade was high. Pauk remembered one manu-

---

60 Franz Bölsker-Schlicht, "Torfgräber, Grasmäher, Heringsfänger . . . – deutsche Arbeitswanderer im 'Nordsee-System,' " in Klaus J. Bade, ed., *Deutsche im Ausland – Fremde in Deutschland: Migration in Geschichte und Gegenwart* (Munich, 1992), 260–61.

factory in which he once had a job as having a reputation as a "pigeon loft" because of the high turnover among the work force.[61]

Pauk's union activities, moreover, were also instrumental in making him go on the tramp. Once, to the annoyance of his employer, he had called in the factory inspector to have working conditions checked and therefore had to leave. And another case illustrates how there was a close connection between his mobility and his militancy. Because of the low wage rate, Pauk and a workmate intended to leave one particular manufactory. However, as Pauk put it: "We wanted to put in a wage demand before we left." The work force was successful, but, as a consequence, he and his colleague got the sack, having (correctly) been regarded as "ringleaders" by the management. Since they had planned to leave anyway before they initiated the dispute, they did not take this dismissal too seriously.

What had made Pauk receptive to new and radical ideas was his mobility and the variety of experience that went with it. This gave him an insight into the miserable conditions in different workshops and the plight of the workers in the cigarmaking trade, as he came into contact with workers from various regions and different trades. On the initiative of tramping cigarmakers agitating for the union, he had joined the labor movement and, later, the Social Democratic Party. Thus, Pauk became one of the untold activists who were to remain widely unknown since they only worked at the local or provincial level or on their travels, far away from the centers of the working-class movement. On his journeys he made use of hostels owned by unions as well as of the union's travel benefits, though he still found it necessary to beg now and then.

To Pauk, trade union structures and personal, informal networks were of equal importance for his travels in search of work. For example, at the first place he arrived at after leaving home, he was lucky to meet "a fellow sufferer and workmate from the place where I had served my apprentice-ship. He set out immediately to lend me a hand and took me to a factory where workers were wanted." Afterward the man helped him to find lodg-ings. Or, in 1907, after having worked in several places, Pauk returned to his birthplace, where an old acquaintance had set up a branch of a cigar company and had offered him employment; but even this job did not hold him for long.

Generally, personal contacts played quite an important role in working men's search for employment. Pauk rarely traveled alone, preferring to take to the road with a colleague. Often they moved to a workshop they had

---

61 The German metaphor of the pigeon loft signifies constant coming and going.

either heard positive "tales" about from other workmates or to a place of work where one of them had already been employed before and where they knew about conditions as well as the master or manager, thus making it easier to get a job. This informal network – along with job placements organized by local union branches and hostel wardens – was of decisive importance in the search for work. And the network helped not only find work but also influenced the places to which the workers directed their migrations.[62]

For years Pauk's travels were confined to the Minden-Ravensburg area, where he easily moved between domestic outwork and factory production in various smaller places in the district. Then, in 1909, on the initiative of a workmate who accompanied him, he moved to a provincial town east of Bremen where he settled down, now leading "a more peaceful life" than before. However, "during this time [i.e., up to the outbreak of World War I] I frequently made shorter journeys," Pauk remembered. Only once, in the spring of 1912, did he take the opportunity of traveling out of mere curiosity to Deventer, Holland, with a Dutch worker.[63]

For Pauk, therefore, the great wide world had been limited to his native region in Westphalia-Lippe and to the northwestern area of Germany he had moved to in 1909. A long time before him, however, particularly in the 1870s and 1880s, other cigarmakers and working men had extended their travels and ventured the trip across the Atlantic to the New World. But this is a different story.[64]

---

62 For this widespread pattern, see also the other autobiographies referred to previously.

63 Pauk, *Jugendjahre eines Tabakarbeiters,* quotations from pp. 18, 21, 29.

64 E.g., in the county of Lübbecke (in the Minden-Ravensburger area) between 1879 and 1881, cigarmakers and their dependents made up 6 to 12 percent of all emigrants heading abroad; Heinz-Ulrich Kammeier, *Deutsche Amerikaauswanderung aus dem Altkreis Lübbecke in der zweiten Hälfte des 19. Jahrhunderts* (Münster, 1983), 151. From the 1890s onward North America ceased to attract any relevant numbers of German cigarmakers; see Horst Rössler, " 'Amerika, du hast es besser' – Zigarrenarbeiter aus dem Vierstädtegebiet wandern über den Atlantik, 1868–1886," *Demokratische Geschichte: Jahrbuch zur Arbeiterbewegung und Demokratie in Schleswig-Holstein* 4 (1989): 87–119.

7

Migration in Duisburg, 1821–1914

JAMES H. JACKSON, JR.

When Napoleon passed through Duisburg in November 1811, he found a
town still much like the provincial market center that had existed on a flat
plain near the confluence of the Rhine and Ruhr rivers 350 years before.[1]
Even though its population had reached about five thousand, its subordinate
economic stature was clearly manifest as the town had fallen into the commercial orbit of the Netherlands. Reflecting its basic economic fortune as
a modest market town, Duisburg's three main roads as well as city streets
and alleyways were in very poor repair. The city walls were hardly visible
through overgrown vegetation. Much to the relief of occupying administrators, Duisburg was a peaceful community and the population hung onto
an old-fashioned morality of hard work and possessed a conservative mentality. Although the Prussians returned in 1815, Duisburg did not change
measurably. With the exception of textiles, tobacco processing, soap manufacturing, and those firms engaged in the transshipment of goods, the city's
economy continued its provincial orientation toward the local market. Demand for Duisburg's products was by no means assured, however. The
1820s and 1830s were particularly difficult years for agriculture in the lower
Rhine, causing economic uncertainty in both town and countryside. Over
the next several decades, however, local businessmen invested in improving
harbor facilities and in several processing plants, hoping to take advantage
of the geographical position of their city. In the 1830s and 1840s, Duisburg
experienced two business cycles, with peak years in 1830–34 and 1842–46.
Each economic advance was led by tobacco processing, textile production,
construction, and harbor activity. Modern technology was evident not only
in the increasing numbers of steamships visiting the port but in the use of
several coal-fired steam engines in local processing plants. The city's stra-

1 The history of Duisburg is covered in Günter von Roden, *Geschichte der Stadt Duisburg,* vol. 1: *Das
alte Duisburg von den Anfängen bis 1905,* 2d ed. (Duisburg, 1973), and Ludger Heid et al., *Kleine
Geschichte der Stadt Duisburg* (Duisburg, 1983).

147

tegic position in the transportation network of the lower Rhine area was confirmed with the coming of the railroad in 1846. These improvements also connected Duisburg more directly to national and international business cycles. Thus, the disruptive agricultural and political events throughout Germany and Europe in 1847–48 were responsible for an abrupt halt to Duisburg's business expansion. In spite of these setbacks, the city's population had more than doubled since the 1820s, reaching over 13,000 by the middle of the nineteenth century.

Economic stagnation was reversed only in the mid-1850s when the industrial era came to Duisburg and major smelting plants were constructed on the banks of the Rhine. In the first decade of industrialization, however, metallurgy was not predominant. Tobacco processing, sugar refining, chemical production, and textiles played a more significant role. In 1858, however, signs of economic recession appeared when the Vulkanhütte was shut down along with several coal mines and the sugar refinery. Full recovery did not come until the late 1860s, when new smelting technology and the founding of new factories meant full employment. In the first two decades of industrialization, Duisburg's population had increased two-and-one-half times, encouraging a construction boom. The city's occupational complexion was now markedly different from preindustrial times. Factory workers became the second largest category of employed persons. In addition, the proportion of casual laborers in the work force grew until more than one of every five employed persons belonged to this group. The worldwide economic depression of the 1870s and 1880s severely affected Duisburg's smelting plants and construction industry.

Even though prosperity returned, the early 1890s was still characterized by uncertainty. The level of metal smelting production remained virtually unchanged over the past twenty years and the rate of business bankruptcy was still high. Nevertheless, city officials and some businessmen looked to the future and launched a major expansion of the harbor, added electrified streetcar lines, founded technical schools, and broke ground for a new city hall. Their efforts paid off handsomely in the early twentieth century. By 1905, Duisburg was the twentieth-largest city in Germany with a population of nearly 200,000. It was a great industrial vortex, drawing into its economic life those persons with the skills it needed, sorting and sifting them into appropriate jobs. This city had become an engine of German economic development, offering increasingly diverse employment choices and greater economic opportunity. But the city also became more exacting and offered fewer options to those with only general skills.

DUISBURG'S MIGRATION RECORDS

Throughout these decades of economic ebb and flow, of political upheaval, and population growth, bureaucrats were keeping track of the comings and goings of Duisburgers. These city officials produced reports that summarized the town's births, deaths, marriages, and migration, yielding the most reliable estimates of vital rates and geographical mobility currently available (see Appendix 7.1).[2] These officials were also required to monitor monthly fluctuations in agricultural commodity prices, including various kinds of grains, meats, and processed agricultural goods. In addition, city magistrates also collected and annually published information on population, budgets, crime, economic activity, schools, public welfare, and taxes. Finally, Duisburg's population was counted and analyzed by census enumerators throughout the nineteenth century.[3] Together, these sources yield some extraordinary insights into the nature of geographical mobility in Duisburg.

QUESTIONS ABOUT MIGRATION IN DUISBURG

Many social observers in the late nineteenth and early twentieth centuries saw the growth of cities and the population shift from the agricultural countryside to the crowded, alien worlds of the city and the factory as the root of contemporary social problems.[4] And the plight of the migrant dramatically illustrated the human cost of urbanization and industrialization for those who already held a captious view of urban life. In their opinion, the moribund, decaying city drained vitality from rural migrants, leaving them hollow vestiges of their former robust selves. They were transformed into quintessential urban persons – impersonal, calculating, strangers to others and to self. Attention was focused on the implications of urban life for German society by the antiurban writings of Wilhelm Riehl, Paul de Lagarde, and Julius Langbehn, by the Wandervogel and other movements to reestablish contact with a more natural, rural heritage, by the national debate

2 Steve L. Hochstadt and James H. Jackson, Jr., " 'New' Sources for the Study of Migration in Early Nineteenth-Century Germany," *Historical Social Research/Historische Sozialforschung,* no. 31 (1984): 85–92; James H. Jackson, Jr., "Alltagsgeschichte, Social Science History, and the Study of Migration in 19th-Century Germany," *Central European History* 23 (1990): 242–63.
3 For an analysis of the development and character of censuses in Prussia to 1900, see James H. Jackson, Jr., "Migration and Urbanization in the Ruhr Valley, 1850–1900," Ph.D. diss., University of Minnesota, 1980, appendix 2.
4 Andrew Lees, *Cities Perceived: Urban Society in European and American Thought, 1820–1940* (New York, 1985); Klaus Bergmann, *Agrarromantik und Grossstadtfeindschaft* (Meisenheim am Glan, 1970); Elisabeth Pfeil, *Grossstadtforschung: Entwicklung und gegenwärtiger Stand* (Hanover, 1972).

over tariff policies in the 1890s and the technical achievements of city administrators, and by the accelerating shift of population from the countryside to the city.

It was in this atmosphere of moral denunciation, political conflict, and a
seemingly relentless demographic shift to the city that three major figures
in German sociology, Ferdinand Tönnies, Georg Simmel, and Max Weber,
gave more systematic treatment to the problem of urban–rural existence,
with special attention to the fate of migrants.[5] These ideas were codified in
the early twentieth century by an American student of Simmel, Robert E.
Park, in his seminal essay, "Human Migration and the Marginal Man."[6]
The pessimism of these critics about the effects of urban existence on peasant
migrants has continued to influence the German view of nineteenth-
century social history.

Before these overarching issues of social change and the meaning of migration for individuals can be addressed, however, four basic questions must
be resolved. First, what was the scope of migration in Duisburg during the
transition to an era of heavy industry? What was the impact of industrialization on the volume and geographical range of migration? Second, what
was the social composition of the city's migration stream? Third, what were
the reasons for migration? And finally, what was the impact of migration
on the city? Clearly, these represent only a first step in assessing the human
consequences of urbanization in Germany. But the answers to these questions will provide a necessary foundation for further research.

MIGRATION BEFORE THE ERA OF HEAVY INDUSTRY

Duisburg's migration system was defined by its increasing volume, by its
steady geographic range, by the symmetry of its flows and counterflows,
and by its selective social composition. First, the total volume of migration
expanded significantly from the early 1820s to the mid-1830s, rising from
an annual rate of almost 3 percent to nearly 16 percent (see Figure 7.1).[7]

5 Ferdinand Tönnies, *Community and Society,* trans. Charles P. Loomis (East Lansing, Mich., 1957);
   Georg Simmel, "Die Grossstädte und das Geistesleben," in Theodore Petermann et al., *Die Grossstädte: Vorträge und Aufsätze zur Städteausstellung* (Dresden, 1903); and Max Weber, "Die Verhältnisse
   der Landarbeiter im ostelbischen Deutschland," *Schriften des Vereins für Sozialpolitik* 55, no. 3 (1892);
   Max Weber, *The City,* trans. Don Martindale and Gertrud Neuwirth (New York, 1958).
6 *American Journal of Sociology* 33 (1928): 881–93.
7 Although they manifest a more dramatic rise than found in other areas of the lower Rhine, these
   rates reflected the basic trends for the entire *Regierungsbezirk* Düsseldorf in the early nineteenth century. Between 1826 and 1835, e.g., the total migration rate in the district rose from 6.3 to 9.3 percent.
   See Johann Wilhelm Georg von Viebahn, *Statistik und Topographie des Regierungs-Bezirks Düsseldorf* (Düsseldorf, 1836), 124. Also see Steve L. Hochstadt, "Migration and Industrialization in

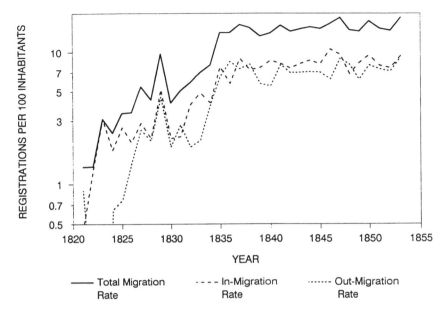

Figure 7.1. In-, out-, and total migration rates, for Duisburg: 1821–53. *Source*: See Appendix 7.1.

The importance of geographical mobility for Duisburg is demonstrated by the fact that, by midcentury, twice as many people moved in and out of town every year as were born or died there. Second, Duisburg's migration catchment basin was increasingly localized, with most migrants coming from no more than sixty-five to seventy kilometers away. Indeed, only one-fourth of all migrants came from or moved beyond the *Regierungsbezirk* Düsseldorf.[8] Third, geographical mobility in Duisburg migration was not a unilinear movement – out of the countryside to the city – as some urban critics surmised. Movement to and from Duisburg mirrored each other fairly closely, with in-migration maintaining a small but persistent surplus over out-migration. Finally, single persons, young adults, and men consti-tuted the bulk of Duisburg's migrants before the advent of heavy industry.

Germany, 1815–1977," *Social Science History* 5 (1981): esp. 445–68. See Figure 7.1, and Friedrich Lenger, *Zwischen Kleinbürgertum und Proletariat: Studien zur Sozialgeschichte der Düsseldorfer Handwerker, 1816–1878* (Göttingen, 1986), table 10.

8 Lenger, *Zwischen Kleinbürgertum und Proletariat,* table 11, shows almost the same proportions for Düs-seldorf. Evidently, Duisburg was not drawn into one of Europe's major seasonal migration systems that was focused on the North Sea coast of Belgium and Holland and on Friesland, Oldenburg, and Westphalia in northern Germany. Jan Lucassen, *Migrant Labour in Europe, 1600–1900* (London, 1987), 23–41.

Migration records for Duisburg unequivocally show that geographical mobility was overwhelmingly for single persons.[9] Only one of every seven
migrants was married, less than half the proportion found in the population
as a whole. When combined with census data, these sources also suggest
that about two-thirds of all migrants were young adults aged fifteen to
thirty-five.[10]

Additionally, demographic information shows that by midcentury, men
were nearly three times as likely to be part of Duisburg's migration stream
as women. For both men and women, migration rates increased rapidly
from 1820, reaching a new plateau by 1835 that was maintained until midcentury. But men experienced a much stronger acceleration of migration
rates, from an annual average of 2.7 percent in the early 1820s to 22.7
percent in the years between 1835 and 1853. Comparable statistics for
women were 2.0 and 8.0 percent. After 1835, the volume of men in motion
was nearly equal to one-quarter of the total male population of Duisburg.
Other evidence suggests that gender not only governed one's chances of
entering the migration stream but also regulated the timing of participation.
The town's highly irregular pattern of age-specific sex ratios shows that by
1843, men predominated in the late teens and in the thirties; women were
in the majority during the early twenties.

Migration not only became a more common occurrence for Duisburgers
in the first half of the nineteenth century; it also changed the texture of
preindustrial life – even for those who were residentially immobile – in at
least three fundamental ways. First, rising levels of geographical mobility
accelerated the city's rate of population increase. Without migration, Duisburg would have been one-third smaller at midcentury.[11] The advantages

----

9 If every married female migrant is presumed to have 2.2 children with her and if that presumed
   number of children was deducted from the total number of single migrants, the proportion of the
   migration stream composed of single persons not traveling with a family unit would average about
   75 percent for in-migrants, 80 percent for out-migrants, and 77.5 percent for all migrants during
   these sample years. Düsseldorf had even higher proportions of single persons in its migration stream
   than Duisburg, over 90 percent (uncorrected) for both in- and out-migrants. See Lenger, *Zwischen
   Kleinbürgertum und Proletariat,* table 12.
10 This rough estimate was derived by making the following calculations in two steps. First, if it is
   assumed that dependent children, fifteen years or younger, did not travel without their mothers and
   that migrant families contained the average number of children for Duisburg, subtracting a number
   equal to 2.2 times the number of married female migrants from the total of single migrants would
   yield an estimate of migrants sixteen years of age and older. Second, from 1843 census data, it is
   likely that there was only a one in ten chance that a person over thirty-five was single. If it is assumed
   that this life-course transition was representative of Duisburg's migrants in the second quarter of the
   nineteenth century, an additional 10 percent of unmarried migrants was subtracted from the figure
   derived from the first step.
11 If Duisburg's growth had depended on vital potency alone, the town's residents would have numbered only 10,500 by 1853 instead of 13,300. This is, of course, a very crude estimate that does not

and challenges of a larger population are clear for construction trades and food suppliers as well as city bureaucrats who were charged with implementing educational, sanitation, and public safety policy. Second, rising levels of geographical mobility combined with the increasing proportion of males in the migration stream to shift decisively Duisburg's sex ratio upward from less than 95 males per 100 females in the early 1820s to nearly 110 males to 100 females at midcentury.[12] This major deviation from the typical preindustrial pattern of western European towns was possibly tied both to a decline in those sectors of the economy that traditionally employed women, such as textiles, and to a demand for brute muscle power along the town's quays and at the railroad depot. And it is likely that the tempo and texture of the city's social life – entertainment, housing, and courtship patterns, for example – began to change as a result. It is important to recognize that the preponderance of males in Duisburg was not due to the labor demands of industrialization.

A third way in which migration changed Duisburg's social framework is revealed by statistics on denominational affiliation. In the early 1820s three of every four Duisburgers were Protestant. By midcentury, however, this majority had been reduced to about 64 percent, a phenomenon that cannot be explained by higher rates of natural increase among Catholics or by a major Catholic effort to proselytize Protestants.[13] From available data, it

separate the natural increase for native Duisburgers from that of migrants. Probably, most migrants were about to enter their reproductive years and contribute to Duisburg's natural increase. If their reproductive contribution was attributed to migration, it would magnify further the significance of geographical mobility for urban growth. For a discussion of these issues, see Nathan Keyfitz and Dimiter Philipov, "Migration and Natural Increase in the Growth of Cities," *Geographical Analysis* 13 (1981): 287–99. Duisburg was not dependent on either net migration or reproductive surpluses for growth, in contrast to larger European towns and cities. See Jan de Vries, *European Urbanization, 1500–1800* (Cambridge, Mass., 1984), 234, for analysis of the contrasting experience of some important administrative and commercial centers, such as Stockholm and Amsterdam, in which growth was dependent primarily on an increasing excess of births over deaths. The experience of another Rhenish city, Düsseldorf, is reflected in the statistics presented in Lenger, *Zwischen Kleinbürgertum und Proletariat,* table 2. Like Duisburg, Düsseldorf grew more by natural increase than migration. Yet the city would have been 20 percent smaller without migration.

12 Changing sex ratios could have been due to sustained higher crude death rates for women than for men. Contemporary demographic records, however, do not reveal any unusual death events for women. In fact, female crude death rates are consistently lower than those for males, with the exception of the 1840s.

13 Jonathan Sperber, *Popular Catholicism in Nineteenth-Century Germany* (Princeton, N.J., 1984), found no large-scale evangelistic effort by Catholics during the first half of the nineteenth century. If Duisburg's population growth had resulted solely from an excess of births over deaths, the proportion of Catholics would have remained virtually unchanged, rising from 23 percent in 1816 to 25 percent by 1853, rather than to 35 percent. This estimate was determined as follows: The absolute increase in the number of Catholics in Duisburg between 1816 and 1853 was 3,318. Available demographic data for the first half of the nineteenth century indicate that the proportion of this increase due to an excess of births over deaths can be estimated at 32 percent (or 1,062 persons). For Protestants, there was an increase of 4,172 residents, 60 percent (or 2,503) of which could be attributed to

appears that Duisburg's Catholics were far more mobile than its Protestants.[14] More important for Duisburg's demographic composition, the net
migration rate for Catholics was five times that for Protestants. This pattern
suggests that a long-standing migration structure in Germany was beginning
to break down, at least in the lower Rhine. Several studies of the Rheinprovinz have concluded that religion was a major barrier that channeled
preindustrial migration streams.[15] In Duisburg and in other majority-
Protestant towns of the lower Rhine region, that hurdle was now being
crossed.[16]

Until the mid-1830s, two factors probably worked to increase migration.
First, the mix of small and medium-sized farms in the lower Rhine encouraged local migration but discouraged long-range seasonal or overseas
migration.[17] Compared with farmers in the rest of Germany, those in the
Regierungsbezirk Düsseldorf had the advantages of a relatively mild climate,
good soil, access to reliable transportation facilities, and proximity to growing markets in the region's towns and cities. But they also experienced the
inefficiencies of relatively small farm size. Although the *Regierungsbezirk*
Düsseldorf contained more large estates than any other district of the Rheinprovinz, fewer of them were contiguous; far more characteristic of this area
were small and medium landholdings, a pattern that was the consequence
of Rhenish peasants' tenacious drive to secure even a small plot at "incred-
ible" sacrifice, according to one observer.[18] But this pattern of landholding

natural increase. Although only a rough approximation, these calculations suggest that Duisburg's
population would have reached about 9,300 by the early 1850s, 2,350 of which would have been
Catholic. Thus, the shift in proportion Catholic was due to migration. For another example of this
same transition, see F. W. R. Zimmermann, "Die katholische Bevölkerung im Herzogtum Braunschweig," *Allgemeines Statistisches Archiv* 4 (1896): 554–94.

14 Between 1834 and 1853, Protestants experienced in-migration rates averaging 6.6 percent per an-
num and out-migration rates of 5.8 percent. The same figures for Catholics were 14.0 percent and
9.5 percent.

15 Hans Heinrich Blotevogel, *Zentrale Orte und Raumbeziehungen in Westfalen vor der Industrialisierung
(1780–1850)* (Paderborn, 1975); Etienne François, *Koblenz im 18. Jahrhundert: Zur Sozial- und Be-
völkerungsstruktur einer deutschen Residenzstadt* (Göttingen, 1982), 49–50; Steve Hochstadt, "Migration
in Preindustrial Germany," *Central European History* 16 (1983): 216–17. In the Rhineland, e.g.,
migration tended to link communities of similar denominational background. Edmund Strutz, "Bin-
nenrheinische Wanderung," *Jülich-Bergische Geschichtsblätter* 15 (1938): 27–30.

16 Sperber, *Popular Catholicism*, 48f.; Annemarie Burger, *Religionszugehörigkeit und soziales Verhalten:
Untersuchungen und Statistiken der neueren Zeit in Deutschland* (Göttingen, 1964), 160–67.

17 Theodor Freiherr von der Goltz, *Geschichte der deutschen Landwirtschaft*, vol. 2: *Das neunzehnte Jahrhundert* (Stuttgart, 1903), 206f.

18 Apparently, it was more economical to lease out divergent holdings than to work them as a single,
far-flung enterprise. Some contemporary observers of local agriculture believed that this fragmentation of large estates prevented rapid assimilation of innovation in planting procedures and animal
husbandry. Alexander von Lengerke, *Entwurf einer Agricultur-Statistik des Preussischen Staates nach den
Zustanden in den Jahren 1842 und 1843* (Berlin, 1847), 181–84; Thomas C. Banfield, *Industry of the*

was also associated with strong out-migration because farmers with small plots could not support themselves solely from their own land.[19] Because there was a mixture of small and medium-sized farms in the lower Rhine, however, seasonal farm migrants could find local employment and did not need to leave their own region, as the Hollandgänger, the Sachsengänger, and the Schwarzwälder did.[20]

A second factor that probably encouraged increased migration in the lower Rhine area was tied directly to the gradual social division of the German peasantry between farmers and agricultural wage laborers during the early nineteenth century.[21] The elimination of feudal duties and changes in land tenure rights was associated with the development of three varieties of rural workers by the late 1830s – *Gutstagelohner, Kleinstellenbesitzer,* and *Einlieger.*[22] For at least two of these new groups of farm laborers, migration was a necessity in order to avoid destitution. Government surveys also noted that by midcentury, there were large increases in the number of migrant farm workers who perhaps rented some land but needed seasonal jobs that required migration to make ends meet.[23]

But these economic realities of the farm economy that encouraged mi-

Rhine, series I: *Agriculture: Embracing a View of the Social Condition of the Rural Population of That District* (London, 1846), 53.

19 Theodor Freiherr von der Goltz, *Die landliche Arbeiterfrage und ihre Lösung,* 2d ed. (Danzig, 1874), 65, 67; Theodor Freiherr von der Goltz, *Die ländliche Arbeiterklasse und der preussische Staat* (Jena, 1893), 145.

20 Von der Goltz, *Die ländliche Arbeiterfrage,* 88–90.

21 This process is described by von der Goltz in *Geschichte der deutschen Landwirtschaft,* 196–203, and `Die ländliche Arbeiterklasse und der preussische Staat,* 85, 92f. Also see Hans Wolfram Graf Finck von Finkenstein, *Die Entwicklung der Landwirtschaft in Preussen und Deutschland, 1800–1930* (Würzburg, 1960), 109–20, and Robert M. Berdahl, *The Politics of the Prussian Nobility: The Development of a Conservative Ideology, 1770–1848* (Princeton, N.J., 1988), 300–10.

22 Hermann Aubin, "Agrargeschichte," in Hermann Aubin, Theodor Frings, J. Hansen et al., eds., *Geschichte des Rheinlandes von der ältesten Zeit bis zur Gegenwart,* vol. 2: *Kulturgeschichte* (Essen, 1922), 137ff.; Alexander von Lengerke, *Die ländliche Arbeiterfrage* (Berlin, 1849); von der Goltz, *Die ländliche Arbeiterfrage,* 14–54. *Gutstagelohner* were laborers on large estates who had the security of annual contracts and led the least precarious existence. *Kleinstellenbesitzer* composed the second group and were characterized by their ownership of small plots and by their freedom to seek wage work where it was available. They might follow the harvest as migrant labor but would have a hometown to which they could return. Summer wages were used to supplement yields from their own small farms. For a representative listing of farm jobs and their compensation in the late 1830s, see Alexander von Lengerke, *Landwirtschaftliche Statistik der deutschen Bundesstaaten* (Braunschweig, 1840), vol. 2, part 1: 32–39. See p. 63–64 for a description of employment conditions for farm workers in the area from Cologne to Düsseldorf. Finally, the most economically marginal group – the *Einlieger* – were those without land or a labor contract on a large estate. The precarious living standard of these farm workers was directly tied to the vagaries of the growing season. They were also the most mobile of the three groups of farm workers.

23 Von der Goltz, *Die ländliche Arbeiterklasse,* 104. Migration as a response to the process of enclosure and farming practices has been found in other European settings. Brinley Thomas, *Migration and Economic Growth* (London, 1954).

gration were probably moderated after the mid-1830s by occupational continuity in Duisburg and increasingly powerful changes in farming
techniques in the *Regierungsbezirk* Düsseldorf. First, the urban economies of
the lower Rhine did not produce a large class of unstable, poorly paid jobs
with limited opportunities for advancement that urban workers shunned
and migrants could fill. This development must wait until the mid-1850s
and the construction boom that accompanied industrialization. Second, migration levels in Duisburg probably moderated after the mid-1830s because
agriculture in the *Regierungsbezirk* Düsseldorf became much more intensive
with the introduction of new crops and a new crop rotation system, ab-
sorbing more and more rural labor, even in the face of an increasing number
of persons living in the countryside.[24] Rising grain prices from the mid-
1820s provided the incentive for a shift from the three-field rotation system
to a more complex one that renewed the soil and placed fallow fields into
production.[25] Consistent increases in agricultural productivity encouraged
further innovation.[26] In the Rheinprovinz, grain production rose about 40
percent in the three decades after the end of the Napoleonic era as a consequence of these developments. But more striking was the growing importance of root crops. Rhenish production of these crops tripled between
1820 and midcentury. Widespread cultivation of root crops and introduction of new crop rotation systems had great implications not only for productivity but also for the rhythms of farm work. Root crops, like potatoes
and turnips, required much more fertilizing, hoeing and weeding than traditional crops. In addition, the introduction of these crops lengthened the
calendar of farming activity. At the beginning of the nineteenth century,
the peak season of agriculture lasted from the hay harvest in July to the
grain harvest in September. But with the introduction of these farming
innovations, agricultural labor was needed for several additional months in
spring and autumn.[27] As a result, *Kleinstellenbesitzer* and *Einlieger* were of-

---

24 Christian Eduard Langenthal, "Geschichte der deutschen Landwirthschaft in Verbindung mit der
    allgemeinen Geschichte von 1770–1850," *Historisches Taschenbuch*, 4th series, no. 4 (1863), 272f.,
    292f.; von der Goltz, *Geschichte der deutschen Landwirtschaft*, 218ff., 234, 236, 270; Aubin, "Agrar-
    geschichte," 140–43. Georg Meyer, *Über die Schwankungen in dem Bedarf an Handarbeit in der deutschen
    Landwirtschaft und die Möglichkeit ihrer Ausgleichung* (Jena, 1893); Steve Hochstadt, "Socioeconomic
    Determinants of Mobility in 19th-Century Germany," Arbeitspapier 1/85, Institut für Europäische
    Geschichte, Abteilung Universalgeschichte, 11–12.
25 By the late 1830s at Monning, a farm near Duisburg, and in Huckingen, just to the south, e.g.,
    grain crops were alternated with clover and root crops in patterns adapted to local conditions.
    Lengerke, *Landwirtschaftliche Statistik*, 356.
26 Langenthal, "Geschichte der deutschen Landwirtschaft," 285; von der Goltz, *Geschichte der deutschen
    Landwirtschaft*, 239, 257. By 1850 the Norfolk system was in widespread use in the Rhine Province.
    Von der Goltz, *Geschichte der deutschen Landwirtschaft*, 225.
27 Von der Goltz, *Geschichte der deutschen Landwirtschaft*, 222.

fered increased opportunity for employment close at hand and did not need to seek out so frequently jobs on distant farms or in towns. So powerful was the need for labor on farms that residents of nearby towns were often drawn to fieldwork during the lengthened harvest season.[28]

Third, geographical mobility in Duisburg was probably moderated after 1835 by the increasingly common practice of stall-feeding farm animals rather than letting them graze in open fields.[29] Rising grain prices in the early nineteenth century were accompanied by rising dairy prices and provided an incentive for increasing cattle production. Between 1816 and 1849, the number of horses, cattle, sheep, and pigs increased dramatically in the lower Rhine.[30] This growth was made possible by using clover, potatoes, and turnips in addition to traditional grains to feed animals throughout the year. Stall feeding permitted farmers to maintain larger herds through the winter months. They also received an additional bonus in the form of increased production of manure that could be used in renewing their soil. This technique of fattening animals for market using clover and root crops required, of course, more labor than use of pastures, dampening the need of rural labor to migrate.[31] Finally, there is some evidence to suggest that the labor demands of the textile trade in the lower Rhineland diminished migratory pressures.[32]

MIGRATION DURING THE INDUSTRIAL ERA

The constant movement of people was a fundamental fact of life in Duisburg, then, even before industrialization. From the 1850s, when Duisburg became the site of some heavy industrial installations, evidence of migration was unmistakable: Total migration rates rose from an average of about 21

28 Ibid., 192.

29 Ibid., 245; Langenthal, "Geschichte der deutschen Landwirthschaft," 282–83.

30 Between 1816 and 1849, the number of horses, cattle, sheep, and pigs in the *Regierungsbezirk* Düsseldorf increased between 30 and 100 percent. *Zeitschrift des Königlichen Preussischen Statistischen Bureaus* (1861), 220–23. There is also evidence that the weight of these animals also increased. See von der Goltz, *Geschichte der deutschen Landwirtschaft*, 265, and Günther Franz, "Landwirtschaft, 1800–1850," in Hermann Aubin and Wolfgang Zorn, eds., *Handbuch der deutschen Wirtschafts- und Sozialgeschichte*, 2 vols. (Stuttgart, 1976), 2:311.

31 For a contemporary discussion of labor requirements for stall feeding, see Lengerke, *Landwirtschaftliche Statistik*, 33–35. Also see Friedrich W. von Reden, *Deutschland und das übrige Europa*, 224–25, for a listing of fodder requirements for various animals.

32 Gerhard Adelmann, "Die landlichen Textilgewerbe des Rheinlandes vor der Industrialisierung," *Rheinische Vierteljahrsblätter* 43 (1979): 260–88, and Herbert Kisch, *From Domestic Manufacture to Industrial Revolution: The Case of the Rhineland Textile Districts* (New York, 1989). The importance of domestic or cottage industry for migration behavior has been stressed by Walter D. Kamphoefner, *The Westfalians: From Germany to Missouri* (Princeton, N.J., 1987), and Myron P. Gutmann, *Toward the Modern Economy: Early Industry in Europe, 1500–1800* (New York, 1988).

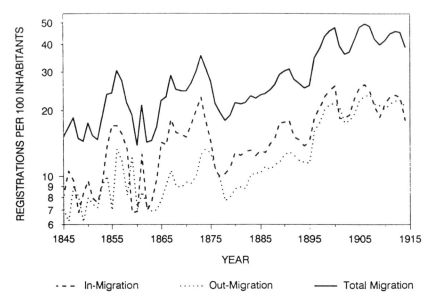

Figure 7.2. In-, out-, and total migration rates, for Duisburg: 1845–1914. *Source*: See Appendix 7.1.

percent to nearly 45 percent per year (see Figure 7.2). This meant that the volume of persons recently in transit, either coming to or leaving the city, was normally equal to between one-fifth and one-half of its total number of inhabitants.[33] The sheer magnitude of this migratory stream can be viewed in another way. From 1845, during the last decade before full industrialization, until 1904, just before the city's expansion through annexation, the total population grew from 10,607 to 106,770, a net gain of 96,163. During the same years, 724,421 individual arrivals and departures

---

33 Many large German cities, including the Ruhr Valley centers of Dortmund and Essen, had equal or greater migration rates in the latter part of the nineteenth century. Dieter Langewiesche, "Wanderungsbewegungen in der Hochindustrialisierungsperiode: Regionale, interstädtische und innerstädtische Mobilität in Deutschland, 1880–1914," *Vierteljahrschrift für Sozial- und Wirtschaftsgeschichte* 64 (1977): 1–40; Steve Hochstadt, "Migration and Industrialization in Germany, 1815–1977," *Social Science History* 5 (1981): 445–68. Residency registers did not record the number of persons who moved in and out of Duisburg, but rather the number of individual moves made by those migrants. Thus, many persons who stayed in town less than a year were counted at least twice (on arrival and on departure). Migration rates given here and in other tables and figures throughout this analysis do not correct for this overcount and are higher than the actual proportion of the population who were migrants. If it is assumed that those migrants whose length of stay was under one year were counted twice, a more accurate estimate of the actual migrant population can be made by subtracting extra out-migration registrations made by in-migrants from total migration. This figure suggests that actual migration rates were about 87 percent of the total number of moves registered for both 1867–68 and 1890.

were recorded by city officials. Clearly, many more persons came and left than chose to settle down in Duisburg.[34]

There is no question that industrial development in the Ruhr Valley after 1850 precipitated one of the greatest mass population movements in German history, drawing thousands from all over the Reich into an industrial cauldron. And it is equally true that Duisburg was not an exception. After the coming of heavy industry, the proportion of migrants coming from beyond the *Regierungsbezirk* Düsseldorf increased dramatically, from about 20 percent to nearly 50 percent before easing back to 40 percent. In addition, changes in the distribution of birthplaces for Duisburg residents in the most migrant-prone age groups between 1890 and 1905 suggest that this trend continued into the early twentieth century.[35] That Duisburg was drawing its migrants from a much wider area by the turn of the twentieth century can be confirmed by two additional observations. First, the average distance that migrants moved increased by 10 percent to 15 percent between 1867–68 and 1890, from 105 kilometers to 118 kilometers for in-migrants and from 86 kilometers to 96 kilometers for out-migrants. Second, Duisburg began to attract large numbers of foreign workers. By 1910, one of every six migrants was foreign-born.[36] In the late nineteenth century, two-thirds were Dutch. But on the eve of World War I, Italians composed the largest group (41 percent), followed by the Dutch (35 percent) and citizens of the multiethnic Austro-Hungarian Empire (21 percent).

But this depiction of the geographical range of Duisburg's migrants is misleading. In an age of mass industrial geographical mobility, Duisburg's catchment basin was surprisingly constrained. The regional distinctiveness of the Rhineland seems to have circumscribed the geographical range of Duisburg's migrants.[37] A quarter of all migrants in 1867–68 and a third in

34 Apparently, migrants became more restless in the last quarter of the nineteenth century because the proportion of Duisburg's migrants remaining behind in the city declined steadily from the mid-1870s to 1910. From 1853 until the mid-1870s, the ratio of net migration to total migration increased, from about +10 percent to +15 percent to over +30 percent. After the period of the depression, this ratio began to decline from about +15 percent to +20 percent levels to under +5 percent.

35 The declining proportion of native Duisburgers between 1890 and 1905 was not due simply to the flight of locals. The Prussian census of 1905 showed that 74.2 percent of fifteen to thirty year olds born in Duisburg were still residents of their hometown. *Preussische Statistik* 206, no. 2 (1908): 51, 274–75.

36 *Statistische Monatsberichte der Stadt Duisburg* (1908–13).

37 The profound impact of regionalism in Germany was manifest in numerous ways. For an overview of regional landholding patterns and their meaning for peasant life, see Gottfried Pfeifer, "The Quality of Peasant Living in Central Europe," in William L. Thomas, Jr., ed., *Man's Role in Changing the Face of the Earth* (Chicago, 1956). Political regionalism in nineteenth- and twentieth-century Germany is analyzed by Heinz Gollwitzer, "Die politische Landschaft in der deutschen Geschichte des 19./20. Jahrhunderts: Eine Skizze zum deutschen Regionalismus," *Zeitschrift für bayerische Lan-*

1890 had moved less than 25 kilometers from their place of birth. In addition, two of every five migrants moved less than 25 kilometers from their last place of residence or to their next place of residence. Less than 25 percent moved more than 150 kilometers to or from Duisburg. The circumscribed character of migration in Duisburg can also be demonstrated by examining the geographic distribution of birthplaces and last and next places of residence (see Maps 7.1 and 7.2). In both 1867–68 and 1890, nearly all of Duisburg's migrants came from or departed for destinations in west-central Germany. In fact, about one-half of them moved within an area bounded on the west by the towns of Geldern and Jülich and by Bochum and Remscheid in the east. Most other migrants originated from or left for towns and villages in the Rhine River valley, from the Tanaus, Hunsrück, and Eifel regions in the south to the Sauerland and plains of the lower Rhine in the north. Although the city had become part of a much larger migration system since preindustrial times, attracting migrants from more distant places, migration in Duisburg retained an intensely local flavor and was composed of countervailing streams. These patterns strongly suggest that massive east–west migration was not typical of late nineteenth-century migration in the established cities of the Ruhr.[38]

desgeschichte 27 (1964): 523–52, and H. Berding, "Staatliche Identität, nationale Integration und politischer Regionalismus," *Blätter für deutsche Landesgeschichte* 121 (1985): 371–93. Economic and currency regions have been noted by Bruno Kuske, *Entstehung und Gestaltung des Wirtschaftsraumes* (Bonn, 1930); H. Kramm, "Landschaft und Raum als ökonomische Hilfsbegriffe," *Vierteljahrschrift für Sozial- und Wirtschaftsgeschichte* 34 (1941): 1–14; Thomas J. Orsagh, "The Probable Geographical Distribution of German Income, 1882–1963," *Zeitschrift für die gesamte Staatswissenschaft* 124 (1968): 280–311; and Frank B. Tipton, Jr., *Regional Variations in the Economic Development of Germany during the Nineteenth Century* (Middletown, Conn., 1976). From the perspective of anthropology and human geography, see Hermann Aubin, *Grundlagen und Perspektiven geschichtlicher Kulturraumforschung und Kulturmorphologie* (Bonn, 1965). Although still controversial, see Wilhelm Brepohl, *Industrievolk im Wandel von der agraren zur industriellen Daseinsform dargestellt am Ruhrgebiet* (Tübingen, 1957), 365f., 371, and K. Köstlin, "Die Regionalisierung von Kultur," in K. Köstlin and H. Bausigner, eds., *Heimat und Identität: Probleme regionaler Kultur* (Neumünster, 1980), on the creation of a "new" region in the Ruhr Valley. For an overview of the significance of regionalism in social history, see Wolfgang Zorn, "Territorium und Region in der Sozialgeschichte," in Wolfgang Schieder and Volker Sellin, eds., *Sozialgeschichte in Deutschland,* vol. 2: *Handlungsräume des Menschen in der Geschichte* (Göttingen, 1986).

38 At the turn of the century, for example, the proportion of Polish-speaking residents, who presumably had made a long-distance move from East Prussia, Posen, or Silesia, amounted to less than 3 percent of the population in the major Ruhr cities of Dortmund (2.7 percent), Bochum (2.8 percent), Mülheim/Ruhr (0.5 percent), and Duisburg (0.5 percent). Only in the towns of Recklinghausen (18.8 percent) and Buer (14.4 percent) did the percentages indicate substantial long-distance migration from the East. Max Broesike, "Die Polen im westlichen Preussen 1905," *Zeitschrift des preussischen statistischen Landesamtes* 48 (1908): 255–56. During the first decade of the twentieth century, new sources of migration opened in the eastern provinces, changing the proportions of Polish-speaking residents in the Ruhr Valley, especially in the boom towns on the northern rim. For the primary core cities of the Ruhr in 1910, the percentages were 4.5 percent for Dortmund,

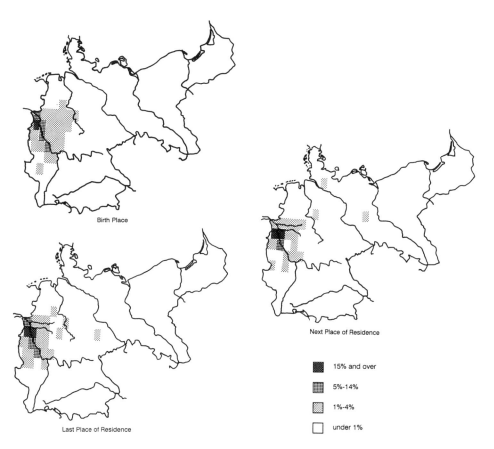

Map 7.1. Geographical distribution of migrants to and from Duisburg: 1867–68

STRUCTURAL ECONOMIC CHANGE IN THE LOWER RHINE

Four factors appear to have contributed to the breakdown of the preindustrial migration equilibrium that had existed since the early 1830s and set the context for mass migration in Duisburg and the lower Rhine after

9.0 percent for Bochum, 6.4 percent for Essen, and 3.1 percent for Duisburg. The highest proportions were found in Recklinghausen (23.1 percent), Herne (21.6 percent), and Gelsenkirchen (17.7 percent). *Statistisches Jahrbuch für den Preussischen Staat* 10 (1913): 28.

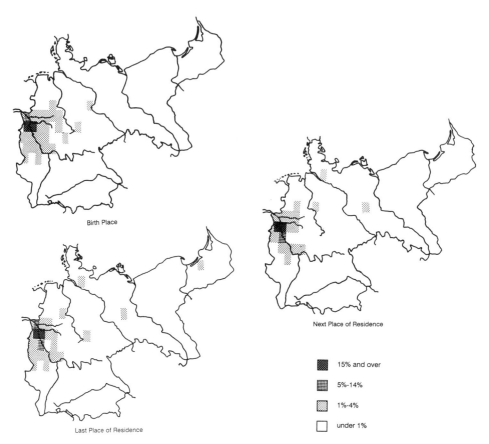

Birth Place

Next Place of Residence

Last Place of Residence

■ 15% and over

▦ 5%-14%

▨ 1%-4%

☐ under 1%

Map 7.2. Geographical distribution of migrants to and from Duisburg: 1890

1850.[39] First, social traditions of geographical mobility that tied Duisburg and other towns in the lower Rhine to their hinterlands were already well established by midcentury. Although held to modest levels for almost two decades by limited urban economic opportunity and by the labor patterns of local agriculture, the process of establishing social mechanisms to cope with geographical mobility was underway. This process of establishing a range of social contacts that reduced the costs of mobility did not halt with the coming of industrialization. Second, Duisburg's industrializing economy began to create a large number of poorly paid, temporary jobs that

39 For an overview of these issues, see Steve Hochstadt, "Socioeconomic Determinants of Mobility." Also, von der Goltz, *Die ländliche Arbeiterklasse,* 123–49.

had little potential for advancement but nevertheless paid better than agricultural work. This was particularly true of unskilled jobs in construction
for which migrants were prime candidates. These building workers had such
marginal jobs that they usually had to supplement their earnings during the
slow winter season by working as butchers, beer brewers, ice cutters, or the
like.[40] Third, laborers on farms in the lower Rhine were not so tied down
by contract or custom. By the 1860s, the farm wage-labor system had become much more fluid, with widespread use of free rather than servile
labor.[41]

Finally, farmers in the lower Rhine became far more responsive to market
forces, fundamentally changing the farming calendar and planting practices.[42] For example, more and more farmers employed chemical fertilizers
that permitted them to escape the need for complex crop rotation schemes
and to plant crops that offered the highest return. Responding to changing
consumer tastes, they planted commodities like fodder root crops and sugar
beets and rationalized livestock raising by stall-feeding animals.[43] Although
many of these new farm practices were labor-intensive, farmers were able
to cope with wage-labor shortages by streamlining their operations, depending increasingly on family members and on new equipment, strategies
that reduced the amount of year-round farm employment but magnified
the need for seasonal workers who were drawn from increasingly distant
locations, including the Polish-speaking east.[44]

---

40 Franz Habersbrunner, *Die Lohn-, Arbeits- und Organisations-Verhältnisse im deutschen Baugewerbe mit
besonderer Berücksichtigung der Arbeitgeber-Organisation: Eine volkswirtschaftliche Studie* (Leipzig, 1903),
38; Wolfgang Renzsch, *Handwerker und Lohnarbeiter in der frühen Arbeiterbewegung: Zur sozialen Basis
von Gewerkschaften und Sozialdemokratie im Reichsgründungsjahrzehnt* (Göttingen, 1980), 44, 207.
41 E. von Kahlden, "Die ländlichen Arbeiter," in August Meitzen, ed., *Der Boden und die landwirtschaft-
lichen Verhältnisse des Preussischen Staates* (Berlin, 1908), 8:383–84; von der Goltz, *Geschichte der
deutschen Landwirtschaft*, 361–70, 393–94.
42 Aubin, "Agrargeschichte," 143–48; J. A. Perkins, "The Agricultural Revolution in Germany, 1850–
1914," *Journal of European Economic History* 10 (1981): 71–118; Robert G. Moeller, *German Peasants
and Agrarian Politics, 1914–1924: The Rhineland and Westphalia* (Chapel Hill, N.C., 1986), 9–21. A
similar transformation of farming near new industrial areas in the Stéphanois region of France and
in the sandy farming areas of the Achterhoek in Holland, adjacent to the lower Rhine area. See
Michael Hanagan, "Nascent Proletarians: Migration Patterns and Class Formation in the Stéphanois
Region, 1840–1880," in Philip E. Ogden and Paul E. White, eds., *Migrants in Modern France:
Population Mobility in the late Nineteenth and Twentieth Centuries* (London, 1989), 89, and Mike L.
Samson, *Population Mobility in the Netherlands, 1880–1910: A Case Study of Wisch in the Achterhoek*
(Uppsala, 1977), 20–21, 34–38.
43 Max Rolfes, "Landwirtschaft, 1850–1914," in Hermann Aubin and Wolfgang Zorn, eds., *Handbuch
der deutschen Wirtschafts- und Sozialgeschichte* (Stuttgart, 1976), 2:498.
44 Von Kahlden, "Die ländlichen Arbeiter," 411–26; E. J. T. Collins, "Labor Supply and Demand in
European Agriculture, 1800–1880," in E. L. Jones and S. J. Woolf, eds., *Agrarian Change and Economic
Development* (London, 1969), 71–73. Also see Otto Auhagen, *Die ländlichen Arbeiterverhältnisse in der
Rheinprovinz und im oldenburgischen Fürstentum Birkenfeld, Schriften des Vereins für Socialpolitik*, 54, no.
2 (1892): 672.

THE CHARACTER OF DUISBURG'S MIGRATION
STREAMS

The close association of farm work, construction activity, and migration strongly suggests that geographical mobility in the late nineteenth century would be socially biased. And, indeed, Duisburg's migrants were highly atypical in both 1867–68 and 1890 (see Table 7.1). Almost three times as many men migrated as women, although the numbers of males and females in the city were roughly equal. Similarly, younger adults between fifteen and thirty years of age made up about two-thirds of the migratory stream but represented only slightly more than one-fourth of Duisburg's popula- tion at large.[45] Unmarried persons were also overrepresented. In addition, Catholics and members of smaller denominations were migrants more fre- quently than would be expected, given their proportion in the city's pop- ulation. The same can be noted for those who did not hold German citizenship. Craftsmen, domestic servants, brickmakers, quarrymen, and those employed in commerce and transportation were relatively more active migrants than those in other economic classifications. Finally, on a rough prestige scale, skilled workers and the most marginal unskilled laborers were more residentially mobile than expected.

Clearly, migration involved much more than the simple physical removal of a cross-section of the population from one place to another. It meant moving through social as well as physical space. Contemporary critics of urban development showed considerable sensitivity toward this fact as they built their theories concerning the nature and consequences of migration. These scholars suspected that geographical mobility would select a unique subset of individuals and have a different meaning for each segment of the population. Social observers presumed that migrants' experiences would be conditioned by those demographic, cultural, and economic characteristics that divided German society as a whole: gender, age, marital status, religion, citizenship, and occupational status. And migration rates for Duisburgers confirm the power of these social constraints (see Table 7.2). Although migration levels for both males and females had increased by two-thirds during the initial decades of industrialization, men entered the migration

---

45 H. Llewellyn-Smith, "Influx of Population," in C. Booth, ed., *Life and Labour of the People in London* (London, 1902), 3:70, noted that migration into London during the nineteenth century took place during the young adult years of fifteen to thirty. These observations were affirmed for Essex in the 1850s and at the turn of the twentieth century by A. B. Hill, *Internal Migration and Its Effects upon the Death Rates with Special Reference to the County of Essex,* Special Report Series, no. 95 (London, 1925).

Table 7.1. *Selected characteristics of migrants and census populations, for Duisburg: 1867–68 and 1890 (percentage)*

| | 1867–68 | | 1890 | |
Characteristic	Migrants	Census	Migrants	Census
Sex				
Male	75.0	52.6	71.0	52.0
Female	25.0	47.4	29.0	48.0
Total	100.0	100.0	100.0	100.0
(N)	(6,212)	(25,757)	(7,564)	(59,285)
Age				
Child (0–14)	13.8	38.3	13.9	40.1
Young adults (15–29)	64.3	27.4	66.0	27.4
Adults (30–59)	21.1	29.8	19.3	28.6
Older adults (60 and over)	0.8	4.5	0.8	4.0
Total	100.0	100.0	100.0	100.1
(N)	(5,762)	(25,757)	(7,565)	(59,285)
Marital status				
Single	85.9	62.2	83.1	64.4
Married	13.8	33.7	15.6	32.5
Other	0.3	4.2	1.3	3.1
Total	100.0	100.1	100.0	100.0
(N)	(6,250)	(25,757)	(7,563)	(59,285)
Religion				
Catholic	60.2	47.4	57.3	52.6
Protestant	36.3	51.7	39.3	46.0
Other Protestant	2.7	0.7	1.6	0.8
Jewish	0.8	0.7	1.6	0.8
Total	100.0	100.5	99.8	100.2
(N)	(6,087)	(25,757)	(7,485)	(59,285)
Citizenship				
Germany	96.6	98.1	93.1	96.6
Other	3.4	2.0	6.9	3.4
Total	100.0	100.1	100.0	100.0
(N)	(5,713)	(25,757)	(7,526)	(59,385)
Socioeconomic level				
Professional and higher white-collar	0.8	3.4	1.4	2.9
Proprietors, managers, and lower white-collar	6.5	12.5	6.0	13.1
Skilled artisans	47.5	27.8	38.5	26.4
Unskilled workers (position specified)	21.4	26.9	22.4	34.1
Unskilled workers (position unspecified)	23.7	29.5	31.7	23.6
Total	99.9	100.1	100.0	100.1
(N)	(6,087)	(5,381)	(7,019)	(7,401)

Table 7.1. *(continued)*

	1867–68		1890	
Characteristic	Migrants	Census	Migrants	Census
Economic branch (employed persons only)				
Mining and industry	65.1	46.1	54.6	54.0
Laborers and servants	25.3	33.6	35.2	29.1
Trade and transport	7.4	15.3	8.1	11.2
Professionals and bureaucrats	1.2	2.3	1.4	3.7
Agriculture	0.4	2.4	0.3	1.5
General office	0.4	0.3	0.4	0.5
Total	99.8	100.0	100.0	100.0
(N)	(4,720)	(2,324)	(5,895)	(2,736)

Source: StADuisburg 80/88, 92–97, 120, 152–53, 167; *Preussische Statistik* 16 (1869): 32–41, 103; *Statistisches Jahrbuch Deutscher Städte* 3 (1893): 274–75, 280–87.

stream to a far greater degree than women, reflecting the constraints of the ideology of *Geschlechtseigentumlichkeit*.[46] Likewise, the extremely high migration rates for young adults reveal the interaction of social values, geographical mobility, and patterns of subservience and opportunity.[47] Entering the young adult years during the late nineteenth century meant exercising greater autonomy but also confronting new challenges and choices. Young adults, aged fifteen to thirty, exchanged a dependent household status for the responsibilities of the adult work world and an independent family. Each of these developmental tasks – exercising adolescent license, entering the

46 This theory of innate gender differences was symptomatic of increasing sex role polarization and profoundly affected the way German sociologists assessed social change during industrialization and urbanization as well. Eda Sagarra, *An Introduction to Nineteenth-Century Germany* (Harlow, Essex, 1980), 231–50; Karin Hausen, "Family and Role-Division: The Polarisation of Sexual Stereotypes in the Ninteenth Century – An Aspect of the Dissociation of Work and Family Life," in Richard Evans and William Lee, eds., *The German Family: Essays on the Social History of the Family in Nine- teenth- and Twentieth-Century Germany* (London, 1981), esp. 64–65; Ingeborg Weber-Kellermann, *Frauenleben im 19. Jahrhundert. Empire und Romantik, Biedermeier, Gründerzeit* (Munich, 1983); Juliane Jacobi-Dittrich, "Growing Up Female in the Nineteenth Century," and John C. Fout, "The Wom- an's Role in the German Working-Class Family in the 1890s from the Perspective of Women's Autobiographies," in John C. Fout, ed., *German Women in the Nineteenth Century: A Social History* (New York, 1984).
47 John R. Gillis, *Youth and History: Tradition and Change in European Age Relations, 1770–Present* (New York, 1974); Michael Mitterauer and Reinhard Sieder, *The European Family: Patriarchy to Partnership from the Middle Ages to the Present* (Chicago, 1982); Ingrid Peikert, "Zur Geschichte der Kindheit im 18. und 19. Jahrhundert: Einige Entwicklungstendenzen," in Heinz Reif, ed., *Die Familie in der Geschichte* (Göttingen, 1982).

Table 7.2. *In-, out-, and total migration rates of selected population groups, for Duisburg: 1867–8 and 1890*

Characteristic	1867–68			1890		
	In	Out	Total	In	Out	Total
Sex						
Male	23.9	13.8	37.8	24.6	17.4	41.9
Female	8.8	5.1	13.8	10.5	7.4	18.0
Age						
Child (0–14)	6.0	3.5	9.5	6.0	4.3	10.4
Young adults (15–29)	39.4	22.7	62.1	41.8	29.6	71.4
Adults (30 and over)	10.7	6.2	16.9	10.7	7.6	18.3
Marital status						
Single	23.2	13.4	36.5	22.4	15.8	38.3
Married	6.9	4.0	10.8	8.3	5.9	14.2
Religion						
Catholic	21.3	12.3	33.6	18.9	13.4	32.3
Protestant	11.8	6.8	18.6	14.8	10.5	25.3
Economic branch (employed persons only)						
Mining and industry	41.1	23.9	65.3	37.0	26.1	63.1
Laborers and servants	22.1	12.7	34.8	44.2	31.3	75.5
Trade and transport	14.2	8.2	22.4	26.5	18.7	45.1
Professionals and bureaucrats	15.2	9.0	24.2	13.8	9.7	23.6
Agriculture	4.9	3.0	7.9	7.3	5.2	12.5
Socioeconomic level						
Professional and higher white-collar	4.0	2.3	6.3	8.4	5.9	14.3
Proprietors, managers, and lower white-collar	8.7	5.0	13.8	8.0	5.6	13.6
Skilled artisans	28.7	16.6	45.2	25.3	17.9	43.2
Unskilled workers (position specified)	13.4	7.7	21.1	11.4	8.1	19.5
Unskilled workers (position unspecified)	13.5	7.8	21.3	23.3	16.5	39.8

Note: Group-specific rates are shown as registrations per 100 population.
Source: StADuisburg 80/88, 92–97, 120, 152–53, 167; *Preussische Statistik* 16 (1869): 32–41, 103; *Statistisches Jahrbuch Deutscher Städte* 3 (1893): 274–75, 280–87.

job market, finding a spouse, and establishing a separate household – was facilitated by geographical mobility. In fact, migration was so advantageous in this process that two-thirds of all lifetime moves were made during these years. Catholics continued to be the most mobile denominational group, perhaps reflecting discriminatory labor recruitment policies of some of Duisburg's major employers or rural demographic pressures.[48] Along with demographic and cultural characteristics, socioeconomic factors created some of the most profound fissures in Germany society.[49] In the late nineteenth century, Germany was still a highly stratified society, retaining its traditional hierarchical structure into the 1870s. And the segregation of social groups by income level, occupational training, and educational attainment remained a prominent feature of German society before World War I. Because of their unique employment life cycle, skilled artisans could be expected to have the highest propensity to move, rivaled only by the most marginal unskilled in 1890. All other groups had substantially lower migration rates.

IMPACT OF MIGRATION ON DUISBURG'S
SOCIAL CHARACTER

Migration not only reflected the profound divisions of German society but was a powerful force that changed social relationships in industrial Duisburg, making the city a more heterogeneous place to live – culturally, demographically, and economically. First, the increasing proportion of foreign-born was due directly to the broadening network of Duisburg's migrants. Between the late 1860s and the early 1910s, the foreign community tripled in size. In the first decade of the twentieth century, for example, nearly one of every ten Duisburgers did not speak German. Second, even more dramatic was the transformation of the city's religious composition. At mid-

---

48 Eberhard Franke, *Das Ruhrgebiet und Ostpreussen: Geschichte, Umfang und Bedeutung der ostpreussischen Einwanderung* (Essen, 1936), 26. Alice Goldstein, "Aspects of Change in a Nineteenth-Century German Village," *Journal of Family History* 9 (1984): 145–57, shows that Catholics in the village of Altdorf in Baden responded to population pressures by migrating, thereby maintaining a stable population. Other religious groups chose to limit family size to achieve the same demographic goal. Also see Conrad F. Taeuber, "Migration to and from Selected German Cities: An Analysis of the Data of the Official Registration System (*Meldewesen*) for 1900–1927," Ph.D. diss., University of Minnesota, 1931, 264–82.

49 For descriptions of the lives and conditions of different classes in late nineteenth-century Germany, see Gerhard A. Ritter and Jürgen Kocka, eds., *Deutsche Sozialgeschichte: Dokumente und Skizzen,* vol. 2: *1870–1914* (Munich, 1974), 243–381, and Alfred Kelly, ed., *The German Worker: Working-Class Autobiographies from the Age of Industrialization* (Berkeley, Calif., 1987). For analysis of these social divisions in historical perspective, see Ralf Dahrendorf, *Society and Democracy in Germany* (Garden City, N.Y., 1967), 78–98; Theodore S. Hamerow, *The Social Foundations of German Unification, 1858–1871: Ideas and Institutions* (Princeton, N.J., 1969), 57–94; Eda Sagarra, *A Social History of Germany, 1648–1914* (New York, 1977), part 2; Barrington Moore, Jr., *Injustice: The Social Bases of Obedience and Revolt* (White Plains, N.Y., 1978), 173–208; Sagarra, *An Introduction to Nineteenth-Century Germany,* 197–230; James J. Sheehan, *German History, 1770–1866* (Oxford, 1989), 730–92.

century, two-thirds of the inhabitants were Protestant. But the strong influx of Catholics over the next half century made them a minority, with only 45 percent of the population.

Third, Duisburg's sex ratio continued to strongly favor males. And the fluctuations in this statistic between 104 and 124 males per 100 females were directly tied to the migration tides. The peaks of the late 1850s and the early 1870s, for example, were also moments of dramatically higher levels of geographical mobility. This meant, of course, that Duisburg continued to be a city of young men, with all of the attendant implications for housing, entertainment, and public order. For contemporary critics of urban life, this pattern was a portent of crisis in marriages. Increasingly, there were simply too many eligible bachelors for the number of potential brides. Did such high sex ratios actually have a negative impact on family formation, however? Apparently not, because marriage rates in Duisburg remained higher than that for the nation as a whole, for the most part. Nor did the high proportion of males in the city's population have a negative impact on the fertility of Duisburg's women. The general fertility rate for Duisburg remained substantially above that for other Prussian cities.[50] Surprisingly, it also exceeded the rate for the Prussian countryside, at least until the birth control revolution of the first decade of the twentieth century.[51] Throughout the late nineteenth and into the twentieth century, Duisburg could not be considered an urban graveyard; it was a center of demographic vitality, full of young families. At the same time, it was a city for young, single men.

Finally, migration fundamentally changed the employment outlook in Duisburg, making the labor market more competitive. In 1867–68 enough migrants arrived to meet one-third of the city's total labor requirements. The arrival of large numbers of skilled craftsmen was primarily responsible for this figure. Sixty percent of the craftsmen needed by the expanding local economy could have been supplied by newcomers. By contrast, migrants could have taken only one-quarter of the available unskilled positions. By 1890 migrants were competing for nearly two of every five jobs in Duisburg, an increase from a generation earlier. The most marked change by the last decade of the century came from the ranks of common laborers, domestic servants, and allied occupations. These kinds of workers arrived

50 Between 1876 and 1910, the number of births per 1,000 women aged fifteen to forty-five in Duisburg declined from 239 to 163. For Prussian cities, the range was 161 to 118; for rural areas in Prussia, it was 183 to 169. *Statistisches Jahrbuch für den Preussischen Staat* 10 (1913): 35–37.
51 Helmuth Jahns, *Das Delikt der Abtreibung im Landgerichtsbezirk Duisburg in der Zeit von 1910 bis 1935* (Düsseldorf, 1938); James Woycke, *Birth Control in Germany, 1871–1933* (London, 1988).

in Duisburg in such increased numbers that they could have filled over half of the positions available, double the proportion of 1867. The transformation of the in-migrant stream suggests that early industrial development was accompanied by a great influx of skilled labor. And in the course of the nineteenth century, the shifting needs of the city's maturing economy attracted more unskilled workers who nevertheless faced an increasingly competitive employment situation.

URBAN AND TRANSATLANTIC MIGRATION IN THE
NINETEENTH CENTURY

To what extent was Duisburg's migration experience representative of other German cities? How did the intensity of geographical mobility in this urban center compare with transatlantic migration? There is some evidence to suggest that in preindustrial times, Duisburg reflected the experience of the region in which it was located. In the second quarter of the nineteenth century, for example, migration rates for Duisburg, the city of Düsseldorf, and the *Regierungsbezirk* Düsseldorf apparently responded to the same pressures and incentives in the mid-1830s when mobility levels jumped appreciably (see Figure 7.3). For the next decade – until the political upheavals of the late 1840s and their agrarian and commercial counterparts – Duisburg's total migration levels also matched those of such diverse cities as the Prussian capital, Berlin, the modest governmental center of Düsseldorf, and the textile town of Krefeld.[52] In the initial decade of industrialization, however, Duisburg broke from this stable pattern when total migration rates reached over 30 percent, nearly double the levels for the other three cities. During the decade of prosperity between 1864 and 1874, industrial expansion in Berlin as well as in Duisburg was accompanied by extraordinary migration levels; in the case of the imperial capital, this experience with geographical mobility was not equaled at any time in the nineteenth or early twentieth centuries. In the three decades preceding World War I, migration in Duisburg achieved its highest rates. These levels were also attained by Düsseldorf as that city assumed a more industrial character. During the same years, geographical mobility rates for all major Ruhr cities were more intense and more volatile than for either regional administrative centers or the textile towns, consistently exceeding the average for all German cities with fifty thousand or more population.[53]

52 Berlin, Düsseldorf, Duisburg, and Krefeld have the longest time-series of migration statistics currently available.
53 See Figure 7.4.

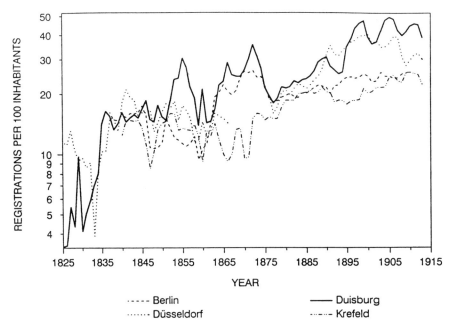

Figure 7.3. Total migration rates for Berlin, Düsseldorf, Duisburg, and Krefeld: 1825–1914.
Source: For Berlin: *Statistisches Jahrbuch der Stadt Berlin* 13 (1888): 18–19, 94; 15 (1890): 104
Statistisches Jahrbuch Deutscher Städte 1 (1890): 53–54; 2 (1892): 37–38; 3 (1893): 293, 300; 4
(1894): 159; 5 (1896): 315; 7 (1898): 266–67; 8 (1900): 315–16; 9 (1901): 252; 10 (1902):
104; 11 (1903): 127; 12 (1904): 478–79; 13 (1906): 481; 14 (1907): 70; 15 (1908): 62; 16
(1909): 39; 17 (1910): 56–57; 18 (1912): 46; 19 (1913): 67; 20 (1914): 70. For Düsseldorf:
Friedrich Lenger, *Zwischen Kleinbürgertum und Proletariat: Studien zur Sozialgeschichte der Düsseldorfer Handwerker, 1816–1878* (Göttingen, 1986), 245–46. For Duisburg: See Appendix
7.1. For Krefeld: *Statistisches Jahrbuch der Stadt Krefeld-Uerdingen* 1 (1927): 72; 2 (1932): 106.

Thus, Duisburg can be used at a minimum as a case study of how those
who lived in the great urban engines of the entire German economy responded to the consequences of urbanization and migration.[54] Although the
timing and magnitude of migration after 1850 were clearly tied to the
unique economic fate and demographic structure of each city, it was equally
true that relatively high migration levels were not confined to cities with

---

54 Duisburg also shared many demographic and occupational characteristics with Hamburg, Bremen,
Frankfurt/Main, some suburbs of Berlin, and towns in Upper Silesia. See Hans Bohm, "Demogra-
phische Strukturen deutscher Mittel- und Grossstädte in der Hochindustrialisierungsperiode," in
Franz-Josef Kemper, Hans-Dieter Laux, and Günter Thieme, eds., *Geographie als Sozialwissenschaft:
Beiträge zu ausgewälten Problemen Kulturgeographischer Forschung* (Bonn, 1985).

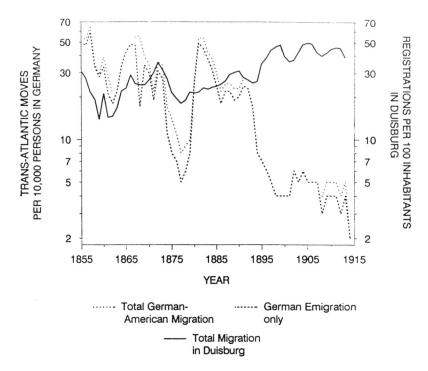

Figure 7.4. German American transatlantic migration and total migration in Duisburg: 1855–1914. *Source*: For Duisburg: See Appendix 7.1. For German American Transatlantic Migration: Peter Marschalck, *Deutsche Überseewanderung im 19. Jahrhundert* (Stuttgart, 1973), 35–37; Günter Moltmann, "American-German Return Migration in the Nineteenth and Early Twentieth Centuries," *Central European History* 13 (1980): 384–85; A. Schulte im Hofe, *Auswanderung und Auswanderungspolitik* (Berlin, 1918), 55–58.

heavy industry. For those urban areas for which data currently exist, the trend of geographical mobility was upward from midcentury through the first decades of the twentieth century.[55] Duisburgers may have been more exposed to the vicissitudes of urban growth and demographic permutation but what they experienced was a formative social experience for their time. This assertion is reinforced by a comparison of urban and transatlantic migration rates. The intensity of internal migration far exceeded that for overseas movement. Migration rates to and from Duisburg were 50–200 times that of transatlantic moves before the 1890s. On the eve of World War I, it was nearly 1,000 times greater (see Figure 7.4).

Duisburg's migration experience also suggests two additional unconven-

55 Hochstadt, "Migration and Industrialization in Germany, 1815–1977."

tional conclusions concerning the relationship of internal migration to industrial centers and emigration. First, it appears that they were not complementary choices; local geographical mobility and overseas movement were directly, not inversely, related from the 1850s until the 1880s.[56] This relationship was redefined after the American boom of the early 1880s and the Panic of 1893. But after the turn of the century, the considerably lower German emigration rates appear to be synchronized once again with the movement of local industrial migration. Second, evidence of stepwise overseas emigration – movement from the countryside to industrial areas and then directly to overseas destinations – cannot be found using Duisburg's demographic data. Apparently, Duisburg did not represent a reservoir of the "uprooted" who were potential overseas migrants.[57]

PRELIMINARY CONCLUSIONS AND FUTURE
DIRECTIONS

This investigation of migration in Duisburg has indicated the need for revision of some important conventional views of geographical mobility in nineteenth-century Europe. First, one of the most enduring stereotypes of European societies before the advent of heavy industry asserts that they were characterized by low rates of geographical mobility.[58] But an alternative view of preindustrial migration that is based on newly explored records is emerging rapidly.[59] It is becoming more and more apparent that Europeans,

56 For a similar conclusion, see J. J. Lee, "Aspects of Urbanization in Germany, 1815–1914," in Philip Abrams and E. A. Wrigley, eds., *Towns in Society: Essays in Economic and Historical Sociology* (Cambridge, 1978).
57 To explore this thesis fully, life-time migration itineraries must be assembled. Cf. Mack Walker, *Germany and the Emigration, 1816–1885* (Cambridge, Mass., 1964), 189–91, and Wolfgang Köllmann, "The Process of Urbanization in Germany at the Height of the Industrialization Period," *Journal of Contemporary History* 4, no. 3 (1969): 61.
58 For the study of migration and social change in the Ruhr Valley industrial area, the work of Wilhelm Brepohl has been highly influential, especially on the research of the demographic historian Wolfgang Köllmann. See Brepohl, *Industrievolk im Wandel*, esp. 137–40; Wolfgang Köllmann, *Bevölkerung in der industriellen Revolution* (Göttingen, 1974), 41–42. Both of these migration scholars repeat the conclusions of the conservative version of the urban anomie school.
59 These "new" sources are discussed by Myron P. Gutmann and Etienne van de Walle, "New Sources for Social and Demographic History: The Belgian Population Registers," *Social Science History* 2 (1978): 121–43; Steve L. Hochstadt, "Migration in Germany: An Historical Study," Ph.D. diss., Brown University, 1983; Hochstadt and Jackson, " 'New' Sources for the Study of Migration"; A.-S. Kalvemark, "The Country That Kept Track of Its Population," in Jan Sundin and E. Soderlund, eds., *Time, Space, and Man: Essays in Microdemography* (Atlantic Heights, N.J., 1979); David Kertzer and D. Hogan, "On the Move: Migration in an Italian Community, 1865–1921," *Social Science History* 9 (1985): 1–24; David Souden, "Movers and Stayers in Family Reconstitution Populations, 1660–1780," *Local Population Studies* 33 (1984): 11–28.

including Duisburgers, have always moved in considerable numbers.[60] Second, migrants did not lose touch with their sustaining rural roots. Local origins and destinations predominated and the migration streams in and out of Duisburg were fairly well balanced. The drama of east-to-west population shifts or the transatlantic migration of a relative few should not obscure the fact that the typical migration experience of Germans in the nineteenth century was much more mundane and localized. Third, continuity marked the demographic character of Duisburg's migration stream at the watershed between preindustrial and industrial times. In spite of the growing heterogeneity of the city's population, the transition of industrialization did not represent such a profound break as contemporary social critics or modernization theorists have assumed. Many of the changes commonly associated with the Industrial Revolution had already occurred by the time the first factories were built on the banks of the Rhine. Duisburg's migration system after midcentury retained its old character, with more of the same kinds of people in motion.

Further research is needed, of course, to confirm the general applicability of these preliminary conclusions to other towns and cities in nineteenth-century Germany. Also, the human consequences of geographical mobility must be more precisely defined if basic questions of "marginality" and "uprootedness" are to be addressed.[61] Equally challenging will be a full analysis of the impact of migration on sending areas. The answers to these

---

60 European populations have never been as sedentary as once thought; rather, several distinct kinds of movement have characterized the countryside since at least the seventeenth century. Those most closely tied to the agricultural seasons were the great annual migrations undertaken by gangs of harvest laborers, construction workers, and peddlers. Aside from these long-distance movements, many of which were seasonal and temporary, rural Europeans regularly traveled shorter distances as well. See D. Gaunt, "Preindustrial Economy and Population Structure," *Scandinavian Journal of History* 2 (1977): 183–210; Alan McFarlane, "The Myth of the Peasantry: Family and Economy in a Northern Parish," in R. M. Smith, ed., *Land, Kinship and Life-Cycle* (Cambridge, 1984); Souden, "Movers and Stayers." The most important form of rural migration involved primarily single folk who worked as farmhands, domestics, or urban day laborers, moving annually from one service position to another. See A. Kussmaul, *Servants in Husbandry in Early Modern England* (Cambridge, 1981); Roger Schofield, "Age-Specific Mobility in an Eighteenth-Century Rural Parish," *Annales de démographie historique* (1970): 261–74; David Souden, "Migrants and the Population Structure of Late 17th-Century Provincial Cities and Market Towns," in Peter Clark, ed., *The Transformation of English Provincial Towns, 1600–1800* (London, 1984); Peter Clark and Paul Slack, *English Towns in Transition, 1500–1700* (London, 1976); Hochstadt, "Migration in Preindustrial Germany."
61 Helpful in this regard may be the techniques of *Alltagsgeschichte*. For an overview, see Peter Borscheid, "Alltagsgeschichte – Modetorheit oder neues Tor zur Vergangenheit?" in Wolfgang Schieder and Volker Sellin, eds., *Sozialgeschichte in Deutschland: Entwicklungen und Perspektiven im internationalen Zusammenhang* (Göttingen, 1987), vol. 3, and Geoff Eley, "Labor History, Social History, and *Alltagsgeschichte*: Experience, Culture, and the Politics of the Everyday – a New Direction for German Social History?" *Journal of Modern History* 61 (1989): 297–343.

questions will inevitably aid our understanding of the meaning of social change and the response of ordinary people to large-scale structural change.

APPENDIX 7.1: SOURCES FOR MIGRATION DATA

1816–47	StA Duisburg 10/2594–95, 2598–99, 2606, 2613
1848–63	HStA Düsseldorf, Regierung Düsseldorf 415, 441, 447–50
1853–63	HStA Düsseldorf, Landratsamt Duisburg-Mülheim 308I–II
1858–63	StA Duisburg 80/87, 93, 152
1864–93	*Bericht über die Verwaltung und den Stand der Gemeinde-Angelegenheiten der Stadt Duisburg*
1894–1911	*Statistisches Jahrbuch Deutscher Städte* 7 (1898): 268–69; 8 (1900): 317–18; 9 (1901): 255; 10 (1902): 105; 11 (1903): 128; 12 (1904): 480, 481; 13 (1905): 482; 14 (1906): 69; 15 (1907): 61; 16 (1908): 61; 17 (1909): 38; 18 (1910): 54; 19 (1912): 44; 20 (1913): 65; 21 (1914): 68
1908–14	*Statistische Monatsberichte der Stadt Duisburg,* vols. 1–7.

8

In-Migration and Out-Migration in an Area of Heavy Industry: The Case of Georgsmarienhütte, 1856–1870

SUSANNE MEYER

The town of Georgsmarienhütte, in what is now western Lower Saxony, is a relatively young industrial community. It was incorporated in 1860 as the result of the establishment of the Georgs-Marien Mining and Foundry Company (Georgs-Marien-Bergwerks- und Hüttenverein, or GMBHV) in 1856. Like many new companies of the period, the GMBHV was based on coal and iron ore; in 1871 the company had about 1,500 employees and the town's population was 1,590. After World War I the GMBHV became part of the Klöckner concern, one of the largest mining and steel companies in Germany. The number of employees steadily increased through mid-century, reaching a peak of about 6,000 in the 1960s. Today, only about 2,000 people work at the Georgsmarienhütte facility.

In the sense that the object of study can be clearly isolated and defined, Georgsmarienhütte represents a kind of laboratory for the historian. The plans for the Georgsmarienhütte factory were drawn up in the distant state capital of Hanover, as were the architectural plans for the village. Practically all of the employees who lived and worked in Georgsmarien-hütte had migrated and settled there at the time the factory was built. And because the community always remained an industrialized island in the midst of an agrarian region, Georgsmarienhütte's isolation was even more complete. These conditions allow us to make unusually clear assumptions in preparing to study Georgsmarienhütte as a community and an industrial site.[1]

The story of the foundry and village's establishment throws light on the as yet poorly studied history of early industrialization in the Osna-

1 This essay is a revised version of one part of my study, *Schwerindustrielle Insel und ländliche Lebenswelt: Georgsmarienhütte, 1856–1933: Werk und Gemeinde, Herkunft, Siedlung und Sozialstruktur an einem ländlichen Industriestandort* (Münster, 1991), which was based to a large extent on computer analysis. I wish to thank Walter Kamphoefner (Texas A & M University) and Klaus J. Bade (Institut für Migrationsforschung und interkulturelle Studien, Universität Osnabrück) for their support and criticism. Thomas Kozak provided the translation.

brück region. It is also an excellent example of industrial policy in the
Kingdom of Hanover, a medium-sized, predominantly agricultural state
within the German Confederation.[2] Above all, the case of Georgsmarienhütte offers us the opportunity to study internal and transatlantic migration from the same area of origin; it also helps us understand the
migration behavior of its inhabitants in the context of the available migration alternatives.[3]

Finally, the evolution of a local industrial work force can be traced within
the same geographic boundaries. This permits two studies with different
orientations to overlap, in effect examining the same object from two different perspectives, exploring the migration process on the one hand and
investigating the origins of the industrial work force on the other.[4] It is thus
possible to understand both processes – the development of different types
and forms of migration and the birth of a (local) work force – by means of
an investigation of regional and social roots.

The members of the evolving local work force had to make choices
among a number of alternatives – not only between "migration to take
advantage of labor markets ('migration of opportunity') and migration out
of necessity ('quicksand'),"[5] but also between staying where they were and
(transatlantic) emigration. The importance of the two latter choices is especially clear in the case of Georgsmarienhütte, where the composition of
the local work force was strongly influenced by in-migration but just as
strongly by a specific type of emigration pattern that developed in the surrounding countryside, which could have been a source of new workers for
the GMBHV.

THE LABOR MARKET AND THE FOUNDING
OF THE GMBHV

The problem of recruiting workers for all types of jobs – diggers, construction workers, teamsters, miners, and foundry workers – was a recurring
theme in the early GMBHV business reports. These reports claimed that

2 Meyer, *Schwerindustrielle Insel,* 15–22.
3 This case study follows Klaus J. Bade's perspective on "sociohistorical migration research," which
   tries to embed the "migration process and migration behavior in the demographic, economic, social,
   and cultural history of the regions of origin and destination." See Klaus J. Bade, "Sozial-historische
   Migrationsforschung," in Ernst Hinrichs and Henk van Zon, eds., *Bevölkerungsgeschichte im Vergleich:
   Studien zu den Niederlanden und Nordwestdeutschland* (Aurich, 1988), 68, 72.
4 Cf. Hartmut Kaelble, "Einführung," in W. Conze and U. Engelhardt, eds., *Arbeiter im Industrialisie-
   rungsprozess: Herkunft, Lage und Verhalten* (Stuttgart, 1979), 19ff.
5 Ibid., 27.

plenty of potential employees lived in the surrounding area but that some emotional objection prevented them from accepting industrial work.[6] In the following two sections, I assess the validity of this claim by the GMBHV management and expose the motivational structures upon which these "emotional" objections may have been based. I first review the contemporary labor situation in the Osnabrück region, considering the situation in agriculture and among the skilled trades as well as the general population trends. In particular, I focus on the campaign undertaken by the newly established GMBHV to recruit workers for heavy industry.[7] In the second section, I study the regional emigration statistics for the period before and after the establishment of the GMBHV, looking for significant differences in the patterns of migration – who left, and who stayed?

AGRICULTURE, TRADE, AND POPULATION

Characteristic for the agrarian structure in the southern part of the Osnabrück region in the middle of the nineteenth century was the presence of a large number of *Heuerleute* (the singular is *Heuerling*). *Heuerleute* were agricultural workers who exchanged a certain number of days' work on the landlord's property, rather than cash or a share of the crops, for the use of some land and a place to live. Despite the fact that tens of thousands of *Heuerleute* had already emigrated, they still made up a majority of the population. Given the inheritance laws, *Heuerling* status offered noninheriting peasants' sons or farmhands at least the possibility, by means of contracts with peasants or even tenant farmers, of establishing their own meager means of existence.[8] In 1850, 2,073 *Heuerleute* families lived in the Osnabrück District (Amt Osnabrück) and 2,157 in the Iburg District, corresponding to 58.44 and 51.47 percent of the total numbers of families, respectively.[9] A comparison of the numbers of primary and secondary residences in 1772 and 1806 shows that the number of households in the Iburg

6 Management report, *Geschäftsbericht des Verwaltungsrates*, of Jan. 13, 1858, Dep. 32b, No. 765. Unless otherwise indicated, these sources are in the Niedersächsisches Staatsarchiv at Osnabrück.

7 For a detailed account of the agricultural situation, see René Ott, *Kohle, Stahl und Klassenkampf: Montanindustrie, Arbeiterschaft und Arbeiterbewegung im Osnabrücker Land, 1857–1878* (Frankfurt/Main and New York, 1982), 41–63.

8 On the nature of the *Heuerling* relationship in the region around Osnabrück, see Ott, *Kohle*, 42–43.

9 Franz Bölsker-Schlicht, *Die Hollandgängerei im Osnabrücker Land und im Emsland: Ein Beitrag zur Geschichte der Arbeitswanderung vom 17. bis zum 19. Jahrhundert* (Sögel, 1987), 89. The following terms are used to differentiate three levels of local and regional administration in the Osnabrück region (*Osnabrücker Land*). On the lowest level, the local village or community (*Gemeinde, Stadt*), on the second level, the district (*Amt* or *Kreis*), and on the third, the "administrative district" (*Regierungsbezirk*, formerly *Landdrostei*).

and Osnabrück districts grew more rapidly than the total of primary and secondary residences.[10] Newly arriving families of *Heuerleute* moved into already existing *Heuerleute* houses, often constructed as multiple-family dwellings or double cottages. They found shelter in barns, stables, bakeries, unused servants' cottages, or tenant-farm buildings, which no longer provided income for a family and had thus been converted into rental property.[11]

The growth of the population and the accompanying housing shortage resulted from a changed reproductive pattern among the *Heuerleute*. This change, in turn, was caused by the coincidence of the *Heuerling* system and protoindustrial development. In regions where peasant holdings were not divided by heritage, late marriage and small families were the rule because a son could only inherit the whole farm and thereby support a wife and a family upon the death or retirement of his father. For the *Heuerling* with a second job, in contrast, early marriage and a large number of children were necessary to secure the family's survival.[12] *Heuerleute* families in the Osnabrück region had several ways of securing their survival. The *Heuerling* contract itself, however, did not provide sufficient income. Although the *Heuerling* shared his landlord's right to use the common lands, such use was "without any personal legal right" and was merely tolerated. To increase the family income, family members did spinning and weaving, and the sons and husbands migrated either to Holland proper to do seasonal agricultural work (mowing grass or cutting peat) or to northern Holland to work as whalers, herring fishermen, brickmakers, or dike builders. Mining work existed for a very few in the Osnabrück region itself.[13]

The breakup of the common lands and the decline in these secondary occupations made the economic situation of the *Heuerleute* unbearable, though their existence had, in fact, always been endangered. The division of the commons led to significant impoverishment among the *Heuerleute*: Until that time, they had shared access to the common lands, "they had lived within the protective framework of communal agriculture (insofar as it continued to exist in the form of the common lands); now, however, the transformation of land holdings to private property robbed them of one of

---

10 Adolf Wrasmann, "Das Heuerlingswesen im Fürstentum Osnabrück," *Osnabrücker Mitteilungen* 44 (1921): 4, 18.
11 Ott, *Kohle,* 42, following Wrasmann, "Heuerlingswesen," 65, 73, 81.
12 Walter D. Kamphoefner, *Westfalen in der Neuen Welt: Eine Sozialgeschichte der Auswanderung im 19. Jahrhundert* (Münster, 1982), 28.
13 Ott, *Kohle,* 43.

their primary means of subsistence, and no substitute emerged to replace it."[14] On the other hand, the division of the commons also made it possible to create additional plots for the *Heuerleute*.

As seen in an overview of the Osnabrück region, the situation of the *Heuerleute* had improved slightly by the late 1840s. According to the statistics compiled in 1852 by the Hanoverian government, with special attention to the situation of domestics, tenant farmers, and peasants during the period 1849–50, several reasons explained this improvement: favorable harvests; frugality; the law of October 24, 1848, regulating the conditions of *Heuerleute* in the Principality of Osnabrück (mainly aimed at avoiding the creation of very small *Heuerling* plots); the decline in the number of *Heuerleute* families due to a high rate of emigration; increased opportunities for work, arising from the introduction of new agricultural technologies and the gradual expansion of industrial activities such as tobacco processing, cotton weaving, and coal mining.[15]

Around 1850 the picture became more differentiated on the district level in Osnabrück and Iburg. At this time, migration to Holland almost completely disappeared in both districts. In 1849 the district of Iburg reported 1,714 *Heuerleute* families, 798 peasants (*Colonen*) leasing *Heuerling* plots (this is not the total number of *Colonen,* however), and 630 hereditary tenant farmers (*Erbpächter*) and new-settler (*Neubauer*) families.

In the Iburg parishes of Glane, Hagen, and Oesede, and in the village of Iburg itself, the conditions of the lower classes, especially wage workers, were "quite poor, although there was no lack of work opportunity." *Heuerleute* in the village of Iburg were reported to own few cattle, and the potential sources of income were said to be "meager," especially in the winter months. The cost of leasing land was comparatively high in these parishes (as well as in Borgloh parish), and the breakup of the common lands was complete except in Hagen. In the other parts of the district, the *Heuerleute* survived on a "more or less subsistence income."

In Osnabrück there were 1,956 *Heuerleute* families, 845 peasants leasing *Heuerling* plots, and 370 hereditary peasant farmers and new-settler families. The division of the common land had also been completed here, but the material situation of the *Heuerleute* improved only in areas close to the city of Osnabrück. Those who could walk to the city in 1.5 hours or less could

---

14 Ibid., 44. Ott bases his description on G. W. L. Funke, *Über die gegenwärtige Lage der Heuerleute im Fürstentum Osnabrück* (Bielefeld, 1847), 28ff.
15 *Zur Statistik des Königreichs Hannover,* Zweites Heft, Anhang (Hanover, 1852) [cited in the following notes as *Statistik*], 66f.

"find a day's work there with certainty"; the situation for those living farther away was worse.[16]

Within the *Heuerleute* group, it seems that those who remained at home
were better off than those who emigrated. The new settlers, who were
present in higher proportions among the rural population of the Osnabrück
and Iburg districts than in other parts of the administrative district,[17] were
exceptional in that almost all of them had secure incomes.[18]

The population of the Osnabrück District increased by about 20 percent
between 1772 and 1801; in Iburg District the figure was about 10 percent.
The census figures from 1821 and 1848 show further increases relative to
1801: 11.12 percent (from 17,176 to 19,327 inhabitants) for Osnabrück and
7.36 percent (21,154 to 22,835) for Iburg, respectively.[19]

The transitional growth of new opportunities, as was the case in many
parts of Westphalia, did not compensate for the effects of the decline in
previously available secondary occupations. The Osnabrück region experienced "temporary and partial deindustrialization";[20] that is, the collapse
of protoindustrial production was not followed by an expansion of industrial, mostly textile, production.[21] Designed for an agrarian society, the Hanover legislation governing rural districts (*Landgemeinderecht*) had the effect
of reinforcing these trends in a negative way by hindering any significant
internal migration.[22]

Very little factory production existed in the Osnabrück region into the
mid-nineteenth century; the situation there was a "grab bag" of transitional
phenomena, where the "textile industry was no longer the pacemaker, but
the mining industry had not yet taken over."[23] The city itself was unable
and unwilling to accept the numerous "idle and underemployed hands" in
the skilled trades and hence in the housing market.[24] Referring to recent

---

16 The description of the Osnabrück and Iburg districts is based on the *Statistik*.
17 Bölsker-Schlicht, *Hollandgängerei*, 320.
18 *Statistik*.
19 On the 1772 and 1801 figures, see Wrasmann, "Heuerlingswesen," 1; the figures for 1821 and 1848
    are calculated from Gustav Uelschen, *Die Bevölkerung in Niedersachsen, 1821–1961* (Hanover, 1966),
    180–82. However, significant emigration led to decreases in population, from 21,752 to 20,301 in
    Osnabrück between 1842 and 1852, and from 23,870 to 23,161 in Iburg between 1845 and 1852.
    See Bölsker-Schlicht, *Hollandgängerei*, 132, 319.
20 See Kamphoefner, *Westfalen*.
21 See Peter Kriedte, Hans Medick, and Jürgen Schlumbohm, *Industrialisierung vor der Industrialisierung:
    Gewerbliche Warenproduktion auf dem Land in der Formationsperiode des Kapitalismus* (Göttingen, 1977),
    302, 305.
22 See Meyer, *Schwerindustrielle Insel*, 33–41.
23 Ott, *Kohle*, 61.
24 Karl Heinrich Kaufhold, "Entstehung, Entwicklung und Gliederung der gewerblichen Arbeiter-
    schaft in Nordwestdeutschland, 1800–1875: Unter besonderer Berücksichtigung staatlicher Mass-
    nahmen," in H. Kellenbenz, ed., *Wirtschaftspolitik und Arbeitsmarkt* (Munich, 1974), 83.

population trends, a socially and geographically limited way of thinking is revealed in a sentence from the Osnabrück city directory of 1853: "Osnabrück would also have grown more rapidly [in population] if the city fathers had not been working, in the interests of tradesmen and lower classes alike, to prevent the influx of strangers and thus ward off the threat of unemployment."[25] This attitude, which came from the guild tradition of the skilled crafts, viewed the city as closed economic space.

In 1849 there were three textile mills with about 240 employees in the city of Osnabrück, along with three cotton mills; by 1857 there were 127 "factory operations" with 22 steam engines (total capacity: 252 metric horsepower) and 1,500 employees.[26] Between 1833 and 1861 Osnabrück experienced an increase in the number of people employed in the trades with a simultaneous drop in the number of shops, indicating strong competition in the craft sector. Among the individual trades, however, it was only the construction industry that experienced above average growth – by more than 100 percent. But this growth merely compensated for lower employment figures in the textile trades, which had previously been by far the largest group, and in woodworking.[27] Changes in the numbers of artisans, actually only shifts, and the initial slow growth of the overall population, which only became rapid after 1860, show that the city did not really offer "an alternative way of insuring one's survival."[28]

In the vicinity of the city of Osnabrück and in the villages that were later annexed to the city, the following industries were in operation in 1849: two paper mills with about 100 employees each, two iron foundries and one forge, several brickworks, and the city-owned mine on the Piesberg to the north, with about 200 workers. There was also a cigar factory with 140 to 200 employees in 1849.[29]

Farther away from the city, there were only a few industrial facilities before the establishment of Georgsmarienhütte in 1856: a state-owned coal mine with 256 employees, a small iron foundry with 50 workers (1849), and two small paper mills. In the southern part of the Osnabrück District, which would later serve as the immediate source of labor for the GMBHV,

---

25 *Osnabrücker Adressbuch von 1853,* 174, quoted in Jörg Jeschke, *Gewerberecht und Handwerkswirtschaft des Königreichs Hannover im Übergang, 1815–1866: Eine Quellenstudie* (Göttingen, 1977), 113.
26 Figures from Ott, *Kohle,* 61; from W. van Kampen and T. Westphalen, eds., *100 Jahre SPD in Osnabrück, 1875–1975* (Osnabrück, 1975), 18; and from *Statistik,* 71. On the city of Osnabrück in the census years 1818 and 1831, see also Jeschke, *Gewerberecht,* 306–09.
27 See Jeschke, *Gewerberecht,* 287–91.
28 Ibid., 28. On population growth in Osnabrück, see van Kampen and Westphalen, *100 Jahre SPD,* 19.
29 *Statistik,* 71; on the cigar factory, see Jeschke, *Gewerberecht,* 308f.

Hagen parish reported 50 wooden shoemakers, 30 other tradesmen, fruit sellers, and broom binders, in addition to flax growers and linen producers. Oesede parish reported 10 wooden shoemakers and 24 other tradesmen in addition to those engaged in linen production.[30]

EMIGRATION BEFORE AND AFTER THE FOUNDING OF GEORGSMARIENHÜTTE

The description given previously demonstrates that the trades offered only very limited alternatives for poor people in the Osnabrück region. This situation and the insufficient chances of economic survival provided by agriculture were the decisive factors leading to mass emigration from the region during the 1830s. The administrative district of Osnabrück, with only about 1 percent of the population of the German Confederation, supplied "over 7 percent of the German emigrants" in that decade. The former Principality of Osnabrück (seven districts and the city itself) had the most intense emigration of all areas ruled by Prussia between 1830 and 1866, with "an average of 1 percent" of the overall population leaving each year.[31]

According to the emigration figures compiled by Karl Kiel, the total number of emigrants from the Osnabrück and Iburg districts from 1832–33 to the founding of Georgsmarienhütte in 1856 was 10,394; over the entire period studied (until 1866), the rates of emigration were 0.95 percent for Osnabrück and 0.75 percent for Iburg.[32]

The recorded occupations of 639 male emigrants from the former Principality of Osnabrück (prefectures Osnabrück and Buer bei Melle) show how the emigration structure reflects the spectrum of poverty in the area:[33]

68.0 percent rural lower class (*Heuerleute*, farmhands, and day laborers)
 7.1 percent tenant farmers and peasants with small holdings
 4.4 percent peasants with medium-size or large holdings
 3.6 percent journeymen and apprentices

30 On the coal mines, see Ott, *Kohle*, 60; the other figures are from *Statistik*, 71.
31 Kamphoefner, *Westfalen,* 23; for Osnabrück, see Karl Kiel, "Gründe und Folgen der Auswanderung aus dem Osnabrücker Regierungsbezirk, insbesondere nach den Vereinigten Staaten, im Lichte der Hannoverschen Auswanderungspolitik betrachtet (1823–1866)," *Osnabrücker Mitteilungen* 61 (1941): 165–76.
32 Kiel, "Gründe und Folgen," 166f., 176. Kiel himself gives a slightly higher estimate of the overall figures. The emigration rate or emigration intensity is the ratio of the number of emigrants in a given year to the total population for the same year, here within the time period 1832–66.
33 Kamphoefner, *Westfalen,* 59. The Osnabrück and Buer prefectures exhibited "average emigration rates relative to the region as a whole." Ibid., 176f.

13.3 percent craftsmen (no further information)
0.0 percent master craftsmen
3.4 percent tertiary sector, industry

The figure for craftsmen most likely concealed many sons of *Heuerleute* who had previously held second jobs in rural linen production and were now anxious to become artisans.[34] Within the rural lower class, it was the *Heuerleute* more than the farmhands and day laborers who emigrated. Walter Kamphoefner describes this group socially as "poor but not miserable."[35] A glance at the family status of the emigrants from the Osnabrück and Iburg districts (see Table 8.1) confirms that there was a generally high rate of family migration in the first waves of emigrants, and that this rate only gradually declined. The year 1856 was chosen as the dividing point because the Georgsmarienhütte was founded in that year. Family emigration outnumbered the unmarried emigrants by far in the first two waves. Daughters and sons left with their parents, however, depriving new industries of potential workers.

High rates of internal out-migration and emigration were associated with the following factors: remnants of rural protoindustry, population growth, relatively high residential density, and a relatively high proportion of *Heuerleute* among the rural population.[36] Here we must ask whether the possibility of finding wage work would have had any effect whatsoever on the decision

Table 8.1. *Family status of emigrants from Osnabrück and Iburg, 1832–56 and 1857–66*[37]

	Unmarried men (%)	Unmarried women (%)	Families	Total no.
Osnabrück, 1832–56	22.16	14.59	63.25	5,723
Osnabrück, 1857–66	28.64	23.96	47.38	1,302
Iburg, 1832–56	28.40	20.05	51.53	4,671
Iburg, 1857–66	36.50	25.58	37.90	1,571

34 See Kaufhold, "Entstehung," 82.
35 Kamphoefner, *Westfalen,* 57–68; with reference to Tecklenburg, see 66; on the Lippe region, see 67.
36 See Kamphoefner, *Westfalen,* 35. Kamphoefner points to the high residential density in the areas studied. It is true that there is a correlation between high residential density and high emigration rate, but the areas with low residential density have not low but average emigration rates. One should also note that the residential density factor is important only in rural areas.
37 Calculated from the data given by Kiel, "Gründe und Folgen," 166f.

to emigrate, and whether the alleged shortage of industrial workers actually existed.

The record shows that the directors of the city-owned Piesberg coal mine north of Osnabrück urgently sought workers in the 1850s. The search had to be extended beyond Osnabrück; and, in 1855, they asked the royal mining authorities in Clausthal to arrange for the transfer of workers from the state-owned mines in the Harz mountains.[38] The hard-rock miners recruited from the Harz, it was reported, demonstrated a strong distaste for coal mining: "We are forced, therefore, to try to teach coal mining to young people who have no experience but are interested in taking up mining." The appeal was thus not only to trained miners but also to every son of a *Heuerling* or day laborer.

The administrators of the state-owned mines in Borgloh and Oesede had also turned to the Hanover royal finance ministry in 1854, to transfer "hard-working miners from the Harz" to the Oesede shaft, which was almost adjacent to the site later occupied by the Georgsmarienhütte. They claimed that the "prospering operation" was faced with a "shortage of workers."[39]

The number of such opportunities to earn wages outside the traditional crafts was not significant in the Osnabrück region. But even these limited opportunities were not seized upon by the local population. And even the few businesses operating at that time were unable to satisfy their needs for new workers. Yet at the same time emigration remained high: During 1854–56, when the Piesberg and Borgloh/Oesede mines were beginning to recruit miners from outside the area, a total of 1,112 people, including many whole families, left the Osnabrück and Iburg districts.[40]

It is surprising that the local population showed no interest in industrial work, including mining, outside that which already existed. They seemed to prefer emigration or internal out-migration despite the fact that work in the coal mines (six to seven hours per shift)[41] made it possible to continue farming as a second job. Naturally, working two jobs was very exhausting. The working conditions for the *Heuerling* economy and the mining industry had adapted to one another, as is shown in the following description of the Borgloh-Oesede mine from the year 1874:

Almost all of the workers have come from the agricultural trades and continue to practice these; 193 are heads of their own households, while 163 are boarding with

---

38 Archiv des Oberbergamtes Clausthal, Fach 165, no. 19: letter from Stüve, Dec. 26, 1855.
39 Report to the Hanover royal finance ministry of February 1855: Archiv des Oberbergamtes Clausthal, Fach 165, no. 18.
40 Kiel, "Gründe und Folgen," 166f.
41 Ott, *Kohle,* 72.

parents or relatives. Of the former, 59 have homes and at least 1.48 hectares of land . . . ; of the latter, 134 are married but nonlandowning workers, 128 are leasing an average of 1.06 hectares. Two-thirds of those leasing land are *Heuerleute* and owe their landlords between 80 and 130 days of labor, but this may now be performed in the afternoon to allow for their mining work.[42]

The miners thus farmed an arable parcel of about 1.06 to 1.48 hectares (4 to 6 morgen or 2.65 to 3.70 acres), which was about average for a *Heuerling* plot.[43] But "liberation" from the status of *Heuerling* or "mining cottager" (*Bergmannskötter*)[44] to that of a "miner only" did not seem desirable to the individual worker, as revealed in the fact that by 1874 only four two-family miner's houses with gardens had been built and occupied. The miners were simply unwilling to trade agriculturally usable land for a garden plot. They showed interest, the mine operators found, only when the size of the plot was half a hectare or greater.[45]

The establishment of the Georgsmarienhütte finally led to temporary, localized, monostructural industrialization in the Osnabrück region – a relatively large protoindustrial region that, overall, was experiencing deindustrialization. Although the industrial expansion was very limited compared with that of other regions such as the Ruhr, there still seemed to be a labor shortage. The southern Osnabrück area now became, to a certain extent, an area of simultaneous in-migration and out-migration.

Using districts in Westphalia as examples, Kamphoefner has demonstrated a connection between a protoindustrial economy and intense transatlantic emigration; the internal migration to the city of Bochum can serve as a comparative figure. For this area, German emigrants were predominantly of rural origin, with "a regular tendency toward higher rates of emigration as one went farther from the city." However, the "choice between internal and transatlantic migration did not depend exclusively on one's nearness to urban areas. At least before the founding of the German Empire in 1871, the protoindustrialized regions were dominant in trans-

---

42 Eugen Hiltrop, "Beiträge zur Statistik des Oberbergamtsbezirks Dortmund, mit besonderer Berüchsichtigung der Ansiedlungsbestrebungen der Grubenbesitzer für die Belegschaft ihrer Werke," *Zeitschrift des Kgl. Statistischen Bureaus* 15 (1875): 279.
43 Statistics from the year 1847, from Wrasmann, "Heuerlingswesen," 28.
44 Klaus Tenfelde, *Sozialgeschichte der Bergarbeiterschaft an der Ruhr im 19. Jahrhundert* (Bonn-Bad Godesberg, 1977), 116–18. Tenfelde points out that the state-operated mining industry in the southern Ruhr area "made a special effort to accommodate the requirements of second jobs in agriculture. It was expected that such a work force would stay healthy and strong and be safe from market and food-supply crises." The average landholding there was also about 5 morgen. The Ibbenbüren mine in the Tecklenburg district, near Osnabrück, also experienced a "special form of mining tenant farmers," who owned property and were thus protected from "general impoverishment." Albin Gladen, *Der Kreis Tecklenburg an der Schwelle des Zeitalters der Industrialisierung* (Münster, 1970), 96ff.
45 According to Ott, *Kohle*, 71.

atlantic emigration." We can surmise that "workers in protoindustry . . . for the most part rejected the alternative of internal migration to centers of heavy industry in favor of transatlantic emigration."[46] Nevertheless, the absolute number of migrants from this area to the Ruhr must have been considerable, probably between 9,000 and 16,000 between 1844 and 1856 (depending on the estimation technique used).[47] Still, the number of emigrants was greater than that of internal migrants to the Ruhr.

But Kamphoefner also warns us not to interpret these findings prematurely on the basis of the Bochum example. Focusing on the immense industrial concentration in the Ruhr, with its variations in appearance and large masses of workers, can lead us to lose sight of other areas of heavy industry; viewing the move to industry as the only alternative to emigration also distorts the picture. Osnabrück was the "Hanoverian Bochum"[48] in the north of the Münster region and had just as much potential as a destination for migration as the developing Ruhr cities. Significant outmigration of rural workers occurred there as well: Many sons of *Heuerleute* from the Ravensberg region, for example, set out for Georgsmarienhütte.

The question of individual motivation in the decision to leave or stay is a difficult one, and we can offer only an approximate answer. In this context, Klaus J. Bade distinguishes "material and immaterial determining factors," each with two levels. "A decision to migrate is made not on the basis of a critical evaluation of the supraindividual motivating factors identified in social history, but according to individual disappointments, hopes, and expectations."[49] Reducing the field of view to a single unit, as happens in the following description of the vicinity of the Georgsmarienhütte, leaves open the final answer to the question. At least it becomes possible to give a more differentiated answer to the question of the choice between alternatives – emigration or "occupational emigration without leaving home."[50]

For this study, all known emigration data for the time period 1856–70 were collected for an area within five to ten kilometers of Georgsmarienhütte.[51] This radius was chosen simply by reckoning the maximum distance

46 Kamphoefner, *Westfalen*, 40–42. For Bochum, Kamphoefner bases his analysis on David Crew, *Bochum: Sozialgeschichte einer Industriestadt, 1860–1914* (Frankfurt/Main, 1980).
47 Tenfelde, *Sozialgeschichte*, 236: "By the beginning of the 1850s there are already reports of 1,000 new workers from the collapsing textile industry in Minden-Ravensberg."
48 Wilhelm Müller-Wille, *Westfalen: Landschaftliche Ordnung und Bindung eines Landes* (Münster, 1950), 2, 311.
49 Klaus J. Bade, "Massenwanderung und Arbeitsmarkt im deutschen Nordosten von 1880 bis zum Ersten Weltkrieg," *Archiv für Sozialgeschichte* 20 (1980): 287.
50 Bade, "Massenwanderung," 306.
51 The computations were performed, in keeping with the structure of the emigrant card file, at the

workers could travel on foot each day to reach their jobs at the Georgsmarienhütte. The area of study thus encompasses about 20 percent of the
total area of the Osnabrück and Iburg districts and 27.6 percent of their
population, based on yearly averages of data from the census taken on December 1, 1871. The percentage of emigrants, in contrast, was a mere 6.15
percent (205 out of a total of 3,336 for the two districts) during the period
1856–66.[52] Emigration was thus lower in the immediate vicinity of Georgsmarienhütte than in the rest of the two districts. One should note, however,
that the figure for the percentage of the population reflects the concentration of people in Georgsmarienhütte (1,056 inhabitants in 1871). The difference should therefore not be given too much weight. Despite the
relatively low number of emigrants from the Georgsmarienhütte area, however, the changes in the waves of emigration over time correspond closely
to the general trends in the districts as a whole: decreases after 1858, increases again after 1864. The proportion of the emigration diverted by the
foundation of Georgsmarienhütte remains unclear. The main reasons certainly came from outside the area: economic crisis, protests against immigrants in North American cities, and delayed realization of the decision to
emigrate because of the American Civil War.[53]

Although the records give the migrants' destinations in all cases, I will
not examine these in detail here. I note only that 91 percent mentioned
America or North America, 3.3 percent mentioned Holland and Denmark,
and 5.3 percent migrated to other areas of Germany. Of the latter group
(sixteen migrants), four said they were going to Bremen, which was a popular embarkation point for emigrants.[54] The high percentage of transatlantic
migration leads one to conclude that there was a strong tradition of emigration.[55] To the extent that more precise information about the destination
of these emigrants was recorded, it fits the scheme developed by Kamphoefner, linking German regions of origin with the distribution of emi-

church parish level – here the Catholic parishes Oesede, St. Johann, Hagen, and Iburg as well as
the Protestant parish St. Katharinen.

52 These figures can be somewhat inexact. For the Georgsmarienhütte area I used all emigrant data
available in the Osnabrück Staatsarchiv, while for the Osnabrück and Iburg districts I employed the
figures of Kiel ("Gründe und Folgen"), who gives a small margin of error for his data.

53 See Kamphoefner, *Westfalen,* 70–72; Peter Marschalck, *Die Deutsche Überseeauswanderung im 19.
Jahrhundert* (Stuttgart, 1971), 40–42; Klaus J. Bade, "Die deutsche Überseeische Massenauswanderung im 19. und frühen 20. Jahrhundert: Bestimmungsfaktoren und Entwicklungsbedingungen," in
Klaus J. Bade, ed., *Auswanderer – Wanderarbeiter – Gastarbeiter. Bevölkerung, Arbeitsmarkt und Wanderung in Deutschland seit der Mitte des 19. Jahrhunderts,* 2 vols. (Ostfildern, 1984), 1:267–69.

54 As determined from the emigrant card file of the Niedersächsisches Staatsarchiv Osnabrück.

55 On the roles of a regionally varying "transatlantic emigration tradition" and of "transatlantic communication" as indirect influencing factors, see Bade, "Massenwanderung," 306.

Table 8.2. *Emigration from 11*
communities near Georgsmarienhütte

Year	Number of emigrants
1856	32
1857	33
1858	11
1859	8
1860	14
1861	10
1862	2
1863	10
1864	33
1865	33
1866	19
1867	36
1868	56
1869	36
1870	5
Total	338

grants in selected American cities and their hinterlands. People from Hanover tended to go to Cincinnati, St. Louis, and the large East Coast cities of New York, Baltimore, and Philadelphia.[56] Among the ninety-three destinations given in detail, Cincinnati is mentioned sixty-five times, St. Louis seven times, and the East Coast cities twenty-one times. The extremely high rate of transatlantic emigration and the low rate of internal migration in the years following the founding of Georgsmarienhütte indicate no significant movement from the Osnabrück region to the developing industrial centers in Westphalia or to large German cities.

Overall, the number of emigrants decreased, and the figures ran parallel to those for German emigration as a whole. I would like to turn to a more detailed examination of the age, family status, and occupation of individual emigrants in order to answer questions with respect to changes in the emigration structure in the immediate Georgsmarienhütte area. Then it will be possible to address the more difficult question of the people's motives for staying home, moving to other areas, or emigrating abroad.

Comparable data for the territory of the former Principality of Osna-

56 Kamphoefner, *Westfalen*, 94f., 100.

Table 8.3. *Ages of emigrants from the*
Georgsmarienhütte area [57]

Age	Number	Percentage
14 or less	1	0.46
15–19	93	43.25
20–29	98	45.58
30–49	18	8.37
50 or more	5	2.32

brück[58] in 1864 show 21.11 percent between 14 and 19 years old, 57.25 percent between 20 and 45 years old, and 21.62 percent between 46 and 60 years old. Comparison with the data of Table 8.3 reveals the above-average mobility of young men and women under 20 in the Georgsmarienhütte area. These people probably emigrated shortly after their church confirmation, before they would have begun working at regular jobs.

The number of emigrants decreased significantly after the opening of the Georgsmarienhütte works, as did the proportion of family emigration. During the period 1821–56 the overall percentages of emigration were very high, 63 percent in Osnabrück District and 51 percent in Iburg District, whereas in 1856–70 the figures were 47.38 and 37.9 percent, respectively. The percentage of family emigrants from the Georgsmarienhütte area, however, decreased to 19.86 percent, while the proportions of unmarried male and female emigrants in the age group 15–19 years rose.

The rate of emigration for the purpose of family reunification in the Georgsmarienhütte area was 14.23 percent in the period between 1856 and 1870. But in interpreting this low value we must recall that this fact was not automatically mentioned when applying for permission to emigrate.

Further differentiation of the emigrant data by occupation leads us closer to answering the question of who emigrated, who remained, and what the determining factors for the decision were (see Table 8.5).

One thing to note in these figures is that the high rate of emigration from the village of Iburg (82 of the total of 338 emigrants) is related to the high proportion in the tertiary sector and the crafts: 32 emigrants (50 per-

57 Ages were recorded in 215 of the total of 338 cases, giving us relatively reliable figures. The data were calculated on the basis of the emigrant card file of the Niedersächsisches Staatsarchiv Osnabrück.
58 See Ott, *Kohle,* 60.

Table 8.4. *Family status of the emigrants*[59]

	Percentage of unmarried emigrants	Percentage of emigrants in families	Absolute no. of families
Georgsmarienhütte, 1856–70	80 Male: 64.55 Female: 15.45	19.86	14
Amt Osnabrück, 1857–70	52.20 Male: 28.24 Female: 23.96	47.38	156
Amt Iburg, 1857–70	62.08 Male: 36.50 Female: 25.58	37.90	149

cent of those in these two groups, excluding the miners, manual laborers, and laborers) came from this village alone.

By comparison with the district of Osnabrück as a whole, there is a marked shift in the occupational structure of the emigrant group from the Georgsmarienhütte area. The figures on emigrants from the prefectures Buer and Osnabrück for the period 1832–60 show that 79.5 percent were in agriculture, 16.9 percent in crafts, and 3.4 percent in the tertiary sector; among emigrants from the Georgsmarienhütte area during the period 1856–70 47.2 percent were in agriculture, 28.2 percent in crafts, and 24.6 percent in the tertiary sector.

Aside from the slightly different time periods covered by these two sets of figures, the differences in occupational structure are surely related to the fact that handicrafts and service work were concentrated in the area near the city of Osnabrück, as compared with the average for the two prefectures. And the numbers in particular crafts increased due to the construction of the Georgsmarienhütte works. The individual occupations listed will not be studied here, but it is clear that a need for above-average numbers of artisans developed. Masons, stonemasons, carpenters, and cabinetmakers were in high demand on account of the fact that not only the industrial facility but also an entire workers' village had to be designed and built. In the case of Georgsmarienhütte, therefore, rural artisans from the building trades were more typical emigrants than shoemakers and tailors, the other major trade

59 The figures for Georgsmarienhütte are calculated from the emigrant card file of the Niedersächsisches Staatsarchiv Osnabrück; for the Osnabrück and Iburg districts, they are based on the data given in Kiel, "Gründe und Folgen."

Table 8.5. *Occupations of emigrants (or their fathers) from Georgsmarienhütte* [60]

	Fathers		Unmarried	
Occupation	Absolute no.	Percent	Absolute no.	Percent
Neuerling, new-settler, day laborer, fieldhand, servant + maid (47 people)	3	2.11	52	36.62
Tenant farmers, farmers (*Ackerman*)	3	2.11	4	2.81
Peasants, hereditary tenant farmers			5	3.52
Journeymen or apprentices	1	0.70	17	11.97
Master craftsmen	2	1.40		
Miscellaneous craftsmen	1	0.70	19	13.38
Tertiary sector			23	16.19
Others (miners, laborers)	1	0.70	11	7.74
Total	11	7.72	131	92.23

group among emigrants. Shoemaking and tailoring needed relatively few tools and could be practiced as second jobs. We can also assume that the workers listed as artisans in the emigrant card file included many former agricultural workers or people who combined agricultural and artisan work.[61]

At the same time, the emigration of unmarried farmhands and maids continued. They were young, mobile, and just then deciding on plans for their lives – as narrow as the range of choices may have been. At least for the young men, job opportunities would have been available in industry.

The situation was quite different for their fathers. According to the Hanover legislation for rural districts, they had been required to demonstrate at least a minimal material standard of living above the poverty level at the time of their marriages. Thus, in the Georgsmarienhütte area it was the *Heuerling*, usually married, who tried to increase his income through industrial work. He and his family could depend on farming as additional income and as a basic source of sustenance in case he lost his job. Since his family could continue working the land, the *Heuerling* tended to live on his plot and in the attached cottage while working in the mine or foundry. In

60 This information is given in 142 of the total of 338 cases, or almost 50 percent, if one subtracts the children from the total number of emigrants. The figures are calculated on the basis of the emigrant card file in the Niedersächsisches Staatsarchiv Osnabrück; the occupations are grouped to match approximately the scheme used by Kamphoefner.
61 Cf. Kamphoefner, *Westfalen*, 59, 62. Kamphoefner uses data on the fathers' occupations to show that these were less likely to be traditional artisan families. Kaufhold ("Entstehung," 82) speaks of "pressure on the crafts as the most available alternative" [to agricultural work].

this way the fact that the wages in Georgsmarienhütte were lower than those paid in the Ruhr made less of a difference.[62] The farm as a primary source of subsistence (usually with income-earning secondary work such as linen production), after a period of extreme poverty and high emigration due to the collapse of the linen industry, had become a secondary income source.[63]

The type of *Heuerling* status that developed remained stable well into the twentieth century. Looking forward two generations, to the period after World War I, we can see how little the condition and self-understanding of these *Heuerleute* had changed. By the turn of the century, the Osnabrück area was heavily industrialized, and had, compared with nearby, less industrialized districts, "by far the largest" ratio of *Heuerling* plots to peasant plots, whereas the individual plots were smaller. The *Heuerling* himself, still highly valued as a strong, healthy industrial worker, served only as the "manager" of his own farm, passing on his agricultural know-how within the family while most of the work was done by his wife, the children, and perhaps a maid. As the operator of a farm, however, the *Heuerling* still had higher status in the country than a laborer. This can be seen in the education of the children, in marriage patterns, in traditional customs, and in the continuing inclusion of *Industrieheuerlinge* in the system of farm neighborhoods. The *Heuerling* families also did well financially. An analysis of the total income of three *Industrieheuerlinge* in the 1920s found, surprisingly, that their agricultural work, figured on an hourly basis, paid more than twice as well as their industrial jobs.[64]

Evaluating the wages offered by the Georgsmarienhütte management during the early years shows why these industrial jobs were unattractive to the sons of farmers who did not inherit the family plot. This was true despite the fact that workers' housing was offered as part of the arrangement, providing the former farmhand with at least some private space and the hope

62 See Ott, *Kohle,* 287, and Tenfelde, *Sozialgeschichte,* 296.
63 See Kriedte et al., *Industrialisierung,* 66f., 311f.
64 Johannes Drees, "Arbeitsausgleich zwischen Industrie und Landwirtschaft dargestellt am Heuerlingswesen im Kreis Osnabrück," manuscript dissertation (no place or date of publication [Osnabrück, 1924]), 19, 27, 73–79, 108. See also Karl Kärger, *Die Verhältnisse der Landarbeiter in Nordwestdeutschland, Württemberg, Baden und in den Reichslanden: Geschildert auf Grund der vom Verein für Sozialpolitik veranstalteten Erhebungen* (Leipzig, 1892); on the Osnabrück administrative district, 57–71. For the study period (around 1890), Kärger notes a strong flow of hired hands from the Osnabrück vicinity, especially Hasbergen, to industrial areas (58–61). The description of the *Heuerleute* agrees with that of Drees from the 1920s. The previous generation also lived in relatively good economic circumstances. Drees even claims that the *Heuerleute* felt themselves to be the "social equals" of the peasants ("Arbeitsausgleich," 70).

of setting up a small household, and thus making it possible for him to marry.

During the construction phase in summer 1857, Georgsmarienhütte employed 2,500 workers, and from the time normal operation began through about 1865 the average number of regular employees ranged between 1,300 and 1,400. Throughout this period it was feasible for the management to limit the "normal day's wages to 14 ggr. or less, although other employers were paying 18–20 ggr. or more." The increased need for craftsmen had a direct effect on wages in the city of Osnabrück. The city building administrator wrote in spring 1857, after a year of construction at Georgsmarienhütte, "The high rise in the demand for workers by the large firms in the process of development in the city and its surrounding area justifies and necessitates a general increase in the wages for the building trades." Wages rose by 2 gute groschen on account of the increased demand, from 8–13 to 10–15 gute groschen for helpers and journeymen stonemasons, respectively.[65]

Continuing to work in the foundry or as a miner at Georgsmarienhütte after the building phase was over would have meant only a slight increase in wages.[66] Converting gute groschen and silbergroschen to pfennig, we arrive at the comparative daily wages shown in Table 8.6. Another indication of the relative wage level is a report from the Georgsmarienhütte village council president in 1865, complaining that unmarried foundry workers who migrated to the town frequently moved on. Another report mentioned "too low wages" as the reason.[67]

The establishment of the Georgsmarienhütte works did, therefore, have an effect on the social composition of the emigrant group. Within the rural lower-class group, the "miserable" were more likely to emigrate than the "poor," reversing the previous trend. On the one hand, for farmhands and day laborers, industrial jobs did not offer a significantly greater chance of securing a livelihood. On the other hand, temporary jobs in the works might enable them to save up enough money for emigration. At the same

---

65 The abbreviations here and in Table 8.6 are for an antiquated type of coinage: ggr. = gute groschen; sgr. = silbergroschen. Business report of the Georgsmarienhütte, Jan. 1858: Dep. 32 b, No. 765, 11. Report of the city building administrator (*Stadtbaumeister*), April 14, 1857: Dep 3b V, No. 518, Stadt Osnabrück, Gilde- und Polizeisachen.

66 This varied from region to region. In the Ruhr, for example, the wages for craftsmen were usually higher than those for miners; in Tecklenburg District, near Osnabrück, the wages for miners in the 1820s were higher than those for craftsmen. See Tenfelde, *Sozialgeschichte,* 115, and Gladen, *Tecklenburg,* 95. Jeschke (*Gewerberecht,* 444) confirms that industrial wages were in general higher than craftsmen's wages in the Kingdom of Hanover in the 1850s and 1860s.

67 Ott, *Kohle,* 228.

Table 8.6. *Comparative daily wages at Georgsmarienhütte*

Type of employment	Wages in gute groschen/ silbergroschen	Wages in pfennig
Other jobs, 1857	18–20 ggr.	171–90
Craftsmen, GMBHV, 1857	14 ggr.	133
Helpers, stonemasons, 1857	10–15 ggr.	95–142.5
Foundry workers, Hagen-Beckerode, 1850	12–16 ggr.	114–52[68]
Warehouse workers, Piesburg, 1863	11 ggr. 4d	136
Miners, Piesburg, 1863	15 sgr. 2d	182
Average wage, Borgloh, 1870	17 sgr. 3d	207[69]

time artisans and tertiary sector workers continued to prefer emigration, feeling that even higher wages did not compensate for the loss of status involved in becoming industrial workers. Another aspect may have played a role as well: There was no sense of the new, the "free air of the city," the attraction of the unknown, which theoretically might have made the break from the countryside and the home village easier. Before making the decision to leave, people knew what kinds of negative experiences awaited them – noise, regimentation, and relatively low wages.

The preceding interpretation of the emigration data is supported by an analysis of the living costs for three *Heuerling* families from the Bersenbrück region in the northern part of the Principality of Osnabrück in 1846 and of two Georgsmarienhütte foundry workers' families in 1877. Because these data are remarkable, I examine them in detail. Data on the income and expenditures of *Heuerling* families in an area with a high rate of emigration were collected by the district administration in Bersenbrück, whereas the household data for the foundry workers were collected in response to an appeal by the director of the Georgsmarienhütte works, Georg Wintzer, to reinstate tariffs on iron in 1878.[70] Although thirty years separates the two sets of data, it is possible to conclude that neither the *Heuerling* position nor the foundry job alone provided an acceptable standard of living, and certainly not a desirable one. This is not to say that the *Heuerleute* did not suffer; on the contrary, the industrial workers suffered just as much. It does seem,

68 For 1857, see note 65; for 1850, see *Statistik*, 70.
69 The data for 1863 and 1870 come from Ott, *Kohle*, 80, 91. The wages increased in the following years.
70 The director of the GMBHV, George Wintzer, was a member of the investigating committee for Lower Saxony; see *Protokolle über die Vernehmungen durch die Eisenenquete-Kommission* (Berlin, 1879), 247–77.

however, that the "total income"[71] of the *Heuerling* family, including earnings from second jobs and seasonal migrant work, was better able to cover
its modest needs than the foundry worker's wages alone.[72]

Wintzer gave the following well-prepared answer to the question of
"workers' conditions" before the investigating committee in 1878:

Question: "What would be the disadvantages of lowering wages?"

Answer: "Lowering wages would impoverish the people and force them to emigrate. . . . I must point out, that for a time our plant did not prevent emigration
but actually tended to encourage it: People worked hard for two, three, or four
years in order to save up the money for passage (often 300 taler) and then emigrate.
Our rural population has now gotten used to factory work, and we have employees
from all around the area, from as far away (1–2 miles) as the villages of Versmold,
Lengerich, etc."

Thus, the managers of the works were conscious of the fact that wages were
as low as they could possibly be without tipping the balance for individual
workers against accepting and remaining in industrial jobs and in favor of
emigration.

At an average wage of 65 marks per month (calculating a month as 25
shifts at a rate of 2.60 marks per shift), Worker A has a monthly surplus of
only 2.37 marks, while Worker B has a deficit of 32.40 marks. In any case,
a five-person household, considered the statistical mean at the time, did not
have enough to cover expenses.[73]

The foundry worker, like the *Heuerling* in the rural lower class of the
earlier period, was on the borderline of poverty and thus tended to opt for
emigration.

This fact must be taken into account when we ask about the motives of
individuals deciding about emigration and when we evaluate the "social
component" of that decision.[74] In our case, three factors must be weighed:
(1) the economic situation in the home region; (2) the hopes and expectations for a better life in North America as a result of emigration; and (3)
the rewards to be gained from internal migration to an industrial location.
Taking these three economic criteria into account, however, makes it
harder to understand psychological motives ("a farmer wants to stay a

---

71 Kriedte et al., *Industrialisierung*, 113.
72 For the foundry workers' household records, see *Protokolle*, 275f. The record of income and ex-
    penditures for the *Heuerleute* families is from Wrasmann, "Heuerlingswesen," 42–47. It is important
    to note that the rates of emigration and of seasonal labor migration in the Bersenbrück region were
    the highest in the Osnabrück administrative district at the time; see Bölsker-Schlicht, *Hollandgängerei*,
    171–87, 317, and Kiel, "Gründe und Folgen," 176.
73 Ott, *Kohle*, 306.
74 Marschalck, *Überseeauswanderung*, 52.

farmer") and the meaning of emigration traditions in the context of an individual's decision-making process.[75] The noneconomic motives of the emigrants in the first two waves from the subpeasant classes of the northeastern Prussian provinces, for example, were determined by three elements: a tradition of emigration, "transatlantic communication," and "emotional bonds to the land."[76]

The same conclusion seems to be valid in the present case, but in a different sense. The *Heuerling* no longer needed to emigrate in order to stay a farmer; instead, he remained at home and found a way to supplement his subsistence level agricultural income through "occupational emigration without leaving home" in the new industry that was developing at his doorstep.[77] Those who rejected this solution tended to emigrate, but not to migrate to other industrial areas of Germany. After some delay, industrial work thus replaced protoindustrial work for those individuals who, before the establishment of the Georgsmarienhütte works, had for some reason not chosen or not yet chosen emigration as an economic solution.

At least for Georgsmarienhütte, it is possible to conclude that a *Heuerling* became an *Industrieheuerling* and a tenant farmer became a "mining cottager," but a farmhand seldom became a factory worker. The farmhand personified the "transition from preindustrial poverty to industrial poverty"; he was the person Director Wintzer had in mind when he spoke of temporary work at Georgsmarienhütte in order to save up for emigration.[78]

The movement of employees from other areas to Georgsmarienhütte during the early years of the GMBHV was necessary, to be sure, but also planned. It was necessary because there were very few experienced industrial workers in the Osnabrück region, and the mine and foundry could not begin operation without trained personnel. It continued to be necessary because the local labor pool would have been unable to supply the 2,500 workers needed during the construction phase. That it was planned is clear from the fact that employees were recruited in distant locations from the very beginning, with no particular emphasis on the immediately surrounding area.[79]

---

75 Bade, "Massenwanderung," 306; Kamphoefner, *Westfalen,* 42.
76 Bade, "Massenwanderung," 305–10, esp. 306.
77 Ibid.
78 W. Fischer and G. Bajore, eds., *Die Soziale Frage: Neuere Studien zur Lage der Fabrikarbeiter in den Frühphasen der Industrialisierung* (Stuttgart, 1967), introd., 7.
79 The primary recruiting areas for Georgsmarienhütte were in three zones: the linen-producing area of northwestern Germany, the mining area in the Harz mountains, and in a few areas where industrialization had begun early on. This division can be seen from the dominant occupational structures. The regional and occupational breakdown of those migrating to Georgsmarienhütte is

The social composition of the Georgsmarienhütte work force was thus influenced strongly by in-migration, but at least as much, as pointed out in the introduction, by the emigration pattern that crystallized in the surrounding districts. For the reasons discussed, people who would have been potential workers for the GMBHV instead chose to emigrate. The new arrivals in Georgsmarienhütte therefore encountered the *Industrieheuerling* and his family, who had decided to remain at home. This confrontation determined the structure of the labor force and of the population; the relationship and its consequences, however, are topics of study in their own right.[80]

based on SPSS and dBase statistical analyses of church records from the Georgsmarienhütte parishes; see Meyer, *Schwerindustrielle Insel*, 195–310.

80 Meyer, *Schwerindustrielle Insel*, esp. 311–73. For the effects on the willingness of workers to strike, see Meyer, "Die Streikbewegungen in der Osnabrücker Montan- und Metallindustrie, 1859–1933: Eine kleine Streikgeschichte," in Ursula Alberts et al., eds., *Vom Deutschen Metallarbeiterverband zur Industriegewerkschaft Metall: Texte und Dokumente zur Geschichte der Metallarbeiter in Osnabrück* (Bramsche, 1990), 70–91.

9

Foreign Workers in and around Bremen, 1884–1918

KARL MARTEN BARFUSS

I

Due to its role as an emigration port, the city of Bremen figures prominently in the historical literature on migration. For millions of European emigrants, Bremen and Bremerhaven were the last places they experienced the Old World on their way overseas. But as the home port of the Norddeutsche Lloyd, Bremen was not only a place to pass through for overseas emigrants but also the destination of a great number of alien immigrants.[1]

At the turn of the century the proportion of foreign-language speaking inhabitants in some communities on the outskirts of Bremen was about one-third. In the community of Delmenhorst, thousands of Bohemians, Poles, Ruthenians, and Croats lived amid the local German population. In 1901 nearly 60 percent of the 840 pupils who attended Blumenthal's Catholic church spoke Polish.[2] Citizens of Bremen considered the so-called jute-quarter to be an enclave of Poles and Czechs until the mid-1930s. In 1913 some 22,000 foreign immigrants were living in Bremen or in the surrounding communities, constituting approximately 7 to 8 percent of the local population.[3] Today, they would be considered *Gastarbeiter* or "guest workers" on account of their status and living conditions.

The migration to Bremen, especially of immigrants from eastern Europe, never reached the scale of the Polish migration to the Ruhrgebiet. As a result, this migration's ethnic composition as well as the political and legal conditions to which it was subject were more diverse. The so-called Ruhr

---

1 For the only study of the immigration of non-German and German-speaking peoples to the Unter-wesergebiet before World War I, see Karl M. Barfuss, *"Gastarbeiter" in Nordwestdeutschland, 1884–1918* (Bremen, 1986).
2 Stadtgeschichtliches Dokumentationszentrum Blumenthal – Schulstatistische Erhebung vom 27. Juni 1901.
3 Cf. Barfuss, *Gastarbeiter*, 122; illustration, no. 1: "Bremen in den Grenzen von 1900."

Poles (*Ruhrpolen*) came almost exclusively from Prussia's eastern provinces.[4] Except for the Masurians, they were Catholic and all were German nationals. Moreover, Prussian anti-Polish regulations absolutely forbade the employment of foreign Poles coming from Russia and Austria-Hungary in industry. Along the Lower Weser, the Unterwesergebiet, the characteristics, structures, and interests of three jurisdictions came together – the Free Hanseatic City of Bremen, the Grand Duchy of Oldenburg, and the Prussian province of Hanover. As a result, different legal regulations concerning foreigners existed side by side with the German Reich's general Polish policy. Above all else, the multicultural character of the Unterwesergebiet makes a historical investigation of immigration into this region before World War I worthwhile.

Within the enormous overseas and continental streams of migration since the 1880s, general push and pull factors explain the influx of foreign workers to Bremen and its environs. The predominantly agricultural countries of origin were experiencing increasing economic and social impoverishment, while the receiving countries were experiencing prosperity and thus presented greater economic opportunity. At the same time, labor as a factor of production was increasingly mobile because of improvements in transportation and communication. In that way, lower costs of production could be achieved. These improvements were associated with the loosening and/ or abolition of legal obstacles to population movements across borders. Thus, the dams that had restrained migrants now opened, creating actual streams of migration.

According to Körner, the migration of alien in-migrants to the Unterwesergebiet can be classified into six groups: as group migration or individual migration; as a result of social and political tensions in the region of emigration; as a voluntary decision; as continental long-distance migration; as a mixture of migration for a short time (of sojourners or itinerant workers), long-term migration (with the intention of returning home with their savings), and permanent emigration; and as a combination of free or regular migration and state-regulated or limited migration.[5]

---

4 On Polish immigration to the Ruhrgebiet, see Christoph Klessmann, *Polnische Bergarbeiter im Ruhrgebiet, 1870–1945: Soziale Integration und nationale Subkultur einer Minderheit* (Göttingen, 1978); cf. Richard C. Murphy, *Gastarbeiter im Deutschen Reich: Polen in Bottrop, 1891–1933* (Wuppertal, 1982); Krystyna Murzynowska, *Die polnischen Erwerbsauswanderer im Ruhrgebiet während der Jahre 1880–1914* (Dortmund, 1979); Valentina M. Stefanski, *Zum Prozess der Emanzipation und Integration von Aussenseitern – Polnische Arbeitsimmigranten im Ruhrgebiet* (Dortmund, 1984). On Polish immigrants to the outskirts of Hamburg, see Elke Hauschildt, *Polnische Arbeitsmigranten in Wilhelmsburg bei Hamburg während des Kaiserreichs und der Weimarer Republik* (Dortmund, 1986).

5 Cf. Heiko Körner, *Internationale Mobilität der Arbeit: Eine empirische und theoretische Analyse der internationalen Wirtschaftsmigration im 19. und 20. Jahrhundert* (Darmstadt, 1990), 13.

II

The Free Hanseatic City of Bremen, arising out of the medieval tradition of the urban republics (*Stadtrepubliken*) and still an independent federal state (*Bundesstaat*) in the German Reich, concentrated for centuries on the export trade and shipping industry with close connections to the United States in particular.[6] In the nineteenth century tobacco, cotton, wool, and coffee were the most important imported goods. The empty cargo holds on their way to America were used, as much as possible, for the transport of emigrants.[7] In Bremen, the great merchants and shipowners set the tone not only in economic but also in political affairs. Until after World War I, these patricians formed a majority in Bremen's *Senat,* the city's main governing institution.

From the founding of the Reich (1871) to 1888, Bremen (and Hamburg) stayed out of the German customs union (*Zollverein*) in deference to its worldwide trading interests. When Germany's industrialization began in the middle of the nineteenth century, the economy of Bremen was both positively and negatively affected. On the one hand, the growing trade in imported raw materials expanded Bremen's industrial sales markets; on the other hand, the increase in protective tariffs vis-à-vis other countries hindered the export of finished goods and agricultural products into Prussia and Oldenburg. These protective tariffs crippled the establishment of a competitive industry in this Hanseatic city.[8] In order to keep pace with industrialization, wealthy merchants and shipowners had, since the 1870s, looked for reasonable opportunities to invest their capital in factories. They located these factories just outside the city limits in the territories of Prussian Hanover and Oldenburg. After the city joined the *Zollverein* in 1888, industrialists also began investing in the city of Bremen itself.

New industry was concentrated in textiles; the processing of other raw materials, especially food; the extraction of iron; and shipbuilding. Bremen's industrial sector had close connections to established commercial firms and shipping lines, above all to the Norddeutsche Lloyd. Their common interests included the safeguarding of markets, the full utilization of transport capacity, and the expansion of shipping tonnage. The close relations among Bremen's economic interests were also clearly visible in the composition of the boards of directors and in the fact that banking houses directed capital

6 Referring to the economic relationship between the United States of America and Bremen, see Ludwig Beutin, *Bremen und Amerika* (Bremen, 1953).
7 Cf. Herbert Schwarzwälder, *Geschichte der Freien Hansestadt Bremen* (Bremen, 1976), 2:156.
8 Cf. Schwarzwälder, *Geschichte der Freien Hansestadt Bremen,* 345–51.

into their own enterprises. The same men sat on many management committees and supervisory bodies and numerous patrician families were related to each other. Through the oligarchic structures of the upper-middle class, reigning families influenced the whole community and shaped the political culture with their traditional, deeply rooted civic pride. In order to enhance Bremen's prestige, they donated generously to public institutions, promoted the arts, and fostered a charitable sense of patriarchal welfare. But they also did everything imaginable to assert their economic privileges against the growing pressure of the new industrial middle and working classes.

The way factories were structured internally reflected both the economic and political relations in the city as well as the trading houses and shipping companies upon which these relations were based. Consequently, an important characteristic of other German enterprises, those founded by self-employed tradesmen, engineers, or tinkers, who built from scratch successful companies through product innovation and from whom companies took their identities, was missing. Bremen enterprises were much more mass producers and appliers of existing technologies. They were established as joint-stock companies outside the city limits and were run for the most part by managers who were principally obliged to satisfy the expectations of the shareholders. Labor relations were conducted along purely rational and pragmatic lines and were marked by great anonymity. This fact remains an important characteristic of companies that have a high percentage of foreign workers.

Bremen's economic and social structures account for the city's political and social polarization and partly explain the bloody suppression of the *Bremer Räterepublik* between January 10 and February 3, 1919. After World War I it became obvious that Bremen's traditional economy would not survive. The secretiveness and lack of public control as well as the one-sided orientation of the industry made it impossible to switch to promising new industries like chemicals or the manufacture of electrical equipment. The merchants' speculative mentality blocked long-term planning and the development of an industrial orientation. Accordingly, Bremen was much more deeply affected by the world economic depression of the 1930s than other German cities.[9]

In the 1870s new factories were founded outside of the city and, beginning in 1888, new industrial plants were established within Bremen itself. Infrastructural improvements were made: new harbors, streets, and public

---

9 For references to the financial and economical crisis of Bremen in the 1930s, see Otmar Escher, *Die Wirtschafts- und Finanzkrise in Bremen 1931 und der Fall Schröderbank* (Frankfurt/Main, 1988).

buildings. The high point was reached in 1884 when two companies were established that would become market leaders of the Reich and, at times, of the whole European continent: the Bremer Wollkämmerei (BWK) in Blumenthal and the Norddeutsche Wollkämmerei and Kammgarnspinnerei, or Nordwolle for short, in Delmenhorst. These two spinning mills used the raw wool imported at Bremen. They delivered semifinished products to the textile finishing industry. In competition with Dundee in Scotland, Bremen became a center of the European jute industry. In contrast, the small cotton spinning mill in Grohn was insignificant. Shortly before the beginning of World War I the industrial giants of the textile industry, situated in Bremen and its surrounding area, employed some ten thousand male and female workers.[10]

The shipbuilding industry of the Unterwesergebiet expanded as well. At first they constructed merchant ships and later, supported by the naval law of 1898, built warships. The number of workers grew dramatically, from approximately two hundred in 1895 to about ten thousand in 1914. The construction industry boomed as thousands of skilled and unskilled workers were needed in order to expand the harbor and to redirect the course of the river. As a matter of course, production at Bremen's brickworks also increased. These industries were dependent on mobile seasonal workers. Trade and services expanded as well.[11]

The rapid expansion of enterprises outstripped the ability of the local labor market to meet the demand. For various reasons, the available manpower was limited: In the nineteenth century the excess of births over deaths was comparatively low in northwestern Germany and the close proximity to ports of emigration encouraged the tendency toward overseas emigration. The greater part of the surplus population, moreover, was needed in the expanding agricultural sector.

In northwestern Germany, the subdivision of farms through inheritance was unknown and, therefore, most farms maintained their integrity. Younger sons set up new farms of their own, married, or stayed as unmarried employees on the farms of their older brothers who had inherited the family farms. Since the agricultural revolution of the eighteenth century, farmers improved their yields significantly, due to the privatization of common lands, the introduction of artificial fertilizer, and new modes of cultivation. At that time, governments supported the so-called internal colonization of uninhabited peat bogs to the north and west of Bremen. As

10 Cf. Barfuss, *Gastarbeiter*, 38.
11 Ibid., 61–79.

a consequence, large parts of the rural population surplus, consisting of a natural increase and people who became unemployed because of new agricultural machinery, settled there. Frequently, they supplemented their incomes with additional jobs. Proof of the region's considerable land reserves lay in its low population density, which in the area between the Dutch border and the Elbe River was about fifty inhabitants per square kilometer in 1900. In some districts, the density was only twenty or thirty inhabitants per square kilometer.

Furthermore, oppressive social dependencies and bondages were kept in check. Certainly, differences existed between the rich and the poor, between landowners and so-called *Heuerleute* – a combination of a tenant farmer and agricultural laborer – as well as between farmers and *Gesinde* (laborers and servants), but these differences were moderate when compared to the manors located east of the Elbe. Consequently, fewer people emigrated. Companies were unable to resort to local unemployed workers with industrial experience as long as the regional economy, with its agricultural orientation, did not experience crises and mass unemployment. The fact that in Bremen and surrounding areas agriculture, trade, and shipping were dominant created a psychological resistance to industrial work. It was frowned upon because of its strict rules, its environmental pollution, its anonymity, and a working cycle dictated by machines. When young women took up factory work, moreover, their chances for marriage befitting their rank worsened.[12]

That is why the industries of the Unterwesergebiet, especially jute processing and wool processing, had little success with the recruitment of native workers. Job notices placed in local papers by Nordwolle and BWK after 1884 met with little response. Although some companies offered wages that were at the top of the local wage scale, the material incentives were not enough to overcome the psychological and social prejudices against factory work. Therefore, the solid agricultural labor market could not be transformed into an industrial one.[13]

The labor force during the industrialization of the Unterwesergebiet was characterized by the fact that labor mobility was necessary for the seasonal work in the construction and in the textile industries, in contrast to industries with year-round production and longer training period requirements, where employers valued low levels of personnel turnover and long-term employment. With few exceptions, prior experience and skills were un-

12 Ibid., 28–35.
13 Ibid., 39–61.

necessary. Training periods were short and, because of the low technical level, even foreign-language workers were eligible for employment. The textile industry in particular expected modesty among its workers when it came to material demands. In order to assert themselves against domestic and foreign competitors, to meet the profit expectations of their share-holders, and to build up reserves for times of economic crisis, employers paid comparatively low wages. Labor reserves were created specifically to guard against possible fluctuations in the prices of raw materials and the consequent rapid shifts in demand. Therefore, the initial wage differential reversed quickly and increases in wages trailed those of other industries. Similarly, the shipbuilding and the construction industries paid unskilled or semiskilled workers badly. The gigantic program to build a blue-water navy at the turn of the century (*Kriegsflottenprogramm*) forced the shipyards to operate on low wages. The expansion of the port was not to increase Bremen's already heavy debt load. This explains the state and national interest in low-paid, foreign workers.[14]

Specific employment policies encouraged the strikingly low wages paid by the textile industry. Workers were recruited from underdeveloped regions, where wages remained substandard. To ward off the tendency of the recruited workers to organize or to switch to other industries, the textile industry established numerous so-called welfare institutions or *Wohlfahrts-einrichtungen*. These included company apartments, crèches, hospitals, churches, and consumer cooperatives. An individual who changed his or her employer or who joined a union ran the risk of losing his or her shelter and all other social services. Lujo Brentano accordingly called these social services, "social fetters." When factories expanded, additional workers were recruited, forcing the residents of the company tenements to move closer together. Foreign workers helped newcomers belonging to their ethnic group to adapt to the new situation. Above all, the social services provided by the company maintained downward pressure on wages and increased structural dependencies.[15]

A further characteristic of the demands placed on workers in these industries was a willingness to endure environmental pollution like dust, noise, or stench and to submit without protest to the management's will. It was assumed that workers were immune to union demands and socialist agitation. The agricultural laborers from eastern European and East Elbian manors were considered to be unenlightened, simple, and accustomed to

---

14 Ibid., 61–72; cf. Rolf Rumschüssel, "Die Lage der polnischen Arbeiter und Arbeiterinnen bei der Wollkämmerei von 1886 und 1914," manuscript, Oldenburg, 1989, 87.
15 Cf. Barfuss, *Gastarbeiter*, 140–43.

subordination; it was widely believed they were therefore predestined to work in the new factories. The textile industry kept wages low by prohibiting union activities and by occasional wholesale replacement of the labor force. As a result, pressures for modernization and rationalization were relieved; and as a consequence, increases in productivity were low and increases in wages became impossible. A vicious circle made factories dependent on low wages and recruitment of workers from the periphery of the labor market, where poverty caused a "self-sustaining migration."[16]

An especially drastic example is that of Hemelingen's jute factory. In 1911 the factory had to stop production temporarily because it could not attract workers even from eastern Europe and was unable to increase wages in order to recruit local workers. The costs of a temporary shutdown were lower than the costs of increased wages. Only when factory owners could no longer resort to foreign workers, following World War I, did the pressure to rationalize become stronger. Companies which neither modernized nor diversified suffered heavy losses, and, in the end, many, like Hemelingen's jute factory, closed their doors for good.

III

The labor market of the Unterwesergebiet was roughly divided into two parts during that time. The first consisted of relatively well-paid jobs that required training, special skills, and mental abilities. The second consisted of unskilled or semiskilled jobs with low social status and poor pay. Germans or German-speaking immigrants worked in the first part; the second part depended on foreign labor.

In contemporary debates, Social Democrats maintained that foreign workers replaced local ones because they had few if any demands and were uninterested in unionization, both of which kept wages low. While this thesis is questionable for a number of reasons, it certainly did not apply to the Unterwesergebiet. Foreign workers were hired for inferior jobs because of a lack of local workers. As will be discussed, this secondary segment of the labor market was characterized by processes of rotation and exchange. Little mobility occurred between the two segments because of the differences in skills as well as for psychological and social reasons. These two labor market segments of local and foreign workers corresponded exactly to Cairnes's economic model of "noncompeting groups."[17] In fact, differ-

16 Cf. Körner, *Internationale Mobilität der Arbeit*, 89–99.
17 John E. Cairnes, *Some Leading Principles of Political Economy Newly Expounded*, 2d ed. (1874; reprint:

ences in income and status were transmitted to the second generation of immigrants and beyond.

Since the establishment of Nordwolle and BWK, foreign workers came from areas with worse living conditions and few opportunities. The effects were especially pronounced in the agricultural regions of the eastern part of the German Reich, in the provinces of Posen, West and East Prussia, and Upper Silesia, as well as in neighboring Polish areas of Russia (Congress Poland) and Austria-Hungary (Galicia). Poverty, dependency, and hopelessness characterized these mostly rural areas.[18]

In 1892 Max Weber described "the living conditions of the agricultural workers in eastern Germany" on behalf of the Society for Social Policy (Verein für Sozialpolitik).[19] Agricultural reforms and industrialization led to changes in the patriarchal estates in the east. Such estates became large farms organized along capitalist principles and labor relations were largely subject to profit maximization. Countless estate laborers were dismissed on account of rationalization measures. Others had to rely on seasonal work to earn supplementary incomes or had to migrate permanently. Conditions in Galicia, where people suffered from hunger, epidemics, lack of freedom, high infant mortality, and hopelessness, were even worse than those in the Prussian East.[20]

The discrepancies between the industrial centers of the western and central parts of the Reich and the eastern regions were so obvious that even low-wage jobs in industries in the German Northwest held a great attraction for East Elbian laborers. This poses the question whether migration overseas provided an alternative and whether Bremen and the Unterwesergebiet were merely temporary stopovers.[21]

Nevertheless, by the 1890s acquisition of free land in the United States was no longer possible. As a result, America lost its attraction for would-be agricultural emigrants. From now on there was no possibility for them to maintain their agricultural way of life. In addition, the economic crisis of 1893 made conditions even worse. Forced to choose between working in

London, 1884). Cf. Gerhard Stavenhagen, *Geschichte der Wirtschaftstheorie,* 2d ed. (Göttingen, 1957), 93–94.

18 Cf. Barfuss, *Gastarbeiter,* illustration, no. 2: "Abwanderungsgebiete."

19 Cf. Max Weber, *Die Verhältnisse der Landarbeiter im ostelbischen Deutschland* (Leipzig, 1892).

20 Cf. Barfuss, *Gastarbeiter,* 112.

21 For some evidence on overseas migration of textile workers, see the files of the registration office of Delmenhorst, Stadtarchiv Delmenhorst; also, see Marlene Ellerkamp, "Textilarbeiterinnen im Kaiserreich – Krankheit, Lebensweise, soziale Sicherung und Protest in Bremen," Ph.D. diss., Universität Bremen, 1988, 544. Ellerkamp's study has since been published as *Industriearbeit, Krankheit und Geschlecht: Zu den sozialen Kosten der Industrialisierung: Bremer Textilarbeiterinnen, 1870–1914* (Göttingen, 1991).

German or American industry, more and more potential migrants decided to stay in Germany where economic development was becoming more dynamic. They saved the money that they would have spent on the passage and avoided the risks of a completely new beginning. At home, moreover, they could remain in close contact with their relatives. Thus, only a small portion of the migrants worked in the industries of the Unterwesergebiet to earn money of the voyage.

In some cases the original intention to emigrate abroad may have been revised by employment experiences and social integration in the Lower Weser region. Labor migrants remained loyal to their homelands and migrants from eastern Europe, according to the reports of Bremen's Emigration Certification Office (Nachweisungs-Bureau für Auswanderer), planned to limit their stay in America to only a few years at a time but repeat their stay often.[22]

Migration to Germany was organized in different ways. In the absence of a public employment exchange, companies recruited either through their own agents, often workers who came from their respective ethnic group, or through other agents; even the agents of the transatlantic shipping companies were sometimes involved. Since 1905 the most important institution to enforce national labor market policies and regulations was the Central Office for Field Hands (Feldarbeiterzentrale). After 1912 the name was changed to Central Office for German Workers (Deutsche Arbeiterzentrale).[23]

Labor migrants came either individually or in groups. German-speaking people and people from neighboring regions usually migrated alone; in contrast, foreign-language migrants preferred to travel in groups. They included gangs of itinerant workers, for example, bricklayers, and were at-

22 Informative insights into cycles and causes of overseas migrations are given by the annual reports of the "Nachweisungsbureaus für Auswanderer Bremen," Archiv der Handelskammer Bremen, Best. A III 3. In the annual report of 1895 you will find the following notices: "The reduction in migration that started in 1892 has been going on till the beginning of this year. . . . The Bohemians and Moravians were the only foreign emigrants who went to the agricultural areas. This migration is getting less and less like the one of the Germans. The other foreign emigrants, particularly Hungarians, Slovaks, Galicians, and Poles, go to the industrial areas. Seldom do they settle down in America. They mostly return home to their families after some years and often they repeat such journeys. These emigrants have a low living standard and consequently they save 800–1,000 marks a year in America. They send their savings home to their family. More than half of these workers are illiterate. If the attempts to expel those people from America were successful, the poor districts of Austria-Hungary, where they come from, would be seriously affected."
23 On the organization of foreigners' recruitment and the political and legal conditions, cf. Klaus J. Bade, "Vom Auswanderungsland zum 'Arbeitseinfuhrland': Kontinentale Zuwanderung und Ausländer beschäftigung in Deutschland im späten 19. und frühen 20. Jahrhundert," in Klaus J. Bade, ed., *Auswanderer– Wanderarbeiter– Gastarbeiter: Bevölkerung, Arbeitsmarkt und Wanderung in Deutschland seit der Mitte des 19. Jahrhunderts,* 2 vols. (Ostfildern, 1984), 2:433–85.

tracted from more distant areas through announcements that advertised the opening or expansion of factories. Ruthenian workers from eastern Galicia migrated in groups under the leadership of Greek Orthodox clerics, who represented the mostly illiterate workers in negotiations, supported them spiritually, and eased their adaptation to the new situation. Beginning in 1905 the Employment Agency for Ruthenian Workers (Vermittlungsstelle für ruthenische Arbeiter) looked after their placement in jobs. Workers who had left a company were generally replaced with in-migrants from the same group or with members of their families. The older the company, the more common was the practice of replacing workers. The final result was that whole families worked for the same company. Employers tried to hire members of the second generation: Young people received gifts and bonuses if they committed themselves to work for these companies after finishing school. In company-owned facilities young people were already introduced to their future job before they actually started work. The costs of their recruitment and of their training were thus lower than for new foreign workers.

Companies frequently complained about high commissions charged by outside recruiting agents. Newly recruited workers often felt that they themselves had been deceived or led astray by misleading or wrong information regarding the living conditions in areas to which they migrated. Illiterate workers were especially prone to become victims of such deceptions.[24]

A comparison of the different colonies of immigrants of the Unterwesergebiet shows differences in the ethnic composition. Migration to Prussian Blumenthal came mostly from Polish East Elbia and was quite homogeneous; migrants to Bremen and, especially, to Delmenhorst, which belonged to Oldenburg, were heterogeneous: Germans from Bohemia and Poland, Poles from eastern Germany and Galicia, Ruthenians, Croats, Hungarians, and Rumanians. Apart from the Poles, Hemelingen, which belonged to Prussia, attracted a great number of Ruthenians. What accounts for the differences in ethnic composition in such a small area during the period of migration from east to the west?

The reasons for the developments in and around Bremen can be gathered into three groups: first, the development of the connections between the areas of emigration and immigration; second, the specific strategies companies pursued to minimize labor costs; and third, the different political and legal structural conditions of worker recruitment.

24 Cf. Barfuss, *Gastarbeiter,* 115–21.

What were the individual connections between the regions of in- and out-migration? Nordwolle received a great share of its workers from Sudetenland, which was situated in Bohemia and, therefore, belonged to Austria-Hungary. The basis for this relationship was that the founders of Nordwolle already owned a company in Neudek, Bohemia. In addition, the resident population of the Sudetenland had experience in industrial work. Furthermore, the level of economic development was lower in Bohemia, a fact that aided recruitment. With appropriate promises regarding wages, people were brought to Delmenhorst and later on to Bremen and to the jute industry of Hemelingen. The German Bohemians formed their own colony in Delmenhorst. After a very short time they had settled in and, as they were German-speaking and skilled workers, they had achieved good social standing. The experience of the very mobile workers coming from Eichsfeld was similar. Situated in the northern part of the Thuringian Forest, this poor region had an excess of labor.[25] Together with the Bohemians they formed a new Catholic parish in an area that originally had been Protestant.

After futile attempts to hire local workers, the Bremer Wollkämmerei sent an agent in 1886 to the sugar beet region in central Germany. His task was to recruit *Sachsengänger,* or itinerant Polish agricultural workers, who were employed as cheap labor in the labor-intensive harvesting of sugar beets in the area around Magdeburg. Because the Polish labor gangs had already departed when the Blumenthaler agent arrived, he followed a group of female workers home to the county of Adelnau (Odolanow) in the Prussian province of Posen. The agent succeeded in concluding labor contracts with more than forty people and brought them back by train to Blumenthal. The arrival of the foreign female workers caused such a sensation that even a novel was written about it. Over the course of many years Adelnau became the main recruitment area for BWK because of chain migration. In the period from 1886 to 1943, 2,700 immigrants coming from Adelnau were officially registered in Blumenthal. "Transplanted villages" arose and Polish colonies developed in Blumenthal, Grohn, and Lüssum. By the turn of the century, in-migrants comprised one-third of the total population.[26] For the companies, the use of existing relationships to recruit workers had

---

25 Cf. Karl Haendly, "Bauern und Weber im Eichsfeld: Geschichte eines deutschen Kleinstaats, seiner Wirtschaft und der Menschen, die ihn bewohnten, 1897–1933," Ph.D. diss., Universität Köln, 1945.

26 Cf. Barfuss, *Gastarbeiter,* 50, 117. On the importance of chain-migration for the cultural adaptability of Germans in America, see Walter D. Kamphoefner, " 'Entwurzelt' oder 'verpflanzt?' Zur Bedeutung der Kettenwanderung für die Einwandererakkulturation in Amerika," in Bade, *Auswanderer – Wanderarbeiter – Gastarbeiter,* 1:321–49.

the advantage of lower recruitment costs; for the immigrants, settlement in a "transplanted village" facilitated integration into migrant society.

The specific relationship between Blumenthal and Adelnau was accidental, but it was part of the general direction of the migration movement. Unlike the BWK, the companies situated in Bremen, Hemelingen, and, above all, in Delmenhorst did not succeed in using a specific regional labor market in the long term. Because of these firms' wage strategies and because of various political and legal factors, the picture we have of their employees is highly differentiated.

Companies' recruitment strategies aimed at minimizing labor costs. Due to continuous economic growth in the German Reich since the mid-1890s, which was only interrupted by short-term recessions, shortages in the labor supply soon became apparent. Workers left the agricultural labor market for industry and the building trades, especially canal construction. As a result, wages for all kinds of labor had to be raised. For this reason Bremen's textile industry, excepting the BWK, increasingly had to recruit people coming from the eastern European periphery of the labor market. In other words, in order to replace workers that had migrated, or to find workers needed for expansion, the textile mills had to extend their recruitment area to eastern Europe.

By the middle of the 1890s the migration from Bohemia and from the Eichsfeld came to an end because well-paid jobs were available locally. As a result, the recruitment of Polish workers from eastern Germany was intensified. Since the turn of the century Poles came from western Galicia in Austria-Hungary, which was a third area of recruitment; and after 1905 Ruthenians from eastern Galicia and Croats came. The ethnic structure of Delmenhorst changed accordingly.

After 1905 the proportion of German immigrants arriving in Delmenhorst also increased, as the expansionary phase of German big industry ended. At the same time, small-scale industries and service enterprises grew up around big industry. Jobs in these two sectors paid well and their workers enjoyed a higher social standing. New industries, which were not subject to the wage policies and recruiting pressures of the textile industry, could offer workers higher pay. Under these conditions, the fluctuation of the foreign workers was not higher than that of native workers. During the early phases of industrialization, the mobility of labor remained high,[27] but when evolving economic structures stabilized and when workers were fi-

---

27 On the term "Durchgangsbevölkerung" (emigrants passing through), see David Crew, "Regionale Mobilität und Arbeiterklasse: Das Beispiel Bochum, 1880–1901," *Geschichte und Gesellschaft* 1 (1975): 99.

nancially able to buy housing, the number of transients and sojourners decreased.[28]

Differences in the ethnic composition of foreign workers were also based
on the legal and political framework of recruitment. Prussian policy toward
Poles had played a significant role in this history since the Bismarck era.
The new nationalism of the late nineteenth century dictated that the Polish
people who had been incorporated into Prussia with the partitions of their
homeland in the late eighteenth century were to be Germanized. Concurrently, Prussia prohibited the migration of Poles from Austria-Hungary or
Russia and, in 1885, expelled about 32,000 foreign Poles from the country.

Legally, Prussian Poles were German citizens and thus enjoyed unlimited
freedom of movement within the Reich; but they were under considerable
pressure to assimilate and this pressure steadily increased. The climax was
reached when the infamous language paragraph or *Sprachenparagraph* was
included in the *Reichsvereinsgesetz* (Reich Association Law) of 1908. This
meant that – with some exceptions – use of the Polish language was prohibited in public meetings. These anti-Polish regulations were enforced not
only in ancestral Polish areas but also in areas of in-migration. The pressure
created resistance on the part of the Polish people and increased Polish
nationalism, which was supported by large colonies, including those in the
Unterwesergebiet.

From the 1890s onward, however, nationalist policies came into conflict
with economic interests. Migration overseas or to the middle and western
parts of the Reich emptied eastern Germany of its surplus labor force. Industry in eastern Germany suffered from a labor shortage (*Leutenot*) and
some officials even briefly thought of "importing" Chinese contracted laborers. Blending national and economic interests, large land owners in
1890–91 forced the creation of a special status: the foreign-Polish seasonal
worker (*ausländischer-polnischer Saisonarbeiter*). Amended over time, this status
permitted Poles from outside the Reich to work as seasonal laborers in
agriculture in Prussia's eastern provinces from spring to late autumn. Later
this permission to work on a seasonal basis was extended to all of Prussia.
But they were forced to return (*Rückkehrzwang*) to their native country in
winter. This system of rotating foreign labor prevented permanent settlement and the so-called Polonization of the eastern provinces. In addition,
seasonal workers had to be single; families were only permitted in exceptional cases.

In 1908 Prussia introduced obligatory identity cards (*Legitimierungszwang*)

---

28 Cf. Barfuss, *Gastarbeiter*, 122–33.

for foreign workers. Only those workers who could give proof of their prospective employment received a "card of legitimacy" and were entitled to enter Prussia. The card possessed a disciplinary function: If a worker left his job without an official termination of the employment contract, he committed *Kontraktbruch* (breach of contract), forfeited his card of legitimacy and his wages, and as a rule, was expelled from the country. The task of legitimizing and controlling foreign workers was assigned to the German Agency for Farm Workers, which, in competition with private agents, also recruited laborers.

Although *Legitimationszwang* applied to all foreign workers, *Rückkehrzwang* or the obligation to return home remained a discriminatory practice restricted to Polish seasonal workers from abroad. In order to identify foreign Poles easily, their legitimacy cards were color coded. One of the effects of these restrictive regulations was the development of a black market for legitimacy papers, involving thefts and counterfeiting. Foreign Poles also tried to pass as aliens of other nationalities in order to circumvent forced repatriation. Discrimination and the disciplined treatment of foreign workers continued, moreover, by restricting their freedom of assembly and association and by special provisions in the labor law.[29]

Non-Polish workers from abroad were neither subject to *Rückkehrzwang* nor limited in their employment opportunities to agriculture. Of special importance in this regard were the Ruthenians and/or Ukrainians from eastern Galicia. For various reasons they were especially appreciated: Economically, their demands were extremely modest and they were immune to union influence; politically, they were antagonistic toward Poles. The political and social tensions in eastern Galicia, where the Poles, although the minority, provided the social upper classes – especially the landed aristocracy – and where the Ruthenians felt themselves oppressed, provided the background for this antagonism. In the interests of Ruthenian workers, the Ruthenian National Committee supported Prussia's anti-Polish agitation and thereby ingratiated itself with German authorities. The enmity between Poles and Ruthenians was carried as cultural baggage into the areas of in-migration. As a result, companies deemed it advisable to separate Poles and Ruthenians in order to maintain peaceful working conditions.[30]

The status of "seasonal worker" for foreign Poles, the *Legitimationszwang,* and the German Agency for Farm Workers were the main foci of Prussia's Polish policy. However, this policy could only succeed if other German

29 Ibid., 79–90.
30 Ibid., 90–93.

federal states did not circumvent it. Prussian authorities suspected that foreign Poles would winter in neighboring German states instead of returning
home during the so-called waiting period or *Karenzzeit*. Therefore, Prussia's
authorities pressured other federal states "in the national interest" to adopt
their regulations.

Companies in Bremen and Delmenhorst already employed hundreds of
Poles from western Galicia. Among them were many seasonal workers who
were obliged by Prussian law to return to their homes abroad but who went
to Bremen and Delmenhorst in order to stay permanently in the area. When
asked by the city senate for its opinion, Bremen's chamber of commerce
argued that application of Prussian regulations would severely hamper the
interests of Bremen's industry. It asked the senate to reject Prussian demands. But in order not to snub all-powerful Prussia the senate came up
with a dual strategy: They agreed to a fundamental loyalty to Prussia but
rejected the expulsion of Galician Poles from Bremen as long as no common
policy had been agreed upon for the Reich. That is why many Galician
Poles continued to work in Bremen's jute industry even after World
War I.

Developments in the Grand Duchy of Oldenburg were quite different.
Here the government adopted a much more rigorous policy and adapted
many of the Prussian regulations, including the deportation of most Galician
Poles. They took this action despite protests from the city of Delmenhorst,
which supported the interests of its big industries. But in other respects
Oldenburg failed to support Prussia's anti-Pole policy because it was foreign
to its tradition.[31] Croats and Ruthenians, who were not obligated to return
home, replaced the Galician Poles. Within a few years, the Ruthenian colony in Delmenhorst increased to more than a thousand people, due to
intense recruitment by the textile industry. Croatian immigrants numbered
in the hundreds; small groups of Hungarians and Rumanians arrived as well.

In Prussian Blumenthal the responsible *Landrat* or chief district administrator enforced the labor regulations from the start. Foreign Poles were
not tolerated. The recruitment of Ruthenians or other foreigners was not
necessary because a sufficient number of workers came by chain migration
from among Poles from eastern Prussia as well as from members of the
second generation. Moreover, we cannot exclude the possibility that management sought the ethnic homogeneity of its employees in order to avoid
the transfer of national rivalries to the shop floor. By contrast, in Hemelingen, which was also Prussian but which was subject to a different *Landrat*,

31 Ibid., 95–102.

the temporary employment of Galician Poles was tolerated. Nevertheless, over the years Ruthenian workers were favored in recruitment here as well.[32]

In sum, the composition of the immigrant colony in the lower, secondary segment of the labor market was a complex expression of different political conditions, specific recruitment philosophies of big industry, and accidental conjunctures. In their totality, however, they reflected the general dynamic and thrust of continental migration.

IV

The living conditions of immigrants depended on worldwide industrial competition. Accordingly, industrial companies tried to minimize their costs and jute factories paid the least of all. The pay level at German jute factories could not exceed – by an appreciable amount – that of their Indian and Scottish competitors, though import duties and greater productivity permitted a somewhat higher wage level. Consequently, the contrast between wages of foreign workers and the local population was quite obvious. The workers of the jute factory formed a special caste, similar to those of the colonial system, and were stigmatized as "jute-proletariat" by native workers. The immigrants were also isolated in company housing, which became enclaves of foreignness.

The immigrant workers were predominantly young single men and women. Due to the private and public housing shortages they were accommodated in company housing, which, owing to their appearance and strict regulations, were called barracks. Married workers had the chance to get a company flat. According to the lease, they had to take in newcomers when no unoccupied flats were available. For a small amount of money, newcomers slept in the corridors or in the tiny rooms of these flats. The tenants thereby added to their low incomes, an especially important supplement when mothers with small children did not work. Not surprisingly, the number of boarders increased with the number of children. The dreadful crowdedness of many flats was a real danger to health and morality. These circumstances caused communities to enact housing regulations for boarders (*Quartiergängerordnung*) in order to remedy the worst problems.[33]

A contemporary statistical inquiry in Bremen verified that the migrant workers usually lodged with fellow countrymen. The company tenements

32 Ibid., 96.
33 Ibid., 144–52.

and barracks developed into colonies that assumed the character of ghettos. Here, inhabitants could speak their own language, cultivate their customs and traditions, and they were able to cushion the cultural transition. Seen in this way the insufficient housing conditions made it easier for immigrants to settle down and stave off pressures to assimilate (Delmenhorst). In 1905 approximately 350 Ruthenian and Croatian workers were crowding together into about fifty flats, twenty-five by forty meters square. At night, the entrance to the flat was locked and the grounds were guarded by a warden and a dog.[34] The effect of these housing conditions was that the number of unmarried couples, illegitimate children, and infanticides, as well as the rates of infant mortality, increased.

The circumstances in Blumenthal were quite different. At first newcomers had to stay in barracks, but the Prussian *Landrat,* supported by the BWK, founded an exemplary housing cooperative. He followed enlightened sociopolitical ideals, but his intent was to have the immigrants settle down and assimilate quickly. In 1912 the Savings and Building Society (*Spar- und Bauverein*) accommodated nearly 3,500 occupants, who worked in the textile and shipbuilding industries. Each house had an extensive garden plot, which corresponded to the needs of the rural immigrants. By cultivating these plots the tenants improved their income as well as their social standing in the rural society of Blumenthal. The effect was a decrease in the personnel turnover in the factories, yielding a more reliably permanent work force. The *Spar- und Bauverein* of Blumenthal was important for the integration of Poles from eastern Germany. There are reasons to believe that the *Landrat* awarded flats only to immigrants considered loyal. That means that the Poles unconditionally had to become Germans.[35]

The working and living conditions had an influence on the upbringing and schooling of the immigrants' children. As infants, they could be sent to the daytime nurseries. As pupils, they normally attended a Catholic denominational school, at which they were largely isolated from native pupils. In 1909 nonsocialist politicians in Bremen defended the grants to the Catholic private school with the argument that the children of foreign-language immigrants could not hinder native children educated in Catholic schools. Private or public Catholic schools had inferior facilities compared with Protestant schools. Teachers were badly paid, often overworked, and had to endure crowded classrooms and badly behaved children. These circum-

---

34 Ibid., 143, 150.
35 Ibid., 148–49.

stances slowed down the integration of the second generation but also eased the pressure for assimilation. Therefore, Catholic immigrants preferred the private Catholic schools to the public schools in spite of the school fees they had to pay.[36]

According to criminal statistics, the crime rate of immigrants was quite high. But offenses were caused by the bad living conditions and not because of a criminal mentality among the immigrants, as the public widely believed. Assaults were frequent, but these were restricted to the immigrant community. Few offenses against natives were reported.[37]

Marriages were usually endogamous given the segregation, the denominational barriers, and the struggle to maintain ethnic identity and relationships in "transplanted villages." An analysis of the marriage registers in Delmenhorst shows that foreign workers of the second generation had cut themselves off from natives as well as from other fellow countrymen. Germans and Czechs from Bohemia typically did not marry Poles or Ruthenians. Even the Poles coming from Posen seldom married Poles from Upper Silesia. If a Protestant married a Catholic, the Catholic would normally abandon his or her denomination. In most cases, the children would have been baptized Protestant. This pattern was logical since if a Catholic individual agreed to a mixed marriage, she or he already signaled a willingness to acculturate.[38]

Due to their peasant backgrounds, immigrant families remained large. Contact with industrial civilization, however, resulted in fewer children in the second and third generations, as these adapted to the conditions found in the host society.[39] The rate of exogamous marriages increased, too, although the second generation mostly married endogamously.

An analysis of social mobility shows the remarkable degree to which those in the immigration generation never rose above the level of worker and, at most, only advanced within their factories. Even the second generation seldom attained skilled positions or reached a higher social status. With time, however, immigrants did establish retail businesses and shops for handicrafts. Although those in the second generation abandoned many of their parents' traditions, they were not completely accepted by the host society. This conflict made it difficult for the second generation to find its own identity and to improve its social position. Lateral mobility – movement to other

36 Ibid., 159–67.
37 Ibid., 157–58.
38 Ibid., 168–71.
39 Ibid., 158.

industries – increased; vertical mobility remained nearly impossible on account of insufficient educational opportunities, uncertainties in behavior, and social prejudices.[40]

Prejudices were based not only on the alien appearance of the immigrants but also on the economic motives behind their recruitment and on their living conditions. Consequently, foreignness and poverty became the ascribed or real marks of the immigrants. The high rate of illegitimate children and the great number of people "living in sin" were regarded as tokens of immorality. In Delmenhorst, the familiar quotation, "They are living in a Polish way" (*se läwt polsch*) stood for the assumedly immoral or "dirty" behavior of unmarried couples. The absence of curtains at the windows was also interpreted as a lack of culture. That is why a quarter of Blumenthal was called "Little Cameroon" (*Klein-Kamerun*). Their unsatisfying progress at school – actually caused by bad school conditions – was regarded as a token of the inferior intelligence of the Slavs. In later decades, Nazi propaganda intensified such prejudices.[41]

The German workers, including social democrats and trade unionists, were not free of prejudices. Although they professed the idea of proletarian internationalism, in their everyday life they considered foreign workers the cause of low wages. According to the Social Democratic newspaper, *Bremer Bürgerzeitung,* the immigrants were ruled by "rotgut and clergymen" (*Fusel und Pfaff*) and were submissive and ignorant. These negative views expressed not only the prevailing xenophobia but also the experiences of previous labor struggles. At first, the newcomers, mostly illiterate, did not unionize or participate in strikes. Over time, the foreign workers became conscious of the unfair treatment. They went on strike, and spontaneously organized protests occurred. Women, especially, were involved in these actions. The management threatened sanctions, fired them, or evicted them from company-owned flats. Such wildcat strikes were inconsistent with industrial disputes organized according to union strategies. Even foreign workers took part in the organized strikes. But their participation was limited to joining the union just before the strike and to quitting it shortly thereafter. All efforts of the union officials notwithstanding, the immigrants never became familiar with the labor movement. Differences in mentalities were great, competition remained difficult. Sanctions of management against unionized and politically active workers threatened their existence. In addi-

40 Ibid., 197–200.
41 Ibid., 167, 201–5.

tion, pressure from the native work force was similar to that of the German nationalists and resulted in the founding of a separate Polish trade union.[42]

V

Although the German economy needed migrant workers urgently for the lower segments of the labor market, neither the native population nor the political institutions were willing to permit their participation in politics and social affairs.

Poles who were Prussian citizens were excepted from this general pattern since they, too, belonged to the Reich. Prussian Polish males were therefore entitled to vote for Reichstag deputies. They also formed a Polish parliamentary party to represent their special interests. These Poles, however, were for the most part excluded from elections to the Prussian *Landtag* because of the socially discriminatory electoral laws (*Dreiklassenwahlrecht*). In national elections, Poles in the Ruhrgebiet tended to support the Catholic Center Party (Zentrum). In the Protestant Unterweserraum, they favored the Social Democratic Party (SPD) because it was allied with the splinter party, the Polish Social Democratic Party (Polska Partia Socjalstyczna or PPS). Apparently, their social democratic orientation did not conflict with their Catholicism. Whereas the latter satisfied cultural and religious needs, the arguments of social democracy helped alleviate problems of caste, as long as social democrats did not pursue dogmatic internationalism and atheism.

The SPD ran well among Poles in the elections in Bremen and in its outskirts. But when Germanization policies were strengthened, Polish nationalism developed into a countermovement. This created a conflict within the PPS. In order not to lose followers whose national consciousness was growing, the party had to become patriotic. It thereby risked estrangement from the internationally oriented SPD. The climax of this conflict was reached in 1913 when the alliance of the two parties broke up. In the meantime, however, most of the naturalized Poles had been integrated into the political culture of the Unterwesergebiet and Bremen. Unlike the Poles living in Prussian eastern Germany and in the Ruhrgebiet, they hardly took any notice of the nationalism policy and stuck to their social democratic orientation.[43]

42 Ibid., 186–96, 203–4.
43 Ibid., 215–25.

As a Prussian official, the *Landrat* of Blumenthal considered Poles untrustworthy as "enemies of the Reich," Catholics, and social democrats.
He did his utmost to hinder any expression of Polish nationalism or prohibited such activities outright. Therefore, politically active Poles moved
from Blumenthal to Bremen or to Delmenhorst in neighboring Oldenburg.
As a result, political pressure from powerful Prussia on its neighboring federal states became stronger. Prussia now wanted them to segregate and
register Poles through legitimacy cards. Bremen and Oldenburg made some
concessions to Prussia but neither state was prepared to change its attitude
toward the Poles completely. They did not want to risk the peace in their
factories merely for the sake of Prussian interests.[44]

Foreign workers had no opportunity to participate in the political system
of their newly adopted home. As a result, they did not identify themselves
with its political culture. Additionally, they lived under the threat of expulsion, which was an arbitrary measure resorted to by authorities without
legal foundation. Moreover, workers who received low wages could not
afford the high fees to become naturalized. But as long as close connections
to their home country existed and hopes for eventual return remained alive,
foreigners had little intention to become naturalized. Many workers in fact
intended to return home and with the help of their savings buy land, as,
for example, the Ruthenians did.[45]

Due to the political and legal discrimination and the urgent need to keep
their identity, national subcultures developed in the immigration areas. The
Catholic church was a place where Prussian Poles met and were able to
maintain their identity. In the parishes they either formed the majority or
represented a large minority. When Prussia intensified its struggle against
the Catholic Church (*Kulturkampf*), the Catholic episcopacy gradually gave
way to nationalist pressures, resulting in a growing estrangement between
Prussian Poles and their church.

Although the Catholic clergies of Bremen and Delmenhorst were not
subject to anti-Polish repression, in Prussian Blumenthal many conflicts
occurred. Customary Polish rites caused the appointment of a German nationalist clergymen at the insistence of the responsible *Landrat*. In another
parish a priest considered to be well disposed toward the Poles lost his
position because of alleged imbecility. Poles reacted by disrupting the service. They were wearing their national emblems "provocatively" as the
Landrat who arrested the leader argued. A great part of the Catholic parish,

44 Ibid., 181–85.
45 Ibid., 91, 172–81.

even some integrated Poles, had refused to accept the involvement of the church in the national struggle. Polish consciousness of identity and Polish nationalism concentrated in associations.[46] All of this demonstrates differences between federal states: In Prussia a policy of supervision and suppression prevailed; in Bremen and Delmenhorst official policies were much more tolerant.

The different Polish organizations were either just social clubs or national associations with political aims. The Polish Sokol gymnastic clubs (*sokol* = hawk), in particular, aroused suspicions among Prussian authorities. According to the tradition of many European peoples, these clubs regarded sport as part of the realization of the national idea of freedom. Bohemians, Czechs, and Ruthenians also had their own clubs, in which they cultivated their identity, held political discussions, and supported national emancipation. Thus, immigrant clubs of the Unterwesergebiet reflected the political tendencies, emancipation movements, and rivalries of Europe of the pre–World War I period.[47]

Within historic Poland itself, Poles founded associations to help elect Polish candidates in local elections. Such associations were established in the years before 1914 because of the increasing number of voters and the strong nationalist upsurge. In addition, a Polish trade union was formed (*Zjednoczenie Zawodowe Polskie* or ZZP) in reaction to unsympathetic German trade unions and as an expression of a national radicalism. The ZZP had 740 members in the district of Blumenthal in 1913. Some members came from the so-called free (social democratic) unions, but the ZZP officials also succeeded in recruiting workers who had not been interested in the German trade unions. The members of the Polish trade union participated unconditionally in industrial disputes, although they were opposed by the local German unions. Thus, they countered the charge of being an organization of strikebreakers.[48]

VI

After World War I migration movements within Europe changed. The Treaty of Versailles created new borders, legal standards were altered, and nationalist sentiment increased, especially in Germany. The economic situation changed as well. During the war the supply of raw material to the textile industries had been stopped, throwing unskilled and semiskilled

46 Ibid., 210–14.
47 Ibid., 231–35.
48 Ibid., 226–30.

workers out of work. Additionally many young men were drafted into military service and had to leave the Unterwesergebiet for the fronts. After the world war and after the reestablishment of an independent Poland, about one-fifth of Prussian Poles emigrated to the new Poland. But disillusionment with conditions there prompted some of them to return to the Unterwesergebiet a few years later. However, this was possible only if they were German citizens. Furthermore, economic and political crises as well as rationalization measures influenced the labor market and encouraged racial attitudes aimed at foreign workers.

Despite the problems of the interwar world, many foreign workers continued to live in and around Bremen, Delmenhorst, and Hemelingen, especially Poles, Ruthenians, Czechs, and Croats. Their decision to stay in Germany meant that they were prepared to give up most of their identity in favor of integration. The third generation of the Polish immigrants did the same, despite and perhaps because of their hostile treatment by the Germans. Somewhat ironically, during World War II most of these foreign workers were granted German citizenship so that they could be drafted into the military.

Immigration to Germany ended with the close of World War I. Nationalist foreign workers returned home, racism and Nazi antiforeign agitation grew stronger, and immigrants had little chance to maintain their cultural identity. An attempt at cultural pluralism failed primarily because it remained limited and because of the geographic segregation of ethnic immigrant colonies. Finally, the assimilation of some immigrants was facilitated by the close confessional and cultural relations among the migrants and natives.[49]

This permanent social integration accelerated the social advancement of former immigrants. Integration took place after World War II, when another wave of immigration of foreigners to Germany began. But the second and third generations preferred to work in the same industries that employed their ancestors at the turn of the century. If one contacts descendants of these immigrants today, one finds that their traditions have almost completely disappeared; the only traces remaining are their foreign names, which are the last reminders of their origin.

49 Ibid., 236–42.

PART III

Women's Migration: Labor and Marriage Markets

10

The International Marriage Market: Theoretical and Historical Perspectives

SUZANNE M. SINKE

In 1860 Julius Lafontaine wrote to the mother of his prospective bride, asking her for her daughter's hand in marriage: "Oh Madam, times have changed. That which I strove for in Stuttgart without success, a good living, so that I could make your daughter happy, I have found here [in America]. I am still single. . . . I have worked up to the present with a special goal in mind. Now it is your choice, Madam, if your daughter still loves me, you can make two people happy."[1] We cannot know whether Lafontaine actually went to America primarily to earn money to marry, or whether this was simply a persuasive argument. The record shows that his plea worked, and Emma Lechler traveled from Stuttgart to San Francisco in order to marry him.

Marriage as a grounds for emigration may appear an exception to normal migration patterns. Yet an international marriage market is not the exception, nor is it confined to any particular period in history. By using examples from the United States immigrant population in the nineteenth and twentieth centuries, with special attention to German immigrants, I will describe this market and some of the many ways in which it operates.

I

Among German immigrants in the nineteenth century, marriage was a common theme in letters to the homeland. Both men and women wrote back to female friends and relatives about the generally good marital prospects in America, or about a certain individual a letter recipient could marry. Emigration manuals occasionally made claims along these lines: "Industrious

---

1 A. Julius Lafontaine to Mrs. Lechler, San Francisco, Feb. 20, 1860, Bochum Auswanderer Briefe Sammlung (hereafter cited as BABS). My special thanks to those in Bochum who allowed me access to the collection and to the German Academic Exchange Service (DAAD) for granting me a fellowship to work with this collection.

and calm girls who are at least reasonably good looking can be sure that they will receive several proposals of marriage in the first year."[2] The statistics on German immigrant marriage patterns bore out the claim that young single female immigrants did not stay single long.

My research utilizing women's letters from the Bochum Emigrant Letter Collection indicated that marriage was not the primary motive for migration for most German female immigrants, but it was for some, and it played a role for many others.[3] Further, it became clear that, as in the case of Lafontaine, a "suitable spouse" lay somewhere in the plans of many German immigrant men. Going to America to advance economically could also mean gaining the chance to marry. Because of migration, the local marriage pool took on international dimensions, and international marriage took on a new meaning.

We cannot consider the international marriage market simply as a way to describe intermarriages of two nationalities.[4] It also encompasses those of the same background who participated in international migration, and eventually even those affected by the changes in marital norms and expectations that resulted from migration. In other words this international marriage market involved not just the couple from different backgrounds who met in a new land, or the man who went back to his homeland to find a spouse, or the woman who answered the advertisement in an ethnic newspaper to marry a countryman in another city, but also the woman who agreed to migrate to marry someone in another land. Further, it had an impact on the family who had to look beyond the confines of its village for a mate for a daughter because so many of the young men had left for another land.[5]

The international marriage market could not take place without the migration of people to take advantage of economic opportunities in other

2 Traugott Bromme, *Hand- und Reisebuch für Auswanderer nach den Vereinigten Staaten von Nord-Amerika* (Bayreuth, 1848), 57; quoted in Wolfgang Helbich, Walter Kamphoefner, and Ulrike Sommer, eds., *Briefe aus Amerika: Deutsche Auswanderer schreiben aus der Neuen Welt, 1830–1930* (Munich, 1988), 499.

3 See Suzanne Sinke with Stephen Gross, "The International Marriage Market and the Sphere of Social Reproduction: A German Case Study," in Donna Gabaccia, ed., *Seeking Common Ground* (Westport, Conn., 1992).

4 Richard N. Bernard refers specifically to marriage markets, which he defines as "the counties in which the individual marriers lived," in his study of intermarriage in Wisconsin: *The Melting Pot and the Altar* (Minneapolis, 1980), 121. While this definition was sufficient for his purposes since the majority of spouses did come from the area, such a localized concept is woefully inadequate to explain immigrant marriage patterns.

5 I did not collect data on this last category, but it appears in some immigrant letters and in studies such as those cited by Judith Smith in *Family Connections* (Albany, N.Y., 1985), 92.

countries. In many ways the marriage market operated like the international labor market.[6] Some persons interested in arranging marriages examined the options and the impediments to possible matches and chose among them. Yet the market functioned also among those who did not think consciously about its existence. Thus the male migrant who, after acquiring a sufficient economic base in another country, decided that he wanted a wife and found that there were few women of his group there, and the woman "labor migrant" who after years in domestic service married in the new country, both fit into the pattern.

Basically, as I define it, the term *international* implies that the decision to marry somehow (consciously or on the practical level) involves international migration. In the most forthright cases one or more of the spouses is involved in international migration. The spouses can be of the same or different ethnic backgrounds – the key is migration.

Marriage has substantially different meaning in different cultures, though most recognize a formalized relationship between members of different genders.[7] In the United States, the most common forms of establishing a marriage are ceremonial (religious), registered (courthouse), and common law.[8] To work within these categories was the lot of immigrants, who sometimes faced restrictions on migration and reentry, as well as miscegenation laws, which tried to avert family formation within or between specific groups.

The last term I need to define is *market,* and it is perhaps the most difficult because it comes out of a body of economic theory in which "economic man" acts rationally to maximize benefits.[9] In the international marriage market the market consists of perceived and actual choices: options and impediments. This illuminates some of the difficulties of using economic theory for either marriage or migration, yet at the same time illustrates that

6 For an overview of this concept, see Dirk Hoerder, "International Labor Markets and Community Building by Migrant Workers in the Atlantic Economies," in Rudolph J. Vecoli and Suzanne M. Sinke, eds., *A Century of European Migrations, 1830–1930* (Urbana, Ill., 1991).
7 See Gary R. Lee and Lorene Hemphill Stone, "Mate-Selection Systems and Criteria: Variation according to Family Structure," *Journal of Marriage and the Family* 42 (1980): 319.
8 I selected these categories and some of the following discussion based on the information in William J. O'Donnell and David A. Jones, *The Law of Marriage and Marital Alternatives* (Lexington, Mass., 1982), 13, 28.
9 The Chicago school illustrates this pattern in its descriptions of "maximizing interests" in marriage. For a bibliography and good critique of this viewpoint, see Marilyn Waring, *If Women Counted: A New Feminist Economics* (San Francisco, 1988), 37–38. A related approach is found in hypergamy theory, which argues people try to marry "up" socially and racially. See for example, Larry Hajime Shinagawa and Gin Yong Pang, "Marriage Patterns of Asian Americans in California, 1980," in Sucheng Chan, ed., *Income and Status Differences between White and Minority Americans* (Lewiston, N.Y., 1990), 225.

a model incorporating the interplay of economic and other factors can offer a better overview of these phenomena. Let me put this briefly into a broader context.

The concept of an international marriage market fits into a category I call social reproduction. The literature on the relations of production to reproduction is diverse. Much of it takes as its point of departure Engels's *The Origin of the Family, Private Property and the State,* which looks at reproduction in terms of physically reproducing individuals and the relations of production.[10] My definition of reproduction is much more inclusive; it entails biological and social components. Biological reproduction includes bearing children and the activities necessary for physical sustenance: nurturance, and meeting basic physical and psychological needs. At this level a person can survive short term, but a society will die out.

Social reproduction refers to some of the same activities as in biological reproduction, but delves more deeply into the way in which one carries out these activities.[11] It also goes beyond meeting basic needs to incorporate activities meant to create or replicate family, community, ethnic, or other cultural patterns.[12] These activities are much harder to tie into an economic model, for while one can label them the requirements for replication of the labor force, they operate in a realm of culture and society that does not base status or even identity merely on economic factors, and in actuality they go much beyond the "needs" of any particular production system.[13] The difference can be as simple as cooking with olive oil rather than lard; both

10 Feminists, especially feminist socialists, have attacked this on a variety of grounds, particularly on the relation of patriarchy to unpaid labor in the home, on sex hierarchy as a system, on the relationship of women to men in a society with gender divisions. See Joan B. Landes, "Marxism and the 'Woman Question,'" in Sonia Kruks, Rayna Rapp, and Marilyn B. Young, eds., *Promissory Notes* (New York, 1989), 15; Zillah Eisenstein, ed., *Capitalist Patriarchy and the Case for Socialist Feminism* (New York, 1979), for a discussion of two systems of oppression; Karen Sacks, "Engels Revisited: Women, the Organization of Production, and Private Property," in Michelle Zimbalist Rosaldo and Louise Lamphere, eds., *Woman, Culture and Society* (Stanford, Calif., 1974), 207–22, looks at women's status as social adults as well as wives and relates their position in society to the degree of exploitation they can tolerate as laborers. For an overview of some of the feminist Marxist literature, see Veronica Beechey, *Unequal Work* (London, 1987).
11 This may be confusing to those familiar with Marxist feminist writing, which uses social reproduction in a more materialistic fashion. I use it in this way because the tasks involved are (re)producing society, though not necessarily in the same form as before. Both genders share these tasks, which immigration historians and others often term cultural adaptation and cultural continuity.
12 Dutch feminist Anja Meulenbelt's "De ekonomie van de koesterende funktie," *te elfder ure* 22 (1975): 638–75, offers a more inclusive model, and serves as a stepping-stone for my own work.
13 Immanuel Wallerstein and Joan Scott provide an economic model that allows for this kind of detail in their "householding." "A household is a unit that pools income for purposes of reproduction. . . . We shall call the multiple processes by which they pool income, allocate tasks, and make collective decisions *householding.*" The stress is on the kinds of income a household possesses and the decisions it makes about them. "Households as an Institution of the World-Economy," in Rae Lesser Blumberg, ed., *Gender, Family, and Economy* (Newbury Park, Calif., 1991), 234, 236.

perform similar tasks, but depending on one's background one tastes "normal." But reproduction is actually a misnomer, because what is going on is social production – that is, it is the creation as much as re-creation of certain cultural settings and societal norms.[14]

From this theoretical basis we can go on to relate social production to migration and, more specifically, marriage to migration. Migration highlights the choices surrounding social reproduction because migrants generally try to maintain or reestablish some of these activities when they establish families and ethnic communities. Likewise they seek to change some things. Because marriage is generally a crucial step in establishing a basis for reproduction, it deserves special attention. However, both marriage and migration are decisions that may be goals in themselves or means to other goals. Migration may be a means to marry, to sustain a marriage, to desert a marriage, or to avoid marriage. Likewise, marriage may be a means to migrate, to remain in a new setting, to return to the land of origin, or to avoid migration. Each of these is obviously an ideal type, and rarely are they totally separate. A woman may want to marry and to migrate, but she may stress one more than the other. Further, these goals and means may change over time. They are, nonetheless, useful to keep in mind. Using American examples, let me illustrate these patterns.

Migration to marry includes those couples who were formally engaged prior to the emigration of one, with the second partner following once the first had settled a bit. Nineteenth-century Germans of bourgeois background, who showed considerable concern for finding mates of "good family," sometimes made such arrangements. The separation, however, usually lasted several years and rarely went without problems. Paula Brenken Rogge, who had waited four years for her sweetheart to return and marry her, advised against a premigration engagement for another: "If Bernard comes [to America] now, he cannot even think about marriage for some time. . . . It would take at least four to six years, in our opinion, for him to reach his goal, by that I mean to be well situated here. Would Toni be able to take it that long?"[15]

For many immigrants, the engagement occurred by correspondence after one suitor migrated. Spouses arranged by correspondence (letter brides and

---

14 Part of this discussion comes from Suzanne Sinke with Stephen Gross, "The International Marriage Market and the Sphere of Social Reproduction," 3–4.
15 Paula Rogge to mother, Aug. 3, 1891, Portland, Ore., BABS. A similar pattern appeared among the petite bourgeoisie of other ethnic groups as well. See, e.g., the letters of August Segerberg to Hertha Schedin in H. Arnold Barton, ed., *Letters from the Promised Land: Swedes in America, 1840–1914* (Minneapolis, 1975), 192.

grooms) commonly fit in this category, especially if the migrants could not afford to return to the old country or if they faced legal restrictions on reentry.

Migration to sustain a marriage appeared in cases where the couple was married prior to migration, and one spouse (most commonly the husband) preceded the other. The couple then reunited after a time. Virginia Yans-McLaughlin noted this pattern among Buffalo Italians, where the husbands usually tried to bring their wives within two years, though it often took longer.[16]

Conversely, migration was sometimes a means of getting out of a marriage; once in America immigrants who originally planned to send for spouses changed their minds: "You got married, [he] took the money, and left you right away to America. Sometimes, he sent for you; sometimes he found somebody else that he liked better, and forgot you. Sent you a divorce."[17]

The use of migration to avoid marriage occurred frequently in cultures practicing arranged marriage. Fannie Edelman was one of six daughters, and after seeing several sisters marry, some against their will, she had second thoughts: "I was nearly sixteen, and I began to fear that one fine day my father would come home with some ready-made human merchandise for me. I therefore began to think more and more frequently about America – where I saw my only refuge."[18] This kind of challenge appeared particularly in cultures where the old ideals of marriage were under stress, as in the eastern European shtetl of the late nineteenth century, Korea in the early twentieth century, and post–World War II Japan.

Edelman's use of the term "human merchandise" to refer to a possible mate exemplified how much she saw this arrangement in its capacity as a market, with dowries and daughters traded for sons and their earning and ecclesiastical potential. One can get the same impression from newspaper personal advertisements: offering a person with certain characteristics and soliciting one with others.[19]

---

16 Virginia Yans-McLaughlin, *Family and Community* (Urbana, Ill., 1971), 97.
17 Fannie Shapiro, quoted in Elizabeth Ewen, *Immigrant Women in the Land of Dollars* (New York, 1985), 53. See also Reena S. Friedman, " 'Send Me My Husband Who Is in New York City': Husband Desertion in the American Jewish Immigrant Community, 1900–1926," *Jewish Social Studies* 44 (1982): 1–18. Women also "escaped" to America, e.g., Maria Hwang, who did not accept her husband having a concubine (a common practice in Korea at the time) and left for America with their children. Eun Sik Yang, "Korean Women of America: From Subordination to Partnership, 1903–1930," *Amerasia* 11 (1984): 1–28.
18 Quoted in Sydney Stahl Weinberg, *The World of Our Mothers* (New York, 1988), 72.
19 The "merchandise" aspect is sadly clear in certain 1990s pornographic magazines which offer to arrange marriages with women from southeast Asia – for a price. In some cases the women involved

Marriage for migration is most blatant in "technical" marriages, where the "spouses" have little or no contact with one another after the ceremony. Glenn Hendricks reported that this was a common means to get a residence permit for Dominican immigrants during the 1960s, with a free trip back to the Republic plus a substantial fee offered to American residents who would agree to it.[20]

Marriage as a means to remain in a new setting was sometimes the choice of a young adult whose parents returned to the old country. On a practical basis, if the couple came from different backgrounds, or even different villages, it made a move "back" difficult. Julianna Puskás, in a study of Hungarian immigrants, noted that nearly all of those who married and began families in the United States stayed there permanently.[21]

I have only scattered evidence on those immigrants who used marriage as a means to return to the Old World. Walter Kamphoefner noted that single German immigrant women rarely returned to the land of origin, but that couples who had recently married were heavily represented among returnees.[22] In this scenario, a woman returning alone was a "failure," but a couple with sufficient resources to start a new life in their homeland had fulfilled their goals in America.

Cases of persons marrying in order to avoid migration included those where a young adult decided not to emigrate, and used marriage as a means of illustrating his or her ties in the homeland. This was a notable option among young German women who began doubting the trustworthiness of their boyfriends in America and decided someone in the homeland might be better after all.

These ideals of marriage and market strategies are subject to qualifications that fall into two broad categories: marriage options and marriage impediments. Both operate in the sending as well as receiving nation (and in between); both can change over time; both are the perception of individuals and groups, and do not necessarily apply to all persons equally. Marriage options depend largely on attitudes toward marriage, types of marriage, and the pattern of arrangement of marriage. Impediments include social and religious proscriptions, economic constraints, political and legal restrictions, and practical obstacles.

---

have no say in the process, but for many the arrangement is a risk they will take in hopes it will be a ticket out of poverty for themselves and their families.

20 Glenn Hendricks, *The Dominican Diaspora* (New York, 1972), 60.

21 Julianna Puskás, "Hungarian Overseas Migration: A Microanalysis," in Vecoli and Sinke, eds., *A Century of European Migrations*.

22 Walter Kamphoefner, "The Volume and Composition of German-American Return Migration," in Vecoli and Sinke, eds., *A Century of European Migrations*. 293–313.

II

A major determinant of marriage patterns is the cultural worth placed on marriage and the cultural options available for those who did not marry. Charlotte Ikels, in a study of ethnic differences concerning marriage, noted that among the Chinese the duty to marry off one's children was paramount. This could go to the extreme of calling back ghosts of dead children to perform a wedding. Among the Irish, the pattern reversed and families sanctioned single life for their children.[23]

Ikels's conclusions found support in other studies of marriage patterns within these groups. Hasia Diner, for example, noted that because of economic conditions in Ireland in the nineteenth century few women could expect to marry. By the 1880s the dowry a woman needed to command to be "on the market" approximated rent for an average landholding for ten to twelve years. Late marriage prevailed for those who could marry, and a sense of family solidarity encouraged young (and not so young) women to work and help support parents and siblings. Coming from this context, Irish emigrant women were less likely to go to the United States looking for a mate. Rather, they could earn their bread and send some back to their families as well. Some married when in their thirties, but, overall, being single was a viable and, for some, preferable option to marriage.[24]

This sense of remaining single (or as some said, independent) and working as preferable to marriage also appeared in the writings of Swedish and Finnish immigrant women. As one Swedish woman wrote: "You asked me if I had a fiancé. I can't say that I don't have one, but I haven't decided on one yet, because I believe that if I get married I won't have things as good as I have them now."[25] For both Swedish and Finnish women the reluctance to marry seems to relate both to old country attitudes about when and if one should marry or work and to the impact of American ideals, which they often acquired through contact with American families. In the

23 Charlotte Ikels, "Parental Perspectives on the Significance of Marriage," *Journal of Marriage and the Family* 47 (1985): 253–54.
24 Hasia Diner, *Erin's Daughters in America: Irish Immigrant Women in the Nineteenth Century* (Baltimore, 1983), 4–12, 50–51.
25 Quoted in Joy K. Lintelman, " 'America Is the Woman's Promised Land': Swedish Immigrant Women and American Domestic Service," *Journal of American Ethnic History* 8 (1989): 19. Among the Finns there were tales of the domestic servants who saved up enough to buy not just furs and pearls, but also apartments with all the furnishings. K. Marianne Wargelin Brown, "The Legacy of Mummu's Granddaughters: Finnish American Women's History," in Carl Ross and K. Marianne Wargelin Brown, eds., *Women Who Dared: The History of Finnish American Women* (St. Paul, 1986), 20.

latter case, the immigrants were less willing to submit to the restrictions of Old World ideals about wives, particularly when the women had (from their perception) favorable work options.

A different view of marriage applied to cultures where the stress was not only on getting married but on virgin brides. Generally this led to strict supervision of girls and young age at marriage for women. The Italian immigrants of the nineteenth century and the Mexicans and Dominicans of the twentieth upheld these ideals. A Sicilian proverb about marriage stated: "The man at twenty-eight, the woman at eighteen."[26] In such cases the stress was on not "shaming" the family by getting pregnant before marriage. Judith Smith, in a study of Italians in Rhode Island, pointed out that young marriage worked against the economic goals of the family since the daughter's wages were lost.[27]

German immigrant women generally fell between the extremes in age at marriage. Most assumed marriage as a part of their lives, but not one they should begin too early. Men generally waited until they had amassed sufficient income to buy a farm or home or at least support a family; women simply saved their earnings until the right prospect came along.

The organization of marriage also played a role in whether immigrants could form official unions or not. Although in the United States the basic options for marriage were ceremonial, registered, or common law for immigrants there were variations based on custom and circumstances. One such variation was proxy marriage, which became a common option for some Asian immigrants who could not return to the homeland in order to marry. In this case one spouse was absent at the wedding ceremony and name registration.

The most well known use of proxy marriage was among Japanese and Korean picture brides, who used this form of marriage to evade immigration restrictions. In Korea it was common to post pictures of potential husbands in port cities, and then collect applications from women.[28] Eun Sik Yang reported that 1,066 Korean picture brides arrived in the United States be-

---

26 Yans-McLaughlin, *Family and Community*, 82–83. Hendricks cited an even younger age at marriage, often at fifteen or sixteen, for Dominican women. *The Dominican Diaspora*, 99–100. For Mexican Americans, Vicki Ruiz documented the ubiquitous chaperones, in charge of watching young women, at early twentieth-century dances. See her "The Flapper and the Chaperone: Historical Memory among Mexican-American Women," in *Seeking Common Ground*, 141–57.

27 Smith also noted that among Italians the double burden of providing a sufficient dowry yet having to get married young led some young women to head for America to marry. Mario Puzo's mother, for example, emigrated to marry a man she barely knew because her family was too poor to provide her with the culturally required bridal linen. *Family Connections* (Albany, N.Y., 1985), 92, 114.

28 Ronald T. Takaki, *Strangers from a Different Shore: A History of Asian Americans* (Boston, 1989), 56.

tween 1910 and 1924. This was small compared with the 20,000 Japanese picture brides between 1911 and 1920,[29] but significant to the Korean community in America, altering the sex ratio from 10:1 to 3:1.[30]

Another form of marriage which immigrant groups practiced was polygyny (commonly called polygamy). Mormon missionaries had considerable success in recruiting converts in the British Isles, Scandinavia, and Germany in the mid-nineteenth century. The church at that time expected converts to leave their homeland and come to "Deseret," where polygyny was common up to 1890.[31] One Swedish immigrant wrote of his visit to Salt Lake City in 1859: "It is said that there are many Swedish and Norwegian girls here. . . . There are also many Swedes who have three and four wives."[32] A somewhat different form of plural marriage resulted specifically from the migration experience. "American marriage," as social workers at the turn of the century labeled this, was a form of bigamy, which came about when married individuals remained separated long enough for additional ties to result. In this case one spouse, usually the husband, pretended he was not married in order to marry and have a family in America. For some, it was a matter of desertion, but for many it was the product of long separation. Andreas Reuter, a blacksmith from Hesse, pleaded for years for his wife to join him in America. Meanwhile he fell in love with a young woman living in the same house, and when she got pregnant the couple married.[33] Sometimes such unions were unofficial, but in Reuter's case, as in many others, the immigrants simply ignored the first marriage and wed officially a second time.

Remarriage was a legal option for those whose spouses had died. In this case, as with most others, the cultural ideals varied as to whether this was proper. German culture generally condoned remarriage, but there often were few options in Germany for women who did not have substantial means. Thus, German immigrant letters sometimes mentioned this possibility for widows: "If Mrs. Palm is not [re]married yet then she can come here; there are many good men who want wives."[34] While common-law

29 Takaki, *Strangers from a Different Shore*, 47.
30 Yang, "Korean Women of America: From Subordination to Partnership, 1903–1930," 3, 8, 10. Until 1917 the government of the United States did not recognize proxy marriages, hence the immigration service remarried new arrivals in group ceremonies. Yuji Ichioka, *The Issei: The World of the First Generation Japanese Immigrants, 1885–1924* (New York, 1988), 167.
31 Dean L. May, "Mormons," in Stephan Thernstrom, Ann Orlov, and Oscar Handlin, eds., *Harvard Encyclopedia of American Ethnic Groups* (Cambridge, Mass., 1980), 722, 729.
32 Letter to *Hemlandet*, reproduced in Barton, *Letters from the Promised Land*, 88.
33 Andreas Reuter to brother Karl, Nov. 18, 1837, Baltimore, BABS. On social work in such a setting, see Joanna C. Colcord, *Broken Homes: A Study of Family Desertion* (New York, 1919), 99–100.
34 Pauline Wendt to brother-in-law, Manson, Iowa, May 15, 1890, BABS.

marriage was officially recognized in the United States, an immigrant who tried to use this as the basis for bringing in a spouse faced difficulties. In the 1970s immigration authorities required a legalization of Dominican "free unions" in order to bring in the spouse or children under a U.S. visa.[35] The Immigration and Naturalization Service was even more diligent in recent years in trying to track down "technical" marriages.[36]

III

Another aspect of marriage options we need to consider is the arrangement of marriage. Who does it, when, how, and what changes does migration make? With either autonomous (self-determined) or arranged (other-determined) marriages there could be substantial differences because of migration. I can barely scratch the surface of the various types of arrangements that individuals and groups used to facilitate marriage, yet I want to illustrate some patterns.

Arranged marriage, whether carried out by parents or by a third party, was the norm for many if not most immigrants well into the twentieth century. The degree to which the persons negotiating the marriage could coerce the potential spouses into such an arrangement varied depending on the culture. In China or Japan, in the nineteenth century, the parents, and more specifically the father, had responsibility for their daughters' future. A poor family might "sell" a daughter into servitude, prostitution, or marriage. There was a Japanese saying about children: "One to sell, one to follow, and one in reserve."[37] This perception of wives and children as the property of husbands or parents, respectively, was by no means limited to parts of Asia. European countries often assumed this stance as well, though many of them, in the face of antislavery agitation, adopted laws by the nineteenth century to restrict sales of people.[38]

---

35 Hendricks, *The Dominican Diaspora*, 95.
36 Barbara Lobodzinska notes this among Polish immigrants in the 1970s in "A Cross-Cultural Study of Mixed Marriage in Poland and the United States," *International Journal of Sociology of the Family* 15 (1985): 94.
37 Quoted in Takaki, *Strangers from a Different Shore*, 49. Eun Sik Yang argues that "there is no evidence that any Korean woman was sold by her father or husband before coming to America." See Yang's "Korean Women of America: From Subordination to Partnership, 1903–1930," 1–28. The Chinese sometimes referred to a daughter as a "thousand pieces of gold," which was more a term of endearment than a reflection of what a daughter would bring if the father sold her. Some sales, however, did occur, though the money functioned to compensate for the loss of labor to the family.
38 In the British Isles wife sales persisted until the twentieth century as a form, albeit rare, of popular divorce. Samuel Pyeatt Menefee, *Wives for Sale* (New York, 1981). One historian told me that he saw an advertisement for this kind of sale in a Boston newspaper from the nineteenth century. Unfortunately, I have not been able to confirm it.

In the United States, having marriage partners arranged or at least suggested by parents or a third party, and a fairly utilitarian approach to marriage, were standard in the early nineteenth century. But the ideal of "romantic love," which began to gain popular support in the late nineteenth century and became enshrined in "mainstream" culture in the twentieth century, soon clashed not only with the older American pattern, but also with the customs of many immigrant groups.[39]

Jewish marriage ideals in shtetl communities underwent a similar shift in the late nineteenth century. The traditional practice was for parents to arrange matches, often with the assistance of a *shadkhen* (marriage broker) for teenage girls. The parents determined the size of the dowry for the daughter and set the date for the wedding, sometimes before consulting their children. As the saying went: "First you marry, then you love."[40] The disruptions caused by severe economic conditions and emigration at the end of the century meant, first, that families could not provide dowries, and hence had difficulty marrying off their daughters, and, second, that many daughters heard of the freedom both economically and in terms of marriage chances in America. The change toward autonomous marriage came first to the working class but soon affected others on the Pale. As a popular song heralded: "In America . . . when a fellow loves his girl, he marries her without a penny!"[41]

Once in America the *shadkhen* did not disappear, but often transformed into a sort of dating service, arranging meetings for potential partners, just as parents encouraged their children to go to Yiddish theater or Jewish summer resorts in order to meet the "right" people.[42] Other groups experienced a similar process: The broker continued to operate in America but in a less formal capacity.

Among many ethnic groups one of the most common patterns of finding a spouse was through correspondence. This allowed an immigrant who wanted a mate of the same background and who could not find someone easily in America to save time and money in the search. With a letter bride (or groom)[43] the choice of a mate and arrangements to marry took place

39 For an overview on the change in marriage customs, see Peter Filene, *Him/Her/Self: Sex Roles in Modern America,* 2d ed. (Baltimore, 1986). On shifting ideals of marriage at the turn of the century, see esp. Elaine Tyler May, *Great Expectations: Marriage and Divorce in Post-Victorian America* (Chicago, 1980).

40 Weinberg, *World of Our Mothers,* 23.

41 Ibid., 72.

42 Ibid., 205–6.

43 Women could also send for husbands, but since the vast majority of cases I could uncover were men seeking women, I use this term.

through the mail and then either the groom married by proxy (as with picture brides), or he returned to the old country to marry, or the woman migrated and the couple married on her arrival (sometimes at the docks, hence the term "wharfside brides").[44] Whether someone arranged the marriage, or the individuals themselves made the decision to wed, spouses by correspondence could be found scattered through the pages of immigrant letters. One mid-nineteenth-century German immigrant wrote his aunt, requesting she find him a wife: "My demands for a young woman are very limited, a developed figure with passable face is sufficient, everyone wants industriousness and a good disposition, social position and class make no difference. Wealth is good and none perhaps better. Concerning religion I could go along with anything except a Catholic."[45]

In some cases the letter writers had potential spouses in mind. Einar M., a widower with one daughter, wrote back to the pastor of a local church in Sweden, asking he forward a letter to a certain woman he had not seen nor corresponded with for twenty-four years. The letter read in part: "Are you married or unmarried? If you are unmarried, you can have a good home with me. . . . If you can't come maybe you know somebody else who wants to become a good housewife."[46]

Relatives encouraged this correspondence process by suggesting potential spouses.[47] But relatives could also control the correspondence process. Among the German bourgeoisie of the nineteenth century it was customary for a young man to get permission from the parents of a young woman before writing to her. August Gildemeister, though "as good as engaged" with his sweetheart in Germany, had to send his loving greetings via his sister until his intended's father agreed to their correspondence (which coincided with agreement to their engagement).[48]

Yet another variation of finding a potential spouse by letter appeared in the pages of newspapers. In various locations around the world the decline of some form of marriage broker coincided with both increasing geographic

---

44 The term "wharfside bride" comes from Price and Zybrzycki, cited in Bernard, *The Melting Pot and the Altar,* xxvi.
45 Quoted in Wolfgang Helbich, ed., " *'Amerika ist ein freies Land' "* (Darmstadt, 1985), 137.
46 Nov. 14, 1907, reproduced in Barton, *Letters from the Promised Land,* 265–66.
47 Ikels reported on a mother in Hong Kong who found a likely candidate and coaxed her son in Boston to write to the young woman. The correspondence eventually resulted in marriage. "Parental Perspectives on the Significance of Marriage," *Journal of Marriage and the Family* 47 (1985): 258.
48 August Gildemeister collection, letters from 1846–50, BABS. In the Azores, Lamphere, Silva, and Sousa note a similar phenomenon. Men must have permission to write, and that generally is coupled with approval for marriage. "Kin Networks and Family Strategies of Working-Class Portuguese Families in a New England Town," in Linda Cordell and Stephen Beckerman, eds., *The Versatility of Kinship* (New York, 1980), 229–30.

mobility and the growth of classified advertisements for spouses, male and female. Two studies done of New York–based papers in the 1970s exemplified this. Both *India Abroad,* the English language weekly of the Indian community, and *Nowy Dziennik,* a Polish language daily, contained matrimonial ads in most issues.[49] These advertisements generally gave some information about the writer and requested correspondence from the potential spouse as a first step toward possible matrimony. Just as with picture brides, an exchange of pictures could also be an early step in the screening process.[50] While the writers might want to marry for love, they still had fairly specific ideas about who they might consider eligible.

IV

Marriage options in the form of cultural ideals and possible arrangements were only one side of the coin. In every case there were impediments to marriage: social and religious, economic, legal, and practical obstacles. Immigrants, even with the assistance of matchmakers and matrimonial ads, could not always overcome these obstacles though they often tried. Impediments, like options, operated at various points during migration. I will concentrate on those within the United States for immigrants, with only cursory attention to regulations in the country of origin or at other locations.

Social and religious grounds for spousal preference exist in all groups, though in varying degree, and are at least related to other impediments. With these we can see clearly the role of migration in causing change. I want to look at a spectrum of choices concerning mates, from within the ethnic group to outside it. In the latter case this draws on the extensive literature concerning intermarriage.

Marriage within the ethnic group was the ideal for many. One Swedish immigrant, when asked if he did not consider American women better than Swedish ones as potential spouses, protested strongly: "I tried the best I could to convince them of their great error and told them that only with the noble Swedish maidens can one seek for true love and faithfulness, those in whom there is no guile or egotistical calculation."[51] Such ideals might be

---

49 Musab M. Siddiqui and Earl Y. Reeves, "A Comparative Study of Mate Selection Criteria among Indians in India and the United States," *International Journal of Comparative Sociology* 27 (1986): 226; Lobodzinska, "A Cross-Cultural Study of Mixed Marriage in Poland and the United States," 98.

50 Ichioka, *The Issei,* 164.

51 The quotation is more biased than some, since the man was writing to his fiancée. August Segerberg to Hertha Schedin, Avon, Ill., Oct. 13, 1884, reproduced in Barton, *Letters from the Promised Land,* 195.

compounded in cases where religious or racial differences existed. Thus it was more common for Dutch Catholic immigrants to marry other Catholics than to marry Dutch Protestant immigrants.[52]

The influence of American ideals on the position of women also contributed to a general disdain for "Americanized" women in some immigrant groups.[53] As one social worker at the turn of the century noted, "it is a popular saying, particularly among young Italian immigrants, that girls who have been in America too long do not make good wives, that when a man wants to marry he had better send for a girl from the old country."[54] Many did arrange such matches, either through a return trip, or through correspondence.[55] Many attempted to find someone from the same village or region, but not all could achieve this degree of *campanilismo*.[56]

Whereas some immigrants saw intermarriage, however they defined it, as undesirable, others sought it. Immigrant men might eschew American women because they demanded better treatment; immigrant women might choose American spouses because they treated their wives better.[57] Women who knew of American legal provisions on domestic abuse, and of the tradition in America of "ladies first," spread this information.

Although marriage outside the group under such circumstances might be more socially desirable for women, men also might be attracted by the social and economic advantages of marriage outside their group.[58] Thomas and Henry Petingale, British immigrants of the 1830s, married into "good" American families, which helped them get government appointments – even from the normally anti-immigrant Know-Nothing Party.[59] While

---

52 See Yda Schreuder, "Ethnic Solidarity and Assimilation among Dutch Protestant and Dutch Catholic Immigrant Groups in the State of Wisconsin, 1850–1905," in Rob Kroes and Henk-Otto Neuschäfe, eds., *The Dutch in North-America* (Amsterdam, 1991), 205.

53 For an overview of women's changing roles and the impact of popular culture on immigrant and second-generation women, see Ewen, *Immigrant Women in the Land of Dollars*.

54 Colcord, *Broken Homes*, 28.

55 E.g., Virginia Yans-McLaughlin indicates that high endogamy was the rule in the Buffalo Italian community. *Family and Community*, 94, 256–57.

56 In the book *Rosa*, the heroine recounted crossing the Atlantic with two mail-order brides, one nervous and the other self-assured: " 'Look at *me*,' said the comical Francesca with her crooked teeth. 'I'm going to marry a man I've never seen in my life. And he's not *Lombardo* – he's *Toscano*. But I'm not afraid.' " Maria Hall Ets, *Rosa* (Minneapolis, 1970), 163. Just as region might play a less significant role in America than in Italy for Italians, according to one study religion and caste played a less significant role for Indian immigrants in the United States than in India. Siddiqui and Reeves, "A Comparative Study of Mate Selection," 226.

57 Elizabeth Pleck noted immigrant and especially second-generation women spread news of American law on domestic abuse, which challenged a man's right to beat his wife. "Challenges to Traditional Authority in Immigrant Families," in Michael Gordon, ed., *The American Family in Social-Historical Perspective*, 3d ed. (New York, 1983), 504.

58 See, e.g., Lobodzinska, "A Cross-Cultural Study of Mixed Marriage," 94.

59 Charlotte Erickson, *Invisible Immigrants: The Adaptations of English and Scottish Immigrants in Nineteenth-*

242 Suzanne M. Sinke

British immigrants of the nineteenth century might justify their marriages, they had fewer problems with marrying into "Yankee" families than some other groups.[60] Scholars sometimes referred to this as cultural affinity, a common point of reference in studies of intermarriage.[61]

Yet even among groups where social pressure against intermarriage was strong, particularly intermarriage which crossed racial lines, such matches might occur given certain circumstances. Asian war brides often fit this pattern. As Evelyn Nakano Glenn propounded, Japanese women who married Americans often had a "rebellious streak." Because of wartime and occupation conditions, they had a taste of independence and did not want to remain tied to traditional Japanese roles. Still, coming out of a culture that stressed obedience to parents made it difficult to challenge parents on such an important decision. Rarely were parents supportive: "You made your own decision. If your husband leaves you, don't come back. Just slit your throat."[62] And even among the women there was some ambivalence about marrying interracially, which Japanese culture strongly condemned: "So I look at him and all the feelings I have get mixed up and make me upset and dizzy: loving him, hating myself for loving a white man."[63]

In addition to more general social impediments there were those such as preferences for younger spouses, those without children, persons without physical or mental impairment, or even those who were not too tall or too short. Ethnic background and religion fit into this list. So too did class, which relates to the economic impediments to marriage. Economic considerations nearly always play a role in decisions about marriage, even of "love matches," but social requirements of how much money one needs to marry have been less prevalent in the United States than in many of the sending countries of immigrants. A standing refrain in the letters of German

Century America (Ithaca, N.Y., 1990), 402: A similar case occurred in the southwest, where Anglos married into "good" Mexican families prior to annexation of the territory to the United States; Edward Murguía, *Chicano Intermarriage* (San Antonio, Tex., 1982), 45.

60 Ronald Takaki argued a similar case for Filipino male workers of the early twentieth century. They considered themselves Americans, had little sense of ethnic purity, and came out of a culture that readily accepted mestizos. *Strangers from a Different Shore*, 341.

61 These affinities translate into groupings, such as Leon's study of Hawaiian intermarriage patterns where Japanese, Chinese, and Korean compose one cluster, and Caucasian, Hawaiian (or part Hawaiian), Filipino, and Puerto Rican make up the second. Panunzio's study of intermarriage in Los Angeles, while biased, found similar patterns there, with one cluster consisting of Mexicans, Filipinos, and "Americans." J. L. Leon, "Sex-Ethnic Marriage in Hawaii: A Nonmetric Multidimensional Analysis," *Journal of Marriage and the Family* 37 (1975): 775; Constantine Panunzio, "Intermarriage in Los Angeles, 1924–33," *American Journal of Sociology* 47 (1942): 690.

62 Evelyn Nakano Glenn and Nisei Issei, *War Bride: Three Generations of Japanese American Women in Domestic Service* (Philadelphia, 1986), 61–63.

63 Akemi Kikumura and Harry H. Kitano, "Interracial Marriage: A Picture of the Japanese Americans," *Journal of Social Issues* 29 (1973): 78.

immigrants was that a woman did not need a dowry to marry in America.[64] Many did save their funds however, just as did the men, who knew they needed some means to support a family.

American employers often took advantage of the separation of workers and their families, paying a wage that would support one person on a bare subsistence level, but not a level that would allow family formation or community development without additional input. By leaving the main reproductive tasks to support systems in the Old World, immigrant workers could survive and even save a bit on these "production only" wages. The cost of bringing over a woman to marry in such a case might be prohibitive.[65] Once in America, however, wives could be an economic advantage. Ewa Morawska calculated the contributions of taking in boarders, raising a garden, sewing, cooking, and selling household products for east central European families in Johnstown around the turn of the century. These earnings could equal or surpass the men's wages.[66]

Among turn-of-the-century Japanese immigrants, the choice of whether to marry before coming to America also related to economic considerations. Whereas the first son expected to inherit and hence return after a short sojourn in America, a second son generally anticipated a longer stay, and thus greater advantage to the double income and household services provided by a wife.[67] The economic consequences of marriage could also work against marriage, as in the case of children whose salaries provided sole support for other family members.[68]

You could fill several books with the political and legal impediments to marriage, even if you only did research on the United States; I will only deal with a few restrictions here. One of the keys to understanding them is to recognize that U.S. immigration policy has consistently addressed both production and reproduction, but that the relationship between them has changed in this century. In the nineteenth century the federal government's concern was primarily with recruiting workers for industry; thus it enacted restrictions against mentally impaired, ill, and destitute migrants. It expounded a more "biological" policy in 1882 with the Chinese Exclusion

---

64 Sinke with Gross, "The International Marriage Market and the Sphere of Social Reproduction," 16–17.
65 In the twentieth century, with the rise of the female majority among immigrants, the pattern included a few women who sent for husbands.
66 Ewa Morawska, " 'For Bread with Butter': Life-Worlds of Peasant Immigrants from East Central Europe, 1880–1914," *Journal of Social History* 17 (1984): 395–97.
67 Takaki, *Strangers from a Different Shore*, 49–50.
68 As Judith Smith writes: "Cultural norms which defined marriage primarily in terms of family needs could be adjusted to support the decision *not* to marry because of familial considerations." *Family Connections*, 116.

Act. This legislation pitted the need for cheap labor against racist attitudes toward the formation of a Chinese community in America. Because migration prior to that time was heavily male, and because after 1882 only the minority of Chinese Americans who were citizens could bring in their wives and children, few Chinese immigrant men could have Chinese wives. In 1930 the Chinese community remained 70 percent male, and not until the repeal of Chinese Exclusion in 1943 did this ratio begin to change much.[69]

The Japanese immigrant experience differed in that there was a lapse between the Gentlemen's Agreement of 1906, by which Japanese laborers could no longer migrate to the United States, and the Ladies' Agreement of 1920. In the meantime the wives of Japanese in America could continue to migrate, which led to the picture bride phenomenon. Within this system, the Japanese consulates, interested in retaining a positive image for the community in America, set rigid economic standards concerning who could bring in a wife.[70]

Because the government also regulated who could marry whom, legal marriage outside one's ethnic group became a stumbling block for many immigrants. Miscegenation laws in California and Oregon, for example, made it illegal for Asian immigrants to marry "whites," though the definition of white changed over time. A striking example of this was the Punjabi–Chicana marriages of the early twentieth century. Though both groups were physically Caucasian by standards of the day, Indians were denied "white" status by a 1923 law. The U.S. census labeled Mexican immigrants white in 1920, a separate race in 1930, and white again in 1940. In any case, Indian men often migrated to California alone, and when a 1917 immigration measure forbade further immigration, those with wives (who usually stayed in India to carry out their roles in the husband's family) could not reunite without losing their immigration status. Others sought wives in America, and found Mexican women, with whom they often worked in agriculture, likely candidates because of physiognomic and culinary similarities. To marry they often had to dodge the law, such as going to Arizona to wed. In some cases they simply lived as common-law spouses.[71] This "Mexican-Hindu" community largely died out after 1946

69 Li, "Fictive Kinship," 49–52; see also Takaki, *Strangers from a Different Shore*, 121–25.
70 Until 1915 a businessman had to show an annual gross income of $1,200 plus $1,000 in savings; a farmer needed an annual profit of $400 to $500 plus the same amount of savings; and a laborer was nearly barred until after 1915 when he could bring a wife if he had over $800 in savings. Takaki, *Strangers from a Different Shore*, 47–48; Ichioka, *The Issei*, 165.
71 Common-law marriage provisions did not usually stand up to challenges under miscegenation law, though within the ethnic community persons might follow this custom and consider themselves

when the law changed and Asian Indians could become citizens and bring over relatives.[72]

Anti-Asian legislation on various governmental levels at the turn of the century reflected a growing awareness of race, which eventually resulted in a national origins quota system. The quota legislation of the 1920s sought to maintain a specific mix of ethnic groups, one that suited the goals of eugenicists. More recent legislation replaced the ethnic quotas with family reunification policies and skills preferences. Partly because of the shift to family reunification as the primary mode of entry for unskilled immigrants, the sex ratio of immigrants has changed to favor women over men.[73]

One of the contributing factors to this preponderance of women is the rise in spouses of American service personnel overseas. Even the war bride legislation illustrated that racial ideals died hard; special immigration laws of December 1945 allowed the entrance of non-Asian war brides, but not until an amendment a year and a half later could Asian war brides come under the same terms. After this legislation the bureaucratic regulations for gaining a passport and U.S. visa for a service person's wife or husband could still take two years. The number of people who took advantage of the legislation, however, was large, with approximately one million persons entering as spouses from the mid-1940s up to 1952.[74]

Under the McCarran–Walter Act of 1952 the government opened the door for the wives and children of aliens to be admitted as nonquota immigrants, and the 1965 Immigration Act placed even higher priority on family reunification. These combined with the repeal of many miscegenation laws to make getting married or reuniting families a possibility for more immigrants.[75] The laws did, however, lead to a change in immigration strategy. Marriage became a key way to migrate once again, with the con-

married (and others might treat them that way). For European migrants who did not face this type of racial discrimination, common-law marriage was an option. Further, the lack of restrictions of citizenship, economic standing, or other qualifications made a more formalized marriage a possibility for many who did have to contend with these laws in the country of origin.

72 Karen Leonard and Bruce LaBrack, "Conflict and Compatibility in Punjabi-Mexican Immigrant Families in Rural California, 1915–1965," *Journal of Marriage and the Family* 46 (1984): 528–29, 533–34; see also Takaki, *Strangers from a Different Shore,* 125.

73 Yet as Donna Gabaccia demonstrated in "Women in the Process of Migration," read at the Bremerhaven conference, the shift also has to do with changing economic conditions whereby the demand for traditional "female" jobs increases.

74 Elfrieda B. Shukert and Barbara S. Scibetta, *War Brides of World War II* (Novato, Calif., 1988), 1–2; Bok-Lim C. Kim, "Asian Wives of U.S. Servicemen: Women in Shadows," *Amerasia Journal* 4 (1977): 97–100, 114.

75 Peter Li, in "Fictive Kinship, Conjugal Tie and Kinship Chain among Chinese Immigrants to the United States" makes the point that immigrants have always used kinship to avoid immigration restrictions, and the type of restrictions determine what type of kinship they choose to claim.

sequence that the Immigration and Naturalization Service increased its efforts to find technical marriages.[76]

Besides legal restrictions on marriage and on the reunification of partners, there were many practical impediments to marriage for immigrants in the United States. The most obvious was sex ratios within the ethnic community. If a Filipino wanted to marry a Filipina in the United States in 1930, he faced a huge problem; men outnumbered women fourteen to one.[77] Even in groups which did not face such extensive immigration or marital restrictions, the sex ratio might pose problems.

A variation on the sex ratio problem occurred in war-ravaged nations where the number of young men killed left a population of young women with few chances of marriage, limited economic opportunities, and strong cultural pressures both to marry and to support their elders. Marriage to an American, in such cases, could provide a solution, albeit one which generally met with strong familial and cultural disapproval.[78]

A distribution problem of the sexes existed for groups where the men worked predominantly in one location and the women in another, as with Finnish immigrants. Finnish men tended to work in rural areas, particularly in the mines of Minnesota and Michigan, whereas the Finnish women went to urban areas to take advantage of domestic work.[79] Under such circumstances autonomous marriages where the couple had time to court were difficult if not impossible.

Illiteracy could prove a particularly difficult obstacle to overcome, especially when a group was geographically dispersed. Hmong immigrants of the 1980s came from a preliterate culture where clans arranged marriages with the assistance of a matchmaker. The geographic dispersal of various clans, combined with illiteracy, broke up the traditional networks of contact. Thus autonomous marriage patterns began to develop.[80] Transportation and communication services formed another category of practical obstacles. In the era before steam transportation, few immigrants could return to the Old World to find a spouse. Likewise, if the postal service failed

---

76 In a series of court cases, the INS sought to define what a "technical" marriage was. The rulings included: 1975 – "evidence of separation, by itself, does not support conclusion that spouses never intended a bona fide marriage." 1977 – "it is not required that a marriage contracted in good faith last any particular period of time." 1979 – "cannot rescind permanent resident status on INS belief that a marriage is factually dead at the time of status adjustment." William J. O'Donnell and David A. Jones, *The Law of Marriage and Marital Alternatives* (Lexington, Mass., 1982), 34.
77 Takaki, *Strangers from a Different Shore,* 337.
78 Kim, "Asian Wives of U.S. Servicemen," 93.
79 Brown, "The Legacy of Mummu's Granddaughters," 18.
80 William M. Meredith and George P. Roue, "Changes in Lao Hmong Marital Attitudes after Immigrating to the United States," *Journal of Comparative Family Studies* 17 (1986): 118–19.

to deliver a letter, the plea for a spouse might go unheeded for years before a correspondent realized the problem. Broken correspondence might mean a broken engagement.[81] Political upheavals of various kinds could also interrupt both transportation and communication. Nearly all contact with the sending nation could be severed by war or political fiat, making either a wedding or a family reunification impossible. All these problems plagued German immigrants at times.

Although transportation advances decreased the time needed to travel back to find a spouse, increasing demands, even within societies that relied on arranged marriage, for the spouses to get to know one another before the ceremony could still pose problems.

The examples in this section highlight the categories of impediments: social and religious, economic, political, and practical obstacles. When looking at impediments, the lines of migration history diverge, for as this collection demonstrates, ethnic and especially racial discrimination resulted in sharply different opportunities, including the opportunity to marry.

V

The international marriage market incorporates not just the persons migrating specifically to marry, but also those whose marriage decisions become intertwined with international migration. This market is part of a larger sphere of social reproduction, which functions concurrently at all times with the productive sphere. Marriage decisions, which form the building blocks of families and households, thus illuminate choices in (as well as interplay between) both spheres. They also highlight that, though much literature points to the gendered nature of spheres, all people inhabited both.

Marriage and migration are two responses to diverse motivations – hence, assuming causality based on a pattern leads to distortion. Thus I argue that labeling some migrants "family" migrants as opposed to "labor" migrants is frequently false. Again, the interconnections need greater attention: The predominance of "economic motivations" in immigration history sometimes obscures the preponderance of chain migration of families and friends.

Options, arrangements, and impediments to marriage illustrate the cultural norms of both immigrants and the receiving society. In this realm the divergence of the reproductive from the productive appears most clearly.

81 In the early nineteenth century German immigrants frequently note lost letters, sometimes several in a row.

248 Suzanne M. Sinke

Discrimination and preference affect both migration and marriage decisions. A study of the international marriage market, thus, links several strands of research. Marriage and migration, two topics of interest in their own rights, offer even greater potential in tandem.

11

Making Service Serve Themselves: Immigrant Women and Domestic Service in North America, 1850–1920

JOY K. LINTELMAN

"Domestic service was clearly considered undesirable by most working women,"[1] reads a remark in the concluding chapter of a study of household employment in industrializing America.[2] This comment is representative of historical and contemporary literature that paints an overwhelmingly negative picture of domestic service. In most studies, women are described as forced into domestic service due to lack of technical skills, gender segmentation of the labor force, and, for immigrants and nonwhites, lack of language abilities and racial or ethnic prejudice.[3]

This view of domestic service is accurate at a general level. Many working-class women viewed their experiences as domestic servants negatively as they toiled in middle- and upper-class homes in the United States and Canada, and many avoided such employment whenever possible. But this negative assessment should not be applied uncritically to all domestic servants. Many female immigrants to North America in the late nineteenth

1 I wish to thank Hartmut Keil, Leslie Moch, and the participants in the Bremerhaven conference for their helpful suggestions and comments. Part of my title, "Making Service Serve Themselves," was inspired by a remark made about Irish domestics by Carol Lasser in her dissertation " 'Mistress, Maid, and Market': The Transformation of Domestic Service in New England, 1790–1870," Ph.D. diss., Harvard University, 1982, 246.

2 David M. Katzman, *Seven Days a Week: Women and Domestic Service in Industrializing America* (New York, 1978), 268.

3 For general studies that depict domestic service in a mostly negative light, in addition to Katzman, see Linda Martin and Kerry Segrave, *The Servant Problem: Domestic Workers in North America* (Jefferson, N.D., 1985); Blaine Edward McKinley, " 'The Stranger in the Gates': Employer Reactions toward Domestic Servants in America, 1825–1975," Ph.D. diss., Michigan State University, 1969; Phyllis Palmer, *Domesticity and Dirt: Housewives and Domestic Servants in the United States, 1920–1945* (Philadelphia, 1989); and Daniel E. Sutherland, *Americans and Their Servants: Domestic Service in the United States from 1800 to 1920* (Baton Rouge, La., 1981). On blacks in domestic service, see Isabel Eaton, "Special Report on Negro Domestic Service," in W. E. B. DuBois, ed., *The Philadelphia Negro* (New York, 1899), 136–37, who referred to domestic service as a "despised calling." On domestic service in recent decades, see Lewis A. Coser, "Servants: The Obsolescence of an Occupational Role," *Social Forces* 52 (1973): 31–40. Coser states: "Domestic employment has lost the shreds of genteel respectability it may once have possessed . . . it is relegated to an underclass of social inferiors who have no place in the respectable scheme of things" (38).

and early twentieth centuries worked as maids, and found in domestic service many positive features. Most of these women perceived domestic service as a sought-after occupation. It met many of their needs as immigrant females and represented a type of employment that they were able to make "serve themselves."

General studies of domestic service note that domestic employment had some positive attributes and even aided assimilation and social mobility for some immigrant women,[4] but little attention has been given to exactly why immigrant women were attracted to domestic service, and why they often perceived the job differently than native-born whites. Recent studies of immigrant and nonwhite North American domestics have begun to detail some of the variations in domestic experience, but they offer little in the way of a conceptual framework for analyzing domestics or encouraging comparisons between domestics in different groups.[5]

This essay addresses some of these central issues about domestic service. It presents a conceptual framework within which to examine domestics, arguing that the experiences of domestic servants were shaped by the interaction of several primary social variables. These variables and their influence upon the domestic's experience can be summarized through the following general principles:

1. The goals and expectations that women hold toward employment influence their perceptions of domestic service. These goals and expectations vary by race and ethnicity, and are shaped by women's social and cultural backgrounds.

---

4 See, e.g., Katzman, *Seven Days,* 3–5, 29, 141, 229–30, 233, 273–74; Allyson Sherman Grossman, "Women in Domestic Work: Yesterday and Today," *Monthly Labor Review* 103, no. 8 (1980): 17. On the Canadian experience, see Marilyn Barber, "The Women Ontario Welcomed: Immigrant Domestics for Ontario Homes, 1870–1930," *Ontario History* 72 (1980): 168; and Genevieve Leslie, "Domestic Service in Canada, 1880–1920," in Janice Acton, Penny Goldsmith, and Bonnie Shepard, eds., *Women at Work: Ontario, 1850–1930* (Toronto, 1974), 85–90.

5 On Finns, see Carl Ross, "Servant Girls: Community Leaders," and Marsha Penti, "Piikajutut: Stories Finnish Maids Told," in Carl Ross and K. Marianne Wargelin Brown, eds., *Women Who Dared: The History of Finnish American Women* (St. Paul, Minn., 1986), 41–54, 55–72; Varpu Lindström-Best, " 'I Won't Be a Slave!' – Finnish Domestics in Canada, 1911–30," in Jean Burnet, ed., *Looking into My Sister's Eyes: An Exploration in Women's History* (Toronto, 1986): 33–53; Varpu Lindström-Best, " 'Going to Work in America': Finnish Maids, 1911–30," *Polyphony* 8 (1986): 17–20; Varpu Lindström-Best, *Defiant Sisters: A Social History of Finnish Immigrant Women in Canada* (Toronto, 1988). On the Irish, see Hasia Diner, *Erin's Daughters in America: Irish Immigrant Women in the Nineteenth Century* (Baltimore, 1983). On the Japanese, see Evelyn Nakano Glenn, *Issei, Nisei, War Bride: Three Generations of Japanese American Women in Domestic Service* (Philadelphia, 1986). On Hispanics, see Vicki L. Ruiz, "By the Day or Week: Mexicana Domestic Workers in El Paso," in Vicki L. Ruiz and Susan Tiano, eds., *Women on the U.S.–Mexico Border: Responses to Change* (Winchester, Mass., 1987), 61–76. On blacks, see Elizabeth Clark-Lewis, "From 'Servant' to 'Dayworker': A Study of Selected Household Service Workers in Washington, D.C., 1900–1926," Ph.D. diss., University of Maryland, 1983.

2. Domestic servants whose primary social network approves of and supports domestic employment are able to counteract many of the negative elements of service.

3. The more closely a domestic servant's appearance, religion, language and culture resembles that of her employer, the more likely her experience as a domestic is positive.

4. The domestic's marital status and life-course stage influence the way in which she experiences domestic service.

5. The immigration policies of the country in which the female immigrant domestic seeks work affect her employment experience.

The interplay of these factors and their variation over time and across space help explain why domestic service was experienced differently by women of different racial and ethnic groups in different social contexts.

I will illustrate the ways in which these variables operated in a positive way in the lives of immigrant domestic servants, with particular emphasis on the late nineteenth and early twentieth centuries, when the largest numbers of immigrant women were active in the occupation. Because my own research focuses on Swedish immigrant domestics, they will be used frequently to illustrate the ways in which the variables operated. However, the applicability of these concepts to domestics of other ethnic and racial groups will also be addressed.

I

The dominant immigrant groups in North American domestic service at the turn of the century came from northern and central Europe, with especially high concentrations of Irish, German, and Scandinavian women (see Table 11.1).[6] The goals and expectations of women in these immigrant groups regarding employment, as shaped by their experiences as women and as workers in their homelands, help explain their attraction to North American domestic service.

Women in all of these ethnic groups sought to improve their economic and social status. As population increased and placed pressure on agricultural resources in nineteenth-century Europe, many families experienced a decrease in standard of living. Daughters in poor rural families might be forced to seek employment at a young age. In Germany and Scandinavia, domestic service represented one of the few wage-work opportunities available to

---

6 Katzman, *Seven Days*, 66–69. Lucy Maynard Salmon, *Domestic Service* (New York, 1897; reprint: 1972), 78–80.

Table 11.1. *Propensity of immigrant women for household labor, 1900*

Place of birth	Servants		Laundresses		Percent in domestic service
	Number	Percent of wage earners	Number	Percent of wage earners	
Sweden	35,075	61.5	3,501	6.1	67.6
Ireland	132,662	54.0	15,925	6.5	60.5
Norway	10,440	45.6	1,385	6.0	51.6
Denmark	3,970	45.3	485	5.5	50.8
Hungary	5,837	46.3	308	2.4	48.7
Germany	58,716	36.3	10,174	6.3	42.6
Austria	7,866	38.6	482	2.4	41.0
Poland	6,292	24.1	1,098	4.2	28.3
England and Wales	13,620	21.9	1,937	3.1	25.0
Russia	4,850	13.8	364	1.0	14.8
Italy	1,840	9.1	505	2.5	11.6

Source: David M. Katzman, *Seven Days a Week: Women and Domestic Service in Industrializing America* (New York, 1978), 67.

young, single, working-class women in the nineteenth century.[7] Faced with economic need yet subscribing to notions of female domesticity, most cultures of northern Europe found single women's employment as servants on farms or in middle- and upper-class urban households acceptable. But domestic service was often difficult and in most countries of northern and central Europe, offered little hope for advancement.

For example, in response to economic pressure on her family's resources

7 By the 1880s and 1890s, some factory work was available for women as these nations became increasingly industrialized. Such opportunities were, however, available mainly in larger urban areas, and involved long hours, low wages, and poor working conditions. See, e.g., Gerda Meyerson's study of Swedish women factory workers *Arbeterskornas Värld: Studier och erfarenheter* (Stockholm, 1917). Some limited opportunities for higher education existed, but schools were usually too expensive for most young women from families with limited means. The experience of a young woman named Ingeborg Frankmar is illustrative: "It was the year 1901. I was 17 years old. My future was to be decided. What should I be? I had seen in a newspaper an announcement about a course at Vinslövs folk high school in Skåne. I stealthily showed my father the announcement and he understood that I wanted to go there. He shook his head. Too expensive.... We were nine children." Source: Autobiography, Ingeborg Frankmar collection, Folklore Archive, Nordic Museum, Stockholm, Sweden. Note: the references here and following listing Folklore Archive are segments of two large manuscript collections. These collections are composed of entries to two contests, one sponsored by a Stockholm newspaper (*Stockholms Tidningen*) and the other by a popular Swedish magazine (*Året Runt*), in the 1940s and 1960s that asked people to submit materials on immigration to compete for several prizes. The entries were then deposited in the Folklore Archive. Within the larger manuscript collections, the entries are arranged alphabetically by entrant's name.

in Sweden, thirteen-year-old Hilda Linder began work in 1909 as a domestic at a neighboring farm. She received no cash wages, only material for a dress and room and board for her first year of employment. The next year she received seventy-five kronor, still only half of the usual domestic's wages, which her employer justified because of her young age.[8]

As migration out of Europe increased in the late nineteenth century, women heard of economic opportunities in other countries. Those who were already familiar with domestic work in the homeland were naturally curious about wages and working conditions in service elsewhere. Specific details about conditions for domestics abroad were widely available, both from formal and informal sources. Most of these sources reported that domestic service in the United States represented a significant improvement from servant work in Europe. Personal letters were probably the most convincing and compelling source of information. One German immigrant woman compared her work as a domestic in the United States with that in Germany: "My dear friends," she wrote, "it's a stark contrast with servants and maids, since they have a lot more rights here than over there, when I'm done with my work then I go anywhere I want to, and they can't even say one word about it."[9] Another German woman wrote that "The maids here [in the U.S.] have it good, one cannot tell anymore who is the wife and who is the maid."[10] A young Swedish man wrote home to his sister from Sioux City, Iowa:

It should perhaps interest you to know how girls have it here. America is . . . the woman's promised land. A domestic has determined work times, they do major cleaning one day a week and wash and iron one day . . . every Thursday they are free to work for themselves or go out where they want.[11]

Photographs sent along with letters provided even further evidence of economic and social opportunities available abroad. Domestics in North America often sent portraits home to friends and family, decked out in their finest dresses and hats. To some women it must have seemed that emigrating to America would transform them, as they saw their friends wearing fancy

---

8 Hilda Linder, Autobiography, Collection 22:1:12:E, Emigrant Institute, Växjö, Sweden, Jan. 1971.
9 Margarethe Winkelmeier, Indianapolis, to her parents, brother, and sister-in-law, Germany, Dec. 15, 1869. Quoted in Walter Kamphoefner, Wolfgang Helbich, and Ulrike Sommer, eds., *News from the Land of Freedom: German Immigrants Write Home,* trans. Susan Carter Vogel (Ithaca, N.Y., 1991), 585.
10 Barbara Monn, Marine City, Mich., to brother, sister-in-law, and their children, Germany, Feb. 16, 1869, Bochum Emigrant Letter Collection (BABS), Bochum, Germany. The author wishes to express her gratitude to Suzanne Sinke for sharing this letter excerpt.
11 Carl, Sioux City, Iowa, to sister Stina, Sweden, April 12, 1910, Svea Jönsson collection, Folklore Archive, Nordic Museum, Stockholm, Sweden.

hats and dresses. Only wealthy upper-class women could afford to dress that way in the home country.[12]

With few economic opportunities at home, and apparently many abroad, young women decided to try their luck in another country. Maja Johansson described her decision to emigrate: "I had a place as a domestic . . . in Halmstad.[13] In five years the wages never got higher than ten kronor a month and there was no set work time, so when I heard how much better domestics had it in America my thoughts went there. . . . In 1909 I left."[14] For many northern European women like Maja, social and cultural background – where patriarchal and relatively rigid class structures limited their economic and social opportunities – encouraged participation in American domestic service. Servant work was considered gender-appropriate employment by the home culture, prior experience in the occupation eased anxiety about ability to perform work tasks, and the comparatively better social and economic conditions of servants in the United States compared with the homeland made the job an attractive employment choice.

Social and cultural background influenced Irish immigrant women's participation in domestic service as well. Like their German and Scandinavian counterparts, they saw little hope for economic advancement in Ireland, and they heard reports of good wages and working conditions in American domestic service. But unlike many other northern European women, most Irish women had not worked as domestics in the homeland. The availability of domestic positions in North America, the inclusion of room and board along with a cash wage, and the "on-the-job" training nature of household labor helped draw them to the occupation. Aspects of their cultural background, which outlined appropriate roles and behavior for women, influenced their choices as well. Hasia Diner has noted that the "rigid sex segregation and late and infrequent marriage" typical of Irish society encouraged single Irish women to view domestic service positively.[15] The sex

12 On the similar impact of Finnish immigrant domestics' photographs, see Lindström-Best, "I Won't," 39.
13 Halmstad is a city located on the southwest coast of Sweden, in Hallands *län*.
14 Autobiography, Maja Johansson collection, Folklore Archive, Nordic Museum, Stockholm, Sweden.
15 See chap. 4 in Diner, *Erin's Daughters in America,* esp. 70–71, 90–91. Interesting parallels can also be found in the experiences of migrating women in other cultures. Cf., e.g., the discussions of Finnish domestic workers by Ross and Penti in Ross and Wargelin Brown, or Lindström-Best, *Defiant,* 84–102. See also Gábor Gyáni's study of Hungarian women's migration to Budapest as domestics: Gábor Gyáni, *Women as Domestic Servants: The Case of Budapest, 1890–1940* (New York, 1989). My thanks to Dirk Hoerder for bringing this essay to my attention. On the role of domestic service employment in nineteenth-century England and France, see Louise A. Tilly and Joan W. Scott, *Women, Work, and Family* (New York, 1978), 22, 31–33, 35–36.

segregation and live-in nature of domestic service, for this group of women, if not employment attractions, were certainly not viewed as obstacles to domestic employment.

The influence of cultural background upon women's goals and expectations for employment in North America is also revealed by immigrant women who chose not to enter domestic service. For example, it was unusual for Italian and Jewish immigrant women to obtain household employment. For both groups the centrality of home and family within the culture discouraged young immigrant women from seeking employment that required them to live and work alone in a stranger's household.[16] These women tended to utilize economic opportunities in areas other than domestic service.

II

The disdain of native-born white North Americans for domestic service from roughly the mid-nineteenth century on has been well documented.[17] This disdain was fundamentally based upon the social stigma associated with servant work. Young white native-born women avoided domestic employment, fearing that it would have negative effects on their social position, personal friendships, and prospects in the marriage market. They complained of isolation, loneliness, and ostracism.

In spite of the negative attitudes about domestic service prevalent in North American society, European immigrant women still entered domestic service in large numbers. According to the 1911 Canadian Census, immigrant women made up 35 percent of all women employed in the category "Domestic and Personal Service."[18] And nearly one-third (32 percent) of the American servant population in 1890 consisted of foreign-born white women.[19] In several immigrant groups the majority of wage-working women were employed as domestics: Over two-thirds (67.6 percent) of

16 Alice Kessler-Harris, *Out to Work: A History of Wage-Earning Women in the United States* (New York, 1982), 127–28.

17 See, e.g., Diner, *Erin's Daughters in America,* 81–82; Katzman, *Seven Days,* 7–43; Sutherland, *Americans and Their Servants,* 3–5; as well as Lillian Pettengill, *Toilers of the Home: The Record of a College Woman's Experience as a Domestic Servant* (New York, 1903), 42, 92–93, 366. For similar attitudes regarding domestic service in Canada, see Barber, "The Women Ontario Welcomed," 150–52, and Leslie, "Domestic Service," 85–89.

18 Leslie, "Domestic Service," 96.

19 U.S. Bureau of the Census, *Statistics of Women at Work* (Washington, D.C., 1907), 159, 185; Joseph Hill, *Women in Gainful Occupations, 1870 to 1920* (Washington, D.C., 1929), 38. Even in 1920, when immigration had decreased for most of the groups likely to enter domestic service, white immigrant women still made up 21 percent of the American servant population.

first-generation wage-earning Swedish American women in 1900 worked in domestic service, along with 60.5 percent of the Irish female wage earners, and over 50 percent of the Norwegian and Danish women (see Table 11.1).[20]

Immigrant women apparently ignored North American attitudes about domestic service, found their own definitions of status and prestige within the context of their ethnic community, and utilized ethnic support networks to overcome some of the difficulties experienced by native-born white domestics. It is clear that Swedish, Finnish, and Irish ethnic communities held more positive attitudes regarding domestic service in the late nineteenth and early twentieth centuries than did native-born white society, and their attitudes and actions helped immigrant women have positive experiences in domestic service. The Swedish ethnic community provides a good case study.

Swedish Americans were aware of American women's avoidance of domestic service and the stigma attached to service within the dominant culture, but were quick to point out that their own attitudes differed. Author Johan Person wrote in 1912 that Swedish "servant girls as a class are not disdained in spite of the circumstance that . . . [America's] own poorer daughters do not want to work as servants."[21]

That Swedish Americans were proud of their "sisters in service" is also evident if one examines the ethnic press.[22] A 1905 editorial in a Chicago Swedish newspaper stressed the esteem Swedish women received as domestics, addressing the question of why "our Swedish sisters in domestic service are so highly respected and gain the good will of their employers?"[23]

The Swedish ethnic community was not merely supportive of domestic service in print, but also sought to improve the domestic's life in specific ways. Perhaps the best indicator of ethnic community support for domestic service was the creation of employment bureaus. The Swedish National Association of Chicago opened a free employment bureau in 1894 to assist job-seeking Swedish men and women. Managed for nearly two decades by a former domestic servant named Othelia Myhrman, the agency helped thousands of young Swedish women find positions in service.[24] The bureau

20 Katzman, *Seven Days,* 67.
21 Johan Person, *Svensk Amerikanska Studier* (Rock Island, Ill., 1912), 103.
22 Much of the material on the Swedish ethnic community's relationship with Swedish domestics is drawn from Joy K. Lintelman, " 'Our Serving Sisters': Swedish-American Domestic Servants and Their Ethnic Community," *Social Science History* 15 (1991): 381–95.
23 "Our Sisters Who Serve," *Svenska Nyheter* (Chicago), March 21, 1905.
24 "Mrs. Othelia Myhrman," in Erik G. Westman, ed., *The Swedish Element in America* (Chicago, 1931), 3:324–27.

focused on the worker rather than employer, and not only located jobs, but tried to meet the applicant's desires in terms of type of domestic work (cook, chambermaid, nursemaid, etc.) and geographic location.[25] For Finnish immigrant domestics in Canada, employment agencies even acted as protectors of newly arrived women, advising them to guard against exploitation by employers, and helping them relocate when necessary.[26]

The ethnic community provided additional institutional support for domestics through the "woman's home." These homes, usually found in urban areas with large ethnic populations, were important resources for domestics. A Swedish Woman's Home in Chicago was founded in 1907 to "create a home for working girls." Particular attention was paid to domestics' needs, because the home was seen as "a retreat during their vacations and time off periods."[27] Swedes in Boston founded the Swedish Home of Peace (Fridhem) in 1914 to house unemployed girls, and also offered an employment bureau for newly arrived immigrant women.[28]

The ethnic community was concerned about the domestic's social life as well as employment experience. Ethnic cultural and social activities were scheduled to allow domestics' attendance. Since Thursdays were usually "the maids' day off," Swedes would schedule dances, performances, picnics, and other recreational activities at these times.[29]

Given the responses of the ethnic community to the domestic's needs, it is easier to understand the immigrant woman's attraction to domestic service.[30] While the domestic lived in her employer's household, and spent the majority of her time there, she still maintained her own social network outside of the employer's home, which in turn influenced her work experience. A study of domestic service in twentieth century Zambia has also highlighted the importance of life outside the workplace in shaping the domestic's experience.

25 See Inge Lund (pseudonym for Ingeborg Lundström), *En Piga i USA: Ett Pennskafts Äventyr* (Stockholm, 1917), 30, and Inge Lund, "Svenska Tjänsteflickor," in K. Hildebrand and A. Fredenholm, eds., *Svenskarne i Amerika* (Stockholm, 1926), 57.
26 Lindström-Best, *Defiant*, 98.
27 Immanuel, *Woman's Home, 1907–1952* (n.p., 1952). Copy located at Swenson Swedish Immigration Research Center, Augustana College, Rock Island, Ill. (hereafter SSIRC)
28 Swedish Congregational Church, Boston, Mass., Swedish Home of Peace corporation papers, 1914, located at SSIRC. Homes for Scandinavian immigrant women were also located in other cities such as Denver and New York City. On Finnish women's homes, see Lindström-Best, "I Won't," 47, or Lindström-Best, *Defiant*, 98.
29 See Joy K. Lintelman, " 'America Is the Woman's Promised Land': Swedish Immigrant Women and American Domestic Service," *Journal of American Ethnic History* 8 (1989): 17.
30 On Finnish community support in Canada, see Lindström-Best, *Defiant*, 97. The ethnic community as a social support network was important for Japanese American domestics, as well. See Glenn, *Issei, Nisei, War Bride*, 177–82.

Servants' behavior while at work is . . . shaped not only by the demands placed on them there but also by processes beyond the workplace. . . . Some of these extra work forces are influenced by cultural practices, others by associations with neighbors, fellow workers, people in other lines of work, and friends and relatives.[31]

Similarly, much of the "new labor history" stresses the necessity of examining the influence of life outside the workplace on the work experience.[32]

Why would the ethnic community embrace an occupation disdained by the dominant society? The benefits that the ethnic community reaped from immigrant women's participation in domestic service provides an explanation. Immigrant males might see domestics as attractive marriage partners because their employment experiences had accustomed them to American ways.[33] Economic status also influenced the relationship between domestics and the ethnic community. Because of the continual demand for domestics in North America, maids generally had steady work, in contrast to immigrant males whose employment might disappear at a moment's notice in response to a market fluctuation or labor strike. And because domestic employment included room and board as well as cash wages, maids often had more money than other immigrant workers to support ethnic businesses or institutions. An investigation of Swedes in Chicago in the early twentieth century revealed that domestics were significant financial contributors to Swedish churches and charity institutions.[34] Another Swedish author wrote of Swedish domestics:

Where some Swedish American enterprise which needs financial backing is concerned . . . one first thinks of the Swedish-American servant girls. . . . The Swedish-American newspapers count them among their best subscribers, and the Swedish-American churches as their best members, and Swedish-America in general, we believe, as their "best girls."[35]

Finnish and Irish domestics also provided economic support for the ethnic community.[36]

The social support network between domestics and their ethnic community could be so strong that domestics might influence the ways in which

31 Karen Tranberg Hansen, *Distant Companions: Servants and Employers in Zambia, 1900–1985* (Ithaca, N.Y., 1989), 17.
32 Leon Fink, "American Labor History," in Eric Foner, ed., *The New American History* (Philadelphia, 1990), 233–50.
33 See, e.g., Person, *Svensk-Amerikanska Studier,* 102–3.
34 E. H. Thörnberg, *Lefnadsstandard och sparkraft: med särskild hänsyn till den svenska befolkningen i Chicago* (Stockholm, 1915), 37.
35 Person, *Svensk-Amerikanska Studier,* 104.
36 On the Irish, see Diner, *Erin's Daughters in America,* 92. On Finns, see Isabel Kaprelian, "Women and Work: The Case of Finnish Domestics and Armenian Boarding-House Operators," *Resources for Feminist Research* 12 (1983): 52.

the ethnic community responded to American society. Carl Ross has described the "substantial economic and social independence that Finnish immigrant women derived from employment as domestic workers," and its effect upon Finnish Americans.[37] Largely as a result of their experiences as domestic servants, argues Ross, Finnish women's social behavior and attitudes were transformed. Domestics' economic power and leadership skills helped to redefine women's roles in Finnish American communities.[38]

III

The social variables examined up to this point have centered on domestics themselves – their attitudes toward service, and their relationship to the immigrant community. But these immigrant women did not live within a vacuum. The broader context of North American society also shaped their experiences. It is in the relationship between the immigrant domestic and the dominant society – the employer–employee relationship – that race and ethnicity have the most influence on the domestic's experience.

The race or ethnicity of the domestic worker influenced her choice of positions as well as her experiences on the job. Employers were sensitive to the differences between themselves and their employees – when women of color or immigrants entered domestic service in increasing numbers in the nineteenth century, differences were accentuated.[39] Employers developed stereotypes depicting the reputations of various nonwhite and foreign-born domestics. The best-known stereotype can be found for the Irish domestics – the "Bridget" or "biddy" image – temperamental, dirty, stupid, and generally difficult to manage.[40] The predominance of the Irish stereotype relates not only to their numbers but also to their degree of difference from employers. Of the major immigrant groups occupying domestic service in the time period we are studying (Irish, Scandinavians, Germans), the rural Catholic Irish woman represented the sharpest contrast to the urban middle-class and predominantly Protestant employer.

Prejudice against ethnic or racial groups could limit job opportunities. Katzman has noted the existence of newspaper advertisements indicating "No Irish need apply."[41] Other employers took a reverse strategy, adver-

37 Ross, "Servant Girls," 42.
38 Ibid., 41–54. Given the existence of several former Swedish American domestics in positions of leadership and influence, it is likely that they may have had a similar impact on their ethnic community. See Lintelman, "Our Serving."
39 Katzman, *Seven Days,* 62–94.
40 Diner, *Erin's Daughters in America,* 66–67, 71–72, 86–88, 117.
41 Katzman, *Seven Days,* 163.

tising for a specific race or nationality. The following notice from the *New York Times* is typical: "Wanted: A North German Protestant Woman as seamstress and nurse to growing children . . ."[42] That ethnic and racial stereotyping was based upon employer opinion rather than employee behavior is obvious, because the same complaints and stereotypes made about Irish domestics were later applied to Scandinavians, blacks, and other nonwhite or foreign-born household workers.[43]

An employer's prejudices might extend beyond hiring practices into the daily routine of the domestic. Some employers of Irish domestics made concerted efforts to convert them to Protestantism, or at least to prevent them from practicing their own Catholic faith.[44]

The impact of race or ethnicity upon the domestic servant's experience is perhaps most profound for black domestics. The racial prejudice held by most middle- and upper-class Americans in the late nineteenth and early twentieth centuries made it difficult for black domestics to make service serve themselves in the same ways that many immigrant women could. Unlike many immigrant women who migrated to North America and saw domestic service as a positive employment choice, many black women had no other options for wage work but domestic service due to racial prejudice that denied them entrance to other forms of employment. Yet black servants should not be considered helpless victims, and their experiences as domestics were also influenced by their cultural background. Unwilling to repeat their experiences as slave women, after emancipation black women in the South demanded and achieved the right to "live out," one of the central differences in the black and immigrant domestic experiences in the early twentieth century.[45]

IV

Nearly all of the immigrant women working as domestics in North America in the late nineteenth and early twentieth centuries were single, and this

---

42 *New York Times*, March 1, 1881, as cited in Silke Wehner, "Auswanderung deutscher Dienstmädchen in die USA, 1870–1920," in Monika Blaschke and Christiane Harzig, eds., *Frauen wandern aus: Deutsche Migrantinnen im 19. und 20. Jahrhundert* (Bremen, 1990), 29–50. Some employers also advertised in the ethnic-language newspapers. With regard to Swedes, see, e.g., Stina L. Hirsch, "The Swedish Maid: 1900–1915," M.A. thesis, DePaul University, 1985, 28.

43 Katzman, *Seven Days*, 222.

44 Douglas V. Shaw, *The Making of an Immigrant City: Ethnic and Cultural Conflict in Jersey City, New Jersey, 1850–1877* (New York, 1976), 2, 119.

45 For an excellent discussion of black domestic servants, see chap. 5, "White Mistress and Black Servant," in Katzman, *Seven Days*, 184–222. See also David Chaplin, "Domestic Service and the Negro," in Arthur B. Shostak and William Gomberg, eds., *Blue-Collar World: Studies of the American Worker* (Englewood Cliffs, N.J., 1964), 527–36.

status was one of the reasons why immigrant women found domestic service so attractive.[46] For newly arrived single immigrant women, household employment could ease the difficulties associated with immigration. Servant work meant a roof over one's head, food on the table, a family environment, and a steady wage. Of Finnish domestics in Canada, Varpu Lindström-Best has written that "domestics usually lived in middle- and upper-class homes in safe and relatively clean neighborhoods. No time was spent looking for housing and no initial investment needed to buy furniture or basic kitchen utensils."[47]

For most immigrant women at the turn of the century, employment as a domestic ended at marriage. Many ethnic cultures as well as the dominant North American culture held a negative view of married women's wage labor. To fulfill properly the accepted roles of wife and mother, it was believed, women should not work outside the home.[48] And on the practical side, live-in domestic work in America was not conducive to married life. Unless the husband was employed in the same household, the lack of time available to build and maintain a relationship with one's spouse would be a major difficulty in continuing domestic employment after marriage. And in a time period where child care facilities were almost nonexistent, a woman with children would find live-in service impossible unless she sent her children away to live with someone else.[49]

The relationship of marital status to the domestic's experience can also be illustrated by examining some of the changes in household service and in the domestic service labor force in the United States in the twentieth century. It has already been noted that European immigrant women tended to leave domestic service upon marriage. As the number of females emigrating to the United States from northern Europe decreased, the supply of available domestics diminished. Black women began to migrate from the South to fill these positions, but because many of them were married or knew they would want to continue domestic employment after marriage,

46 Katzman, *Seven Days*, 80–82. In my research I have come across a few married couples who both worked as household employees, a fascinating area of domestic service that thus far has not been the focus of scholarly study. For further evidence of domestic employment of married couples, see Hirsch, "Swedish Maid," 28–29.
47 Lindström-Best, "I Won't," 37.
48 On Swedish attitudes toward married women's wage work, see Murray Gendell, *Swedish Working Wives* (Totowa, N.J., 1963), 45–60.
49 In a study of working-class Swedish American women in Minneapolis who sought help from charity organizations, domestic service was not considered an employment option by married women, despite the extreme economic need that most of them faced. See Joy K. Lintelman, " 'She Did Not Whimper or Complain': Case Records and Swedish-American Working-Class Women in Minneapolis, 1910–1930," paper presented at the conference Swedes in America: New Perspectives, Växjö, Sweden, May 31 to June 3, 1991.

they were unwilling to follow the immigrant's practice of live-in service. As a result of these changes in labor force composition, a gradual transformation in domestic service from live-in to day labor took place.[50] After this change had taken place, immigrant women from different ethnic groups and at different stages in the life course were attracted to domestic service. For example, it was only as day labor that many married Japanese immigrant women were able to make service serve themselves.[51]

V

The immigration policies of receiving countries have also influenced domestics' experiences. For the time period of this study, 1850–1920, European women desiring to come to the United States as domestics were subject to the same restrictions applied to other European immigrants. Most of the women who wanted to enter the United States were allowed to do so. Once they entered the country they were free to seek employment as they wished and, after a period of time, to become citizens if they so desired.[52]

During approximately the same time period in Canada, women seeking employment as domestics were actually given preferential treatment. Responding to the shortage of women willing to enter domestic service, the provincial government of Ontario, as well as the Canadian government, actively recruited immigrant women for domestic service. Agents were sent to European countries (primarily Britain, but also Scandinavia and northern Europe) to encourage the emigration of household workers to Canada. And female domestics were allowed to emigrate to Canada when other workers were not. The domestic's journey to Canada was eased through low fares and bonuses; employment bureaus assisted them in finding jobs, and some regions even established hostels for domestics' temporary lodging and recreation.[53] Many immigrant women took advantage of these Canadian policies, worked as domestics for a time, and eventually settled as Canadian citizens. These Canadian institutions were actually formalizing some of the

50 Katzman, *Seven Days,* 87, 94. For an example of this process in Washington, D.C., see Elizabeth Clark-Lewis, " 'This Work Had A' End'. The Transition from Live-In to Day Work," in *Southern Women: The Intersection of Race, Class, and Gender,* Center for Research on Women, Working Paper No. 2 (Memphis, Tenn., 1985).
51 See Glenn and Issei, *War Bride,* 99–166.
52 For an overview of U.S. immigration policy in this time period, see Michael C. LeMay, *From Open Door to Dutch Door: An Analysis of U.S. Immigration Policy since 1820* (New York, 1987).
53 See Leslie, "Domestic Service," 99–104, and Barber, "The Women Ontario Welcomed."

elements of the social support network that helped to make domestic service a positive experience.

VI

The literature on contemporary domestic service is developing rapidly, and it would be impossible to attempt an incorporation of all recent scholarship into this conceptual framework at this point.[54] Some useful observations can, however, be made. The racial and ethnic groups entering domestic service have changed – the largest group of immigrant domestics in the United States today is Latin American.[55] But the framework presented here is still applicable. The social variables that interacted to make domestic service a positive experience for many immigrant women in the late nineteenth and early twentieth centuries are still important determinants of the ways in which women experience domestic service.

Unlike at the turn of the century, immigration policy at present has a negative effect on the experiences of many domestics in the United States. Shellee Colen has studied women in one of the primary immigrant groups employed in domestic work in New York City – West Indians. For an immigrant woman to work in the United States today, she must obtain a "green card" verifying permanent resident status. But it is not easy to obtain a green card, so most of these women enter the United States on visitor's visas and stay on as illegal workers.[56] Their goal is to find an employer who will be willing to sponsor them in their application for resident worker status. Once they have the green card, they can bring other family members to the United States, find other employment, and proceed to build their lives in a new homeland. But their citizenship status influences their domestic experience by making them more exploitable by employers. It usually takes a while to find a sponsor, so many women work for a time as illegal domestics. Their illegal status makes them vulnerable. If an illegal domestic complains about problems at a place of employment or seeks another position (traditionally the ultimate weapon of the domestic against employer mistreatment – if things get too bad, the domestic can quit), she might risk being discovered by immigration authorities. And even once a

54 The most complete bibliography to date on contemporary domestic service in the United States and elsewhere can be found in Elsa M. Chaney and Mary Garcia Castro, *Muchachas No More: Household Workers in Latin America and the Caribbean* (Philadelphia, 1989), 456–80.
55 Martin and Segrave, *The Servant Problem,* 104.
56 A "green card" indicates permanent resident status and allows foreign workers to reside in the United States.

green card is obtained, there is strong disincentive for leaving even very difficult positions because discontinuing employment with a sponsor would mean starting all over again in the quest for a green card.[57]

Marital status and goals and expectations also continue to influence domestics' work experiences, with varied effects. The experience of the West Indian domestics in Canada interviewed by Makeda Silvera is illustrative.[58] The cultural background of West Indian women draws them to domestic service. In the Caribbean, the immigration of women to the United States to work as maids is considered a socially acceptable behavior. The economic situation in their homeland is poor, and most of these women have children to support. They learn of economic opportunities abroad in much the same way as the Swedish or Irish women of the past. For example, one woman recalled:

I was about six or seven when I started hearing about England, Canada, and the U.S. Is [It's] like everybody in the Caribbean [was] talking about foreign [places]. I remember sometime my uncle . . . use to send us old newspapers from the States and we use to read them from back to cover . . . I remember the first year when he was away, he would send and tell us all how wonderful America was.[59]

But emigration for mothers and/or married women, leaving children and family behind, makes domestic service difficult. Separation from children accentuates feelings of isolation and loneliness. One of the women in Silvera's study talked about her youngest daughter, age ten. She had not seen her since she was twelve months old.[60] And these women's need to maintain economic support of dependents decreases their flexibility and employment options. They cannot afford to be unemployed for long, without their families suffering the consequences.

The social support network also continues to influence contemporary domestics' experiences. Colen found that women she interviewed living in isolated suburbs complained most of loneliness and isolation, while those "who got away on days off to their 'own' community fared better."[61]

57 Shellee Colen, " 'With Respect and Feelings': Voices of West Indian Child Care and Domestic Workers in New York City," in Johnnetta B. Cole, ed., *All American Women* (New York, 1986), 46–70.
58 Makeda Silvera, *Silenced: Talks with Working-class West Indian Women about Their Lives and Struggles as Domestic Workers in Canada* (Toronto, 1983).
59 Ibid., 63.
60 Ibid., 83.
61 Colen, " 'With Respect and Feelings,' " 52.

VII

My purpose in this essay has been to present a conceptual framework for analyzing the experiences of women in domestic service and to apply this framework to immigrant domestics in North America in the late nineteenth and early twentieth centuries. I have argued that the interplay and inter-action of five central social variables in the domestic's life influenced whether her experience was negative or positive. In the case of many Irish, German, Swedish, and Finnish immigrant domestics, the variables of in-dividual goals and expectations about employment, social support network, similarity to employer, marital status and life-course stage, and immigration policies operated in ways that made domestic service a positive experience and allowed them to make service serve themselves. For immigrant do-mestics today, the situation is otherwise.

The topic of immigrant women and domestic service entered the public and political realm in the United States in the 1990s with the Clinton administration's rejection of attorney general candidates Zoë Baird and Judge Kimba Wood. Both candidates had hired illegal immigrant women as household workers. Baird had done so in spite of a 1986 immigration law that forbid the hiring of illegal immigrants as household workers. The continued willingness of feminists and professionals to exploit female im-migrants working in child care and household labor points to the need for further research about immigrant domestics in historical and contemporary society. Areas of study that might help to shape positive responses to the problems of contemporary immigrant women include: study of the racial and cultural interaction between immigrant domestics and their employers; examination of ways in which domestic workers have struggled to organize and improve conditions (including the professionalization of household la-bor); the employment of married immigrant domestics (including the im-pact that such employment has on both the immigrant woman's family and that of her employer); and global comparisons of legislation designed to improve the situation of immigrant domestics (ranging from immigration regulations to the application and enforcement of social security and tax laws).

12

German Domestic Servants in America, 1850–1914: A New Look at German Immigrant Women's Experiences

SILKE WEHNER

In immigration history studies,[1] the prevailing characterization of women has been as "dependents, migrants' wives or mothers, unproductive, illiterate, isolated, secluded from the outside world and the bearers of many children."[2] Only in the past twenty years have ethnic history studies challenged this view by demanding that immigrants' experiences should be differentiated according to class and gender. These studies stated correctly that many immigrant women were not as helpless and unable to acculturate as previously assumed and took into account particularly their participation in the American labor market.[3] In German American immigration history as well, the understanding of German immigrant women's experiences was, until the 1980s, oriented toward the predominant representation of women as "the repository of the past, the preserver of custom."[4] This stereotype was based on the assumption formed in the nineteenth century that the

1 This essay is taken from my dissertation, "Deutsche Dienstmädchen in Amerika, 1850–1914," Ph.D. diss., Universität Münster, 1993. Research for this project was supported by grants from the German Marshall Fund of the United States and the German Historical Institute, Washington, D.C.

2 In her essay, "Women in Migration: Beyond the Reductionist Outlook," in Annie Phizacklea, ed., *One Way Ticket: Migration and Female Labour* (London, 1984), 13, Mirjana Morokvasic criticizes this stereotype in view of contemporary female migration to industrial countries.

3 For a criticism of this stereotype, see H. Arnold Barton, "Scandinavian Immigrant Women's Encounter with America," *Swedish Pioneer Historical Quarterly* 25, no. 1 (1974): 37–42; Maxine S. Seller, "Beyond the Stereotype: A New Look at the Immigrant Woman, 1880–1924," *Journal of Ethnic Studies* 3 (1975): 59–70; Janice Reiff Webster, "Domestication and Americanization: Scandinavian Women in Seattle, 1888–1900," *Journal of Urban History* 4, no. 3 (1978): 275–91; Hasia R. Diner, *Erin's Daughters in America: Irish Immigrant Women in the Nineteenth Century* (Baltimore, 1983); Carl Ross and K. Marianne Wargelin Brown, *Women Who Dared: The History of Finnish-American Women* (St. Paul, Minn., 1986); Susan A. Glenn, *Daughters of the Shtetl: Life and Labor in the Immigrant Generation* (Ithaca, N.Y., 1990).

4 Dale R. Steiner, *Of Thee We Sing: Immigrants and American History* (Orlando, Fla., 1987). The same image is prevalent in Carol Hymowitz and Michaele Weissman, *A History of Women in America* (New York, 1978), 206–7, in which immigrant women are generally characterized as the "spiritual centers of their families" and "the heart and soul of family life." Some newer studies contradict this image and take into account single German immigrant women's experience. See, e.g., Wolfgang J. Helbich, Walter D. Kamphoefner, and Ulrike Sommer, eds., *Briefe aus Amerika: Deutsche Auswanderer schreiben*

267

268   *Silke Wehner*

possibilities for German immigrant women – regardless of their specific sociocultural background – were limited due to their family, child care, and household responsibilities.[5] While this image certainly applied to some women, it underestimated the fact that many married and single German women from the lower social classes had to earn a living and were thereby forced to confront American society on different levels.[6] In this essay, I will widen the scope of experiences investigated to date by examining the lives of young, single German immigrant women working as domestic servants in America between 1850 and 1914. Scrutiny of the working and living conditions of German domestics between the ages of fourteen and thirty years old, as described in their letters home, will conclude that the German women's experiences in America have to be reevaluated. In raw numbers, they represented more than one-quarter of all immigrants traveling alone at the end of the nineteenth century.[7] By investigating the particular motives and conditions of emigration of some of the many young German women belonging to the lower social classes who emigrated – not as accompanying family members, but as independent individuals or daughters traveling without their parents – it will be shown that their experiences are too important to be ignored. My argument contends that the experiences of young German women could in fact have had an accelerating influence on the process of acculturation of these young women and their future children.

aus der Neuen Welt, 1830–1930 (Munich, 1988): Monika Blaschke and Christiane Harzig, eds., *Frauen wandern aus: Deutsche Migrantinnen im 19. und 20. Jahrhundert* (Bremen, 1990); Agnes Bretting, "Frauen als Einwanderer in der Neuen Welt: Überlegungen anhand einiger Selbstzeugnisse deutsche Auswanderinnen," *Amerikastudien/American Studies* 33, no. 3 (1988): 324–27. To date, no monograph on single German immigrant women in America has been written.

5 In his book, *Das Deutschtum in den Vereinigten Staaten in seiner Bedeutung für die amerikanische Kultur* (New York, 1909; reprint, Leipzig, 1912), Albert Bernhard Faust points out that for German women, the destination "in den schlichten Künsten der Fürsorge für Haus und Familie . . . wenn sie stets fleissig spann und nähte und koch und wusch und eine stattliche Kinderschar nicht als Last, sondern als Segen empfand" (1912: 419). For a similar opinion, see Rudolf Cronau, *German Achievements in America* (New York, 1916).

6 For an account of married German women's financial problems in America, see Dorothee Schneider, " 'For Whom Are All the Good Things in Life?' German-American Housewives Discuss Their Budgets," in Hartmut Keil and John B. Jentz, eds., *German Workers in Industrial Chicago, 1850–1910* (DeKalb, Ill., 1983), 145–60; and Christiane Harzig, "The Role of German Women in the German-American Working-Class Movement in Late Nineteenth-Century New York," *Journal of American Ethnic History* 8, no. 2 (1989): 87–107.

7 One of the few statistics on the number of German women emigrating alone can be found in Wilhelm Mönckmeier, *Die deutsche überseeische Auswanderung: Ein Beitrag zur deutschen Wanderungsgeschichte* (Jena, 1912), 148–49. According to this source, more unmarried than married women emigrated alone between 1899 and 1910: 51,254 compared with 7,412. Mönckmeier states their percentage with 29.2 percent for the years between 1883 and 1894. A. Schulte im Hofe calculates their share for the years 1901 to 1913 with 23.2 percent in his *Auswanderung und Auswanderungspolitik* (Berlin, 1918), 26.

Because of their situation as self-supporting individuals, mostly living at a great distance from their families as "live-in" servants in America, the conditions of adaptation of young German domestics to American life-style, cultural habits, and a foreign language differed substantially from those of married German women who did not come into such close contact with American daily life and society. By choosing domestic service, the young single immigrants adhered to the cultural values of their homeland in which the work of women in another household was highly valued as a perfect preparation for a woman's future life. But by fulfilling these traditional female tasks in a foreign environment, the young German women's lives and attitudes changed since they were prepared to participate in urban America with the rapid technological changes in the households and cities. Life in the cities challenged their traditional social values by requiring a more independent and self-confident behavior in a modern, urban environment characterized by a heterogeneity of races, languages, and customs. The experience of domestic service, which according to Carol K. Coburn represented a "great educator," could serve to ease the assimilation of the next generations by being transmitted to the servants' future children.[8] Despite the crucial role that these "average" women played in the process of acculturation, historical studies of German immigrant women have, with few exceptions, ignored them.[9] Instead, these concentrate exclusively on the achievements and exceptional contributions in the fields of art, literature, education, political activism, and emancipation of a few "heroic" German immigrant women.[10] Although most of the young German women working as domestics did not plan to pursue a professional career or to abandon their traditional gender-expectations concerning their future roles as wives and mothers,[11] they could nevertheless become active agents of assimilation by consciously deciding to work in an American household, where they submitted themselves to new sets of values, unknown customs, and a new language, and where contact with other German immigrants was necessarily limited on account of the work they did.

---

8 Carol K. Coburn, "Learning to Serve: Education and Change in the Lives of Rural Domestics in the Twentieth Century," *Journal of Social History* 25, no. 1 (1991): 128.

9 See n. 4.

10 Cf. Cecyle S. Neidle, *America's Immigrant Women: Their Contribution to the Development of a Nation from 1609 to the Present* (New York, 1975); Faust had already differentiated between the "heroic" and the "domestic" type of German woman in America. For a critique of the stereotype of the female immigrants on the American frontier, who are mostly portrayed as "heroic in many cases, but silent and accepting of the new environment into which they had been thrust," see Adolf Schroeder, "Eden on the Missouri: Immigrant Women on the Western Frontier," *Yearbook of German-American Studies* 18 (1983): 197–215.

11 Bretting, "Frauen als Einwanderer in der Neuen Welt," 327.

Besides growing accustomed to American culture and society, young German domestics could at the same time foster cultural understanding between Germans and Americans on a private, personal level. They thereby contributed to the formation of a positive image of the German among Americans. The process of acculturation[12] was bilateral since German domestics also brought a "piece of a strange world"[13] into their American employers' homes by working as cooks or children's maids. This exchange was particularly intense in the years between 1850 and 1914, when German single women immigrated in large numbers and made up an important part of the servant population in America. World War I, which cut off German immigration, and the increasing migration of black women after the turn of the twentieth century to the northern states, where they took over servant positions formerly occupied by immigrants, ended this period of intense firsthand cultural contact between German domestics and American employers.

I

An evaluation of the process of acculturation of German female domestic servants in America has to take into account the conditions of emigration. What was the situation of German single domestic servants in their home country and what motives led to their emigration? The majority of the emigrating young German domestics belonged to the lower social classes, most of them coming from rural areas.[14] They were used to poor living conditions, which Dorothee Wierling has characterized as "proletarian." Their lives were "shaped by extreme insecurity, little authority in decision making, and the need to integrate all family members into the labor [force]."[15] The young German girls were used to primitive, narrow living accommodations with few rooms and little privacy. Their clothes were simple and functional, their nutrition usually centered on potatoes and bread unless they were fortunate enough to have their own small vegetable gar-

12 My use of the term "acculturation" follows the definition given by Åke Hultcrantz in *General Ethnological Concepts* (Copenhagen, 1960). It is understood as "the process of change in complete culture-contact . . . between two cultures leading to increasing similarities between them in most cultural fields" (17). Hultcrantz points out "that every phase of acculturation also corresponds to an attitudinal change" (35).

13 Georg R. Schroubek, "Die böhmische Köchin: Ihre kulturelle Mittlerrolle in literarischen Zeugnissen der Jahrhundertwende," in *Dienstboten in Stadt und Land* (Berlin, 1981), 69.

14 Dorothee Wierling, "Vom Mädchen zum Dienstmädchen: Kindliche Sozialisation und Berufsvorbereitung," in *Dienstboten in Stadt und Land*, 74.

15 Wierling, "Vom Mädchen zum Dienstmädchen," 74.

den.[16] As daughters of the lower peasantry or land workers in the rural areas, or as daughters of small store or restaurant keepers in the cities, they worked since early childhood in the households, on the fields and in the garden. After school completion, around the age of fourteen, they were usually sent off to work in domestic service, following a migration pattern that was common throughout Germany.[17] By leaving their families at an early age, they spent an important part of their socialization phase in an environment of strangers.

As domestic servants in Germany, young women had to obey *Gesindeordnungen* – laws regulating the relationship between master and servant that mostly favored the master's position. Until 1918, fifty-nine different *Gesindeordnungen* were in effect in Germany,[18] some of them unchanged since the seventeenth and eighteenth centuries. The *Gesindeordnung für sämtliche Provinzen der preussischen Monarchie,* originating in 1810, covered the largest part of Germany: East and West Prussia, Silesia, Pomerania, Brandenburg with Berlin, Saxony, and Westphalia. Paragraph 77 of this law even allowed physical punishment in the case of disobedience: "If the servants cause anger on the part of the employer due to improper behavior, and are therefore treated with scolding words or minor violence, they cannot ask for legal satisfaction."[19] *Gesindeordnungen* excluded domestic servants from the legal and social rights that other employees in the German labor market had managed to acquire. They provided the employer with nineteen different reasons to discharge his servant, such as disobedience, robbery, carelessness, sickness, and reasons relating to moral issues like "cursing" or "sexual excesses," but allowed the servant to leave his position only in the case of danger to health and life or financial damage through the employer.[20] Whereas they gave detailed orders as to the tasks of servants, who were incessantly reminded of their lower social status and their duty to be obliging and willing, they hardly mentioned any legal obligations of employers toward their servants. Regulations concerning, for example, the nutrition, living conditions, and health of the servants remained vague and were mostly subject to the individual discretion of the employer. Most important

16 Günter Wiegelmann, *Alltags- und Festspeisen, Wandel und gegenwärtige Stellung* (Marburg, 1967). For the particularly bad food of the servants as reflected in terms like *Gesindebraten* and *Dienstbotenkaffee,* see Oscar Stillich, *Die Lage der weiblichen Dienstboten in Berlin* (Berlin, 1902), and Reinhard Sieder, *Sozialgeschichte der Familie* (Frankfurt/Main, 1987), 52.

17 Michael Mitterauer, "Gesindedienst und Jugendphase im europäischen Vergleich," *Geschichte und Gesellschaft* 11 (1985): 177–204.

18 Wilhelm Kähler, *Gesindewesen und Gesinderecht in Deutschland* (Jena, 1896).

19 Ibid., 158.

20 Dorothee Wierling, *Mädchen für alles: Arbeitsalltag und Lebensgeschichte städtischer Dienstmädchen um die Jahrhundertwende* (Berlin and Bonn, 1987), 88.

was the fact that because of *Gesindeordnungen,* servants were not free to change their positions whenever they wanted. If they left their positions without the employer's consent or a legally accepted reason, they could be forced by the police to return.

Another way to restrict the work conditions of domestic servants in Germany were the *Dienstbücher* – service logs controlled by the local police that listed all former positions, with commentaries by the employers. Legally introduced in 1846,[21] they did not, as many employers claimed, serve to inform about the social background of the servant when shown to a prospective employer, but rather helped to discipline the servants and to keep them from changing positions under the threat of a negative review.[22]

Domestic servants in Germany were used to working under very restrictive conditions; they also faced a life after the work experience that did not offer any opportunities for major changes of their economic situation. The perspectives for the future of single lower-class women in the cities as well as in the rural areas of Germany were limited by the barriers created by social norms and by the few opportunities they had, due largely to a fragmented education and the need to earn a living. In rural areas, the meager land resources were diminished by an increasing population whose needs could no longer be satisfied by farming, crafts, or a mixture of the two as in the case of the rural workers. Already used to a low standard of living, these laborers' hopes for financial stability decreased, due to the effects of a highly competitive industrialized world.

These circumstances also influenced the women's lives since on the one hand, their own work was not sufficiently rewarded, and on the other hand, their prospective husbands did not earn enough to start a family and were forced from their land. Marriage, the only opportunity for women of the lower social classes to advance socially, was carried out within rigid social boundaries, so that most of the domestics could never escape their miserable economic situation.[23] The hierarchical structure of the rural villages was dependent upon land possession and social status, forming a traditional social system that, as Ingeborg Weber-Kellermann states, stabilized the "old peasant order" (*altbäuerliche Ordnung*),[24] and restricted the marriage opportunities

21 Wierling, *Mädchen für alles,* 16.
22 Cf. Else Conrad, *Das Dienstbotenproblem in den nordamerikanischen Staaten und was es uns lehrt* (Jena, 1908), 37. *Dienstbücher* and *Gesindeordnungen* helped, according to Wolfgang Kaschuba, to keep the servants in a "state of subjugation" (*Unmündigkeit*) and "incapacity to act socially and politically." See Kaschuba, *Lebenswelt und Kultur der unterbürgerlichen Schichten im 19. und 20. Jahrhundert* (Munich, 1990), 36.
23 See Ingeborg Weber-Kellermann, *Die deutsche Familie: Versuch einer Sozialgeschichte* (Frankfurt/Main, 1974), 147.
24 Ibid., 86.

of the lower classes. Despite the hope that migration to the cities would improve the chances for marriage, the majority of urban domestics married unskilled or skilled workers, a fact proving that the chances of marrying into a higher social class were limited there as well.[25]

To these young single women, America offered better working conditions, with higher wages and a higher standard of living. Neither *Gesindeordnungen* nor *Dienstbücher* were in effect in America. Although even there, domestic servants were exempted from social insurance laws and unions,[26] they nevertheless had much more freedom to choose and change positions. The relief that German servants might feel once they had escaped the restrictive working conditions in Germany is expressed in Wilhelmine Wiebusch's first letter home. In 1884 she wrote from New York to her friend Marie, also a domestic: "We are living like savages in the land of freedom, so far we haven't needed any papers, nobody has asked for our names or background."[27] Another servant, Elisabeth Kleinegesse from Varensell in Westphalia, stated in 1859 in a letter from New York: "Here one is respected as a human being."[28]

America particularly raised hopes for improved marriage opportunities and social mobility. As Merle Curti and Kendall Birr have pointed out, this idea was one of the "attractions" America offered women: "The opportunities in the Old World for humble girls with inadequate dowries to marry advantageously in the New was a factor in forming the American image."[29]

This image had been shaped by descriptions in immigrant guides emphasizing the good chances for domestics on the American marriage and labor market. Many women of the lower social classes could have been stimulated to emigrate by Traugott Bromme's *Hand- und Reisebuch für Auswanderer,* which appeared around 1850 and stated:

The treatment of the servants, who are generally called "help" here – the terms "Knechte" and "Mägde" are totally unknown – is excellent, and the social distance between master and servant is hardly noticeable concerning the names as well as

25 Wierling, *Mädchen für alles,* 251.
26 Donna Van Raaphorst, *Union Maids Not Wanted: Organizing Domestic Workers, 1870–1940* (New York, 1988), 222.
27 Wilhelmine Wiebusch's domestic service experience in Hamburg prior to emigration can be followed through her Dienstbuch. Her letters have been published in Helbich et al., *Briefe aus Amerika,* 554–69, 563. They are originally part of the collection of emigrants' letters, the Bochumer Auswanderbriefe-Sammlung (hereafter cited as BABS), located at the Universität Bochum. I want to thank Prof. Helbich and Ulrike Sommer for helping me use this archive.
28 Letter dated Aug. 21, 1859: "Hir wirt man noch cheachtet wie ein Mensch." Elisabeth Kleingesse's letters are part of the collection of the Westfälisches Freilichtmuseum in Detmold. Also see Regina Fritsch, "Briefe aus Amerika: Zur Lebensgeschichte einer Frau im 19. Jahrhundert," *Beiträge zur Volkskunde und Hausforschung* 2 (1987): 145–50.
29 Merle Curti and Kendall Birr, "The Immigrant and the American Image in Europe, 1860–1914," *Mississippi Valley Historical Review* 37 (1950): 221.

the behavior. There you don't hear any scolding or cursing, you are not aware of bad moods of inspectors or foremen, and still the work gets ahead very well. A few years suffice to make them independent. . . . Female servants never work in the fields, but take care of the homes, the dairy and at most the garden; industrious ones are very much sought after, and fair-minded maids have often found their luck as housewives in America. Industrious, settled girls, who are comely of body can be sure to receive marriage offers in the first year.[30]

Although these uncritical and very optimistic views of conditions of domestic service in America applied primarily to the situation of service in the rural areas around the middle of the nineteenth century, this and other descriptions in immigrant guides as well as in letters of already settled immigrants had a general tremendous impact on domestics in Germany who compared the promising situation in America with work and life in Germany. Even the contemporary German American literature used the idea that young German servants could find a "heaven on earth" in America by marrying an artisan.[31] Descriptions such as in Karl Friedrich Wilhelm Wander's *Auswanderungs-Katechismus* could be very enticing. In answering the question: "Should girls be encouraged to go to America with the prospect of finding a good opportunity to marry?" [*Ist es Mädchen anzurathen, nach Amerika zu gehen, in der Absicht, bald eine gute Heirathsgelegenheit zu finden?*], Wander informed the reader:

Girls who are used to the heavy rural and farm work, or who know how to run a middle-class kitchen and family business [*Familienwirthschaft*], are allowed to expect a good position and can find soon, if they are fortunate enough to possess a liking bodily expression, an opportunity to marry. . . . It is true that German housewives, under the condition that they have kept their characters over there, are very honored; and in some places there is still a great demand for marriageable persons of the female sex; since one tends to prefer a strong, German girl in full bloom to a pale American through whom the sun seems to shine.[32]

The deplored scarcity of women in the American West and the fact that in America, the balance between German single men and women was uneven, underlined the impression that in America the factor of class ceased to hinder the opportunities of single German women on the marriage market. Hedwig Schindler, for example, a widow who emigrated with her two children and mother in 1891 and worked as a domestic on a farm, wrote

30 Traugott Bromme, *Hand- und Reisebuch für Auswanderer,* 6th ed. (1848; reprint, Bamberg, 1850), 434–35.
31 See G. Stürenberg, *Klein-Deutschland: Bilder aus dem New Yorker Alltagsleben* (New York, 1886), 218–25: "Gretchen, oder: Mächtiger als der Reichskanzler."
32 Karl Friedrich Wilhelm Wander, *Auswanderungs-Katechismus: Ein Ratgeber für Auswanderer, besonders Diejenigen, welche nach Nordamerika auswandern wollen* (Glogau, 1852), 161.

to a friend that she can even be selective in view of the favorable situation in which she found herself living among German immigrants in rural America: "I could have married already; many young German men visit us, one from [Hanover] calls himself my fiancé, but I am not going to agree so soon, I can always make a good catch, since German women are *very popular here.*"[33]

A letter by another German domestic, Barbara Meister (born Ruess), who, like many others, organized her emigration through the help of relatives living in Illinois, shows that marriage was not restricted by social norms in America, which required bride and groom to have a sufficient dowry, as was often the case in Germany:

A rich farming woman who wanted to have me for a long time took me into her house where I soon got to know her son Jackob Meister; I stayed there for some time and she asked me to marry him but I refused to do so at the beginning; I was supposed to marry one of her sons earlier but could not understand it and always said that I did not have anything whereas she answered that I did not need anything; that would never be possible in Germany but here the girl does not need anything, if the boy has a little something they get along.[34]

The feeling of having more freedom and being treated better in America referred not only to the status as servants or to the lack of marriage restrictions but also to the apparently different status of women. Immigrant guides as well as letters of male and female immigrants inform us about the different status of women in America and Germany. Georg Treu, for example, informed potential immigrants in his *Buch der Auswanderung,* published in 1848:

Women are, by the way, highly respected in America, at most taking care of the house, but never working in the fields. This would rather be considered a high disgrace and cause mockery for husband and brothers in the neighborhood. In the cities, the woman does not go to the market like in Germany, but this is exclusively done by the men, who, with baskets at their arms, go to get the groceries every day.[35]

Another guide described the situation in almost identical words:

---

33 Letter dated Dec. 26, 1891: ". . . ich hätte mich längst verheirathen können; es kommen immer Deutsche junge Männer zu uns; einer aus [Hanover] nennt sich meinen Bräutigam, aber ich werde nicht so schnell einwilligen; ich kann jederzeit noch Parthie machen, da deutsche Frauen sehr beliebt sind hier." Hedwig Schindler's letters are part of BABS.

34 Letter from Metamara, Ill., dated Sept. 20, 1869. Letters from Barbara Meister née Ruess, originally part of BABS, have been published in *"Alle Menschen sind dort gleich . . .": Die deutsche Amerika-Auswanderung im 19. und 20. Jahrhundert,* ed. Wolfgang J. Helbich (Düsseldorf, 1988), 100–107.

35 Georg Treu, *Das Buch der Auswanderung* (Bamberg, 1848), 132.

For the women, Americans have great respect that could almost be called awe . . . no woman works in the fields, since this would be considered a disgrace for her sex; and if one sees a newly arrived German farmwife, who can not tame her diligence so quickly and adapt to the American customs, working outside, the whole American neighborhood gets angry and gossips about it for a long time.[36]

These descriptions did not necessarily intend to encourage the German immigrant women to adapt to this behavior, but, in fact, served mostly to keep them away from it by emphasizing the alleged virtues of the German female – diligence and submissiveness in comparison with the negative stereotype of the American woman.[37] But positive reactions documented in the letters of German women about the treatment of women in American society show that the women indeed enjoyed their new role in society: "I have it very nice now, here one is a different woman than in Germany, the name 'woman' [*Weib*] is seldom heard."[38]

After comparing the perspectives of their new life with the restrictive life in Germany, most young German immigrant women decided to stay forever, even those who had only planned a temporary stay in order to earn some money, learn the language, or satisfy their curiosity. Once they got accustomed to the new circumstances, even feelings of homesickness could be overcome in view of the opportunities that America offered young German women from the lower social classes. Barbara Meister, for example, tried to soothe her family's concern for her well-being in 1868: "Dearest parents, do not worry I can get along very well in the New World and homesickness does not bother me; if it should bother me though, I always think about your positions in service."[39]

Although repeated pleas for photographs and more information about family members, friends, and neighbors nevertheless point to the strong wish for continued participation in the family life in Germany and, thereby, to the importance of maintaining contact with their families after emigration, the consciously made decision to stay in America, away from family and friends, also points to the readiness of the young single German woman

---

36 Friedrich Vulpius, *Amerikanische Erfahrungen, Winke und Warnungen für Auswanderungslustige* (Belle Vue, 1847), cited in Ruth Roebke, "Informationen für Frauen und das Frauenbild in Auswanderratgebern aus dem 19. Jahrhundert," in Arbeitsgruppe Volkskundliche Frauenforschung, ed., *Frauenalltag   Frauenforschung* (Frankfurt/Main, 1988), 102.

37 On the negative stereotype of the American woman, who is usually portrayed as lazily sitting in her rocking chair, see Roebke, "Informationen für Frauen und das Frauenbild," 102ff.

38 Letter dated Sept. 20, 1869.

39 Letter dated Oct. 25, 1869, from Springbay: "Liebste Eltern seid ausser Sorgen ich kann in der neuen Welt gut durchkommen und das Heimweh plagt micht nicht wenn es mich quelen sollte denke ich jedesmal an Eure Dienstplätze . . ."

to confront the new culture and society rather than to return to the old familiar environment.

II

Young single German women's choice of a place of work was influenced by several factors – ethnicity, social background, acquired skills, and education – that together formed the emigrant's "cultural baggage," along with the opportunities offered by the American labor market.[40] Ethnicity and social background determined whether a woman was supposed to work at all or for how long during her life cycle; they shaped the values and expectations that accompanied her on her search for a job. In the case of a single young German woman arriving in America, all of these factors led to domestic service as a transitional phase in her life.

According to the *Reports of the Immigration Commission,* 61.1 percent of all German women (married and single) immigrating to America at the turn of the twentieth century had not worked prior to their emigration; for an additional 14.9 percent, the work experience had been limited to domestic service.[41] As can be concluded from an analysis of immigrant ship passenger lists, the majority of the single German women aboard gave domestic service as their occupation, which means that they had either worked in that profession in Germany, or that they were looking forward to doing so in America.[42]

The alternatives that a newly arrived and thus inexperienced immigrant, especially a woman, had on the labor market were not numerous. The lack of English-language knowledge and the generally low skill requirements for American industry left most unmarried German female workers with the choice between unskilled factory work and domestic service (many married German women took in boarders to earn extra income).[43] A majority of the single German women found employment in domestic service: In 1900, 54.6 percent of all wage-earning women were working in that field, compared with 25.1 percent in manufacturing and mechanical pursuits, 8.3 percent in trade and transportation, and only 3.0 percent in professional

40 See Dirk Hoerder, ed., *The Immigrant Labor Press in North America, 1840s–1970s* (Westport, Conn., 1987), 16.
41 *Reports of the Immigration Commission,* vol. 1: *Abstracts* (Washington, D.C., 1911; reprint, 1970]), 359–60.
42 This statement refers to an analysis of passenger lists included in my study of German servant women's emigration to the United States. See n. 1.
43 See U.S. Dept. of Labor, *The Immigrant Woman and Her Job,* by Caroline Manning (Washington, D.C., 1930), 50ff.

services.[44] Only a small minority of German women – 7.9 percent – continued to work after marriage;[45] wage-earning outside of the household was, in effect, an experience mainly shared by young, unmarried German women.

In the choice between unskilled factory work or household work in America, the balance was tipped by the social and gender expectations imbedded in the German women through their ethnic upbringing, domestic service being considered the consequent and unquestioned result of the transmitted values of the German women's native culture. According to the opinion of the peasantry in Germany, a factory was not considered an appropriate workplace for a young woman, but rather a step down the social ladder, whereas domestic service offered more social security, independence from the family, and a stronger emphasis on the traditional female tasks.[46] As Heidi Müller points out, the "higher prestige" of domestic service also resulted from the close contact with the upper social classes.

Particularly female servants in middle-class homes . . . identified to a high degree with the life-style of their employers. In the eyes of these girls, factory work was a step down socially and not considered as a professional alternative.[47]

In German culture as well as in northern European cultures in general – as studies of Scandinavian[48] and Irish[49] women prove – the work of women in the households was highly valued. It was considered an ideal preparation for the young woman's future role as wife and mother (and it was also one of the few workplaces available to women in nonindustrialized societies). In her study of female attitudes in Germany, Esther Schönmann indicates that the teaching of domestic skills, obedience, and how to give up personal interests for the comfort of others by focusing on female roles in home and marriage was seen as a way to improve a woman's virtues.

Daughters were trained in an almost militaristic way for their threefold fate as wife, housewife, and mother and at the same time for the unquestioned acceptance of

44 *Reports of the Immigration Commission*, vol. 28: *Occupation of the First and Second Generation of Immigrants to the United States*, 74.
45 According to the U.S. Bureau of Labor, 88.9 percent of all German female employees were single. *Report on the Condition of Woman and Child Wage-Earners in the United States*, vol. 18: *Employment of Women and Children in Selected Industries* (Washington, D.C., 1913), 30.
46 Kaschuba, *Lebenswelt und Kultur der unterbürgerlichen Schichten*, 20; Wierling, "Vom Mädchen zum Dienstmädchen," 83.
47 Heidi Müller, *Dienstbare Geister: Leben und Arbeitswelt städtischer Dienstboten* (Berlin, 1981), 109.
48 See Joy K. Lintelman, " 'America Is the Woman's Promised Land' – Swedish Women and American Domestic Service," *Journal of American Ethnic History* 8 (1989): 9–23; Varpu Lindström-Best, " 'I Won't Be a Slave!' – Finnish Domestics in Canada, 1911–1930," in Jean Burnet, ed., *Looking into My Sister's Eyes: An Exploration in Women's History* (Toronto, 1986), 33–53.
49 See Diner, *Erin's Daughters in America*.

authorities. An important goal of the education was the foundation of gentleness and charm, obedience and diplomacy in the interest of enabling the girls to enter into a harmonious marriage.[50]

Combined with limited formal education, these goals also served to prepare girls from the lower classes for their roles as obedient, submissive servants.

The importance of ethnic and social values for the choice of a woman's workplace after emigration becomes evident in a comparison with immigrant women of other nationalities. Although the lack of language knowledge applied to the majority of female immigrants of all nationalities, their participation in the labor market was highly differentiated. The possession of advanced industrial skills permitted a wider variety of job choices, as in the example of Jewish women.[51] But differing cultural norms and the general distaste for domestic service, considered "menial" labor, were the main reasons why, for example, more Italian and Jewish women avoided domestic service and looked for employment in industry.[52] Only every eleventh Italian woman and every seventh Russian woman (most of the Russian immigrants were Jewish) went into domestic service – compared with every second Irish and Scandinavian woman and every third German woman.[53] Mainly employed in the garment industry, Italian and Jewish women worked at home in family-run sweat shops or in the ethnically concentrated factories. The case of the Italians, in particular, points to the impact of ethnic values on the work experience of women. As Virginia Yans McLaughlin has highlighted in her study of Italians in Buffalo, New York, the cultural attitude toward "female honor" kept Italian women away from domestic service.

Buffalo's Irish, Polish, Swedish and German women commonly sought employment as domestics in middle-class homes, but jealous Italian men would not permit

50 Esther Schönmann, "Es allen recht machen, sich selbst vergessen – Einübung weiblicher Verhaltensweisen in Anstandsbüchern vor 1930," *Jahrbuch für Volkskunde* 13 (1990): 80.
51 Of Jewish women from Russia, 61.7 percent had been engaged in manufacturing prior to emigration. See *Reports of the Immigration Commission,* vol. 1: *Abstracts,* 361.
52 For an example of a Jewish woman who considered domestic service too menial to be taken up by her daughter, see Rose Cohen's commentary of her mother's reaction in David Katzman, *Seven Days a Week: Women and Domestic Service in Industrializing America* (1978; reprint, New York, 1983), 12.
53 Joan Younger Dickinson, *The Role of the Immigrant Women in the U.S. Labor Force, 1890–1930* (New York, 1980), 76–81. According to *Occupations of the First and Second Generations of Immigrants to the United States* (Washington, D.C., 1911), 76–77, 37.7 percent of the Italian women and 41.2 percent of the Russian women worked in the needle trades. See also Thomas Kessner and Betty Boyd Caroli, "New Immigrant Women at Work: Italians and Jews in New York City, 1880–1905," *Journal of Ethnic Studies* 5, no. 4 (1978): 19–31.

their wives to work under another man's roof, no matter how serious the family's economic circumstances.[54]

In the case of single German women, domestic service dovetailed with the social and gender expectations of their society, by representing an ideal profession that was supposed to be pursued in a transitional phase until marriage. This work offered these women, newcomers in a foreign country, many advantages since it provided them with board and lodging plus high wages in comparison with rates in Germany. While domestics in Germany around the turn of the twentieth century were paid between 150 and 250 marks per year (beginners received only 60 to 100 marks; cooks received the highest wages),[55] the average yearly wages in America, as reported by the employees in a study prepared under the direction of the U.S. Industrial Commission, ranged from $78 in the South to $286 in the West.[56] This meant that even the lowest-paid servant in America earned up to four times as much as a servant in Germany. German domestics were enthusiastic about the higher wages and repeatedly commented on the much better financial situation in America, like Karoline Pacher, who in her first letter home in 1891 stated that "I like it very much here, I have all that I want to eat and to drink and earn 48 M. per month – what would I have at home?"[57] Descriptions of higher wages also served as an invitation to emigrate for the female readers of these letters. In 1884 Wilhelmine Wiebusch tried to interest her friend Marie, who was a maid in Hamburg, to join her and another friend in New York: "Anna is the second girl and I cook; we both receive 12 dollars (50 marks) per month, what do you think Marie, wouldn't you like to come to America as well?"[58]

The higher wages enabled the German domestics to save their money for a dowry, to send part of the wages to Germany to supplement the income of their families as they used to in Germany,[59] or to help finance the emigration of other family members. The letters also point to the fact

---

54 Virginia Yans McLaughlin, "Patterns of Work and Family Organization: Buffalo's Italians," in Theodore K. Rabb and Robert I. Rotberg, eds., *The Family in History. Interdisciplinary Essays* (New York, 1971), 111–26; see also Franc Sturino, "The Role of Women in Italian Immigration to the New World," in Burnet, *Looking into My Sister's Eyes,* 21–32.

55 Müller, *Dienstbare Geister,* 226.

56 Gail Laughlin, *Domestic Service, Report of the U.S. Industrial Commission,* vol. 14 (Washington, D.C., 1902), 748.

57 Letter dated Sept. 2, 1891, from Philadelphia: "Es gefällt mir sehr gut, ich habe zu essen und zu trinken was ich verlange und hab den Monat 48 M. was hät ich zu Hause." Karoline Pacher's letters are part of BABS.

58 Letter dated Sept. 12, 1884.

59 Karoline Pacher, e.g., regularly sends home more than half of her month's wages, but, at least at the beginning, defends her brother who does not send any money by saying "er denkt auch . . . an Euch aber wenn er Geld hat dann hats doch kein Bode er trinkt so gern den Bier."

that many women enjoyed their new consumer freedom by buying clothes they could never have afforded (or were not allowed to wear because of social norms) in Germany. Because domestic service in America offered more advantages than disadvantages, they mostly ignored the fact that over the years, this profession had acquired a low social status.

From the middle of the nineteenth century, domestic service in American cities began to change. On the one hand, the relationship of employer to employee was being reworked, and, on the other, the status of domestic service as a profession was shifting.[60] Starting with the influx of the Irish immigration in the 1840s, domestic service had increasingly developed into a profession for immigrants. American women shunned domestic service because of the social disadvantages associated with it, including lack of privacy, interference in the servant's private life, isolation, and the constant reminder of status differences while at work.[61] Lucy M. Salmon, the author of the first thorough study on domestic service, stated in 1897 that another reason was the "competition with the foreign born and Negro element that seems objectionable to the American born."[62] With the widening of the female labor market, American women increasingly left domestic service and moved to other, newly developed occupations such as clerking in the new department stores, or in work as telephone operators and secretaries.[63]

In total, these developments created the social stigma accorded to domestic service, since it did not require any education or special skills and could be carried out by any newly arrived female immigrant. Because most immigrant servants belonged to a lower social class than their employers and sometimes did not even speak the same language, the social gap between employer and employee widened and the relationship became more impersonal.

Many German women were nevertheless attracted by the promises of America, a situation that was met by a high demand for servants in American society, which could not be filled. Increasing urbanization and industrialization plus the reluctance of American women to go into domestic service had created a scarcity of domestic servants. Urban families in particular depended on immigrant domestics,[64] who in 1900 represented 38.3 percent

---

60 See Katzman, *Seven Days,* 44ff.; Faye E. Dudden, *Serving Women: Household Service in Nineteenth-Century America* (Middletown, Conn., 1983).
61 Lucy Maynard Salmon, *Domestic Service* (New York, 1897; reprint, New York, 1972), 151ff.
62 Ibid., 150.
63 See Dickinson, *The Role of the Immigrant Woman in the U.S. Labor Force,* 209; Barbara Mayer Wertheimer, *We Were There: The Story of Working Women in America* (New York, 1977), 151ff.
64 According to the statistics given by the U.S. Bureau of the Census, Dept. of Commerce and Labor, *Statistics of Women at Work* (Washington, D.C., 1907), 43–44, native women of native parentage

of all servants among female breadwinners in the United States.[65] Among
the many immigrant women in domestic service, the Irish and German
women represented a majority. Of the 590,084 foreign-born domestic servants around 1900, 195,000 came from Ireland and 160,939 from Germany,
together almost two-thirds of all foreign-born servants in the United States
(the Scandinavian countries additionally supplied 75,180 servants).[66]

Besides the cultural and social reasons that led to domestic service mentioned already, American attitudes toward the German female immigrants
also influenced the choice of work. Although in constant need of servants,
American employers proved to be very selective in their choice of the
servants. Books and articles in family and women's magazines mention
strong prejudices of Americans against Irish women – mainly because they
were Catholic[67] (despite the fact that they had the advantage of the language) – and also against Italian women, of whom it was said in one article:

> The great majority of Italian women lack a sense of order, or of time, and with
> them, as with other women, the absence of these two mental essentials is the cause
> of waste. . . . It is impossible to teach an Italian the dampers of a stove. . . . Econ-
> omies in using, so natural to an American housewife, are unknown to the Italian,
> their economies are negative, they go without.[68]

In contrast, Americans not only retained German women to work as
servants, but they even encouraged them to do so. An analysis of advertisements in the *New York Times* between 1870 and 1920 reveals that the
German servants were closely associated with the American ideal of the
"Protestant native white servant."[69] Advertisements looking for "a neat,
tidy girl, Protestant, German or American" were very common.[70] Together
with other Protestant domestics from Scandinavia, Germans seemed to fit
best the assertion: "Housework is natural and easy for the hardy women of
northern European countries," and represented perfect substitutes for the
American girls.[71]

represented a large number of the servant population only in cities with less than 50,000 inhabitants,
whereas immigrant women primarily served in bigger cities.

65 Ibid., 45. This number only represents the foreign-born servants; the native-born servants with one
or both parents being foreign-born made up an additional 20.5 percent of all servants.

66 Ibid., 47.

67 For prejudices against Irish women, see Oscar Handlin, *Boston's Immigrants: A Study in Acculturation*
(Cambridge, Mass., 1941; reprint, New York, 1972).

68 Lillian Betts, "Italian Peasants in a New Law Tenement," *Harper's Bazaar* 38 (1904): 804.

69 Daniel E. Sutherland, *Americans and Their Servants: Domestic Service in the United States from 1800 to
1920* (Baton Rouge, La., 1981), 26.

70 *New York Times,* May 1, 1886.

71 Izola Forrester, "The 'Girl' Problem," *Good Housekeeping* 54, no. 9 (1912): 381–82. In this article,

The popularity of German women as servants was further supported by the long-time experience of Americans with German immigrants since colonial times, when Germans had come as "indentured servants" and worked on American farms.[72] Since the middle of the nineteenth century, an ever larger number of Americans came into contact with German or German American women as neighbors or servant girls and were accustomed to their culture. According Frederick C. Luebke, the German woman was seen as a "model of cleanliness and efficiency; her daughter was valued as a reliable houseservant or maid."[73]

While German "live-in" servants were daily confronted with the customs of American culture, they might also transfer some of their native customs to the new environment in which they worked and lived – besides being the representatives of a lower social class than their employers, a foreign language, and often a different religion. Cooks who were allowed to work without interference from their mistresses could introduce German recipes, like Friederike Rübeck, who gained admiration for her puddings and cakes, adding: "I told them [i.e., her employer] that [they might think this was good but that] it was really nothing and that they should see what they cook in Germany!"[74] In professional child care as well, German domestics might play an influential role, since Friedrich Fröbel's idea of the "kindergarten" had been exported to America. Advertisements in the American daily press around the turn of the century show a particular popularity for German "Kinderfräuleins" trained after the "Fröbel-Kindergarten-System."[75] It is difficult to document specific evidence of German domestics' influence on, for example, American food habits, education, or holiday celebrations, since the range of influences depended very much on the liberty that was given to the domestics to fulfill their tasks as cooks, childmaids, or governesses. Nevertheless, it might be asked if the experiences of Americans with their German servants did not improve the cultural un-

Forrester states: "We have found that housework, especially for the eastern European girl, offers many difficulties, because the better class of homes do not know the girl from eastern Europe as they do the girl from Scandinavia or Germany and therefore hesitate to employ them. Many of them have no housekeeping experience, and do not make desirable servants in good homes."

72 See Sharon V. Salinger, " 'Send No More Women' – Servants in Eighteenth-Century Pennsylvania," *Pennsylvania Magazine of History and Biography* 107 (1983): 29–48.

73 Frederick C. Luebke, "Images of German Immigrants in the United States and Brazil, 1890–1918," in Frank Trommler and Joseph McVeigh, eds., *America and the Germans,* 2 vols. (Philadelphia, 1985), 1:209.

74 "Ich habe Ihnen gesagt, dass das noch nichts wäre; in Deutschland kochten sie noch ganz anders!" Letter from Friederike Rübeck, Aug. 1, 1927, from Brooklyn. I would like to thank Dr. Heinz-Ulrich Kammeier (Bielefeld) for lending me this letter.

75 Cf., e.g., *New York Times,* May 18, 1894.

derstanding between both societies to a great extent and help to promote the creation of the generally positive image of the German immigrant in America.

The German servants' popularity was also connected to the image of the German immigrant woman working side by side with her husband on the farm; it is still present in the cliché of the efficient, industrious, clean German woman as portrayed in literature, movies, and advertisements.[76] The idea of a "large, red-armed, strong German girl,"[77] waiting to serve others, gave rise to hopes for a solution to the "servant problem" at the turn of the century.[78] In newspaper advertisements, servant agencies offered a large number of German girls as prime choice; some farmers even traveled from the Midwest to the immigrant ports to secure a supply of German girls.[79]

Not only American, but also German employers looked forward to employing German servants. "Greenhorns" – newly arrived and thus inexperienced immigrants – were particularly popular because, still being used to less wages and freedom, they could be exploited more than American or "Americanized" domestics. The many "wanted" advertisements in the German American daily press of the time especially asking for a "German girl, preferably one just arrived,"[80] point to the fact that language and culture affinity were only important factors in the selection of domestics as they also guaranteed them to be willing, obliging, and ready to work for low wages. This attitude is shared by Hanna Sellschopp, who, in 1891, wrote from San Francisco:

I have a new girl now, my old one did not function any more, a Rhinelander, a so-called greenhorn, who has only been in the country for four months. She does not understand a word of English which is good, on the one hand, in terms of gossiping, running away, etc. but poses a hindrance, on the other hand, if we have visitors or she is supposed to get some things; but one has to be satisfied, particularly in this country, when it comes to domestic servants.[81]

76 See, e.g., the famous "Dutch Cleanser."
77 M. E. W. Sherwood, "The Lack of Good Servants," *North American Review* 153 (1891): 551.
78 Despite an actual increase in the number of servants between 1870 and 1920 from 901,954 to 1,356,531, due to a fast-growing middle class, the demand could never be satisfied. The situation was considered a problem by those employers who could not afford to pay high wages or to hire more than one servant. They also complained about the difficulty of finding the ideal willing and faithful servant. See Salmon, *Domestic Service.*
79 David E. Schob, *Hired Hands and Plowboys: Farm Labor in the Midwest, 1815–1860* (Urbana, Ill., 1975), 193.
80 See, e.g., *New Yorker Staatszeitung,* May 6, 1900, with several advertisements of this type.
81 Letter dated April 5, 1895: "Ich habe nun auch ein neues Mädchen bekommen, meine Alte taugte nicht mehr, eine Rheinländerin, ein sogenanntes Greenhorn, die erst vier Monate im Lande ist. Sie versteht noch kein Wort englisch, eines theils ganz gut in Bezug auf schwatzen, ausrennen usw.,

It is also prevalent in the comment of another German employer from Portland, who envied her German neighbor for having a "real German girl and so undemanding, she does everything [that the employer wants]."[82] But despite the fact that some German employers tried to take advantage of their German domestics' lack of knowledge about their new rights as servants, the scarcity of servants in America, combined with the particular popularity of German (and other northern European) servants and the fact that domestic service not only complied with the social and gender expectations of their home country but also offered many advantages to young German women, altogether constituted favorable conditions for their emigration to America that could not be paralleled by another German immigrant group.

III

The intensity of the reactions to the new circumstances depended upon several factors: whether a woman served in rural, ethnically concentrated areas or in the multinational, modern cities; and whether she had a position among Germans or Americans. While American and German historians have argued[83] that German domestics' chances on the servant market were limited by their poor English, and that they therefore mostly went into German households, one should not conclude that they stayed in these positions.[84] Even in cases where German women served in the households of relatives or friends, until they had paid off the debts incurred in order to afford passage to the United States, a good, lasting relationship was not guaranteed, as Barbara Meister's depiction of being treated by her uncle "like a dog" shows.[85] The letters moreover prove that the decision to choose between a German and an American employer was not necessarily made in favor of the German. On the one hand, a German family might be preferred until the domestic got acquainted to the new situation, partic-

anderseits aber auch hinderlich, wenn mal Leute kommen oder sie mal etwas holen soll; doch der Mensch soll ja zufrieden sein, besonders hier zu Lande, in Bezug auf Dienstboten." Letters of Hanna Sellschopp are part of BABS.

82 Letter dated May 10, 1890: "Frau Storp die hat wirklich Glück gehabt mit ihrem Mädchen es ist die Cousine von unserer Gertrud [a former domestic] auch so echt deutsch u. so anspruchslos thut Alles u. Jedes." Paula Rogges's letters are part of BABS.

83 See Agnes Bretting, *Soziale Probleme deutscher Einwanderer in New York City, 1800–1860* (Wiesbaden, 1981), 95; Dudden, *Serving Women*, 162; Christine Stansell, *City of Women: Sex and Class in New York, 1789–1860* (New York, 1986), 157.

84 Cf. the analysis of Census records of Milwaukee, St. Louis, and New York City in my forthcoming study. See n. 1.

85 See Barbara Meister née Ruess's letter from Sept. 11, 1870.

ularly by young German girls who hoped to find a "substitute family."
Americans, on the other hand, were very popular because they had the
reputation of paying higher wages. Anna Maria Klinger, for example, noted
this advantage in 1849 in a letter from New York.

On the same day that I arrived here I went into service at a German family; right
now I am very satisfied with my wages compared to Germany, I have 4 dollars per
month, 10 gulden in our money, once one speaks English it goes much better,
since the English give good wages, there the maid earns 7 to 10 dollars, per month,
but who does not speak or understand English cannot ask for these wages.[86]

The lack of English language skills was not necessarily regarded as an
insurmountable obstacle (by employers and servants alike), as the example
of Wilhelmine Wiebusch, who curiously and self-confidently went into
service in an American family right after arrival, shows. She humorously
described the misunderstandings and problems she had with the language,
adding examples of her increased knowledge in each letter. In 1884, she
wrote to her friend that "You should hear us speak English, we repeat
everything like little children whether it is right or not, sometimes the lady
says she almost dies laughing at us."[87]
     Whereas the knowledge of English was not essential in the rural areas
with their isolated farms or ethnic communities, in the cities it was required
to get along. Due to the conditions of work, German domestics did not
have the opportunity to learn English at school or in special English classes
like other immigrants; they learned the language on the job. The degree of
the language learned in service depended on the contact established with
the employer and with other servants in the same household, and on
whether the environment was ethnically German. Anna Maria Klinger, for
example, suffered because, while serving among Germans, she could not
learn English.

The only problem is the language, which is not as easily learned as you might think,
since until now I can not speak a lot and so it goes with many who don't learn in
six or eight years, but when one goes to Americans right away, then one learns as
much as in ten years among Germans.[88]

Not only was the way in which German women learned English influenced by the particular circumstances of the workplace, but so too was the
treatment the domestics received, regardless of the nationality of the em-

86 Letter dated March 18, 1849 from New York. Anna Maria Klinger's letters are to be found in
    BABS, but have also been published in Helbich et al., *Briefe aus Amerika,* 500–535.
87 Letter dated Sept. 12, 1884.
88 Letter dated around the middle of the year 1850.

ployer. The relationship very much depended upon the social status of the employer: In households of restaurant or store owners, where the whole family participated in the work, domestics did not feel as isolated and lonely as in middle-class families where social norms emphasized the need to re-inforce the class differences between employer and servant and where the household work was fully delegated to the servants. But particularly in these households they could at the same time also develop pride in view of the tasks they were given. This was the case with Wilhelmine Wiebusch, who worked in the family of a businessman in Brooklyn:

Certainly we have more work, since the Americans live very refined, here one eats warm meals three times a day, and then we have all the laundry in the house because it is so terribly expensive to give it away [to others to do], we even have to iron shirts and cuffs . . . but we organize it the way we want it, the ladies care very little about the housework, they don't do anything but dress themselves up three to four times a day and leave the house.[89]

She identified with her employer's household by defending the decision not to give the laundry to the dry cleaner, as if it were her own money, but she also points out that because of her experience in household work, she can run the household, contrary to the "ladies" who are incapable of doing so. Studies of Scandinavian domestics prove that this pride often characterized the servants' attitude.[90]

The difference of status between employer and employee was often re-inforced by a very common attitude toward servants who had to pass so-called honesty tests. By leaving money lying about the house in order to test the degree of honesty of their newly employed servants, employers not only showed mistrust, but they also underestimated the reaction of the servants, who often already knew this trick. Engel Winkelmeier, for ex-ample, commented on her employer's attempt to test her by "strewing money": "My goodness, I was not even thinking about keeping the money. Once the woman saw that, she was willing to give me more freedom. She was always afraid that I might leave her again."[91] In contrast, her sister

89 Letter dated Sept. 12, 1884.
90 See Lindström-Best, "I Won't Be a Slave," 40.
91 Letter dated Aug. 21, 1868 from Indianapolis: "Als sie nun man sah, das man Ehrlig war, den sie hatte auch zu erst Geld gestreuet. Man das vält mier da gewis nicht ein zu behalten. Da die Frau das man sah, da lies sie sich was gevallen. Da waer sie immer bange, das ich wieder wech ging." Letters by Margarethe and Engel Winkelmeier, sisters who emigrated together to Indianapolis, have been published in Hans-Ulrich Kammeier, *"So besinnt euch doch nicht lange und kommt herrüber . . ." Briefe von Amerikaauswanderern aus dem Kreis Lübbecke aus zwei Jahrhunderten* (privately published, n.d.), 62–73. For other examples of these common tests in Germany and America, see Wierling, *Mädchen für alles,* 211; and Lillian Pettengill, *Toilers of the Home: The Record of a College Woman's Experience as a Domestic Servant* (New York, 1903), 215.

Margarethe was treated very well by her American mistress, who cared for her "as my mother" when she fell sick. Another servant, Karoline Pacher, encountered a caring mistress as well: "I have already been to the theater with my mistress when they played something German, she paid for it, I would not have gone for my own money, it cost 2 M."[92] Used to having very little money and the need to spend the earned wages for matters related to the family rather than to one's personal wishes, Karoline Pacher was to experience a self-determined leisure culture for the first time in her life. By confronting social activities that were offered in America, German domestics could thereby develop a new attitude characterized by independence from the family and self-confidence.

Besides these individual differences of service experiences, the descriptions in the letters particularly point to the better food as well as the better legal status that German domestics enjoyed in America. By dealing with topics that had characterized their poor standard of living and status in Germany, the young German domestics could best prove that their lives had indeed improved and that their emigration was successful.

The descriptions of food make up a big part of the letters sent home. They yield detailed accounts of the sometimes unimaginable abundance, particularly for Germans of the lower classes, for whom the supply of food had always been bad. Karoline Pacher's account, in a letter from Philadelphia in 1891, exemplified the enthusiasm over food:

We get three meals per day, in the morning we have beef steak or baked ham with eggs or sausage or ground meat or fish and all the other things I cannot describe to you all the kinds of food; this we have in the evenings as well, sometimes with soup, I even ate oyster soup and liked it very much.[93]

Next to the material conditions of food and wages, the unlimited possibilities of changing positions whenever they wanted proved to be very enticing, as Elisabeth Kleinegesse commented:

Servant girls are in great demand here, one does not have to put up with everything here like in Germany and the employers know that very well, here no employer dares to treat a servant roughly since they can not insist on the servant's staying, even if a servant here does not have any reason for not staying, I can go at any

92 Letter dated Nov. 4, 1891: "Ich war auch schon mit meiner Madamme im Theader wie Deutsch gespielt worden ist sie hat mirs bezahlt für mein Geld wäre ich nicht hinein gegangen es kostet 2 M."
93 Letter dated Nov. 4, 1891: ". . . es gibt drei mal zu essen morgens bekommen wir Büfsteck oder gebackten Schinken mit Eier oder Bratwurst oder Hackfleisch oder Fische und das andere wo noch dazu komt die sorten kan ich Euch nicht alle schreiben und das giebts auch abends manchmal auch noch Suppe zwar Austersuppe habe ich gegessen die hat mir sehr gut geschmeckt . . ."

time if I don't like it anymore, here one can get 100 positions every day and is more needed by one than the other and one position is better than the other.[94]

Wilhelmine Wiebusch adapted quickly to her new rights and frequently changed positions, defending her behavior with the comment: "You see this is the way it goes, today I am here but might be gone again by to-morrow if I don't like it any more, this is the land of freedom."[95]

The changes of positions, of course, did not please the employers, who had hoped that foreign domestics could help them to solve the "servant problem." But the German domestics were not interested in becoming life-long, faithful, and obliging servants, they rather quickly got used to the new system of more rights, a fact that Catherine Beecher deplored in a commentary in 1869:

The German and Irish servants . . . become more or less infected with the spirit of democracy. They came to this country with vague notions of freedom and equality . . . they repudiated many of those habits of respect and courtesy which belonged to their former condition, and asserted their own will and way in the round var-nished phrase which they supposed to be their right as republican citizens.[96]

Although many American mistresses nevertheless tried to mold their foreign servants according to their individual wishes and middle-class norms, they had to realize that the immigrants were no "raw material" that could be molded as they wanted.[97] Immigrant women brought with them their own fixed set of values, shaped by culture, class, and gender, to their expectations and behavior in America. They had their specific ideas about how and when to spend their money, how to dress, and how and when to associate with men. As Christine Stansell points out in her book *City of Women: Sex and Class in New York, 1789–1860:* "Despite their poverty, however, these young immigrant women, with their gaudy costumes, promenades and evenings at the theater, had their own notions of where to seek the makings of womanhood."[98] Most of all, the young German women did not plan to stay domestic servants forever, but rather understood

94 Letter dated March 15, 1860: ". . . den die dinstmetchen werden hir soh sehr chesucht hir braucht man sich nicht alles chefallen lasen wie man bai aich und das wisen die Herschaften auch recht chut hir wacht sich kaine Herschaft ainen Dinboten edvas chrob zubehandeln den sih könen sih hir durch aus nicht befehlen das sie Blaiben sohlen wen hir der Diestbode auch char kaine Ursache weswechen ernicht blaiben wil wens mir hir nicht chanz chut chefählt soh kan ich chehen zu iederzait und man hir (kan) hir jeden Tache wohl 100 Dienstekrigen den ainen komtman noch chelegender wie den andren und der aine dinst ist alle noch schöner wider andre."
95 Letter dated Feb. 27, 1887.
96 Catherine Beecher, cited in Carol Lasser, "The Domestic Balance of Power: Relations between Mistress and Maid in Nineteenth-Century New England," *Labor History* 28 (1987): 14.
97 Sherwood, "The Lack of Good Servants," 557.
98 Stansell, *City of Women,* 168.

their work experience as a temporary stage until they could start their own families.

I V

Although it is difficult to make general statements about the effects of serving in an American household upon the future life of a German domestic, some conclusions can be drawn from the available sources. In view of the poor standard of living and restrictive working conditions they had been used to, German domestics did not hesitate to adapt to those patterns of American culture and society that symbolized an improvement of their situation. They quickly got used to their new rights as servants, looked forward to learning the English language, and delightedly accepted the much better food and fashionable and refined clothing styles. These changes of material patterns of culture and of attitudes were either the result of a generally higher standard of living in America (sometimes further improved by marriage), or the consequence of an identification with the American household in which they had served. Wilhelmine Wiebusch, for example, proudly informed her friend Marie about her living conditions after marriage. She boasted of carpets in two rooms, place settings for twelve (and napkins for twenty-four), dark red plush furniture, and, as wedding presents from her last employer, a silver basket, silver sugar pot, and silver butter dish.[99]

The identification with a middle- or upper-class life-style could even lead to the wish of not wanting to be recognized as German, with domestics valuing class status over ethnicity. In a letter advising her mother how to organize her forthcoming visit to America, Karoline Pacher asked her to wear a "nice black dress" and a hat that had been sent to her from America, in order to "not look so German."[100] But this attitude is not shared by all German immigrant women, and Wilhelmine Wiebusch, for example, even complains about the Germans in New York who "do as if they didn't understand German any more and didn't know anything about their fatherland."[101]

The adaptation of certain values or ideas of the upper social classes represents a behavior that characterized the role of domestic servants in Germany as well. As Ingeborg Weber-Kellermann argued, domestic servants were living in a "world between values and norms" (*Zwischenwelt der Werte*

---

99 Letter dated March 18, 1887, from Secaucus, N.J.
100 Letter dated March 24, 1906, from Philadelphia.
101 Letter dated Sept. 12, 1884.

und Normen),[102] transmitting middle- and upper-class values and habits to the lower class, but always realizing the differences between their employer's status and their own peasant or working-class background. Nevertheless, they did not, as has been stated,[103] completely identify with their submissive role as servants and give up their expectations in view of the insurmountable differences. In America as well as in Germany, they consciously made up their minds by a comparison between their employer's life-style and their own ideas concerning the role and work of women, material desires, and the expected behavior according to their social class and gender.

The "intermediate" role between two classes was also taken up by the German domestics in America who went into middle-class homes, but here this role was extended by the confrontation with another culture. David Katzman correctly stated that life as a "live-in" servant in American households "removed them from their ethnic culture and threw them into direct contact with a more Americanized, more modernized environment," thereby accelerating the process of acculturation.[104] Life and work in an American household confronted the German domestics with new sets of values and habits. They learned about household innovations such as electricity, gas ovens, central heating, vacuum cleaners, to name only a few.[105] The American family also brought them into contact with the role of women in American society, with different social norms and goals and different ways of behavior. The cities confronted them with modern technology like streetcars, elevated trains, elevators in skyscrapers, and movie theaters – developments that changed the way they behaved in public and during their leisure time. They were taught how to deal with the modern American city with its masses of immigrants from different countries – as employers, fellow servants, or urban dwellers – thereby making them a part of the developing urban society. With the wages they received, they took part in the American culture of consumption.[106]

---

102 Ingeborg Weber-Kellermann, " 'Wie der Herr, so's Gescherr' – Normen und Wertvorstellungen einer abhängigen Gruppe," in *Dienstboten in Stadt und Land,* 54.
103 Wierling, "Vom Mädchen zum Dienstmädchen," 85.
104 Although his argument that domestic servants' social mobility was less possible in America than in Europe must be rejected in view of the German domestics' social background given earlier. Katzman, *Seven Days,* 171.
105 See Susan Strasser, *Never Done: A History of American Housework* (New York, 1982); Susan J. Kleinberg, "Technology's Stepdaughters: The Impact of Industrialization upon Working-Class Women," Ph.D. diss., University of Pittsburgh, 1973.
106 For an excellent study of immigrant women's confrontation with America's culture of consumption, see Elizabeth Ewen, *Immigrant Women in the Land of Dollars: Life and Culture on the Lower East Side, 1890–1925* (New York, 1985).

All of these challenging and sometimes unavoidable changes in a woman's life represent a picture of the German single immigrant woman that strongly contrasts with the acculturation-hindered stereotype so far portrayed in histories of German Americans and/or in women's studies. The experiences of German domestic servants in American culture and society call for a reevaluation of the role that German immigrant women played in the process of acculturation, particularly the effect that these women had on their children.

In matters of their private lives, German servants were more reluctant to abandon their ethnic ties. Although they might come into close contact with American or other cultures on the private level through fellow servants, like Wilhelmine Wiebusch who shared her work with servants from Ireland and Wales, they also continued to spend their scarce leisure time with other Germans. They participated in the social activities offered by the "little Germanies," by going to dances or to the theater, where they might also meet their prospective husbands. Still, due to the character of their work, their participation in the ethnic communities, which helped to ease their integration into American society, was limited compared with that of other German immigrants.[107]

Since marriage was such an important step in the lives of German women at that time, much weight was put upon the choice of the marriage partner. The majority of the German domestics whose lives are documented, like the majority of German women in America in general, married German or German American men.[108] This choice expresses their wish to foster the values of their own culture, although the fact that the husband was German does not necessarily imply that he was not "Americanized." Depending on their occupation, male German immigrants also learned about new forms and attitudes of the American labor system, such as new technologies, a different value of skills in an industry that functioned through division of labor, a freedom of trade unknown to them, and a different work ethic, all of which influenced their future life.[109] The social status that the prospective husband offered to his bride might have had an impact on the choice of a marriage partner as well.

The idea that German single women's opportunities improved in Amer-

---

107 On the function of ethnic communities as "pressure chambers," see Agnes Bretting, "Die Konfrontation der deutschen Einwanderer mit der amerikanischen Wirklichkeit im 19. und 20. Jahrhundert," *Amerikastudien/American Studies* 27 (1982): 247–57.

108 See U.S. Bureau of the Census, *Immigrants and Their Children*, by Niles Carpenter (Washington, D.C., 1927), 234–35, 243–44.

109 See Daniel T. Rodgers, *The Work Ethic in Industrial America, 1850–1920* (Chicago, 1974; reprint, 1979).

ica has been connected to government statistics proving that the propensity of German women going into domestic service decreased. Only 35.7 percent of the second generation of German women chose domestic and personal service as a profession, compared with 54.6 percent of the first.[110] Nevertheless, these numbers should not lead to the impression that German women born in America shunned domestic service. In fact, 35.7 percent was still a very high number compared with only slightly more – 38.8 percent – of the second generation of German women working in manufacturing and mechanical pursuits, 16.1 percent in trade and transportation, and only 6.5 percent in professional service.[111] The conclusion drawn from these statistics can be interpreted to show that these women clung to German ethnic ideas as to the expected work of women and the role of women in family and society. An analysis of the census records, as well as other local studies of German immigrants, reveals the same impression.[112]

Although the adherence to cultural norms after emigration and after the transitional phase of domestic service depended on many different circumstances, the experiences of German domestic servants in American households nevertheless should not be underestimated. Because they used domestic service as an ideal "springboard" into life in America, their social position and opportunities as young single women had changed tremendously compared with their situation in Germany, even if they did not pursue a professional career or reach an upper-class life-style. The important role that domestic service played for these women can only be understood if we realize the differences between the opportunities of a lower-class woman in the nineteenth century, on the one hand, and those of women living nowadays, on the other. Only by ignoring their class background and their gender, and the expectations and restrictive norms associated with these two factors, can we come to the superficial assumption that the experiences of German domestic servants in America are not important enough to warrant further studies.[113]

110 *Occupations of the First and Second Generations of Immigrants in the United States,* 74.
111 Ibid.
112 See Kleinberg, "Technology's Stepdaughters"; Laurence A. Glasco, "The Life Cycles and Household Structure of American Ethnic Groups: Irish, Germans, and Native-Born Whites in Buffalo, N.Y., 1855," in Nancy F. Cott and Elizabeth H. Pleck, eds., *A Heritage of Her Own: Towards a New Social History of American Women* (New York, 1979), 268–89.
113 Maxine S. Seller was the first to criticize the subsumption of female immigration experiences into those of their male counterparts in *Immigrant Women* (Philadelphia, 1981). See also Morokvasic, "Women in Migration."

13

Acculturation of Immigrant Women in Chicago at the Turn of the Twentieth Century

DEIRDRE M. MAGEEAN

I

The research reported in this essay grows out of the project "Women in the Migration Process" – a comparative analysis of German, Irish, Swedish, and Polish women in Chicago at the turn of the century.[1] The aim of the project has been to determine the role of women in the migration process in the second half of the nineteenth century. Its emphasis throughout has been on the transfer of culture. Hence the project follows the women from Europe to North America and analyzes the structures of the sending as well as the receiving culture, the options open to them, the incentives and structures that fostered the decision to migrate, and the adaptations and change of their roles in the process of migration.

The geographical focus of the study is Chicago, the second largest metropolitan area of the United States at the beginning of the twentieth century. This city experienced rapid industrial development during the latter half of the nineteenth and the early twentieth centuries. The consequent number and range of job opportunities in the city were a magnet for male and female migrants. By 1860 almost half of the city's population was foreign-born and by 1900, the period of this study, 77.3 percent of the white population comprised immigrants of the first and second generations. The four ethnic groups studied represent the four largest groups in the city at the turn of the century. The Germans were by far the largest group with 31.5 percent, followed by the Irish with

1 The project "Women in the Migration Process: A Comparative Perspective" was funded by the Volkswagen Foundation. The project, which was coordinated by Christiane Harzig of the Labor Migration Project of the University of Bremen, involved the collaborative research of Monika Blaschke, Christiane Harzig, Marianna Knothe, Deirdre Mageean, and Margaret Matovic. The results of this research are to be published in *Peasant Maids – City Women: The Movement of Women from Rural Europe to Chicago,* forthcoming.

15.7 percent, the Poles with 9.3 percent, and the Swedes with 8.3 percent. Together they accounted for 64.8 percent of the immigrant population.[2]

The justification for focusing on these four groups lies not only in their numerical representation but also in the fact that all four countries of origin experienced significant out-migration to the United States. The demographic and socioeconomic composition of the migrant streams from these countries differed as did their reasons for leaving, though there were a number in common. The timing of their arrival in Chicago varied as well. By 1900 both the Germans and Irish were well established and into the second generation while the Poles were only at the beginning of their history in Chicago. Hence the ethnic communities were at different stages in their development and occupied different niches in Chicago's occupational and social structure. How these differences and those in the culture of origin affected the acculturation of the four different groups of female migrants is the main focus of the study.

In contrast to traditional community studies, which frequently overlook or give scant attention to the role of women in the community and their role in the acculturation process (most concentrate on the formal organizations of men), the project seeks to see women (as well as men) within the formal and informal structures of social relations. Particularly important are the worlds of family and kinship networks, the organization of everyday life by women, and the organizations that they formed in their new worlds.

While the role of women in that key vehicle of acculturation, the family, is recognized as important, the project also looks at women as individuals. The overwhelming majority of the female migrants studied here migrated as young and single individuals. For some of these women, particularly the Swedes and Irish, marriage and family was an option that was not always pursued. Therefore the emphasis here must be on their position in the labor force, their premigration skills, attitudes toward emancipation, and possible conflicts between work and family.

Overall the project aims at a conceptual framework that integrates the productive (paid employment) and reproductive (housework) experiences, relates the individual to the family, and examines the opportunities open to the women. It also aims to investigate how emigrant women weighed these opportunities relative to their expectations, contemporary ideas, and ethnic background.

---

2 Source: U.S. Census, 1900.

II

Given the emphasis of the project on the influence of the cultures of origin, a brief description of the respective sending societies is in order here. The four areas examined – Mecklenburg in Germany, the province of Munster in Ireland, the province of Dalsland in Sweden, and the parish of Zaborow in Poland – vary considerably in size but each represents a distinct culture and tradition. All are essentially rural societies where agricultural economy and society strongly shaped the worlds of family and work.

Mecklenburg. From the 1860s onward, the grand duchies of Mecklenburg supplied most of the German migrants who went to Chicago. The region was tightly controlled by the manorial lords who owned three-quarters of all the land. They controlled not only the economic system but also the social relations of the people. The opportunities to marry and to find work and a place to live were all dependent on the landowners. Given this tight control of marriage possibilities, it is not surprising that Mecklenburg had the highest proportion of illegitimate births in Germany in the second half of the nineteenth century. From this closed and inflexible system left those for whom it had no room.

Most of the women who left Mecklenburg for the United States did so as members of families – with parents or with husbands and children. Some left with those they intended to marry and for whom emigration was the only chance to get married. There were also a significant number of single women, some of whom had an illegitimate child or children, and for whom emigration represented opportunities for themselves and their children – opportunities that did not exist in the closed society of Mecklenburg.

Munster. During the period 1851–1911 some 1,460,032 people emigrated from the province of Munster.[3] From the Great Famine (1847–49) onward the dominant characteristic of Irish emigration was the large number of young, single Irish women. In no other migrant population was there such a high proportion of women. Immediately after the famine and during the years 1891–1911 women dominated migration from Munster (52.7 percent during 1901–11). The effects of "postfamine adjustment" were acutely felt in Munster.[4] Changes in landholding patterns, inheritance, marriage and

3 W. E. Vaughan and A. J. Fitzpatrick, *Irish Historical Statistics, 1821–1971* (Dublin, 1978), 346–48.
4 The period after the Great Famine was one of considerable economic, demographic, and social change in Ireland. There was considerable consolidation of land, and partible inheritance gave way to impartible inheritance; the age at marriage increased and the rate of marriage decreased. Economic

family patterns, and the roles of women resulted in a reduction in the status of women and their economic importance. There were greater restrictions and controls over marriage as the consolidation and retention of land became paramount. Changes in the agricultural economy were generally detrimental to women. As a result the options for women became increasingly narrow and unattractive. In the words of one commentator, the choices for women were "to be matched, to be dismissed as unmatchable, or to emigrate."[5] Increasingly women looked to America in order to achieve personal and economic independence.

Zaborow. The parish of Zaborow in Galacia, composed of five villages, is the smallest area of origin being considered. At the turn of the century it was a homogeneous rural community. The inhabitants were all ethnically Polish and Roman Catholic, untouched by industrialization or urbanization. It was an area of small farms where the desire for land was strong but where little was available. A family's wealth and its position in the social strata were judged by the amount of land it owned. The population rise during the nineteenth century increased the pressure on those seeking land and kept wages low. Seasonal migration to Germany and Denmark was common but emigration to America offered better economic incentives.

Most of the emigrants to the United States went with the intention of earning money and returning to buy more land or build new houses. Some went several times, spending an average of three to five years in America. For unmarried women emigration offered the chance to earn money for a dowry, which on their return provided better marriage prospects. Some also went with the hope of finding a husband abroad. Married women usually had the farm's needs in mind when they decided to emigrate. During the period 1890 to 1919, some two hundred women from the five villages of the parish of Zaborow left for the United States.[6] Given the close familial connections in the parish this meant that nearly every family in Zaborow had a female relative in Chicago.

Dalsland. One of Sweden's smallest provinces in the western part of the country close to the border of Norway, Dalsland was, like most of Sweden,

considerations increasingly determined the choice of marriage partner and the economic position of women in marriage was eroded. For more, see Cormac O'Grada, *Ireland before and after the Famine* (Manchester, 1988).
5 David Fitzpatrick, "Marriage in Post-Famine Ireland," in Art Cosgrove, ed., *Marriage in Ireland* (Dublin, 1985), 120.
6 Marianna Knothe, "Polish Women in Chicago at the Turn of the Century," in Blaschke et al., *Peasant Maids – City Women.*

dependent on traditional agriculture. Parts of the area were close to subsistence thresholds and were periodically threatened by crop failures. Population pressure forced men and women to rely on migration, industrial work, or handicraft for survival. Land and marriage were closely linked and marriage rarely preceded the acquisition or inheritance of land. Seasonal migration of men and women was common. Young women found employment as domestic servants in the cities or in Norway, and for many the acquaintance with urban life was a first step to emigration. Seasonal migration provided a living but allowed people to stay in their home parishes. Crises as a result of overpopulation, however, forced initial migration to America. Later in the century "betterment migration" was common and many Dalslanders returned home after years in the United States.

The majority of emigrants consisted of young, unmarried men and women, sons and daughters of farmers, whose future prospects were uncertain. For the young women emigration to the United States was an attractive alternative to employment as a farm servant, work that was arduous, entailed long hours, and was increasingly exploitative. Throughout the 1890s these servant maids dominated the migration stream.

III

From these four areas of origin came female migrants who settled in the neighborhoods of Chicago. Because of the importance of the neighborhood in ethnic life – where everyday life took place and culture changed and developed – it is the unit of analysis for this study of acculturation. At the turn of the century Chicago was truly a city of neighborhoods. Although the Germans, Irish, Swedes, and Poles differed in their degree of residential clustering, for all four groups there were neighborhoods where that ethnic group dominated. These areas were defined as, for instance, "Irish" or "Polish" not only by dint of numerical representation but also because of the preponderance of Irish or Polish businesses, churches, schools, and other institutions in the area. These neighborhoods were simultaneously ethnic communities and part of Chicago's urban environment. The neighborhoods chosen for study were the seventeenth ward on the north side of the city for the German women; two different parishes on the west and south sides of the city for the Irish women; the settlement of Lake View to the north of the city for the Swedes; and Polish Downtown and the parish of St. John Cantius on the west side for the Poles. More than just physical entities, these neighborhoods were also the social, economic, and cultural worlds for the migrants and the locus of interaction between the Old World and the New. Further, the neighborhoods, like the migrant women themselves, were constantly evolving.

The emigration of women from four rural areas to the urban center of Chicago heralded great changes in their lives. For some, such as the Polish women, the move may have been perceived as a temporary move with the intent to return to Zaborow. For the Irish women it was inevitably a permanent move and a new life to be made. For all four ethnic groups, however, it was no longer a life punctuated and marked by the events of an agrarian society (those elements of culture were immediately lost) but adaptation to an urban way of life. Lives once dominated by the seasons and an agricultural economy were now governed by the clock and an industrial economy. The adaptations made by the migrants, the traditions preserved, and the sense that they made of their new lives were determined by their cultural background as well as the timing of their arrival and the niches they found in Chicago society.

Clearly in the short space of this essay it is not possible to discuss in detail the changes and experiences of the respective groups.[7] My intent here is to highlight some of the findings, the issues that have emerged, and questions raised by the research.

For very many of the women who emigrated to Chicago the decision to leave their cultures of origin was prompted by opportunities for economic betterment. Thus, like their male counterparts, these female migrants responded to the "push" forces of their home region (population pressure, structural constraints, and economic pressures) and the "pull" forces of a rapidly expanding American city. However, unlike men, these women's migration decisions and experiences were shaped by marriage decisions. Further, for female migrants there is a close relationship between the labor market and the marriage market. German, Irish, Polish, and Swedish women in Chicago had to make rational choices between marriage and economic independence for, as we shall see, marriage usually curtailed the economic activities of women outside the home.

What can the study of the ethnic neighborhoods in Chicago tell us about the worlds of reproduction and production? Census and church register records provide some insight into these aspects of the lives of the migrant women. Some common themes emerge from the four groups. First, the marriage patterns reveal high rates of endogamy – not just to partners from the same country, as might be expected if language were the only issue, but to partners from the same region, parish, or town land. For instance,

7 For a full report of the findings of the project, see Blaschke et al., *Peasant Maids – City Women.*

among the Zaborowian women in St. John Cantius parish 46.5 percent of the partners were from within Zaborow Parish.[8] Among the Mecklenburg women one-third of all marriages recorded in the church records are cases where both partners came from Mecklenburg.[9] Irish and Swedish marriage patterns reveal similarly high rates of endogamy.[10] There is no evidence as to whether these partners were known to each other before emigration or whether the social contacts and chain migration between the sending and receiving societies gave rise to these patterns. At any rate, these migrants of the first generation preferred to stick to "their own kind" and the strong ethnic outlook of the respective churches strengthened this behavior. Cross-national or cross-religious marriages were very rare for all the groups.

As might be expected, when marriage is not restricted by access to land or inheritance, as was the case in the four regions of origin, the age at which marriage can occur is lowered. German, Irish, and Polish marriage ages were, on average, reduced by three to four years. The exception is the Swedish experience, where ages in Chicago correspond closely to the age at marriage in Sweden. There was even a tendency for Swedish men in Chicago to marry somewhat later than in Sweden. Their inclination to marry older women was, however, less than in Sweden. While the reduction in age at marriage may well be a common feature of urbanization the rates of marriage among the groups reflect both the sex ratios within the ethnic communities and the way in which the marriage market operated. For instance, over 80 percent of the young Zaborowian women in Chicago were married within four years of arriving in the city.[11] In part these high rates might be explained by the high ratio of men to women in Chicago but it is also due to social contacts maintained through the chain migration from Zaborow to Chicago and the extent to which men "sent home" for future brides, paying their tickets to America. The behavior of the Zaborowian women in Chicago exemplifies the interplay of different forces. The urban environment of Chicago, unlike the peasant culture of Zaborow

---

8 Marriages with partners from Zaborow and neighboring villages within ten kilometers accounted for 76.2 percent of all marriages. Although fewer people in Chicago chose their partners from the same village as in the old country, the desire to marry a husband at least from a neighboring village remained very strong. See Knothe, "Polish Women in Chicago," in Blaschke et al., *Peasant Maids – City Women.*

9 Christiane Harzig, "Women From Mecklenburg Living in the German-American Community in Chicago, 1860–1900," in Blaschke et al., *Peasant Maids – City Women.*

10 In the Irish parish of Visitation on the south side of the city, a quarter of the marriages were between people from the same county in Ireland, and half of these involved people from the same parish. The Swedish figures reveal an endogamy rate (as measured by both partners being Swedish) of 95 percent.

11 Knothe, "Polish Women in Chicago."

where social and economic forces constrained the rate of marriage, permitted marriage at an early age. Hence, urbanization of these women
brought about change in marriage behavior. However, they retained the
strong traditional regard for the high position of marriage and the status of
wife. Thus the desire for marriage remained strong. The Swedish community, like the Polish community, had a "surplus" of young men but here
the rates of marriage are lower. Instead we find a surprising number of
women remaining unmarried. Admittedly the sample size is small (based
on thirteen single Dalsland women) but there is the suggestion that what
we see here is the influence of the home culture of Dalsland – a province
with one of the lowest rates of marriage in Sweden. If so, then might the
Swedes be doing what the Irish have been noted for in carrying over their
marriage patterns from the culture of origin?

For the overwhelming majority of the women, marriage meant the end
of paid employment outside the home. Even if we allow for the underre-
cording of women's occupations in the census, what is striking for all four
groups is the paucity of working married women. Among German wives
the figure was lowest, with less than 1 percent of wives working outside of
the home; among the Poles the figure was 4.2 percent and among the Irish
5 percent. Although these women all came from rural economies with a
tradition of family labor, where the economic contributions of women and
children were significant, they all appear to conform to the urban model of
the family maintained by the male wage earner. The question here is how
much of this behavior can be attributed to acceptance of or conformity to
an ideology and how much to the practical difficulties of women working
in an urban-industrial setting when they had young children to care for.
Figures alone cannot help us here and we lack the rich ethnographic information available for the cultures of origin. However, we do know from
the records of charitable organizations that male employment was far from
steady and that the meager wages of laborers and unskilled workers were
often insufficient to provide adequately for a family.

For all four groups of immigrant women married life was often marked
by insecurity and hardship. Unemployment, strikes, and the illness or death
of a husband all resulted in the loss of vital income and, as a consequence,
brought about crises for families. Drunkenness and desertion also threatened
family life, leaving women and children in an extremely vulnerable position.
Swedish, German, and Irish records all allude to the problems thus created.
In particular the German and Irish charity records make frequent mention
of husbands who depart "looking for work" and who are never heard of

again.[12] Divorce was not frequent among the Swedes in Chicago but it was at least an option (not open to the Catholic Irish or Poles) and the records show that it was usually sought by women on the grounds of desertion, cruelty, and/or drunkenness.

Clearly, reliance on a single wage could leave a family in a vulnerable situation. Women could, however, contribute to the household income in various ways, for example, performing tasks that could be done at home, such as washing, sewing, and mending, and taking in lodgers. This latter strategy was adopted by all four groups to varying degrees. Among the Poles the practice was strongest with 30 percent of households containing boarders (many of whom were young single girls). It was least favored by the women from Mecklenburg who preferred, instead, to care for relatives.[13] Interestingly, the Mecklenburg women had the smallest household size (an average of 4.2 persons) and the smallest family size of the four groups (56 percent of families had one to two children). Here we seem to be seeing an attempt to limit both family and household numbers to an "ideal size."

We stated earlier that the reasons for married women not working may well lie in a combination of ideology and simple lack of opportunities. Given the still high levels of fertility, it was simply difficult for mothers of young children to leave the home – at least until the development of child care centers at the turn of the century. Even then the number of spaces available in such centers was woefully inadequate. Yet we are faced with the fact that, even where there were no children present, some wives remained "at home" and were not employed in wage labor. For instance, among the Polish women fifteen of the ninety-five wives in the sample were childless and yet stayed at home. In interpreting this behavior, we have to recognize that in the home cultures of all four groups women attained "adult" status through marriage. Among the Zaborowian women in particular, the status of wife was much desired and the married woman was distinguished from the unmarried woman by the cap she wore.[14] Mar-

---

12 Harzig, "Women from Mecklenburg in the German-American community in Chicago, 1860–1900," and Deirdre M. Mageean, "Irish Women in Chicago," in Blaschke et al., *Peasant Maids – City Women.*

13 It is not always possible to tell from the census returns which individuals are relatives and which are not related. A common surname gives some indication of family relationship but it is not a reliable measure. Harzig concludes that many of the nonkin in the Mecklenburg households studied were probably employees of the household business such as bakers, carpenters, and clerks. See Harzig, "Women from Mecklenburg Living in the German-American Community in Chicago, 1860–1900," in Blaschke et al., *Peasant Maids – City Women.*

14 Marianna Knothe, "The Life of Polish Women before Emigrating," in Blaschke et al., *Peasant Maids – City Women.*

riage was also a prime reason for coming to Chicago – either to find a marriage partner or to acquire sufficient money for a decent dowry. Given this importance of marriage for Zaborowian women, it may well be that, having acquired the desired status of married woman, they demarcated themselves from the single women by no longer working outside the home. The strands of influence on the decision to remain "at home" are not easy to disentangle. However, it is safe to say that urbanization – be it expressed in ideology or in practical constraints – forced Irish, German, Polish, and Swedish women to adapt their working behavior to their newfound situation.

For single women Chicago offered a range of employment opportunities and a chance for economic independence unmatched in their home countries. For migrant women, the city's diverse economy provided employment in domestic service, factory employment, retail trade, restaurants, and white-collar work. Given the rural background of the women, it is not surprising to find them strongly represented in the one sector in which they had experience – domestic service. American-born women scorned domestic service but migrant women, such as the Swedish and Irish, took the jobs in preference to factory work. Domestic service paid reasonably well, provided accommodation and a uniform, and allowed a taste of civilized living as well as the opportunity to learn of "American ways."

A sample from the 1900 census of Chicago provides an example of the representation of various ethnic groups. The area of Prairie and Calumet Avenues was, in 1900, still among the most fashionable in the city. It was an area of big houses and prominent families, where foreign-born servants worked for Chicago's wealthy. The census records 341 servants, 269 female and 72 male. Among the female servants, the Irish constituted the majority (26.7 percent) followed by the Swedes (20.8).[15] Almost all of these women were single and in their twenties and early thirties. For the Swedish women domestic service offered an opportunity to capitalize on their skills as servants, which they had acquired at home. Swedish maids were held in high regard and many women were able to make a career in domestic service. Irish women had less experience in domestic service but they were able to exploit the ever high demand for servants, knowing the worth of their labor. Domestic service often entailed a lonely and isolated life and, frequently, a celibate one. However, given the often unattractive aspects of married life among these first-generation women – poverty, desertion, and frequent

15 The data were taken from an indexed listing of servants compiled by Thomas Golembowski and printed in *Chicago Genealogist* 21, no. 2 (1988–89): 39–46.

childbearing – life as a domestic servant was an attractive alternative. The conditions of service in America were a decided improvement on those at home and the steady employment offered the opportunity to save and to send tickets or remittances back home. Still, for all its advantages, domestic service was very much the job of first generation women – a "first foot in the door" in Chicago's economy and a chance to adapt to the New World. All the women in the 1900 sample, for instance, were foreign-born. As soon as opportunities arose for these women and their children, they moved out or up.

Although domestic service was pursued by all four groups, the reasons for choosing this female sphere of work differed. For the Swedes and Irish, domestic service was a career that represented an alternative to marriage. It offered economic independence and a degree of autonomy that could not be found in married life. Indeed, as Joy Lintelman has argued, the personal and financial freedom that many Swedish immigrant women obtained through immigration may have been a deterrent to marriage.[16] The same held true for the Irish who had left in pursuit of economic autonomy. For the Germans, on the other hand, domestic service was valued because it served as training for their role as housewife.[17] Among the Polish women "service" was defined and pursued not in the homes of middle-class Americans but in boardinghouses and restaurants in the Polish community. Hence, each group used the opportunities in the domestic service sector to their own advantage – some as an alternative to marriage and others as a preparation for it.

IV

The census provides us with useful cross-sectional data but it tells us little of the dynamics of family life or the social networks of the immigrant women in their respective neighborhoods. A problem faced by all the investigators in the project was how little ethnographic information was available compared with that for the home country. However, the search for new sources that could shed light on the process of migration and the acculturation of these migrant women did result in new information and insights into the formal and informal organizations of the immigrant women. Parish histories and archives of women's clubs and organizations

16 Joy K. Lintelman, " 'On My Own': Single, Swedish and Female in turn-of-the-century Chicago," in Philip J. Anderson and Dag Blanck, eds., *Swedish-American Life in Chicago: Cultural and Urban Aspects of an Immigrant People, 1850–1930* (Urbana, Ill., 1992), 89–99.
17 See Christiane Harzig, introduction to Blaschke et al., *Peasant Maids – City Women*.

were particularly valuable in providing insight into the worlds of female influence that German, Irish, Polish and Swedish women created – worlds that allowed them to work within their own ethnic communities and also to enter public life. Here we find women involved in charity work, cultural activities, education, and self-help groups. In the orientation of their activities we see the influence of the home culture but we can also trace how they left their mark on the city.

As noted earlier, the Germans and Irish arrived early in the city and, thus, were able to participate in the creation of its social structure. They built and developed institutions and associations that met their daily needs and served important functions in the new environment. Until recently historians have concentrated on the formal organizations of men and have neglected the key role women's organizations have played in this process. Yet examination of these organizations in Chicago shows that they shaped and contributed to the organized life of the communities. Associations of all shapes and sizes – churches, schools, orphanages, old people's homes, and hospitals – were supported or organized by women who took responsibility for the leisure, charity, insurance, and education functions of their communities.

From the early development of the German American community in Chicago, women had participated in its development. As with many immigrant communities in the United States, voluntary associations took over important functions in structuring the immigrants' lives and in tending to their needs. Women were active in these organizations either by participating together with men in the many social organizations and benevolent groups or by creating their own groups. Such groups ranged from gymnastic societies to choirs and combined fund raising and entertainment. Others, like the Columbia-Damen Club (Columbia Club for Ladies), organized in 1893, was an association with purely intellectual aims. A highly exclusive, middle-class organization, it organized cultural programs to educate and entertain. Increasingly though, the focus of women's groups was charity. Women came together to promote a particular cause and to raise the funds necessary to support that charity. Outstanding among such organizations was the Frauenverein Altenheim (Altenheim Women's Club), which decided to establish a charitable institute that would be of lasting social value to the community. They founded the German Old People's home in 1885, one of the most successful German American charity endeavors, which still exists today.

Among the Irish communities in Chicago, which grew rapidly from the mid-nineteenth century onward, the needs for charitable work were many.

Throughout most of Chicago's history, Irish women – both lay and religious – were major figures in benevolent work, caring for the poor and disadvantaged in general, and for women in particular. Their influence on Irish migrants' lives can be measured not only in the success of their various establishments but also in their success in recruiting many second-generation Irish women, who saw the religious life as a chance to do valuable and significant work, to their ranks. Lay women, particularly those in the middle classes, played an active role in such societies as the Catholic Women's League and the Visitation and Aid Society. The Catholic Women's League, which was founded in 1893, was largely Irish but also had German Catholic members. The league conducted a wide range of activities, including direct relief, protection of unmarried girls who were new to Chicago, and cultural and educational programs. A major focus, the development and support of settlements, was a concerted effort to duplicate the work of Hull House and the University of Chicago Settlement. An organization with a more working-class base was the Women's Catholic Order of Foresters, a life insurance company. Before the inception of the society in 1891, few Catholic women belonged to any insurance society. In addition to its insurance functions, the society gave liberally to charity and helped poor women in parishes throughout Chicago.

As with the German and Irish women, Swedish immigrant women's organizations were largely oriented toward charity. Before 1880 most Swedish organizations had been all male but from the end of the nineteenth century onward there developed female organizations, whose concern was charitable work. The work of these groups ranged from financing an immigrant hostel to running temperance organizations. The temperance societies were active in trying to establish "dry neighborhoods" and in running nondrinking social clubs. Many of the groups were church-based and provided their members with opportunities to socialize as well as to perform socially useful services. These church organizations were particularly useful for the large number of young single Swedish women who made their way to Chicago, caring for their social and spiritual needs. In the decade after 1900 Swedish women sought to gain greater equality within Swedish social organizations and to establish their own lodges and beneficiary societies – a movement that led to the mushrooming of twenty-five women's lodges between 1903 and 1916.

Although the Polish community was the youngest of the four communities studied, by 1900 it had already developed a number of women's groups. These groups, like those of the other three ethnic groups, provided a female public sphere. Initially many of these groups were parish based and catered to the particular needs of a community, but over the years a number of women recognized the need to pull together members to pursue the common goal of a Polish women's association. From the 1880s a number of groups were formed, most of which had similar aims – mutual aid and the preservation of national sentiments and, eventually, in 1898, the Polish Women's Alliance was formed. The aims of this organization were to unite Polish women in the United States into one organization; to pay death benefits and to preserve the national spirit among its members. Hence, although the alliance had aims in common with the other ethnic groups, it was unique in its overtly nationalist sentiments. Indeed, at its first convention in 1900, a resolution was passed that recommended to members that they speak only Polish to their children, defining that as the duty of every Polish woman.

Although the format, organization, and aims of the assorted women's groups in the German, Irish, Polish, and Swedish communities differed to varying degrees, they shared a number of important aspects. Through their charitable, social, cultural, and educational activities, they contributed to the organized life of the community and shaped the community. The organizations served the daily needs of the community, influenced the material living conditions of the members of the community, and shaped their acculturation process. Hence, they helped to mitigate the often harsh process of adjusting to life in a foreign land. For the women themselves membership in the many associations provided a chance to become involved in community affairs and to move beyond the confinements of the house. Especially among the larger and more successful societies the offices were full-time jobs and provided the officeholders with an entry into the public forum. The sense of unity, strength, and public presence that women derived from membership in societies was important and provided a spur to action in other domains. As Margaret Haley, leader of the Chicago Teachers' Federation, testified:

Someone has said that the fraternal beneficiary insurance organizations of women did more to pave the way for women toward public life than did the actual Nineteenth Amendment. Possibly it's true. I made my own entrance into the courts and the newspapers through membership in one of these organizations, the Women's Catholic Order of Foresters.[18]

Through their participation in the labor force, through their role as family members, and through their activities in voluntary organizations, German, Irish, Polish, and Swedish women helped to shape the city of Chicago at

18 R. L. Reid, ed., *Battleground: The Autobiography of Margaret A. Haley* (Chicago, 1982), 29.

Acculturation of Immigrant Women in Chicago   309

the same time as they adjusted their own lives to life in an urban setting. In their cultures of origin the everyday lives, domains, and activities had been shaped by a rural economy and culture. Clearly in an urban environment their lives were no longer influenced by these forces, and all four groups felt this impact of urbanization equally. But rather than viewing these women as mere passive participants in the acculturation process, we should see them as active agents who took advantage of their newfound situation to pursue the opportunities Chicago offered. The forces that propelled the women to leave their homelands influenced their choice of labor market or marriage market. For the Irish and Swedish, this entailed the pursuit of economic independence and security. For the German and Polish women, it meant greater opportunities for marriage. For all the women it meant taking active roles in building their ethnic community. Thus the story of these migrant women in Chicago is one not of cultural decay (although they lost or abandoned elements of their home culture) but one of reconstruction and re-creation.

PART IV

Acculturation in and Return from the United States

14

Communicating the Old and the New: German Immigrant Women and Their Press in Comparative Perspective around 1900

MONIKA BLASCHKE

That women were an important part of the German American reading public is suggested by the female-oriented materials that began to proliferate in the late nineteenth century.[1] This segment of the immigrant press included women's magazines as well as women's pages. During the course of the nineteenth century a combination of demographic and social factors had worked to expand the reading public. Mirroring the development of the English-speaking press's historical changes over time, the German American press adopted its products to court the woman consumer.

Yet it is only now that researchers of German immigration have begun to analyze the role of gender.[2] Little tribute has been paid to the role of the ethnic press specifically designed for women and only some isolated issues have been addressed.[3] This state of historical research on the Ger-

---

1 This essay presents specific results of my forthcoming thesis on the German American women's press, 1890–1914 (Ph.D. diss., Universität Bremen, 1995). I would like to thank Reinhard Flessner, Christiane Harzig, Dirk Hoerder, and Horst Rössler for their critical comments on earlier versions. Research for this project was funded, in part, by a grant from the German Marshall Fund of the United States.

2 Only in recent years have the lives of German immigrant women in the United States received closer attention. That this subject has been neglected disregards the fact that women made up more than 40 percent of the total German immigration to the United States. For a local study of German American women's experience, see Christiane Harzig, *Familie, Arbeit und Weibliche Öffentlichkeit: Deutschamerikanerinnen in Chicago, 1880–1900* (Ostfildern, 1991); see also Monika Blaschke and Christiane Harzig, eds., *Frauen wandern aus: Deutsche Migrantinnen im 19. und 20. Jahrhundert* (Bremen, 1990), for an overview of research currently underway.

3 See Ruth Seifert, "The Portrayal of Women in the German-American Labor Movement," in Hartmut Keil, ed., *German Workers' Culture in America* (De Kalb, Ill., 1988): 109–36; and by the same author, "Women's Pages in the German-American Radical Press, 1900–1914: The Debate on Socialism, Feminism, and the Suffrage," unpublished paper, 1988; Dorothee Schneider, "For Whom Are All the Good Things in Life? German-American Housewives Discuss Their Budgets," in Hartmut Keil and John B. Jentz, eds., *German Workers in Industrial Chicago* (DeKalb, Ill., 1989): 145–62; Harzig, *Deutschamerikanerinnen in Chicago*, see esp. chap. 6; Agnes Bretting, "Frauenleben in New York City, 1890–1910: Ein Vergleich der Frauenseiten in der bürgerlichen Staatszeitung und der sozialistischen Volkszeitung," unpublished paper, 1989; Blaschke, "Die deutschamerikanische Presse für Frauen: Bestand, Prognosen, und Probleme," in Blaschke and Harzig, *Frauen wandern aus*, 97–112.

man American women's press reflects a phenomenon common to all ethnic groups in the United States. While considerable progress has been
made in the study of the immigrant press during the past ten years,[4] even
the newer studies fail to acknowledge the crucial role of the ethnic
women's press.[5] By considering it mainly to be a by-product of the male-
dominated ethnic press, they not only lose sight of the immense commercial success and longevity of several ethnic women's magazines, but
they also miss a chance to follow up on issues offered by the women's
press that defy easy categorization and go beyond the set of questions traditionally asked.

This essay sets out to serve a double purpose: first, to introduce a variety
of ethnic women's magazines and pages into the discussion; and second,
to demonstrate their value for an analysis of the lives of immigrant women.
Exploring the role of gender and probing into some of the changes taking
place in the late nineteenth century can add significantly to our understanding of the foreign-language press. Specifically, this essay is divided
into three parts. Part 1 lays out in some detail the relationship between
women and the German American press. Attracting the woman reader
emerges as one of the most successful strategies devised by the German
American press to ward off the coming decline after immigration figures
began to drop in the early 1890s. Part 2 pays particular attention to the
ways the immigrant press promoted divergent visions of women's roles.
The socialist press serves as a special case in point. Part 3 takes a closer look
at the women involved. It highlights interests and activities of women
readers as well as the options for immigrant women to take up careers in
journalism themselves. While the German American women's press will be
at the center of this brief and necessarily incomplete survey, comparisons
to other ethnic groups will be drawn throughout. It will then be possible
to point to obvious parallels as well as significant variations between the
individual ethnic groups, reflecting the inner chasm of the groups and divergent ethnic role traditions.

4 New studies have taken up where Robert Park left off with his pioneering monograph, *The Immigrant Press and Its Control* (New York, 1922; reprint: Westport, Conn., 1970).

5 See Sally M. Miller, ed., *The Ethnic Press in the United States: A Historical Analysis and Handbook* (New York, 1987), for a compilation of articles on the press of twenty-six foreign-language groups in the United States plus one on the Irish press; see also Dirk Hoerder and Christiane Harzig, eds., *The Immigrant Labor Press in North America, 1840–1970s: An Annotated Bibliography*, 3 vols. (New York, 1987), and Christiane Harzig and Dirk Hoerder, eds., *The Press of Labor Migrants in Europe and North America, 1880s to 1930s* (Bremen, 1985), which includes two articles on the women's page in the socialist *Jewish Daily Forward* and the Finnish American women's magazine, *Toveritar*, plus a short report on the Lithuanian women's press; see also Hanno Hardt, "The Foreign-Language Press in American Press History," *Journal of Communication* 39, no. 2 (1989): 114–31.

A PERIOD OF CHANGE: THE GERMAN AMERICAN PRESS
AND WOMEN, 1890–1914

Over an extended period of time, the German American press was foremost among the ethnic press, comprising 79 percent of all the foreign-language publications in 1885 and still claiming 46 percent in 1914.[6] Between 1892 and 1894, 790 German American newspapers and journals were being published, the climax of that group's journalistic production.[7] Yet immigration from Germany had been steadily declining after 1893 and the forces of Americanization were pulling the first and second generations apart. This posed a very real threat not only to the ethnic group's coherent identity but to its foreign-language press as well. Moreover, the very nature of publishing was changing. Advertising became the main source of income, constituting 55 percent of the total income of all journals published in the United States in 1900 and 60 percent by 1910.[8] It accounted significantly for the phenomenal growth and increase in circulation occurring after 1890.[9]

Yet the pool from which advertisements – or, for that matter, readers – could be drawn was not unlimited. According to Carl Gustav Wittke, "only publishers who learned to emulate the methods of the American commercial dailies could expect to meet their competition, and then only if they shifted from the exposition of a specific doctrine to the dissemination of news and advertising."[10] In an attempt to secure its piece of the pie, the German-language press entered upon a period of significant change. Utilizing American technology (cheaper newsprint, high-speed presses, and type-setting machinery), various means of communication (telegraphs and newspaper syndicates), as well as expanded distribution and advertising net-

---

6 James M. Bergquist, "The German-American Press," in Miller, *The Ethnic Press in the United States,* 131–59; see also Park, *The Immigrant Press and Its Control,* 310.

7 The figure for 1840 is 40 and for 1860, 250; Anne Spier, "The German Peoples," in Harzig and Hoerder, *The Immigrant Labor Press in North America,* vol. 3: *Migrants from Southern and Western Europe,* 308–51; see also Carl Gustav Wittke, *The German-Language Press in America* (Lexington, Ky., 1957).

8 Park, *The Immigrant Press and Its Control,* 364.

9 Dorey Schmidt notes that "whereas in 1885 there were only four magazines with 100,000 or more circulation, there were twenty in 1905 with a total circulation of over 5.5 million. And advertising expenditures kept pace with this expansion, increasing from $360 million in 1890 to $821 [million] by 1904." Dorey Schmidt, "Magazines, Technology, and American Culture," *Journal of American Culture* 3, no. 1 (1980): 3–16.

10 Wittke, *The German-Language Press in America,* 2. In general, Wittke elaborates, the German press emerges as basically an "American press published in a foreign language," 6. James Bergquist summarizes: "From the days of its founding by struggling and resourceful eighteenth-century printers down into the twentieth century, the evolution of the German-American newspapers paralleled the history of American journalism as a whole and was influenced by the same changes in technology, communication, and society." Bergquist, "The German-American Press," 131.

works, the German American publishers fought against signs of demise. In a further attempt to guarantee the press's survival they introduced so-called American features, including sensational coverage and illustrations, to keep their papers attractive.[11] But only the financially stable would survive. Nationwide, mergers of daily publications and suspensions of others cleared the way for the ethnic press's adaptation process.[12]

Reaching out to the woman reader formed an integral part of that process. Women's pages and women's magazines fulfilled a crucial role in the editors' endeavor to ward off an ongoing decline of sales and circulation by recruiting a whole new group of (female) readers. They thus followed the example successfully set by the American mainstream press. A variety of women's magazines had come into being since the 1880s and newspapers commonly began to carry women's pages in the 1890s. Commercially, the new women's press proved to be highly successful. In 1903 the *Ladies' Home Journal* (Philadelphia, 1903–),[13] for instance, was the first American magazine to reach one million subscribers. Capitalizing on women's new roles as major shoppers in a rapidly expanding consumer society, publishers across the nation began courting the woman consumer. Building on the growing recognition that the average woman "buys, or directs the buying of, or is the fundamental factor in directing the order of purchase, of everything from shoes to shingles," they sought to attract women to their publications and thus to their advertisements.[14] Alongside other manifestations of a new urban life-style, the women's press thus helped lay the foundations for a quickly evolving consumer culture and facilitated what John Kenneth Galbraith has defined as women's essential role in industrial society: "a continuous or more or less unlimited increase in consumption . . . disguised as service to the family."[15]

---

11 According to Miller, this was a trend notable among all ethnic groups around that time; "Introduction," in Miller, *The Ethnic Press in the United States,* xvii. Robert Park noted that in general the foreign-language press lagged behind about forty years, yet he and Sally Miller also argue that a trend toward faster takeover set in around 1900; Park, *The Immigrant Press and Its Control,* 364.

12 The total number of periodicals published in the German-language press dropped to 750 in 1900, 702 in 1905, and 634 in 1910. Park, *The Immigrant Press and Its Control,* 319.

13 Salem Steinberg, *Reformer in the Marketplace: Edward W. Bok and the "Ladies' Home Journal"* (Baton Rouge, 1979); see also Michael Dennis Hummel, "The Attitudes of Edward Bok and *The Ladies' Home Journal* toward Women's Role in Society, 1889–1919," Ph.D. diss., North Texas State University, 1982.

14 Nathaniel C. Fowler, quoted in George Juergens, *Joseph Pulitzer and the New York World* (Princeton, N.J., 1966), 137. See also Marion Marzolf, *Up from the Footnote: A History of Women Journalists* (New York, 1977), 205; Helen Damon-Moore and Carl F. Kaestle, "Gender, Advertising, and Mass-Circulation Magazines," in Carl F. Kaestle et al., eds., *Literacy in the United States: Readers and Reading since 1880* (New Haven, Conn., 1991): 245–71.

15 John Kenneth Galbraith, "How the Economy Hangs on Her Apron Strings," *Ms* (May 1977): 74–77 and 112. See also Kathy Peiss, *Cheap Amusements: Working Women and Leisure in Turn-of-the-*

For the editors of the German-language press, securing advertisements and drawing women to its publications also became inextricably intertwined. Mainstream and socialist papers alike began to tailor their products to appeal to the female reader. In 1891 the *New Yorker Staatszeitung* appears to have been the first German-language publication to introduce a woman's page; next came the Chicago papers, and others followed suit. Clearly, the American press served as a model for its foreign-language press as German American newspapers published women's pages before the national German papers did.[16]

Publishers enlisted various techniques to promote their advertising value. While some emphasized their national readership in advertisers' manuals,[17] others alerted advertisers to women's special buying power. The German Jewish women's magazine, *The American Jewess,* for example, argued that "women buy soap, china, glassware, flour, baking powder, carpets, and all other household articles" – and that "Jewish women buy the best."[18] For the financially unstable socialist papers in particular, securing advertisements became a daily and often frustrating routine. To prove that socialist papers were a medium for buying power, publications like the *Wisconsin Vorwärts* (Milwaukee, 1887–1932) and the *Cleveland Echo* (1911–20) appealed directly to their women readers by admonishing them to buy the local merchandise offered in the paper and thus to support the socialist cause.[19]

Reaching out to the woman reader implied crossing the bridge to the rural reader as well. In that process, the national magazine rose to success. Part of a larger pattern, it was representative of a time when modern industrial America was taking shape. Toward the end of the nineteenth century new technologies made mass printing relatively inexpensive and revenues from advertising helped guarantee financial surplus. Three federal

Century New York (Philadelphia, 1986); Susan Strasser, *Satisfaction Guaranteed: The Making of the American Mass Market* (New York, 1989); and Susan Strasser, *Never Done: A History of American Housework* (New York, 1982).

16 See, e.g., Sylvia Lott-Almstadt, *Brigitte, 1896–1986: Die ersten 100 Jahre* (Munich, 1986).

17 See Frank Luther Mott, *A History of American Magazines* (Cambridge, Mass., 1957), 3:32.

18 *The American Jewess* was published in the 1890s by Rosa Sonnenschein. See Charlotte Baum, Paula Hyman, and Sonya Michel, *The Jewish Woman in America* (1974; reprint: New York, 1977), 32f.; see also Selma Berrol, "Class or Ethnicity: The Americanized German Jewish Woman and Her Middle-Class Sisters," *Jewish Social Studies* 47 (1985): 21–32; for information on advertisements and the women's column in the Baltimore *Jewish Comment,* see Arthur A. Goren, "The Jewish Press in the U.S." in Miller, *The Ethnic Press in the United States,* 210.

19 E.g., *Wisconsin Vorwärts,* Jan. 5, 1902. On the role of advertisements in the German American socialist press, see also Anne Spier, "The German Peoples," 335: "For labor newspapers, which were generally not profit-oriented, as for other newspapers, advertisements were the most important source of revenue, since subscriptions could not even cover the costs of paper, let alone the production costs"; and Meta Berger, "Autobiography of Mrs. Victor Berger," unpublished manuscript, State Historical Society of Wisconsin Manuscript Collection, MSS 65, 11ff.

acts stimulated the growth of magazines even further. The Postal Act of March 3, 1879, introduced a special second-class mail rate – marking the "true birthday of the modern magazine" – and in 1885 that rate was reduced to one cent per pound. And after 1897, Rural Free Delivery opened up the world of printed matter to the rural public and paved the way for a national mail-order boom.[20] In due course, the rural population became part of a national public and the magazine the first national medium of its kind, speaking to native-born and newcomers alike.

Not surprisingly, ethnic magazines fared best among rural German Americans[21] and the Scandinavian peoples[22] in the United States. German American magazines began in the late 1870s when weekly Sunday editions to the daily newspapers started to be distributed among the rural population. Modeled on the U.S. example, they came increasingly to combine human interest sections – including the by then established and well-known women's columns – with the latest news.[23] After 1900, however, farm and family magazines began to take their place and quickly reached the highest circulation figures of the German American press.

Among them the monthly women's magazine *Die Deutsche Hausfrau* (Milwaukee, 1904–) ranks as the most outstanding example. Originating from a women's page in the agricultural weekly *Acker- und Gartenbauzeitung* (Milwaukee, 1870–1917) in the 1890s, the *Hausfrau* held its strongest appeal among rural Germans, selling a majority of subscriptions in the states of Wisconsin, Illinois, Texas, Minnesota, Nebraska, and New York.[24] Carefully crafted as a practical helpful-hints magazine geared to a middle-class audience, it featured a colorful mixture of sentimental Old World memories, serialized German fiction, news of the world, introductions to Amer-

20 Susan Waugh McDonald, "From Kipling to Kitsch: Two Popular Editors of the Gilded Age: Mass Culture, Magazines, and Correspondence Universities," *Journal of Popular Culture* 15, no. 2 (1981): 50–61. The boom included mail-order catalogs that combined a variety of ads with specialty departments, and fared incredibly well until the Post Office required that subscriptions be paid in advance, thus putting a halt to mail-order magazines.

21 Although only 33 percent of all German Americans lived in rural areas as of 1920, no more than 28 percent of all German papers were published in the ten largest cities. That same year there were twenty-seven towns that supported local German papers with a circulation of less than one thousand. Park, *The Immigrant Press and Its Control,* 298; see also table XII, 302.

22 According to Park, while 53 percent of the Norwegian population was rural, 75 percent of the press circulation was in rural communities in 1906. Also, the combined Danish, Norwegian, and Swedish papers held second place after the German American publications. *The Immigrant Press and Its Control,* 320ff.

23 Bergquist, "The German-American Press," 141.

24 In 1907 it sold 15,387 subscriptions in Wisconsin, 12,532 in Illinois, 7,587 in Texas, 7,214 in Minnesota, 6,031 in Nebraska, 5,829 in the state of New York, and 5,803 in the city of Milwaukee, N. W. Ayer & Son, *Newspaper Annual and Directory,* 1907. See also Karl J. R. Arndt and May E. Olson, *Die deutschsprachige Presse der Amerikas,* 3 vols. (Munich, 1980).

ican life-style, household hints and domestic advice, a fashion section, plus extended space for letters to the editors and other avenues for reader participation. The *Hausfrau* quickly climbed the circulation ladder and reached a remarkable circulation of 132,000 in 1907. It held on to an average of 90,000 in the early 1910s, lost half of its subscriptions after 1914, but managed to keep a circulation between 40,000 and 50,000 after World War I. The magazine continues to be published today making it the commercially most successful German American magazine of the twentieth century.[25]

For the Scandinavian women, the monthly *Kvinden og Hjemmet* (The woman and the home) performed a similar role. Published since 1888 by two Norwegian-born sisters (Ida Hansen and Mina Jensen) out of Cedar Rapids, Iowa, in a Danish Norwegian and a Swedish version (*Kvinnan och Hemmet*), the magazine reached a peak circulation of 82,650 in 1907. For many years, *Kvinden og Hjemmet* ranked among the very top of all Danish-language publications and surpassed all others with regard to longevity (fifty-two years). Like its German counterpart, it mixed Scandinavian fiction and homemaking advice or copied materials from the *Ladies' Home Journal*.[26]

VISIONS OF WOMANHOOD

Setting out to interpret the various types of womanhood displayed in the ethnic women's press, one has to bear in mind that communication acts as a process "through which a shared culture is created, modified, and transformed."[27] It has also been argued that communication functions as an "act of constructing reality itself, rather than simply a picture of reality."[28] Thus, while all groups and fractions within them seek to advance their own particular ideas on women's proper roles, any form of female identity portrayed will necessarily remain an artificial design paying tribute to singular aspects of women's lives only while leaving out others.

In general, the ethnic women's press can be said to have advanced two

---

25 Today, the *Hausfrau* is published in Athens, Georgia. After almost fifty years of publication in Milwaukee, it was sold to a Chicago publishing company in the early 1950s. When that owner saw its readership dwindle in the late 1970s, he sold it to its current owner. The magazine still sells about 25,000 copies a month. Interview of the author with Roswitha Shapland, current editor, April 6, 1992.

26 Marion Marzolf, *The Danish Language Press in America* (New York, 1979), 103ff., 229; Marzolf, "The Danish Language Press," in Miller, *The Ethnic Press in the United States,* 64; Ulf A. Beijbom, "The Swedish Press," ibid., 384; Lilly Setterdahl, "Adjusting to America," *The Palimpsest: Iowa's Popular History Journal* 68, no. 3 (1987): 136–44.

27 Summarizing here the European viewpoint, see Jennifer Tebbe, "Print and American Culture," *American Quarterly* 32, no. 3 (1980): 272.

28 Gaye Tuchman, *Making News: A Study in the Construction of Reality* (New York, 1978), 2, quoted in Tebbe, "Print and American Culture," 275.

different visions of womanhood. One exclusively promoted women's roles as guardians of family life and cultural traditions, especially as represented in language and religion. The other saw its primary role in fostering political energies and strove to educate women to become participants in the working men's struggle. Both operated within a context of the growing influence of the American environment. For the researcher today, it is these conflicting images that make the women's press essential reading. And its special value lies in highlighting both ethnic role traditions and challenging notions as well as arrangements sought to combine the two. The following examples yield an overview of this development.

If we are to understand fully the magazines' attraction, we need to go beyond pure circulation statistics and traditional forms of content analysis. Both German Americans and Scandinavians placed high value on women's domestic roles, encouraging them to stay at home to fulfill their reproductive duties. Yet while the ethnic society liked to portray women's special role as one of duty to husband, family, and the ethnic community as a whole, the impact of acculturation significantly threatened these very pillars of immigrant life. By and large, German and Scandinavian women were assuming a larger part in public life, claiming their share of what modern-day American society could offer. Declining rates of fertility, a gradual rise in female employment especially among the second generation, and varied female club activities gave testimony of changing lives. Combining a backward view to the Old Country and a contemporary outlook on women's issues in the United States, the women's journals attempted to speak to the traditional immigrant housewife as well as the American woman. Moreover, *Hausfrau* and *Kvinden og Hjemmet* helped make sense of the new environment in very practical terms. Recipes described in detail how to prepare the new foods, Butterick fashion patterns with German translations enabled immigrant women to dress just like American women, and the personal editor's advice repeatedly addressed some of the most common problems of acculturation, thus easing the tensions of trying to create a new home.[29] Readers bought the magazine for its entertainment value and its practical advice yet also treasured the sense of identification it awarded them in their specific ethnic roles. By bringing the outside world to the individual household, these journals transcended geographical and ethnic isolation. Serving as agents of Americanization, they helped ease the transition from a rural to an urban society and provided for immigrant women what the *Ladies'*

---

29 This analysis is based on a thorough examination of the *Hausfrau* (1904–14). See also Setterdahl, "Adjusting to America."

Home Journal offered to the American-born, namely, "security at a time of uncertainty threatening the security of familiar customs."[30]

In the case of the urban socialist press, differences are more pronounced and conclusions are less easily drawn. How to combine the dual interests of women's emancipation and liberation of the working class proved to be a source of constant discussion and a problem not easily solved. German American socialist men in particular tended to sentimentalize women's specific roles as wives and mothers and favored relegating them to a distinctively female sphere.[31] One correspondent for the *New Yorker Volkszeitung* put it quite bluntly by remarking that the greatest hindrance for women to taking part in political life was the socialist husband.[32] It was only after 1908 that the socialist platform incorporated a demand for universal suffrage and accepted the foundation of a separate Women's National Committee, and that the socialist press began to pay closer attention to the women's cause.

In early 1900 the *New Yorker Volkszeitung* (1878–1932) became the first to introduce a permanent Sunday half-page for women. The *Wisconsin Vorwärts,* the *Cleveland Echo* (1911–20), and others followed this example by offering their own women's pages in the succeeding years.[33] Yet while the women's page in the *Volkszeitung* was supported by the local socialist women's club and intended to free women from the bonds of lethargy and thus awaken them to political activism,[34] papers like the *Wisconsin Vorwärts* pursued a far less ambitious goal. It bore little or no connection with its famous local predecessor, the *Deutsche Frauenzeitung* (Milwaukee, 1852–54). Mathilde Franziska Anneke had been the very first to connect the emancipation of women and the social question in the German American press.[35] Instead,

---

30 Steinberg, *Reformer in the Marketplace,* xvi. See also Patricia Searles and Janet Mickish, "A Thoroughbred Girl: Images of Female Gender Role in Turn-of-the-century Mass Media," *Women's Studies* 10 (1984): 261–81. They argue that the final role of the women's press was in helping readers "interpret and cope with reality at a time when social change was prevalent and conception of women's roles and women's rights was in flux."

31 E.g., see Mari Jo Buhle, *Women and American Socialism, 1870–1920* (Urbana, Ill., 1983); Sally M. Miller, *Flawed Liberation: Socialism and Feminism* (Westport, Conn., 1981); Bruce Dancis, "Socialism and Women in the United States, 1900–1917," *Socialist Revolution* 6 (Jan.–March 1976): 81–144.

32 Quoted in Seifert, "Women's Pages in the German-American Radical Press," 12.

33 All papers made extensive use of materials first printed in the *Volkszeitung,* the German social democratic women's paper *Die Gleichheit,* the organ of the German Bund für Mutterschutz, *Die Neue Generation,* the American *Appeal to Reason,* and the socialist women's *Progressive Woman.* Buhle, *Women and American Socialism, 1870–1920,* 148; Seifert, "Women's Pages in the German-American Radical Press."

34 *New Yorker Volkszeitung,* Jan. 7, 1900.

35 On Anneke see, e.g., Maria Wagner, *Mathilde Franziska Anneke in Selbstzeugnissen und Dokumenten* (Frankfurt/Main, 1980). Almost twenty years later, Auguste Lilienthal and Mathilde Feodora Wendt of the weekly *Die Neue Zeit* (New York, 1869–72) envisioned true equality of the sexes, refused to sacrifice women's rights to the socialist cause, and supported the U.S. women's movement.

the women's page in the *Vorwärts* featured a variety of contributions on women's topics most of which could be found in the mainstream press as well. Boilerplate press and nationwide syndicates made for an easily accessible joint source.[36] So it happened that the *Vorwärts* and its Catholic rival, the weekly *Milwaukee Seebote* (1851–1924), repeatedly came to publish identical materials on their respective women's pages. Struggling for market acceptance, the bid for the woman reader in this case appears to have paid little more than lip service to women's expanding roles.

Dedicated to the cause of socialism and Americanism alike, the *Jewish Daily Forward* (New York, 1897–) followed yet a different line.[37] When a women's page was finally established, it gave belated testimony to the rising significance of Jewish women in the Socialist Party after 1910.[38] At the same time, however, it addressed the attempt to reconcile conflicting women's roles. As Maxine Seller has pointed out, the women's page illustrates how "reality interacted with ideology to enrich – and complicate – the columnist definition of socialist womanhood." The columns favored a politically active, yet unassuming type of woman who, at best, was to sacrifice her participation in public life as a single wage earner for a concentration on family affairs after marriage. Seller concludes that the *Forward,* in "giving Americanization priority over feminism and socialism . . . walked a fine line between leading and following public opinion."[39]

In striking contrast, the Finnish Socialist Women's journal *Toveritar* (Woman comrade, 1911–1930) assumed a much more progressive stance. If compared with other immigrant women, Finnish women enjoyed an unparalleled active and independent role in the ethnic community's social and political life on both the local and national level. Having been granted suffrage in their home country in 1906, Finnish women were granted voting rights by Finnish churches, workers' clubs, and ethnic societies in the host society as well. To develop women's potential further, socialist women started the *Toveritar* in Astoria, Oregon, to reach out to immigrant women all over the United States and Canada. The *Toveritar* was most successful

---

36 On the boiler-plate press, see Alfred McClung Lee, *The Daily Newspaper in America: The Evolution of a Social Instrument* (New York, 1947); Eugene Harter, *Boilerplating America: The Hidden Newspaper* (Lanham, Md., 1991).

37 It became the leading Yiddish newspaper of the world with a circulation of 200,000 in 1920; Maxine Seller, "Defining Socialist Womanhood. The Women's Page of the *Jewish Daily Forward* in 1919," *American Jewish History* 77 (June 1987): 416–38.

38 Buhle, *Women and American Socialism,* 124; Goren, "The Jewish Press," 206; Baum et al., *The Jewish Woman in America,* 126ff.

39 Seller, "Defining Socialist Womanhood." See also Seller, "The Women's Interests Page of the *Jewish Daily Forward:* Socialism, Feminism, and Americanization in 1919," in Harzig and Hoerder, *The Press of Labor Migrants,* 221–42.

when Selma Jokela McCone, editor since 1915, changed the journal's outlook from one propagating strictly political theory to one that mixed political education with entertainment and practical advice. In addition, she
set in motion a grass-roots campaign to encourage reader input and to make
the journal "woman's own paper, which would become a close friend, one
who is needed every week."[40]

To gain a richer understanding of the socialist press, we need to assess
the appeal that middle-class culture held for many of the working-class
women. Maxine Seller has argued that the absence of homemaking advice
in the *Jewish Daily Forward* stems from the fact that the paper presented itself
as "unburdened by middle-class romanticism of the women's sphere" and
did not consider housework a "source of feminine fulfillment."[41] Similarly,
the German American socialist *Cleveland Echo* renounced the dispensing of
any and all domestic advice. Still, it appears that those papers that broadened
their scope to encompass practical information could claim the greatest
success. One letter to the editor of the *Volkszeitung* pointed out that only
a mixture of contents would make the women's page attractive.[42] For the
time being, we can only speculate as to the "Cinderella qualities" of those
articles serving supposedly middle-class needs.[43] On this point, a comparison
of features in the socialist and mainstream press promises to be instructive.
Much can be learned from a perspective that seeks to integrate the two.

A FORUM OF COMMUNICATION

Sending letters to the editor constituted one of the few ways ordinary
women and men could make themselves heard. Whether their primary role
was to articulate protest or to simply raise one's voice on matters of everyday
life, letters opened up a new arena of communication beyond the immigrant
household. Readers responded emphatically to the *Hausfrau*'s calls for reader
participation, for instance, indicating a clear demand for the new magazine.
Letters to the *Hausfrau* cover a range of topics, from private quarrels between spouses at home, homesickness, and rebellious children to problems

40 Selma J. McCone, quoted in Buhle, *Women and American Socialism,* 299; see also Varpu Lindström-
    Best and Allen Seager, "Toveritar and Finnish-Canadian Women, 1900–1930," in Harzig and
    Hoerder, *The Press of Labor Migrants,* 243–78; Carl Ross and K. Marianne Wargelin Brown, eds.,
    Women Who Dared: The History of Finnish-American Women (St. Paul, Minn., 1986).
41 Seller, "Defining Socialist Womanhood," 428.
42 *New Yorker Volkszeitung,* Sept. 23, 1900.
43 Juergens, *Joseph Pulitzer and the New York World,* 149. See also Lizabeth A. Cohen, "Embellishing
    a Life of Labor: An Interpretation of the Material Culture of Working-Class Homes,
    1885–1915," *Journal of American Culture* 3, no. 4 (1980): 752–75.

caused by the husband's unemployment or alcoholism. So, too, the "Bintel-Brief" (Bundle of Letters) column in the *Jewish Daily Forward* served as a repository of the most common problems.[44] The issues reflected here not only provide key indicators of changing cultural values but also illustrate the female perspective, demonstrating the ways in which immigrant women tried to deal with their lives. Examples include German women searching for relatives via queries in the *Hausfrau,* Finnish immigrants attempting to find a mate by responding to marriage ads, and deserted Jewish women claiming their rights in the *Forward*'s "Gallery of Missing Husbands." Having few other means available to compensate for the geographic diffusion of the ethnic group all over the continent, they made ample use of space offered to them in the immigrant press.

By the same token, circulation drives, originating with the native press, worked to encourage reader participation. *Hausfrau* and *Toveritar* alike sought to solicit women readers as local agents in order to promote circulation. The record was impressive indeed, as many a woman developed remarkable promotional techniques. In 1907, for example, the winner of the *Hausfrau*'s nationwide competition for the largest number of new subscribers had alone managed to secure over a thousand new subscriptions. In short, such circulation drives performed a dual function: first, to involve women readers actively in the publication process and to bestow a kind of group identity upon those striving to achieve the goal of increasing subscriptions; and second, to help guarantee the journal's commercial success.

There is also clear indication that only when women were given the chance to participate actively in the design of the women's page did it begin to reflect their concerns. It is from the letters to the *New Yorker Volkszeitung,* for example, that we learn the most about the women's personal perspective. Rather than echoing the dominant male view, women editors and correspondents as well as female readers made extensive use of this space to discuss their own gender-specific attitudes on women's proper roles. Fresh contributions on varied issues such as birth control, venereal disease, child labor, and socialist women's activities offered a female perspective. Simultaneously, women's letters to the editors called for a reformation of gender relations and the sharing of household labor and demanded an end to the suppression of the working class and the patriarchal suppression of women.[45]

---

44 Baum et al., *The Jewish Woman in America,* 126ff.; Goren, "The Jewish Press," 217; see also Mordecan Solters, *The Yiddish Press: An American Agency* (New York, 1925); Isaac Metzker, ed., *A Bintel Brief* (Garden City, N.Y., 1971); Abraham Cahan, *The Education of Abraham Cahan* (Philadelphia, 1969); Mosches Rischin, ed., *Grandma Never Lived in America: The New Journalism of Abraham Cahan* (Bloomington, Ind., 1985).

45 See p. 321 and n. 32 above.

In establishing a personal bond between readers and publications, women editors fulfilled an important function. For the longest time, of course, women were welcome only as occasional spectators in the world of German American journalism, joining their journalist husbands on social occasions or preparing special meals for festivities.[46] And while in other cases only the combined labor of husband and wife kept many a publication alive, only men received the proper recognition. But at the turn of the century, women's page editors, frequently referred to with such fictional names as "Frau Greta" or "Frau Anna," came to be permanent figures on the German American newspapers' staffs.[47] Their columns ranked among the most popular features. Readers turned to these writers for practical advice and were often given substantial information. In fact, most writers took pains to respond to all questions in great detail, whether digging up song lyrics from the Old Country and attempting to cure obvious signs of homesickness or advising potential migrants on routes and destinations.[48] Most important, however, readers valued the "dignity of recognition" these columns awarded them in their daily lives.[49]

For women to succeed in the male-oriented field, it took considerable talent, the courage to challenge conventional stereotypes, a creative personality, and the willingness to either forgo or postpone family life.[50] Few immigrant journalists managed to have a career and be a mother and housewife at the same time.[51] Those who had received an American education yet still maintained close ties to the ethnic community were the most successful. In addition, family connections and a stimulating intellectual climate at home played an important role in encouraging women's professional careers.

---

46 *Verhandlungen des Vereins der Deutschen Presse von Wisconsin,* 1895ff. See also Deutscher Presse Club, *Fünfundzwanzigjähriges Stiftungsfest, 1882–1907* (Milwaukee, 1907), and *47. Jahrbuch des Deutschen Press Klubs Milwaukee, Wisconsin, 1882–1929* (Milwaukee, 1929).

47 In the United States as a whole, women journalists had been gaining considerable ground by 1900. Their total number rose from 35 in 1879 to 2,193 in 1900 and 5,730 in 1920. Barbara Salomon Miller, *In the Company of Educated Women: A History of Women and Higher Education in America* (New Haven, Conn., 1985), 240.

48 Due to high demand, "Frau Anna" of the *New Yorker Staatszeitung,* in real life E. Dittmar, even published a monograph advising young German women on different aspects of migration to the United States, *Die Einwanderung gebildeter weiblicher Erwerbsbedürftiger nach den Vereinigten Staaten* (Bielefeld, 1909).

49 Seller, "The Women's Interests Page," 231.

50 According to Susan Henry, a proper understanding of women journalists must take into consideration a variety of biographical data as well as a thorough investigation of class and social status. Susan Henry, "Private Lives: An Added Dimension for Understanding Journalism History," *Journalism History* 6, no. 4 (1979–80): 98–102.

51 If they did, however, they only received the ethnic community's praise for fulfilling their reproductive duties. Ida Hansen, extraordinarily successful editor and publisher of *Kvinden og Hjemmet* as well as a mother of seven, e.g., was praised for being an "excellent housewife and mother" without giving any further clues as to her professional life. Quoted in Marzolf, *The Danish Press,* 104.

Marie Jüssen Monroe, for example, editor of the *Hausfrau,* was the niece of Carl Schurz, the renowned journalist and German American politician. Born in Madison in 1862, Marie Jüssen grew up in Wisconsin and Chicago, profiting no doubt from her parents' active participation in that city's elite society. Together with her parents, she spent extended periods of time in Europe where her father served as a consul general. Marie Jüssen continued to live with her mother after her father's death in 1891 and became *Hausfrau* editor in 1904. She did not marry until after her mother's death in the early 1920s. At the time of her marriage to American-born lawyer Charles Monroe, she was sixty-two years old.[52]

Meta Stern Lilienthal's biography reflects a different political background, yet offers a similar perspective. Her parents ranked among New York's most famous socialists and her mother, Auguste, had actively campaigned for women's rights. But it was only after her marriage and after she had started a family that Meta Stern began to develop an interest in socialism and journalism. After studying the socialist classics in great detail, she became a writer for the *New Yorker Volkszeitung* and several New York–based American magazines.[53]

Yet while some women achieved remarkable success, ethnic and gender boundaries operated to keep most in their place. Pondering the situation of women writers who were both socialist and Jewish, Norma Fain Pratt concluded that "if men found it difficult to earn a living by writing, women found it impossible," as "not one woman was permanently employed on a radical paper as part of its editorial staff."[54] Instead, a majority of women writers from all ethnic groups took refuge in family life, focused their energies on other activities (politics, lecture tours, teaching), or consciously kept "a low public profile."[55] For example, the Irish-born "Kit" Kathleen Blake Coleman, an internationally known Irish-born women's page editor, war correspondent, and travel journalist in Canada, kept aloof from all radical concerns of women and emphasized her maternalism instead.[56] Few

52 Marie Jüssen Monroe, "Biographical Sketch of Edmund Jüssen," *Wisconsin Magazine of History* 12, no. 2 (Dec. 1928): 146–75; see also *Directory and Club List of the Elite of Chicago, 1886–87* (Chicago, 1886); *Milwaukee Journal,* May 13, 1931.
53 Buhle, *Women and American Socialism,* 128; Sally M. Miller, "Other Socialists: Native-Born and Immigrant Women in the Socialist Party of America, 1901–1917," *Labor History* 24, no. 1 (1983): 95f.
54 Norma Fain Pratt, "Culture and Radical Politics: Yiddish Women Writers in America, 1890–1940," in Lois Scharf and Joan M. Jensen, eds., *Decades of Discontent: The Women's Movement, 1920–1940* (Boston, 1986).
55 Dorothea Diver Stuecher, "Double Jeopardy: Nineteenth-Century German-American Women Writers," Ph.D. diss., University of Minnesota, 1981, 81.
56 Barbara M. Freeman, "Kathleen Blake Coleman: An Irish Woman Becomes a Canadian Pioneer Journalist, 1889–1915," *Journal of Newspaper and Periodical History* 6, no. 2 (1990): 27–30.

dared to challenge male supremacy, and those who did remained outsiders of the ethnic group. Thus Mathilde Franziska Anneke gained a favorable reputation among her fellow German Americans only after opening a girls school in Milwaukee and concentrating on her role as an educator.[57] Quite clearly, the ethnic group's approval was not easily gained.

Coming of age in the 1890s, the women's press quickly took on a life of its own. In that process, readability, outlook, and practical value marked the road to success. Speaking to real and imagined needs of women readers, women's pages and magazines offered instruction, advice, and entertainment, an introduction to American culture, and a source of unfailing support. In creating a medium of contact, they successfully encouraged women to take on an active part in the publication process. Women sent in letters, solicited new readers, or otherwise used the press for their particular purposes. Once scholars cross the boundaries between public and private spheres and begin to inquire about aspects of ordinary life and their relation to the political realm, the ethnic women's press proves to be a rich source for probing into the immigrants' daily lives and patterns of acculturation. Equally important, by examining the economic factors underlying the rise of the women's press, we can trace the beginnings of a consumer society that eventually eroded the foundations of ethnic life. As Elisabeth Ewen has accordingly argued, "Americanization . . . is also the initiation of people into an emerging industrial and consumer society."[58]

---

57 Stuecher, "Double Jeopardy," 72.
58 Elisabeth Ewen, *Immigrant Women in the Land of Dollars: Life and Culture on the Lower East Side, 1890–1925* (New York, 1985), 15; see also Stuart Ewen and Elisabeth Ewen, *Channels of Desire: Mass Images and the Shaping of the American Consciousness* (New York, 1982); Neil M. Cowan and Ruth Schwartz Cowan, *Our Parents' Lives: The Americanization of Eastern European Jews* (New York, 1989).

15

Return Migration to an Urban Center: The Example of Bremen, 1850–1914

KAREN SCHNIEDEWIND

The history of German return migration has been a neglected subject. Migration has been considered as a one-way stream to the United States where most migrants were supposed to find a better life than at home. International research on return migration only started in the 1950s and 1960s and by the end of the 1970s numerous studies of return migration of various ethnic groups were published.[1] International research concentrates on two major questions: Did the process of migration lead to a significant degree of social mobility? In which way did return migration have effects on the culture of origin, that is, did migrants influence the local society they went back to in a conservative or innovative way? Had migration changed their political attitudes or did they try to introduce new techniques of production or did they just reinforce the existing social and political structure of the areas they went back to?

STATE OF RESEARCH

In Sweden, Lars Göran Tedebrand and the Uppsala Migration Research Project have been able to analyze the relationship between the volume of emigration and return migration, the impact of American economic developments on both, and a positive or negative correlation between social trends and remigration. They found out that rural areas were more affected by return migration than urban areas since most migrants returned to their places of birth. Upward social mobility was very rare.[2]

---

1 E.g., see Theodore Saloutos, *They Remember America: The Story of the Repatriated Greek-Americans* (Berkeley and Los Angeles, 1956), and Wilbur S. Shepperson, *Emigration and Disenchantment: Portraits of Englishmen Repatriated from the United States* (Norman, Okla., 1965).
2 Lars-Göran Tedebrand, "Remigration from America to Sweden," in Dirk Hoerder, ed., *Labor Migration in the Atlantic Economies: The European and North American Working Classes during the Period of Industrialization* (Westport, Conn., 1985), 378–79.

With regard to Norwegian return migration, Ingrid Semmingsen noted that 40 percent of the migrants had been employed in industry and mining prior to their departure from the United States, while 10 percent had been farmers. After their return to Norway 40 percent became farmers, while only 11 percent worked in factories and mines. She therefore argued that working in American industries had provided a substantial number of these migrants with the necessary capital to become farmers in Norway.[3]

Although most Finnish migrants returned to rural areas, Keijo Virtanen did not consider them to be conservative. While their influence on the culture of origin remained limited because of their small numbers, they invested considerably into the local economies, advanced mechanization, and initiated new industries. In addition, many migrants became socially and culturally active and played a leading role in rural radical movements.

Many Italian migrants – usually referred to as birds of passage – came to the United States in order to earn enough money to go back and live a better life in their home towns. Francesco Cerase argued that migration was a crucial factor in conserving the existing structure of Italian society and thus had a different impact than in Finland. The activities of innovative return migrants were blocked by the local elites who feared competition.[4] George Gilkey, however, stressed the Italian return migrants' loss of traditional respect for the local elites. He argued that they improved the situation in the rural areas of southern Italy by introducing new work techniques and by increasing the number of medium-sized properties.[5] Dino Cinel, too, emphasized the loss of authority, but he described return migrants as "new men," as individualists with a desire for competition. They were mainly interested in preserving the social position of their families. They did not try to introduce new forms of cooperation.[6]

Donna Gabaccia, in contrast, pointed out that political attitudes and the willingness to become members of radical political organizations depended

3 Ingrid Semmingsen, *Veien mot West: Utvandringen fra Norge til Amerika, 1825–1915* (Oslo, 1941), quoted in Dirk Hoerder, "Immigration and the Working Class: The Remigration Factor," *International Labor and Working Class History* 21 (1982): 31.
4 See the work of Francesco Cerase, "A Study of Italian Migrants Returning from the U.S.A.," *International Migration Review* 1 (1967): 67–74; "Nostalgia and Disenchantment: Considerations on Return Migration," in Silvano M. Tomasi and Madeline H. Engel, eds., *The Italian Experience in the United States* (New York, 1970); "Expectations and Reality: A Case Study of Return Migration from the United States to Southern Italy," *International Migration Review* 8 (1974): 245–62.
5 George Gilkey, "The United States and Italy: Migration and Repatriation," *Journal of Developing Areas* 2 (1967): 23–36.
6 Dino Cinel, "Land Tenure Systems, Return Migration and Militancy in Italy," *Journal of Ethnic Studies* 12 (1984): 55–76.

on the political situation in the places the migrants went back to.[7] No significant upward social mobility could be noted among Sicilian return migrants. Most of the men remained in occupations their fathers had already held while women got married to men with the same occupational status as their fathers.[8]

The subject of *German* return migration, however, has been generally neglected. With the exception of two studies by Moltmann and Kamphoefner,[9] dealing mainly with the volume of German return migration during the nineteenth century, there is only one case study on remigration from the United States to two German North Sea islands.[10] This stream of migration included neither those people who could be considered "real failures" nor the legendary "rich uncles from America." Apart from a low degree of social mobility, innovative behavior of the migrants was a scarce phenomenon. Kortum stressed the fact that the traditional socioeconomic structure of the islands had not altered during the migrants' absence. Thus there was little room for innovative action even if the migrants were willing to run any risks. Like Gabaccia, Kortum emphasized the importance of the economic and political situation in the culture of origin.

International and German research on return migration so far has focused on rural areas. Urban centers were of interest only for comparative reasons. In this essay, I will concentrate on urban return migration to the city of Bremen, an important port of emigration and commercial center in northern Germany. This study is largely based on the files of applicants for Bremen citizenship from 1870 to 1918. At the end of the nineteenth century Bremen citizenship was mandatory for some professions such as civil servants, priests, lawyers, and notaries. Only Bremen citizens were, of course, entitled to vote for the parliament of Bremen, being a free and Hanseatic city with a government and administration of its own. The right to get support from the local authorities according to the German poor law and the use of state institutions by the elderly required citizenship as well. As Bremen citizenship was not obligatory, this source does not furnish a rep-

---

7 Donna R. Gabaccia, *Militants and Migrants: Rural Sicilians Become American Workers* (New Brunswick, N.J., 1988), 162.

8 For Polish return migration, see the essay by Adam Walaszek in this volume.

9 Günter Moltmann, "American-German Return Migration in the Nineteenth and Early Twentieth Centuries," *Central European History* 4 (1980): 378–92; Walter D. Kamphoefner, "Umfang und Zusammensetzung der deutsch-amerikanischen Rückwanderung," *Amerikastudien/American Studies* 3 (1988): 291–307.

10 Gerhard Kortum, "Migrationstheoretische und bevölkerungsgeographische Probleme der bei nordfriesischen Amerikarückwanderung," in Kai Detlev Sievers, ed., *Die deutsche und skandinavische Amerikaauswanderung im 19. und 20. Jahrhundert* (Neumünster, 1981).

resentative and complete sample of return migration to Bremen.[11] Unfortunately, we know nothing about the total amount of return migration to Bremen. Data on emigration of Bremen inhabitants to the United States are also sparse: From 1867 to 1914, 27,383 people emigrated, but no information exists about the social and occupational composition of this group.[12] Thus, applications for citizenship are the only possible source to study return migration to Bremen. The files contain precise information on date and place of birth, year of emigration, place of residence in the United States, length of stay, year of return, and occupation after return. They refer to reasons for emigration and remigration and in some cases describe the migrants' lives abroad. I was able to single out a group of 459 return migrants who had come back from the United States to Bremen between 1850 and 1914. Using these files as my main source and supplementing them by additional German as well as American sources, the occupational careers of the migrants could be reconstructed.[13]

It was then found that merchants and clerks returned in considerable numbers, as well as artisans and workers, innkeepers, and grocers, who either continued to work in their occupations or looked for other jobs in Bremen (see Table 15.1).

The careers of the largest occupational groups of the sample were closely analyzed during the whole process of migration: the situation in the culture of origin and the occupations held before emigration, the migrants' stay in North America, and their experiences after return to Bremen during a period of ten years. These results were interpreted in the framework of the economic, political, and demographic developments in both societies to examine the underlying motives and to study the character of return migration to Bremen. Thus, it was possible to answer questions pertaining to the consequences of this specific form of migration on the individual migrants and to a certain extent on the city's economy.

In the following, the experiences of merchants, clerks, artisans, and industrial workers will be presented in a general perspective and be illustrated by some examples. The remainder of the article will then focus on the

---

11 Only some male return migrants in the sample were forced to apply for citizenship because of the military service they had avoided by emigrating from Germany. See Karen Schniedewind, "Migrants Returning to Bremen: Social Structure and Motivations, 1850 to 1914," *Journal of American Ethnic History* 2 (1993): 35–55, esp. 48ff.

12 Arno Armgort, unpublished paper, Bremen 1988.

13 The results of this research have been published in my thesis *Begrenzter Aufenthalt im Land der unbegrenzten Möglichkeiten: Bremer Rückwanderer aus Amerika, 1850–1914* (Stuttgart, 1994). Apart from the Applications for Citizenship (*Bürgerrechtsakten*), city directories in Bremen and the United States were used to document the occupational careers of the return migrants.

Table 15.1. *Occupations of return migrants in Bremen, 1850–1914*

	U.S.	Bremen 1	Bremen 2
Commercial occupations	137	238	128
Merchants	(58)	(118)	(61)
Clerks	(58)	(107)	(22)
Industrial employment	20	45	37
Artisans	19	36	23
Others	41	121	44
Total	217	440	232[a]

Note: U.S.: First occupation noted in the United States. Bremen 1: Occupation immediately after return. Bremen 2: Occupation after ten years of residence in Bremen.
[a]The different total numbers of migrants are due to the fact that not all of them could be found or identified in the different sources.

savings and fortunes earned in the United States and the way migrants made use of them after their return in order to reveal one aspect of the consequences of return migration on the culture of origin.

MERCHANTS

More than 70 percent of the merchants held this occupation throughout the whole process of migration. Their occupational status and position in society remained unaffected. More than 54 percent continued to be merchants after ten years of residence in Bremen after their return. The decrease in the overall number of merchants, however, does not indicate a change of occupation or downward social mobility but a high degree of further geographical mobility. Of 118 migrants, 49 (41.5 percent of the merchants) could not be found in the city directories of Bremen ten years after their return: They had left the city either going back to the United States or to other German or European destinations.[14]

The migration of merchants to foreign countries was not a new phenomenon or peculiar to the second half of the nineteenth century. Bremen merchants had always been very mobile and were heavily involved in overseas or European trade. Traditionally, sons of merchants were sent for a limited period of time to foreign commercial firms where they became

14 Unfortunately it was not possible to find out where exactly they migrated to as the files of the registration office were destroyed in Bremen.

acquainted with different forms of business. At the beginning of the nineteenth century this migration concentrated on England and the Netherlands. But from 1830 onward an increasing number of young merchants
went to the important commercial centers on the American East Coast.[15]
Members of all established Bremen merchant families were working in the
United States during this period, where they built up subsidiaries or were
involved in already existing branches of Bremen firms. As early as 1846,
176 Bremen firms could be counted in the United States.[16] Obviously,
Bremen had developed very close commercial links to the United States.
The importation of American tobacco and cotton was a prominent branch
of commerce. Thus, temporary migration of Bremen merchants to the
United States can be explained not in terms of social conditions unfavorable
to this occupational group in the culture of origin but in terms of a traditional migration to foreign commercial centers. Occupational interests and
supplementary qualification, which could be gained during a stay in the
United States, accounted for the high number of young merchants going
abroad. Evidently, this form of migration was not free from economic pressure: Foreign work experiences and contacts improved the merchants' com-
petitiveness at home. Compared with the clerks, workers, and artisans who
migrated, however, this group held a special position.

For the great majority of the merchants, then, their stay in the United
States turned out to be very profitable. This success did not become visible
in terms of a change of occupation but in the very fact of remaining merchants during the whole process of migration. Upward social mobility was
still possible by enlarging their fortunes and business activities. Downward
social mobility was rare.

The close cooperation between Bremen and American firms included
intensive business contacts as well as a vivid exchange of commercial personnel: Merchants and clerks were sent back and forth across the Atlantic.
This fluctuation led to a frequent change of property holders in American
commercial businesses, but it also proved that various Bremen merchants
were continually involved in these businesses.

In 1839, for example, Georg Wilhelm Krüger, the son of a merchant in
Bremen, became a partner in the business of the Bremen merchant Hermann Oelrichs in New York. Krüger had held the position of an American

15 Franz Josef Pitsch, *Die wirtschaftlichen Beziehungen Bremens zu den Vereinigten Staaten von Amerika bis zur Mitte des 19. Jahrhunderts* (Bremen, 1974), 197.
16 Rolf Engelsing, "England und die USA in der bremischen Sicht des 19. Jahrhunderts," *Schriften der Wittheit zu Bremen* (1957): 44.

agent for another Bremen firm since 1836. In 1837 Edwin Adalbert Oelrichs, a brother of Hermann Oelrichs, arrived in New York; he also became a property holder in his brother's business in 1844. The same year, Gustav Schwab arrived in New York and started working as a clerk for Oelrichs & Krüger. After having finished his apprenticeship in the business of H. H. Meier in Bremen (one of the most well known merchants in the city), he had been recommended for this job.

Oelrichs & Krüger was highly successful in New York: The firm took over the agency of the first regular shipping line between New York and Bremen organized by the Ocean Steam Navigation Company, founded in 1846. During the same year Krüger retired and went back to Bremen. In 1850 Edwin Adalbert Oelrichs was nominated Bremen consul in New York and succeeded his brother in this office. That same year Schwab got married to a granddaughter of Caspar Meier and thus established very close contacts to the Bremen firm of H. H. Meier. Business interests on both sides may have influenced this choice of marriage partner to a great extent. Schwab finally became a partner of Oelrichs in 1859 and the firm took over the agency of the North German Lloyd, founded in 1857 in Bremen. In 1861 Oelrichs returned to Bremen; his younger brother Henry continued to work in New York and Schwab became consul of Bremen.[17]

This example illustrates the confusing variety of commercial and family networks that Bremen merchants built up in Bremen and the United States. Taking into consideration knowledge and experiences gained in the United States, return migrants were highly efficient in organizing the transatlantic cooperation with American firms. Not all merchants, however, specialized in trade with the United States after their return; others restricted their business to Germany or the European context. American business experiences could also successfully be applied in activities not connected to the German–American trade.

Max Wilhelm Ueltzen, for example, was born in Bremen in 1870, the son of a merchant. For seven years he worked in the United States, Mexico, and Spain. In 1899 he settled down in Germany, first in Hamburg and then, in 1902, he moved to Bremen. He opened up a commercial firm in Hamburg with a branch office in Bremen, specializing in export and import. Four years later, he became a partner of a general agent of a fire insurance company in Breslau. In 1912 he was involved in a third business: insurance

---

17 Alfred Vagts, "Gustav Schwab, 1822–1880: Ein deutsch-amerikanischer Unternehmer," *Bremisches Jahrbuch* 50 (1965): 327–60; Franz Josef Pitsch, *Die wirtschaftlichen Beziehungen,* 82, 200; State Archive of Bremen, 2-8.A.10.c.5.

and transportation.[18] Ueltzen personified the image of a successful Bremen merchant whose business contacts were not limited to the city itself. International activities, however, were not necessarily included.

Unlike Ueltzen's, the career of Heinrich Constantin Knoop was more intimately connected to his migratory experiences. Also the son of a merchant, he was born in Bremen in 1850. When he was twenty-one years old, he went to Manchester in England to work as a clerk. There he stayed for six years before he crossed the Atlantic and worked in Wilmington, North Carolina, for two years, in Charleston, South Carolina, for three years, and in New Orleans, Louisiana, for six more years. Back in Bremen, he became a partner of a cotton merchant.[19] Eleven years of residence in the centers of cotton production of the southern United States had qualified him for the career of a cotton merchant in Bremen.

Return migrants invested in a wide variety of businesses. Most of them either opened up new firms in Bremen or worked for companies with American branches. Some of them simply retired. All investments, however, concentrated on the commercial area and not a single merchant invested his American money in establishing new industries in Bremen. Thus, return migration of merchants did not lead to an innovation or modernization of the economic structure of the city but rather played a conservative role.

CLERKS

Toward the end of the nineteenth century, the number of clerks in the sample increased. In contrast to the situation during the first half of the century, clerks could no longer expect to end their careers as merchants or grocers. The number of clerks in Germany had considerably increased during the last decades of the century and they consequently had to face tough competition on the labor market and even unemployment. Migration to the United States offered them many opportunities. First, it could prevent unemployment; second, clerks could make use of their American business experiences and knowledge of the English language to move into more qualified and better paid positions after their return. Third, they could still aspire to open up their own businesses either in the United States or after returning to Germany by earning enough money during their stay.

18 State Archive of Bremen, 2-8.A.6.a.5, 1902/125; Adressbücher der Freien Hansestadt Bremen (City Directories of Bremen), 1902–12.
19 State Archive of Bremen, 2-8.A.6.a.5, 1890/169; Adressbücher der Freien Hansestadt Bremen, 1898–1905.

Yet overall, the clerks in the sample experienced very little social mobility during their stay in the United States. Three-fourths of the migrants who had succeeded in finding a job as a clerk remained in that occupation during their stay. The position of a clerk in an office of a commercial firm, however, should not be underestimated, since these positions were usually unavailable for the majority of first-generation immigrants. These jobs required a good knowledge of English, which most immigrants did not have after only a short stay in the United States. A visible upward social mobility, however, remained the exception among clerks during their sojourn. Change in occupational status occurred to a considerable degree only after their return to Bremen.

The term "clerk" comprised a wide range of different occupations: shop assistants in small groceries, employees in the offices of important commercial businesses, and sons of merchants whose apprenticeship made it necessary to work in inferior positions for a limited time. These sons of merchants formed the most privileged group among the clerks. They could count on taking over the family business one day or rely on a future inheritance to start businesses of their own.

Gustav Carl Brauer was one of these merchants' sons. Born in Bremen in 1864, he went to Texas in 1885. One and a half years later he headed for New York City where he stayed for five years. Applying for citizenship in Bremen in 1892, he argued that he had worked as a clerk in the United States and now wanted to open up a commercial firm in Bremen. Lacking the necessary capital, he had to wait for an inheritance. Only one year later he opened up an agency and, in 1895, he became a partner of a broker who subsequently started a branch office in Leipzig in 1898. In 1901 he got involved in yet another business dealing with cotton trade.[20] The kind of change in social status experienced by Brauer was typical of the career of a Bremen merchant's son. These sons very often developed their own business activities after some years' work as a clerk. Therefore, this career pattern cannot be considered as upward social mobility.

The starting position of Heinrich Alexander Christian Theye, however, shows yet another picture. He was born in Bremen in 1864. His father worked as a cashier. When Theye was sixteen years old, he went to Indiana for one year. Having emigrated as a commercial apprentice, he claimed to be a clerk when he applied for Bremen citizenship in 1883. At that time he held a job as a trainee in a commercial firm where he did not receive

---

20 State Archive of Bremen, 2-8.A.6.a.5, 1892/115; Adressbücher der Freien Hansestadt Bremen, 1893–1913.

any salary at all and hoped to be able to find a job as a clerk one day. Sixteen years passed before he established his own agency in Bremen.[21]

Although Theye's father obviously had the financial means to support his son during his training, his occupation as a cashier belonged to the lower scale of commercial activities. In fact, Theye experienced a significant upward social mobility, but sixteen years had passed after his return from the United States before he could start his own business. Thus a causal connection between his migration and the change of social status is not at all apparent. Especially in Theye's case it seems rather doubtful that such a connection existed as he had spent only one year in the United States. To the contrary, American experiences could hardly result in an immediate upward social mobility since these clerks lacked – in contrast to the sons of merchants – the necessary capital. Most of them returned with only small amounts of savings, could not count on an inheritance and thus had to continue working in inferior positions hoping eventually to save enough money. In any case, the example of Theye convincingly shows that changes of social status took place over long periods of time and were not (and could not be expected to be) an immediate result of migration.

For the majority of clerks, however, migrating to the United States did not imply a significant improvement of their social status: They did not come back as merchants or start a business of their own after returning. Rapid industrialization in Germany and the United States had led to an increase of commercial employees in both countries; most of them had to remain in this career. About one-fifth of the returning clerks continued to work in this occupation.

A good example is Heinrich Grewe, born in Bremen in 1857. His father was a shoemaker. When Grewe was fifteen, he emigrated to the United States. He worked in various places, eventually in New York City. There he became an American citizen in 1879 and worked as a clerk. That same year he returned to Bremen. In 1897 he applied for Bremen citizenship and was still working as a clerk for Friedrich Missler, the main agent of the North German Lloyd in Bremen.[22] Grewe's migration to the United States did not result in a significant change of social status but provided him with a very qualified and well paid job where he could use his experiences gained from living abroad.

Many clerks profited from migration by moving into higher and more

21 State Archive of Bremen, 2-8.A.6.a.5, 1883/179; Adressbücher der Freien Hansestadt Bremen, 1883–1909.
22 State Archive of Bremen, 2-8.A.6.a.5, 1897/111; Naturalization Records of the Superior Court, New York County, May 14, 1879.

diversified jobs. In this context their migration shows similarities to the merchants' migration. But this was not the rule – some clerks actually had to face downward social mobility after their return. Johann Ferdinand Brand, for example, who had worked for five years as a clerk in New York City, could not find a job as a clerk in Bremen and had to accept a job as a worker in a sawmill.[23] Karl Christian Heinrich Sprute, too, had worked as a clerk in New York City for eleven years before he returned to Bremen. He remained in this position for another five years, after which he was registered as a worker in the city directories.[24] Thus, in some rare cases return migration was followed by downward social mobility. It remains doubtful, however, if this decline of status implied a lower level of income as well, since the salaries of clerks could be considerably lower than the wages of qualified workers. The individual clerk may have been more frustrated by leaving a white-collar job, as these were highly valued in nineteenth-century Germany.

ARTISANS

At the end of the nineteenth century the occupational situation of artisans mirrored that of clerks. Becoming a master artisan was no longer a necessary result of apprenticeship and obligatory migration. Instead, artisans as well as clerks more often remained qualified employees throughout their occupational careers. Moreover, industrialization initiated a process of deskilling in the trades. Artisans could circumvent these developments by migrating to the United States only to a very limited extent. As Bodnar points out, artisans who had finished their apprenticeship at home and who had worked in their trade for several years before leaving their country were in a more advantageous position than those without any occupational experiences.[25] Experienced artisans were at least able to find a job in their trade although they did not succeed in rising above the position of wage earners.

Joseph Schumacher, born in Bremen in 1851, left the city when he was eighteen years old and went to Osnabrück, later on to Frankfurt am Main. During the following years he worked as a carpenter in Stuttgart and Düs-

23 State Archive of Bremen, 2-8.A.6.a.5, 1899/113.
24 State Archive of Bremen, 2-8.A.6.a.5, 1903/442; City Directories of New York City, 1901–3; Naturalization Records of the New York Court, New York, N.Y., Sept. 2, 1898; Adressbücher der Freien Hansestadt Bremen, 1904–11.
25 John E. Bodnar, *The Transplanted: A History of Immigrants in Urban America* (Bloomington, Ind., 1985), 171.

seldorf. In 1879, when he was already twenty-seven years old, he migrated
to New York City and continued to work as a carpenter.[26] The locksmith
Friedrich Petermann, born in Saxony in 1836, worked in various German
towns for several years before he went to New Orleans and St. Louis. He,
too, found a job as a locksmith during his stay.[27]

Both migrants were very qualified artisans when they decided to leave
their country. Not only had they finished their apprenticeship in Germany,
but they had also gained migratory and occupational experiences before
arriving in the United States. These qualifications certainly helped in finding
a job in their occupation. Nevertheless, their further histories give rise to
the assumption that they were not satisfied with the opportunities offered
there. Schumacher returned to Bremen after five years; Petermann only
stayed for three years.

Another locksmith, Heinrich Eggers, was still an apprentice when he
went to New York City in 1894. He succeeded in working in his occupation for two years but then joined the American army for another three
years before he returned.[28] Thirty years later than the previously mentioned
Petermann, Eggers emigrated to the United States. He most likely ended
up working in a factory. He was not as qualified as Petermann because he
had not finished his apprenticeship. Both factors may have led to the change
of occupation that occurred after two years of residence. After returning to
Bremen he planned to work in the shipbuilding industry. Thus, the occupational change in the United States was not a definite one but probably
resulted from unfortunate conditions in the American labor market. His
intention to work in an industrial plant in Bremen may suggest that he had
worked in comparable factories in the United States and had acquired additional qualifications there.

On the whole, the migration of artisans to the United States bears striking
similarities to the older tradition of migrating artisans in Europe. Instead of
working in Germany and Europe, however, they looked for further qualifications in the United States or simply happened to enlarge their area of
migration. Younger and less qualified artisans who had not finished their
apprenticeship often had to work in other occupations, mainly as workers.
Only after their return did some of the artisans achieve the position of a
master artisan and start small businesses. Similar to the situation of clerks,

26 State Archive of Bremen, 2-8.A.6.a.5, 1900/163. He was not registered in the city directories of
     New York City, but became an American citizen in 1885 as a carpenter. Naturalization Records
     of the Common Pleas Court, New York, May 8, 1885.
27 State Archive of Bremen, 2-8.A.6.a.5, 1870/192.
28 State Archive of Bremen, 2-8.A.6.a.5, 1899/122.

the artisans' savings rarely sufficed to start their own businesses immediately following their return.

WORKERS

In general, German migration to the United States toward the end of the nineteenth century was largely made up of unskilled workers hoping to earn enough money to return eventually. The Bremen case demonstrates, however, that returning as a "rich man" was to remain a vain hope for most. Take Friedrich Wilhelm Krieter, for example, who was born in Bremen in 1876, the son of a worker. In 1891 he emigrated to New York and worked on several American and English vessels and in different factories. After eight years of residence in New York City he went back to Bremen. On his return he had saved thirty marks – a sum an average worker could earn during less than two weeks of work in Bremen.[29] Like Krieter, most workers came back without, or with only very little, money. Ordinary workers in the United States usually did not earn enough money to save – in this respect the German and American situations hardly differed. Although American wages were generally higher than German ones,[30] workers were always threatened by periods of unemployment when savings were urgently needed to survive.[31]

Only very rarely could qualified workers improve their situation and make use of their experiences gained from migration. Johann Matthias Schnackers was one of them. Born in Aachen in 1827, he left Germany in 1846 when he was nineteen years old. He went to Holland and some years later to France. Finally, in 1870, he arrived in the United States – already forty-three years of age. Via Cuba he returned to Bremen in 1876 and immediately found a job as a molder in the shipbuilding industry. He received extraordinarily high wages. When he applied for citizenship in Bremen, the authorities were impressed by his abilities: Not only was he highly qualified, but he also spoke three languages fluently.[32]

Schnackers was an exception among the returnees not only with regard to the money he earned but also considering his advanced age. Generally, the age of forty was a critical turning point in the life cycles of industrial

29 State Archive of Bremen, 2-8.A.6.a.5, 1899/132.
30 Hartmut Keil and Heinz Ickstadt, "Elemente einer deutschen Arbeiterkultur in Chicago zwischen 1880 und 1890," *Geschichte und Gesellschaft* 5 (1979): 110.
31 See the example of the return migrant Matthias Dorgarten in Wolfgang Helbich, Walter Kamphoefner, and Ulrike Sommer, eds., *Briefe aus Amerika: Deutsche Auswanderer schreiben aus der Neuen Welt, 1830–1930* (Munich, 1988), 397–436.
32 State Archive of Bremen, 2-8.A.6.a.5, 1876/344.

workers. It became more difficult to find a new job and wages started to decrease slowly but steadily.[33] Schnackers, however, had no trouble finding a job at once and was the best-paid return migrant holding an industrial occupation. Being already forty-nine years old turned out to be completely irrelevant. His qualification as a molder after thirty years of migration to several countries ranked much higher than his age. Qualified workers in general had better opportunities of improving their situation by earning higher wages upon return. Very rarely did they leave their positions as workers and start small businesses like groceries or inns. Almost 70 percent of all the workers of the sample experienced downward social mobility compared to the occupations held by their fathers. This was the highest percentage reached within the sample.

SAVINGS AND FORTUNES

The amount of savings and fortunes return migrants brought back from the United States can, on the one hand, serve as an indicator of economic success during their stay overseas. On the other hand, the ways the migrants made use of this money reveal different motives for their return. The majority of return migrants came back to Bremen without any savings at all; only 87 out of 459 brought any money back. The actual amount of savings could vary to a great extent (from 20 to 175,000 marks) according to occupational status. (A well-paid clerk for example could earn up to 2,000 marks annually.)

Albert Andreas Land, for example, sold his pharmacy in St. Louis in 1899 in order to return to Bremen with his wife, who had fallen seriously ill. Immediately after his return, he bought a site upon which to build a house. The purchase left him with the considerable amount of 15,000 marks. At the age of thirty-two, he could afford to retire.[34] Carl Engelbert Harttig, on the contrary, could not live on his American savings for very long. At the age of fourteen he had emigrated to New York City in 1891 and had worked as a bookkeeper before he returned in 1899. A month after his return, he was still looking for a job and had to spend his savings (200

---

33 See Heinz Reif, "Soziale Lage und Erfahrungen der alternden Fabrikarbeiter in der Schwerindustrie des westlichen Ruhrgebiets während der Hochindustrialisierung," *Archiv für Sozialgeschichte* 22 (1982): 1–94; and Josef Ehmer, "Lohnarbeit und Lebenszyklus im Kaiserreich," *Geschichte und Gesellschaft* 14 (1988): 448–71.
34 State Archive of Bremen, 2-8.A.6.a.5, 1899/134.

marks) to make ends meet during this period of unemployment.[35] In contrast to Land, Harttig was forced to find a job rather quickly because his savings would not last long enough. In general, it appears that savings up to 500 marks were mostly eaten up by expenses during unemployment and could not be used as investments for the future.

Furthermore, the investment of savings in businesses of any kind was not the rule: Only sixteen returnees were able and willing to make use of their money this way.[36] Other return migrants did not plan to invest their money but came back with the intention to retire and live on their American savings. Johann Albert Dierks was forty-seven years old when he returned to Bremen in 1903. He lived on the interest of his fortune (75,000 marks) and rents he kept receiving from Savannah where he had run several grocery stores during his stay.[37] The former innkeeper August Johann Helmken was only thirty-eight years old when he returned to Bremen in 1901. He decided to stop working because of his bad health. He had amassed 175,000 marks, 70,000 marks in Bremen and the rest in the United States.[38] Thus, while both migrants had been very successful during their stay in the United States, they used their savings to retire early and did not invest their capital in private enterprises in Bremen.

In those cases where American savings brought back to Bremen actually helped to establish new firms, these were commercial ones: small groceries as well as more important firms specializing in export and import, for example. This was not always easy to realize and sometimes the savings were not sufficient to start a business immediately. Johann Heinrich Otto Precht was born in Bremen in 1873 as the son of a worker. When he was fourteen years old, he went to New York and worked as a waiter. He returned to Bremen in 1898; he had saved 1,500 marks during his stay. He planned to open up a grocery later on but was looking for a job as a clerk to earn the necessary money.[39]

Compared with the situation of other return migrants of other nationalities, the low rate of returnees with savings in Bremen is fairly striking at

---

35 State Archive of Bremen, 2-8.A.6.a.5, 1899/129.
36 For these migrants investments are documented in the source material. The number sixteen is probably too small since it can be assumed that a lot of merchants invested money earned in the United States in new businesses in Bremen. For them, however, this was not a decisive turning point in their careers. Artisans and clerks for example changed their social position to a considerable degree if they established small shops or businesses.
37 State Archive of Bremen, 2-8.A.6.a.5, 1903/433.
38 State Archive of Bremen, 2-8.A.6.a.5, 1902/117.
39 State Archive of Bremen, 2-8.A.6.1.5, 1898/164.

first sight. Only one-fifth of Finnish return migrants came back without any savings at all. They bought houses or land or enlarged existing property.[40] Only eighty-seven return migrants in Bremen claimed to have savings or any other sort of capital. Therefore, the relation between those who had savings and those who had not is turned upside down when compared with the Finnish case. These findings point to a fundamental difference between urban and rural return migration. If rural migrants emigrated with the clear intention to earn enough money to enable them to buy land later on, they had to keep to their original goal once in the United States, that is, they had to earn and save as much money as they could. Return was a sensible decision once this goal had been achieved. Urban migrants, in contrast, may have had different aims when leaving their country for a period of time: Many remigrants in Bremen may have had the intention to obtain further or completely new qualifications. From this point of view their migration can be considered successful, although they did not have any savings when they returned.

CONCLUSION

This study of Bremen returnees shows that emigration and return migration played a differing role in the career trajectories of the different occupational groups. For a considerable number of merchants and clerks it meant gaining supplementary qualification in the United States that improved business connections and – this is only true for clerks – improved their situation in the German labor market. In this context it is not important if it was a planned goal or if it only proved to be an advantage after their return. In any case, their occupational position had definitely improved after their sojourn in the United States. Although this is not true for all the commercial personnel, especially not for all clerks, this result shows a special form of migration – comparable with the traditional form of artisans' migration in Europe. Although this old tradition may also have influenced the artisans' decision to spend some years in the United States, most were not as successful as merchants and clerks had been. Only older migrants who had already acquired some qualifications and practical experience in their trade succeeded in finding an appropriate job.

Yet this study does not point to any significant degree of innovative potential resulting from the migrants' return – whether immediately after

---

40 Keijo Virtanen, *Settlement or Return: Finnish Emigrants (1860–1930) in the International Overseas Migration* (Helsinki, 1979), 195.

their return or ten years later. This result, however, needs to be closely linked to the migrants' occupational careers and their investments in Bremen. It may partly stem from the inherent limitations of the source materials used. Thus, it is to be hoped that additional studies will shed more light on the migrants' behavior, determining, for example, whether the stay in the United States was of any influence on the migrants' political consciousness; whether, too, they had lost respect for local elites; and whether they preferred a democratic political system to the situation in Prussian Germany. Only then will we be able to evaluate finally or fully the characteristics of return migration.

Differences between rural and urban migrations in Germany should form an integral part of this analysis. Return migration to Bremen constituted a very specific form of migration: The majority of migrants emigrated from Bremen, worked in American industrial cities, and went back to an urban center. There was no interchange between agricultural and industrial occupations during this process of migration. Since the economic structure of the city of Bremen was more complex, it offered a wider choice to the migrants of how to make use of American experiences and savings than a rural community could have done. To a higher degree than rural return migrants, urban remigrants could choose between different sectors of the economy. Bremen being a commercial center, however, offered different opportunities than industrial cities. Only a comparison of various case studies will enable us to determine the conditions that caused certain areas of remigration to transform into innovative ones and left other areas unchanged.

16

Migration, Ethnicity, and Working-Class Formation: Passaic, New Jersey, 1889–1926

SVEN BECKERT

In the spring of 1919 thousands of textile workers in a small New Jersey town went on strike, demanding the eight-hour day.[1] It was not their first walkout. What was unprecedented, however, was the participation of skilled workers. During the previous thirty years, these workers had sided with the millowners during industrial conflicts and had refused to join the action of their less skilled colleagues. In a radical shift in policy, the employers had now laid them off, leaving them with few alternatives but to join the struggle. The workers went to the union and asked "if they could join." After stressing "that they have to come to us now," the union accepted the new members.[2]

Divisions between skilled and less skilled workers are not uncommon, but in Passaic, New Jersey, they acquired a particular twist. The worsted mills were owned by German entrepreneurs who had hired most of their skilled work force directly from Germany, while staffing the unskilled positions largely with eastern and southern European immigrants.[3] This essay demonstrates how an alliance between German immigrant capital and German immigrant workers was successfully fostered through the preferential treatment of skilled workers and through the support of the German employees' religious, educational, and cultural institutions by the millowners. It analyzes the relationship between the social organization of migration, the making of ethnicity, and working-class formation and also attempts to understand the German immigrants' experience in relation to other migrant groups as well as the internal structure of the immigrant community itself.

1 For their encouragement and help, I would like to thank Richard Bensel, Elizabeth Blackmar, Joshua Freeman, Victor Gotbaum, Michael Hanagan, Lisa McGirr, Dieter Plehwe, James Shenton, Charles Tilly, the members of the Proseminar on State Formation and Collective Action at the New School for Social Research, and the fellows at the Center for Labor Management Policy Studies.
2 *Passaic Daily News (PDN)*, Feb. 10, 1919.
3 For a good discussion of the dynamics of alliances between skilled and unskilled workers, see Michael Hanagan, "Solidarity Logics – Introduction," *Theory and Society* 17, no. 3 (1988): 309–27.

347

Although immigrant capitalists have often exploited their compatriot immigrant workers to an extent they could not have exploited others, this
essay shows how the common national origin of employers and a segment
of the work force could result in preferential treatment.[4] In the Passaic mills,
skill divisions, expressed in ethnic terms, weakened the potential for the
success of collective action by the thousands of unskilled immigrant workers. Only changes in immigration patterns, mill ownership, and in the structure of the city's working class fostered by World War I created the space
necessary for workers' unified challenge to the overwhelming power of the
millowners.

I

The history of Passaic's industrialization provides the background for conflicts that emerged between manufacturers and workers. Passaic's industrial
growth began in the late 1880s. Although its location ten miles from New
York City and its supply of water had attracted some textile companies
during the boom years of the Civil War, it was only later that investments
reshaped the face of this largely residential town. Two smaller textile enterprises opened their gates in 1888; a year later, in 1889, one of the largest
German woolen textile firms decided to locate their North American operations there.[5]

Like many German textile companies, the Kammgarnspinnerei Stöhr &
Company of Leipzig had a history of involvement in international trade
and was highly integrated into the world economy. The largest company
in Leipzig, it was to expand into Holland, Hungary, Czechoslovakia, Italy,
and Latvia in the early twentieth century.[6] Saxony, the state where the
company originated, was one of the woolen industry's centers in Europe
and exported about sixty million marks worth of textiles in 1890 to the
United States. Importers were so successful that the National Association
of Wool Manufacturers pressured Congress to increase duties on woolen
goods, a move that in turn motivated Kammgarnspinnerei owner Edward
Stöhr to travel to the United States in 1888 with plans to establish a modern
woolen and worsted mill. Passaic's proximity to New York City's markets
and the availability of international communication links convinced Stöhr

4 See, e.g., Charles Tilly, *Transplanted Networks,* New School for Social Research, Working Paper
  Series 35 (New York, 1986), 8.
5 *PDN,* May 7, 1889; Passaic's industrial district also included the towns of Garfield, Wallington, Lodi,
  and parts of the city of Clifton.
6 Karl Juckenburg, *Das Aufkommen der Grossindustrie in Leipzig* (Leipzig, 1913), 70.

that it was advantageous to locate here. In Passaic he set up one of the largest and most modern woolen mills in the world, concentrating yarn spinning, dyeing, and finishing in one place. Raw wool would enter the buildings at one end and finished cloth would emerge out the other. When Congress enacted the McKinley tariff in 1890, which increased duties on woolen goods imports from 40 to 50 percent, the Botany Worsted Mills – as the American branch of the Kammgarnspinnerei was known – was poised to take up production in Passaic.[7]

The city's boom years had begun. Passaic's Mayor Wolstan R. Brown proclaimed that "our mills have been pushed to their capacity, our merchants are prosperous . . . and property is in active demand."[8] In 1891 Edward Stöhr formed a partnership with two wool manufacturers in Germany, Friedrich Arnold in Greiz and Ludwig Hirsch in Gera, in an effort to enlarge his Passaic operations.[9] With this added capital, Stöhr's investment in the United States proved extremely successful. Botany grew steadily in the years following its incorporation. It employed 300 workers in 1890, 1,600 in 1899, more than 4,500 in 1912, and in 1920, after the war, it listed over 6,400 employees on its payroll.[10] The growth of employment went hand in hand with the modernization of production, though the number of spindles rose faster than the number of workers. As it grew, Botany became the nation's largest worsted textile producer and provided excellent returns to its stockholders. The company paid dividends ranging from 6 percent in 1900 to 30 percent in 1906. The cumulative profits between 1889 and 1924 amounted to forty million dollars or eleven times the company's original investment. Throughout this time, the company remained firmly controlled by German stockholders, important decisions being made at the German end of the concern.[11]

"The decision of the Botany mills to locate in Passaic," wrote the *Passaic Daily Herald* in 1913, "brought the city to the attention of many other

---

7 Michael Ebner, "Passaic, New Jersey, 1855–1912: City-Building in Post-Civil War America," Ph.D. diss., University of Virginia, 1974, 47; "History of the Organization and Development of the Botany Worsted Mills," *Passaic Daily Herald (PDH)*, Fiftieth Anniversary and Business Review (Passaic, N.J., 1922); Rutgers University Urban Design Studio, *Botany Mills Redevelopment Plan* (Passaic, N.J., 1977), 1.

8 Wolstan R. Brown, *Annual Message of the Mayor of Passaic, 1893* (Passaic, N.J., 1893), 5.

9 Friedrich Arnold produced wool goods and was among the largest entrepreneurs in Greiz, Saxony. Ludwig Hirsch was owner of a dyeing and finishing plant in Gera, Saxony.

10 Rutgers University, *Redevelopment Plan,* 3; William J. Pape, *The News History of Passaic: From the Earliest Settlement to the Present Day* (Passaic, N.J., 1899), 281; Ebner, "Passaic," 50; Beulah Amidon, "Old-Fashioned Strike," *Survey* 56 (April 1, 1926): 11.

11 Rutgers University, *Redevelopment Plan,* 2; Kammgarnspinnerei Stöhr, *Handbuch deutscher Aktiengesellschaften* (Berlin, 1907–8), 580; "History of the Botany Worsted Mills," *Alien Property Custodian,* National Archives (hereafter NA), Record Group (hereafter RG) 131, entry 155, box 44.

manufacturers, with the result that the big industries began to appear as though by magic." Four additional German textile mills located in Passaic after 1889, all of them in some way connected with Stöhr's European textile empire. In 1902 the Gera Worsted Mills – a venture of the Brothers Weisflog from Gera in Germany – opened its doors. It was one of the more specialized plants in Passaic, concentrating on weaving and finishing while receiving yarn from the larger spinning mills. In 1906 the Gera Mills employed 600 workers. The business proved so successful that in 1905 the same investors founded the New Jersey Worsted Spinning Company to provide them with their own yarn. In 1909 the two companies were integrated into the Passaic Worsted Spinning Company.[12]

By 1910 two additional German mills had come to Passaic. In 1902 Paul Haberland and Ernst Pfennig founded the Garfield Worsted Mills with a capitalization of $125,000. The mill was located in Garfield, an emerging industrial suburb of Passaic. By 1918 the Garfield Mills employed 1,100 workers and was engaged in weaving and finishing, and it bought its yarn from the other companies.[13]

In 1904 the Forstmann & Huffmann Company of Weiden, Germany, built the second largest woolen and worsted plant in the city. For half a century Forstmann & Huffmann had been closely connected to the United States. Having opened a store on New York's Broadway as early as 1853, it expanded quickly and exported a large part of its textile products across the Atlantic. At first, the new mill was a venture between the Kammgarnspinnerei Stöhr in Leipzig and the Forstmann und Huffmann Aktiengesellschaft in Weiden. A large part of the initial $750,000 capitalization was contributed by Stöhr. The board of directors of the German and American ends of both concerns became interwoven.[14] In 1908, the factory expanded dramatically when a worsted spinning mill was erected to supply the company with its own yarn. Now divorced from its ties to the Botany Worsted Mills, by 1912 the company employed 2,510 workers.

12 "Passaic, New Jersey," *PDH*, 1913, 39; Board of Trade and the United Brotherhood of Carpenters and Joiners of America, *Passaic of Today, Official Industrial Review and Souvenir* (Newark and New York, 1906), 31; David Goldberg, "Immigrants, Intellectuals and Industrial Unions: The 1919 Textile Strikes and the Experience of the Amalgamated Textile Workers of America in Passaic and Paterson, New Jersey and Lawrence, Massachusetts," Ph.D. diss., Columbia University, 1984, 138; Ebner, "Passaic," 50; Morton Siegel, "The Passaic Textile Strike of 1926," Ph.D. diss., Columbia University, 1952, 9.

13 Ebner, "Passaic," 50f.

14 *Handbuch der deutschen Aktiengesellschaften*, 157; Ebner, "Passaic," 51. Edward Stöhr was elected vice-president of the company, Ferdinand Kuhn, the treasurer of the Botany Worsted Mills, became director, and G. Roechling, Stöhr's superintendent, became a member of Forstmann & Huffmann's board. See Board of Trade, *Passaic of Today*, 30. In turn, Justus Forstmann was elected vice-president of the Botany Mills and joined the board of directors of the German end of Stöhr's concern.

Passaic had become by 1904 one of the worsted manufacturing centers in the United States and a center of German foreign investment. The Botany Worsted Mills was one of the largest of all pre-1914 European direct investments in the United States.[15] Although this New Jersey town also produced handkerchiefs, cotton textiles, and rubber goods, the woolen textile industry clearly dominated the local economy. But not only German capital, technology, and managers migrated to Passaic. From 1889 onward thousands of immigrants from Europe poured into the city. Some of them had already worked for the same textile companies in Germany; others were drawn from the European rural periphery. A pattern of working-class formation emerged that was in some ways peculiar to Passaic yet in other ways typical of many contemporary American industries.

II

After the worsted mills opened, large numbers of workers migrated to Passaic. While in 1880 there had only been approximately 2,000 workers in the city, the number grew to 16,144 in 1909 and to 30,000 in 1927.[16] The rapid concentration of capital and the advancement of mill technology, moreover, restructured the work process. Skill requirements rapidly diminished. Only a few highly skilled workers were needed to run a mill employing thousands.

While economic developments in Europe contributed to the changing face of Passaic's proletariat, at the core of this process were the recruitment strategies of the worsted companies. Given their need for a large work force, labor procurement was a central issue for the millowners. Yet, neither skilled nor unskilled workers were to be found in Passaic in sufficient numbers. Traditional recruitment strategies of Passaic's older industries no longer worked as the flow of immigrants from Ireland, Holland, and England to the New Jersey town had all but ceased at the end of the 1880s.[17] "Practically every authority familiar with textile conditions predicted [the] failure [of the Forstmann & Huffman Mills because of] . . . the lack of skilled workers on these shores."[18]

15 Peter J. Buckley and Brian R. Roberts, *European Direct Investment in the U.S.A. before World War I* (New York, 1982), 50.
16 *Reports of the Immigration Commission,* Immigrants in Industries, part 21, Diversified Industries, Community D, Senate Documents vol. 79, 61st Congress, 2d session (Washington, D.C., 1911), 299, and Passaic Chamber of Commerce, *Bulletin* (June 1927), 2.
17 See also *Reports of the Immigration Commission,* 303–7.
18 "Forstmann & Huffmann Co.," advertisement in *PDH,* Fiftieth Anniversary and Business Review, 1922.

The worsted companies tapped two distinct labor markets. Unskilled positions in the mills were mostly filled with eastern European immigrants who arrived in large numbers in the nearby port of New York. Because there were few skilled workers among the new immigrants, the companies decided to induce Germans to leave their country and to migrate to Passaic. Capital networks between the Old and the New World created corresponding networks of migration. Company internal labor markets induced migration to the United States at a time when German emigration had substantially declined and in areas like Saxony was at a virtual standstill. In Passaic, German immigration became closely tied to the investment cycle of German capital. It was at its height in the five years after Botany Mills had opened and again after Forstmann & Huffmann Mills had been set up in 1904. While there were only 437 Germans in Passaic in 1886 this number climbed to 1,172 ten years later, and to 2,097 in 1910.[19]

A large number of German immigrants in Passaic came from Saxony, home of the Kammgarnspinnerei Stöhr, with others migrating from Neuss and the state of Thuringia.[20] In the Saxon city of Leipzig the millowners directly recruited workers from the German end of the concern, a pattern that was repeated by the Forstmann & Huffmann Mills in 1904.[21] The U.S. Immigration Commission reported in 1911 that "all who left Germany were assured positions in the mills." Robert H. Dittrich, for example, born in Werdau in 1868, was a foreman in the spinning department of the Stöhr Company in Leipzig. "In 1889 he came to the United States," where "he accepted a position at once with the Botany Worsted Mills, as foreman of the spinning department."[22] Albin Junge, born in 1865 in Chedewitz and employed in the "worsted spinning business" in Leipzig, began working "in the Botany Worsted Mills as a manager of the spinning and twisting departments."[23] While still in Europe, Peter Wollersheim, a Belgian who had worked in the Forstmann & Huffmann plant in Werdau, received a letter from Ernst Huffmann in 1906. A nephew of Julius Forstmann, the owner of Passaic's second largest plant, Huffmann wrote that he had "re-

19 Fritz Joseephy, "Die deutsche überseeische Auswanderung seit 1871," Ph.D. diss., Universität Erlangen, 1912, 79. See also the pensión lists in NA, RG 131, entry 155, boxes 44–50; *Reports of the Immigration Commission*, 303–7; Ebner, "Passaic," 77.
20 *Reports of the Immigration Commission*, 306; Philipp Maas, *Deutsche Evangelische-Lutherische St. Johannes Gemeinde in Passaic, N.J., 1891–1906* (Passaic, N.J., 1906), 5.
21 Forstmann Woolen Company, Passaic, N.J., *Skilled Hands* (Passaic, N.J., 1954), 14–15. This was not a unique pattern, as work on Paterson's silk weavers shows. See Richard Dobson Margrave, *The Emigration of Silk Weavers from England to the United States in the Nineteenth Century* (New York, 1986).
22 William W. Scott, *History of Passaic and Its Environs* (New York, 1922), 1:483.
23 Ibid., 494.

ceived yesterday morning from my uncle . . . in Passaic the telegraphic information to engage you." Wollersheim arrived in New York City in May of the same year. "His passage was purchased by Forstmann and he was met at the dock in New York. . . . Mr. Wollersheim then came to Passaic and was employed as head dyer." A Bureau of Investigation agent reported that these recruitment strategies "are indicative of all the German woolen firms in Passaic." Wollersheim named eighteen workers who "were engaged in Germany by his firm [Forstmann & Huffmann] to work in this country" – among them five finishers, a weaving master, and a dyer.[24] And Julius Forstmann himself stated that he had staffed the new mill with "skilled and loyal technicians brought over from Europe."[25]

While skilled workers were of central importance to the mills, the overwhelming majority of employees were unskilled. No other industry at the time had been as successful as the textile industry in dividing the work process and in deskilling tasks. "A worsted mill needs only few skilled workers," noted a German economist in analyzing the situation of the industry in the second half of the nineteenth century, "[o]f greatest importance are . . . efficient and cheap hands . . . and the cheapness of them is more decisive than their abilities."[26]

The Passaic worsted mills procured unskilled workers from three different sources. Passaic's old work force was one of them. The Rittenhouse Manufacturing Company, for example, had closed in December 1890 and left its workers with little alternative but to seek employment in the mills.[27] A more central source of labor for the mills was immigrants from southern and eastern Europe, especially women, who arrived in the city after 1889. Slovaks and Hungarians were the first to come, followed by Poles and Ruthenians. Passaic's working class was further diversified after the turn of the century, when large numbers of Italians migrated to the city. In 1909 the Immigration Commission reported that 4,500 Poles, 4,000 Slovaks, 3,200 Ruthenians, 3,000 Hungarians, and 1,750 Italians lived in the city.[28]

All in all, by 1910 approximately 23,000 immigrants had found their way from southern and eastern Europe to Passaic. Migration patterns corresponded to economic development – networks of familial and communal relationships provided a sensitive regulatory mechanism for migration.

---

24 NA, RG 65 (Bureau of Investigation), Investigative Case Files, Case File No. 205831.
25 Forstmann Woolen Company, *Skilled Hands*, 25.
26 Werner Hitz, *Entwicklung und handelspolitische Lage der deutschen Kammgarnspinnerei* (Würzburg, 1933), 24.
27 Ebner, "Passaic," 45.
28 *Reports of the Immigration Commission*, 303ff.

Thus, the small number of Poles, Slovaks, and Italians who had settled in Passaic before the industrial takeoff in 1889 played a central role in catalyzing the future flow of immigrants. The majority of the Slovak community, for example, originated from the county Spis, a small area in Slovakia.[29] The first seven members of this community came in 1879 when a Passaic entrepreneur "personally brought [them] from Castle Garden."[30] Later, hundreds followed, as they told their relatives, old villagers, and friends about the new economic opportunities in the United States and more specifically in Passaic. Hungarians, Poles, and Italians showed similar patterns.[31] These relationships not only directed the population movement, they also facilitated acculturation, survival, and labor market strategies.[32]

When immigrant networks of communal and familial relations failed to ensure the companies a sufficient supply of workers, the woolen mills commissioned a privately owned labor agency based in New York City to hire immigrants directly after arriving in the United States. Here, labor recruitment and labor policy merged. Access to a huge pool of workers made the mills relatively independent of their unskilled labor force. It facilitated their policy of hiring different immigrant groups, as allegedly they "asked the agents to collect for them as many diverse nationalities as possible."[33] And it secured a labor supply that, according to the Chamber of Commerce, was "particularly good because of the mixture of races."[34]

III

The process of class formation in Passaic was shaped by the correspondence between capital and human migration. For German workers, this relationship was direct; for others it was only mediated. The social organization of migration, however, had an impact on all workers. National origin and sex shaped their access to different segments of the labor market.

Upon arrival, most German immigrants took skilled jobs in the worsted

---

29 Goldberg, "Immigrants," 142–43. Most Poles came from western Galicia, most Russians from Ukraine, and most Ruthenians from only a few provinces of Galicia. See David Goldberg, *A Tale of Three Cities: Labor Organization and Protest in Paterson, Passaic, and Lawrence, 1916–1921* (New Brunswick, N.J., 1989), 49.
30 Scott, *History*, 494.
31 See M. Gaudentia, "The Polish People of Passaic," *Polish-American Studies* 3 (July 1948): 76. See also *Reports of the Immigration Commission,* 303. For Ruthenians and northern Italians, see *Reports of the Immigration Commission,* 304, 306.
32 See Tilly, *Transplanted Networks.*
33 *Senate Committee on Education and Labor,* 69th Congress, 1st session (May 26, 1926), testimony of Henry T. Hunt.
34 "Pertinent Points Pertaining to Passaic," *Passaic Chamber of Commerce Bulletin* (Sept. 1927): 8.

mills. They came "with trades"; 86 percent had experienced wage labor in their home country, many of them in the textile industry.[35] Among a sample of eighty-eight Germans employed in 1918 in the Botany Worsted Mills, twenty-eight worked in clerical occupations, ten as skilled engineers or mechanics, nine as mill hands, eight as foremen, six as firemen, five as loom fixers, five as spinners, and one as weaver and examiner.[36] The remainder worked in nonskilled jobs. Not only were most skilled workers of German origin but also most supervisors and managers. In 1918 every single head of the different departments at the Botany Worsted Mills was a male German immigrant. Most had come to work in Passaic after years of experience in the German, French, and Belgian textile industry.[37] "These mills," the Alien Property Custodian reported in 1919, "have always kept their distinctively German organization, both as to executives and employees."[38] Passaic's woolen mills were indeed so dominated by German immigrants that German became the managerial language of Passaic.[39]

There were a number of reasons why the millowners were procuring textile workers from Germany. For one, they were skilled employees and had already adapted to the mills' technology and management style. This was a central factor, as all worsted mills in Passaic had virtually transplanted a German work setting to the United States. Moreover, because the small skilled labor force was of critical importance to the production process and skilled workers were difficult to replace, the companies saw an opportunity to build strong bonds to its German workers in the environment of the New World, first and foremost by paying high wages and providing continuous employment.[40] That owners and skilled workers were of the same national origin was not essential to this process – indeed, it is far from exceptional that skilled workers are comparatively privileged – but it did strengthen the alliance.

As a result, the material situation of German workers, foremen, and managers was secure. In 1909 they earned an average of about $800 a year – $300 more than the average male Passaic immigrant and double the sum of Polish, Ruthenian, or Slovak men. Only 23 percent of Germans in Passaic

---

35 *Reports of the Immigration Commission,* 315: 83.2 percent of all German men and 11.5 percent of all German women in Passaic worked in the woolen and worsted industry.

36 NA, RG 65, Case File No. 74457.

37 NA, RG 131, entry 155, box 47. Report of April 30, 1918.

38 *Alien Property Custodian Report,* 65th Congress, 3d session, Senate Document No. 435, vol. 8 (Washington, D.C., 1919), 129.

39 The "use of English among the working organization is the exception rather than the rule." Letter of Frank Lawson to Mitchell Palmer, NA, RG 131, entry 155, box 114, correspondence.

40 *Reports of the Immigration Commission,* 329.

had an income of less than $600 a year, whereas only 6 percent of all Southern Italians or Ruthenians could count on a higher income.[41]

While German men held the highest-skilled and best-paying jobs in the mills, Polish, Hungarian, and Ukrainian women and Hungarian, Polish, Ruthenian, and Slovak men were employed as unskilled workers.[42] The worsted mills showed a clear preference for hiring workers from Hungarian and Polish backgrounds in general and women in particular. These immigrants labored in one of the more than one hundred jobs involved in the process of making raw wool into cloth: the carding, combing, drawing, spinning, twisting, reeling, winding, and weaving of the raw material. Their background was different from those of the Germans – most had no experience in industrial work. A large number were recruited from the rural proletariat. Fifty-seven percent of all Hungarian men and 76 percent of all Polish men had worked as farm laborers prior to their migration. The women shared similar backgrounds – 76.5 percent of all Ruthenian women, for example, had worked as farm laborers while in Europe. Only northern Italian men had some experience as factory operatives – 14.3 percent of them – while a mere 3 percent of the Hungarian and none of the Polish immigrants looked back on similar careers.[43] For some, migrating to Passaic was only a further stop in a chain of prior migrations that had taken them from Galicia and Slovakia to other regions of the Austro-Hungarian Empire or to Germany.[44]

The immigrants' background shaped their attitudes toward their stay in the United States. Many workers saw migration as a temporary move to earn money in order to improve their lot in their home country. For them, migration was an attempt to escape permanent proletarianization. This was reflected in the large return migration to Europe. During the crisis of 1907–8, for example, a large number of immigrants left Passaic for Europe.[45] Italians frequently labored during the fall and winter in the worsted industry and returned for the harvest to Italy.[46] For some immigrants, then, improving their situation in the United States was not in itself a high priority.

Immigrant women were the most exploited workers in Passaic.[47] More

---

41 Ibid., 318.
42 Ibid., 302, 304f., 307.
43 Ibid., 312, 314.
44 Goldberg, *Tale,* 49f.
45 *Reports of the Immigration Commission,* 303ff.
46 Ibid., 303.
47 Working-class women in Passaic generally worked for wages. Every second woman fourteen years and older was employed. Three out of four labored in factories, the others either worked in their own homes – most of them providing for boarders – or had domestic jobs.

than half of all unskilled jobs in the mills were held by women.[48] Indeed, women often arrived in Passaic on their own.[49] Sixty-eight percent of all Polish and 53 percent of all Ruthenian women were employed for wages, most of them in the weaving and spinning departments of the worsted mills.[50] They did not receive the same pay as unskilled immigrant men. In 1897 two-thirds of all women employed were paid less than five dollars a week, while four-fifths of all men made more than this amount.[51] A Hungarian man's income was around 50 percent higher than that of a Hungarian woman.

The wide differences in wages paid to distinct groups in the work force, hence to different ethnic and gender groups, strengthened divisions. Often pay differences resulted from different skill requirements but sometimes they were arbitrarily applied as a means of stratifying a work force that increasingly encompassed workers of similar skill levels.[52] Wage data for the whole of New Jersey's woolen industry from 1895 offer evidence of this stratification. Forty-four percent of all workers made less than five dollars a week, while at the same time 3 percent made three to five times as much, that is, between fifteen and twenty dollars.[53] And by 1918 not much had changed. While a female twister tender, probably of Hungarian heritage, earned $12.23 per week, a male loom fixer, who was very likely a German immigrant, made nearly three times this amount, or $30.45 per week.[54]

National origin and sex determined which jobs were available to which workers. This, in turn, strengthened already existing cultural identifications and, at the same time, changed them, as nationality and gender were reconstructed with new meaning. To be German meant being a skilled, well paid, and privileged worker. To be a Polish worker implied being unskilled and poor. To be a woman worker meant either living at the margins of absolute poverty or depending on other sources of family income. Work, income, and, as we will see later, living patterns and culture, separated a "labor aristocracy" from the majority of Passaic's proletariat. This model of labor relations worked so well that the Dillingham Commission lauded the

48 *Reports of the Immigration Commission,* 320.
49 Goldberg, *Tale,* 50.
50 *Reports of the Immigration Commission,* 316.
51 The data refer to the woolen and worsted industry in the state of New Jersey. Bureau of Statistics of Labor and Industries in New Jersey, *21st Annual Report* (Trenton, N.J., 1899), 46.
52 Goldberg, "Immigrants," 157; David Gordon, Richard Edwards, and Michael Reich, *Segmented Work, Divided Workers: The Historical Transformation of Labor in the United States* (Cambridge, Mass., 1982), 138.
53 Bureau of Statistics of Labor and Industries in New Jersey, *19th Annual Report* (Trenton, N.J., 1897), 97.
54 Goldberg, "Immigrants," 157–58.

new immigrants in 1911 as "tractable."[55] And seven years later, in 1918, the management consulting firm of Ford, Bacon, and Davis commended Passaic as a manufacturing center. Despite "the presence of 28,000 workers with all the inherent racial and geographical antagonism employed . . . , no labor disturbance, of any consequence, has ever occurred."[56]

IV

The spatial patterns and social life of Passaic mirrored the ethnic and class divisions that structured the workplace. On the most obvious level, the social geography of the town was structured along class lines. On the west side, the wealthiest of the city's four wards provided pleasant surroundings for the mill officials, businessmen, lawyers, doctors, and other professionals.[57] The eastern parts of town were a different world – a largely immigrant-dominated working-class neighborhood, where factories and dwellings stood door to door. The dilapidated houses were crowded and the rooms small. Women wearing "broad shoes, full gathered skirts," and gray shawls made their purchases in the tiny stores which flanked the streets – from the Jewish tailor, the German butcher, or the Italian grocer.[58] Many of the men wore the little flat peaked cap, the hat which had become the international badge of male workers.[59]

The conspicuous class stratifications that structured the town, however, had ethnic fault lines. The strong correspondence of class position and national origin for immigrants from eastern and southern Europe situated them firmly in the poor neighborhoods. In 1910, 98.4 percent of all Hungarians, 98.7 percent of all Austrians, and 85.2 percent of all Italians lived in these areas. Moreover, while most working-class residents lived in close proximity to each other, individual street blocks were dominated by distinct groups. In some streets, virtually all people spoke Hungarian, in others they argued in Polish, and a block further down they communicated in Italian.[60]

55 *Reports of the Immigration Commission,* 335.
56 Report by Ford, Bacon, and Davis to the *Alien Property Custodian* concerning the Gera Mills (Nov. 11, 1918). NA, RG 131, entry 155, box 122.
57 Siegel, "Passaic Textile Strike," 86.
58 Data concerning the ownership of stores can be found in the manuscript census. Passaic, Passaic County, *Census of Populations,* 12th Census of the United States, 1900, Records of the Bureau of the Census, NA, RG 29. See also Eloise Shellabarger, "The Shawled Women of Passaic," *Survey* 44 (July 3, 1920): 463.
59 Eric Hobsbawm discusses this for Great Britain in *Workers* (New York, 1984), 186. For Passaic, see, e.g., the picture in Michael Ebner, "Strike and Society: Civil Behavior in Passaic, 1875–1926," *New Jersey History* 72 (1979): 19.
60 See Passaic, Passaic County, *Census of Populations,* 12th Census of the United States, 1900.

But these clusters did not necessarily evolve around modern national identities as, for example, northern and southern Italians settled in completely different sections of town.[61]

The relationship between class position, national origin, and the social geography of Passaic can be seen most clearly in the case of German immigrants. German mill managers, technicians, and some shopkeepers dwelled in the wealthier parts of town, far away from the 66 percent of Passaic Germans who lived in working-class areas. Though German workers lived closer to other immigrant workers than to the German management, they still clustered in distinct areas within the immigrant district. It was here that the Botany Worsted Mills had erected houses for some of its skilled factory workers. Segregated, but in close proximity, skilled German immigrants enjoyed living conditions very different from most other immigrants. They had an average of three times the living space of Polish immigrants. While a German family paid an average of $3.06 per person for rent, a Polish family spent only 90 cents. And Germans seldom had boarders in their homes, something which few other immigrants could afford to do without.[62]

Like the spatial patterns of life in Passaic, the social life of the city was organized along ethnic and class lines. Workers migrating to Passaic brought with them their individual and collective memories: their traditions, their religion, and often their political orientations. Life in Passaic reshaped those beliefs. Ethnic identity, far from being a primordial concept brought across the Atlantic, went through an extensive process of organization, culminating in the institutionalization of ethnicity as a complex system of cultural and political references.[63]

Religion was the focal point of this process. Immigrants established a wide variety of congregations that catered to narrowly defined groups.[64] Associated with these congregations were schools that taught immigrant children in their parents' language, dramatic societies that presented popular plays, and nationalist groups. As churches and synagogues became focal points of ethnic life, they also became places of prolonged struggles over the control of the ethnic community.[65] In 1912 a controversy in the Polish

---

61 *Reports of the Immigration Commission,* 333.

62 Ibid., 337, 340, 344.

63 Also see Katherine O'Sullivan and William J. Wilson, in Neil Smelser, ed., *The Handbook of Sociology* (Newbury Park, Calif., 1988), 237f.

64 Gaudentia, *The Polish People,* 77, and "Passaic, N.J. 1913, Achievement," *PDH,* 1913, n.p.

65 For a good study of this process in another New Jersey community (Bayonne), see John Bukowczyk, "The Transformation of Working-Class Ethnicity, Corporate Control, Americanization, and the Polish Immigrant Middle Class in Bayonne, New Jersey, 1915–1925," *Labor History* 25 (1984): 60ff.

community over who would head the parish mobilized thousands of people, disrupted church services, and even led to strikes. In this case, the ethnic lines were sharply drawn. A Polish priest with a German name and probably of German heritage was opposed by Polish churchgoers. In another case, a Slovak priest was berated by some of his parishioners for having adopted Hungarian culture and for failing to support Slovak nationalism.[66]

Aside from the congregations there was a whole range of other immigrant organizations whose number has been estimated at more than one hundred in 1922. Large numbers of saloons, often dominated by one ethnic group, served as places for informal as well as organized meetings. Ethnic halls became a locus for immigrant workers' activities, providing space for cultural events, political discussions and, later, the organization of strikes. There was the Polish Peoples' Home, the Russian National Home, and Maciag's, the meeting place of many Polish immigrants. Germans, in turn, had their gymnastic clubs, the "Turnvereine," the "German Young People's Society," the "German-American Central Verein of Passaic and Vicinity," and "Concordia." Slovaks joined together in four benevolent societies before 1895. The Polish people of Passaic had by 1910 founded twenty-eight organizations, ranging from the Polish National Union to the Polish Workmen's Alliance of America and the Society of St. Stanislaus.[67] While most organizations of Polish and Slovak immigrants were closely associated with churches, many Hungarians joined groups distant from or even hostile to religion.

Since most immigrants were workers, most ethnic organizations were also working-class institutions, the activities of which were largely focused on mutual aid. The organizational principle was common ethnicity, yet since ethnicity and class position strongly intersected they provided the embryo for class politics as they equipped workers with skills and resources useful for working-class collective action. While ethnic organization did not make cross-ethnic collective action impossible, it rendered it more difficult as ethnicity became culturally institutionalized.

The growing organization of ethnic identities initiated prolonged struggles over their content, fought along the class stratifications of the different immigrant communities. Congregations and organizations, though dominated by workers, encompassed all strata of immigrant groups, including the better-off middle class. This group of shop owners and proprietors,

---

66 Goldberg, "Immigrants," 144–45.
67 On the saloons, see *PDN*, July 9, 1895, and *PDN*, July 5, 1899. Goldberg, "Immigrants," 143–45. *PDN*, Jan. 8, 9, 10, 1917. For information on these clubs and organization, see Scott, *History*, 421–23, and Gaudentia, *The Polish People*, 81. *PDN*, July 19, 1895. Gaudentia, *The Polish People*, 80f.

while small in numbers, frequently struggled over the control of "their" community and in this process transformed the meaning of ethnicity into a coherent ideology, often focused on nationalism. The Polish community of Passaic, for example, staged vigorous anti-Bolshevik demonstrations during the 1920 Russian-Polish War. Although the protests were motivated by the opposition to Russian territorial claims, they gave the Polish middle class an opportunity to define Polish ethnicity as strongly anticommunist.[68] In addition, a "buy Polish" campaign, initiated by the Polish immigrant elite in the first half of 1919, resulted in the strengthening of anti-Semitism as another element of ethnicity-as-ideology. The Polish Merchants and Tradesmen's Association set up a boycott of shops owned by Jews and organized anti-Jewish demonstrations.[69] Both elements, anticommunism and anti-Semitism, later resulted in the opposition of many Polish workers to the Jewish, socialist leadership of the textile union.

The relationship between ethnic elites and the working class was, however, not one-sided. The immigrant middle classes had numerous economic contacts with the working class, as their stores, saloons, and insurance agencies were dependent on the support of their compatriots. Consequently, they were vulnerable to pressure by workers. During strikes they frequently provided workers with political and material support. This, in turn, gave them a voice in solving conflicts. Immigrant shopkeepers, for example, tended to be in the forefront of demands for compromise solutions and opposed outside involvement in local labor struggles.

The German immigrant community experienced these struggles from a different vantage point. From the moment they settled in Passaic, the German millowners and managers controlled life in the German community. They exerted great efforts to foster the loyalty of German workers to the companies. In 1891, a year after the first mill opened, St. John's German Lutheran Church was established by employees of the Botany Worsted Mills. The church "was dependent for its existence upon subscriptions from the mills."[70] The congregation created a choir, a Sunday school, German-language instruction for children, and a women's club.[71] Mill managers believed these institutions would stabilize the work force and strengthen ethnic bonds outside the workplace. In 1918 one of the directors of the

---

68 Yet, orientation toward Europe could also result in different political assessments as Hungarian immigrants were staunch defenders of the socialist revolution in their home country.

69 For a more elaborate treatment, see Goldberg, "Immigrants," 510–17.

70 *Minutes of the Meeting of the Board of Directors, Botany Worsted Mills* (June 28, 1918), NA, RG 131, entry 155, box 47.

71 Maas, *Deutsche Evangelisch-Lutherische St. Johannes Gemeinde.*

Botany Worsted Mills defended financial support for the church "for the purpose of keeping up the morale of the mill."[72] Most important among the institutions of the German immigrant community was the German school that instructed the children of woolen mills employees. It was financed by the companies and was a point of constant attention in the board meetings. In 1895 a special meeting of the board of directors of the Botany Worsted Mills reported that "the German School maintained for the benefit of children of employees of the company required funds."[73] It was decided to donate $750, a payment that would become a yearly feature, slowly being increased to $4,000 by 1909. These donations were even more significant given that they were one of the very few charity donations the company made.

The influence of the millowners over German immigrant culture led to the formation of a German community in Passaic that was nationalist in tone and that favored nonpolitical activities. The gymnastic association or Turnverein, founded in 1892, supported financially by the mills, and led by a foreman, constructed an imaginary past by organizing events like a *Bauernball* – a peasants' dance. The Concordia Society put on a masked ball that was characterized by the *Passaic Daily News* as "real German." And the Botany Singing Society presented its repertoire at a 1912 meeting of the German-American Alliance.[74] It appears that during World War I some of these organizations articulated pro-German attitudes.[75] In contrast, the small Passaic Socialist Party counted few employees of the worsted mills – hence few Germans – among its members.[76]

The privileges of German workers in Passaic were not limited to the funding of their religious, educational, and cultural organizations. The mills were careful to provide their skilled work force with favors unknown to other workers. Already in December 1889, only six months after the company had started construction of the mill, the board of directors noted that "six houses for employees had been built."[77] In 1891, the *Passaic Daily News*

72 *Minutes of the Meeting of the Board of Directors, Botany Worsted Mills* (June 28, 1918), NA, RG 131, entry 155, box 47.
73 *Minutes of the Board of Directors Special Meeting of the Botany Worsted Mills* (Oct. 8, 1895), Minutes of Stockholders' and Directors' Meetings, vol. 1, May 13, 1889–Aug. 16, 1904, 171, Botany Worsted Mills, Inc. Records, MC 51. Special Collections and Archives, Rutgers University Libraries.
74 The Botany Worsted Mills supported, e.g., the statewide meeting of the German-American Alliance in Passaic. *PDN,* April 15, 1912; March 1 and 4, 1912; Jan. 8, 1917; April 15, 1917.
75 See the numerous anonymous letters to the Bureau of Investigation, denouncing the German immigrant community of Passaic. For example, NA, RG 65, File No. 34689.
76 Goldberg, "Immigrants," 168.
77 See *Minutes of the Meeting of the Board of Directors, Botany Worsted Mills* (Dec. 31, 1889), Minutes of Stockholders' and Directors' Meetings, vol. 1, May 13, 1889–Aug. 16, 1904, 107.

disclosed that "forty handsome brick houses contiguous to the mills for occupancy by some of the employees" had been finished.[78] Five years later the "treasurer reported that the company had agreed to sell certain lots of its property . . . to some of its employees for the purpose of homesteads thereon."[79] The lots were sold to six German workers. Two of them, Walter Haessner and Franz Werner, worked as foremen.[80] Similarly, the first pensions the company ever paid out went to three of its German employees.[81]

The peculiar process of class formation divided Passaic's workers along lines of skill and national origin. This fragmentation was not an outcome of existing cultural differences; it expressed the unequal positions of workers within the labor market. Migration networks, hiring practices, and the domination of German ethnic life created a strong bond between German mill managers and German skilled workers. This alliance, combined with a uniquely flexible labor market for unskilled workers, made the success of workers' collective action extremely unlikely.[82]

V

Throughout their history, Passaic's textile manufacturers were aware of the potential of workers to challenge management's control. Until a prolonged strike in 1926 they prided themselves on their ability to sustain "labor peace." They were conscious of the basic foundation of their success – the structure of their work force as well as of the labor market. Nevertheless, after the turn of the century and especially with the cessation of immigration during World War I, the millowners utilized not only an elaborate spy system, the "Wool Council," but also welfare plans in order to contain labor unrest.

Passaic's working class was far from docile. Wages and working conditions provoked repeated protests. Earnings in the woolen and worsted industry were extremely low. Average wages rose only slightly in the period

---

78 *PDN*, Jan. 17, 1891.
79 *Minutes of the Semi-Annual Meeting of the Board of Directors of the Botany Worsted Mills* (Feb. 17, 1896), Minutes of Stockholders' and Directors' Meetings, 174.
80 Only two names could be identified in a Passaic City Directory. See *Richmond's Twelfth Annual Directory of Passaic, Clifton, Garfield and Wallington* (Passaic, N.J., 1918). That the houses were built for skilled workers is also stressed in "History of the Botany Worsted Mills," NA, RG 131, entry 155, box 44.
81 *Minutes of the Meeting of the Board of Directors, Botany Worsted Mills* (Dec. 19, 1911), Minutes of Stockholders' and Directors' Meetings, 297.
82 See also Gordon et al., *Segmented Work*, 161f.

from 1896 to 1912, from \$280 to \$406 a year.[83] They were well below the
state's average income for workers, 35 percent below in 1900. Of forty-
two New Jersey industries reporting in 1897, only nine paid less than the
woolen and worsted industry.[84] The cost-of-living increase virtually paralleled wage increases so that the absolute standard of living of these workers
remained stagnant.[85] Moreover, employment for unskilled workers was unstable and fluctuated sharply with the economic cycles of the textile economy.

Apart from a small minority of skilled workers, working conditions were
– even in the eyes of contemporaries – terrifying. Most work was related
to feeding and tending machines. It was repetitive and extremely fatiguing.
In the huge halls, cramped with machinery, noise and heat was often unbearable. Ventilation was poor and occupational diseases plagued the workers.[86] "Because of the massing of machinery," wrote the editors of the
Journal of Industrial Hygiene in 1919, "the noise was deafening. . . . No seats
were provided. The workers looked beaten and crushed under the combined strain of noise, heat, and constant standing."[87] The effect of these
conditions on the health of workers was grave; accidents were frequent.
Because night work for women was legal in New Jersey until 1924, the
mills employed them especially for night shifts. Due to the harsh working
conditions women faced during pregnancy, and the poverty of many families, Passaic held claim to the highest infant mortality rate in the United
States between 1906 and 1917.[88]

Although faced with numerous obstacles in their struggles for higher
wages and better working conditions, the workers early on challenged the
overwhelming power of the millowners. Yet, aside from some craft and
short-lived textile workers' unions, there was no industrial labor organization in Passaic in the thirty-six year period after the emergence of a
large-scale proletariat. The specific process of class formation in Passaic had
created two strongly interlinked challenges for any organizing efforts: inequality and ethnicity. How could inequality in the textile work force be

83 *Annual Reports of the Bureau of Statistics of Labor and Industry of New Jersey,* vols. 19ff., (Trenton, N.J.,
   1896ff.). These numbers refer to the woolen and worsted industry in the state of New Jersey. Since
   Passaic was by far the most important location in New Jersey for this industry, one can assume that
   the statewide data have significance.
84 Ibid., vol. 21 (Trenton, N.J., 1899), 32.
85 Ibid., vol. 21ff.
86 Testimony of W. Jett Lauck before the Senate Committee on Education and Labor, *Senate Committee
   on Education and Labor,* 23.
87 "Wage Earning Women in War Time," *Journal of Industrial Hygiene* (Oct. 1919).
88 *New York Sunday Call Magazine,* June 25, 1916. Children suffered from malnutrition. *PDN,* May
   5, 1920.

translated into collective action and how could different ethnic identities be transformed into class unity? Since the state's policy, migration networks, and the transformation of the meaning of ethnicity were central processes in the making of Passaic's working class, changes in these patterns resulted in changing patterns of workers' collective action.

When the first worsted mill opened its gates in 1889, Passaic scarcely had a tradition of labor organization. Short-lived benevolent societies existed in 1873 as well as in 1885.[89] Beginning in 1875 and peaking in 1886, some strikes involving textile workers had been recorded.[90] Yet, in 1889, the year the Botany Worsted Mills located in Passaic, the city knew only one union, the Brotherhood of Carpenters, a small local of skilled workers that did cater to the needs of new immigrants. Even though the city's proletariat expanded rapidly after 1889, no lasting labor organization emerged during the next thirty years, and only a few very short strikes occurred.[91]

The first labor conflict at the Botany Worsted Mills, which by then had 1,900 workers on its payroll and was the largest employer in town, took place in 1899. When a group of workers demanded a 25 percent wage increase,[92] 60 workers, mainly from the dye house, walked out, "complaining that they were underpaid."[93] The following day, 150 additional workers followed the strike call. All of the strikers were of Hungarian heritage, a group of workers with a strong affinity to radical organizations.[94] After a three-day walkout they returned to work, defeated. Mill executives refused to meet with their representatives and conceded no wage increase.[95]

The defeat of this strike illuminates the dynamics of workers' mobilization in the mills. Only a small minority of the work force had walked out, all of them from one national background. Workers who, according to the *Passaic Daily News,* "get good wages" refused to join the movement, as they earned already about $1.65 a day compared with the $1.20 a day the strikers made. No cross-ethnic alliances developed and the higher paid and better skilled workers who were central for the maintenance of the production process, stayed on the job and "urged the workmen to return."[96] By importing strikebreakers to replace unskilled workers, the mills were able to

89 Ebner, "Passaic," 128, 132.
90 Ibid., 129.
91 Ibid., 136.
92 For information on the strike, see *PDN,* July 13, 14, 15, 1899.
93 *PDN,* July 13, 1899.
94 Bureau of Industrial Statistics, *Labor and Industries of New Jersey: 22d Annual Report* [1899] (Trenton, N.J., 1899), 203.
95 Goldberg, "Immigrants," 162.
96 *PDN,* July 13, 1899.

break the strike. The flexible labor market accommodated such a policy and the Botany management proclaimed that "the strike did not bother them" because "it will be an easy matter to fill [the strikers'] places."[97]

Workers' weakness in these early conflicts reassured Passaic's elite that "a union here will never succeed among that class of people for the reason that they are not of the same religion or country and are therefore antagonistic to each other."[98] In 1902 and 1906 two ill-fated strikes underlined this assessment as both walkouts involved only a small percentage of the total work force. Indeed, until twenty-three years or one generation after the worsted mills had opened their gates, no major labor conflict had occurred. In this period the total workdays lost due to strikes amounted to as little as 2,258.

In 1912, however, it seemed as if Passaic's textile workers would be able for the first time to challenge the power of their employers. In late winter the Industrial Workers of the World began organizing Passaic's immigrant proletariat.[99] Under the leadership of the "Detroit" Industrial Workers of the World (IWW) – a faction opposing William D. Haywood's organization – 500 Forstmann & Huffmann weavers walked out on March 14. In the following two weeks nearly 4,000 others joined in, amounting to 40 percent of the total textile labor force.[100] Although the strike was the largest so far in Passaic's history, it never closed down any of the mills, as usually only workers of single departments struck.[101] Strike participation varied, in some mills 75 percent of all employees walked out, in others only 8 percent. All of them were unskilled.[102] In the Botany Mills, 800 out of 4,500 workers struck, many of them women. Most strikers were Polish, Slovak, Italian, Hungarian, and Russian women and men, whereas the skilled workers, who again stayed in, were of German and English heritage.[103] The workers demanded an end to fines for imperfect work, the abolition of the four-loom system, pay for periods in which looms were idle through no fault of their own, abolition of bonuses and fines, a 50 percent increase in the price per yard for weavers, double pay for overtime, and recognition of the IWW.

Yet, what began so promisingly ended in almost complete failure. A split

97 *PDN,* July 14, 1899.
98 *PDN,* March 11, 1902.
99 *PDN,* March 14, 1912.
100 Philip Newman, "The First I.W.W. Invasion of New Jersey," *Proceedings of the New Jersey Historical Society* 58 (1940): 268–83.
101 Michael Ebner, "The Passaic Strike of 1912 and the Two I.W.W.'s," *Labor History* 11 (1970): 456.
102 Bureau of Industrial Statistics, *Labor and Industries of New Jersey: Thirty-fifth Annual Report* [1912] (Camden, N.J., 1913): 238.
103 Ibid., 235. Skilled workers of English heritage worked in the other branches of the textile industry.

in the union leadership, ethnic conflicts, and the resistance by employers made the strikers' demands impossible to achieve. At first it seemed as if the movement could overcome tensions between ethnic groups. Workers were organized along company lines rather then by nationalities, and rallies were frequently addressed in Polish, Hungarian, Russian, and Italian. But a power struggle between the leader of the local IWW and the leader of the Italian workers resulted in the withdrawal of the Italians from the strike front.[104] They "paid little attention to our needs," declared the Italian workers. They joined William D. Haywood's "Chicago" IWW, which had come to Passaic on March 27.[105] While more and more workers, especially the more radical Italian and Hungarian immigrants, protested Daniel DeLeon's "Detroit" IWW leadership and advocated militant actions comparable with those which led to success in the Lawrence Bread-and-Roses Strike, the two factions of the IWW began openly attacking each other. Political conflicts intermingled with ethnic identifications. The strike front crumbled; the weavers of Forstmann & Huffmann returned to work on April 9 under an independent settlement leaving only two companies on strike.[106] With no financial means to carry on, the remaining strikers were forced to capitulate.[107] The Botany Mills's optimism – "we have never dealt with a union and never will" – remained intact.[108] The consequences of the "very costly failure" for the organizers were grave.[109] The Botany Mills fired ninety-seven workers who participated in the movement, the Gera Mills fired all who did not return to work immediately, and Forstmann & Huffmann laid off the strike committee.[110]

VI

The outbreak of World War I and the corresponding war boom was a turning point in Passaic's labor history. Labor markets contracted and workers enjoyed more power in challenging the millowners than ever before. In the spring of 1916 a nationwide wave of strikes affected the city. The weavers at the Forstmann & Huffmann mills were the first to act. Seven hundred of them walked out demanding a 25 percent pay increase, pay for idle looms, greater respect from loom fixers, and a weekly minimum wage

104 Ebner, "Passaic," 155. See also Ebner, "Passaic Strike," 458f.
105 William D. Haywood addressed a rally himself the following week.
106 Ebner, "Passaic," 156.
107 Newman, "Invasion," 283.
108 *PDH*, March 25, 1912.
109 Bureau of Industrial Statistics, *Labor and Industries of New Jersey: Thirty-fifth Annual Report*, 238.
110 Goldberg, "Immigrants," 166.

of fourteen dollars instead of the piecework system. Colleagues, especially weavers from the Gera Mills, the Passaic Worsted Mills, the New Jersey Worsted, and the Garfield Worsted, followed. Because the management granted the strikers' demands, Botany's workers stayed in. A union was immediately formed, numbering 4,000 members and relying on local leadership.

For the first time ever, Passaic's workers were able to celebrate significant gains when the mills offered pay increases between 5 and 10 percent. The general economic climate as well as the cessation of immigration accounted for this success.[111] Moreover, attitudes of immigrant workers had changed as they realized that they would not return to their home countries and second-generation workers had begun to join the textile work force. These workers oriented their future toward the improvement of their lot as workers, seeing their status as proletarians as permanent.[112]

Though the newly founded union quickly disintegrated, the strike demonstrated to the wool industrialists that their time of unchallenged power had come to an end. Traditional means of regulating class relations – discharging workers and building upon divisions among them – had begun to lose some of their power. Workers were able to force employers into a defensive position.[113] Passaic's woolen and worsted manufacturers decided to prepare for future challenges and organized the "Industrial Council of Passaic Wool Manufacturers," which had the task of developing and standardizing wages.[114] A tight labor market was an issue of great concern for the directors of the mills and frequently it was reported in board meetings "that labor was still scarce and restless."[115] The focal point of the Wool Council became the Central Bureau of Employment, which opened its gates in early 1917. Organized by a New York City labor agency that "normally specialized in breaking strikes," it screened workers' job applications and kept files on all employees of the woolen mills in Passaic.[116]

In the last days of 1917 a short and very limited strike occurred, dem-

---

111 Department of Labor, *Thirty-Ninth Annual Report of the Bureau of Industrial Statistics of New Jersey for the Year Ending Oct. 31st 1916* (Trenton, N.J., 1917), 237; Goldberg, "Immigrants," 169, 176.

112 The importance of this phenomenon is discussed at length in Hartmut Zwahr, *Die Konstituierung des Proletariats als Klasse* (Munich, 1981), 9ff.

113 U.S. Department of the Interior, Bureau of Education, "The Problem of Adult Education in Passaic, N.J.," *Bulletin* 4 (1920): 4–26.

114 Goldberg, "Immigrants," 179. Members were the Botany Worsted Mills, the Forstmann & Huffmann Mills, the Gera Mill, the New Jersey Worsted, and Passaic Worsted.

115 *Minutes of the Meeting of the Board of Directors, Botany Worsted Mills* (July 10, 1917), in *Alien Property Custodian*, NA, RG 131, entry 155, box 48. See also the Minutes for the meetings on June 18, 1917, and Aug. 21, 1917.

116 Goldberg, "Immigrants," 180.

onstrating once again the basic dynamics of collective action in the mills and the problems that would have to be overcome. A group of boiler house stokers went on strike. The walkout created "no problem for production" as the strikers were immediately replaced by strikebreakers. "[T]his movement did not materially affect the firemen in the various plants," argued one mill manager confidently; "owing to the fact that it did not represent the actual firemen but only their helpers, the various manufacturers in general paid no attention whatever."[117] The participants in this organizing effort included twenty-three Hungarians, twenty-one Poles, four Slavs, three Italians, and only two Germans.[118] Without solidarity from skilled workers, the power of the boiler house stokers was limited.

The war not only brought changes to workers but to the companies as well. The federal government and its Bureau of Investigation kept a close watch on the German-owned corporations. In 1918 the Alien Property Custodian took control of the Botany Worsted Mills, the Gera Mills, the Passaic Worsted Mills, and the Garfield Worsted Mills, though leaving untouched the directors and managers, who had acquired U.S. citizenship.[119] For workers, the identification of their employers as "national enemies" gave them an important tool in mobilizing against the "Kaiser-like" attitudes of the owners.[120]

The immediate postwar years demonstrated that the situation for Passaic's workers had irreversibly changed. Unions nationwide fought to mitigate the effects of a deep economic depression by demanding the eight-hour day. Those sentiments reached Passaic in January 1919. The Gera Mills reported in mid-January that "there is some agitation for an eight hour day."[121] When the American Woolen Company, the most important competitor of Passaic's wool industry, announced the forty-eight-hour week, "it was deemed wise" by the Botany directors and all the other mills "to adopt the same measure."[122] They insisted, however, that workers would still work fifty-five hours a week, their only improvement being time and a half for overtime.[123] Their demands unfulfilled, on February 3 the weavers

117 NA, RG 65, File No. 34689, Anonymous letter to H. Drukker (Dec. 4, 1917). See also *Minutes of the Regular Monthly Meeting of the Board of Directors of the Botany Worsted Mills* (Dec. 21, 1917), NA, RG 131, entry 155, box 47.
118 NA, RG 65, File No. 34689.
119 NA, RG 131, entry 155, box 47, statement of Edward Hiler.
120 Ebner, "Strike and Society," 19.
121 *Weekly Letters to the Directors of the Gera Worsted Mills* (Jan. 11, 1919), NA, RG 131, entry 155, box 124.
122 *Minutes of the Meeting of the Board of Directors, Botany Worsted Mills* (Jan. 30, 1919), NA, RG 131, entry 155, box 48.
123 Goldberg, "Immigrants," 183.

in the Gera Mills "suddenly threw off the power on their looms and announced they had worked eight hours."[124] By the end of the following
week, more than 15,000 workers had walked out, which amounted to the
first general strike in the worsted industry of Passaic. The workers con-
tended that the mills had made their profits on both sides of the Atlantic
and now the employees on the German end worked shorter hours than the
workers in Passaic.[125]

The reaction of the larger Passaic community, the municipal government, and the ethnic middle classes was important for the outcome of the
strike. While the city government adopted a policy of repression against
outside organizers, it remained impartial toward the local workers' organizations. An important source of strength for the striking workers was the
support of the larger immigrant community. Relief money was provided
by the city's immigrant middle classes, immigrant churches gave moral as
well as material support, and ethnic organizations provided strikers with
meeting halls.[126] For shop and saloon owners support was economically wise
as strikers threatened to boycott uncooperative stores. Later, the support of
the ethnic middle class found its limits in the exclusion of outside radical
organizations.

Divisions in the work force were no longer as deep; and for the first time
the predominantly German loom fixers, foremen, and clerks either joined
the union or formed their own, albeit weeks after the 1919 strike began.[127]
The closing of the ranks between the 250 to 300 skilled and highly paid
loom fixers and the unskilled workers evolved out of a rather peculiar process. One of the strikers' demands was to be treated "like human being[s]"
by the loom fixers who reportedly "have handled them roughly and on
many occasions used profane language and regarded themselves above us
in everything and we were nothing to them." In all previous strikes the
loom fixers "remained at work, fixed up machines where necessary and
received their pay as usual."[128] Yet during the 1919 strike they had been
laid off by the millowners, a change from their employers' previous policy
of strengthening the loyalties of their skilled work force.

A somewhat interesting situation presented itself at the meeting of the union in
Glita's Hall yesterday when a representative of the loom fixers appeared and an-

---

124 *PDN,* Feb. 4, 1919, and *PDH,* Feb. 4, 1919.
125 Goldberg, "Immigrants," 186, 196.
126 Ibid., 200, 207, 208.
127 *PDN,* Feb. 17 and 27, 1919.
128 *PDN,* Feb. 10, 1919.

nounced that all members of that branch of the industry had been laid off and they wanted to know if they could join the new union.

"At last," said one of the officers of the union, "they realize that they are workingmen too. Well, as such, they are eligible to join the union but they have to come to us now. We won't go after them."

The workers decided to accept into the union all workers of the worsted and woolen mills.[129]

Why did the mill owners sacrifice the alliance with their skilled workers? There is no direct evidence for what motivated the lockout, but it appears that the economic downturn may well have convinced employers that shutting down the mills for some weeks was not all that damaging, considering the savings in wage costs. Moreover, the intense rupture that the war represented for the German worsted mills and for German American immigrant culture in Passaic, along with the growing acculturation of German immigrants of the first and especially the second generation, made the cross-class alliance of the type that had existed for the past thirty years more and more anachronistic. Particularly the mills that the federal government now controlled became suspicious of alliances with a group of workers that had been stigmatized as national enemies. The one mill that the government did not control, Forstmann & Huffmann, however, still continued a special relationship to at least a small group of German workers. When in 1925 they nominated fifty-three representatives for the "employees assembly," a company union, they chose thirty-nine Germans, most of them highly skilled workers.[130]

There is little evidence of ethnic conflict during the strike in general, and the workers, many of whom had rushed to obtain citizenship during the war, coped with the diversity of their ranks by addressing strike meetings in Polish, Hungarian, Slovak, Italian, and German. Reflecting the radical changes taking place in Europe, conflicts between different immigrant groups did indeed spill over into Passaic. But for now they did not threaten the unity of the strikers. For the first time in the city's history, the mills actually had to shut down with 80 percent of all workers joining the walkout. After seven weeks, the union and the employers under federal mediation agreed to the forty-eight-hour week and a wage increase corresponding to a pending settlement in Lawrence. And although the companies refused to recognize the union, they accepted shop committees. On March 25 workers returned to the mills. Only hours later, however, the

---

129 Ibid.
130 This conclusion has been drawn from their names. *F & H News* 6 (Nov. 12, 1925): 1, Robert W. Dunn Papers, Library of the University of Oregon, Eugene.

Garfield Worsted Mills fired sixteen workers because of their involvement in the strike. Nine hundred workers struck immediately in solidarity. On the following day, all mill employees joined the protest.[131]

Given its knowledge of the extreme difficulties involved in organizing a second strike, this second walkout may have been deliberately provoked by the Wool Council.[132] In the following days the factors that previously had given the union strength turned against the workers. Now, the intense localism of the newly founded union, the reliance on the city's cooperation, and the anti-Bolshevism of some union leaders weakened the strikers' cause.[133] The federal government and city officials condemned the strike and blamed "Bolshevik agitators" for new developments. Moreover, the ethnic middle class and the churches now refused to give the strikers any support. With local solidarity undercut and no access to any other networks, the union faced a highly organized opponent without adequate resources of its own.

The strike front held for barely one week. It collapsed slowly as workers and even some strike leaders returned to work, attracted by the mills' offer to introduce the forty-eight-hour week with fifty-five hours pay, a wage increase of 15 percent.[134] However, no shop committees were to be recognized. By April 10 the industry was producing at normal levels.

The 1919 strike once more alerted the millowners to the increasing instability of their labor relations. Although the Wool Council had succeeded in breaking the walkout, employers turned to new strategies. During the war the mills had done little in terms of "Americanization" programs, which had been so popular in many American industries. The German origin of the factories did not encourage such moves, as they had their own fears of being confronted with demands for the Americanization of management and labor policy. However, owners of the Botany Mills had introduced paternalistic "welfare work" in 1917, with pensions paid to some disabled or retired workers.[135] The concept expanded after the 1919 strike, when the Botany founded a committee "to consider the question of the relations of the company to its employees."[136] By May the stockholders had approved

---

131 See Goldberg, "Immigrants," 218, 219.
132 Ibid., 220.
133 *PDH,* March 8, 1919.
134 *Minutes of the Meeting of the Board of Directors, Botany Worsted Mills* (April 11, 1919), NA, RG 131, entry 155, box 49.
135 NA, RG 131, entry 155, box 47.
136 *Minutes of the Meeting of the Board of Directors, Botany Worsted Mills* (April 25, 1919), NA, RG 131, entry 155, box 49.

a life insurance scheme and the following summer the erection of a lunch room was decided upon.[137] The Forstmann & Huffmann Mills endorsed similar schemes, even creating a company union.[138] These programs, however, made only little use of Americanization language and even the organizer in charge was hired directly from Germany.[139] The combination of welfare work, the antiunion stand of the local government, the Wool Council, and the spy network did succeed in making it difficult for labor organizations to operate in Passaic.

In the last moments of the 1919 strike the leadership of the local union had intensified contacts with the Amalgamated Clothing Workers. In May, these contacts resulted in the formation of the Amalgamated Textile Workers Union (ATWA) in which the Passaic local played a major role. Soon the ATWA counted five thousand dues-paying members in Passaic. For the first time a union had gained a foothold in the city, though it was not recognized by any company. This level of organization was only short-lived, as the union was unable to overcome ethnic divisions. It received its most active support again from Hungarian workers, who were less focused on the church, thus less sensitive to antiunion sentiments of the clergy. Polish workers, in contrast, remained distant from the organization because the anti-Semitic campaign of the spring of 1919 also targeted the Jewish leadership of the ATWA. Polish halls were closed to union meetings and the Polish church spoke out against the organization, fearing for its hegemony in the Polish community. In addition, the anti-Soviet demonstrations that moved through Passaic in 1920 accused organized labor of Bolshevism and undermined the strength of the ATWA. As the Polish middle class increasingly dominated their ethnic community and its working-class conationals, their reformulation of ethnic ideology ultimately targeted workers' autonomous struggles. By 1924 these conflicts, combined with repressive measures by the city and hostile employers, resulted in a situation in which the union could only "recruit secretly."[140]

The postwar experience of Passaic's workers corresponded to that of the majority of American workers. The strike wave of 1919, the following loss

---

137 *Annual Meeting of the Stockholders of the Botany Worsted Mills* (May 28, 1919), NA, RG 131, entry 155, box 49; *Special Meeting of the Board of Directors of the Botany Worsted Mills* (Aug. 6, 1920), NA, RG 131, entry 155, box 49.

138 *F & H News* 6 (Nov. 12, 1925): 1, Robert W. Dunn Papers, Library of the University of Oregon, Eugene. See also *Minutes of the Meeting of the Board of Directors, Botany Worsted Mills* (April 25, 1919), NA, RG 131, entry 155, box 49.

139 *F & H News* 6 (Nov. 12, 1925).

140 This account follows Goldberg, "Immigrants," 231–34, 501, 512–15, 534.

of union strength, the employers offensive in defense of "workers' rights," and the new designs of corporate management left deep imprints.[141] Yet, while the decade brought "labor peace" nearly everywhere until the early 1930s, Passaic was to witness the largest labor conflict in its history in 1926. Here workers finally overcame the obstacles that had frustrated their struggles for so long.

In the 1920s decreased demand and idle production capacities in the mills resulted in a declining profitability of investments in textiles. The Botany Mills sought the solution to its problems in announcing a 10 percent wage cut in September 1925. All other Passaic mills, except the Forstmann & Huffmann Company, followed suit.[142] Soon afterward, a young communist, Albert Weisbord, came to Passaic and began organizing workers into the United Front Committee.

On January 25, 1926, a committee of workers demanded that the management of the Botany Worsted Mills rescind the wage cut. The mill refused and immediately discharged all forty members of the committee. Before the workers left the factory they called upon their colleagues to join the strike.[143] On this and the following days four thousand workers of the Botany Worsted Mills walked off their jobs and were joined by employees of other mills. The strike spread fast and in March sixteen thousand workers were out. They organized huge picket lines, blocked the entrances to the factories, and effectively closed out all strikebreakers.[144] They demanded a 10 percent wage increase, time-and-a-half for overtime, decent sanitary working conditions, no discrimination against union workers, and, most important, recognition of the union.[145]

Passaic's workers stood together as never before. Divisions along ethnic, skill, and gender lines had diminished. Women actively participated in the leadership of the strike and set up institutions that specifically addressed the needs of female strikers. And although some immigrant groups, particularly Hungarians, were still decidedly more radical than others, there is no evidence of ethnic conflicts. Since the decrease of immigration during World War I, few new Europeans had arrived in Passaic. Most immigrants, and especially their children, now planned for their future in the United States. They spoke English and the second generation provided the missing links

---

141 David Montgomery, *The Fall of the House of Labor* (Cambridge, Mass., 1987), 464.
142 Siegel, "Passaic Textile Strike," 136.
143 "The Passaic Strike," *Christian Century* 43 (Aug. 5, 1926): 972.
144 Ibid., 976.
145 Albert Weisbord, *Passaic: The Story of a Struggle against Starvation Wages and for the Right to Organize* (1926; reprint: San Francisco, 1976), 28.

of communication. This unity was enforced by the union, which promoted active strike participation of all workers and their families, and addressed the special needs of ethnic groups through the distribution of foreign-language newspapers and through the use of foreign-language speakers at rallies. Observers agreed that the strike was the largest "Americanization" campaign ever conducted in Passaic.[146] Moreover, the small immigrant middle class, many priests, and most immigrant organizations supported the strikers.[147] Even the German Catholic clergy of Passaic led demonstrations of striking workers. The common goal to improve living conditions in Passaic outweighed tensions between different immigrant groups. "The terrific obstacles which immigration put in the way of organizing are much less than before," commented the strike leadership on the new situation.[148] If national origins played any role in the strike, it was only by the workers denouncing the foreign ownership of Passaic's woolen mills. Albert Weisbord fought allegations of being a Soviet agent by "counter[ing] . . . with the German question."[149]

Not only did ethnic divisions diminish, but the overwhelming correspondence between skill and national origin also gradually lessened. Although most skilled workers were probably still of German heritage, it appears that some other groups, particularly northern Italians, had gained access to these positions. At the same time many children of German immigrants found only unskilled positions open to them in the mills. The bonds between German capital and German workers had further loosened as skilled workers were hit by wage cuts and layoffs. Combined with the further undermining of their craft privileges by the introduction of new machinery, the skilled workers had numerous reasons to join the struggles of their less skilled colleagues and to unite in one local union.[150]

While the mobilization of Passaic's workers was unprecedented, the policy of the mills and the Wool Council did not change since the last labor dispute. Categorically refusing to meet the strikers, they argued that the "present labor controversy . . . [is] a skillfully fomented Communist revolt."[151] They threatened to move south and hired African American

146 Ibid., 43.
147 "Passaic Strike," *Christian Century*, 977.
148 Weisbord, *Passaic: The Story of a Struggle*, 3.
149 Albert Weisbord, *Passaic Reviewed* (San Francisco, 1976), 31.
150 Weisbord, *Passaic: The Story of a Struggle*, 4; Martha Stone Asher, "Recollections of the Passaic Textile Strike of 1926," *Labor's Heritage* 2 (1990): 19.
151 For the reduction in the number of skilled workers, see U.S. Dept. of Labor, Bureau of Labor Statistics, *Monthly Labor Review*, vol. 46: *Mechanical Changes in the Woolen and Worsted Industries, 1910 to 1936*, 60. See also NA, RG 60, U.S. Dept. of Justice, Bureau of Investigation, File No. 16–167, Passaic textile strike; and Weisbord, *Passaic: The Story of a Struggle*, 53.

strikebreakers from the South in a dramatic yet unsuccessful effort to create racial conflicts.[152]

The local government, which had come under the direct influence of the worsted companies in 1919, supported these efforts. The local police broke up picket lines, clubbed "men, women and children . . . into insensitivity,"[153] closed meeting halls, and arrested hundreds of strikers. Courts supported the effort by issuing injunctions that were among the "most sweeping . . . in American labor history."[154]

Despite the determined resistance by the millowners, the walkout lasted more than one year and resulted in significant gains for Passaic's workers. After Albert Weisbord and, with him, the Communist Party had left the scene in early August, as a result of enormous outside pressure the American Federation of Labor (AFL)-affiliated United Textile Workers gave up its opposition to the strike and took over the leadership.[155] Yet, despite widely held expectations that the mills would agree to negotiate with the United Textile Workers, they still refused. Only one of the mills, the Passaic Worsted Company, agreed to a mediation effort. The subsequent settlement included recognition of the union, the right to collective bargaining, and no discrimination in the reinstatement of strikers.[156] This first agreement finally broke the resistance of the largest company, the Botany Worsted Mills. On December 13, 1926, a contract was signed that included restoration of wages to levels prior to the 10 percent wage reduction, the right to collective bargaining, the recognition of the union, and the reinstatement of the striking workers.[157] Only one company, Forstmann & Huffmann, refused to negotiate at all. Their striking workers admitted defeat on February 14, 1927. Gera Worsted and New Jersey Worsted workers went back to work on February 16, after the companies agreed to respect their right to affiliate with the AFL. By March 1, 1927, the longest strike in Passaic's history had ended.[158]

Although many of the strikers' demands remained unfulfilled, the strike had resulted in the recognition of a union for most Passaic workers. This was an important achievement in light of the long battle, including four defeated strikes, that had been waged for this goal. Moreover, the Central

152 *New York Times,* April 5, 1926; *Nation* 123 (July 7, 1926): 2.
153 "Passaic Strike," *Christian Century,* 974.
154 Weisbord, *Passaic: The Story of a Struggle,* 40.
155 Siegel, "Passaic Textile Strike," 203; letter of William Green, President of the AFL (July 6, 1926), cited in "Passaic Strike," *Christian Century,* 980.
156 Siegel, "Passaic Textile Strike," 264.
157 *Nation* 123 (Dec. 29, 1926): 679.
158 John R. Commons, *History of Labor in the United States* (New York, 1935), 3:557.

Employment Bureau was dissolved, thus taking one of the most powerful tools out of the hands of the employers.[159]

Even if the settlements of 1926 fell short in some respects, the strike itself signified an important change for labor in Passaic and in the United States. Workers of different ethnicity, skill, and gender had held out for many months and thus had overcome divisions that had kept so many of their struggles from succeeding. Diversity did not result in fragmentation. The alliance between German capital and German skilled workers that had characterized labor relations in the mills for decades after their arrival had been replaced with an alliance between skilled and less skilled workers. For all ethnic groups, including the Germans, class became the determining social fault line. This laid the basis for a more permanent organization in the following decade. For the nation as a whole, the Passaic strike of 1926, along with strikes in Gastonia and New Bedford, was a harbinger of workers' militancy in mass-production industries in the 1930s. Their tactics and their demand for union recognition became the cry of workers in the years to come.[160]

159 Robert W. Dunn, "Textile Union Breaks Passaic Employers Association," *Federated Press Eastern Bureau,* sheet 1, no. 2091 (March 7, 1927), Robert W. Dunn Papers, Library of the University of Oregon, Eugene. In the same year federal, state, and municipal authorities joined in creating an employment bureau. Siegel, "Passaic Textile Strike," 347.
160 Siegel, "Passaic Textile Strike," 367.

17

Changing Gender Roles and Emigration: The Example of German Jewish Women and Their Emigration to the United States, 1933–1945

SIBYLLE QUACK

I

In 1939 an American social worker, who worked with German Jewish refugee boys, expressed her frustration: "The boys looked upon women as housekeepers and could not imagine requesting guidance from a woman." The refugee boy, her report went on to say, "has contempt for women as anything but the mother and housekeeper."[1] At about the same time, another social worker described two adult emigrants from Germany standing in the hall of a refugee aid organization and talking: "Go into the last room," one of them insisted, "there you will find a man."[2]

Those reports from the late 1930s provide eloquent testimony as to how American professional women viewed the newly arrived refugees from Germany and how they expressed their astonishment, sometimes anger, about certain attitudes that those refugees held. They call out for a focus on the gender relations in German Jewish families in the 1930s. Was it really the old traditional and patriarchal family as one would expect from these statements? How were gender roles defined? Did women take care of their children and households while men worked and made all major decisions?

In this essay, I will show that during the Nazi era, specifically the period from 1933 to 1939, gender roles in the Jewish community and in Jewish families underwent a process of change. I will also argue that these changed

---

1 Quoted by Amelia Igel, "Case Work with Refugees" (New York, 1939), 4; see Papers of the National Refugee Service, File 112, YIVO Institute for Jewish Research, New York City. This essay is part of a social history of German Jewish women who emigrated from Germany to the United States between 1933 and 1945. See Sibylle Quack, "Verfolgung, Vertreibung, Einwanderung: Ihre Auswirkungen auf das Leben von Frauen: Ein Beitrag zur Sozialgeschichte der deutsch-jüdischen Emigration in den Vereinigten Staaten von Amerika nach 1933," Habilitationsschrift, Universität Hannover, 1993.

2 Ruth Mann, "The Adjustment of German Refugees in this Country in Relation to Their Backgrounds." Paper given at the Jewish Conference of Social Work held in Buffalo, June 16, 1939. See Papers of the National Refugee Service, File 112, YIVO Institute.

gender roles were carried along during their emigration to the United
States. In fact, this change played a decisive role in the social history of
German Jewish immigrants in the United States and their successful ad-
justment to this country.

But if we focus only on the fate of refugee men, as most studies do, we
fail to provide a differentiated picture of that group's adjustment. In particular, studies on the emigration of academics and cultural figures from Nazi
Germany to the United States not only lack discussion of everyday life but
also to a large extent neglect women. One easily gets the impression that
German refugees to America were mostly intellectuals and exclusively men.[3]
Other studies with a broader approach, however, mention the immigrant's
family situation.[4] They show that the wife often had to become the sole
breadwinner in emigration while the husband studied for an examination
or learned the language or looked desperately for a job. How depressed he
was, how hard it was on him not to abandon hope, and how heroic the
wives were who supported their families, managed everything, and, most
important, "helped out" by working in low-paying jobs – such are the
findings of most studies, as well as subjects of exile literature.[5] Nevertheless,
the important role of women in the economy of the refugee community
was early on pointed out:

3 To name only a few from recent years: Anthony Heilbutt, *Exiled in Paradise – German Refugee Artists
  and Intellectuals in America from the 1930s to the Present* (New York, 1983); Michael Groth, *The Road
  to New York: The Emigration of Berlin Journalists, 1933–1945* (Munich, 1984); Claus Dieter Krohn,
  *Wissenschaft im Exil: Deutsche Sozial- und Wirtschaftswissenschaftler in den USA und die New School for
  Social Research* (Frankfurt/Main and New York, 1987).
4 Most useful data on women émigrés are found in Maurice Davie, *Refugees in America: Report of the
  Committee for the Study of Recent Immigration from Europe* (New York and London, 1947), 124–26.
  Also, see Ruth Neubauer, "Differential Adjustment of Adult Immigrants and Their Children to
  American Groups: The Americanization of a Selected Group of Jewish Immigrants of 1933–1942,"
  Ed.D. diss., Columbia University, 1966; Herbert Strauss, "Zur sozialen und organisatorischen Ak-
  kulturation deutsch-jüdischer Einwanderer der NS-Zeit in den USA," in W. Frühwald and W.
  Schieder, eds., *Leben im Exil: Probleme der Integration deutscher Flüchtlinge im Ausland, 1933–1945*
  (Hamburg, 1981), 244. Also by the same author, "Kontinuität im Wandel: Der deutsch-jüdische
  Einwanderer seit 1933," in Frank Trommler, ed., *Amerika und die Deutschen: Bestandsaufnahme einer
  300 jährigen Geschichte* (Opladen, 1986), 592. The author's earlier studies, which laid the groundwork
  for the history of the German Jewish emigration from Nazi Germany, did not contain data on women
  émigrés at all. See "The Immigration and Acculturation of the German Jew in the United States of
  America," in *Leo Baeck Institute Year Book* 16 (1971): 63–94; and "Jewish Emigration from Germany
  – Nazi Policies and Jewish Responses," pt. 1: *Leo Baeck Institute Year Book* 25 (1980): 313–61; and
  pt. 2: *Leo Baeck Institute Year Book* 26 (1981): 343–409. The most important study on the refugee
  family remains that of Gerhard Sänger, a psychologist and himself a refugee. His work was the first
  to provide a sensitive look into the refugee family, though based on the psychological situation of
  the refugee man. E.g., see *Today's Refugees, Tomorrow's Citizens: A Story of Americanization* (New
  York, 1941).
5 About the image of the heroic women in the novels of exile writers, see the excellent study by Heike
  Klapdor, *Die Gestalten der Frauen im Drama deutscher Exilautoren, 1933–1945* (Weinheim and Basel,
  1985).

It is a matter of honor in this connection to point out expressly women's significance for the reconstruction of our economic independence. This was a case of
good luck, which one absolutely could not have predicted. Spoiled in comparison
to German women generally and to American women, these women were the
ones who demonstrated the greatest strengths in the new conditions.[6]

Spoiled women? Later on, we will see that this judgment was prejudicial.
Those statements focused on men, and when talking about women they
did so from the male perspective.

Recent studies, however, have emphasized the contradiction between
refugee literature and reality,[7] and have focused on the life conditions of
women refugees,[8] especially women writers. This approach has helped to
bring out some of the untold story of refugee women. But there is still
much work to be done.

Toward this end, it is necessary to concentrate on the experiences of
Jewish emigrant women before they left Germany, and, particularly, to look
at them as a minority group of women.[9] For the social historian, it is also
important to bring together women's and men's experiences in order to
compile a complete picture, with all its diversity. As feminist historians in
recent years have suggested, the gender perspective enables us to discover
interconnections between the gender system and politics, society, and culture.[10] When we use gender as a social category in the study of the German
Jewish emigration from Nazi Germany, we have to examine gender relations not only within the individual refugee family but also within the whole
group. This must be done first in the German Jewish community, and then

6 Julius and Edith Hirsch, "Berufliche Wiedereingliederung und wirtschaftliche Leistung der deutsch-
jüdischen Einwanderung in die Vereinigten Staaten (1935–1960)," in *Twenty Years: American Federation of Jews from Central Europe, Inc. 1940–1960* (New York, 1961), 53.
7 Klapdor, *Die Gestalten der Frauen;* Gabriele Kreis, *Frauen im Exil: Dichtung und Wirklichkeit* (Düsseldorf, 1984).
8 Christine Backhaus-Lautenschlaeger, . . . *Und standen ihre Frau: Das Schicksal deutschsprachiger Emigrantinnen in den USA nach 1933* (Pfaffenweiler, 1991).
9 In her recent study of German Jewish women in the *Kaiserreich,* Marion Kaplan points out that studies
on women's history in Germany have largely neglected Jewish women. Unlike studies in the United
States and Great Britain, which focus on ethnic identity as central to women's experiences, German
studies have concentrated on "German" women rather than on women in Germany. Kaplan states
that most German historians have allowed Jewish women to disappear from German history as Jews
– either because they felt uneasy with their country's history regarding Jews or because they wanted
to emphasize that Jews were Germans, neglecting their specific historical experiences within an ethnic minority group. See Marion Kaplan, *The Making of the Middle Class: Women, Family, and Identity
in Imperial Germany* (New York, 1991), viii. Many thanks to Marion Kaplan for sharing her findings
with me before her book was published. Her statement is particularly true for studies of the Nazi
era. But the studies mentioned previously, which deal with women in the emigration, also fail to
focus on Jewish women, although this was predominantly an emigration of Jews.
10 See Hanna Schissler, "The Meaning of Gender for Historical Analysis," paper delivered at the
German Historical Institute, London, Dec. 2, 1986, 14.

in the host country. For example, how did the situation of oppression between 1933 and 1939 influence gender relations within the German Jewish
community, and what were the consequences for men and for women?
How, then, did gender influence the desire to emigrate, and finally, what
role did gender play in the emigration and immigration process itself? Those
questions are a challenge for the understanding of the social history of
German Jewish immigrants in the United States. As yet, they have not been
answered. In the following, I will make some suggestions.

II

The roughly 500,000 German Jews (*Glaubensjuden*) living in Germany before Hitler came to power were part of a heterogeneous group, which
varied in geographic distribution, occupation, customs, and intellectual
characteristics.[11] Nevertheless, the demographic and economic profile of
the Jewish population, which made up only 0.77 percent of the general
population in 1933, was distinctive. Because of their historical exclusion
from certain professions and occupations, as well as from buying land, a
large part of the Jews were engaged in trade and commerce (61.3 percent
compared with 19.4 percent). Fewer Jews were employed in industry or
crafts (23.1 percent compared with 40.4 percent), and in agriculture or
forestry (1.7 percent compared with 28.9 percent). Their percentage was
relatively high in the free professions (including public and private service
jobs: 12.5 percent compared with 8.4 percent). Their social status differed
from the majority of Germans: 46 percent of the Jewish population was
self-employed (compared with 16.4 percent), one-third comprised white-
collar workers (compared with 17 percent), and only 8.7 percent was
classified as manual or industrial workers (compared with 46.4 percent).[12]

Jews were predominantly a middle-class group, of which 70 percent lived
in big cities. One-third of all Jews lived in Berlin, where they made up
about 4 percent of the population. High intermarriage rates, which were
on the rise until 1933 (especially common among Jewish men and in big
cities) together with low fertility rates and the aging of the population (*Über-
alterung*) caused the Jewish community to fear for its survival.[13] Although

---

11 Strauss, "The Immigration and Acculturation of the German Jew in the United States," 76.
12 Ibid.
13 The following studies analyze the demographic and economic situation of Jews in Germany in 1933:
    Erich Rosenthal, "Trends of the Jewish Population in Germany, 1910–1939," *Jewish Social Studies*
    6 (1944): 233–74; Monika Richarz, ed., *Jüdisches Leben in Deutschland: Selbstzeugnisse zur Sozialge-
    schichte, 1918–1945* (Stuttgart, 1982), introd.; Usiel Schmelz, "Die demographische Entwicklung
    der Juden in Deutschland von der Mitte des 19. Jahrhunderts bis 1933," *Zeitschrift für Bevölkerungs-*

Jews in Germany had adapted to the social, cultural, and political environment of the majority society, they "also preserved a sense of ethnic solidarity and religious cohesion," as Marion Kaplan has pointed out.[14] Kaplan's findings suggest that Jewish women played a very active role in the process of acculturation to German culture in the *Kaiserreich* by maintaining religious and ethnic characteristics.[15]

To a very large degree, Jewish women had not participated in the labor market. Most of them were housewives. Until 1933 their employment had increased only to 27 percent in comparison with 34 percent of women in the general population who were employed.[16] A Prussian census of 1925 showed that more than half of all employed Jewish women worked in trade and commerce (53.04 percent, as compared with 14.37 percent of employed women), 23.1 percent worked in industry and crafts (22.87 percent), and 10.34 percent in administration and free professions (3.49 percent). Only 3.46 percent of Jewish women worked in agriculture (compared with 43 percent). Finally, 9.35 percent of Jewish and 14.23 of non-Jewish women worked in domestic service. Of Jewish women who worked outside the home, 36.9 percent were salaried employees (compared with 13.4 percent), 23 percent were self-employed (compared with only 6.4 percent), and 22.5 percent of them worked in family enterprises as *mithelfende Familienangehörige* (34 percent of non-Jewish women). Only 9.8 percent of Jewish but 32 percent of non-Jewish women were laborers.[17]

III

From the very beginning of the Third Reich, the Jewish population faced economic, political, and social discrimination, and its living conditions grew ever worse. One of the consequences was that Jewish women were forced in greater numbers to work outside the home in order to earn money. In the first years of the Nazi regime, a great number of Jewish businesses and stores had to close or to be scaled down because of boycotts organized by the Nazi Party. Government employees and civil servants, university teachers, lawyers, doctors, and journalists either lost their jobs or had to continue

wissenschaft 8 (1982): 31–72; Esra Bennathan, "Die demographische und wirtschaftliche Struktur der Juden," in Werner Mosse, ed., *Entscheidungsjahr 1932: Zur Judenfrage in der Endphase der Weimarer Republik* (Tübingen, 1966).
14 Marion Kaplan, "Jewish Women in Nazi Germany: Daily Life, Daily Struggles, 1933–1939," *Feminist Studies* 16 (1990): 582.
15 This is one of the central themes in Kaplan's *The Making of the Jewish Middle Class*.
16 Richarz, *Jüdisches Leben in Deutschland*, 19.
17 See Bruno Sommerfeld, "Die jüdische Frau im Beruf," *C.V. Zeitung*, May 3, 1935. See n. 20.

under severe restrictions. Very often women started to work in order to supplement reduced incomes, and, in many cases, they became the sole breadwinners in the family. This all happened within the German Jewish community. They got jobs in Jewish welfare institutions or worked, together with their husbands or other relatives, in family businesses and offices. After the Nuremberg Laws (1935) prohibited the employment of so-called "Aryan" female servants under the age of forty-five in Jewish households, many, mostly younger Jewish women started work as domestics. A report of the Berlin Jewish Employment Service (*Jüdischer Arbeitsnachweis*), for example, showed that after 1933, job placement of women outnumbered that of men. In 1933, 4,518 women but only 2,507 men had been placed; in 1934, 7,133 women and 4,141 men; in 1935, 7,760 women and 4,725 men; and in 1936, 8,286 women and 5,954 men.[18] Most of the women were placed in offices and trades; but in rising numbers they also worked in domestic service, which had previously been uncommon for Jewish women as we have seen from the numbers of the Prussian census. Of course, all of them were directed to so-called "typical women's jobs." Because of Nazi policies, academic training was impossible for them – as Jews and as women. All their hopes of an academic career were gone, their career development was destroyed. By 1935 every second Jewish girl who would have chosen a business or professional career before 1933 now wanted to become a seamstress.[19]

Unfortunately, there are no statistics that show the exact percentage of Jewish women in the labor market in the years between 1933 and 1939. As we have seen, before Hitler came to power, only about 27 percent of Jewish women (in comparison with 34 percent of all German women) had been gainfully employed. Although many Jewish women – professional women as well as those who worked in stores and factories – lost their jobs in the first year of the Nazi dictatorship, their employment rate rose in the following years with the growing economic needs of the Jewish community. In 1935, before the Nuremberg Laws were decreed, an article in the *C.V. Zeitung* (organ of the Central-Verein deutscher Staatsbürger jüdischen Glaubens) estimated that the percentage of employed Jewish women had risen at least by 3 to 4 percent since 1933.[20]

18 Numbers derived from the statistics of Gertrud Prochownik, "Die jüdische Arbeitsvermittlung in Berlin," *Jüdische Wohlfahrtspflege und Sozialpolitik: Zeitschrift der Zentralwohlfahrtsstelle bei der Reichsvertretung der Juden in Deutschland*, n.s. 7 (1937): 7–13.
19 Report of the apprenticeship office for Jewish girls; see Kaplan, "Jewish Women in Nazi Germany: Daily Life, Daily Struggles," 588. As Kaplan points out, choices available for Jewish girls, besides housework, and sewing-related jobs, were much more limited than those for boys, who could consider more options.
20 See Bruno Sommerfeld, "Die jüdische Frau im Beruf." The *C.V. Zeitung* was the main organ of

This growing employment of women constituted a substantial change in the dynamic of Jewish families. Before Hitler came to power, the average married Jewish woman in Germany typically had been a middle-class housewife; most of these women had lived in cities, had fewer children than the average Christian woman, employed domestic servants, and possessed a good level of *Bildung*. From the very start of National Socialist rule, then, there was a change in women's roles in many Jewish families, which broadened their burden of responsibilities and also their power of decision making.

At the same time, the image of women in the Jewish community underwent important changes. As in earlier times of oppression, the community claimed the women as mothers and wives to keep the family together, to heal the wounds of humiliation, and to comfort husbands and children. At the same time that Jewish newspapers were full of articles on the tasks of the Jewish women as mothers and housewives, there were also voices stating that the emancipation of women in the period before Hitler, when universities and schools of higher education had opened up for women, had actually threatened the Jewishness of women and families.[21] Many men in the Jewish community believed (not surprisingly, considering the National Socialist environment) academic careers for women had been a mistake, and that, in addition, they had alienated Jewish women from their faith. Some articles, written to comfort Jewish women because they had had to give up their careers and all future hopes of academic professions, resorted to exaggeration and repeated hostile prejudices toward women in academic fields.[22] And, while Jewish men also were forced out of the universities in Germany and had to find new occupations and training, for them articles in the Jewish press expressed hope that at least "the best among them" would be able to enter academia in the countries of emigration again. For women, this prospect was often categorically denied.[23]

At the same time that the Jewish community insisted upon greater devotion to the family, Jewish women were forced to start working outside the home in ever larger numbers. We can only imagine how hard it was

the Central-Verein deutscher Staatsbürger jüdischen Glaubens (1893–1938), or the Central Union of German Citizens of Jewish Faith.

21 Jewish women had been pioneers at institutions of higher education and at the universities in the *Kaiserreich*. They had also been highly represented at the universities in the Weimar Republic. E.g., in 1932, Jewish women comprised 29 percent of all Jewish students in comparison to 17.9 percent of women in the Gentile student body. See Marion Kaplan, *Die jüdische Frauenbewegung in Deutschland: Organisation und Ziele des jüdischen Frauenbundes, 1904–1938* (Hamburg, 1981), 303.

22 See, e.g., the article "Fest im Leben stehen," *C.V. Zeitung*, July 26, 1934.

23 See Otto Toeplitz, "Die Zukunft unserer jungen Generation," *C.V. Zeitung*, March 18, 1937. See also the comments of the editorial group of that newspaper at the end of the article, which shows that there was some discourse about the author's opinion.

for them to try to fulfill all tasks at the same time. In 1934 the *C.V. Zeitung* wrote that "The present has created a type of married Jewish woman that the past hardly knew: the woman as cobreadwinner or even as single income-earner in the family."[24] That was true not only for married women but also for countless single women, who very often supplied the only income for their parents and siblings through their work as maids in other Jewish families. Many Jewish women from smaller towns and villages migrated to bigger cities to look for jobs. In 1937, for example, 60 percent of the biggest group of that *Binnenwanderung,* the *Hausangestellten,* were women.[25] Of course, the search for jobs was not the only reason for that migration. Jews from smaller cities and towns, suffering tremendous anti-Semitism, tried to find protection and support in the larger Jewish communities in the bigger cities.

While Jewish migration to bigger cities in those years was higher as a percentage for women, at least until 1938, more men than women emigrated to other countries.[26] The proportion of women in the German Jewish population rose from 52.3 percent in 1933 to 57.5 percent in 1939 because of the rising numbers of emigrating men, and also because of the higher mortality rate of Jewish men, caused by exposure, maltreatment, and imprisonment in concentration camps.[27]

IV

The lower rate of emigration of Jewish women was the subject of an article in the *C.V. Zeitung* in 1938.[28] Interestingly enough, the article demanded that more women should emigrate because single Jewish men could not find suitable spouses in the countries of emigration, in order to start Jewish

24 "Die jüdische Frau in der Wirtschaft," *C.V. Zeitung,* Nov. 22, 1934.
25 See Bruno Blau, "Die Entwicklung der jüdischen Bevölkerung in Deutschland von 1800–1945," unpublished manuscript (New York, 1950), part 2, 318, in Leo Baeck Institute, New York City.
26 See, e.g., the sex distribution of Jewish emigrants from Munich: Among the 3,574 people who emigrated to different countries between 1933 and 1938, 1,938 or 54 percent were men. See Peter Hanke, *Zur Geschichte der Juden in München zwischen 1933 und 1945* (Munich, 1967), 126.
27 See Erich Rosenthal, "Trends of the Jewish Population in Germany, 1910–1939," *Jewish Social Studies* 6 (1944): 246. Although it is certain that more women than men died in the Holocaust, I have not yet been able to find exact figures that prove that the total of German Jewish men who were able to emigrate during the whole Nazi period outnumbered that of Jewish women. But because of the higher percentage of women in the German Jewish community, the absolute number of women who emigrated would have been much higher than that of men. To find the percentage of women among the emigrants from Nazi Germany is a subject for further investigation. My impression is that, with the large wave of emigrant families that started in 1938, the number of women who emigrated rose significantly, whereas for the earlier period between 1933 and 1937–38 women's emigration was more restrained than men's.
28 See "Mehr Frauen für die Auswanderung!" *C.V. Zeitung,* Jan. 20, 1938.

families, and the continuation of the Jewish community in those countries seemed to be in danger.

Clearly, gender played an important role in the decision of Jewish women not to leave Germany, even if they wanted to leave, often earlier than men. The Jewish Women's Federation (*Jüdische Frauenbund*) had demanded women's emigration much earlier, but its arguments were not heard until the Jewish community leaders became conscious of the need of women in the countries of emigration, and until emigration became absolutely urgent.[29] Before that, Jewish women obviously were needed too much in Germany. The emigration of other groups, like children and younger single men, or married men, who emigrated before their families, was more at the center of the activities of the Jewish institutions. Of course, the decision to emigrate was made individually, and, as Herbert Strauss has pointed out, organized Jewish policies and publicity concerning emigration were not a major motive in the decisions of Jews in Germany to emigrate.[30]

Nevertheless, this delay in trying to recruit women for the emigration is a good example of the interrelation of gender, policies, and social demands. As we have seen, Jewish women had a better occupational situation than men and were often the only ones who could secure their families' incomes. Another reason was that the community as well as the families expected women, especially single women, to take care of their old parents or sick relatives. Besides that, a large number of women worked in the Jewish welfare organizations, which were desperately needed by the community. In 1938 an article in the Jewish press demanded the greater emigration of women, explaining that until then it had been thought that the emigration of single women was too dangerous. Now, international Jewish women's organizations were asked for help. Why did that not happen earlier? This gives an example of how gender roles were defined by social needs, and how gender then became a decisive factor in questions of survival – in staying or going.

As memoirs and autobiographies of emigrants suggest, many women had desired to leave Germany early on. This was also influenced by their gender. Very often, women wanted to leave, and men hesitated. What were the reasons for those differences in the attitudes of men and women toward emigration?

---

29 In 1936 the *Jüdische Frauenbund* was concerned not only that fewer women than men emigrated but also that many Jewish men of marriageable age left the country and more and more Jewish women stayed behind with no chance at all of marrying. See Kaplan, "Jewish Women in Nazi Germany," 597.

30 See Strauss, "Jewish Emigration from Germany," pt. 2, 389.

For women, the well-being of their children was an important factor. Once they discovered that their children would have no future in Germany, women wanted to leave. Because they were traditionally responsible for the emotional welfare of the family, women especially suffered with their children when they experienced daily humiliation in schools and on the streets. It was mostly women who had to go to school and argue with teachers and directors. It was mostly they who had to console children, and often their parents, too. The fact that many women worked in Jewish social agencies also accelerated their decision to emigrate. Here they witnessed the concrete consequences of the inhuman Nazi policies. Yet, those experiences sometimes dissuaded them from emigration. They decided to stay in Germany in order to continue their important work.

For many Jewish men, their patriotic feelings caused them to hesitate to emigrate. This might have been true for women as well but it was especially difficult for conservative Jewish men who had been soldiers in World War I to realize that the Nazis treated Jews as if they were no longer Germans. This was even more the case because, in the first years of the Nazi regime, Jewish combat soldiers from World War I and their sons were protected from some of the harsher Nazi anti-Jewish policies. In those families, women's desire to emigrate often did not prevail for many years. A woman described in her memoirs how her husband did not take seriously her anxiousness to leave Germany: "You are a child, said he. . . . You mustn't take everything so seriously. Hitler used the Jews very skillfully as propaganda to gain power – now that his goal is achieved, you'll hear nothing more about the Jews."[31] The woman had wanted to leave the moment Hitler had come to power. It took the sad lessons of years of Nazi policy before her husband was ready to leave. In other cases, women tried to make arrangements without their husbands' knowledge and contacted relatives in the United States: "It was in the middle thirties and she wrote to them behind my father's back, hoping to get an affidavit so we could come to the United States. She was more of a realist than my father in this respect."[32]

For both Jewish men and women, their integration into German culture and their *Bildung* caused them to hesitate before finally deciding to emigrate.

---

31 See Edith Bielschowsi, "My Life in Germany before and after January 30, 1933," 5. Harvard University's Competition in 1940. Records are kept in the Houghton Library, Harvard University, Cambridge, Mass. For other examples, see Kaplan, "Jewish Women in Nazi Germany: Daily Life, Daily Struggles, 1933–1939," 592–94.

32 See Sylvia Rothchild, *Voices from the Holocaust* (New York, 1981), 40. For other examples, see Kaplan, "Jewish Women in Nazi Germany," 605.

Because, however, in assimilated Jewish families it was often the women who maintained religious traditions, one must ask whether this made it easier for women to choose to break with Germany. As Claudia Koonz has suggested, Jewish women were less assimilated than men into the German economy and culture.[33]

The decision to emigrate had also to do with many other factors, such as Nazi policies and regulations and foreign visa requirements. For emigration to the United States, obtaining an entry visa was not a question of social class or wealth, but much more one of having relatives or friends who would give an "affidavit of support" for the emigrant. Still, immigration laws in the United States privileged the immigration of whole families, which made it more difficult for single women to obtain a visa.[34]

Besides choosing to emigrate, Jewish women made other fundamentally important decisions. Many of them decided not to have any more children under the Nazi regime. Birthrates fell significantly during the 1930s.[35] Although statistics do not reveal motives and although the Jewish birthrate was in decline even before 1933, subjective sources, such as interviews and letters, show that there was a tendency among the Jewish population not to have children under the Nazi regime. "I do not have to tell you how astonished I am that you have got a baby," wrote a woman who had already emigrated to Palestine to her friend in Berlin in 1936.[36] Interviewees have told of opting to have abortions during this decade.[37] They describe how dangerous abortions were for Jewish women, who until 1938 were subject to the same antiabortion laws as non-Jews, laws that had been made stricter

33 See Claudia Koonz, "Courage and Choice among German Jewish Women and Men," in Arnold Paucker, ed., *The Jews in Nazi Germany, 1933–1938* (Tübingen, 1986), 285. See also the chapter on Jewish women in her *Mothers in the Fatherland: Women, the Family, and Nazi Politics* (New York, 1987).

34 As a reaction to earlier mass immigration from eastern and southern Europe, restrictive immigration laws were passed in the United States between 1917 and 1924, and amended in 1929. They created a quota system, which was based on "natural origin as reflected in the number of nationals of a given country enumerated in the U.S. census at a given time" (Strauss, "Jewish Emigration from Germany II," 358). There were several categories of visas: nonimmigrant visas, for visitors or travelers in transit; nonquota immigrant visas, for clerics, university teachers, students, former residents, and relatives of qualifying individuals; quota immigrant visas, with preference visas for parents of U.S. citizens, and wives and children under twenty years of age of legal residents; and ordinary immigration visas. The quota for German nationals (25,000) included many more immigrants than those of other countries, e.g., Poland or Italy (6,000). All immigrants had to prove that they were not "likely to become a public charge." They had to provide an "affidavit of support" from relatives or close friends in the U.S. See Strauss, "Jewish Emigration from Germany," pt. 2, 358–59. See also Davie, *Refugees in America*, 16–17.

35 See Rosenthal, "Trends of the Jewish Population," 262.

36 See Hertha Lieb collection, box 3, folder 3, Archives of the Leo Baeck Institute, New York City.

37 Interviews with Ellen H., New York, Feb. 24, 1988, and with Margo M., Washington, D.C., Jan. 22, 1991. Recordings of all interviews done for this essay are in the possession of the author.

and harsher in 1933. As Jews, they were especially in danger. Later on, in emigration, the situation often was so hard that they no longer had enough strength to have a child, or they had grown too old. Many emigrants, therefore, remained childless or had only one child, and they rightly blame the Nazis for forcing this choice upon them. One woman, who emigrated to the United States in 1937, told me: "Nobody could afford to become sick. And this is why we said: We do not want children. The risk was too high."[38]

Those Jewish women who could emigrate only after the November pogrom of 1938 suffered horrible experiences: Their husbands, brothers, fathers, and teenage sons were sent to concentration camps, their apartments were vandalized, their children terrorized. During that time, thousands of Jewish women struggled with the Nazi bureaucracy, sent their children out of the country, broke up their households, succeeded in obtaining visas for emigration, and even obtained the release of men from the camps. "In the mornings, Mom would go to the Gestapo," remembered a Jewish woman. She had been listening to conversations between her mother and other women whose husbands had been imprisoned during the *Kristallnacht* (pogrom against the Jews on November 9–10, 1938).

At first in their desperation the women had gone to the Gestapo. There they had been thrown down the stairs. They did not give in, but instead returned again and again. . . . Nobody dared to speak. And when somehow they made only the slightest noise, some stupid rascal would come and scream.[39]

Between 1939 and 1943 about 30,000 women emigrated from Germany and Austria to the United States.[40] What lay behind them (and their families) were often nightmares of oppression and suffering. We can only imagine how exhausted they were when they finally reached America. In addition, thousands of immigrants had to make long journeys through other countries before they arrived.

V

It is hard to say how many Jewish women, men, and children actually emigrated from Nazi Germany to the United States. Only estimates can be

38 See Hilda Epstein, "Panik war ein Dauerzustand," in Henri Jacob Hempel, ed., *Wenn ich schon ein Fremder sein muss . . . Deutschjüdische Emigranten in New York* (Frankfurt/Main, 1984), 4.
39 See Annemarie Wolfram, "Mein Leben in Deutschland vor und nach dem 30. Januar 1933" (1940), published in Andreas Lixl-Purcell, ed., *Women of Exile: German Jewish Autobiographies since 1933* (New York, 1988), 83.
40 Calculations are based on data provided by the Statistics Dept. of the Immigration and Naturalization Service, Dept. of Justice, Washington, D.C. In the following cited as INS, "unpublished immigration statistics" (1933–44).

made. The quotas for Germany, including Austria after 1938, were not always filled. Especially during the first years of the Nazi regime, refugees from Germany did not enter the United States in any appreciable number.[41] Altogether, between 129,000 and 132,000 people emigrated from Germany and Austria to the United States.[42]

Statistics of the Immigration and Naturalization Service (INS), which report on sex distribution and other demographic characteristic of immigrant arrivals, are based on the categories of "last residence" and "races and people," but not on "country of birth." Thus, those tables do not include figures on thousands of refugees from Germany who had been in other countries for years before they entered the United States.

The INS listed 104,815 persons as "immigrant aliens admitted" between 1934 and 1944 who gave Germany as "last residence." Among the 88,168 adult persons (over sixteen years old) of that group, there were 46,549 women and 41,619 men (53 percent women and 47 percent men).[43] Although it was possible to calculate the general proportion of immigrants from Germany who identified themselves as "Hebrew" or as "German," it was not possible to break down the sex ratio of both Jews and non-Jews. Therefore, only tentative conclusions can be drawn: It seems that within the non-Jewish "German" emigration to the United States between 1933 and 1936, the percentage of women was particularly high (between 62 and 64 percent), whereas the "Hebrew" (sex rates are available only for all countries, not from Germany alone) immigration at the same time shows another picture: Here the proportion of men and women was about equal, or women were in a slight minority.

But the following numbers for the years 1938, 1939, and 1940, when the Jewish emigration from Germany to the United States reached its highest point (the proportion of immigrant aliens from Germany who identified themselves as "Hebrew" in 1938 was 70 percent; in 1939, 88.7 percent; and in 1940, 92.4 percent), show a higher proportion of women:[44]

	Total	Male	(%)	Female	(%)
1938	13,566	6,627	(48.9)	6,939	(51.1)
1939	27,803	13,804	(49.6)	13,999	(50.4)
1940	18,590	8,540	(45.9)	10,050	(54.1)

41 See Herbert Strauss, "The Immigration and Acculturation of the German Jew in the United States," 65.
42 Ibid., 69.
43 See INS, "unpublished immigration statistics" (1933–44).
44 These figures include Austria since 1939. Calculations are based on absolute numbers provided by "unpublished immigration statistics" (1933–44).

Of the 6,939 women immigrants in 1938, 3,294 (or 47.5 percent) were married, 2,975 (42.9 percent) were single, 531 (7.6 percent) were widowed, and 139 (2.0 percent) were divorced. That same year, 51.6 percent of the men were married, 46.1 percent were single, 1.4 percent were widowed, and 0.9 percent were divorced. The percentage of married men and women grew significantly in 1939: 62 percent of the women and 60.7 percent of the men were married; 26.5 percent of the women and 36.5 percent of the men were single; 9.3 percent of the women and 1.7 percent of the men were widowed; and 2.2 percent of women and 1.1 percent of men were divorced.

In 1940 the trend toward married immigrants grew even more: 65.2 percent of the women were married and 70.5 percent of the men; 21.5 percent of the women and 25.9 percent of men were single; 11.4 percent of women and 2.2 percent of men were widowed; and 1.9 percent of women and 1.3 percent of men were divorced.[45] The high number of female widows was a result of World War I; the higher mortality rate of men mentioned previously also played a role.[46] The higher divorce rate of women was a phenomenon known already from the Jewish community before 1933.[47]

VI

In New York, of course, there was no rest. In the months after arrival, many emigrant women worked as domestic servants, regardless of their education or training. They peeled potatoes, served as private nurses, worked on the line in factories, went into office jobs as clerks and secretaries, or opened little stores with their husbands or relatives. At the same time, they had to care for their children, find places in schools and kindergartens, rush through New York in awful heat or cold to their poorly paid jobs, do the shopping after work, go home, cook, clean, and wash, all the while being expected to console and encourage their dislocated and depressed husbands. Single women often lived in with their employers. "It was very hard, because we had very little time for ourselves. Only one

---

45 All calculations are based on absolute numbers given by the tables of the INS, "unpublished immigration statistics" (category last residence).

46 Rosenthal, "Trends of the Jewish Population."

47 See Heinrich Silbergleit, *Die Bevölkerungs- und Berufsverhältnisse der Juden im Deutschen Reich: Erster Band Freistaat Preussen* (Berlin, 1930), 68–69. See also Rosenthal, "Trends of the Jewish Population," 248. The author explains the phenomenon by the high percentage of Jews living in big cities, where also in the general population the proportion of divorced women was higher than that of men.

afternoon, on Saturday, would we have free time," said one woman, who got the job through the National Council of Jewish Women.[48] She described how at the same time all of them suffered from their separation from relatives and friends they had left in Germany and from the knowledge of the dangers to those left behind.

There were, however, organizations and institutions that helped. The National Refugee Service (NRS), a joint effort of several American refugee aid organizations, coordinated the different tasks or activities. Selfhelp, a refugee help organization founded in 1936 by Paul Tillich, Tony Stolper, Friedrich Pollack, Else Staudinger, and others,[49] was in the beginning a very small institution but grew ever bigger and later on became an important social agency, typifying the acculturation process of the refugee community.[50]

Men émigrés often had more difficulties adjusting to the American environment. It was harder for them to find jobs than it was for the women. America was still in the Depression, and a job as a domestic servant was often the only kind of job that could be found. The records of the refugee aid organizations show that there were many more job placements for women than for men. For example, the statistics department of the NRS showed under employment placements for April, May, June 1940 the following numbers:[51]

	April	May	June
Male	101	143	88
Female	310	281	199

Other tables on the employment placements showed similar numbers.[52] A great part of those jobs for women were placements in domestic service, as private nurses, or in textile factories.

Women's work, especially married women's work, was considered by most of the participants, and by the refugee organizations, to be just temporary, whereas men sought more long-term positions in their old occupations or at least in a related field. Of course, there were also many men

48 Interview with Anneliese R., New York, Oct. 16, 1987.
49 See Selfhelp Papers, kept in the archives of Selfhelp, Community Services, Inc., New York.
50 On the acculturation of organizations founded by the refugee community, see Herbert Strauss, "Jüdische Emigrantenverbände in den USA: Perioden ihrer Akkulturation," in Manfred Briegel and Wolfgang Frühwald, eds., *Die Erfahrung der Fremde* (Weinheim, 1988), 121–40.
51 See "Table: Basic Statistics Covering Major Operations of National Refugee Service, Inc.," *National Refugee Service, Quarterly Report of the Executive Director,* April–June 1940.
52 See the reports during the months of July–Sept. 1940, Jan.–March 1941, April–June 1941, and July–Sept. 1941. This situation was true until America entered World War II, when more jobs for both men and women became available.

among the refugees who held jobs as gardeners, clerks, janitors, elevator
men, and peddlers, and most changed these jobs frequently, as did the
women. But the attitude – the consensus in most cases – was that after a
while men would be able again to be the sole breadwinner, and that women
would again become housewives. That is why women could often endure
very difficult working conditions: It was only temporary, it would be over
soon.

In the meantime, many refugee men took retraining and language courses
for which they drew financial support from their wives' work or from
refugee aid organizations. Another reason for difficulties in adjustment was
that men often spoke no English. Many of the women had had a different
education in Germany, with an emphasis on modern languages, and it had
also been common in Germany to send middle-class daughters on vacation
trips to England.

But the changing role of women does not tell the whole story. Men's
role in the family changed as well. In the Jewish community in Germany,
there had already been some discussions about the possible help of men in
the household. In 1938 an article in the *Blätter des Jüdischen Frauenbundes*
had cautiously stated: "It won't always be avoidable that our men will have
to take part in the household duties, as is customary in North American
homes."[53] Just how controversial such thoughts were is shown in another
article, published at about the same time in the *Israelitisches Familienblatt*:
"Personally, I don't like making the husband work in the household. . . .
How wonderful if he offers to help on his own! Herein, I would see the
new chivalry! But to engage him in drying dishes and dusting I find entirely
unnecessary."[54]

Probably quite a few middle-class women felt the same way. Although
women's economic role had changed dramatically, their feelings and attitudes often could not follow as fast. How did the men feel? We have a
statement of a "house-husband," published in 1939, in the *New Yorker*. The
article described a language class of adult refugees. One of them gave a
report on his past and current life:

In the old country, I was a director of a large corporation, which employed many
thousands of workers. Here, my occupation is somewhat different; my work takes
place in the household. I am no longer a director, since my wife directs the household. I am a combination of butler and housemaid. Every day I dust the furniture,
clean the carpets, wash and dry the dishes, and finally I go shopping. Formerly I

53 *Blätter des Jüdischen Frauenbundes,* Oct. 1938, 4, cited in Kaplan, "Jewish Women in Nazi Germany,"
591.
54 Lotte Schoenheim, "Der Ehemann im Haushalt," in *Israelitisches Familienblatt,* May 19, 1938, 19.

made long journeys to France, Switzerland, Italy, and so on, but this time, the journey is short. I take with me the briefcase which I always had with me when attending a conference. Now the briefcase does not contain important commercial documents any longer, but apples, cream cheese, sweet butter, pickles, sausages, and other useful things.[55]

Very often, the situation in refugee families was tense. "Real difficulties in refugee families arise," wrote the psychologist and author Gerhard Sänger, a refugee himself, in 1941, "when the wife supports the family and the husband is unable to find work and does not know whether he will ever be able to find a job."[56] Sänger stated that male unemployment in families where the wife worked created tension in the United States as well as in Europe. But he believed that those tensions were more pronounced in refugee families because of the more patriarchal pattern that refugee men brought with them. Considering the expectations of these men, Sänger wrote:

It becomes clear how much greater the difficulties of adjustment are. . . . Forced to live on the income of his wife and children, he no longer holds the authority which was formerly his. He is ashamed of his inability to support the family and feels guilty. . . . He feels insecure and retires into himself, or worse, hides his insecurity behind an aggressive and quarrelsome behavior.[57]

Sänger's description of the refugee women's everyday life is also revealing:

In the evening, she returns from the unaccustomed work in another household or in a factory. Exhausted by the heavy work, she needs a rest. But her work continues. After she has greeted the children and consoled her husband over his bad luck in not finding a position, she has to cook dinner, for most European men do not know how to cook. After dinner is over, she must look after the children, who have missed her care; father did not know what to do for them. Finally, after the children have been put to bed, the laundry has to be washed and the husband instructed what to buy the following day.[58]

Thus, in many cases circumstances forced women to adjust, while men remained for a longer time in the private and stable environment of the family until they were able to make their own adjustment. Then, after they found their own occupations, it was sometimes astonishing how quickly they were able to reach almost the same social level that they had occupied previously in Germany.

From a social historical viewpoint, it is important to keep in mind that

55 *New Yorker,* June 3, 1939.
56 Sänger, *Today's Refugees, Tomorrow's Citizens,* 171.
57 Ibid., 177.
58 Ibid., 178.

it was this changing of roles that permitted the refugee families' adjustment to their new country. Women's work made possible the conditions for upward social mobility.

A significant question is whether married German Jewish emigrant women stopped working outside the house after their families were once again settled, a process that often took years. Did they return to their old roles with restricted responsibilities? The answer is very difficult to provide. The result is a diverse picture, depending upon the age of the women emigrants. It would be wrong, however, to conclude that giving up low-level positions meant necessarily giving up freedom to make decisions. The kind of work that married and unmarried immigrant women were forced to do was certainly not likely to build new self-confidence. The experience of being strong and able to survive gave Jewish women a new feeling of their own abilities and self-confidence. And it is my impression that they retained this even if they did not work outside the house. Many of them, however, remained in their occupations and made careers. Others worked as volunteers in Jewish organizations until they were quite old.

Gender relations in the German Jewish emigrant families never became what they had been in Germany before Hitler. This is particularly true for the second generation, but it was already noticeable among the older generation. It is an important development, without which we cannot understand the successful adjustment of this group to the United States.

The observations of the American social workers, quoted at the beginning of this essay, which were made in the middle of the process of change, show us that attitudes are tenacious and do not change quickly, even under the pressure of new conditions. Children from German middle-class families were accustomed to viewing the father as the main authority and the mother as second in command. That is how they had been brought up in Germany.

The changes of roles were not at all voluntary but dictated by the living conditions of the refugees, first in Germany under Nazi policies, and then during the first years of their emigration and immigration to the United States.

According to the evidence I have gathered, many refugee women attempted, even under the changed circumstances, to give their men the feeling that they continued to be the ones who made the decisions. Many were all too ready to subordinate their own interests if their husbands' interest could thereby be advanced. The records of the refugee aid organizations give testimony of this tendency. The wife of an unemployed chemist, for example, found a job as a secretary, which she liked very much, almost immediately. She earned enough money for both of them. Her husband could not tolerate this situation. As a social worker described it: "He did not want to be dependent upon her, he wanted to be the one to earn. . . . Finally, they were both able to accept general resettlement on the basis of its opportunity for him, with his acceptance that she might find work first, but that her work was only temporary and that he soon would again be the head of the family."[59] Only later could many German Jewish women immigrants develop their own, self-chosen careers, separate from their "temporary" labors.

Some, but not all, express their deep feelings when they speak about what they gained in coming to America. As one immigrant woman has said: "I feel like I was liberated, released from prison. [In Germany] I could never have taken a job without damaging my husband's reputation."[60]

59 See Amelia Igel, "Case Work with Refugees" (New York, 1939), in Papers of the National Refugee Services, File 112, 8, YIVO Institute.
60 Neubauer, "Differential Adjustment of Adult Immigrants and Their Children to American Groups," 83.

Conclusion: Migration Past and Present – The German Experience

KLAUS J. BADE

In united Germany, as in other European countries, the public debate on migration in the early 1990s is haunted by apocalyptic visions of "Fortress Europe," a continent threatened by new mass migrations. Such visions create or at least strengthen defensive reactions and a widespread attitude of denial among those who view immobile populations as an indication of peace and movement across borders as a sign of danger. This is especially true for united Germany, although the history of the Germans has been strongly influenced by manifold migration movements.[1]

GERMAN CONTINENTAL AND TRANSATLANTIC MIGRATIONS

Early continental emigrants from German-speaking areas were, for example, the ancestors of the *Siebenbürger Sachsen* who went to live in what is now Romania. Their roots reach back to the Kingdom of Hungary in the middle of the twelfth century. They were called "Saxons" by their Hungarian neighbors, but, as a matter of fact, they came mainly from the Rhine and Moselle regions of western Germany. Starting in the eighteenth century other settlers from German-speaking areas followed: the *Banater Schwaben* from southwestern and central Germany and the *Sathmarer Schwaben* from Upper Swabia and Baden. Their purpose was to open up, to develop, and to secure through settlement new regions in these areas of eastern Europe. In return, they were offered attractive economic and cultural privileges.[2]

---

1 For emigration from and immigration into Germany as well as for alienation and segregation toward "strange" ethnic, religious, and cultural minorities (Jews, Gypsies) inside German borders, see Klaus J. Bade, ed., *Deutsche im Ausland – Fremde in Deutschland: Migration in Geschichte und Gegenwart* (Munich, 1992); Klaus J. Bade, ed., *Population, Labor and Migration in Nineteenth and Twentieth-Century Germany* (Leamington Spa, England, 1987); Klaus J. Bade, *Homo Migrans: Wanderungen aus und nach Deutschland – Erfahrungen und Fragen* (Essen, 1994).
2 For the history of German settlements in southeastern Europe, see the contributions of Holm Sund-

399

Privileged German settlements also existed for a long time in other parts
of southeastern, east-central, and eastern Europe. In Russia, for example,
this was true for the German settlements in Wolhynia, along the Black Sea,
in the Caucasus, and finally in the Volga region, that is, in what between
1924 and 1941 was called the Autonomous Soviet Republic of the Volga
Germans.[3] Until the 1830s, German continental emigration to eastern and
southeastern Europe, especially to Russia and the Habsburg countries, was
still stronger than transatlantic emigration. In many areas of eastern and
southeastern Europe where Germans settled, the German element and its
cultural traditions, often centuries old, disappeared only during the century
of the world wars. Because of forced resettlements, deportation and expulsion, and cultural repression, and because of the "remigration" of ethnic
Germans dreaming of "coming home" to the land of their fathers and, as
many of them are reported to have said, living "in the Reich as Germans
among Germans," the German settlements in these areas were dramatically
and irrevocably changed.[4]

Since the 1830s, continental emigration to eastern Europe was surpassed
by the rising transatlantic mass emigration to the Western Hemisphere, 90
percent of which headed to the United States. Traces of the older type of
transatlantic group emigration could still be found in the early nineteenth
century.[5] The secular transatlantic mass exodus of the nineteenth century,
however, was characterized by family as well as individual emigration for
predominantly socioeconomic reasons. The overall driving force on the
German side was the imbalance between population growth and employment opportunities during the crucial period of transition from an agrarian
to an industrial society. From the hunger crisis of 1816–17 until the eve of
World War I in 1914, about 5.5 million Germans emigrated to the United
States. The period was marked by three waves of emigration, in 1846–57,
1864–73, and 1880–93. More than 100,000 people emigrated annually dur-

haussen (Romania, Yugoslavia) and Günter Schödl (Hungary), in Bade, *Deutsche im Ausland – Fremde in Deutschland*, 36–84.
3 Detlef Brandes, "Die Deutschen in Russland und der Sowjetunion," in Bade, *Deutsche im Ausland – Fremde in Deutschland*, 85–134.
4 Klaus J. Bade, "'Remigration' to Their Fathers' Land? Ethnic Germans from the East in the FRG," *European Journal of International Affairs* 4 (1991).
5 Frank S. Beck, *Christian Communists in America: A History of the Colony of Saint Nazians, Wisconsin, during the Pastorate of Its Founder, Father Ambros Oschwald, 1854–1873* (St. Paul, 1959); Hubert Treiber, "'Wie man wird, was man ist': Lebensweg und Lebenswerk des badischen Landpfarrers Ambros Oschwald (1801–1873) im Erwartungshorizont chiliastischer Prophezeiungen," *Zeitschrift für die Geschichte des Oberrheins*, no. 136 (1988): 293–348; Hermann Schempp, *Gemeinschaftssiedlungen auf religiöser und weltanschaulicher Grundlage* (Tübingen, 1969); Hartmut Lehmann, "Endzeiterwartung und Auswanderung: Der württembergische Pietist Johann Michael Hahn und Amerika," in Hartmut Boockmann et al., eds., *Geschichte und Gegenwart: Festschrift für Karl D. Erdmann* (Neumünster, 1980), 177–94.

ing the 1850s; and during the 1880s the number reached more than 200,000 people per year.

Calling these significant fluctuations in the emigration curve "emigration waves" may be misleading and has led to misinterpretations. Among these is the tendency to attribute the abrupt rise of such a wave to an intensification of constellations of push and pull at the same time. In reality, there was only one large "wave" of German emigration from the rapid rise of the transatlantic mass movement during the 1840s until its final decline in the early 1890s. This "wave" comprised various peaks and sudden breaks caused by disruptive events, for example, the outbreak of the American Civil War in 1861 and the economic crisis of 1873–79, which hit the German economy as severely as it did the American. And this was also true of the economic crisis of 1893 in the United States (the "Panic of 1893"), which finally led to the abrupt decline in the secular transatlantic mass exodus from Germany to the New World.[6]

Due to the lack of sufficient data, the extent of German American return migration can only be estimated. The group of returnees by no means consisted only of those who had failed or who were not able to integrate. There were also those who had made their fortunes and wanted to live conspicuously in the places where they were from or, at least, to die in the old home country. In the second half of the nineteenth century, the number

6 A new, comprehensive study of German emigration to the United States is needed because of the new research findings published since Mack Walker's still helpful study, *Germany and the Emigration, 1816–1885* (Cambridge, Mass., 1964); for comprehensive surveys on German emigration, see Klaus J. Bade, "Die deutsche überseeische Massenauswanderung im 19. und frühen 20. Jahrhundert: Bestimmungsfaktoren und Entwicklungsbedingungen," in Klaus J. Bade, ed., *Auswanderer – Wanderarbeiter – Gastarbeiter: Bevölkerung, Arbeitsmarkt und Wanderung in Deutschland seit der Mitte des 19. Jahrhunderts*, 2 vols., 2d ed. (Ostfildern, 1986), 1:259–99; Reinhard R. Doerries, "German Transatlantic Migration from the Early 19th Century to the Outbreak of World War II," in Bade, *Population, Labor and Migration*, 115–34; Ingrid Schöberl, *Amerikanische Einwandererwerbung in Deutschland, 1845–1914* (Stuttgart, 1990); Agnes Bretting and Hartmut Bickelmann, *Auswanderungsagenturen und Auswanderungsvereine im 19. und 20. Jahrhundert* (Stuttgart, 1991); for case studies on German immigration to the United States, see Frederick C. Luebke, *Bonds of Loyalty: German Americans and World War I* (Dekalb, Ill., 1974); Kathleen N. Conzen, *Immigrant Milwaukee, 1836–1860: Accommodation and Community in a Frontier City* (Cambridge, Mass., 1976); Kathleen N. Conzen, "Germans," in Stephen Thernstrom, ed., *Harvard Encyclopedia of American Ethnic Groups* (Cambridge, Mass., 1980), 405–25; Wolfgang von Hippel, *Auswanderung aus Südwestdeutschland: Studien zur württembergischen Auswanderung und Auswanderungspolitik im achtzehnten und neunzehnten Jahrhundert* (Stuttgart, 1984); Reinhard R. Doerries, *Iren und Deutsche in der Neuen Welt: Akkulturationsprozesse in der amerikanischen Gesellschaft im späten 19. Jahrhundert* (Stuttgart, 1986); Walter D. Kamphoefner, *The Westfalians: From Germany to Missouri* (Princeton, N.J., 1987); cf. the contributions of Agnes Bretting, Horst Rössler, Monika Blaschke, and Karen Schniedewind on Germans in the United States in Bade, *Deutsche im Ausland – Fremde in Deutschland*, 135–85; Agnes Bretting, *Soziale Probleme deutscher Einwanderer in New York City 1800–1860* (Wiesbaden, 1981); and the following research reports: Klaus J. Bade, "Trends and Issues of Historical Migration Research in the Federal Republic of Germany," *Migration: A European Journal of International Migration and Ethnic Relations*, no. 6 (1989): 7–27; Klaus J. Bade, "German Transatlantic Emigration in the Nineteenth and Twentieth Centuries," in Pieter C. Emmer and Magnus Mörner, eds., *European Expansion and Migration* (Oxford, 1991), 121–55.

of German immigrants employed temporarily in American cities increased, and, toward the end of the century, a growing number of industrial workers even became transatlantic "commuters," migrating back and forth several times during their lives without long-term planning.[7]

In the 1890s emigration from eastern and southeastern Europe to the Americas developed into a mass movement in inverse proportion to the abrupt decline of German mass emigration. This was of crucial importance for German transatlantic shipping lines, whose agents even stimulated the "emigration fever" in eastern and southeastern Europe. Since the decline of German transatlantic emigration, German transatlantic liners carried ever more transit migrants from these regions. Until the beginning of World War I, more than five million emigrants from Russia (especially Jews and Poles) and Austria-Hungary passed through the Reich on their way to embarkation harbors. In Hamburg and Bremen, most of them boarded ships bound for the United States.

This transit migration took place under strict control in special trains, or separate compartments were used. The rigorous German Prussian "transit migration control" (*Durchwandererkontrolle*) was supposed to offer protection against epidemics and illegal immigration from the East.[8] Out of the approximately two million Jews crossing Germany's eastern frontier between 1880 and 1914, only 78,000 stayed in the Reich, representing, however, about 12 percent of the Jewish population in Germany. Of the approximately 100,000 Jews from the East (*Ostjuden*), who, on account of pogroms and acts of violence, fled from the Ukraine and Poland to the Reich between 1914 and 1921, about 40 percent eventually left.[9] German anxiety about foreigners from across the eastern borders showed not only anti-Semitic but also anti-Polish overtones. This provided the background for the strict control of labor migrations from eastern European countries to Prussia and other German states since the early 1890s.[10]

7 For an early, mainly biographically oriented study, see Alfred Vagts, *Deutsch-Amerikanische Rück-wanderung: Probleme, Statistik, Politik, Soziologie, Biographie* (Heidelberg, 1960); Günter Moltmann, "American-German Return Migration in the Nineteenth and Early Twentieth Century," *Central European History* 13 (1980): 378–92; cf. Dirk Hoerder, "Immigration and the Working Class: The Remigration Factor," *International Labor and Working Class History*, no. 21 (1982): 28–41; Walter D. Kamphoefner, "Umfang und Zusammensetzung der deutsch-amerikanischen Rückwanderung," *Amerikastudien/American Studies* 33, no. 3 (1988): 291–307; Karen Schniedewind, *Begrenzter Aufenthalt im Land der unbegrenzten Möglichkeiten: Bremer Rückwanderer aus Amerika, 1850–1914* (Stuttgart, 1994).

8 Michael Just, *Ost- und Südosteuropäische Amerika-Auswanderung, 1881–1914: Transitprobleme in Deutschland und Aufnahme in den Vereinigten Staaten* (Stuttgart, 1988).

9 Jack Wertheimer, *Unwelcome Strangers: East European Jews in Imperial Germany* (New York, 1987); Trude Maurer, *Ostjuden in Deutschland, 1918–1933* (Hamburg, 1986).

10 Klaus J. Bade, "Arbeiterstatistik zur Ausländerkontrolle: Die 'Nachweisungen' der preussischen

In addition to continental emigration to the East and transatlantic emigration, numerous smaller migrations from Germany to other European countries took place. In the nineteenth century, Germans were destined for Holland and Belgium as well as France and Switzerland. These movements were part of different "migratory systems" that changed over the centuries.[11] These emigrations overlapped with seasonal and labor migrations. The grass-cutting and peat-digging crews who moved to Holland (*Hollandgänger*) from northwestern Germany, for example, were all seasonal migrants. German labor migrations to France and, especially, to Paris, however, resulted in the establishment of a subproletarian social milieu that had been stable for generations since the time of the restoration. It differed noticeably from the famous Paris colonies of German cabinetmakers and even more strongly from the Germans in a courtly, and later "upper-class" milieu.[12] Street sweepers from Hesse-Darmstadt, migrants from the Palatinate working in factories, doing excavation, or collecting rags, and Alsatian maids lived in a kind of "guest-worker" milieu with all the problems and functions of a foreign subproletariat. They all suffered low wages and bad working conditions as well as socioeconomic buffer functions during times of crisis on the labor market. The remigration of most of the German street sweepers from Paris back to Germany has to be seen against the background of an economic crisis during which foreigners were no longer employed by the municipal sanitation services.[13]

Among earlier immigrants to Germany were Netherlanders, Huguenots, Waldensers, and Salzburgers – all of whom came for religious reasons. This often led to what would be called a technology transfer. For example,

Landräte über den 'Zugang, Abgang und Bestand der ausländischen Arbeiter im preussischen Staate,' 1906–1914," *Archiv für Sozialgeschichte* (hereafter cited as *AfS*) 24 (1984): 163–283; see also n. 22 in this chapter.

11 Jan Lucassen, *Migrant Labor in Europe, 1600–1900: The Drift to the North Sea* (London, 1986), 129–94; cf. Martin P. Bossenbroek, " 'Dickköpfe und Leichtfüsse': Deutsche im niederländischen Kolonialdienst des 19. Jahrhunderts," and Franz Bölsker-Schlicht, "Torfgräber, Grasmäher, Heringsfänger . . . – deutsche Arbeitswanderer im 'Nordsee-System,' " both in Bade, *Deutsche im Ausland – Fremde in Deutschland*, 249–54 and 255–63.

12 Michael Stürmer, *Handwerk und höfische Kultur: Europäische Möbelkunst im 18. Jahrhundert* (Munich, 1982), 135–64; cf. Klaus J. Bade, "Altes Handwerk, Wanderzwang und Gute Policey: Gesellenwanderung zwischen Zunftökonomie und Gewerbereform," *Vierteljahrschrift für Sozial- und Wirtschaftsgeschichte* 69 (1982): 1–37; Hans-Ulrich Thamer, "Grenzgänger: Gesellen, Vaganten und fahrende Gewerbe," and Klaus J. Bade, "In Europa zu Hause: grossbürgerliche Kultur und höfisches Leben," both in Bade, *Deutsche im Ausland – Fremde in Deutschland*, 231–36 and 236–42.

13 Wilfried Pabst, "Subproletariat auf Zeit: Deutsche 'Gastarbeiter' im Paris des 19. Jahrhunderts," in Bade, *Deutsche im Ausland – Fremde in Deutschland*, 263–68; cf. J. Grandjonc, "La presse de l'émigration allemande en France (1795–1848) et en Europe (1830–1848)," *AfS* 10 (1970): 95–152; J. Grandjonc, "Etat sommaire des dépôts d'archives français sur le mouvement ouvrier et les émigrants allemands de 1830 à 1851/52," *AfS* 12 (1972): 487–531; Charles Brucker, *L'étranger en France et en Allemagne* (Nancy, 1991).

French refugees to the Palatinate caused an enormous increase in the municipal production of fabric, silk, and velvet. They arrived during the last third of the sixteenth century in an immigration wave that also included Calvinists from the Netherlands. Since 1682, the "Huguenot privileges" granted by German princes offered a special economic status as well as cultural autonomy to the refugees. In a second large wave of immigration, tens of thousands of French Huguenots settled in the cities or on the outskirts of closed settlements. The Waldensers, who had been expelled from France and from Savoy, mainly had a rural background. King Friedrich Wilhelm I (1688–1740) invited to Brandenburg approximately eighteen thousand Protestants who had been expelled from Salzburg. The king's invitation aimed not only to demonstrate his protection of persecuted Protestants but also to develop Prussian territories through planned settlement of peasants from Salzburg in the Prussian East. As in other cases, those who had fled their country or had been expelled for religious reasons strongly contributed to the development of cities and villages in the receiving country.[14]

In the course of its history, however, the country that often offered refuge to foreigners itself caused flight and forced migrations. In the nineteenth century, this was true for the "persecution of demagogues" following the Karlsbad Decrees of 1819 as well as for the flight of persecuted revolutionaries of 1848–49, who came to be called "Forty-Eighters" in the United States but who also emigrated to Australia.[15] And it was true for German socialists who, during the period of Bismarck's antisocialist law (1878–90), went to other European as well as to overseas countries. All these movements, however, cannot be compared with the emigration from Nazi Germany caused by political, ideological, and racial discrimination and persecution. Refugees from Germany fled to approximately eighty countries worldwide, among which the United States played the most important role. Hoping that their emigration would be only temporary, many emigrants first went to nearby European countries and only left the continent when the threat to them increased due to the expansion of the area under

---

14 Heinz Duchhardt, "Glaubensflüchtlinge und Entwicklungshelfer: Niederländer, Hugenotten, Waldenser, Salzburger," in Bade, *Deutsche im Ausland – Fremde in Deutschland,* 278–87.

15 Adolf E. Zucker, ed., *The Forty-Eighters: Political Refugees of the German Revolution of 1848* (New York, 1950); Carl Wittke, *Refugees of Revolution: The German Forty-Eighters in America* (Philadelphia, 1952); E. W. Dobbert, *Deutsche Demokraten in Amerika* (Göttingen, 1958); Walter D. Kamphoefner, "Dreissiger and Forty-Eighters: The Political Influence of Two Generations of German Political Exiles," in Hans L. Trefousse, ed., *Germany and America: Essays on Problems of International Relations and Immigrations* (Brooklyn, 1980), 89–102; Johannes H. Voigt, "Deutsche in Australien und Neuseeland," in Bade, *Deutsche im Ausland – Fremde in Deutschland,* 215–30.

German control or influence. For many, especially for the Jews, flight into exile meant salvation from impending death.[16] Due to this history the right of asylum for all refugees persecuted for political reasons is guaranteed in the constitution of the Federal Republic.

In this century of world wars, however, refugee movements involved not only foreigners migrating to Germany and Germans leaving their country but also the flight and forced migrations of other peoples caused completely or at least partly by Germany. Among these are the flight and forced resettlements from areas annexed by Germany and the Soviet Union after the Hitler–Stalin Pact of 1939. World War II set in motion forced resettlements, expulsions, and deportations in areas occupied by Germany, for example, the "Warthegau," as well as in the Soviet Union, for example, the "Volga Republic."[17] Germany's loss of the war resulted in the imprisonment of German POWs, who were forced to labor in Siberia, and their subsequent reintegration into society as "late returnees" (*Spätheimkehrer*), a process that lasted well into the 1950s.[18] The end of the war also brought about the flight and expulsion of millions of Germans from the East, which amounted to the largest forced mass migration in European history.[19]

FROM EMIGRATION TO IMMIGRATION

In the course of just one century, from the 1880s to the 1980s, Germany changed from a "classical" emigration country to a new type of immigration country.[20] The abrupt decline of the secular transatlantic mass exodus in the early 1890s marked a first step in this development. The preceding dispro-

---

16 Evelyn Lacina, *Emigration 1933–1945: Sozialhistorische Darstellung der deutschsprachigen Emigration und einiger ihrer Asylländer aufgrund ausgewählter zeitgenössischer Selbstzeugnisse* (Stuttgart 1982); Institut für Zeitgeschichte, Munich, Research Foundation for Jewish Immigration, New York, eds., *Biographisches Handbuch der deutschsprachigen Emigration nach 1933*, 3 vols. (Munich, 1980–83); Horst Möller, *Exodus der Kultur: Schriftsteller, Wissenschaftler und Künstler in der Emigration nach 1933* (Munich, 1984); Werner Röder, "Die Emigration aus dem nationalsozialistischen Deutschland," in Bade, *Deutsche im Ausland – Fremde in Deutschland*, 345–53.

17 Michael R. Marrus, *The Unwanted: European Refugees in the 20th Century* (New York, 1985), 122–295.

18 Albrecht Lehmann, *Gefangenschaft und Heimkehr: Deutsche Kriegsgefangene in der Sowjetunion* (Munich, 1986).

19 Rainer Schulze et al., eds., *Flüchtlinge und Vertriebene in der westdeutschen Nachkriegsgeschichte: Bilanzierung der Forschung und Perspektiven für die künftige Forschungsarbeit* (Hildesheim, 1987); G. Krallert-Sattler, *Kommentierte Bibliographie zum Flüchtlings- und Vertriebenenproblem in der Bundesrepublik, in Österreich und in der Schweiz* (Munich, 1989).

20 Klaus J. Bade, *Vom Auswanderungsland zum Einwanderungsland? Deutschland 1880 bis 1980* (Berlin, 1983); Klaus J. Bade, "Vom Export der Sozialen Frage zur importierten Sozialen Frage: Deutschland im transnationalen Wanderungsgeschehen seit der Mitte des 19. Jahrhunderts," in Klaus J. Bade, *Auswanderer – Wanderarbeiter – Gastarbeiter*, 1:9–72.

portion between population growth and employment opportunities changed dramatically in the late nineteenth century because of economic growth and a corresponding increase in employment opportunities. Instead of migrating to overseas countries, migrants now joined the internal migration streams from rural to urban employment areas.[21]

Furthermore, the surplus of labor, which had been the most important push factor of nineteenth-century mass emigration from Germany, was replaced by an increasing labor shortage in the course of the enormous economic growth of the two decades before World War I. These developments formed the background to mass employment of foreign workers, whose numbers amounted to about 1.2 million on the eve of World War I.[22] This shift from the transatlantic mass exodus of German emigrants to the continental mass influx of foreign labor marked a second step in the long-term change from German emigration to foreign immigration.

In early twentieth-century Germany, however, this change was not synonymous with a shift from an emigration to an immigration country for two reasons. First, Germany remained an emigration country, even though emigration sharply declined to a very low level during the two decades before World War I; second, it did not change into a true immigration country but into what in contemporary debates was called the second largest "labor importing country" (*Arbeitseinfuhrland*), surpassed only by the United States.[23]

This situation continued until the end of the Weimar Republic when employment of foreign labor nearly disappeared due to mass unemployment as a result of the world economic crisis.[24] In Nazi Germany, the employment of foreigners between 1933 and 1939 continued on a low level. But during World War II millions of foreign workers, mainly from Poland and the Soviet Union, were deported and forced to labor for Germany.[25] At

21 For a research report, see Dieter Langewiesche and Friedrich Lenger, "International Migration: Persistence and Mobility," in Bade, *Population, Labor and Migration*, 87–100.

22 Klaus J. Bade, " 'Preussengänger' und 'Abwehrpolitik': Ausländerbeschäftigung, Ausländerpolitik und Ausländerkontrolle auf dem Arbeitsmarkt in Preussen vor dem Ersten Weltkrieg," *AfS* 24 (1984): 91–283; Klaus J. Bade, "Labor, Migration, and the State: Germany from the Late 19th Century to the Onset of the Great Depression," in Klaus J. Bade, ed., *Population, Labor and Migration*, 59–85.

23 *Verhandlungen der Budapester Konferenz betr. Organisation des Arbeitsmarktes, 7./8. Oktober 1910* (Leipzig, 1911), 81; Imre Ferenczi, *Kontinentale Wanderungen und die Annäherung der Völker* (Jena, 1930), 21. On the history of foreign workers in Germany, see the contributions by Barfuss and Rössler in this volume.

24 Klaus J. Bade, "Arbeitsmarkt, Bevölkerung und Wanderung in der Weimarer Republik," in M. Stürmer, ed., *Die Weimarer Republik: Belagerte Civitas* (Königstein, 1980), 160–87.

25 Ulrich Herbert, *Fremdarbeiter: Politik und Praxis des 'Ausländereinsatzes' in der Kriegswirtschaft des Dritten Reiches* (Berlin, 1985); Ulrich Herbert, ed., *Europa und der 'Reichseinsatz': Ausländische Zivilarbeiter, Kriegsgefangene und KZ-Häftlinge in Deutschland, 1938–1945* (Essen, 1991); Ulrich Herbert, " 'Aus-

the end of the war, these workers formed the largest contingent of DPs or "displaced persons," amounting to about twelve million people.[26]

In the postwar period, transatlantic emigration remained quite strong until the mid-1950s. The movement included a large number of German expellees and refugees from the East. Since that time, transatlantic emigration declined steadily and the long-term change of Germany from an emigration country to a new type of immigration country became increasingly apparent. We must therefore distinguish three larger processes of immigration and integration for the postwar period.

The first process was the integration of German expellees and refugees from the former German East.[27] This integration process is usually regarded as having been completed as early as the mid-1950s. But this is both true and false. It is true with regard to the process of acculturation in the sense of economic and social integration, though many problems went unsolved even in the mid-1950s. It is false with regard to problems of identity and collective mentalities. In this context, "integration" often turned out to be an intergenerational process. For many expellees and refugees, this so-called integration took on the dramatic features of a true immigration problem.[28]

Many refugees and expellees were still strangers in the Federal Republic when the German–Italian treaty of 1955 was signed. It marked the beginning of officially organized recruitment of foreign labor for the expanding West German economy. Thus began the second immigration and integration process. It started with the "guest worker question" of the 1960s and continued with the growth of the immigration issue since the late 1970s, the existence of which, however, was officially denied for a long time.[29]

The "guest worker period" ended in 1973 with the "recruitment stop" (*Anwerbestop*) of foreign labor during the economic crisis. Since then, foreign workers who were not willing to live separated from their families had to decide between two courses of action. They could either return to their home countries and forgo the chance to come back to Germany later, or

länder-Einsatz' in der deutschen Kriegswirtschaft, 1939–1945," in Bade, *Deutsche im Ausland – Fremde in Deutschland,* 354–67.

26 Wolfgang Jacobmeyer, *Vom Zwangsarbeiter zum Heimatlosen Ausländer: Die Displaced Persons in Westdeutschland 1945 bis 1951* (Göttingen, 1985); cf. Wolfgang Jacobmeyer, "Ortlos am Ende des Grauens: 'Displaced Persons' in der Nachkriegszeit," in Bade, *Deutsche im Ausland – Fremde in Deutschland,* 367–73.

27 Wolfgang Benz, "Fremde in der Heimat: Flucht – Vertreibung – Integration," in Bade, *Deutsche im Ausland – Fremde in Deutschland,* 374–86; Schulze et al., *Flüchtlinge und Vertriebene.*

28 Klaus J. Bade, "Sozialhistorische Migrationsforschung und 'Flüchtlingsintegration,' " in Schulze et al., *Flüchtlinge und Vertriebene,* 126–62.

29 Bade, *Vom Auswanderungsland zum Einwanderungsland,* 96–124; Karl-Heinz Meier-Braun, *Integration und Rückkehr?* (Munich, 1988); Ulrich Herbert, *A History of Foreign Labor in Germany, 1880–1980: Seasonal Workers, Forced Laborers, Guest Workers* (Ann Arbor, Mich., 1991).

they could have their families join them in Germany. Many chose this second course, and, thus, a paradoxical situation developed. In Germany today, a large part of the foreign minority population originated as "guest workers" and exists as an immigration minority but without an immigration perspective.[30]

Economically and socially, several links existed between the integration of expellees and refugees and the immigration of foreign workers. For example, foreign workers replaced expellees and refugees at the lower end of the labor market, who after the war very often had to accept jobs far below their qualifications.[31] This even led to talk of the expellees as "Homo barackensis" and a "new proletariat."[32] The entrance of foreign laborers into the job market therefore benefited many Germans who then moved up the economic opportunity ladder.

The replacement function of the "guest workers" could also be observed in the housing market. Even in the 1950s and 1960s, "guest workers" often moved into camps previously inhabited by expellees and refugees, camps that, in some cases, had already served as "foreign workers' camps" (*Fremdarbeiterlager*) in Nazi Germany. When the Germans and Italians signed their 1955 labor agreement, about 185,000 expellees and refugees were still housed in such camps. Today, foreign workers and their families often live in rundown, cheap apartments, which had previously been called "refugee flats."[33] Nevertheless, by the late 1970s and especially by the early 1980s the foreign minority had already become a permanent and stable element within West Germany, which was slowly changing into an immigration society.

THE NEW IMMIGRATION ISSUE IN UNITED GERMANY

Since 1945 about 15 million German expellees, refugees, residents of the former GDR, and ethnic Germans from Eastern Europe and the former Soviet Union (*Aussiedler*) have entered West Germany, where on the eve

30 Friedrich Heckmann, *Die Bundesrepublik: Ein Einwanderungsland? Zur Soziogenese der Gastarbeiterbevölkerung als Einwandererminorität* (Stuttgart, 1981).
31 For the following as well, see Peter Marschalck, "Demographische Anmerkungen zur Rolle der Flüchtlinge und Vertriebenen in der westdeutschen Nachkriegsgeschichte," and Toni Pierenkemper, "Einige Bemerkungen zu Vertriebenen und Flüchtlingen in arbeitsmarkt-theoretischer Perspektive," both in Schulze et al., *Flüchtlinge und Vertriebene*, 163–79 and 168–70.
32 Peter Waldmann, "Die Eingliederung der ostdeutschen Vertriebenen in die westdeutsche Gesellschaft," in Josef Becker et al., eds., *Vorgeschichte der Bundesrepublik Deutschland: Zwischen Kapitulation und Grundgesetz* (Munich, 1979), 163–92.
33 Ulrich Herbert, "Zwangsarbeiter – Vertriebene – Gastarbeiter: Kontinuitätsaspekte des Wanderungsgeschehens in Deutschland," in Schulze et al., *Flüchtlinge und Vertriebene*, 171–74.

of unification in 1990 about 4.8 million foreigners lived. Excepting Israel and Australia, comparable dimensions for immigration in relation to population size can hardly be found for the same period, neither among industrialized countries nor among "classical" countries of immigration.[34]

At the present time, united Germany faces a new process of immigration, one that differs considerably from the two preceding great integration processes. This new process is more complicated and much more difficult to comprehend than its predecessors.[35] It encompasses five overlapping and mutually exacerbating problem areas.

First, the paradox that an officially declared nonimmigration country faces a serious immigration issue is the problematic legacy of the past decades. Most families that are part of the former "guest worker population" and often consist of three generations must live with this paradoxical situation – as "domestic foreigners," as "foreign inlanders," or as "Germans with foreign passports." They are torn between frustrated immigration perspectives, multicultural visions, and internal ethnosocial tensions.[36]

Second, in the 1980s the number of refugees coming to the West from Eastern Europe and the Third World has grown tremendously. This holds true for asylum seekers as well as for illegal immigrants.[37] In addition, a growing number of Jews from Russia are currently emigrating to Germany. Since the restrictive new asylum law of 1993 went into effect, the number of new asylum seekers has dropped sharply while the number of illegal foreigners seems to be increasing.

Third, starting in the late 1980s, a mass influx of ethnic Germans from eastern and southeastern Europe (*Aussiedler*) into West Germany began. In a sociocultural and mental sense, the "integration" of these "new citizens" takes on the dimension of a true immigration process, even though they immediately receive citizenship and all civil rights. The immigration process is complicated even more by the mentalities, religious views, and traditional attitudes of ethnic Germans toward family and society, and, very often, by language barriers.[38]

34 Klaus J. Bade, ed., *Neue Heimat im Westen: Vertriebene – Flüchtlinge – Aussiedler* (Münster, 1990).
35 For the following, see Klaus J. Bade, *Ausländer – Aussiedler – Asyl in der Bundesrepublik,* 3d ed. (Hanover, 1994).
36 Friedrich Heckmann, *Ethnische Minderheiten, Volk und Nation: Soziologie inter-deutscher Beziehungen* (Stuttgart, 1992); Claus Leggewie, *Multi-Kulti: Spielregeln für die Vielvölkerrepublik* (Nördlingen, 1990); Jürgen Micksch, ed., *Deutschland – Einheit in kultureller Vielfalt* (Frankfurt/Main, 1991).
37 Herbert Spaich, ed., *Asyl bei den Deutschen* (Reinbek, 1981); Ulrich O. Sievering, ed., *Politisches Asyl und Einwanderung* (Frankfurt/Main, 1984); Johannes Müller, ed., *Flüchtlinge und Asyl: Politisch handeln aus christlicher Verantwortung* (Frankfurt/Main, 1990); Klaus Barwig et al., eds., *Das neue Ausländerrecht* (Baden-Baden, 1991).
38 Barbara Malchow et al., eds., *Die fremden Deutschen: Aussiedler in der Bundesrepublik* (Reinbek, 1990);

The fourth area includes the abating but still clearly discernible problems of integration as well as identity for refugees and legal immigrants from the former GDR. They came from the collapsing East into the supposedly "golden" West and suffered a "German–German" culture shock. It resulted from the realization of how far East and West had diverged, not only in material culture and ways of life but also in mentalities.[39]

And finally, the fifth area involves a dilemma resulting not from people crossing borders but from borders moving across people. It concerns the substantial problems of adaptation in the five "new federal states," where many people became strangers in their own land due to the one-sided remodeling of their country's economy, society, and political culture by the West. Problems and difficulties related to this process of alienation at home not only reduced the willingness of "East Germans" to integrate aliens from abroad, but even increased a strong and general hostility toward foreigners and strangers as such. Animosity was especially widespread toward those who sought asylum, up to 20 percent of whom had been sent to live in eastern Germany after reunification according to the regulations of the unification treaty. This development ultimately culminated in violent attacks on asylum seekers, which looked like dry runs for pogroms.[40]

Hostility toward strangers now presents a severe social danger all over united Germany. It is, however, neither "fascist" nor particularly "German." It exists also in other European countries facing similar problems. But behind the new hostility toward strangers, the world sees the "ugly German" rising again because the shadows of the German past make brutality toward helpless minorities appear even more terrible.

On the one hand, hostility toward strangers has in most cases – in united Germany as well – much less to do with the strangers than with the natives and their genuine problems. On the other hand, in Germany the fear of ever increasing immigration pressure and a growing irritation caused by the lack of comprehensive and long-term perspectives for policies toward migration, integration, and minorities exacerbate the problem. Finally, frustration is transformed into aggression. The government's commissioner for foreigners, Liselotte Funcke, resigned from her office in July 1991 in order

Lothar Ferstl and Harald Hetzel, eds., *"Wir sind immer die Fremden": Aussiedler in Deutschland* (Bonn, 1990); Karl A. Otto, ed., *Westwärts – Heimwärts? Aussiedlerpolitik zwischen "Deutschtümelei" und "Verfassungsauftrag"* (Bielefeld, 1990).

39 Volker Ronge, "Die soziale Integration von DDR-Übersiedlern in der Bundesrepublik Deutschland," *Aus Politik und Zeitgeschichte* (Jan. 5, 1990): 39–47; Volker Ronge, *Von hüben nach drüben: DDR-Bürger im Westen,* 2d. ed. (Wuppertal, 1985).

40 Hans-Joachim Maaz, *Der Gefühlsstau: Ein Psychogramm der DDR* (Berlin, 1990); Irene Runge, *Ausland DDR: Fremdenhass* (Berlin, 1990).

to protest the federal government's disinterest in and the lack of political will to confront this social danger.[41]

According to evaluations and estimates of current trends, barring unpredictable events, the following courses of development can be expected in Germany: (1) continued immigration of ethnic Germans from the East; (2) low-level internal East to West migration from the new German federal states with a continuation of integration difficulties of these refugees from the former GDR; (3) to a lesser degree, depending on the development of the economy and the labor market in the German East, an internal West to East migration, including return migrations of refugees from the former GDR; (4) migration movements within the European Union, which will cause more immigration into Germany than German emigration to other states of the union; (5) East to West immigration pressure resulting from differences in economic development within Europe, the dissolution of the former Soviet Union and other political, economic, and social trouble spots in eastern and southeastern Europe; (6) South to North immigration pressure caused by worldwide differences in economic development and the dramatic worsening of the economic, ecological, social, and political situation in the Third World.[42]

Against a background of these scenarios, concepts for workable and effective policies have to be rethought. Long-term plans are needed, not short-term attempts at balance and repair. Migration and integration are existential experiences. They impinge upon all aspects of societal life, and, therefore, all social sciences. A policy on migration, integration, and minorities for this reason must be seen as a task integral to social policy. Its perspectives must not be shaped by considerations of laws alone but should be based on a broad social consensus and developed in accordance with already extant, though often unused, research findings.[43]

As regards such overall and long-term concepts toward migration, integration, and minorities in united Germany, at the moment one can talk

41 Klaus J. Bade, "Ein verlorenes Jahrzehnt: Zum Rücktritt der Ausländerbeauftragten Liselotte Funcke," *Deutsches Allgemeines Sonntagsblatt* (July 19, 1991); cf. Klaus J. Bade, *Ausländer – Aussiedler – Asyl,* 1: introd., 5.
42 For a prospective scenario based on extrapolations of data of population, migration, and the labor market, see Wolfgang Klauder, "Deutschland im Jahr 2030: Modellrechnungen und Visionen," in Bade, *Deutsche im Ausland – Fremde in Deutschland,* 455–64.
43 On the various positions taken in the current public debate in Germany, see Lutz Hoffmann, *Die unvollendete Republik: Einwanderungsland oder deutscher Nationalstaat* (Cologne, 1990); Dieter Oberndörfer, *Die offene Republik: Zur Zukunft Deutschlands und Europas* (Freiburg, 1991); Micha Brumlik and Claus Leggewie, "Konturen der Einwanderungsgesellschaft: Nationale Identität, Multikulturalismus und 'Civil Society,' " in Bade, *Deutsche im Ausland – Fremde in Deutschland,* 430–42; Klaus J. Bade, *Politik in der Einwanderungssituation: Migration – Integration – Minderheiten,* 442–55.

more about what we need than what we have. It may be a dangerous mistake to postpone the political decisions on the national level and to wait for European solutions to national questions. Aggravating the common way into the future by unsolved national questions could cause additional turbulence in the process of European unification. There is no doubt that the problem areas of migration, integration, and minorities include national as well as supranational tasks, but the national ones cannot be replaced by supranational ones.

As the reality of European economic and political unification draws nearer, the German government still has not yet fully answered the challenge of the new immigration issue within the German borders. This new challenge marks the end of a century-long process of change from a country of emigration to a new type of immigration country.[44]

Looking for answers to this challenge, the Germans in fact should look forward to the common European future but, at the same time, revisit their own history and learn the lessons of the past. The message of these lessons is that, in the past, millions of Germans were involved in immigration processes in overseas countries just as foreigners are in Germany today. But there is one crucial difference between past and present: As a rule, German immigrants abroad were welcomed or at least accepted in the countries where they went; they were not viewed as untrustworthy strangers. As this survey of the secular change from the nineteenth-century continent of emigration into what came to be called "Fortress Europe" suggests, however, the mistrust toward foreigners in Europe seems to be widespread.

---

44 For a statement by sixty German scholars on the paradox of allowing immigration without having an immigration policy, see Klaus J. Bade, ed., *Das Manifest der 60: Deutschland und die Einwanderung* (Munich, 1993); cf. Klaus J. Bade, "Immigration and Social Peace in United Germany," *Daedalus* 123, no. 1 (1994): 85–106.

Research on the German Migrations, 1820s to 1930s: A Report on the State of German Scholarship

DIRK HOERDER

German researchers of emigration received their first organizational support in 1977 at a conference in Stuttgart. At this meeting, scholars already active in the field met together with interested librarians and archivists.[1] Peter Marschalck's general survey of German emigration, Wolfgang Helbich's survey of German emigration to the United States, and a third survey of immigration to and emigration from Germany since 1880 provide starting points for research and teaching.[2] In 1982, Klaus J. Bade organized a major symposium on emigration, migrant labor, and labor migrants in the context of demography and labor market theory. This methodologically broad, interdisciplinary approach established a model for migration research by going beyond the confines of social history and by linking empirically the different forms of migration.[3] Since that time, five larger research projects have advanced knowledge on German migration to North America.

Begun at the University of Hamburg under the direction of Günter Moltmann, the first project aimed to write a social history of German emigration to North America.[4] It dealt with themes as diverse as Germans in New York, "Little Germanies," Germans and the frontier, Americanization, and the cul-

---

1 Willi Paul Adams, ed., *Die deutschsprachige Auswanderung in die Vereinigten Staaten: Berichte über Forschungsstand und Quellenbestände* (Berlin, 1980). Little work was done between 1945 and the 1960s. During the Third Reich emigration research was tainted by nationalist or National Socialist ideas. In the early years of the Federal Republic, this legacy went unchallenged.

2 For the most recent update on scholarship, see Klaus J. Bade, "Trends and Issues of Historical Migration Research in the Federal Republic of Germany," *Migration* 6 (1989): 7–28. Peter Marschalck, *Deutsche Überseewanderung im 19. Jahrhundert: Ein Beitrag zur soziologischen Theorie der Bevölkerung* (Stuttgart, 1973); Klaus J. Bade, ed., *Population, Labour and Migration in 19th and 20th Century Germany* (Leamington Spa, England, 1987); Klaus J. Bade, *Vom Auswanderungsland zum Einwanderungsland? Deutschland 1880–1980* (Berlin, 1983); for students, Wolfgang J. Helbich, *"Alle Menschen sind dort gleich . . .": Die deutsche Amerika-Auswanderung im 19. und 20. Jahrhundert* (Düsseldorf, 1988). An older publication is Mack Walker, *Germany and the Emigration, 1816–1885* (Cambridge, Mass., 1964).

3 Klaus J. Bade, ed., *Auswanderer – Wanderarbeiter – Gastarbeiter: Bevölkerung, Arbeitsmarkt und Wanderung in Deutschland seit der Mitte des 19. Jahrhunderts*, 2 vols. (Ostfildern, 1984).

4 This project as well as those at the universities of Munich, Bochum, Berlin, and Bremen were funded by the Stiftung Volkswagenwerk in its special program for North American Studies.

ture of emigration in Germany. Researchers paid especially close attention to places of origin. They raised questions about how the notion of emigration spread in southwestern Germany, to what degree convicts were transported, and how emigrants were recruited. One research topic, including eastern European transit migration and the emigrant aid societies, concerned the voyage from the place of origin via the two large German emigration ports, Hamburg and Bremen. However, this project placed little emphasis on gender and class.[5] Other scholars addressed similar questions and used similar approaches, while concentrating on emigration from southwestern Germany[6] and from Schleswig-Holstein,[7] and the depiction of emigration in popular German literature in the nineteenth century.[8] Many of these studies have been published and the late Günter Moltmann was editor of the series *Von Deutschland nach Amerika*.[9] More recently, the desire to include all types of in- and out-migration induced Klaus J. Bade to plan a second series.[10]

While the University of Hamburg project assembled the fruits of individual research – dissertations, theses, and essays – within a general framework, the project at the University of Munich, directed by Hartmut Keil, developed a comprehensive research program to study the social history of

5 Birgit Gelberg, *Auswanderung nach Übersee: Soziale Probleme der Auswanderungsbeförderung in Hamburg und Bremen von der Mitte des 19. Jahrhunderts bis zum ersten Weltkrieg* (Hamburg, 1973); Günter Moltmann, ed., *Deutsche Amerikaauswanderung im 19. Jahrhundert: Sozialgeschichtliche Beiträge* (Stuttgart, 1976); Hartmut Bickelmann, *Deutsche Überseeauswanderung in der Weimarer Zeit* (Wiesbaden, 1980); Agnes Bretting, *Soziale Probleme deutscher Einwanderer in New York City, 1800–1860* (Wiesbaden, 1981); Günter Moltmann, ed., *Germans to America: 300 Years of Immigration, 1683– 1983* (Stuttgart, 1982), and the German version: "Germantown, 300 Jahre Auswanderung in die USA, 1683–1983," *Zeitschrift für Kulturaustausch* 32 (1982): 305–452; Reinhard R. Doerries, *Iren und Deutsche in der Neuen Welt: Akkulturationsprozesse in der amerikanischen Gesellschaft im späten 19. Jahrhundert* (Wiesbaden, 1986); Michael Just, *Ost- und südosteuropäische Amerikawanderung, 1881– 1914: Transitprobleme in Deutschland und Aufnahme in den Vereinigten Staaten* (Stuttgart, 1988); Barbara Lang, *The Process of Immigration in German-American Literature from 1850 to 1900: A Change in Ethnic Self Definition* (Munich, 1988); Günter Moltmann, ed., *Aufbruch nach Amerika: Die Auswanderungswelle von 1816/17,* 2d ed. (Stuttgart, 1989), and the German version; Hans-Jürgen Grabbe, "Die europäische Einwanderung in die Vereinigten Staaten von Amerika, 1783–1820," a 1990 *Habilitationsschrift* soon to be published; Ingrid Schöberl, *Amerikanische Einwandererwerbung in Deutschland, 1845–1914* (Stuttgart, 1990); Agnes Bretting and Hartmut Bickelmann, *Auswanderungsagenturen und Auswanderungsvereine im 19. und 20. Jahrhundert* (Stuttgart, 1991); Michael Just, Agnes Bretting, and Hartmut Bickelmann, *Auswanderung und Schiffahrtsinteressen/"Little Germanies" in New York/Deutschamerikanische Gesellschaften* (Stuttgart, 1991).
6 Wolfgang v. Hippel, *Auswanderung aus Südwestdeutschland: Studien zur württembergischen Auswanderung und Auswanderungspolitik im 18. und 19. Jahrhundert* (Stuttgart, 1984).
7 Kai D. Sievers, ed., *Die deutsche und skandinavische Amerikaauswanderung im 19. und 20. Jahrhundert . . . mit Fallstudien aus Schleswig-Holstein und Hamburg* (Neumünster, 1981).
8 Juliane Mikoletzky, *Die deutsche Amerika-Auswanderung des 19. Jahrhundert in der zeitgenössischen fiktionalen Literatur* (Tübingen, 1988).
9 Franz Steiner Verlag, Wiesbaden, ten volumes to date, with several more projected.
10 Edited by Klaus J. Bade and Gerhard Hirschfeld, the series is entitled *Studien zur historischen Migrationsforschung* and is published by Klartext Verlag, Essen.

the German American working class in Chicago. Inspired by the Philadelphia Social History Project, the Chicago Project went beyond the use of quantitative methods in urban history in order to relate working-class life, urban space, the labor movement, and ethnic culture. The project sought to mold all of these elements into a new historical framework of ethnic working-class culture. Codirected for several years by John Jentz, the scholars working on the project cooperated closely with scholars in the United States. Furthermore, a group of literary historians (Heinz Ickstadt et al.) joined the team. Whereas the research conducted at Hamburg concerned itself mainly with emigrants from southwestern Germany, the Chicago Project dealt with people coming from the regions east of the Elbe River. Publications of the Chicago group include a documentary history of German working-class culture (also published in English) and a collection of essays in which the Chicago experience was compared with experiences of other cities. Moreover, this project began to pay attention to the particular role of women in the process of community formation. The primary emphasis, however, continued to be the historical development of working-class culture and the participation of German American workers in the emerging labor movement in the United States.[11]

At the University of Bochum, Wolfgang Helbich, joined later by Walter Kamphoefner, took a different approach. Starting with the hypothesis that letters from emigrants must still be available, he initiated a publicity campaign aimed at German descendants of emigrants to North America. The result was the collection of about six thousand letters (1992), organized into an archive for emigrant letters. A small selection of letters as well as a larger scholarly edition have been published. For the latter, Helbich provided an analysis of the possible impact of these letters on village society at home. With the help of postal statistics, he was able to gauge the truly phenomenal volume of emigrant mail. He argued that letter writers usually refrained from painting too rosy a picture, since this would induce other villagers to follow with the expectation that the author could help them find jobs and accommodations. Thus, a built-in corrective against tall tales – and the potential chain migration – was contained within the means of communication lest the recipient of the letter end up at the letter writer's doorstep.[12]

11 Hartmut Keil and John B. Jentz, eds., *German Workers in Industrial Chicago, 1850–1910: A Comparative Perspective* (DeKalb, Ill., 1983); Hartmut Keil, ed., *German Workers' Culture in the United States, 1850 to 1920* (Washington, D.C., 1988); Hartmut Keil and John B. Jentz, eds., *Deutsche Arbeiterkultur in Chicago von 1850 bis zum Ersten Weltkrieg: Eine Anthologie* (Ostfildern, 1984), and the English-language edition: *German Workers in Chicago: A Documentary History of Working-Class Culture from 1850 to World War I*, trans. Burt Weinshanker (Urbana, Ill., 1988).
12 Wolfgang Helbich, ed., *"Amerika ist ein freies Land . . .": Auswanderer schreiben nach Deutschland*

The fourth project, under the direction of Willi Paul Adams at the Free University of Berlin, analyzed the emergence and decline of the German American ethnic group in the context of ethnocultural pluralism and the development of an American national consciousness. In particular, researchers looked at schooling and the impact of religious institutions on the German American communities in Baltimore and Milwaukee. Both topics have not received sufficient attention in recent research on ethnic groups. Furthermore, within this project scholars are analyzing the role of the ethnic community's leadership in its history.[13]

The fifth project, the Labor Migration Project at the University of Bremen, directed by Dirk Hoerder, is concerned with a comparative approach to western and eastern European migration to North America. The project's particular focus is on the migration of skilled and unskilled workers from the 1840s to the 1930s. Scholars from the various cultures of origin teamed up with American and Canadian scholars to work on questions of which cultural and economic surroundings determined the cultural baggage of the migrants, what their expectations and hopes amounted to, how they experienced the trip, and how they interacted with the North American labor movement and the indigenous working-class culture.[14] Within this larger perspective, Christiane Harzig directed a comparative project on German, Swedish, Irish, Polish, and Italian women in Chicago around 1900.[15] Harzig and her colleagues compared in detail the cultures of origin with the re-

---

(Darmstadt, 1985); W. Helbich, Walter D. Kamphoefner, and Ulrike Sommer, eds., *Briefe aus Amerika: Deutsche Auswanderer schreiben aus der Neuen Welt, 1830–1930* (Munich, 1988); the English edition is entitled *News from the Land of Freedom: German Immigrants Write Home*, trans. Susan Carter Vogel (Ithaca, N.Y., 1991). An edition of letters from the Civil War period is under preparation.

13 Forthcoming doctoral dissertations by Annelie Edelmann and Bettina Goldberg; and leadership study authored by Willi Paul Adams. Several essays with partial results of the project have already appeared.

14 Dirk Hoerder, ed., *American Labor and Immigration History, 1877–1920s: Recent European Research* (Urbana, Ill., 1983); Dirk Hoerder, ed., *Labor Migration in the Atlantic Economies: The European and North American Working Classes during the Period of Industrialization* (Westport, Conn., 1985); Dirk Hoerder, ed., *"Struggle a Hard Battle" – Essays on Working-Class Immigrants* (DeKalb, Ill., 1986); Christiane Harzig and Dirk Hoerder, eds., *The Press of Labor Migrants in Europe and North America, 1880s to 1930s* (Bremen, 1987); Dirk Hoerder and Christiane Harzig, eds., *The Immigrant Labor Press in North America, 1840s to 1970s: An Annotated Bibliography*, 3 vols. (Westport, Conn., 1987); Dirk Hoerder and Horst Rössler, eds., *Distant Magnets: Migrants' Views of Opportunities in Industrializing America and Europe* (New York, 1992); Dirk Hoerder, Inge Blank, and Horst Rössler, *Roots of the Transplanted*, 2 vols. (New York, 1994); Dirk Hoerder and Leslie Page Moch, eds., *Global Moves, Local Contexts: European Migrants in International Perspective* (forthcoming); and forthcoming studies of ethnic cooperation and conflict in Budapest (Laszlo Katus) and Cleveland (Adam Walaszek, David Hammack, et al.).

15 Christiane Harzig, *Familie, Arbeit und weibliche Öffentlichkeit in einer Einwanderungsstadt: Deutschamerikanerinnen in Chicago, 1880–1910* (Ostfildern, 1991); Christiane Harzig et al., *Peasant Maids – City Women* (forthcoming). See Deirdre Mageean's summary of this project's research in this volume. Also see the anthology on women's migrations edited by Monika Blaschke and Christiane Harzig (see n. 41 in this chapter).

ceiving neighborhoods. In this urban context, a considerable loss of peasant culture was evident.

Another important aspect of the Labor Migration Project is the research being done on Bremen and Bremerhaven as ports of emigration. From early on, Bremen shipping companies treated transit migrants fairly, hoping that as a port of departure, their city would be recommended to other migrants. The speculation succeeded and about seven million people left the continent via Bremen between 1820 and the 1950s.[16] Similar research is also being done for Hamburg.[17] A special issue of the *Journal of American Ethnic History* dealt specifically with emigration ports in Europe, supplementing the emphasis on Ellis Island in its centennial year.[18] Additionally, a project on migrants from Lower Saxony has been in progress for a number of years at the University of Oldenburg.[19]

Since the late 1980s, scholars at the East German universities of Rostock and Jena have also researched the history of emigration. Three younger scholars have begun detailed studies of Mecklenburg, Brandenburg, and Pomerania in the nineteenth century, concentrating mainly on migration to North America.[20] But they are also looking at eastward migration to Poland and Russia. Moreover, Peter Schaefer and Ulrike Skorsetz at the University of Jena have started a project on emigration from Thuringia. Localized research such as this will help historians understand not only the causes of emigration but the social composition and routes of migration movements as well.[21]

On both sides of the Atlantic, recent work of American and German

16 Peter Marschalck, comp., *Inventar der Quellen zur Geschichte der Wanderungen, besonders der Auswanderung, in Bremer Archiven* (Bremen, 1986). Several older works cover the period from the 1820s to the 1930s. A popular work is Arno Armgort, *Bremen-Bremerhaven-New York: Geschichte der Auswanderung über die bremischen Häfen* (Bremen, 1992). In a broader context, see Dirk Hoerder and Diethelm Knauf, eds., *Aufbruch in die Fremde: Europäische Auswanderung nach Übersee* (Bremen, 1992), published in English under the misleading title *Fame, Fortune and Sweet Liberty: The Great European Migration* (Bremen, 1992). See also the reference to Karen Schniedewind's doctoral dissertation on return migration in n. 37 in this chapter.

17 Günter Moltmann, "Hamburg als Auswandererhafen," in Jürgen Ellermeyer and Rainer Postel, eds., *Stadt und Hafen: Hamburger Handel und Schiffahrt* (Hamburg, 1986), 166–79. See also the studies by Birgit Gelberg and Michael Just cited earlier.

18 *Journal of American Ethnic History* 13 (1993): 3–118, with essays on Copenhagen, Liverpool, Bremen, Irish ports, and Genoa.

19 Under the direction of Antonius Holtmann. Presently, a study of the passenger lists is planned and services are being offered for German Americans in search of their roots.

20 Rainer Mühle, Axel Lubinski (Rostock), and Uwe Reich (Potsdam). See their respective essays in this volume.

21 The studies at the Friedrich Schiller Universität are done by graduate students. The results will be available as theses on the M.A. level. A more substantial study is Ulrike Skorsetz's "Auswanderung aus Thüringen und Integration der Einwanderer in den USA in der 2. Hälfte des 19. Jahrhunderts" (working title).

scholars has reached a new level of sophistication. Earlier group histories and histories of emigrant organizations have via social history become a much broader and richer history of society with full attention paid to concepts of class, ethnicity, and gender as well as to theories of acculturation and to accounts of individual experiences. Research in the United States will only be summarized briefly. Several studies of acculturation are underway or have already appeared in print. Stanley Nadel's fine study on German Americans in New York City extends Agnes Bretting's work into the 1880s.[22] David A. Gerber's work on ethnic pluralism in Buffalo is complemented by Andrew P. Yox's analysis of the development of Buffalo's German East Side.[23] Frederick Luebke has investigated the Germans in Nebraska and is one of the few scholars who aims, by taking German immigration to North and South America into account, at a comparative approach.[24] Walter Kamphoefner and Kathleen N. Conzen have done the most detailed social historical work. Kamphoefner's study of emigration from Westphalia to Missouri is the best social history of emigration available anywhere.[25] Conzen's project on the acculturation of German rural immigrants in Minnesota and Wisconsin places ethnicity and agrarian structures in a new conceptual framework. In writing about the American rural frontier and the retention of ethnic culture in isolated regions, she provides a counterpoint to the social history of Germans in Chicago.[26] Moreover, Conzen shows the connections between family networks, religious affiliations, and landholding patterns, and she contrasts the German experience with that of Irish and Swedish settlers.[27]

To date research on German immigration to Canada is not as highly

22 Stanley Nadel, *Little Germany: Ethnicity, Religion, and Class in New York City, 1845–80* (Urbana, Ill., 1990). Agnes Bretting, covering the period 1800–60, cited earlier.
23 David A. Gerber, *The Making of an American Pluralism: Buffalo, New York, 1825–1860* (Urbana, Ill., 1989); Andrew P. Yox, "Decline of the German-American Community in Buffalo, 1855–1925," Ph.D. diss., University of Chicago, 1983.
24 Frederick C. Luebke, *Immigrants and Politics: The Germans of Nebraska, 1880–1900* (Lincoln, Neb., 1969); F. C. Luebke, *Germans in the New World: Essays in the History of Immigration* (Urbana, Ill., 1990); see also earlier studies by the same author.
25 Walter D. Kamphoefner, *Westfalen in der neuen Welt: Eine Sozialgeschichte der Auswanderung im 19. Jahrhundert* (Münster, 1982), rev. and enlarged English edition under the title *The Westfalians: From Germany to Missouri* (Princeton, N.J., 1987).
26 *Immigrant Milwaukee, 1836–1860: Accommodation and Community in a Frontier City* (Cambridge, Mass., 1976). Her work has been done in conjunction with the Berlin-based project on German immigrants in Milwaukee and Baltimore.
27 Kathleen N. Conzen, *Making Their Own America: Assimilation Theory and the German Peasant Pioneer,* German Historical Institute, Annual Lecture Series, no. 3 (Oxford, 1990); Kathleen N. Conzen, "Peasant Pioneers: Generational Succession among German Farmers in Frontier Minnesota," in Steven Hahn and Jonathan Prude, eds., *The Countryside in the Age of Capitalist Transformation: Essays in the Social History of Rural America* (Chapel Hill, N.C., 1985), 259–92; and Kathleen N. Conzen, *Up Sauk Valley: The Minnesota World That German Peasants Made* (forthcoming).

developed. For a long time scholars simply bypassed this topic, in part because the German-language group there is very heterogeneous. Recently, however, Gerhard P. Bassler published a general survey for the German-Canadian Congress and Hartmut Froeschle compiled a bibliography of research.[28] The high-quality but somewhat nationalist-minded studies of the 1930s, partly written under the influence of the McGill school of sociology, have found no postwar successors.[29]

Whereas the bulk of German migration specialists still focus on emigration, and more attention has been given to internal migration following the publication of a seminal essay by Dieter Langewiesche, interest in immigration to Germany (since the 1880s) has been considerable.[30] Polish scholars, for example, Krystyna Murzynowska, have devoted considerable energies to older Polish migrations.[31] Several West German and American scholars have also dealt with the question of the acculturation of Polish workers in a hostile society. Italian immigrant workers, in contrast, have received less attention.[32] The center of German-language research on imported labor was the Institute for the Study of Foreign Labor at the University of Rostock directed by Lothar Elsner (and temporarily by Joachim Lehmann). In addition to editing a biannual journal,[33] the institute published a survey on the history of labor migration into Germany.[34] A similar survey was prepared by the leading West German historian of foreign labor in Germany, Ulrich Herbert.[35] Both studies agree in fact but differ in interpretation, in particular about the continuity of policies concerning labor migrants before and after 1945. As this survey demonstrates, despite a number of remaining lacunae, especially concerning Italian, western European,

28 Gerhard P. Bassler, *The German Canadian Mosaic Today and Yesterday: Identities, Roots and Heritage* (Ottawa, 1991); *German-Canadian Yearbook,* vol. 11: *German Canadiana: A Bibliography,* ed. Hartmut Froeschle and Lothar Zimmermann (Toronto, 1990); Dirk Hoerder, "German-Speaking Immigrants: Co-Founders or Mosaic? A Research Note on Politics and Statistics in Scholarship," *Zeitschrift der Gesellschaft für Kanadastudien* 14, no. 2 (1994).

29 Albert Moellmann, *Das Deutschtum in Montreal* (Jena, 1937).

30 "Wanderungsbewegungen in der Hochindustrialisierungsphase: Regionale, interstädtische und innerstädtische Mobilität in Deutschland, 1880–1914," *Vierteljahrschrift für Sozial- und Wirtschaftsgeschichte* 64 (1977): 1–40.

31 *Polskie wychodzstwo zarobkowe w Zagłębiu Ruhry, 1880–1914* (Wrocław, 1972; German ed.: Dortmund, 1979). For further literature, see the notes in the essay by Barfuss in this volume.

32 An exception is René Del Fabbro's *Die willkommenen Ausländer: Italienische Arbeitsmigranten im deutschen Kaiserreich, 1871–1918* (Florence, 1993).

33 *Fremdarbeiterpolitik des Imperialismus,* vols. 1–20 (Rostock, 1976–88); since 1989, *Migrationsforschung.*

34 Lothar Elsner and Joachim Lehmann, *Ausländische Arbeiter unter dem deutschen Imperialismus, 1900 bis 1985* (Berlin, 1988).

35 Ulrich Herbert, *Geschichte der Ausländerbeschäftigung in Deutschland 1880 bis 1980: Saisonarbeiter, Zwangsarbeiter, Gastarbeiter* (Berlin, 1986). The English translation appeared under the title, *A History of Foreign Labor in Germany, 1880–1980: Seasonal Workers – Forced Laborers – Guest Workers,* trans. William Templer (Ann Arbor, Mich., 1991).

and northern European foreign workers, the field is generally well covered.[36]

A new, more comprehensive approach to migration has been advanced by research on two important themes: return migration and the roles of women. For a long time, return migration was represented by one older study and two essays, which, because of problematic data, came to different conclusions. Detailed research on return migration to Bremen has disclosed merchants' and commercial clerks' round-trip migration.[37] The second theme, the participation of women in migration and their role in the processes of acculturation, has recently received considerable attention. Women in Chicago have been studied both in their German American neighborhoods, in their areas of origin, and from a comparative perspective.[38] Christine Backhaus-Lautenschläger studied women who left Germany for the United States after 1933.[39] Another scholar is currently completing a dissertation on the press for and by German American women.[40] In March 1990 Monika Blaschke and Christiane Harzig organized a symposium at the University of Bremen on the history of women's migration. They employed a global perspective and looked at women in their everyday lives, whether in Brazil or New York City, whether at home or in the public sphere, and whether in Jewish urban culture or in agrarian colonies.[41]

Finally, Klaus Bade recently directed a project that surveyed, analyzed, and interpreted German migrations worldwide. The resulting publication encompasses eastward migrations from the late Middle Ages to the nineteenth century, transoceanic migrations westward, and intra-European migrations. Even more important, it covers the whole range of in-migration and immigration to Germany, whether by religious refugees or gypsies, courtiers or merchants. The authors give special attention to the movement

---

36 The essays presented in this volume range nearly across the whole scope of research. Also see Steve Hochstadt, "Migration and Industrialization in Germany, 1815–1977," *Social Science History* 5 (1981): 445–68. An older study is Wolfgang Köllmann, *Bevölkerung in der industriellen Revolution* (Göttingen, 1974). For further literature, see the references in Jackson's and Meyer's essays in this volume.

37 Karen Schniedewind, *Begrenzter Aufenthalt im Land der unbegrenzten Möglichkeiten: Bremer Rückwanderer aus Amerika, 1850–1914* (Stuttgart, 1994); G. Kortum, "Untersuchungen zur Integration und Rückwanderung nordfriesischer Amerikaauswanderung," *Nordfriesisches Jahrbuch* 14 (1978): 45–91; Kortum, "Migrationstheoretische und bevölkerungsgeographische Probleme der nordfriesischen Amerikarückwanderung," in Sievers, *Amerikaauswanderung,* 111–201.

38 See the work by Christiane Harzig, cited earlier, partly done in collaboration with Monika Blaschke, Marianna Knothe, Deirdre Mageean, and Margareta Matovic.

39 Christine Backhaus-Lautenschläger, *. . . Und Standen ihre Frau: Das Schicksal deutschsprachiger Emigrantinnen in den USA nach 1933* (Pfaffenweiler, 1991).

40 Monika Blaschke, "Idylle und Alltag: Die deutsch-amerikanische Presse für Frauen," Ph.D. diss., University of Bremen, forthcoming.

41 Monika Blaschke and Christiane Harzig, eds., *Frauen wandern aus: Deutsche Migrantinnen im 19. und 20. Jahrhundert* (Bremen, 1990).

of labor into Germany during the century from the 1880s to the 1980s. Foreign workers arrived under a system of rotating labor, forced workers were brought in during the wars, and "guest workers" from many cultures were invited in after 1945. In-migration to Germany was but part of the intra-European south-to-north migrations in the 1960s.[42]

42 Klaus J. Bade, ed., *Deutsche im Ausland – Fremde in Deutschland: Migration in Geschichte und Gegenwart* (Munich, 1992).

Index

Italicized page numbers refer to figures or maps.

heavy industry; *see* industrialism
Helbich, Wolfgang, 413, 415
Helmken, August Johann, 343
Herbert, Ulrich, 419
Hesse, Nicholas, 29
Heuerleute, 23; in Bremen, 206; in
  Georgsmarienhütte, 179–84, 185–8,
  193–4, 196–8
Hippel, Wolfgang von, 37
Hirsch, Ludwig, 349
Huffmann, Ernst, 352
Hull House, 307
"Human Migration and the Marginal
  Man" (Park), 150
Hupka, Stanisław, 113

Ikels, Charlotte, 234
illegitimate birth: and emigration, 27; in
  Mecklenburg, 71
immigrant guidebooks, 29–30
immigrant press; *see* women's press
immigration laws, U.S., 389n
impartible inheritance, 19–20
industrial capitalism, effect on skilled trades,
  129
Industrial Council of Passaic Wool
  Manufacturers, 368, 372, 375
Industrial Workers of the World (IWW),
  366–7
industrialism: Duisburg migration during,
  157–60, *158*, 162–3, 168; effect on
  eastern Germany during, 209;
  Georgsmarienhütte migration during,
  7–8, 177–99; history of in Passaic, 348–
  51; and migration, 400; women's role
  in, 316
inheritance of land, 19–20, 39; in
  Germany, 205
intermarriage; *see* marriage: intermarriage
internal migration, 1, 6; in Bremen, 8,
  201–24; in Duisburg, 7, 147–75; in
  Georgsmarienhütte, 7–8, 177–99; and
  population growth, 139; and skilled
  workers, 6–7, 127–46; *see also*
  continental migration; overseas
  migration; return migration
Irish immigrants to Chicago, 295–309
  passim

Iwan, Wilhelm, 92
IWW, 366–7

Jentz, John, 415
Jewish Daily Forward, 322–4
Jewish Women's Federation, 387
Jews, emigration of, 31
Johansson, Maja, 254
Journal of Industrial Hygiene, 364
journeymen; *see* skilled workers
Jüdischer Frauenbund, 387
July Revolution, France (1830), 130

Kammgarnspinnerei Stöhr & Co., 348–50,
  352
Kaplan, Marion, 383
Karlsbad Decrees (1819), 404
Katzman, David, 259, 291
Keil, Hartmut, 414
Kleinegesse, Elisabeth, 273, 288
Klinger, Anna Maria, 286
Know-Nothing Party, 241
Konsensakten, 36–7
Körner, Heiko, 202
Kortum, Gerhard, 331
Krefeld migration rates, *171*
Krieter, Friedrich Wilhelm, 341
Krüger, Georg Wilhelm, 334–5
Kurmark, mercantilistic settlement policy
  in, 47
Kvinden og Hjemmet, 319–20

labor markets, and migration, 3
Labor Migration Project, 416–17
laborers: contracted, in Frankfurt/Oder, 99;
  as East Elbian emigrants, 38, 83; as
  Frankfurt/Oder emigrants, 83; free, in
  Frankfurt/Oder, 88, 99; lack of in
  Poland, 109; and land acquisition, 44–5,
  77, 87–8; in Mecklenburg-Strelitz, 68–
  77; mobility of, 202; population growth
  among, 46, 83; recruitment of, 211–14;
  returnees to Bremen, 341–2; rural, in
  Duisburg, 155, 157; *see also* contracted
  laborers; free laborers; guest workers;
  Heuerleute; skilled workers
Ladies' Home Journal, 316, 319–21
Lafontaine, Julius, 227–8